KURSK

THE GERMAN VIEW

KURSK

THE GERMAN VIEW

Eyewitness Reports of Operation Citadel
by the German Commanders

Translated, edited, and annotated

by Steven H. Newton

DA CAPO PRESS
A Member of the Perseus Books Group

Designed by Brent Wilcox

Cataloging-in-Publication data for this book is available from the Library of Congress.

ISBN 0-306-81150-2

Published by Da Capo Press
A Member of the Perseus Books Group
http://www.dacapopress.com

Da Capo Press books are available at special discounts for bulk purchases in the U.S. by corporations, institutions, and other organizations. For more information, please contact the Special Markets Department at the Perseus Books Group, 11 Cambridge Center, Cambridge, MA 02142, or call (617) 252-5298.

1 2 3 4 5 6 7 8 9—05 04 03 02

CONTENTS

v

PART 2

Tactical Aspects of Operation Citadel
Eyewitness Accounts by German Commanders

PART 3

Operation Citadel

An Analysis of Its Critical Aspects

Steven H. Newton

ACKNOWLEDGMENTS

From an institutional perspective it would be exceedingly difficult to find the time for research and writing without the active support of my department chair, Dr. Sam Hoff, and the provost of Delaware State University, Dr. Johnny Tolliver.

Research assistance at the National Archives was provided by Andrew Heilmann and Jonathan Scott, who always work enthusiastically. I just hope that next time they'll ask for a price quote before they place an order for full-size map copies.

My discussions on battlefield tactics with Lieutenant Colonel Dave Wrenn, Virginia Army National Guard and (as of this writing) Operations officer of the 29th Infantry Division (Light) have been, as always, invaluable.

No books would ever issue from the Newton household without the unwavering support of my wife, Faith, as well as our children, Marie, Alexis, and Michael. I get toleration if not encouragement from Momma and Buddy, the cats who let us share their house, as long as writing doesn't interfere with the important things in life—like dinner.

Introduction

Operation Citadel, part of the battle of Kursk, continues to attract interest as the renowned Greatest Tank Battle of All Time. It took place at Prokhorovka, Russia, near the border of Ukraine far south-southwest of Moscow. It followed on the heels of Nazi Germany's thrust into the Soviet Union during the 1942–1943 winter campaign and the Soviets' subsequent counterthrust that spring and summer. Recent historical treatments have scaled down the size of the action, and some memoirs, such as those penned by German commanders Erich von Manstein and Friedrich Wilhelm von Mellenthin, along with German unit histories, have dominated our understanding of the battle for far too long.[1] These were the sources primarily utilized by Paul Carell née Schmidt for his rousing, well-written Kursk segment in *Scorched Earth* (1966).[2] These same sources have continued to dominate the German side of the battle through the publication of Geoffrey Jukes's *Kursk: The Clash of Armour* (1968), Martin Caidin's *The Tigers Are Burning* (1974), Mark Healey's *Kursk 1943: The Tide Turns in the East* (1992), and Robin Cross's *Citadel: The Battle for Kursk* (1993). Janusz Piekalkiewicz's *Operation "Citadel," Kursk, and Orel: The Greatest Tank Battle of the Second World War* (1987), George M. Nipe Jr.'s *Decision in the Ukraine, Summer 1943: IISS. and III. Panzerkorps* (1996), and Walter S. Dunn's *Kursk: Hitler's Gamble, 1943* (1997) have each in their own way attempted to expand the universe of German source material, but none produced a comprehensive history of the battle.[3] Even so, with such a wide variety of easily accessible books on the battle in print in English, it might be thought that very nearly the last word on that campaign has been spoken.[4]

When David M. Glantz and Jonathan House published *The Battle of Kursk* (1999), written with unprecedented access to the Soviet archives, many reviewers suggested that the definitive history of the operation had finally been written. Strangely enough, this has not turned out to be the case. Although Glantz and House deserve high marks for the scholarly perspective and research brought to bear on the Red Army side of the battle, their account of the German conduct of operations is disappointingly thin and relies on many outdated secondary sources while ignoring significant archival material that most historians knew for years had existed. As a result, when the authors set out to debunk the myths surrounding Kursk, their conclusions are at once unsatisfying and based on incomplete data. One almost wishes that the book had been entitled *Kursk: The Soviet Perspective*, for that of the Germans is strangely lacking.[5]

There is significant German material on Kursk and its aftermath in the German Archives (Bundesarchiv) and our own National Archives, both in the Foreign Military Studies section and in the Captured German Records section. Much of the statistical information contained therein has recently been published by Niklas Zetterling and Anders Frankson in their landmark study, *Kursk 1943: A Statistical Analysis*.[6] Yet Zetterling and Frankson, and most of the other authors cited above, have not delved deeply into the postwar accounts written by former German officers of their battles and campaigns at the behest of the United States Army, which in the late 1940s was assessing its own performance and gearing up for a potential confrontation with the Red Army in Central Europe. Especially as these essays relate to the Russian front, their quality varies widely. Frequently officers lacked official papers and maps and had to work from memory: Errors in times, dates, places, and units abounded. Although some officers—Fritz Bayerlein, Gunther Blumentritt, Franz Halder, and Lothar Rendulic among them—made virtual second careers of churning out these works, others wrote only one or two papers. Those who wrote few essays tended to fall at the extremes of the spectrum: either meticulously detailed and accurate, or poorly conceived and sloppily written. Worse still, the translators were company- and field-grade officers with what appears to have been a very limited proficiency in German and almost no understanding of the structure and nomenclature employed by the army of their former enemies.

This state of affairs was rendered doubly unfortunate when, a few years later, two separate cadres of U.S. Army and U.S. Air Force officers, along with several civil servants, reworked, modified, excerpted, and—in the most extreme cases—completely rewrote some of these essays for official government publication. In that process, the U.S. editors (one is tempted to classify them as coauthors) introduced additional errors and, despite all protestations to the contrary, changed the original intent of the German authors in key passages. Several of these, most notably studies attributed to Hans von Greiffenberg, Franz Halder, Hermann Plocher, and Erhard Raus, have survived many reprintings and have become staple sources for many historians writing about the Russian front who lack either the linguistic skills or physical access necessary to work with original German material in the National Archives. As David Glantz has perceptively noted, reliance on these documents as essentially primary sources has severely skewed the Western view of the military events of the Russo-German war.

The tragedy has been compounded by the fact that many of the lesser-known (and untranslated) studies contain a tremendous wealth of information—as long as they are accurately translated and crosschecked, literally paragraph by paragraph, against contemporary documents. Among the most potentially valuable entries in this series is a six-part, multiauthor study of Operation Citadel, nearly the equivalent of the recently published Soviet General Staff study of the battle from the other side of the lines. The effort was coordinated by General of Infantry Theodor Busse, who had been Army Group South's chief of staff during the battle. Busse contributed an overview while five coauthors with relevant personal experience wrote individual chapters on *Armeeabteilung* Kempf, Fourth Panzer Army, Second Panzer and Ninth Armies, Luftflotte Four, and Luftflotte Six. Curiously, the two best available histories of Kursk—the efforts of Walter Dunn and of Glantz and House—neither cite nor acknowledge the existence of this work. There are two main reasons for this strange omission. First, other than Busse, the manuscript does not identify the coauthors, which seriously compromises their authority; and second, the English translation of this work is particularly horrible, often literally reversing the meaning of entire sentences.

A modicum of research, however, reveals that Busse selected an extremely capable and knowledgeable cadre of authors.[7] Listed in the order in which they appear in this book, they are:

Armeeabteilung Kempf	Erhard Raus, commander XI Corps
Fourth Panzer Army	Friedrich Fangohr, chief of staff
Second Panzer and	Peter von der Groeben, operations officer,
Ninth Armies	Army Group Center
Luftflotte Six	Friedrich Kless, chief of staff
Luftflotte Four	Hans Seidemann, commander, VIII Flieger Corps

The German versions of the manuscripts, moreover, are much cleaner and clearer than the existing translations (though the maps are poor in both editions).

Chapters 1–6 of this book are a new translation of that study, heavily annotated with new material in the footnotes and appendices.[8] In preparing these chapters for publication the attempt has been made to take into account the fact that none of the authors expected their work ever to receive commercial publication. They wrote in clear but often pedantic German, relying far too much on passive verb tenses and convoluted grammatical construction, without specific reference to the names of commanders and other officers. Sentences within paragraphs often appear out of order (as if inserted by afterthought), while transitions and contrasting conjunctions are often implied or simply omitted. Attempting to reconstruct the sense of what these officers meant to say, therefore, has in many places required a departure from a strictly word-for-word translation, much at the same level that any good copy editor suggests structural revisions to a manuscript accepted for publication. The difference here has been the impossibility of consulting the authors directly when more subtle questions arose, but that is an issue that editors must regularly tackle. In addition, unit designations have been corrected and rendered in a consistent format, while the names of commanders and other individuals mentioned in the text have been supplied wherever possible. Extensive use of archival materials has been made to support or challenge statements made in narratives. All of the footnotes and appendices represent new work.

A separate manuscript on railroad transportation in the Army Group Center area (included here as Chapter 7) was not technically a part of the Busse study but easily could have been. Written by Hermann Teske, the officer in charge of rail transportation in the sector, this study has long been known and used as a major source by authors researching the Soviet partisan movement. Teske, unlike many other officers in the postwar program, did enjoy access to his working papers and crammed his study with table after table of statistical information.

Taken as a whole, the seven chapters in Part 1 represent a major source regarding German operations at Kursk. Although there is, of course, considerable repetition of the basic chronological framework of the battle, new and sometimes controversial material awaits within. For example, most of the army officers attribute the German failure not to lack of tanks or planes but to a shortage of infantry. Fangohr challenges what has heretofore been the consensus view of Hermann Hoth's plans with respect to advancing on Oboyan or Prokhorovka, and Raus throws new light on von Manstein's decision to continue the battle after the attack in the north had obviously failed.

Chapters 8–11 (Part 2) present detailed pictures of tactical combat—primarily infantry combat—during the summer of 1943 directly related to the battle of Kursk. In a brief narrative drawn from a larger study, Lothar Rendulic recounts the defensive stand of his XXXV Corps east of Orel. Erhard Raus's account of his XI Corps in the battles of Belgorod and Kharkov, during the Soviet counteroffensive, once existed as a continuous manuscript before military editors chopped it into pieces and dropped the fragments into several different publications. The original manuscript appears to have been irrevocably lost, but the overwhelming majority of it—probably 90–95 percent—has been reconstructed and annotated here. Adding to the slim literature available on the battles fought by Army Group Center in the summer and fall of 1943, during and after the evacuation of the Orel salient, is the study of XX Corps operations by its commander, Rudolf Freiherr von Roman. Finally, in an extensive work that has been mined by capable historians but never available to the general public, Martin Francke (who kept the headquarters war diary) details the defensive battle fought by Sixth Army along the Mius River in late July–early August. This was the site of the first Soviet diversionary attacks, which successfully drew the II SS and XXIV Panzer Corps away from Kursk.

Part 3 consists of original essays on several critical topics regarding Operation Citadel. Chapter 12 examines key decisions made by Hoth and von Manstein before and during the battle. Chapter 13 utilizes contemporary German records to assess the effect of the repeated postponement of the offensive on the relative combat strengths of Ninth Army and the Soviet Central Front. Chapter 14 utilizes much of the new material unearthed in the rest of this book to cast new light on the disappointing results of Army Group South's initial assault on 5 July. The concluding chapter of the book (Chapter 15) attempts to grapple with the question of Kursk as a decisive battle, responding to one of the more original provocative challenges to that viewpoint.

PART 1

Strategic Analysis
of Operation Citadel

Eyewitness Accounts by German Commanders

1

Operation Citadel Overview

by General of Infantry Theodor Busse
Chief of Staff, Army Group South

Editor's Introduction

Despite the fact that Field Marshal Erich von Manstein characterized Theodor Busse as "my closest collaborator" and that he rose to command one of the last armies defending Berlin, he has attracted very little attention either from historians or German officers composing their memoirs.[1] The primary reason for this neglect appears to be the fact that Busse, capable as he undoubtedly was, came across as overbearing, excessively optimistic, zealously protective of his relationship with von Manstein, and far too closely tied with members of Hitler's personal entourage for anyone's comfort. Put simply, nobody liked him.

Alexander Stahlberg best captures the feelings of the other officers toward Busse. Having just drawn his billet as von Manstein's adjutant in the critical days when the Sixth Army still held out at Stalingrad, Stahlberg made the requisite courtesy calls—"in precise order of seniority, according to custom"—on Army Group Don's chief of staff, Major General Friedrich Schulz, and Busse, the operations officer. "I at once felt trust and liking for General Schulz," Stahlberg recalled, but "things were quite different" with Busse. "When I went to his office, he offered me a chair facing him, turned the light of a standard lamp on me and questioned me about everything he was interested in without my being able to see his face," the young adjutant later wrote, noting that as a result "there was a wall between us from the start."[2]

Theodor Busse was a Prussian, born at Frankfort on the Oder (the town he would later defend as an army commander) on 15 December 1897. He entered the army as an officer cadet in December 1915 and received his commission as a lieutenant in the 12th Grenadier Regiment in February 1917. Young Busse must have impressed someone during the final year of World War I, because he received one of the 4,000 prized officer slots allowed in the post-Versailles Reichswehr (German army). By July 1937, Major Busse had risen to become the Ia (operations officer) of the 22nd Infantry Division, the post in which he gained promotion to lieutenant colonel in February 1939. During the Polish campaign, the 22nd Infantry Division found itself relegated to a reserve role but played a much more active part in the conquest of the Netherlands in May 1940. Although Busse appears to have performed well, he also rankled General of Artillery Franz Halder, chief of the Army General Staff, by circulating a tactless report that harshly criticized the Luftwaffe's (Germany's air force) interservice cooperation even before the campaign ended. This unfortunate lapse probably contributed to Busse missing out in the major round of promotions and decorations following France's defeat.[3]

Knowing that he could not afford to let his peers get too far ahead of him, Busse jumped at the chance to become operations officer for the newly formed Eleventh Army in September 1940. Eleventh Army had been activated to train new divisions raised for the invasion of the Soviet Union, and when Busse joined the staff there were no plans to utilize it in the campaign. Fortunately for Busse, his new commander, Colonel General Eugen Ritter von Schobert, was a committed national socialist (Nazi) and preferred like-minded men around him. Though Busse was not a Nazi, he strongly supported Hitler's leadership and apparent success as a warlord. Even more critical to Busse's career was the fact that Twelfth Army headquarters, in the wake of the successful Balkan campaign during the late spring of 1941, could not be released from garrison duty to participate in Operation Barbarossa. On short notice, Eleventh Army headquarters was shipped to Romania to control German forces there.[4]

Arguably the biggest break of Busse's life came on 12 September 1941, when the airplane carrying von Schobert crashed, killing everyone aboard. His successor—and the man to whom Busse would be linked throughout the rest of the war—was Erich von Manstein. Busse served von Manstein as operations officer during the Eleventh Army's conquest of the Crimea and held the same post at Army Group Don during the Stalingrad campaign. In March 1943 von Manstein chose Busse over Henning von Tresckow (another gifted staff officer who happened to be a ringleader in the anti-Hitler conspiracy within the army) to become chief of staff, a position he held through the battles for Kursk, the Dnepr River line, the Cherkassy debacle, and the encirclement of the First Panzer Army in early 1944.[5]

Relations between the two men did not start amicably. Busse admitted to R. T. Paget, von Manstein's postwar defense attorney and earliest biographer, that "during the first two weeks I hated his guts; I never left his presence without smarting. But in spite of myself I admired his amazing grasp" of the strategic and operational situations. Eventually Busse found the key to working with his new commander; as Paget wrote, von Manstein "hated paperwork and rarely read papers that were put before him. He expected his officers to report concisely upon their contents and he then initialed the papers to indicate that they had been reported upon. His officers were not encouraged to be verbose." Busse also learned that von Manstein preferred optimism to gloom, and though other staff officers ridiculed his trademark assurance ("It's a bad business, Sir, but we'll manage somehow!") the young Prussian understood the field marshal more completely than they.[6]

Unfailing optimism and personality quirks represented only the smaller part of the reason many of Busse's fellow officers mistrusted him. Busse had married a woman whose sister had married Lieutenant General Wilhelm Burgdorf, who rose to become one of Hitler's adjutants and ultimately the chief of the army's personnel office. If officers close to the front viewed Busse with disdain, their feelings toward Burgdorf reached the level of revulsion. Hard-drinking and politically ambitious without being constrained by any hint of a conscience, Burgdorf routinely wrecked careers, cheerfully turned over accused officers to the mercies of the People's Court, and earned himself a grisly footnote in history as the man dispatched to ensure that Field Marshal Erwin Rommel committed suicide in 1944 following the failed assassination attempt against Hitler. Heinz Guderian characterized Burgdorf as "oafish," which was about the most polite description applied to him. It was a measure of Busse's social ineptitude that he never realized that his practice of spending an hour or so on the telephone with Burgdorf every evening added more bricks to the wall between himself and his peers. Ironically, Busse does not seem to have used these conversations with Burgdorf to advance any particular agenda. In fact, Busse actively supported the idea of the army forcing Hitler to name von Manstein or Gerd von Rundstedt as effective commander-in-chief for the Russian front, something he obviously did not communicate to his brother-in-law.[7]

Busse received the Knight's Cross in January 1944, based on his work as Army Group South's chief of staff, and when Hitler sacked von Manstein in March, Busse remained in place to provide continuity as Colonel General Walter Model took over. He was transferred to command the 112th Infantry Division on 20 July 1944—ironically the very day Hitler survived the famous assassination attempt. In the purges of the army's senior leadership that followed the failed plot, an indisputably loyal and nonpolitical officer like Busse (especially one whose brother-in-law now controlled the personnel office) enjoyed excellent career prospects: After commanding his division for less than two weeks (he may or may not have actually reported for duty), Theodor Busse received command of the I Corps in Army Group North. Promotion to command of the Ninth Army in front of Berlin followed six months later.[8]

In the waning days of the Third Reich, Busse demonstrated an aptitude for operational command and a firmness of resolve that astounded his critics. Initially Busse believed that if he could hold the Oder River line long enough, the Americans would take Berlin and save the bulk of Germany from Soviet occupation. When that idea proved chimerical, Busse steadfastly covered the retreat of German refugees as long as he could, then fought his way west to link up with General of Panzer Troops Walter Wenck's Twelfth Army, managing to salvage 40,000 of his initial 200,000-man command from the final conflagration. Accomplishing these feats required Busse to ignore or even defy orders from Hitler, the German Army High Command (OKH), and his army group commander; only Burgdorf's patronage, the unyielding support of Heinz Guderian (the current chief of the Army General Staff), and Busse's ability to establish an informal relationship with *Reichsminister* Joseph Goebbels allowed him to remain in command long enough to do so.[9]

Busse, who would later resurface as West Germany's director of civil defense, contributed to only three projects under the auspices of the U.S. Army's historical program. He was one of six coauthors of study P-143(a)(11) ("Selected [Ninth] Army Operations on the Eastern Front") and one of thirty-three participants in the turgid P-211 study (a 315-page work entitled "Weather Information for Army Tactical Operations") for which he penned a mere fifteen pages.[10] Busse's primary accomplishment involved coordination of the Operation Citadel study: He selected the five coauthors, created the general guidelines, and, having read the individual chapters, wrote the overview and introduction. Fully aware of the impediments to research (lack of maps, reports, etc.), Busse admitted that the study could not "lay claim to being a first-rate work of analytical military history," but he had obviously taken pains to verify his information as thoroughly as possible.

The introductory chapter to the Citadel study is vintage Busse and provides some unintended insights into his personality. Only Theodor Busse, three years after the fall of Berlin, could refer to the battle of Kursk as a "victory" while simultaneously admitting that the offensive had "neither denied the Soviets a base of operations around Kursk nor destroyed sizeable enemy forces, or even eliminated STAVKA's [the Russian general headquarters] intention to conduct a major offensive in 1943." Writing well before much of the later mythology regarding the Kursk operation had developed, Busse supported the idea that most field commanders favored the so-called backhand blow rather than a set-piece preemptive assault. This later became the standard mantra of German memoirs—Hitler's insistence on striking first. But Busse subtly undercut many self-serving postwar accounts (including those of Guderian and von Manstein) with his contention that those generals had agreed with Hitler that Germany could not afford to relinquish the tactical initiative in Russia, something most of them later took pains to deny. Busse inconveniently asserted that "everyone, including Hitler, OKH, and the army group and army commanders, thoroughly agreed on this point."

In passing (because he had no idea that it would later become a point of debate), Busse also rebutted the idea that Fourth Panzer Army's commander, Colonel General Hermann Hoth, had fatally changed the axis of his attack around 9 July, when he sent the II SS Panzer Corps toward Prokhorovka instead of continuing to drive directly for Oboyan and then Kursk. Busse's understanding of Hoth's tactical plans (obviously influenced by Friedrich Fangohr's essay, but not dissenting from it) was that the panzer general had *from the outset* intended to engage Soviet armored reserves near Prokhorovka. That key point will be developed in Chapter 12.

But this Chapter 1 also represents something more than an overview and summary of the operations detailed in the analyses that follow. Busse provides a grand strategic perspective and insight into the conclusions (and limitations) of German military intelligence during the planning phase of the offensive. It is also from Busse that we receive the first hints of the extent to which von Manstein's decisions during the battle were influenced by his subordinates, especially the commander of III Panzer Corps, Hermann Breith. In total, this chapter provides a sound summary of Operation Citadel from the German perspective and manages to raise a number of important historical questions.

Operation Citadel Overview
by General of Infantry Theodor Busse
Chief of Staff, Army Group South

Introduction

There were no situation maps or files available for the preparation of this study. The various contributors had only their memory and a few personal notes upon which to rely. This study, therefore, cannot lay claim to being a first-rate work of analytical military history. In many instances, its treatment must unfortunately remain superfluous. In the material that it does offer, however, this work is historically accurate, though minor errors of detail may have occurred.

This overview sketches the overall inception and development of Operation Citadel. Because the operations of the field armies and the Luftwaffe are discussed individually, the description of the battle itself has been kept brief and confined to those events that decisively affected the course of the entire operation. The activities of the Luftwaffe are not discussed in this overview, because they will be examined in detail in subsequent chapters. Suffice it at this point to pay special tribute to the Luftwaffe's large share in the victory. Considering the relative disparity in ground force strength, this victory could not have been won without the gallant efforts of the men of the Luftwaffe.

In organization and content, the study of the action fought by the Ninth Army departs from the pattern set in the studies of *Armeeabteilung* Kempf (commanded by General of Panzer Troops Werner Kempf) and Fourth Panzer Army. The reason for this difference is the absence of a writer who could have described details by drawing on his personal experiences. The study, however, remains valuable because its description of the battle within the Orel salient (which adjoined the area encompassed by Operation Citadel) shows how justified were Field Marshal Gunther von Kluge and Colonel General Walter Model when they objected to the decision to schedule the operation for as late a date as was actually set.

As directed, all authors who collaborated in writing the chapters on the operations of individual field armies and the Luftwaffe have expressed their opinions regarding the reasons for the failure of the operation. They did so in order to illustrate the perspective of each participating major command.

The maps available for the preparation of this study were inadequate. The following maps were available:

A. German map, scale 1:3,000,000, reduced from 1:1,000,000
B. U. S. map, scale 1:2,000,000
C. U. S. and German maps, scale 1:1,000,000
D. Assorted German Army and Luftwaffe maps, scale 1:300,000

The Situation on the Eastern Front, Spring, 1943

The German victory in the battle of Kharkov (5–31 March) brought the great Soviet winter offensive to a complete standstill and deprived the enemy of freedom of action. The effects of this victory were felt along the entire Eastern Front, though they were noticed primarily in the sector of Army Group South and in the southern part of the sector of Army Group

Center. A defensive line—continuous, though as yet not entirely consolidated—had again been established by both army groups. The enemy's exhaustion and the onset of the muddy season provided the time necessary to eliminate the existing deficiencies in manpower and equipment. Potential Eastern Front operations for 1943 had therefore been returned to a sound military basis despite the German defeat at Stalingrad and the ensuing loss of territory that followed.

The strategic and political situation of the Third Reich, on the other hand, was extremely unfavorable at this time, having taken a general turn for the worse for the first time since the start of the war. The growing superiority of the Western Allies became initially evident in the course of heavy bombing raids on Berlin. The Axis powers had lost Tunisia; the impact of this defeat on Italy and on Mussolini's position was not as yet clearly discernible, but it was bound to have a negative effect. Romania had lost two field armies during the winter battles of 1942–1943. The position of Marshal Antonescu [of Romania] (who derived his power solely from the military) had been severely shaken. The limit of his country's military capabilities had undoubtedly been reached. Thus the principal European allies of the Third Reich had turned into very uncertain factors. Germany therefore needed a tangible victory if this situation was to take a turn for the better, which meant that the political situation would necessarily influence command decisions on the conduct of military operations on the Eastern Front.

Soviet military strength had for the moment been exhausted by the winter offensive and by the German counterattack at Kharkov. The Russian winter offensive nonetheless achieved a larger measure of success than the STAVKA had perhaps anticipated at the outset, though losses in men and material—particularly in tanks—were heavy. It would certainly take longer than the duration of the muddy season to restore front-line Red Army units to full fighting strength. OKH calculated that the Soviets were not going to be ready to launch a new offensive until perhaps the end of June.

By the end of April it was impossible to forecast a clear picture of Soviet intentions. It remained to be seen whether the Soviets were going to seize the initiative again by launching an all-out offensive at the earliest possible moment, or whether the Red Army would remain on the defensive until the expected German attack had been repulsed, and then inaugurate a counteroffensive. One thing was certain: The Soviets would not remain passively on the defensive. This assumption was borne out by the demands of the Allies and by Soviet successes during the winter offensive.

By the beginning of May certain dispositions of Soviet strategic reserves and potential points of main effort became clear (see Map 1.1):

1. Three groupings opposite the right flank and center of Army Group South, in Areas A, B, and C.
2. One major grouping (five or six armies), containing numerous tank units, located opposite the northern flank of Army Group South and opposite the southern flank of Army Group Center, in Area D.
3. One strong grouping opposite the eastern and northern sectors of the Orel salient, in Area E.
4. One grouping opposite the center of Army Group North, in Area F.
5. One group of strategic reserves controlled by the STAVKA, located in the vicinity of Moscow, in Area G.

Foreign Armies East [*Fremde Heer Ost*—German military intelligence] evaluated the strength of the Red Army forces in each of these areas, concluding that the Soviet main effort could be expected against Army Group South.[11] The STAVKA's objective was apparently to penetrate between Army Groups Center and South in order to push Army Groups South and A into the sea. In conjunction with this offensive, the enemy was expected to attack Army Group Center from Area E. The objective of this subsidiary operation was probably to cut off the Orel salient and thereafter create a final, conclusive rupture of the German front. By comparison, any operations that could be expected from the remaining assembly areas were of minor significance.

Hitler was determined to regain the initiative on the Eastern Front completely. The counteroffensive at Kharkov represented the first step in this direction. Maintaining the initiative against the Soviet Union in 1943 had become critical, because this was bound to be the last year that the Third Reich could reasonably expect to be operating unencumbered by the threat of a second front established in the West. Everyone, including Hitler, OKH, and the army group and army commanders, thoroughly agreed on this point, though opinions on the solution to the problem at hand naturally differed. The following were presumed to be the alternatives:

1: Offensive-defensive action, which meant allowing the Soviets to attack first, and then switching to a counterattack. This solution was advocated by Colonel General Kurt Zeitzler, the chief of the Army General Staff; Lieutenant General Adolf Heusinger, chief of the operations detachment at OKH; and Field Marshals Gunther von Kluge and Erich von Manstein, the commanders of Army Groups Center and South.[12] These officers emphasized that the issue was not to hold terrain but to defeat the Red Army in an offensive-defensive action. They believed this course of action would more likely lead to success, in view of the existing strength ratio between the combatants. Once the Soviet forces had been irrevocably committed in attack, the counterattack would strike the enemy while he was in motion, following a period of elastic defense. The superior quality of German leadership and troops, which had again been proven in the battle of Kharkov, would more likely neutralize Soviet numerical superiority and produce a victory than the prospect of holding the entire length of an overextended front while simultaneously attacking and penetrating a belt of enemy fortifications before the armies could come to grips in open terrain.

2: Strike the first blow in order to smash Soviet attack preparations decisively at an early date, which would thereby make it impossible for the Red Army to launch a major offensive during 1943.

Hitler decided on the second solution, time and again dismissing the first solution because he flatly rejected the idea of any voluntary loss of territory. Always suspicious when this question arose, he feared that defensive-offensive action would begin with a calculated loss of territory that would start the entire front into a retrograde movement that could never be arrested again. He argued further that he did not have time to wait for Stalin to oblige him by launching an offensive, especially in view of the coming invasion in the West.

Thus the decision to strike the first blow had been made. The question then became where to strike. The following factors assumed decisive importance in the solution of this problem:

1. Where could we most effectively strike at Soviet attack preparations?
2. Where could we find an area/objective that corresponded to the limited size of the forces we would have available for the attack?
3. When should the attack take place?

Our appreciation of Red Army concentrations at that time strongly suggested that the point of main effort should be placed in the vicinity of Kharkov and north thereof. That was where it would be possible to hit Soviet offensive preparations most effectively, with the best prospect of ruining the enemy's own offensive plans. The Kursk salient encompassed a limited area that corresponded to the strength of the forces at our disposal. Once this salient had been pinched off, the objective could be considered to have been achieved while simultaneously conserving German strength as a result of shortening the front line.

As to the timing of the operation, everyone agreed that it had to be launched as soon as possible. We could only hope to strike a successful blow while Soviet forces had not yet regained their full fighting power—while their strategic concentrations were incomplete and the terrain remained insufficiently fortified. An early attack might also secure a certain degree of surprise, though other factors would eventually render it useless to hope for this.

During the muddy season major operations by either side were precluded, and we could not hope to attack immediately after its end. The muddy season could only be expected to last through the end of April or beginning of May, even in the event of unfavorable weather. In view of our heavy losses during the winter battles, it would be impossible to reorganize the German divisions earmarked for the attack by that time. The major stumbling block was the speed at which the panzer divisions could be reequipped with tanks. Thus the jump-off date for the operation was tentatively set for the earliest date considered practicable: on or about 25 May. Delays immediately occurred in the provision of new tanks to the panzer divisions, particularly the new Pzkw V Panthers. When it became necessary to postpone the first tentative date, OKH and the front-line headquarters agreed that the operation would have to be launched by mid-June at the latest in order to retain the essential prerequisites of success. Hitler nonetheless postponed the deadline once again during early May, primarily in consideration of arguments made by Colonel General Model, commander of the Ninth Army. The Soviets had persistently strengthened their fortifications opposite the Ninth Army sector and moved new forces into the depth of the projected attack zone. Model demanded additional infantry and panzer units to match these enemy increases, as well as more tanks for the panzer divisions already at his disposal. Moreover, as the result of the inadequacy of the communications net and the partisan threat to its rear areas, Ninth Army had also lagged considerably behind *Armeeabteilung* Kempf and Fourth Panzer Army with regard to strategic buildup, reorganization, troop training, and the stockpiling of supplies. Field Marshal von Manstein, with OKH approval, firmly voiced his opposition to any further postponement of the operation. He believed that additional delay would melt away the essential prerequisites for the success of the attack, but Hitler ultimately designated 5 July as the start date for Operation Citadel.

Forces and Missions

The OKH plan of operations provided for a concentric attack against Kursk by Army Group South (issuing from the shoulder on both sides of Belgorod) and Army Group Center (issuing from the sector west of Malo-arkhangel'sk). The objective was to seal off the salient along the line Belgorod-Kursk-Malo-arkhangel'sk; to establish a new, shorter defensive line; to destroy Red Army forces cut off in the salient; and to engage and defeat the strongest possible Soviet forces from STAVKA's strategic reserves.

The following forces were available:

ARMY GROUP SOUTH
Five corps headquarters
Eight infantry divisions
Nine panzer/panzergrenadier divisions
Various Army troops
Luftflotte Six

ARMY GROUP CENTER
Five corps headquarters
Fifteen infantry divisions
Six panzer divisions
One panzergrenadier division
Various Army troops
Luftflotte Four

TOTAL
Twenty-five infantry divisions
Sixteen mobile divisions.

Six of the infantry divisions (two with Army Group South, four with Army Group Center) were still holding front-line sectors at the time the attack commenced. They could only be released for commitment after the offensive had started.

The army groups received the following missions within the scope of this plan (see Map 1.2):

Army Group South: break through enemy positions out of the line Belgorod-Gertsovka (sixteen kilometers north-northeast of Borisovka); drive a sharp wedge toward Kursk via Oboyan; aggressively screen the eastern flank; and seek contact with Ninth Army on the heights north of Kursk. All available forces were to be concentrated for the destruction of Red Army units sealed off in the salient, following the establishment of a new main battle line as follows: course of the Koreniyo and Rayevka Rivers—west bank of the Don Simina up to its mouth; along the heights east of the Seim River to a point east of Kursk.

Army Group Center (Ninth Army): break through between the Orel-Kursk highway and railroad (and on both sides of the railroad); penetrate to Kursk while driving spearheads sufficiently far to the east so that the new front established guaranteed use of the railroad. The seizure of Malo-arkhangel'sk would secure contact between the

Ninth and Second Panzer Armies. After achieving these objectives, Ninth Army and Second Panzer Army were to be committed in a concentric attack for the purpose of eradicating any Soviet forces remaining in the salient.

Estimates of the Soviet Situation Through the Beginning of July

By the beginning of July the enemy situation on the southern part of the Eastern Front had clarified significantly. The picture of grouped strategic reserves, which had first emerged in April, had been confirmed in its basic outline. That assembly areas appeared to have moved closer to the front indicated that many units had completed their reorganization and were ready for combat.

Foreign Armies East provided the following appreciation of the location and strength of individual groupings in the Soviet strategic reserves (see Map 1.3):

AREA A
   Two army headquarters
   Two rifle corps headquarters
   Thirteen rifle units
   Five tank/mechanized units

AREA B
   Three army headquarters
   Five rifle corps headquarters
   Five tank/mechanized corps headquarters
   Twenty-four rifle units
   Twenty-five tank/mechanized units

AREA C
   One army headquarters
   One tank army headquarters
   Six rifle corps headquarters
   Twenty-six rifle units
   Seven tank/mechanized units

AREA D
   One army headquarters
   One tank army headquarters
   Two rifle corps headquarters

Two tank/mechanized corps headquarters
Twenty-eight rifle units
Seventeen tank/mechanized units

AREA E

Two army headquarters
One rifle corps headquarters
Five tank/mechanized corps headquarters
Five rifle units
Twenty-five tank/mechanized units

AREA F

One tank army headquarters
Two tank/mechanized corps headquarters
Seven rifle units
Fourteen tank/mechanized units

AREA G

Five rifle units
Eight tank/mechanized units

AREA H

One tank army headquarters
Two rifle corps headquarters
One tank/mechanized corps headquarters
Five rifle units
Eight tank/mechanized units

AREA I

Six army headquarters
Two rifle corps headquarters
One tank/mechanized corps headquarters
Thirty-three rifle units
Eight tank/mechanized units

TOTAL

Fifteen army headquarters
Four tank army headquarters
Twenty rifle corps headquarters
Seventeen tank/mechanized corps headquarters
146 rifle units
121 tank/mechanized units

A well-constructed, heavily mined defensive system, echeloned in depth, had been developed along the entire front. In some sectors, as in the Belgorod area and the salient south of Orel, this defensive system had attained a depth of up to twenty-five kilometers; these sectors in particular were heavily mined and contained numerous antitank obstacles. Red Army strength in these sectors had, moreover, grown substantially since April and May. The city of Kursk itself was heavily fortified. Details of the Soviet defenses in the forward areas of each of the field armies are contained in those individual chapters.

OKH derived the following estimate of Soviet strategy:

1: The Soviets were ready for action.

2: They expected a German attack aimed at cutting off the Kursk salient.

3: They planned to wait for this attack to be launched and would only counterattack after determining its full extent.

4: They wanted to hold the Kursk salient under all circumstances, for it would have to serve as the springboard for the main attacks of their own offensive. Aside from the increased commitment of troops to the front lines and the feverish construction of defensive positions, the grouping of strategic reserves behind this sector can be argued as evidence for this conclusion. These reserves were so deployed as to allow the Red Army to counteract the German attack both in the northern and southern half of the Kursk salient. The Soviets had positioned themselves to do this by having the Steppe Front attack from the east while the Central and Voronezh Fronts attacked from the west.

5: Once the Soviets felt that they had contained the German attack, they would commence offensive operations against the Donets Basin and the Orel salient. Judging by enemy preparations, it was reasonable to assume that the Soviets would launch their attack against the Orel salient first. Foiling this plan would require the Ninth Army's attack to smash through with such impact that the Red Army would be forced to employ sizable elements from its Bryansk Front and STAVKA reserves to contain the German attack.

6: Whether the forces of the Southwestern Front were going to strike south of Kharkov or counterattack the southern flank of Army Group South's attack force remained, in the final analysis, to be determined by the course of the German attack.

Both OKH and the front-line headquarters expected the attack to succeed, provided it could be launched before mid-June. This would allow the German offensive to strike and defeat substantial elements of the Soviet reserves that certainly would not yet have recovered their full combat strength. If Red Army forces in the Kursk salient could be quickly sealed off and destroyed by a series of rapid assault penetrations by the panzer divisions, the Soviets would also be deprived of their most important base of operations at Kursk, which would have thoroughly disrupted their own offensive plans.

This confident expectation changed along with the enemy situation and the postponement of the date of attack beyond 10 June. Toward the end of June, this change in the general outlook, along with the impossibility of changing Hitler's with regard to striking the first blow, led to deliberations about the advisability of quickly regrouping to launch a surprise attack from the west, possibly on both sides of Rylsk. This attack had the potential to split the salient in two, followed by the reduction of each segment individually. OKH and the army groups eventually rejected this solution due to terrain factors such as road connections in the assembly area; numerous defiles and waterways running perpendicular to the direction of attack; and the belief that the time required to redeploy troops and supplies would necessitate a further postponement of the attack. Such a solution would have constituted a very artificial operation and would certainly not have led to the desired shortening of the front lines. Moreover, this operation would have required a frontal assault, which would have rendered it nearly impossible to batter and obliterate a desirable number of Soviet forces. This option did not advance beyond a state of deliberation, and the original attack plan was maintained despite the doubts that had arisen in many places.

During the rest period prior to the offensive, the state of training, equipment, and morale of the units earmarked to participate reached the highest peak ever attained heretofore and thereafter during the entire Russian campaign. The assault divisions and army troops moved quickly and efficiently into their assembly areas.

Within Army Group South's sector, *Armeeabteilung* Kempf's XI Corps (320th, 106th, and, subsequently, 198th Infantry Divisions) was assigned to screen aggressively along the right flank of the main effort of Fourth Panzer Army once the offensive began. To this end, *Armeeabteilung* Kempf had to push its right wing to the Koren River, with the pivotal point of this move being located south of Toplinka Station. If events developed favorably, the XI Corps advance would be extended to the Korocha River, allowing the *Armeeabteilung* to screen its own panzer forces against the enemy concentration at Kuplansk.

After breaching the Soviet defenses, *Armeeabteilung* Kempf's III Panzer Corps (6th, 7th, and 19th Panzer Divisions) would penetrate in the direction of Korocha as rapidly as possible. These divisions were to engage and defeat the strong reserve force located and identified there in order to gain freedom of movement for further operations. According to the development of the battle, this would come either in the form of a thrust northeast or north in conjunction with the right wing of the Fourth Panzer Army. In anticipation of such an opportunity, III Panzer Corps initially deployed its right wing astride the Razumnaya sector and its left to the west of the Belgorod-Kursk highway.

The main attack against Kursk and responsibility for quickly establishing contact with Ninth Army fell to Fourth Panzer Army. We anticipated that enemy reserves (chiefly tank units) could be expected to approach rapidly from the east before the linkup could occur. That these forces would have to be engaged in the vicinity of Prokhorovka had been recognized as a prerequisite for the overall success of the operation. Thus II SS Panzer Corps on the right flank of Fourth Panzer Army (consisting of elements of the 167th Infantry Division and the *Liebstandarte Adolf Hitler*, *Das Reich*, and *Totenkopf* SS Panzergrenadier Divisions) was deployed in a parallel echelon to the right on both sides of Volkhovets, ready to push to Prokhorovka.

Fourth Panzer Army's XLVIII Panzer Corps (consisting of elements of the 167th and 332nd Infantry Divisions; 3rd and 11th Panzer Divisions; *Grossdeutschland* Panzergrenadier Division; and 10th Panzer Brigade) had to break through enemy positions on both sides of Butovo and execute a swift thrust to the south bank of the Pena River while maintaining contact with II SS Panzer Corps. XLVIII Panzer Corps's primary mission, upon reaching the Pena River, was to cover the left flank of II SS Panzer Corps against strong Soviet tank forces presumed to be in the vicinity of Oboyan.

In addition to staging a diversionary attack on the left flank of Fourth Panzer Army, LII Corps (consisting of the 255th and 57th Infantry Divisions) had to cover the western flank of XLVIII Panzer Corps on the day prior to the attack. After pulling its elements out of XLVIII Panzer Corps's sector, LII Corps would then follow in the wake of the armored attack, echeloned to the left.

In the area of Army Group Center, XLVII Panzer Corps (consisting of the 6th Infantry Division and the 2nd, 9th, and 20th Panzer Divisions) had been deployed to deliver Ninth Army's main blow. The corps would break through between the highway and railroad leading to Kursk, then advance swiftly to the high ground south of the city, there establishing contact with Army Group South.

The flanks of this narrow-chested wedge were protected in the following manner:

Right flank: XLVI Panzer Corps, consisting of 7th, 31st, 102nd, and 258th Infantry Divisions; and *Gruppe* von Mantueffel.

Left Flank: XLI Panzer Corps, consisting of 86th and 292nd Infantry Divisions; 10th Panzergrenadier Division; and 18th Panzer Division.

XLVI Panzer Corps, maintaining close contact with the XLVII Panzer Corps main attack, had to push its left flank to the line Chern Criik-Patesh. Thereafter the right wing of XLVI Panzer Corps would be advanced to its first objective—the Svapa sector—together with XX Corps as soon as the attack had progressed far enough to permit such an action.

Similarly, XLI Panzer Corps, its main effort placed astride the railroad, would push south approximately to the vicinity of Olkhovatka. Veering sharply to the east, XLI Panzer Corps had to reach the heights east of the Snova sector, establishing a new line as it halted.

To the far left flank of Ninth Army, XXIII Corps (consisting of 78th Assault Division, 216th and 385th Infantry Divisions) was to take Maloarkhangel'sk and establish a new line east of the railroad, though leaving its left wing in its existing position.

Located on far right flank of Ninth Army, XX Corps (45th, 72nd, 137th, and 251st Infantry Divisions) initially had only to hold its position. As soon as Soviet forces began withdrawing in front of its sector as a result of the main attack, XX Corps was to form three groups and strike out toward Dmitriy-Lgovski, Deryugino, and Mikhaylovka.

The 36th Infantry Division and 12th Panzer Division both remained in Army Group reserve behind the XLVII Panzer Corps sector.

The Course of the Battle, 5–9 July

Fourth Panzer Army opened the battle with a preliminary attack at 1500, 4 July, in order to seize certain absolutely necessary observation sites for use during the artillery preparation prior to the main attack. The attack seized these points in every instance. The offensive itself commenced on the morning of 5 July, though the actual hour of attack differed in various sectors.

The attack penetrated the enemy line at all but a few points. In slugging their way through the enemy defense system, German troops experienced great difficulties. Clinging tenaciously to their positions, the Russians everywhere defended themselves stubbornly. The lack of a sufficient number of infantry divisions in the attack—which had been pointed out repeatedly by army and army group headquarters—became painfully evident on the very first day as our troops began fighting their way through the Soviet defenses.

Enemy countermeasures on 5 July were confined to counterthrusts by tactical reserves. On 6 July the Red Army launched powerful counterattacks with reserves located close to the front lines (rifle divisions and tank brigades). These tactics confirmed that the Soviets intended to hold the Kursk salient at all costs for use as an operational base. This determination manifested itself particularly in front of Ninth Army.

Repulsing numerous counterattacks while engaged in a fierce battle on 7 July, *Armeeabteilung* Kempf's XI Corps reached the terrace six kilometers west of the Belgorod-Volchansk railroad. In some places XI Corps spearheads had penetrated into the tree belt on the west bank of Koren Creek before repeated, tank-supported Russian attacks forced the corps to assume the defensive. Upon this line XI Corps stood like a rock wall, fulfilling its mission although holding position further to the west than called for in its attack orders.

During the night of 5–6 July, III Panzer Corps moved its elements to the west bank of the Donets, with the 6th Panzer Division moving up behind the 7th Panzer. The main body of the 168th Infantry Division launched a combined attack with the 19th Panzer against Soviet positions on the heights northeast of Belgorod, from whence it had so far been impossible to dislodge the enemy. This attack was likewise unsuccessful; the heights were not secured until 9 July, when the combined 6th and 19th Panzer Divisions crashed through to the heights in the vicinity of Melekhovo. This thrust, staged from the northwest, resulted in the complete capture of Belgorod heights, wiping out two Red Army divisions. Employing mobile defensive tactics during this period, the 7th Panzer Division—adjoining XI Corps—repulsed strong attacks from the east in the area southeast of Melekhovo; though successful, the division was thus tied down in this area.

Thus *Armeeabteilung* Kempf was still fighting within the Russian defensive system at the end of July 9. The final position of this system ran approximately along a line extending east and north of Melekhovo to Sasnoye Station, through which the *Armeeabteilung* had not managed to reach open terrain before Soviet reserves began to participate in the action. The Germans had been engaging these reserves out of the Korocha area since 7 July.

On 5–6 July, II SS Panzer Corps, deployed on the right wing of Fourth Panzer Army, battled through two Russian defensive belts in bitter fighting. The SS advance was especially hampered by the flanking threat from the east that had developed when *Armeeabteilung* Kempf's left wing had been halted. Continuous enemy attacks—first by infantry and, starting 7–8 July, by tanks—tied down the SS *Totenkopf* Panzergrenadier Division until the 167th Infantry Division arrived, setting back the corps's schedule. Since 8 July, II SS Panzer Corps had been engaged with two or three newly arrived Russian tank corps (II Guards Tank Corps and the XVIII and XXIX Tank Corps). By the evening of 9 July, SS *Liebstandarte Adolf Hitler* and *Das Reich* were just north and northeast of Belenikhino Station, slowly fighting their way forward on either side of the railway leading to Kursk, as *Totenkopf* slowly closed up along their left flank.

The XLVIII Panzer Corps had to overcome thundershowers, a muddy creek bed, and soggy ground while fighting bitter individual engagements in the enemy's defensive system. On 6 July the corps finally broke through the first belt of enemy defenses and at one point penetrated the second belt. The following day XLVIII Panzer Corps found its efforts finally crowned with success, as the 11th Panzer Division and *Grossdeutschland* Panzergrenadier Division thrust along either side of the highway to Oboyan to a point just eleven kilometers south of the town. The 3rd Panzer Division trailed behind the spearhead units while the 332nd Infantry Division, echeloned in depth, advanced northeast on both sides of Zavidovka.

Powerful Russian counterattacks launched from the northeast, north, and west hit XLVIII Panzer Corps's spearheads on the morning of 8 July. These attacks continued with undiminished fury throughout 9 July, requiring the 11th Panzer and *Grossdeutschland* to make maximum efforts to repulse them. Simultaneously, dug-in Soviet infantry supported by tanks holding out stubbornly in the Pena River bend north of Zavidovka forced the Germans to stage a deliberate assault. Elements of LII Corps relieved the 332nd Infantry Division from its position on both sides of Zavidovka, allowing it to conduct a coordinated attack with the 3rd Panzer Division from 8–10 July that ejected the Russians from the Pena River bend but could not eliminate them completely. By the evening of 9 July, therefore, XLVIII Panzer Corps's position had somewhat improved.

Ninth Army succeeded in effecting a fourteen-kilometer penetration at its point of main effort during the initial assault. This attack carried XLVII and XLI Panzer Corps to the line Zaborovka-Ponirts-Poniri on 6 July. Unfortunately, XLVI Panzer Corps gained little ground, and the XXIII Corps attack on Malo-arkhangel'sk failed. Newly arrived Russian forces (one tank corps, three rifle divisions) engaged the German panzer spearheads on 6 July. The fury of these counterattacks intensified, their number multiplied, and the Soviets finally struck all along Ninth Army's wedge on 7 July. Nonetheless, the German attack continued to gain ground toward the south, where they slowly advanced on a ten-kilometer-wide front before grinding to a halt on 9 July in front of a new, heavily occupied position on the high ground around Olkhovatka.

The Course of the Battle, 10–17 July

Colonel General Model wanted to complete his breakthrough of the enemy defensive belt on 12 July by shifting the main attack effort to XLVI Panzer Corps, which was to receive the 36th Infantry Division and 12th

Panzer Division from Army Group Center's reserve. The Soviets thwarted this plan on 11 July by attacking the Second Panzer Army on the eastern face of the Orel salient, chalking up considerable success. The resulting situation forced Field Marshal von Kluge to discontinue Ninth Army's Kursk attack in order to make elements available for use in the defensive battle within the Orel salient.

Meanwhile, by the evening of 11 July, the situation in Army Group South's sector had developed as follows:

1: On the front of *Armeeabteilung* Kempf, XI Corps had achieved a great defensive success in destroying all of sixty Russian tanks that had broken through in its sector. The corps had a firm hold on its position.

2: The III Panzer Corps had stalled in front of the last enemy position along a line running west and north of Melekhovo to Sasnoye Station. The 198th Infantry Division finally relieved the 7th Panzer Division in the evening of 10 July. With the 168th Infantry Division now closing up the left flank of the corps, the command was now in a position to consider the consolidation of all its force for an assault on the enemy line.

On the morning of 11 July, Field Marshal von Manstein held a conference with General of Panzer Troops Werner Kempf, commander of the *Armeeabteilung*, and Colonel General Hermann Hoth, commander of Fourth Panzer Army. The field marshal proposed the following question: Should the attack be continued, considering the condition of the troops, the ever-increasing strength of the Russians, and—particularly—the fact that Ninth Army's assault had ground to a complete halt by 9 July? General Kempf favored suspending the attack. General Hoth advocated a continuation of the operation with the more limited objective of destroying the Red Army units south of the Psel River by a coordinated attack of both armies. Sharing Hoth's opinion, von Manstein reserved his final decision pending a conference with General of Panzer Troops Hermann Breith, commander of III Panzer Corps, so that the army group commander could personally study the situation and observe the condition of the troops. This visit confirmed von Manstein's point of view, and he ordered the attack resumed on the basis of Hoth's proposal.

Pursuant to this order, III Panzer Corps attacked enemy positions in the afternoon of 11 July, breaking through and—by evening—advancing to the vicinity of Oskotshnoye. On the right flank, 7th Panzer attacked east of Razumnaya, while the left flank (19th Panzer) was on the Donets River; the 168th Infantry screened the extended flank along the Donets against tank-supported Red Army units attacking the eastern flank of Fourth Panzer Army.

German arms had won a great victory, and III Panzer Corps was at last on open ground, prepared to bring the maneuverability of its three panzer divisions into play.

Meanwhile, on 10 July Fourth Panzer Army had started assembling II SS Panzer Corps for the attack on Prokhorovka, while the XLVIII Panzer Corps successfully repulsed continuing heavy attacks and cleared the Pena River bend of the enemy (which was accomplished on 11 July).

Liebstandarte Adolf Hitler and *Das Reich* gained but little ground toward Prokhorovka on 11 July, but with the addition of *Totenkopf* to the attack, II SS Panzer Corps managed to establish a bridgehead across the Psel River bend southwest of Dmitriyeskoye. XLVIII Panzer Corps spent the day in heavy defensive fighting, repulsing all attacks, inflicting heavy losses, and even capturing over 100 encircled tanks despite the enemy's best efforts to prevent them from doing so.

That evening, however, Field Marshal von Manstein received word of the adverse developments in Army Group Center's sector. He understood immediately that the entire offensive was threatened when Ninth Army's attack bogged down, enabling the Soviets to turn south with full force. Left to its own devices, Army Group South must expect more days of bitter fighting. Nevertheless, von Manstein adhered to the decision to continue with the limited-objective attack. This was the only way we could hope to hurt the Russian forces with which we were already in contact, as well as those that, according to all intelligence reports, we would encounter within the next few days. The field marshal hoped that by continuing the battle our divisions might gain the freedom of action necessary to withdraw to their original jump-off positions—a move that was certainly going to become necessary later on.

Thus nothing was changed in the order that had just been issued: *Armeeabteilung* Kempf would wheel around and move against the flank and rear of the Soviet Sixty-ninth Army, which was heavily engaged with German units on the eastern flank of Fourth Panzer Army. The Red Army committed fresh forces (V Mechanized Corps against *Armeeabteilung* Kempf; XVIII and XXIX Tank Corps, 13th Guards Rifle Division, and 219th Rifle Division against Fourth Panzer Army) and launched a coordinated attack against both armies on the morning of 12 July. *Armeeabteilung* Kempf repulsed all attacks on 12–13 July but remained tied down in defensive fighting to such an extent that it could not as yet consider wheeling northwest; however, the necessary bridgeheads over the Donets River were secured.

By the morning of 14 July, 6th and 7th Panzer Divisions had defeated the Russians in their front, driving them off toward the north and opening the road to Korocha. In our desire to capitalize on this success, we were tempted to take this important traffic center, but considering the overall situation, Field Marshal von Manstein decided that the thrust to the northwest would be carried out as originally ordered. While 6th Panzer Division remained behind in the area west of Novaya Sloboda, 7th and 19th Panzer Divisions debouched from the bridgehead southeast of Oskochnoye, advancing to take Zhilomostnoye and the terrain east of the town by the evening of 14 July. This reestablished contact with the right wing of Fourth Panzer Army. At the same time, 168th Infantry Division pulled out from its position along the Donets and was moving toward Novaya Sloboda to relieve 6th Panzer.

Fourth Panzer Army repulsed all attacks on 12–13 July without losing a foot of ground. A local crisis on the western flank in the area of Bogaty—caused by the attack of a Russian tank corps—was also mastered. On 14 July, II SS Panzer Corps resumed its attack, pushing to the outskirts of Prokhorovka. Simultaneously while pursuing the enemy, XLVIII Panzer Corps forced its left wing so far to the north that it gained observation points overlooking the Psel River valley west of Oboyan.

For Army Group South, 14 July brought complete success along the entire front, and the enemy's offensive power appeared to have been broken. The requirements for cleaning out the southern bank of the Psel from Prokhorovka to a point north of Peny had been established. Pertinent orders for this operation had been issued, when the situation in Army Group Center and—within the area of our own army group—along the lines of Sixth Army and First Panzer Army now forced the abandonment of the attack. The Red Army had achieved such great success in the Orel salient that Army Group South had to transfer some of its forces to that area. On 17 July the enemy also launched the long-anticipated attack against Sixth Army (*Schwerpunkt* at Kubyhevo) and First Panzer Army (*Schwerpunkt* at Izyum). With the incomplete successes of 14 July, then, Operation Citadel had come to its end.

Conclusions

Operation Citadel did not produce the results desired by Hitler. The battle neither denied the Soviets a base of operations around Kursk nor destroyed sizable enemy forces, nor even eliminated the STAVKA's intention to conduct a major offensive in 1943. The German Army did not achieve freedom of action, could not establish a shorter line designed to conserve its waning strength, and—quite the contrary—the operation used up almost all reserves on the Eastern Front.

This failure must not be ascribed to the troops or to front-line leadership; both gave their all and demonstrated that they could cope with any situation.[13] Particularly the spirit, bearing, and selfless devotion of the men were beyond praise. Untroubled by decisions affecting higher strategy, our soldiers went confidently into battle, and—despite the battle's outcome—the men of Army Group South came out of the operation with a feeling that they had remained victors over an enemy vastly superior in men and material. The reasons for the failure are to be found elsewhere.

One fact must be established. Hitler was correct in arguing that 1943 would be the last year in which the absence of an actual threat in the West permitted a maximum effort in Russia. As far as time was concerned, this was the last opportunity to deliver a crushing blow to Soviet offensive power before an invasion occurred in the West. But did this plan have to be carried out by striking the first blow, especially considering the disparity in German and Russian strength?

During the winter of 1942–1943, the severe battles in the course of the retreat from Stalingrad and the Caucasus had demonstrated the superiority of our operational leadership and our troops in mobile warfare. However, to force the enemy into an open battle by means of a breakthrough was an erroneous decision considering our limited forces, and in particular our inadequate number of infantry divisions. One did not have to wait for the experiences of this war to appreciate the drain on military strength that attends any breakthrough of well-fortified positions even if vast amounts of supplies are available. Time and again the commanders of armies and army groups, in agreement with OKH, urgently called attention to this most vulnerable point of the operation. The panzer and panzergrenadier divisions—nineteen if the uncommitted reserves of both army groups are counted—would have sufficed to gain a major victory—but only if they succeeded in reaching open terrain.

Appraising the situation in retrospect, we find that there is no doubt but that we could have employed a defensive-offensive action as had been urgently requested by OKH and the combat commanders. The overall strategic picture (in fact, the situation in the Mediterranean theater alone) forced the Red Army to attack in the summer of 1943, regardless of whether we did them the favor of making the first move. Hitler's fear that perhaps Stalin might not oblige him by launching an offensive, and that he himself would lose the last year in which freedom of action existed on the Eastern Front, would never have materialized.

Compared to the major reasons for the failure of the attack, other factors were only secondary in nature. These factors were:

1: The lack of sufficient infantry divisions forced us to employ the mobile units from the outset. The panzer and panzergrenadier divisions, therefore, expended their strength in the course of unaccustomed fighting in the system of fortifications before they could develop their primary assets—mobility and speed—in open terrain.

2: Furthermore, the panzer and panzergrenadier divisions had to protect their own extended flanks as the attack progressed, instead of having infantry available to relieve them of this mission.

3: By tying down the panzer units on the flanks, the attack wedges of both army groups (which were already extremely narrow because of our inadequate forces) were further reduced in width as the operation progressed, thereby critically diminishing the fighting power of these divisions.

4: The late timing of the operation played a critical role. All the dark forebodings of OKH and the combat commanders came true. Time worked for the Red Army in every respect. It could strengthen local defenses, refit its units (particularly with tanks), and divine our intentions. An operation that could be ventured against an unprepared enemy at the end of May or beginning of June amounted to a drastic mistake at the beginning of July in the face of a completely prepared enemy.

5: As a result of the late timing of the operation, every element of surprise had been eliminated. Had the attack begun sooner, under the prevailing circumstances, the location of the main effort would hardly have been a surprise to the enemy; now even the timing was no longer a surprise. By the employment of an excellent espionage system in his own country, the enemy was not only aware of our operational plan by the beginning of July, but he had also clearly been informed about many details. A rapid shift in the strategic concentration of troops and in deployment would have resulted in major disadvantages without ensuring a satisfactory measure of surprise.

In summary, the following can be established:

Operation Citadel failed because it was carried out with insufficient forces, considering the late timing of the operation. Furthermore, the Soviets had anticipated our line of action and had fully prepared for defensive and offensive maneuver. The year 1943 could have taken a different turn had the Red Army been made to expend its forces in a direct assault on our unbroken front, backed up by powerful mobile reserves. Instead, the Soviets were able to conduct their own offensive as a counterattack, with the main effort directed against our unsuccessful assault—a maneuver that expended all of our mobile forces.

APPENDIX 1A

German Military Intelligence and Soviet Strength, July 1943

The intelligence estimates cited by Busse in the text were admittedly drawn from memory and stated inexactly, but they do allow for some rough comparisons with actual Red Army strength in order to assess the effectiveness of German military intelligence activities. In the table below Busse's estimates have been matched against the highly detailed Soviet order of battle provided by David Glantz and Jonathan House in *The Battle of Kursk*.[14] Several items should be clarified. Army and tank army headquarters require no explanation. Corps headquarters have been interpreted as rifle corps headquarters, and "mobile corps" headquarters translated into tank, mechanized, or cavalry corps headquarters. "Rifle units" are assumed to refer to rifle divisions, and "mobile units" to mechanized brigades (but not motorized brigades) and tank brigades or separate regiments.

Front	German estimate	Soviet strength
Bryansk	Six army HQs	Three army HQs
	Two corps HQs	Five corps HQs
	One mobile corps HQ	One mobile corps HQ
	Thirty-two rifle units	Twenty-four rifle units
	Eight mobile units	Thirteen mobile units
Central	—	Five army HQs
	One tank army HQ	One tank army HQ
	Two corps HQs	Ten corps HQs
	—	Four mobile corps HQs
	Ten rifle units	Forty-two rifle units
	Sixteen mobile units	Twenty-nine mobile units
Voronezh	Two army HQs	Four army HQs
	One tank army HQ	One tank army HQ
	Two corps HQs	Eleven corps HQs
	Three mobile corps HQs	Five mobile corps HQs .
	Twenty-eight rifle units	Thirty-six rifle units
	Seventeen mobile units	Twenty-six mobile units
Steppe	Two army HQs	Five army HQs

—	One tank army HQs
One corps HQ	Seven corps HQs
Five mobile corps HQs	Ten mobile corps HQs
Five rifle units	Thirty-two rifle units
Twenty-five mobile units	Twenty-eight mobile units
	(plus nine cavalry units)

If the estimates that Busse recalled were approximately accurate, they reveal considerable information about the German failure at Kursk. As a general comment, the Germans apparently missed—almost completely—the extent to which the Red Army had managed to reintroduce corps headquarters as an intermediate level of command. This error had little actual impact on strength estimates but a tremendous influence on any appreciation of Soviet operational and tactical flexibility.

With respect to Bryansk Front, the Germans somewhat underestimated Russian strength, but not to a decisive degree; the same is also true of the Voronezh Front. Regarding the Central Front, facing Ninth Army, the Germans attacked an enemy at least four times as strong in terms of infantry, and nearly twice as strong in terms of tanks, than they expected. The fact that this was case, and not merely a failure of Busse's memory, is borne out by the artillery intelligence estimates presented in the appendixes for Chapter 4. The German forecast concerning Steppe Front's tank holdings proved to be relatively accurate, but they missed the concentration of nearly twenty rifle divisions.

Two provisional conclusions about these comparisons therefore emerge. The rapid failure of Ninth Army's attack from Orel becomes quite understandable when it is realized that even the suspicious Walter Model failed to credit the strength of the Soviet buildup there; not only were the Germans heavily outnumbered, but they were ignorant of just how badly the odds had been stacked against them. Along the Belgorod sector, by contrast, Army Group South appears to have had a good grasp of the Russian strength immediately opposed to it and of available armored units in strategic reserve. What von Manstein and Busse missed was the weight of additional rifle divisions that could be thrown into the defensive lines or used to threaten their extended flanks, especially that of *Armeeabteilung* Kempf.

To what extent did these German underestimates result from Russian deception measures? It is difficult to tell. In his groundbreaking study of Soviet military intelligence, David Glantz concludes that STAVKA "ordered strict measures to conceal the assembly and redeployment of the strategic reserve—the Steppe Military District," but he does not make an argument with respect to Central Front.[15] Now that Glantz and House have so carefully documented Soviet strength at the beginning of the campaign, intense forays into the existing files of German military intelligence are in order.

2

Armeeabteilung Kempf

by Colonel General Erhard Raus
Commander, XI Corps

Editor's Introduction

Considering the critical nature of its mission—covering the right flank of II SS Panzer Corps's drive toward Oboyan—*Armeeabteilung* Kempf suffered under arguably the greatest handicaps of the three major assault commands. General of Panzer Troops Werner Kempf not only possessed the weakest force (three panzer and three infantry divisions in the attack sector) but also had been saddled with the requirement of forcing three bridgeheads across the Donets River on the opening day of the offensive and penetrating five to eight kilometers into the Soviet defensive system. This would have been a difficult assignment under the best of conditions, but the *Armeeabteilung* barely possessed parity with its initial opponent, Lieutenant General Mikhail S. Shumilov's Seventh Guards Army. Under such conditions it is hardly surprising that the *Armeeabteilung* failed to achieve the goals set for it. Thus a major key to understanding the German defeat in Operation Citadel is necessarily an appreciation for the struggle of *Armeeabteilung* Kempf.[1]

When Theodor Busse assembled his team of writers for the Kursk study in 1947 he had four possible choices to tackle the chapter on the *Armeeabteilung*: Hans Speidel (chief of staff), Hermann Breith (commander, III Panzer Corps), Erhard Raus (commander, XI Corps), and Franz Mattenklott (commander, XLII Corps). Speidel would seemingly have been the first choice as the officer with the most relevant knowledge of the operation. Busse and Speidel, however, did not get along well together, and—equally important—Speidel's time was consumed with the preparation of studies on the anti-Hitler resistance in the German army, Field Marshal Erwin Rommel, and the Battle of Normandy. Among the corps commanders, Mattenklott did produce several manuscripts for the historical program, though his XLII Corps had such a peripheral role in the battle of Kursk that he would have brought little firsthand knowledge to the project.

Hermann Breith, leading the *Armeeabteilung*'s panzer spearhead, would therefore seem to have been a natural choice as the primary author, and it is probable that the single manuscript he produced for the U.S. Army (D-258) was a preliminary background contribution to the Operation Citadel project. This work itself, however, suggests several reasons why Busse would not have wanted Breith to expand the narrative to cover the operations of the entire command. As I observed in my introduction to Breith's essay, his "narrative of the battle is succinct, in places to the point of degenerating into a list of villages and daily troop movements." Moreover, as additional research on III Panzer Corps's operations since 1994 has shown, Breith's account of the initial assault is riddled with inaccuracies, a fact of which Busse would have been aware with even a superficial reading.[2]

Busse then found himself left with Erhard Raus, an officer who—like Speidel—contributed thousands of words to the historical program. Unlike Speidel, Raus had served exclusively in the east from 1941 to 1945 and preferred to write detailed tactical narratives rather than sweeping historical analyses. A close comparison of this chapter of the Kursk study with other writings by Raus reveals striking textual similarities (particularly compelling in the German version of the texts), as well as several places in which the author must have had especially detailed knowledge of XI Corps operations.

Comparison between this manuscript and others by Raus also led to an exciting discovery. It is no secret that Raus himself coordinated several groups of writers who turned out detailed publications on tactical aspects of the war in Russia. These studies, as David Glantz has noted, became exceptionally influential on U.S. views of the Russo-German war; they have recently been republished. Historians have also realized that significant portions of these studies covered actions in which Raus himself commanded, chopped by his U.S. editors into small bits and pieces to be scattered throughout. What has escaped general notice, even by Raus's biographer, is that the original German drafts underlying the later heavily edited and revised studies actually constitute a complete narrative memoir covering the war in Russia.[3]

The original manuscript remains lost, and may not still exist, but by taking the longer segments that lay behind the already published material, combining them with unpublished studies totaling nearly five times their length, and supplementing these with the text from several articles Raus published in *Allegemeine Schweizerische Militarzeitschrifte*, nearly the entire document can be reconstructed. In its scope and value as a historical source, the Raus memoir rivals the books of Guderian, von Manstein, and von Mellenthin. In some ways it is more valuable because Raus remained a field commander throughout the war, entering Russia at the head of a motorized brigade and working his way up to army command.

I am currently in the process of editing and annotating the entire Raus memoir for publication, and what appears below and in Chapter 10 can be considered an advanced excerpt, covering the period between February and August 1943. It should be noted that Chapter 2 differs somewhat from the draft originally included in the Busse study in that it is considerably longer and, in places, more detailed. All of the authors in the Kursk study touched on von Manstein's counteroffensive in February–March 1943, and it seemed appropriate to include the more extensive account that Raus wrote. Likewise, additional material that obviously belonged within this period in the larger memoir has been interwoven with the existing draft.

As can be seen in both excerpts in this book, Erhard Raus was an entertaining writer with a keen tactical eye—his narrative is easily more readable and less self-serving than Guderian's. His work is very much a Cold War period piece, in which the Germans fought hard but honorably against the malevolent Soviet hordes. He is at times incorrect in his chronology, and his anecdotes occasionally confuse similar events, people, and units. Such discrepancies are covered in the notes and when taken into account do little to harm the historical importance of his recollections.

The primary limitation (and at the same time the greatest strength) in the Raus memoir is its unrelenting focus on tactical warfare. Readers will not find character sketches or extended analyses of von Manstein or Model, and despite the best efforts of this editor, many of the junior officers fighting their small, intense battles for nameless Russian villages remain anonymous themselves—knowable only through their actions. That portion of the original work thus far unrecoverable appears primarily to be framing or transition material, wherein Raus could be expected to place the operations he commanded into the greater perspective of the war. This lack is not a significant problem with the segments presented here and will be handled in the larger publication with bridging material provided by the editor.

One final note is appropriate. Although there is significant overlap between material in the Raus memoir and sections of the related U.S. Army publications, careful readers will notice differences in syntax and translation. The U.S. officers who edited Raus for government publication did a considerable amount of smoothing, homogenizing, and sanitizing; despite protestations to the contrary, they sometimes altered his observations or conclusions. Where possible, this translation returns to the German manuscript materials and tries to recapture the original style and feel of his writing. Only when (and if) someone recovers the uncut manuscript text of Erhard Raus's memoirs will a final judgment on the accuracy of that process be possible.

Armeeabteilung Kempf
by Colonel General Erhard Raus
Commander, XI Corps

Defense and Recovery, February–March 1943

By 23 November 1942, the Red Army had closed the ring around Stalingrad and started the most powerful winter offensive of the war. Advancing rapidly, the Russians annihilated in quick succession the Romanian, Italian, and Hungarian armies along the Chir and Don Rivers, opening a 560-kilometer gap in the German front. This breach equaled the length of the entire Western Front in World War I. Initially, only isolated German divisions, committed in support of the allied and satellite forces, stood in the way of the Russians, like the stays of a corset. The bulk of German reserves—including five fully equipped panzer divisions—remained tied down in Western Europe because of the Allied invasion of North Africa, although some of these divisions later appeared on the Eastern Front. Army Group A, in the Caucasus, found itself in danger of being cut off, forcing an immediate withdrawal. The army group's motorized units (mainly First Panzer Army) redeployed along the Donets River in order to strengthen the southern wing of Army Group Don, while the Seventeenth Army remained for the time being in the Kuban area and formed a bridgehead there. North of the gap, Second Army had been forced to evacuate Voronezh and the Don Front, with its southern wing being pushed far back to the west. Gradually, two-thirds of the entire Russian front began to sway and crumble.

The front lines built up on the southern flank and along the Donets could not withstand the Russian pressure in the long run, and the only solution was to withdraw farther and farther to the west. The Kuban bridgehead was abandoned, the Seventeenth Army withdrawn without losses to the Crimea and—save two German and one Romanian corps—thrown by divisions into action in support of the new Sixth Army (formed from *Armeeabteilung* Hollidt) fighting desperately north of the Crimea along the Mius. The Red Army always had more units available than Field Marshal von Manstein's Army Group Don, and these were remanned and reequipped in case of need to fuel the continuing thrust to the west. By mid-February 1943 three Soviet armies were striving to reach Kharkov to take that important railroad junction in a concentric offensive. The Russians intended no less than to overcome the formidable obstacle represented by the Dnepr River before any German troops could establish themselves there. Signs of exhaustion among the Soviet spearhead formations had increased to such an extent, however, that it was possible for Field Marshal von Manstein to detach several panzer divisions from the front lines to the south at the same time that OKH sent up several more, completely rearmed and reequipped, from the West (most significantly the II SS Panzer Corps with the overstrength panzergrenadier divisions *Liebstandarte Adolph Hitler*, *Das Reich*, and *Totenkopfhr*).

In the wake of this impending disaster, the staff of XI Corps, which had been lost at Stalingrad, was reconstituted from an unassigned corps staff that was hastily organized in the beginning of February 1943. Formed in the area north of Kharkov, it originally consisted of Lieutenant General Hans Cramer and several General Staff officers who happened to be in this area on an inspection trip. The staff had to assume command over the 168th, 298th, and 320th Infantry Divisions, which had all been committed to cover sectors formerly held by Hungarian and Romanian forces.[4] These divisions lacked a higher headquarters after the collapse of Germany's allies on the Stalingrad front. The lower echelons of the staff were picked from the field units, and a Hungarian signal battalion (later replaced by a small German unit) took care of signal communications. The initial difficulties were being gradually overcome when I took command on 10 February, though it took six months and required numerous reassignments and organizational changes to transform the improvised corps staff into a regular one. Both the XI Corps (known officially as Provisional Corps Raus until midsummer) and II SS Panzer Corps were assigned to another improvised headquarters, *Armeeabteilung* Kempf.[5]

Some of the units assigned to XI Corps had been recently transferred from France, but others had been forced to fight their way out of repeated encirclements. For example, the 320th Infantry Division, which had held a sector on the Don Front with Italian divisions on its flanks, suddenly found itself behind Russian lines because of the rapid disintegration of our allied armies.[6] Major General Georg Postel, the division commander, decided to fight his way back to German lines. En route all of the 320th motor vehicles ran out of gasoline and had to be destroyed. The horse-drawn batteries and field trains also lost a tremendous number of animals in battle and from exhaustion. The division's fighting power and mobility were both thus severely impaired. To avoid the fate of so many other divisions at Stalingrad and along the Don, General Postel had to resort to desperate improvisations. What the division needed either had to be wrested from the Russians or taken from the land.

First, the troops procured hundreds of the small peasant *panje* horses for the light vehicles. Oxen pulled the medium artillery, while cattle and oxen served as draft animals for transporting radio and signal equipment. Even General Postel himself decided to use such a team as a sure means of transportation. The loss of many machine guns, antitank guns, and artillery pieces could be offset only by weapons captured from weak Red Army detachments in sporadic raids; the ammunition for these weapons also had to be taken from the enemy. Similar methods were employed to obtain rations. Small radio sets and other sensitive equipment had to be carried on litters. Infantrymen atop the *panje* horses were charged with reconnaissance and security. The difficult retreat of the 320th Infantry consumed several weeks and was an uninterrupted series of marches, combat actions, and improvisations.

As General Postel's division approached Kharkov on 13 February, it suddenly made radio contact with II SS Panzer Corps, defending the city, and asked for assistance in its attempt to break through to friendly lines. *Obergruppenfuehrer* Paul Hausser, commander of the II SS Panzer Corps, coordinated a strong panzer thrust out of his own lines with a simultaneous attack to the west by the 320th Infantry Division. Achieving tactical surprise, this attack pierced the Russian lines at the designated point, and the division was able to slip back into German lines.

The 320th Infantry Division's appearance hardly resembled that of a German army unit. A strange conglomeration of weapons, equipment, vehicles, and litters; small and large shaggy horses, oxen, and cows; all accompanied by soldiers in such a strange variety of winter clothing that the overall impression was that of a traveling circus on parade. Yet what General Postel led into Kharkov was a battle-tested unit with excellent morale that had courageously fought its way through enemy territory, had returned to its own lines, and was to be considered a precious addition to the *Armeeabteilung*'s strength.[7] By 14 February the 320th Infantry once again stood shoulder to shoulder with the *Liebstandarte Adolf Hitler* and *Das Reich* SS Panzergrenadier Divisions, as well as the *Grossdeutschland* Panzergrenadier Division, in the Kharkov defenses, facing east. The strong will to survive and the skillful improvisations demonstrated by General Postel and his soldiers had enabled the division to avoid destruction.[8]

Unfortunately, by 14 February, Kharkov itself had been surrounded by three Russian armies and its defenders ordered to hold out in a hopeless situation. In his last telephone message, *Obergruppenfuehrer* Hausser called attention to the seriousness of the situation and stated emphatically that the only choice was between losing the city alone or losing the city with all the troops in it. The reply was that "Kharkov must be held to the last man." On the following morning a second order came through by teletype stating that "Kharkov must be held to the last man, but the defenders must not allow themselves to be encircled." On the strength of this ambiguous order, the second part of which precluded the first, the encircled II SS Panzer Corps, the *Grossdeutschland* Panzergrenadier Division, and the 320th Infantry Division took immediate steps for a breakout to the rear without the knowledge or approval of the *Armeeabteilung*. After two days of hard fighting, which ended with the loss of several hundred motor vehicles, Hausser rejoined the German lines, having saved five divisions. His decision to evacuate the city would soon be proven correct.

The next Soviet thrust, aimed at Poltava, ground to a halt about fifty kilometers short of that city because the Russian troops had become too exhausted to continue. Now the Soviets placed all their hopes in the Third Tank Army, commanded by their most capable tank expert, Colonel General Markian M. Popov.[9] Throughout mid-February, Popov had advanced practically without resistance in the direction northwest of Dnepropetrovsk with the apparent intention of reaching the Dnepr bend. His objective was to cross the Dnepr before the Germans could build up their defenses along the river. Soon, however, it became obvious that his forces lacked the necessary drive. XI Corps employed improvised truck transports to place regiments of the 167th and 168th Infantry Divisions in place to block the enemy's attempt to push forward against Poltava from Zenkhov and Oposhnya; after heavy fighting these regiments threw the Russians back across the Vorskla River.

During this fighting an incident occurred that proved the fact that it was not at all unusual for women to fight in front-line Red Army units. A Soviet T-34 was apparently rendered immobile by a direct hit, but when German tanks approached, it suddenly reopened fire and attempted to break out. A second direct hit again brought it to a standstill, but in spite of its hopeless position the T-34 defended itself until a tank-killer team advanced on it. Finally it burst into flames from a demolition charge and only then did the turret hatch open. A woman in a Red Army tanker uniform climbed out. She was the wife and crewmember of the Russian tank company commander who, killed by the first hit, lay beside her in the turret. So far as Russian soldiers were concerned, women in uniform were superiors or comrades to whom respect was paid.

Meanwhile, we were building up strength for a frontal counterattack (see Map 2.1). Divisions arriving from the west detrained at Poltava behind the defensive screen established by XI Corps. We held this line with our three infantry divisions and the reconnaissance battalion of the *Totenkopf* SS Panzergrenadier Division. *Totenkopf*'s other motorized elements, as well as the *Grossdeutschland* Panzergrenadier Division and the *Fuehrer Begleit* Panzergrenadier Battalion, had moved to rest areas west of Poltava but still close to the front. These units formed a mobile reserve to be committed in the event that the Red Army attempted to capture Poltava by an enveloping thrust through the gap to the north. The Russians actually tried to outflank Poltava through the Merla Valley, but our infantry divisions, supported by the *Totenkopf* battalion and tactical Luftwaffe units, eliminated this danger. During these actions the enemy showed definite signs of weakness and exhaustion, and the time for a major counterattack seemed to be approaching.

Quick action was indicated because the snow was beginning to thaw. Mud formed on the ground, and soon all movements would become impossible. But deep down the soil was still solidly frozen. Cold nights prevented a quick thaw and favored movements during the early morning hours. Meanwhile, *Armeeabteilung* Kempf's battle-weary front-line troops had been granted a short breathing spell and the opportunity to integrate newly arrived replacements and equipment. By 10 March the *Armeeabteilung*'s counterattack forces stood ready to jump off; their morale was excellent.

The XI Corps main effort had been placed on the southern wing of its front, where terrain conditions favored the employment of panzers. There *Grossdeutschland* was assembled and given the mission of attacking toward Valki. Adjacent on the left, 320th Infantry Division was to attack after an artillery preparation delivered by all guns in two divisions, supported by corps artillery. The two divisions had formed themselves for a *Schwerpunkt* attack, leaving in their broad front sectors only thin protective screens, which after the start of the offensive were to be withdrawn and follow the forward movement as reserves. Still very weak, the 168th Infantry Division remained around Mirograd, refitting.

After a formidable ten-minute artillery preparation, the grenadiers of the 320th Infantry Division penetrated the Russian positions, mopped up a strongpoint on the main Poltava-Kharkov highway, and threw the enemy back beyond a flooded brook on the other side of Valki. This normally insignificant watercourse had suddenly grown into a raging torrent, which brought the attack to a halt after a gain of less than two kilometers. *Grossdeutschland*'s panzers attempted to overcome the swift current farther upstream and finally succeeded in crossing several hours later. More than eighty panzers broke through the second Russian position on the east bank of the brook and rolled toward Valki. Soon our engineers threw an improvised bridge across the brook, and the attack regained its momentum.

Farther north, the 167th and 168th Infantry Divisions also penetrated Soviet positions on their front after heavy fighting. These divisions captured a number of villages and attempted to establish contact with LI Corps of Second Army to the far left of the *Armeeabteilung*. The reinforced *Totenkopf* reconnaissance battalion, committed between the 320th and 167th Infantry Divisions, closed in on the Soviet positions situated in the woods and penetrated deeply into the forest. The battalion's light tanks advanced in heavy fighting along the railroad tracks running parallel to the woods. By afternoon, XI Corps had made progress along its entire front and kept the crumbling enemy on the move.

On 11 March XI Corps committed all its forces to a concentric attack on Bogodukhov. For this purpose the corps zone had been narrowed to sixteen kilometers (its width had already been reduced from ninety-five to forty kilometers at the end of the first day). The Russians defending Bogodukhov could not resist the onslaught of our ground troops, which were closely supported by the Luftwaffe. Bogodukhov fell after brief house-to-house fighting, and XI Corps then established contact with the spearheads of II SS Panzer Corps, which had just entered Olshany, twenty-four kilometers southeast. After annihilating strong Soviet forces in the Olshany area, *Obergruppenfuehrer* Hausser turned the corps he had saved from encirclement to the east, enveloping Kharkov and cutting off any Russian route of withdrawal to the north.

While XI Corps's main force received orders to advance northward in an attempt to establish contact with LI Corps and thereby isolate the enemy in the Akhtyrka area, I ordered the 320th Infantry Division to screen the pivoting movement of II SS Panzer Corps. Ever-increasing mud and floods slowed the advance at every step. Although all bridges across the swollen Vorskla, Udy, and Lopan Rivers had been destroyed, our infantry and panzer units nonetheless continued to reach their daily objectives. Many motor vehicles and horsedrawn artillery pieces, however, bogged down along the way. On the other hand, the considerably lighter artillery of the Russians and their *panje* wagons pulled through everywhere and escaped our pursuit.

Grossdeutschland carried the main effort and reached the upper Vorskla, with the 167th Infantry Division following closely behind. Since LI Corps on the southern wing of Second Army had lagged so far to the west, no contact with it could be established, and the Russians around Akhtyrka escaped encirclement. In order to continue the operation by a thrust on Tomarovka, our panzer elements had to pivot to the east, changing the direction of their attack. I replaced them with elements of the 167th Infantry Division, which formed a line facing north to provide flank cover. The advance on Tomarovka was delayed because territorial gains to the east automatically led to an extension of the open flank that our limited forces could not easily support.

By the second day of the thrust toward Tomarovka, the strong 167th Infantry Division had been almost entirely immobilized along the flank. I decided that we would have to await the arrival of LI Corps before the eastward thrust could be resumed. Unfortunately, OKH—which was responsible for coordinating the operations of the two army groups—was too far removed from the scene, and its decisions therefore failed to keep abreast of the fast-moving events at the front. When OKH finally ordered LI Corps to relieve the 167th Infantry, we continued our advance and *Grossdeutschland* entered Tomarovka. On its approach to the town, *Grossdeutschland* destroyed a considerable number of Russian tanks while many undamaged ones that had bogged down in the mud were retrieved and turned against the Red Army.

It was in this action that Pzkw VI Tigers engaged the Russian T-34s for the first time, and the results were more than gratifying to us. For example, two Tigers acting as a panzer spearhead destroyed an entire pack of T-34s. Normally the Russian tanks would stand in ambush at the hitherto safe distance of 1,200 meters and wait for the German tanks to expose themselves upon exiting a village. They would then take the tanks under fire while our Pzkw IVs were still outranged. Until now this tactic had been foolproof. This time, however, the Russians miscalculated. Instead of leaving the village, our Tigers took up well-camouflaged positions and made full use of the longer range of their 88mm main guns. Within a short time they knocked out sixteen T-34s that were sitting in open ground and, when the others turned about, the Tigers pursued the fleeing Russians and destroyed eighteen more tanks. Our 88mm armor-piercing shells had such a terrific impact that they ripped off the turrets of many T-34s and hurled them several yards. The German soldiers witnessing this event immediately coined the phrase: "The T-34 tips its hat whenever it meets a Tiger." The performance of the new Tigers resulted in a great morale boost.

Further to the south, Kharkov was recaptured by the *Liebstandarte Adolph Hitler* SS Panzergrenadier Division after four days of street fighting in which Tigers again played a decisive role. The *Das Reich* SS Panzergrenadier Division turned north, advanced on Belgorod, captured the city, and linked up with *Grossdeutschland*, which had now thrust beyond Tomarovka. Between these two points two German infantry divisions slowly struggled through the mud in their effort to reach the west bank of the river. When our counteroffensive had begun there was still some snow on the ground, but just before the *Armee-abteilung* reached the upper course of the Donets a sudden rise in temperature created a severe muddy condition. All vehicles except those on the only hard-surfaced road in the area, leading from Kharkov to Kursk, became helpless. Our infantry could still slog forward, but heavy weapons and artillery were delayed and finally moved up only with great effort. Even the T-34s of the Russian rear guards had become embedded to such an extent that we could not retrieve them until warm weather.

Entering Zolochev, a small city twenty miles north of Kharkov, our troops had occasion to discover the extent to which the Russians sought to intimidate their own population through atrocities. The inhabitants told the German military police that Russian security troops, before their retreat, had herded and whipped a large number of local boys between the ages of fourteen and seventeen years naked through the streets in intense cold. Afterward, they were said to have disappeared into the firehouse where the NVKD [the Soviet Security apparatus] had its headquarters, never to be seen again. During a subsequent search, all of the missing boys were found in a deep cellar of the firehouse, shot through the neck and covered with horse manure. The bodies were identified and claimed by relatives. Nearly all had frostbitten limbs. The reason for this particular atrocity was assumed to have been the alleged aid rendered to German occupation forces.

The Russians also apparently sought to impress German troops and lower their morale by committing numerous atrocities directly against them. One such case occurred in Second Panzer Army's sector several hundred kilometers to the north. During fighting over the village of Zhizdra in early March, a battalion of the 590th Grenadier Regiment, 321st Infantry Division, was assigned the mission of mopping up a sector overgrown with brush. The attack failed. When, on 19 March, the sector again passed into our hands after a counterattack, forty corpses of soldiers were found with their eyes gouged out, or their ears, noses, and genitals cut off. Corpses found in another sector of the battlefield bore signs of similar mutilations.

Despite atrocities like these, such Russian elements as escaped across the Donets were badly mauled, and our reconnaissance units advancing beyond the river met little resistance. Even though our attack divisions appeared fully capable of continuing their drive, the overall situation and the prevailing mud made such a decision inadvisable. Moreover, the objective of the frontal counterattack had been achieved. The breach in the German lines, open for four months, had been closed, and the greatest Russian winter offensive fought to a halt. After suffering a defeat of gigantic proportions at Stalingrad, the German army once again held a continuous line anchored on the Donets River.

Situation, 10 April 1943

After Army Group South had concluded its 1943 spring offensive, the enemy in front of *Armeeabteilung* Kempf primarily remained on the defensive. The Russians, though generally quiet, demonstrated greater activity in the northern sector of the front, between Belgorod and the army group boundary. Lively reconnaissance efforts, artillery reinforcements, the arrival of reserve forces, and the improvement of the natural terrain features for defense all suggested that the Soviets intended to strengthen their defenses in this new sector of the front as quickly as possible. In rear areas, lively traffic of all kinds indicated a rapid and intense reorganization of heavily battered units. Although intelligence identified no new Red Army units at the front, it seemed entirely possible that railroad traffic (in excess of normal troop replacement and supply requirements) had delivered at least three new rifle divisions into the Kursk area and two into the area of Valuiki–N. Oskol–St. Oskol. Aside from this observation, we received indications that significant forces had shifted from the sector opposite the German Sixth Army, as well as from the sector facing Army Group Center, into the N. Oskol–Korocha–St. Oskol area. It proved impossible to determine then whether these units were being concentrated for offensive or defensive purposes.

Armeeabteilung Kempf's main line of resistance and disposition of forces is indicated in Map 2.2. In addition to the 106th, 167th, and 320th Infantry Divisions and the *Totenkopf* SS Panzergrenadier Division already committed at the front, the following units had been assigned to the *Armeeabteilung* at that time for "reorganization and training in local areas": Headquarters, III Panzer Corps; Headquarters, II SS Panzer Corps; 6th and 7th Panzer Divisions; *Grossdeutschland* Panzergrenadier Division; *Das Reich* SS Panzergrenadier Division; and *Liebstandarte Adolf Hitler* SS Panzergrenadier Divisions. Beginning in late April, the following units arrived: Headquarters, XLVIII Panzer Corps; 11th Panzer Division; 168th Infantry Division; and Army troops (armored and self-propelled antitank gun units, flak, artillery, engineers, bridge trains, road construction battalions, etc.). The *Armeeabteilung* placed reorganizing units in the vicinity or west of Kharkov. Units committed at the front rotated one-third their strength (one reinforced regimental *Kampfgruppe*) at a time, for purposes of reorganizing near the front. Because the original attack date had been set for 4 May, maximum efforts were made to move up required personnel and material.

As soon as the *Armeeabteilung* realized that the Red Army had moved additional forces into the area northeast of Belgorod, a panzer *Kampfgruppe*—established by rotating elements of the panzer divisions refitting farther to the rear—was placed on alert north of Kharkov. This deployment prepared us to meet any Soviet attempt to launch a surprise attack on Kharkov.

During this period of protracted position warfare, the 106th Infantry Division, south of Belgorod, managed to take a large number of prisoners. These prisoners were taken in midday raids, because it had been ascertained from deserters that the Russians in this sector—which could be readily observed from the western bank of the river—were allowed to move only at night and therefore slept during the day. The prisoners admitted that many of their comrades were dissatisfied and would like to desert; however, they were afraid of being fired upon by our troops and would have difficulties crossing the deep river that separated them from the German lines. Contact with the company of malcontents was soon established and the necessary arrangements made. Unobtrusive light signals on the chosen night informed the Russian company that the necessary ferrying equipment was ready and that German weapons stood ready to cover their crossing. All necessary precautions had been taken in case of a Soviet ruse. Just the same, the company really dribbled down to the banks of the river and in several trips was ferried across the Donets in rubber boats. The company commander, an Uzbek first lieutenant, was the first man to reach our lines. Part of the company, unfortunately, ran into Russian minefields, suffering considerable losses from exploding mines as well as from the fire of the alerted enemy artillery. The result of this undertaking was that, having become unreliable, the 15th Uzbek Rifle Division was immediately withdrawn from the front, disciplined, and committed elsewhere.

Situation About 30 June 1943

Enemy forces moving into previously identified assembly areas since May had been increasing to such an extent that we had to plan on facing a heavy concentration of Soviet reserves in the area of Korocha–Volokonovka–N. Oskol, as well as the Kursk area. Though we observed no general forward movement of Russian units during May, June brought a continuous strengthening of the enemy front, particularly in terms of artillery, heavy weapons, dug-in tanks, etc. We concluded that the Soviets intended to maintain a defensive stance, however, because they were undoubtedly aware of the numerous panzer divisions in the Kharkov area, while the course of our front line strongly suggested the potential for a large-scale attack. On the other hand, the prospect of a pending Russian offensive could not be completely dismissed given the manifestation of increasing enemy strength throughout June.

Large-scale and well-planned construction of field fortifications accompanied the Russian buildup, which the Luftwaffe monitored through aerial photographs taken during daily flights. Opposite Belgorod, where the main weight of the German attack would fall, the Russian defensive system consisted of three successive fortified belts, extending by the end of June to a depth of forty kilometers. We documented in great numbers the following features: positions on reverse slopes; switch positions; dummy installations; alternate artillery positions (up to four per battery); and alternate positions for dug-in tanks. Mines not only covered the approaches but had been laid to an unprecedented depth. Towns located within and behind the Soviet defensive system—to a distance of sixty kilometers—had been evacuated and transformed into what were practically fortresses, coupled with covering detachments. Most positions appeared already occupied, and reserves had bivouacked in dugouts near the forward areas.

No changes had occurred in the *Armeeabteilung*'s main battle line since 10 April. West of Belgorod, Headquarters, Fourth Panzer Army, assumed command of II SS and XLVIII Panzer Corps, while Headquarters, III Panzer Corps; 6th, 7th, and 19th Panzer Divisions; and a number of army troops had been attached to the *Armeeabteilung*.

After units had been reorganized and refitted, the *Armeeabteilung* concentrated on intensive training for the attack and on the tactical instructions of the subordinate commanders—both in practice and in theory—with particular emphasis placed on the types of missions the troops would be expected to perform. Field exercises with live ammunitions, as well as demonstrations in which the Luftwaffe and other elements participated, contributed to the achievement of a high standard of combat readiness. Map exercises and terrain orientation meetings occurred concurrently, while special courses taught military bridge construction and minefield clearing. Simultaneously, in order to deceive the Soviets regarding German intentions, new large-scale defensive positions were constructed at the front and in forward areas.

In connection with this training effort, XI Corps staff made a thorough study of the problem of crossing the extensive minefields on the east side of the Donets. The usual procedure of sending engineer detachments to clear narrow lanes for the advance of the infantry spearheads was not considered satisfactory because the terrain offered no cover and the enemy could inflict heavy casualties upon engineers and infantry by concentrating his fire on these lanes. Several improvised methods for overcoming this obstacle were therefore under consideration.

The identification of the mined area was the first prerequisite because the infantry had to know its exact location prior to the crossings. This was possible because the German-held western bank commanded the Russian positions on the other side of the river. Another prerequisite was that the infantry should be able to spot the location of individual mines at close range with the naked eye. In many places small mounds or depressions, dry grass, differences in the coloring of the ground, or some other external marks facilitated the spotting. The engineers had made a number of experiments in mine-detecting. In the early days of the war, the infantry sometimes crossed narrow minefields after individual engineers lay down beside the mines as human markers, taking great care not to set them off by pressure. Although neither engineers nor infantry troops suffered losses during these early experiments, the procedure was risky and could be applied only on a small scale. It was therefore of little consequence in the later stages of the war.

A second, more promising method that fulfilled expectations consisted of marking individual mines by placing small flags or other simple markers next to the mines. This was done by engineers or infantrymen who were trained in the recognition of mines. This procedure was applied repeatedly and showed better results than the first, but its large-scale use presented difficulties. The third and best method was to thoroughly instruct all infantrymen in enemy mine-laying techniques and in spotting mines by using captured enemy minefields as training grounds. This procedure required that all infantrymen be sent to rear areas in rotation and was therefore rather time-consuming.

These requirements could be met in the case of Operation Citadel because the time of the attack had been twice postponed with an ensuing delay of several weeks. The divisions committed in the narrow attack zone had moved two-thirds of their combat forces to the rear, where the daily training schedule featured tanks passing over foxholes and the crossing of Russian-type minefields. This training paid off because it helped the soldiers overcome their fear of tanks and mines.

The Mission of *Armeeabteilung* Kempf

The plan of attack assigned *Armeeabteilung* Kempf the mission of providing an aggressive screen along the eastern flank of Fourth Panzer Army, which was to advance across the line Malino-Oboyan. Specifically, the *Armeeabteilung* had to hold the Donets Front from the right boundary of Fourth Panzer Army to the mouth of the Nezhegol River while advancing to the Nezhegol-Korocha line to screen its own panzer elements for a push in the general direction of Skordnoye. After breaking through the

Donets position, III Panzer Corps would take over responsibility for aggressively screening the flank of the entire operation in the sector Korocha-Seim River (see Map 2.3).

The *Armeeabteilung* had to calculate on meeting the following Red Army forces (see Map 2.4).[10]

Day One: four rifle divisions in the first line between the mouth of the
　　　Nezhegol River and Belgorod;
Day Two: all other divisions located in forward areas (estimated at four
　　　rifle divisions);
Day Three and beyond: considerable tank and mechanized forces from
　　　the Ostrogozhsk region.

That the STAVKA intended to hold the shoulder of the Kursk salient with all available forces became increasingly apparent from troop dispositions and the extent of the defensive system in the Belgorod area. We projected that the Soviets had three alternatives from which to choose in committing their strategic reserves:

1. Piecemeal commitment during a defensive battle (this would have been best for us).
2. A concentric counterattack (starting the third or fourth day).
3. A counteroffensive of major proportions.

The following German units were available to the *Armeeabteilung*:

1. For defense along the Donets sector: XLII Corps with 39th, 161st, and 282nd Infantry Divisions (one division, composed of just two infantry regiments, had to be spread over a front line 145 kilometers long);
2. For gaining the Nezhegol-Korocha line: XI Corps (also known as "Corps Raus") with 106th and 320th Infantry Divisions.
3. For the panzer attack on Skordnoye: III Panzer Corps with 6th, 7th, and 19th Panzer Divisions, as well as 168th Infantry Division.

Considering Russian dispositions, defenses, and terrain, German strength could be considered only minimally sufficient for the assigned mission. Clearly, there could not be any major losses at the outset of the operation.

The offensive would occur in three phases. First, the Donets would be crossed and the first Russian defensive belt penetrated. Given the weakness of our force, tactical surprise at least in terms of timing and the choice of river crossings would be essential. Next, the *Armeeabteilung* had to break through the enemy's second and third defensive belts as rapidly as possible to avoid giving the Soviets enough time to commit their strategic reserves. Finally, enemy strategic reserves would be engaged on open ground. With the large number of Red Army tank corps standing by, we could reasonably expect major armored battles, during which our panzer divisions would have the opportunity to demonstrate their superior leadership and weapons.

However, long before the panzer divisions could enter what we hoped would be the battle's final, decisive stage, they had to accomplish a mission strictly relegated to infantry divisions in normal operations: attack across a river against a prepared enemy deployed in depth. Flat bridgehead terrain, barely 100 meters in depth, was available only at the western outskirts of Belgorod.

Because the *Armeeabteilung's* primary mission required safeguarding the eastern flank of Fourth Panzer Army's advance, the closest possible contact between that army and III Panzer Corps had to be maintained. This meant that III Panzer Corps would have to execute an almost immediate thrust to the northeast, disregarding any threats to its own flank. For XI Corps, strung out across a thirty-five-kilometer sector with just two reinforced infantry divisions, there would therefore be no panzer support available. Instead, XI Corps had to establish its screen along the Koremye sector by forming narrow wedges. A diversionary Red Army attack against Kharkov from the Donets bend (on either side of Chuguev and astride the Chuguev-Kharkov highway) remained a threat to the overall success of the operation; we had no reserves available to counter such an attack. Upon repeated requests by the *Armeeabteilung*, Army Group South eventually consented to assemble some of its own reserve forces in the area.

As far as possible, the enemy had to be kept from detecting the movement of German forces into their assembly areas. By spacing the assembly areas far apart and occupying them at staggered intervals, the *Armeeabteilung* attempted to deceive the enemy about the attack's timing and the locations of contemplated crossing sites. Movement forward into the assembly areas by the panzer divisions had to be confined to the hours of darkness. Movement into assembly areas and artillery positions had been completed by 4 July.[11]

In the Chuguev area additional and extensive deception measures attempted to convince the Russians that we contemplated attacking in the Donets bend toward the line Izyum-Kupiansk. Motorized columns advanced toward the front lines in daylight, artillery moved into positions and conducted registration fire, and simulated reserves practiced river crossings.

We had to remain aware of the fact that the Russians made consider-able use of the civilian population for intelligence missions. A favorite practice was the employment of boys eight to fourteen years old, who were first trained for this work and then allowed to infiltrate at suitable front sectors. Immediately before the offensive opened, more than a dozen such children were picked up in the Belgorod area alone. They gave detailed reports on the kind of training they received and their modus operandi. The training of these children had been supervised by Russian officers, it had lasted four weeks, and there had been sixty par-ticipants. The youths came from communities near the front on both sides of the battle lines and therefore were thoroughly familiar with the locale. Many were staying with relatives or acquaintances in German-occupied localities and [were] therefore not easy to discover and appre-hend. Their talent for observation and skill at spying were remarkable. For this reason, civilians in localities near the front (within six to ten kilometers of the front line) had to be evacuated, not only because of the danger from enemy artillery fire but also as a preventative measure against espionage.

The Penetration, 5 July

The Russians became aware of the date of the attack, probably because of a venture by the unit on the left in the afternoon of 4 July. From 0200 to 0220 the Soviets laid down a destructive fire on suspected crossing sites around Belgorod, resulting in considerable German casualties. At 0225, following a short artillery concentration, the *Armeeabteilung* commenced the Donets crossing on a wide front. This assault succeeded at all cross-ing sites in a surprisingly short time, though at some locations only after bitter hand-to-hand fighting. The attack took place without Luftwaffe support, which had been totally committed to Fourth Panzer Army. In addition to organic divisional artillery, the following units were commit-ted to deliver supporting fire (note that flak units had a dual mission of fire support and air defense):[12]

XI CORPS SECTOR
  Artillery Command 153
  I Battalion, Artillery Regiment 77 (105mm)
  II Battalion, Artillery Battalion 54 (105mm)
  I Battalion, Artillery Battalion 213 (105mm)
  Flak Regiment 4
  Flak Regiment 7
  Flak Regiment 48

Assault Gun Battalion 905

Self-propelled Panzerjaeger [Antitank] Battalion 393

.

The three flak regiments, fielding a total of seventy-two 88mm and approximately 900 smaller flak guns, had been attached to XI Corps to serve as a substitute for missing medium artillery. According to Luftwaffe policy, the subordination of flak officers to army unit commanders was forbidden; the corps artillery commander therefore depended on the voluntary cooperation of the senior flak commander. This led to repeated minor frictions but worked out quite well in general.

The flak regiments' first mission was to take part in the artillery preparation under the direction of the corps artillery commander. For this purpose the flak regiments were echeloned in depth and committed in three waves. The first echelon was in position in the main line of resistance and closely behind it; its mission was to place direct fire on enemy heavy weapons and pillboxes. In addition, it had to form flak assault detachments for antitank combat to give close support to the advancing infantry. Together with the corps artillery, the two other regiments were to shatter the first enemy line of defense and paralyze his infantry by delivering sustained concentrations. After that, elements of the first echelon, with the exception of the assault detachments, as well as the entire second echelon, were to support the advancing infantry. The third echelon was to take over the antiaircraft protection of the entire artillery area and was also to participate in counterbattery missions.

III PANZER CORPS SECTOR

Artillery Command 3

Artillery Regimental Staff 612[13]

Assault Gun Battalion 228

II Battalion, Artillery Regiment 71 (150mm)

Heavy Artillery Battalion 875 (210mm)

II Battalion, Artillery Regiment 62 (105mm)

Flak Regiment 99

Flak Regiment 153

The 6th Panzer Division, III Panzer Corps sector, supported the attack of the 168th Infantry Division with its heavy weapons and was assigned the mission of crossing the river and pushing beyond the 168th Infantry lines toward St. Gorodische as soon as the 168th succeeded in widening the narrow bridgehead at Belgorod.[14]

For purposes of deceiving the Russians, XLII Corps conducted a feint attack across the Donets along its northern wing while in reality its combined artillery (which had been concentrated in the area) supported the XI Corps attack.

Soviet intelligence found out that the attack was to start on 5 July at dawn. The Russians laid down intensive harassing fire on the jump-off positions, but this interference ceased as soon as the German artillery concentration started. In XI Corps area these fire concentrations were placed so well and the initial shock so great that the first assault wave was able to cross the enemy minefields, penetrate his main line of resistance without delay, and thrust a few hundred yards beyond it. Thousands of tracers fired by the numerous small flak guns proved particularly effective.

The beginning of the attack had been set for sunrise so that the infantry would be able to detect enemy mines without difficulty. The 106th and 320th Infantry Divisions quickly thrust their spearheads across the minefields and suffered practically no casualties. Only one battalion acted contrary to orders and attacked before daybreak, its commander being afraid that he might otherwise suffer heavy casualties from enemy fire while his men were crossing the extended open terrain in his zone. In the dark, this battalion ran into the previously uncovered minefields, and the two advance companies suffered approximately twenty casualties from mine explosions. When the battalion continued its advance by daylight it had no further losses.

Because the Russians had abandoned their trenches during the artillery concentration and fled into their deep dugouts, the advancing infantry surprised them and had no difficulty in ferreting them out. But when the infantry reached the three-to-five-kilometer-deep zone of battle positions prepared in the preceding months, they had to make extensive use of hand grenades in order to mop up the maze of densely dug-in trenches and bunkers, some of which were a dozen or more feet deep. At the same time, artillery and flak fired counterbattery missions against enemy heavy weapons that had resumed fire from rear positions, and on reserves infiltrating through the trench system, as well as against Russian medium artillery. The third echelon of the flak regiments was fully occupied with defense against Soviet bombers, which attacked the XI Corps area incessantly. During the first two hours of the attack they downed more than twenty enemy aircraft.

We encountered strong enemy forces offering stiff and bitter resistance in their deeply echeloned, amply fortified, and heavily mined battlefield. This remained the case throughout the process of widening the initial bridgeheads as well as during the battle for the area between the Donets and the railroad line, which was also located within the first defensive belt. Throughout the morning, Russian artillery, automatic weapons, and aircraft began to participate in the battle with ever-increasing intensity. Both the tactical reserves of the forward units and elements of rifle divisions and independent tank brigades located just behind the front launched counterthrusts against our penetrations. By early afternoon these efforts had become systematic counterattacks. Even so, after costly see-saw fighting, XI Corps's main body reached the railroad line by evening, and some elements even crossed it.

Suddenly a fierce Russian counterattack, supported by forty tanks, threw back our covering force from the woods on the south flank and hit the 320th Infantry Division, which was echeloned in depth on the corps right wing. Defensive fire of the divisional artillery and a concentration of all medium flak batteries stopped the enemy counterattack at the edge of the forest. Then the medium flak was directed against tank concentrations, which had been recognized in the underbrush, and dispersed them. Repeated Soviet attempts to resume the attack from this area failed without exception; flank protection was soon restored and the threat eliminated.

During this counterattack about 150 men from the 320th Infantry Division were taken prisoner. Shortly thereafter we monitored a telephone conversation between Russian lower and higher headquarters (probably regiment and division), which went about as follows:

Regimental commander: "I have 150 Fritzes (derogatory term for German soldiers) here. What shall I do with them?"
Division commander: "Keep a few for interrogation, and have the others liquidated."

That evening, the presumed regimental commander reported the order executed, stating that the majority of the Fritzes had been killed immediately, and the remainder after they had been interrogated.

In III Panzer Corps sector, 7th Panzer Division crossed the Donets at Solomino and succeeded in effecting a deep penetration of the enemy defenses, though only after a bitter tank fight. This penetration extended to the high ground north of Krivoy Log. Forcing the Donets in the southern part of Pushkarnoye, 19th Panzer Division encountered strong resistance and extremely unfavorable terrain (swamps and minefields) in the wooded area southeast of Mikailovka. Nonetheless, after repulsing a strong Russian tank attack, the 19th managed to cross the railroad line. Neither the 168th Infantry Division nor the 6th Panzer Division succeeded in penetrating the enemy's main defensive belt in the Belgorod area, which meant that the *Armeeabteilung's* mission for the next few days would involve blasting this stronghold open from the east.

By capitalizing on the element of tactical surprise, the *Armeeabteilung* was fortunate enough to breach the first defensive belt between the Donets and the railroad line; after bitter fighting we were even able partially to roll up this line. Only the 7th Panzer Division achieved a penetration of the second defensive belt; at all other points the enemy stood his ground, employing an offensive-defense in many areas.

Threats to both flanks became apparent as the *Armeeabteilung* pushed northeast. The large wooded area northwest of Shevekino provided a well-concealed jump-off point for Russian counterattacks. Costly fighting in the woods was to be expected in any attempt to break through to the Koremye sector. After the losses on the first day (almost 2,000 men in XI Corps alone) it appeared doubtful that this objective could be attained without the help of additional forces.

The Belgorod bastion, seizure of which was bound to tie down major forces for the next few days, had expanded as a result of the *Armeeabteilung's* continued advance toward the line Korocha-Skordnoye, until it formed a deep wedge pointing south and lodged between *Armeeabteilung* Kempf and Fourth Panzer Army. Fresh enemy forces were already pouring into this wedge, which would represent an ever-increasing threat to our left flank.

Higher headquarters had been hoping the troops would encounter an enemy weakened in his power of resistance. This proved to be a delusion. The Russians appeared to be materially prepared (good rations, equipment, and arms) as well as morally inoculated against all symptoms of deterioration (high degree of patriotism; confidence in victory aroused; failure of our efforts to induce enemy troops to desert).

Breaking Through the Second and Third Lines, 6–7 July

The initial success of the first day required immediate exploitation of the breach at Kurtsoi Log, where the 7th Panzer Division had punched through. All our forces concentrated to this end, and the *Armeeabteilung* even abandoned the nonessential and costly Bezlydovka bridgehead on the southern flank. On the west bank of the Donets, elements of the 106th Infantry Division assumed the defensive. The 6th Panzer Division redeployed from Stary Gorod for commitment behind the 7th Panzer, in order to reinforce the assault spearhead. After bitter fighting with Russian tanks, the combined armored strength of these two divisions sufficed to break through the deep defense system, gaining the high ground at Myasoyedovo and even pushing on toward Melekhovo. Coordinating its attack with elements of the 7th Panzer Division, XI Corps seized the commanding heights between Koren and the Donets, then established a screen facing east. The *Armeeabteilung* likewise gained ground with an attack launched from the south and southwest against the area immediately east of Belgorod. Extremely stiff Soviet resistance characterized the fighting in this area, especially around the enemy stronghold of Kreida, which was heavily manned and well supported by automatic weapons and artillery.

The Russians attempted to counter our breakthrough attack by launching numerous thrusts and attacks from the woods west of Koren, where they had assembled three of their front-line rifle divisions, which had been reinforced by two new rifle divisions and two independent tank brigades. Attacking with strong infantry elements and the two tank brigades, the enemy focused his main effort in front of the 106th Infantry Division. In the resulting engagements, XI Corps scored a considerable defensive victory, thanks primarily to the excellent performance of our infantry in permitting the Soviet tanks to roll over them (a procedure that had been especially stressed during training), which succeeded in separating the enemy tanks from their own infantry supports. The tanks pushed up to and beyond the Shevekino-Belgorod road, but the Russian infantry attack broke down in front of our lines, which now held without budging (see Map 2.5).

The enemy tanks struck the corps center, behind which several flak assault detachments and numerous medium antitank guns were sited in a mutually supporting formation. As the Russian tanks ran headlong into this dense network of antitank defenses, I personally led the reserves of the 106th Infantry Division, with support from thirty-two assault guns, antitank guns, and flak assault detachments, to envelop and ultimately knock out all sixty tanks that had penetrated the sector. The last Soviet tank, which had penetrated to the divisional command post, was surprised by an assault detachment carrying gasoline cans and set on fire. On the whole, though determined, the Russian attacks lacked coordination, and because they were unsuccessful, the enemy moved to concentrate his forces for an offensive main effort between Polyana and the woods east of Shcholokovo. Even here the screen would be held in bitter fighting after the arrival of a continuous flow of reinforced *kampfgruppen* from the 198th Infantry Division, which had been brought up from Chuguev in motorized columns.

The Soviets attempted to break up the *Armeeabteilung*'s panzer thrust to the northeast by committing two newly arrived rifle divisions and elements of the II Tank Corps against III Panzer Corps. Simultaneously, the Russians pressured the western flank in the area Blis, Igumenka-Hf., Postikov. While repulsing strong attacks from Melekhova, we managed to encircle the forces opposite the western flank, destroying one rifle division and heavily mauling another; elements of the latter withdrew along the Syev Donets valley to the northeast after abandoning its heavy equipment.

The enemy position had thus been breached to a depth of thirty kilometers; six Soviet rifle divisions, two tank brigades, and three tank regiments had been battered. Evaluation of aerial photographs revealed one last defensive belt along the line Ushakovo-Sheyno-Sobyshno. In continuing its advance, the *Armeeabteilung* had to expect an encounter with three additional groupings of Russian forces:

1. Five or six mauled rifle divisions and tank brigades opposite the western flank.
2. Three or four rifle divisions of the Sixty-ninth Army.
   (Both of these groups could potentially receive reinforcements from the St. Oskol area, including two tank corps and one cavalry corps.)
3. One tank corps and elements of three rifle divisions located in the triangle formed by the Syev Donets and Lipovy Donets, which could operate against either the western flank of the *Armeeabteilung* or the eastern flank of Fourth Panzer Army.

The Drive on Prokhorovka, 11–16 July

In order for III Panzer Corps to achieve freedom of movement toward the northeast to cover the right flank of Fourth Panzer Army, we would have to break through the Russian Sixty-ninth Army between Ushakovo and Sobyshno. After breaking through the last enemy position between Razumnoye and Syev Donets, the drive on Skordnoye would require the concentrated strength of III Panzer Corps. Such a maneuver would be possible only if enemy forces in the Donets triangle (which threatened our own flank) could be thrown back or destroyed. Neither of these maneuvers could be allowed to jeopardize the execution of the other, and it did not appear possible to tackle both enemy groupings simultaneously without Fourth Panzer Army's assistance in cleaning out the Donets triangle.

At this time, however, Fourth Panzer Army faced a bitter struggle with Soviet infantry and strong tank forces along the length of its front. Crossing sites on the Psel River could be gained only after costly fighting, and Russian strength in front of the bridgeheads increased by the hour. A breakthrough toward Kursk, upon which the entire operation hinged, seemed doubtful unless Fourth Panzer Army could be reinforced, and diverting any elements to assist in mopping up the Donets triangle might cause the forward attack of II SS Panzer Corps's right wing to cease altogether.

In his concern over Fourth Panzer Army's attack bogging down, Field Marshal von Manstein considered the following course of action: discontinuation of *Armeeabteilung* Kempf's attack and redeployment of III Panzer Corps on the eastern wing of Fourth Panzer Army. Such a solution became the subject of a conference between von Manstein, Hoth, and Kempf in Dolbino at the *Armeeabteilung's* headquarters on 11 July. Emphasizing the *Armeeabteilung's* dwindling combat strength, the mounting threat to the eastern flank, and the absence of all reserves, Kempf favored discontinuing the attack. Field Marshal von Manstein postponed his final decision pending the outcome of a projected visit with General of Panzer Troops Hermann Breith, commander, III Panzer Corps. Presumably due to the tactical successes of the past few days, Breith presented von Manstein with an optimistic view of the situation, and the field marshal ordered III Panzer Corps's attack to continue (see Map 2.6).

The III Panzer Corps broke through the Russian positions between Ushakovo and Sobyshno, penetrating quickly into the Alexandrovka area. At the same time, the *Armeeabteilung* secured several bridgeheads over the Syev Donets on either side of Rehavel. "Open terrain" beckoned: freedom of movement for the operation against Skordnoye had been won, a jump-off position for the drive on Prokhorovka had been gained, and—as a result—coordinated action with Fourth Panzer Army's flank became possible.

The next challenge grew out of the overall situation. The Russians committed additional strong tank forces against Fourth Panzer Army's eastern flank, and heavy defensive battles raged. Now the *Armeeabteilung* received the most important mission within the scope of the overall operation: defeat Soviet tank forces in the area south of Prokhorovka and forcibly clear the road to Kursk. This would still require enemy resistance in the Donets triangle to be eliminated as a prerequisite.

The recently won penetration near Alexandrovka had to be held in order to serve as a jump-off point for the thrust toward Prokhorovka. The XI Corps defensive screen, therefore, had to be lengthened along the Razumnoye toward the northeast, even though we were holding existing positions only with elements whose strength dwindled rapidly. Only the 6th Panzer Division could be made available as a covering force for the screen toward the north, which it managed by aggressive tactics. That the other two panzer divisions of III Panzer Corps were enabled to maintain their attack could be ascribed to the heroic defensive stand of the XI Corps along a dangerously wide sector.

Confronted by strong Russian defenses and counterattacks by the II Guards Tank Corps, the panzer *Kampfgruppen* of the 7th and 19th Panzer Divisions nonetheless attacked Shashovo from their bridgeheads across the Syev Donets (beginning on 12 July). Elements of four rifle divisions in the Donets triangle attempted to evade the encirclement and break out toward the north. Assisted by the 167th Infantry Division (which had been holding position on the western side of this enemy bastion), III Panzer Corps cleared the wooded section south of Gostishchevo of the enemy—an action yielding over 1,000 prisoners and large amounts of weapons and equipment.

Our continued drive toward the high ground on either side of the line Ivanovka-Maloye-Tablonovo collided with strong Soviet tank forces. The German panzers, however, demonstrated their superiority in the course of several heavy armored battles. Suffering heavy losses, the Russians retreated north, and we established contact with the western wing of Fourth Panzer Army north of Teterevino. High tank losses had so thoroughly weakened the Soviets that Army Group South could now undertake the decisive thrust toward Prokhorovka; the appropriate field orders were immediately issued.

In the meantime, however, the Red Army attacked the far southern wing of Army Group South along the Mius River and at Izyum. As a result, the strategic reserve that was to have been allocated to the drive on Kursk—XXIV Panzer Corps with *Wiking* SS Panzergrenadier Division and 17th Panzer Division—never arrived. On the southern wing of Army Group Center, not only had Ninth Army's assault been unsuccessful, but the Russians had launched a major attack against the Orel salient. Simultaneously, XLVIII Panzer Corps (on the western flank of Fourth Panzer Army) had been halted by strong enemy tank forces (at least one tank army). Army Group South intended to respond to this threat by temporarily assuming the defensive on Fourth Panzer Army's eastern flank in order to crush the Soviet tank army and resume a coordinated drive on Kursk. Meanwhile, after 7th Panzer Division had been detached, *Armeeabteilung* Kempf received only the weakened 167th Infantry Division in exchange to assist in covering its long eastern flank (code-named "Roland"). The crisis point of the entire operation had been reached: There were no reserves remaining that could be thrown into the battle.

Ultimately, it was the Red Army attack along the Mius River and at Izyum that kept Fourth Panzer Army's intended attack toward the Psel-Pena area from materializing. Once XXIV Panzer Corps had been committed there, no strategic reserves remained to Army Group South, and the Russians held the initiative. The attack toward Kursk was called off, and as early as 17 July II SS Panzer Corps would be redeployed from the Kursk salient; an additional panzer division would follow a few days later. Army Group South nevertheless intended to leave *Armeeabteilung* Kempf and Fourth Panzer Army in their existing line as long as no serious attacks materialized or new concentrations of enemy forces became noticeable.

The large-scale attack code-named Operation "Citadel" had not attained its strategic objective, even though great tactical success had been achieved. During the period 5–20 July, Army Group South captured or destroyed 412 tanks, 11,862 prisoners, 132 artillery pieces, 530 antitank guns, and a large number of heavy weapons of all types. The Red Army could certainly have used these troops and weapons in the major offensive that had just opened.

Withdrawal to the Enlarged Belgorod Bridgehead, 18–22 July

As a consequence of the recall of the 19th Panzer Division on 18 July, *Armeeabteilung* Kempf's front had to be withdrawn to an intermediate position; the Soviets followed closely behind. On 21 July, in order to meet a threatening attack against Army Group South's west wing, both 6th Panzer Division and 167th Infantry Division had to be transferred to Fourth Panzer Army. The front withdrew again, this time to the enlarged Belgorod bridgehead. This position had twice the frontage of the old Donets position and had to be held solely by the remaining elements of XI Corps. Heavy losses since 5 July had reduced the fighting power of XI Corps to less than half.

Armeeabteilung Kempf made repeated requests to move the front back to the line of departure—which would have shortened the front considerably while allowing us to take advantage of the excellent, strongly fortified positions on the Donets. These requests were all refused, because such a withdrawal was "intended" only in the face of a major Russian attack. Over the coming weeks, this decision embroiled XI Corps in a series of costly see-saw battles for the control of the enlarged Belgorod bridgehead, which were marked by excessively wide defensive sectors; diminishing combat strength; disappearing moral and physical strength of the troops; lack of reserves; enormous superiority of Soviet personnel and material; and the fact that our position had never been fortified. XI Corps was finally permitted to retire into the heavily fortified defensive system anchored on Belgorod on 22 July.

Conclusion

Operation Citadel had the avowed purpose of gaining the Kursk area, destroying the enemy forces in the salient facing Second Army, and—above all—shortening our lines by about 270 kilometers. In order to conserve German strength, the attack was conceived as a swift follow-up operation and climax to the successful pre-spring battles of *Armeeabteilung* Kempf and Fourth Panzer Army around Kharkov. The recapture of Belgorod had created a favorable jump-off point for this purpose. *Armeeabteilung* Kempf submitted its first proposal for such an operation on 1 April, intending to attack by mid-April or early May at the latest. We reasoned that the four-week pause in the fighting necessitated by the muddy season would allow us to reorganize our troops but would be too brief for the battered Russians to make adequate defensive preparations.

The *Armeeabteilung* repeatedly voiced grave concern over ensuing postponements of the operation. That last time this concern was evidenced by a particularly urgent manifestation, in the form of a verbal report from General Kempf to Colonel General Zeitzler, chief of the Army General Staff. Kempf argued that the enemy would make use of the time not only to regroup his units and fortify his defenses in depth but also to assemble a strategic reserve that could be utilized to repulse our assault, launch diversionary attacks, or even spearhead a planned counteroffensive. Nevertheless, the operation was repeatedly postponed. The reason given for this action was the fact that the new weapons (above all the Pzkw V "Panther" and Pzkw VI "Tiger" battalions) would so reinforce our offensive power as to offset the defensive preparations of the enemy.

Armeeabteilung Kempf received no such weapons or units.

Repeated postponement of the attack is one of the primary reasons that led to the operation's failure. The combat efficiency of our units could be brought up to a very high standard but would not keep up with that of the enemy, who—in the same period of time—was able to make gains in strength greatly exceeding our own thanks to his considerably greater economic war potential. The Red Army had the time and opportunity to bring its defensive measures to a level heretofore unknown. Behind this protective curtain strategic reserves could be assembled without interference.

Other reasons for the failure of the operation included the adherence to a battle plan that had been formulated in anticipation of other events and conditions. This plan provided for an attack to be launched from the shoulder of the Belgorod sector. Once we learned in May and June that this was precisely the area in which the Russians were prepared to offer their stiffest resistance, we should have modified our plans. Either we should have refrained from attacking at all, or the operation should have been carried out to strike the enemy not at his strongest but at his weakest point: in this case the front sector east of Sumy. Our panzer divisions would have achieved freedom of movement much earlier, unlike the actual battle, in which they were hamstrung in fighting through the Soviet defensive system against a numerically superior enemy.

Our plans also suffered from the diverging commitment of the forces in the attacking armies. This led to the breakup of the operation into a series of individual battles and, combined with the disparity of forces, caused our command to forfeit freedom of action. What was to have been a "smooth operation" degenerated into a "slugging match."

That disparity of German and Russian strength was critical in its own right. German numerical inferiority, particularly in infantry, forced our panzer divisions, from the beginning, to expend their strength on tasks that were strange to them before they had the opportunity to engage the enemy in open terrain, making full use of their mobility.

Likewise, the German forces assigned to screen the flanks of the attacking armies (which became longer each day) were clearly insufficient.

The failure of the operation is not to be ascribed to front-line leadership or to the troops. In heavy, continuous fighting against a stubborn, numerically superior enemy, our soldiers suffered heavy losses but proved their superior spirit both in the attack and defense. The difficulty of this struggle can be measured at least in part by casualties figures of XI Corps divisions from 5 to 20 July:

106th Infantry Division	3,244 (46 officers)
320th Infantry Division	2,839 (30 officers)
168th Infantry Division	2,671 (127 officers)
	8,754 total

It is tragic that these troops were not successful, but it would be a historical error to reproach them for their failure.

APPENDIX 2A

Order of Battle: Corps Raus (Special Employment), 2 March 1943[15]

Lieutenant General Erhard Raus

320th Infantry Division
Major General Georg Postel
  Grenadier Regiments 585, 586, 587
  Artillery Regiment 320
  Reconnaissance Company 320
  Panzerjaeger Battalion 320
  Engineer Battalion 320

Attached:

  SS Panzergrenadier Regiment *Thule* (*Totenkopf*)
  Armored Train 62
  II/Panzergrenadier Regiment *Grossdeutschland*
  (plus one battery, light infantry guns)
  Panzer Battalion I, *Grossdeutschland*
  Heavy Panzerjaeger Company *Grossdeutschland*
  Sturm Battalion 393
  III/Artillery Regiment 111
  I/Artillery Regiment 213
  Staff, Mortar Regiment 3
  I/Mortar Training Regiment 1
  II/Mortar Regiment 3
  Flak *Gruppe* Becker
  Light Flak Battalion 81
  Three heavy flak (88mm) battalions

167th Infantry Division (minus detachments)
Lieutenant General Wolf Trierenberg
  Grenadier Regiments 315, 331; Staff, II, III/339
  Staff, I, III Artillery Regiment 238

Panzerjaeger Battalion 238
Engineer Battalion 238

Attached:

13/Panzer Regiment *Grossdeutschland* (Pzkw VIs)
III/Mortar Regiment 55

168th Infantry Division
Major General Dietrich Kraiss

Grenadier Regiments 417, 429, 442
Artillery Regiment 248
Reconnaissance Battalion 248
Panzerjaeger Battalion 248
Engineer Battalion 248

Attached:

Bicycle Battalion 238 (167th Infantry Division)
I/Grenadier Regiment 339 (167th Infantry Division)
III/Artillery Regiment 238 (167th Infantry Division)
3/Assault Gun Battalion 190 (one StG III)
Panzerjaeger Co., 106th Infantry Division
Panzer Co., *Grossdeutschland* (5 Pzkw IVs; 3 Pzkw IIIs)

Corps Troops

Gruppe Strachwitz (*Grossdeutschland*)
Colonel Hyazinth Graf Strachwitz
Panzer Reconnaissance Battalion *Grossdeutschland*
Assault Gun Detachment, *Grossdeutschland*
IV/Artillery Regiment *Grossdeutschland*
6/Flak Battalion *Grossdeutschland*
Kampfgruppe, Fuehrer Begleit Battalion

This order of battle illustrates several key facets of the tactical situation during von Manstein's counteroffensive, especially the manner in which an amalgamation of smaller units was cobbled together to create a potent offensive force out of three badly worn infantry divisions. *Grossdeutschland* had not completely arrived by 3 March, as is indicated by the scattering of divisional units among the other divisions of the corps. Corps Raus filed the following report of unit strength and combat strength on 8 March 1943:[16]

Division	Unit strength	Combat strength
167th Infantry	17,500	3,500
168th Infantry	7,900	1,000
320th Infantry	11,670	2,700
Grossdeutschland	20,415	3,800

Rifle company strengths confirmed the relative fighting power of the three infantry division and SS Panzergrenadier Regiment *Thule*. On 7 March Corps Raus filed this report:[17]

167th Infantry Division
Rifle company average: 115

168th Infantry Division
Rifle company average: 46

320th Infantry Division
G. R. 585 company average: 35
G. R. 586 company average: 41
G. R. 587 company average: 55

SS Panzergrenadier Regiment Thule
Rifle company average: 132

Rough calculations suggest that the combinations employed by Raus had equalized unit infantry strength at about 3,500–3,800 men per division.

APPENDIX 2B

Order of Battle: *Armeeabteilung* Kempf, 5 July 1943[18]

General of Panzer Troops Werner Kempf
Chief of Staff
Major General Hans Dr. Speidel

III Panzer Corps
General of Panzer Troops Hermann Breith
6th Panzer Division (minus Panzer Observation Battery 76)
Major General Walther von Huenersdorff
  II Battalion, Panzer Regiment 11
  Panzergrenadier Regiments 4, 114
  Panzer Artillery Regiment 76
  Panzer Reconnaissance Battalion 6
  Panzerjaeger Battalion 41
  Panzer Engineer Battalion 57

  Attached:
  Regimentsgruppe, 168th Infantry Division
  (Grenadier Regiment 417)
  (One company, Engineer Battalion 248)
  Reconnaissance Battalion 248
  Assault Gun Battalion 228
  II and III/Artillery Regiment 248 (168th Inf. Div.)
  III/Mortar Regiment 54

19th Panzer Division (minus Panzer Observation Battery 19)
Lieutenant General Gustav Schmidt[19]
  Panzer Regiment 27
  Panzergrenadier Regiments 73, 74
  Panzer Artillery Regiment 19
  Panzer Reconnaissance Battalion 19
  Panzerjaeger Battalion 19
  Panzer Engineer Battalion 19

Attached:

Regimentsgruppe, 168th Infantry Division
(Grenadier Regiment 429)
(One company, Engineer Battalion 248)
I/Artillery Regiment 248 (168th Inf. Div.)
Mortar Regiment 54 (-III)
One company, Tiger Battalion 503

7th Panzer Division (minus Panzer Observation Battery 78)
Lieutenant General Hans Freiherr von Funck
Panzer Regiment 25
Panzergrenadier Regiments 6, 7
Panzer Artillery Regiment 78
Panzer Reconnaissance Battalion 37
Panzerjaeger Battalion 42
Panzer Engineer Battalion 58

Attached:

Regimentsgruppe, 168th Infantry Division
(Grenadier Regiment 442)
(One company, Engineer Battalion 248)
IV and V/Artillery Regiment 248 (168th Inf. Div.)
One company, Tiger Battalion 503

Headquarters, 168th Infantry Division
Major General Walter Chales de Beaulieu[20]

(All infantry, reconnaissance, engineer, and artillery units attached out to the 6th, 7th, and 19th Panzer Divisions, or Artillery Commander 3)

Artillery Commander 3
Staff, Artillery Regiment 248 (168th Inf. Div.)
Artillery Battalions 857, II/62, II/71
Panzer Observation Batteries 19, 76, 78
Engineer Regimental Staff 4 (in 6th Pz. Div. area until 6 July)
Engineer Battalion 127
Bridge Construction Battalion 531
Bridge Column 110
Tiger Battalion 503 (minus two companies)
Panzer Signal Battalion 43
Military Police Troop 403
Cossack cavalry company

Cooperating Luftwaffe units
Corps Flak Commander (Commander, Flak Regt. 153)
Flak Regiment 153
(Flak Battalions II/43, I/61, 91)
Flak Regiment 99
(Flak Battalions I/38, IV/38)

Corps Raus (Special Employment)
General of Panzer Troops Erhard Raus

106th Infantry Division
Lieutenant General Werner Forst
　　Grenadier Regiments 239, 240, 241
　　Artillery Regiment 106
　　Reconnaissance Battalion 106
　　Panzerjaeger Battalion 106
　　Engineer battalion 106

320th Infantry Division
Major General Georg Postel
　　Grenadier Regiments 585, 586, 587
　　Artillery Regiment 320
　　Reconnaissance Company 320
　　Panzerjaeger Battalion 320
　　Engineer Battalion 320

Artillery Commander 153
　　Artillery Regimental Staff 781 (Special Employment)
　　Artillery Battalions I/77, I/273, II/54
　　Observation Battalion 31
　　Assault Gun Battalion 905
　　Self-Propelled Panzerjaeger Battalion 393
　　III/Heavy Mortar Regiment 1
　　Mortar Battalion 48
　　Engineer Regimental Staff 601 (Special Employment)
　　Engineer Battalion (Motorized) 62
　　Bridge Construction Battalion (Motorized) 923
　　Bridge Construction Sector Staff 8
　　Bridge Columns 7, 8, 20, 2/50, 102, 297, 2/407, 2/410, 610, 666
　　Road Construction Battalion 41

Cooperating Luftwaffe units
　　Flak Regiments 4, 7, 48

XLII Corps
General of Infantry Franz Mattenklott

282nd Infantry Division
Major General Wilhelm Kohler
　　Grenadier Regiments 848, 849, 850
　　Artillery Regiment 282
　　Fusilier Battalion 282
　　Panzerjaeger Battalion 282
　　Engineer Battalion 282

39th Infantry Division
Lieutenant General Ludwig Loeweneck

Grenadier Regiments 113, 114
Artillery Regiment 139
Reconnaissance Battalion 139
Panzerjaeger Battalion 139
Engineer Battalion 139

161st Infantry Division
Lieutenant General Heinrich Recke
Grenadier Regiments 336, 364, 371
Artillery Regiment 241
Reconnaissance Company 241
Panzerjaeger Battalion 241
Engineer Battalion 241

Artillery Commander 107
Artillery Battalion II/71
Artillery Battery 2/800
Mortar Regiment 77
Heavy Panzerjaeger Battalion 560
Heavy Panzerjaeger Battalion "C"
Heavy Mortar Battalion 580
Light Observation Battalion 13
Engineer Regimental Staff 520 (Special Employment)
Special Staff *Dauber*
Construction Battalions 26, 219
Construction Battalions (POW) 112, 153

Cooperating Luftwaffe units
Flak Regiment 77
Army Troops:
Senior Artillery Commander 310
Artillery Regimental Staff 612 (Special Employment)
Artillery Battalion II/Artillery Regiment 52
Commander of Mortar Troops 1
Mortar Regiment 52
Engineer Regimental Staff 674
Engineer Battalion (Motorized) 70
Bridge Column Sector Staff 925
Bridge Columns 9, 2/411, 1/505, 603, 842, 843

3

Fourth Panzer Army

by General of Infantry Friedrich Fangohr
Chief of Staff, Fourth Panzer Army

Editor's Introduction

Perhaps the most significant contribution of the postwar Kursk study—albeit one that has been unrealized until now—was Busse's fortunate selection of Friedrich Fangohr to write the chapter on Fourth Panzer Army operations. Fangohr penned only two other manuscripts for the historical program: P-031b (volume 6) on the training of General Staff officers and P-071 ("Region, Climate, Population, and Their Influence on Warfare in the Soviet Union"), which was later subsumed into the Raus study ("Effects of Climate on Combat in European Russia"). The attribution of this chapter to Fangohr is strong. First, he was the only senior member of Fourth Panzer Army staff to do any work for the U.S. Army (though the XLVIII Panzer Corps's Otto von Knobelsdorff and II SS Panzer Corps's Paul Hausser both produced studies on the 1944 campaign in France). Second, it is obvious from the context of the document itself that the author enjoyed direct personal access to army commander Hermann Hoth, and the segment covering the author's introduction to Operation Citadel simply could not have been written by anyone else. Thus we have a valuable lost memoir of sorts from a key participant on the battle of Kursk.

Fangohr himself has nearly been lost to history. Born in Hannover on 12 August 1899, he received a lieutenant's commission in Infantry Regiment 129 on 20 November 1917. Retained in the postwar army, he had risen by October 1937 to become a major and the operations officer of the 13th Infantry Division (Motorized), a position he held through the Polish campaign. On 5 February 1940, Lieutenant Colonel Fangohr became operations officer of the XLI Panzer Corps in Panzer Groups Kleist and Guderian, where he remained throughout the conquest of France and the abortive planning for an invasion of England. Almost exactly one year later (15 February 1941), Fangohr advanced to become chief of staff, LVII Panzer Corps (with a promotion to colonel on 1 March), which was assigned to Panzer Group 3. There his wartime working relationship with Hermann Hoth began, though not until 15 July 1942 did the two men become close collaborators, when Fangohr became chief of staff, Fourth Panzer Army, a position he would hold throughout all the critical southern campaigns, from the initial drive toward Stalingrad through the unsuccessful defensive battle west of the Dnepr in mid-1944.[1]

Colonel General Hermann Hoth could best be described as a panzer general in the mold of Heinz Guderian or Erwin Rommel, that is, he believed that mobile warfare could not be effectively directed from a map room somewhere miles behind the battle lines. In Fourth Panzer Army, noted F. W. von Mellenthin, "All senior officers, including corps commanders handling several panzer divisions, travelled in the forefront of the advance. Even General Hoth was more often with the leading tank units than with his staff, although army headquarters was always uncomfortably close to the front."[2] This style of operational leadership succeeded only when there was a chief of staff or operations officer back at headquarters who had the assertiveness to act in the name of his commander when necessary and who enjoyed such implicit trust on the part of that commander that his orders would invariably be sustained. Such officers became not so much the backbone as the spinal cord of German mobile operations, and such staff officers (Theodor Busse, Otto Woehler, Walter Wenck, and others) often rose to make names for themselves as senior commanders.

It is clear that Fangohr should be included in this category. Hoth's memoirs made clear the extent to which he relied on his chief of staff, a picture that Paul Carell sketched even more fully, and even von Manstein commented on the contributions of this "admirable" officer. Yet in many ways Fangohr remains almost invisible, without any discernable sense of color or personality. The most widely available sources, such as Guderian, von Mellenthin, Fridolin von Senger und Etterlin, and others, omit any mention of him, even though all of these officers knew and interacted with him on a regular basis during key periods of the war.[3]

Fangohr began his journey into obscurity even before the war ended. Once Hitler decided to remove Hoth from Fourth Panzer Army, characterizing him as a "bird of ill omen," Fangohr's days were numbered. On 25 August 1944, apparently after having been relieved of his position some weeks earlier, Fangohr took command of the 122nd Infantry Division in Army Group North, advancing to command of I Corps in the Courland pocket on 20 January 1945. Apparently evacuated from that strategic backwater in late March, he escaped Soviet captivity, serving for two weeks in mid-May as the head of the German liaison staff responsible for coordinating the disarmament and internment of Wehrmacht prisoners after the surrender at Rheims.[4]

What accounts for the pervasive obscurity of an able officer? Only speculation is possible at this point, but it seems to have been Fangohr's fate to have consistently served under officers who either drew Hitler's wrath (Hoth and Gustav von Wietersheim at XIV Panzer Corps) or those who were competent but not well-connected in the world of German army politics (Georg-Hans Reinhardt at XLI Panzer Corps and Friedrich Kirchner at LVII Panzer Corps). Lacking a powerful enough mentor, even competent officers like Fangohr could fall by the wayside.

In a personal sense little can be directly gleaned about Friedrich Fangohr from the text that follows, primarily because the work is technical in nature, and when it does concentrate on the contributions of any single individual, that person is Hoth, not Fangohr. In this regard Fangohr's study provides substantial information for broadening our understanding of the thought and actions of the officer who commanded Army Group South's panzer spearhead at Kursk to a far greater extent than even Hoth's own recollections.

Fangohr argues strongly that Fourth Panzer Army's operational plan of attack came from Hoth, not von Manstein, and that Hoth, in fact, managed to talk the field marshal into substantial changes to the original guidelines set by OKH. Critical among these changes is Fangohr's assertion that Hoth had always intended to divert the II SS Panzer Corps toward Prokhorovka to deal with the Fifth Guards Tank Army rather than thrust directly toward Oboyan and Kursk. The significance of this interpretation of Hoth's intent will be discussed in a later chapter.

During the course of the battle, when critical decisions were made between 11 and 13 July, Fangohr reveals several telling details about the relationship between Hoth and von Manstein. In particular, Hoth comes across in this narrative as consistently more aggressive and more operationally flexible in comparison to his army group commander. Given Fangohr's perspective and obvious loyalty to his own chief, this section of the manuscript must be used very carefully. But a consistent picture begins to emerge when this information is taken together with that from Busse and Raus. Fangohr's account of the battle itself is detailed down to division level, though it is rather devoid of tactical detail. He occasionally provides glimpses of the relationship between Hoth and his corps commanders, and he certainly substantiates his conclusion that a major reason for the battle's failure was lack of infantry, not a shortage of tanks. Within its limitations, therefore, Fangohr's analysis of Operation Citadel deserves to take its place as a major German source.

Note: Only a few personal notes were available for the preparation of this study, which was otherwise written from memory. The available maps—partly Luftwaffe editions (scale 1:300,000)—were not adapted for use in a critique of ground operations because elevations, towns, and many roads are not indicated.

Fourth Panzer Army
by General of Infantry Friedrich Fangohr
Chief of Staff, Fourth Panzer Army

Situation Through the End of June 1943

Between 21 February and 23 March 1943, Fourth Panzer Army and *Armeeabteilung* Kempf broke the strength of the Russian winter offensive of 1942–1943. The gap between Army Groups South and A had been closed again, and the west bank of the Donets (with the exception of a small Russian bridgehead northwest of Izyum) had been cleared of the enemy. The important industrial area in the Donets Basin was thereby protected against a threat from the north, while Kharkov and Belgorod were back in German hands. The portion of Army Group South's front immediately east of the Belgorod-Sumy sector was protected by the Don, but the area to the north lacked all natural obstacles and required permanent, strong forces to defend it.

The German command initially intended to push the lines of the Donets sector forward to the Oskol River in order to achieve a more favorable defensive line, which would both conserve our forces and hamper any Soviet attempt to encircle the Donets industrial area from the north. Attacks were planned both from the vicinity of Izyum and the area east of Kharkov. These undertakings had to be abandoned, however, because it seemed doubtful that the desired objectives could be gained, and the disadvantages of failure were disproportionate to what might be achieved (see Map 3.1).

Even so, we had to take into consideration that the Russians, when their units had been completely reorganized, would certainly undertake a large-scale offensive against the Dnepr River–Zaporozhe–Kiev line, probably launched from the Kursk salient as well as the east and north (through Stalino and Kharkov). Such an attack could be expected by the end of summer at the latest and could only be counteracted by preceding it with an attack of our own at the earliest possible moment.

In the meantime, the Russians remained generally inactive following the German recapture of Kharkov and Belgorod in March, though livelier combat activity appeared on the northern sector between Belgorod and the boundary with Army Group Center. Behind the lines the reinforcement of enemy artillery and the passage of reserves toward the front continued unabated. The Red Army particularly applied itself to constructing fortified defensive belts and improving the natural terrain. All ground and aerial reconnaissance reports agreed that the Soviets—at least for the time being—had concentrated exclusively on increasing the defensive strength of this sector as rapidly as possible.

On the other hand, heavy two-way traffic near the front indicated intensive reorganization of the units that had been battered in March, while large numbers of new forces continued to move into the Kursk–N. Oskol–St. Oskol area. This traffic far exceeded the normal requirements for reorganization and supply; we identified two new major concentrations of Soviet forces: into the Kursk salient from the east, and into the Starobelsk area from the Caucasus via Rostov. This led to the suspicion that the Red Army eventually intended to launch a wide envelopment of the Kharkov-Belgorod area, so that, after slicing off that salient, the enemy would possess the option of turning south against the Donets Basin or continuing west against the Dnepr. At least four tank and three mechanized corps assigned to the Twenty-first and Sixty-second Armies were positively identified in the main assembly areas. Thus, while enemy preparations in the Kharkov-Belgorod area appeared on the one hand to be purely defensive, it did not seem entirely unlikely that the Russians would attempt to regain the initiative and anticipate any German offensive by launching their own at the earliest possible date.

The following units had been drawn out of the front line in April for purposes of reorganization and training:

III Panzer Corps, consisting of the 6th and 7th Panzer Divisions and the *Grossdeutschland* Panzergrenadier Division;
II SS Panzer Corps, consisting of the *Liebstandarte Adolf Hitler* and *Das Reich* SS Panzergrenadier Divisions.

Once we realized the extent to which the Soviets had reinforced northeast of Belgorod, we kept a panzer *Kampfgruppe* ready at all times just north of Kharkov, so that any Russian surprise attack on Kharkov could be met immediately. This deployment was achieved by continually rotating the panzer divisions in the reorganization area with those at the front.

Fourth Panzer Army took over its new sector on 25 April . . . assuming command of the following units:

LII Corps (commanded by General of Infantry Eugen Ott), consisting of the 57th, 167th, 255th, and 332nd Infantry Divisions, all of which were committed to the front line;

II SS Panzer Corps (commanded by *Obergruppenfuehrer* Paul Hausser), consisting of the *Liebstandarte Adolph Hitler*, *Das Reich*, and *Totenkopf* SS Panzergrenadier Divisions. This corps had been committed to the front line—in whole or in part—since the end of the winter operation. Now Fourth Panzer Army had these divisions pulled out of the front and stationed in the Kharkov-Udy area for badly needed reorganization of personnel and equipment.

XLVIII Panzer Corps (commanded by General of Panzer Troops Otto von Knobelsdorff), consisting of the *Grossdeutschland* Panzergrenadier Division and the 11th Panzer Division. The 3rd Panzer Division was transferred from the 1st to the 4th Panzer Division only after the attack force for Operation Citadel had been assembled, thereby coming under command of XLVIII Panzer Corps. The corps was quartered southwest of the line Bogodukhov-Akhtyrka.

In order to allow the panzer divisions to be removed from the front line, Fourth Panzer Army had to assign LII Corps's infantry very wide defense sectors. Moreover, this was precisely the part of the front upon which the Russians remained the most restless, which made it difficult for the infantry itself to reorganize. Eventually the infantry had to be relieved by progressively replacing individual regiments with a reinforced panzergrenadier regiment from II SS Panzer Corps. Colonel General Hermann Hoth, commanding Fourth Panzer Army, realized that by taking this action he might inadvertently disclose his future plans to the Soviets but nonetheless decided to resort to this expedient, which was the only way for the divisions of LII Corps to rest their battalions for a few days by rotating them with those at the front.

Meanwhile, in their billeting areas both panzer corps prepared for their impending missions with numerous exercises ranging from small-unit to division-level problems. Training the senior leadership went hand-in-hand with training the troops; both included joint exercises with the Luftwaffe. Fourth Panzer Army placed particular emphasis on the tactics for breaking through a fortified position, breaching antitank ditches, and fighting against antitank strongpoints. Officers and noncommissioned officers both trained for the attack through sand-table exercises, map problems, and tactical terrain orientation meetings. In mid-June General Hoth conducted a command post exercise at his Bogodukhov headquarters for the corps commanders, division commanders, and leaders of special detachments. Based on the actual situation, this exercise had the primary purpose of demonstrating the intended course of action for the first days of Operation Citadel. (It should be noted that the results of the first days of the battle roughly conformed to those predicted by Hoth's exercise.) Thus the veteran divisions of the two panzer corps had been again brought to top-notch condition as far as personnel, equipment, and training were concerned.

The fighting spirit among the infantrymen of LII Corps was by no means inferior to that of the panzer troops. Long and continuous commitment to the front line had left these divisions in dire need of reorganization and rehabilitation. Within the constraints of the situation, General Hoth removed all possible obstacles and placed all possible means at General Ott's disposal, but the reorganization of the infantry, as compared to that of the panzer corps, remained a patchwork affair. It had to be admitted that just prior to deployment for battle the condition of these four infantry divisions was only "satisfactory."

General Hoth's Plan of Attack

I originally learned of the intention to carry out Operation Citadel while at Army Group South headquarters on 27 March. On 6 May, after various changes necessitated by the development of the situation and several postponements of the offensive, we received the first formal order to prepare for the attack. Along with Major General Hans Speidel, chief of staff of *Armeeabteilung* Kempf, I was given a detailed oral briefing at army group headquarters. We received the final attack order at army headquarters on 27 June, which specified that the main attack would jump off on 5 July. As proposed by General Hoth, these orders set aside the afternoon of 4 July for a preliminary attack to seize the observation posts needed by our artillery observers in order to direct fire on the main Russian line. Once this had been accomplished, the army group's operations order envisioned an attack to cut off and destroy all Soviet forces within the protruding Kursk salient in order to gain a shorter defensive line running directly from Belgorod to Orel. Fourth Panzer Army would attack out of the area west of Belgorod along a straight line running due north via Oboyan to seek contact with Ninth Army near Kursk. (Ninth Army would simultaneously attack south toward Kursk from the vicinity of Orel.)

Field Marshal von Manstein and General Hoth discussed the commitment of forces and the execution of the attack in detail on 10–11 May when the army group commander visited Fourth Panzer Army headquarters. General Hoth had developed several new ideas regarding the attack, and Field Marshal von Manstein accepted them as the basis for all further operational planning. General Hoth took into consideration several apparent changes in Soviet dispositions when he advanced these suggestions. It now appeared, for example, that the X Tank Corps had assembled in the vicinity of Oboyan, and during mid-June several days of noticeably heavy vehicular traffic had been observed moving from Voronezh to Kursk. Significant enemy concentrations remained along the Oskol River east of Kursk as well. General Hoth concluded that the Russians had presumably become aware of our intention and had shifted elements of their strategic reserve toward the west in order to have them more readily available.

On the basis of this estimate, General Hoth decided that the order to attack due north along a straight route via Oboyan was not to be interpreted literally. In Hoth's opinion, the terrain and enemy dispositions prohibited such a movement. From the region about twenty kilometers south of Oboyan the terrain sloped down toward the northeast and north to the Psel River and gradually rose again on the other bank of the river, affording the Russians excellent observation. The Psel River crossing sites in and around Oboyan were extremely narrow due to numerous ponds that could not be bypassed because of the river's course. Behind the Psel, on either side of Oboyan and southeast of the town, any Russian divisions thrown back in the attack out of Belgorod would therefore reach a natural fallback position and rallying point.

General Hoth also had to assume that Soviet strategic reserves—including several tank corps—would enter the battle by pushing quickly through the narrow passage between the Donets and Psel Rivers at Prokhorovka (about fifty kilometers northeast of Belgorod). If Fourth Panzer Army's spearheads were engaged in a difficult fight for the Psel crossing sites around Oboyan, then a Russian tank attack would hit our right flank at exactly the moment in which the panzer divisions had their freedom of movement extremely limited by the Psel River. Because such a situation could quickly turn into a disaster, General Hoth realized that his plans must anticipate an engagement with Soviet armored reserves near Prokhorovka prior to continuing the attack toward Kursk. He considered it vital to employ the strongest possible force in such a fight, so that we could compel the enemy to meet us on terrain of our choosing in which the panzer divisions could fully exploit their superior mobility, unhampered by the Psel River. Accordingly, following our penetration of the enemy's defensive belt, II SS Panzer Corps would not advance due north across the Psel but veer sharply northeast toward Prokhorovka to destroy the Russian tank forces we expected to find there. Such a maneuver had the advantage that it would place us much nearer to the intended thrust of *Armeeabteilung* Kempf's III Panzer Corps, raising the possibility of the coordination of the two interior army wings on the battlefield. Such a prospect also led General Hoth to modify the mission of XLVIII Panzer Corps on our left flank. After its initial breakthrough on either side of Cherkasskoe, the corps would not push north to the Psel but keep abreast of II SS Panzer Corps as it wheeled northeast. Such a maneuver would cover *Obergruppenfuehrer* Hausser's flank as he advanced toward the decisive battle and potentially provide additional reinforcements for that engagement. To be sure, we could not as yet determine the manner in which XLVIII Panzer Corps might be committed around Prokhorovka, though in no event would we commit General von Knobelsdorff's corps to an attack west of this objective. No plan of battle could be made for the continuation of the operation after achieving a victory at Prokhorovka, but such a success would place us in the strategic divide between the Oskol, Donets, Psel, and Seim Rivers, from which we would be able to continue the advance in any desired direction (see Map 3.2).

General Hoth also called Field Marshal von Manstein's attention to the fact that breaking through the Russian defensive system would be difficult, costly, and time-consuming. He did not expect Fourth Panzer Army to achieve strategic freedom of movement until we had penetrated the line Teterevino-Novenkoye, roughly twenty-seven to thirty kilometers southeast of Oboyan, where the third and final Soviet defensive belt was located.

The map exercises ordered by General Hoth during June embodied this concept of the forthcoming battle; the general emphasized it in every conversation he held with his subordinates. Every officer from General Hoth down to the youngest lieutenant was so thoroughly indoctrinated with these ideas that the course of the first few days of the operation actually conformed to our expectations.

Nevertheless, the general continued to worry about whether or not our forces could measure up to this difficult task. He felt that two panzer corps with six panzer and panzergrenadier divisions between them constituted an attack force too weak to accomplish their mission. On the other hand, we all believed that the quality of these divisions and their equipment justified visualizing an intangible factor that might restore the balance. The allocation of two battalions deploying between them 188 of the new Pzkw V Panthers appeared to support such a view and brought us up to a total of 700 tanks available to the army during the operation. More distressing in some respects was the nagging doubt—repeatedly expressed to higher headquarters—that the infantry divisions assigned to Fourth Panzer Army simply did not possess sufficient strength to carry out their vital role: protecting the army's ever-lengthening flanks. Eventually, army headquarters found itself forced to employ a variety of auxiliary measures and improvisations to secure our flanks, but these expedients were never able to compensate for the weakness of the infantry. Finally, General Hoth remained convinced that the Germany Army had lost the element of surprise through the repeated postponement of the offensive. Accumulating and reorganizing six panzer divisions south of the Kharkov-Akhtyrka area over a period of several months simply could not have escaped Soviet detection despite all deception measures.

Even so, General Hoth appeared confident of achieving at least a limited victory. With regard to the breakthrough attack against the Russian defensive system, he anticipated complete success. Given our tank strength and state of training, he had confidence as well in the outcome of the expected collision at Prokhorovka, though he never doubted that this would come at the cost of heavy casualties both in personnel and equipment. Whether our remaining forces would suffice for the long, contested drive into the area east of Kursk remained to be seen. Few if any troops would be available to bolster Fourth Panzer Army's strength, even at that critical juncture. Army Group South was the only possible source of reinforcements, and it moved up XXIV Panzer Corps (*Wiking* SS Panzergrenadier Division and 17th Panzer Division) for this purpose. By the time Fourth Panzer Army had become embroiled at Prokhorovka, this corps had arrived behind the army west of Kharkov, but, as a result of the early termination of the attack, it was never committed.

The troops faced this new effort with great expectations. After all, every soldier in Fourth Panzer Army had worked toward its preparation since the first days of spring. For them, all prerequisites for a successful breakthrough appeared to be at hand, and they tackled their assigned missions with enthusiasm.

On 1 July, Adolf Hitler summoned the participating commanders of the army and Luftwaffe—down to corps commanders—to his headquarters. He explained the military and political reasons for the attack and why it had been postponed several times. A *Fuehrerdirectiv*, issued shortly before the start of the offensive, emphasized the importance of the operation, which was to demonstrate to the Russians that despite the reverses suffered during the winter of 1942–1943 the German spirit of attack had not been broken.

Missions, Objectives, and Deployment

By early July no essential changes by the enemy in our front had been noticed. The Russians had apparently committed an additional rifle division in the front line near Belgorod, and during late June we noticed for the first time the presence of Red Army troops in the Pena River sector northeast of Rakitnoye. According to our best intelligence, however, only local reserves had been involved in these changes. The presence of a tank corps at Oboyan (tentatively identified as the X Tank Corps) had been repeatedly confirmed. The Soviets spared no effort to improve their defensive system, even employing female personnel. Aerial photographs suggested that the Russians had substantially improved their position in front of the narrow strip of land at Prokhorovka. Meanwhile the enemy attempted with every means at his disposal to lift the veil that hung over German intentions. Throughout June, enemy reconnaissance activity both on the ground and in the air had increased in intensity and scope. On at least two occasions we discovered enemy agents within the bivouac areas of our panzer divisions.

The disposition and mission of the two assault corps was as follows:

Both corps had been reinforced with infantry: II SS Panzer Corps receiving elements of the 167th Infantry Division, while XLVIII Panzer Corps had the remainder of the 167th as well as the 332nd Infantry Division assigned to it. In addition to its three panzer or panzergrenadier divisions, XLVIII Panzer Corps received Brigade "Decker" (10th Panzer Brigade) with its 188 factory-new Pzkw V Panthers. This brigade consisted primarily of newly trained personnel without battle experience. The Panthers, likewise, had not yet been tried in battle and during the buildup had already evidenced serious technical defects. Brigade headquarters lacked communications equipment and the appropriate armored command vehicles. The brigade, therefore, suffered from all the ills that are associated with hastily organized and unblooded units. Generals Hoth and Knobelsdorff both knew that the brigade (which had to be committed under *Grossdeutschland* at the *Schwerpunkt*) was not going to measure up to the great hopes that Hitler had placed in it.

Breaking through the primary and secondary Russian defensive belts between Belgorod and Tomarovka fell to the II SS Panzer Corps, with the main effort to be located at the interior wings of *Das Reich* and *Liebstandarte Adolf Hitler*. A predawn attack on 4 July would eliminate enemy combat outposts on the high ground opposite *Das Reich* and allow us to place our own artillery observation posts there. Two heavy artillery battalions and one *Nebelwerfer* (rocket artillery) brigade augmented II SS Panzer Corps during the breakthrough phase. *Obergruppenfuehrer* Hausser's divisions would then drive forward and secure the dominant ridge southeast of Prokhorovka.

XLVIII Panzer Corps would make its main effort in the right half of its sector, breaking through Soviet positions on either side of the Butovo-Cherkasskoe area. The corps would launch a limited-objective attack in the afternoon of 4 July, prior to the opening of the main offensive, in order to seize the dominating heights of Sybino (southwest of Butovo). This ridge would be a critical position for our artillery observers on 5 July to utilize in directing fire on the enemy's main battle line. XLVIII Panzer Corps had also been allocated additional artillery assets for the breakthrough phase. Following its breakthrough, General von Knobelsdorff would not continue due north and cross the Pena River as his original operations orders had envisioned but instead pivot to the northeast and keep abreast of the II SS Panzer Corps as it drove toward Prokhorovka. Such a deployment was intended to protect our spearhead element's left flank from the X Tank Corps, still presumed to be in the Oboyan area.

Both panzer corps would attack simultaneously on 5 July after a brief, two-hour artillery preparation. In his attack order, General Hoth emphasized that both corps must pay particular attention to providing constant and adequate protection for their exterior wings and flanks. Additional infantry elements had been attached to each corps headquarters for this purpose.

LII Corps received orders to detach those elements of the 255th Infantry Division located west of Vorsklitsa by extending the 57th Infantry Division's sector as the attack progressed. Those elements of the 255th thus removed from the line would be organized into a *Kampfgruppe* to operate in the XLVIII Panzer Corps area as soon as possible. This *Kampfgruppe* would screen the panzer corps's wing and flank, taking up echeloned positions on the left. The remainder of LII Corps was to stage a feint attack on its right wing during the afternoon of 4 July, at the same time XLVIII Panzer Corps started its attack; on 5 July the corps had the mission of following in the wake of the panzer corps attack, in the area east of Vorsklitsa. Those elements of the 255th Infantry Division still under corps control would join the 332nd Infantry Division in this subsidiary advance; we instructed General Ott to retain the 57th Infantry Division in an exclusively defensive stance.

Army Group South had assigned *Armeeabteilung* Kempf to protect the right flank of Fourth Panzer Army. The attack orders issued by the *Armeeabteilung*, in accordance with agreements made with Fourth Panzer Army, required III Panzer Corps to debauch from the Belgorod bridgehead and the area immediately to the south to jab through the Soviet defensive system and then drive toward Korocha. This panzer attack had to defeat whatever Russian forces might be found there or might be expected to arrive in that vicinity later. Provisional Corps Raus, deployed on the *Armeeabteilung*'s right, would cover the southern and western flank of III Panzer Corps by concentrating its forces for an attack on its northern wing.

The Course of the Battle

XLVIII Panzer Corps's preliminary attack on 4 July commenced at 1500. For this initial attack, the corps committed its infantry without tank support. The morning had been quiet, but an extraordinarily heavy thunderstorm struck just as the attack opened. The downpour was torrential, lasting until the late afternoon. Nevertheless, the operation progressed without interference thanks to excellent preparation. Attack elements of the 167th Infantry Division, 11th Panzer Division, and *Grossdeutschland* Panzergrenadier Division had all reached their objectives by 1800. The 3rd Panzer Division and the 332nd Infantry Division, however, took heavy flanking fire from the Sybino heights, and the 332nd proved unable to secure that ridge during the day. Forward elements of both divisions had to endure Russian counterattacks, which lasted into the night.

The weather improved that night, but the roads remained muddy and Russian artillery was very active. Under these conditions, the main elements of XLVIII Panzer Corps still accomplished the difficult move into their assembly areas on time. Colonel Decker's 10th Panzer Brigade, however, ran into extreme difficulties with the suddenly swampy terrain. Mechanical defects accounted for the loss of 25 percent of his vehicles during the night. Though most of these defects were minor, forty-five Panthers did not manage to ride into action on the first day of the attack. Combat losses incurred subsequently made it impossible to make up for this initial loss.

II SS Panzer Corps succeeded in wiping out the Soviet outposts on its front after bitter fighting. Rainfall in that sector had not been as severe, and the corps's attack echelon was therefore able to move into its assembly area with considerably less difficulty.

The LII Corps's feint attack in the afternoon of 4 July misfired. After suffering substantial losses, the corps had to discontinue the operation.

On 5 July both panzer corps jumped off at 0600 after the planned two-hour artillery preparation. We subsequently established that, though brief, this barrage had been very effective.

The II SS Panzer Corps rolled over countless antitank ditches, knocked out antitank weapons in large numbers, and fought its way through the first and second Soviet defensive belts on 5–6 July. VIII Fleiger Corps had to carry out several missions with powerful bomber formations to subdue the enemy artillery completely. Here it must be acknowledged that General of Fliers Hans von Seidemann, the VIII Fleiger Corps commander, and his pilots supported Fourth Panzer Army brilliantly throughout the course of the offensive. On 7 July, *Obergruppenfuehrer* Hausser noticed, with considerable apprehension, that his right flank had become exposed because *Armeeabteilung* Kempf had so far been unable to make substantial gains northeast across the Donets. Fierce and repeated Russian counterattacks along the Prokhorovka-Belgorod railway, as well as from the north against II SS Panzer Corps's left wing, forced the detachment of major elements for flank protection. To be candid, despite the efforts of the *Armeeabteilung*, II SS Panzer Corps's right flank never ceased to be exposed and threatened until the moment the offensive was suspended. We therefore found it hardly possible to gain ground on 7 July, and the day passed in mopping up individual positions in the Russian defensive system and regrouping for a continuation of the attack the following morning. By evening the corps had consolidated a line running roughly from Teterevino to a point northeast of Rozhdesdevskoye.

Fourth Panzer Army now transferred the entire 167th Infantry Division to II SS Panzer Corps to provide security along its eastern flank. This division immediately moved to the right wing, where it relieved the *Totenkopf* SS Panzergrenadier Division, which could then be employed to strengthen the main attack. This transfer was not an improvisation; we had intended from the very beginning to attach the 167th Infantry to the II SS Panzer Corps, and the measure had been thoroughly discussed during our map exercises. Although it would have been preferable to transfer the division at an earlier date, this was not possible, for without the additional infantry XLVIII Panzer Corps would have been insufficiently strong to breach the Russian defenses.

The advance of XLVIII Panzer Corps suffered major delays as it struggled not just against the Russians but also with formidable terrain obstacles. Specifically, a creek bed ran south and southeast of Butovo that could not be bypassed; the mud in this creek bed defies description. At the same time, enemy flanking fire from the positions still held atop the Sybino heights made itself felt. Because the main effort of VIII Fleiger Corps had to be concentrated in support of II SS Panzer Corps on 5 July, General von Knobelsdorff received little air support. Moreover, enemy tactical reserves launched continuous if often disjointed counterattacks. All in all, XLVIII Panzer Corps had a tough fight on the first day of the attack, suffering losses that were far from negligible. By evening the corps held a line that ran generally from Dragunskoye to a point east of Cherkasskoe and then to a point southwest of Korovino.

On 6 July the Russians unexpectedly cut loose with a cannonade of defensive fire: They brought all arms into play, including long-range artillery. This occurred as the German advance entered an area in which countless enemy tanks had been dug in, hull-down; they were camouflaged and cleverly distributed over the terrain. Each tank represented a strongpoint in itself, the destruction or capture of which was costly and time-consuming. Our maneuvers had to be executed in loose formations (which was already being done), and it was virtually impossible to use roads. Thus added to the time lost in knocking out these buried tanks were the delays incurred when it became necessary for German troops to move off the roads into the exceptionally muddy ground. As was to be expected, the Panthers of the 10th Panzer Brigade suffered most as a result of this situation.

Elements of the 167th Infantry Division were the only corps units to make good progress, gaining ground slowly but steadily. The division reached the area of Dmitriyeskoye that afternoon, following which it was attached to the II SS Panzer Corps. The 11th Panzer Division captured numerous localities and reached the Pena River north and northeast of Cherkasskoe. Immediately to the west of the town, XLVIII Panzer Corps even managed to advance farther north. Despite two days of difficulties, by the evening of 6 July General von Knobelsdorff's corps had succeeded in breaching the Soviet defensive system, penetrating along the general line Teterevino-Novenkoye.

XLVIII Panzer Corps regrouped during the night, a measure that had become necessary as the advance east of the Pena River created both dangers and opportunities. General von Knobelsdorff ordered the 11th Panzer Division and *Grossdeutschland* Panzergrenadier Division to continue the attack on both sides of the road to Oboyan. This advance was effected in relatively close contact with the SS divisions on the right. The 3rd Panzer Division was to follow *Grossdeutschland*'s left flank, while 332nd Infantry Division received instructions to continue its screening mission on XLVIII Panzer Corps's left flank south of the Pena.

Leading elements of both spearhead divisions clashed with major Soviet tank forces attacking from the north almost immediately (apparently the advance elements of X Tank Corps). General von Knobelsdorff's divisions won a complete victory after overcoming initial difficulties; he ordered a pursuit of the Russians as they fled to the north and gained ground quite extensively. By evening advance elements of 11th Panzer and *Grossdeutschland* had arrived just south of the line Shipy-Gorki. Achieved on the third day of the offensive, this represented the northernmost line gained during Operation Citadel. By this juncture, however, the flanks of both 11th Panzer and *Grossdeutschland* were overextended and exposed; hardly any troops remained to throw out a defensive screen. Meanwhile, General von Knobelsdorff had been advised that the main body of X Tank Corps, along with elements of other Russian tank units, was approaching from the north and northeast. All that could be done to reinforce XLVIII Panzer Corps's advance positions was to move 3rd Panzer Division behind *Grossdeutschland* in the Syrtsevo area; the 332nd Infantry made only negligible changes in its defensive sector.

Even with this exposure and the prospect of a strong Red Army counterattack, 7 July marked a complete victory for General Knobelsdorff's men. They had not only routed Soviet tank forces in a meeting engagement but—more critical from the overall perspective of the offensive— had succeeded in slogging their way close enough to Oboyan to bring the Psel River crossing under artillery fire. This now allowed us to render the commitment of fresh enemy units into the area more difficult, though the Russians drew the same conclusion and immediately began constructing new bridges on either side of Oboyan.

Until the evening of 7 July, the progress of the attack by our two panzer corps conformed to General Hoth's expectations, though the threat to the flanks of both corps remained substantially greater than had been originally anticipated. Rain and difficult terrain had delayed our timetable considerably, but XLVIII and II SS Panzer Corps had both gained ground to the north and northeast with sufficient speed and to such an extent that we could look forward with confidence to an encounter with the Soviet strategic armored reserve—an event that seemed to be pending at any moment. On the other hand, it must be mentioned that most of the Russians' emplaced artillery had been able to withdraw behind the Psel and Pena Rivers; major enemy elements were cut off and taken prisoner in one place only. The Red Army attacked on our flanks again and again, stubbornly resisting all attempts to extend the width of our penetration wedge. Resolute enemy resistance and heavy defensive artillery fire against *Armeeabteilung* Kempf allowed the Soviets to maintain heavy pressure against Fourth Panzer Army's right wing. Elements of II SS Panzer Corps, as a result, still remained on the defensive immediately north of Belgorod, which diminished *Obergruppenfuehrer* Hausser's strength for the main effort.

The enemy staged probing attacks against the greatly weakened left flank of Fourth Panzer Army at Krasnopolye. So far these attacks had been repulsed without difficulty, but adjoining Second Army on our left made no appearance on the scene. North of the Kursk salient, Ninth Army continued to struggle against the Russian defensive system, defending itself against heavy armored attacks, mounted by as many as 200 tanks at a time.

For the moment, there was nothing that could have caused General Hoth to change the direction of the attacks as he had originally planned them. But the meager successes of *Armeeabteilung* Kempf and Ninth Army raised doubts in his mind as to whether it was going to be possible to cut off the "Kursk bend." Because we had no indications that the Soviets intended to give up this area voluntarily, we had to expect powerful diversionary attacks along the entire Fourth Panzer Army front, particularly in II SS Panzer Corps's sector.

On 8 July the *Liebstandarte Adolf Hitler* SS Panzergrenadier Division wiped out major enemy tank units that had been holding out near Prokovskoye, in the area between the two panzer corps. On 9–10 July *Liebstandarte Adolf Hitler* and *Das Reich* continued their attack, advancing slowly on both sides of the railroad and highway leading to Prokhorovka (see Map 3.3). Until that moment, major elements of *Totenkopf* had been tied down protecting the corps's right flank; with the arrival of the 167th Infantry Division, *Totenkopf* fell in behind the left wing of the attack. II SS Panzer Corps jumped off for its direct attack on Prokhorovka on 11 July. *Totenkopf* attempted to force a crossing of the Psel near Prelestroye and succeeded in establishing a bridgehead. *Liebstandarte Adolf Hitler* and *Das Reich* continued to struggle against stiff resistance along the railroad and were ultimately unable to push beyond the area southeast of Bogorodits. This initially prevented the corps from exploiting the advantage gained near Prelestroye.

Meanwhile, on 8 July XLVIII Panzer Corps underwent heavy attacks by the Russian X Tank Corps and other newly arrived units, including the III Mechanized Corps. Against these attacks, General von Knobelsdorff's troops held their positions with difficulty. Soviet resistance on the corps's extended western flank had also increased, preventing us from widening our breach in the enemy defenses. The 3rd Panzer Division did succeed in crossing the creek near Valdimirovka to take Kruglik, but it became increasingly obvious that Russian strength in the Pena River bend necessitated a deliberate assault before the situation there could be declared as being consolidated and before we could think of continuing an attack to the north.

Prisoner-of-war statements, intercepted radio traffic, and reports from ground reconnaissance suggested to army headquarters that we faced the following enemy tank units: II Guards Tanks Corps and one unidentified corps on our eastern flank; III Mechanized Corps, V Guards Tank Corps, and X Tank Corps directly in front of our advance; and VI Tank Corps on the western flank in the Pena bend. Although radio intercepts indicated that additional enemy units continued to arrive, a considerable part of the Soviet strategic reserve had already been committed.

Bitter defensive fighting characterized the situation on 9 July in XLVIII Panzer Corps's northern sector, just south of Oboyan. General von Knobelsdorff's troops managed to advance only a short distance in that area. On the other hand, 3rd Panzer Division staged a determined and spirited attack in the Pena bend, advanced southwest, and breached the sector from the rear in the vicinity of Berezovka, forcing the Russians to evacuate the area north of the Pena bank up to the area southwest of Bakovo. The 332nd Infantry Division immediately followed up this success, attacking across the Pena and seizing an area extending north up to the southern edge of Melovoye. Unfortunately, the 332nd Infantry lacked the strength to annihilate the enemy, and his main body escaped to the north. Engineers began throwing up a sixty-ton military bridge at Bakovo, which they completed by noon on 11 July. On 10 July, XLVIII Panzer Corps mopped up strong enemy units in the woods in the Pena bend north of Bakovo and east of Melovoye, an action entailing bitter tank battles with both sides suffering considerable losses—German tank formations, however, won every engagement. One large group of enemy tanks found itself bottled up and unable to escape to the north due to lack of fuel; the Russian crews defended their immobilized vehicles quite stubbornly. The situation on the northern sector was rich in critical moments that day. Superior enemy tank and infantry units repeatedly assaulted XLVIII Panzer Corps's weak defensive positions. Only a supreme effort and repeated counterthrusts served to repulse these attacks. In the course of these counterattacks, General von Knobelsdorff's troops succeeded in somewhat improving their hasty positions, and by evening not one inch of ground had been yielded anywhere in the corps sector. Fortunately, in its own bitter fight in front of Prokhorovka, II SS Panzer Corps had engaged major Soviet forces, thus to some small extent relieving the pressure against XLVIII Panzer Corps's eastern flank.

XLVIII Panzer Corps realized that it would have to be prepared for further heavy enemy counterattacks along its frontal sector and in the Pena bend. Given the extent to which his units were already stretched, General von Knobelsdorff did not believe he could hold his ground on 11 July with such forces as he had at his disposal. In the face of the overall situation, General Hoth found himself forced to agree. A *Kampfgruppe* of the 255th Infantry Division had been freed from the line in LII Corps sector as the 57th Infantry Division extended its own defensive sector; the necessity of employing this *Kampfgruppe* in the XLVIII Panzer Corps sector had been contemplated from the beginning. Now these elements of the 255th Infantry moved up to screen the corps's left flank south of the Pena River. The 332nd Infantry was thus enabled to transfer its own remaining elements north of the river, which in turn allowed part of the 3rd Panzer Division to be relieved, which General von Knobelsdorff could then use to reinforce his northern frontal sector. General Hoth realized full well that he had accepted a calculated risk in so widely extending the 57th Infantry's line, but as the Russians opposing LII Corps had shown no aggressive intentions so far, he believed he could take this chance. It turned out that he was right.

Even more intense fighting occurred on the northern and western sectors of General von Knobelsdorff's line on 11 July, with Russian efforts chiefly centered on liberating the immobilized tank force. Corps headquarters intercepted radio traffic instructing the Soviet tank crews to "stick it out" and stand by their vehicles—relief was on the way. Accordingly, the crews and whatever infantry had happened to be trapped along with them conducted a stubborn defense. These Russians abandoned their stranded tanks only after fierce fighting; nearly 100 undamaged enemy tanks fell into our hands. At nearly the same moment, elements of 3rd Panzer Division jabbed into a Soviet tank assembly area, taking the enemy completely by surprise. The division chalked up a quite respectable victory and brought in both prisoners and captured equipment. Most of the elements of the 332nd Infantry had meanwhile crossed the Pena, allowing corps headquarters to effect the intended regrouping of its forces during the night of 11–12 July. In this manner General von Knobelsdorff reinforced his northern sector and simultaneously strengthened his flanks.

Fourth Panzer Army had reached the end of the second phase of its offensive by the evening of 11 July. During the initial phase, we had broken through the enemy defensive system, advancing north and northeast and capturing many hundreds of prisoners and large amounts of booty. This portion of the attack had, in general, progressed well. Defensive actions against enemy forces—some from their tactical reserves and some newly arrived—characterized the second phase, while XLVIII Panzer Corps mopped up Russian forces in the Pena River bend. We had again won a considerable success, destroying or seizing in usable condition over 900 tanks while also inflicting heavy losses on the enemy's air assets. The Russian air forces continuously flew sorties whenever the weather permitted, pounding our units much more heavily than we expected; even so, by the evening of 11 July the Soviets had lost nearly 1,000 aircraft south of Kursk. Nevertheless, considered as a whole, the offensive no longer appeared to be progressing in a satisfactory manner. Our forces were simply not strong enough to win a decisive battle facing a host of Russian tank units while our own troops had their strength sapped in costly defensive fighting that gained little ground.

The northern wing of *Armeeabteilung* Kempf continued to make slow and unsatisfactory progress and remained unable to relieve any of the pressure against Fourth Panzer Army. For the offensive to succeed, we badly needed such relief. In an attempt to aid the *Armeeabteilung*, Field Marshal von Manstein briefly considered the idea of employing one panzer and one infantry division of Fourth Panzer Army across the Donets in the *Armeeabteilung*'s northern sector. Pushing south, this force would grip the enemy in the flank and rear where it threatened the *Armeeabteilung*'s front. General Hoth countered with the idea of turning the entire II SS Panzer Corps south after taking Prokhorovka, and Field

Marshal von Manstein did not turn a deaf ear to this proposition. He did, however, reserve to himself the right to make the final decision; as events unfolded, further developments removed the need for deciding on such a proposition.

Ninth Army's attack in the north had virtually ground to a halt by this time. Although the troops were fighting hard, they could barely hold the positions already won.

On 12 July, the Russians staged an offensive along Army Group South's entire sector, under unified command, bringing up additional units to participate in the attack (see Map 3.4). The Soviets threw the V Mechanized Corps against the *Armeeabteilung*'s III Panzer Corps south of Prokhorovka, hitting that corps as it advanced from the area northeast of Belgorod. The XVIII and XXIX Tanks Corps attacked II SS Panzer Corps in the vicinity of Prokhorovka, penetrating German positions in several places. We identified the newly arrived 9th Rifle Division on the defensive west of Prokhorovka. Supported by an independent tank brigade, the 13th Guards Rifle Division (brought up from the area of St. Oskol) continuously assaulted XLVIII Panzer Corps's right wing in the area east of the Belgorod-Oboyan highway. In the Pena bend, the battered X Tank Corps doggedly attempted to push south. The 219th Rifle Division, which had previously been committed near Krasnopolye, now attempted to force back General von Knobelsdorff's attenuated left wing. Some of these attacks continued throughout 13–14 July and may well have been executed in coordination with the counteroffensive staged by the Russian Third Army against the Second Panzer Army southeast and east of Orel, which itself had been inaugurated with an exceptionally heavy artillery preparation on 12 July.

Through bitter and indecisive fighting, II SS Panzer Corps held its positions. Casualties—particularly those of the Russians—were high. Valiant German soldiers literally sacrificed themselves but succeeded in eliminating all enemy penetrations without losing ground. In these battles, our antitank weapons bagged an exceptionally high number of Russian tanks. Despite Soviet pressure, the corps actually managed to expand its Prelestroye bridgehead. Yet faced with such superior Red Army forces, *Obergruppenfuehrer* Hausser could no longer think of continuing the attack on 12 or 13 July. Moreover, a sizeable gap still remained between II SS Panzer Corps and *Armeeabteilung* Kempf, even though III Panzer Corps had been able to fight its way into the Sobyshno area. Soviet troops caught in the gap between our two armies repeatedly launched attacks against the SS divisions' open flank.

No important changes took place in XLVIII Panzer Corps sector on 12–13 July. The Russians attacked the corps's northern front with rising fury but were repulsed along the entire line. General von Knobelsdorff's troops slowly pressed on behind the withdrawing enemy each time, improving their defensive positions. Nowhere did the Soviets succeed in regaining lost terrain. On the western flank, near Novenkoye, heavy tank battles raged, and the X Tank Corps was able to win a temporary victory; XLVIII Panzer Corps had to throw the very last of its available units into this breach. Colonel Decker's Panther brigade had to be pulled out of the front lines on 13 July after it had lost most of its tanks due to mechanical defects. This brigade had started out—at least on paper—as a formidable outfit. Hitler and the chief of the Army General Staff both had placed their faith in this unit, but the brigade unfortunately turned out to be a disappointment in most respects.

In the afternoon of 14 July, II SS Panzer Corps attacked again and gained the area south of Prokhorovka. *Obergruppenfuehrer* Hausser's tanks were about to break into the city, while enemy attacks on all other corps sectors were being repulsed. On the same afternoon, XLVIII Panzer Corps scored another victory in the Psel River bend near Novenkoye, inflicting heavy losses on the Russians who had penetrated our positions. General von Knobelsdorff's left wing fought its way into the area north of Novenkoye, gaining artillery observation posts commanding the Psel River valley west of Oboyan.

Such was the situation. There was well-deserved satisfaction with Fourth Panzer Army's latest victories and with the knowledge that we stood on the brink of forcing a final decision over the Soviet strategic tank reserve at Prokhorovka. At this moment of opportunity, however, Army Group South notified General Hoth that Fourth Panzer Army would not continue its advance on 15 July. He was informed that Ninth Army's attack had been discontinued to deal with the Soviet offensive against Second Panzer Army in the Orel salient and that massive Russian attacks against Sixth Army and First Panzer Army were imminent at Izyum and along the Mius River (see Map 3.5). Army Group South ordered Fourth Panzer Army to make all preparations necessary to hold its gains, to clear the Pena and Psel River bends, and to be in a position to advance on the enemy rear south of the Psel. This operation—codenamed "Roland"—appeared quite promising, but we were never permitted to carry it out. The combined enemy offensives against Second Panzer Army, Ninth Army, Sixth Army, and First Panzer Army required the immediate transfer of almost all of our panzer divisions. On 17–18 July Fourth Panzer Army lost all three divisions of the II SS Panzer Corps (redeployed to Stalino); *Grossdeutschland* Panzergrenadier Division (transferred to Army Group Center); and 3rd Panzer Division (transferred to First Panzer Army). We retained only the following units: 11th

Panzer Division and the 57th, 167th, 255th, and 332nd Infantry Divisions. With such reduced forces, our army was not in a position to hold our extended line; it was thus necessary for army headquarters to order a retirement to a shorter, prepared position.

German troops had chalked up tremendous achievements against prohibitive odds. Yet despite the fact that the soldiers and their combat leaders had given their very best, the objective could not be achieved, nor had the Red Army's offensive strength been noticeably diminished. The four rifle divisions that had been initially struck by Fourth Panzer Army's attack had certainly been so badly mauled that they had to be pulled out of the line for reorganization; the X Tank Corps had likewise suffered heavy losses. Two other Soviet mobile corps had lost countless tanks trying to break through at Prokhorovka and between that city and Belgorod. By the same token, German losses had been anything but negligible. Equipment losses might be replaced as time went by, but our manpower losses were irreplaceable. This loss of strength became increasingly apparent during the following weeks and months as our front rolled back toward the Dnepr River.

Yet final, decisive Russian defeat had been in the offing at the very moment that it became necessary to discontinue the offensive.

Conclusions

Any attempt to discover the reasons for the failure of Operation Citadel will reveal the following:

The forces committed were inadequate for the mission and objectives assigned. The two panzer corps were in superb condition—words cannot adequately praise their fighting spirit. Yet fighting trim and martial spirit could not compensate for severe numerical inferiority. The narrow wedge driven into the enemy defenses by the XLVIII and II SS Panzer Corps never achieved sufficient width. German infantry strength was far too low; this has been remarked upon previously and may be deduced by the most superficial examination of the operation. We did not commit enough infantry to enable us to make the panzergrenadier regiments available for their primary mission at critical points in the battle. This shortage of infantry forced General Hoth and *Obergruppenfuehrer* Hausser to commit one third of the panzergrenadiers and artillery of the *Totenkopf* SS Panzergrenadier Division in the outpost line west of Belgorod for several crucial days.

The German offensive did not strike the Russians in a vital spot. The Red Army would probably have sacrificed the few units it had in the Kursk salient without hesitation in order to win a victory on another sector of the front. Nor did our attack force the Soviets to throw the bulk of the reserves being held for subsequent attacks into the area of the German penetration. One must therefore conclude that Operation Citadel lacked a truly decisive strategic objective.

The two major attack groups—Fourth Panzer and Ninth Armies— were too far apart. Ninth Army was never in a position to derive any benefit from the victories scored by Fourth Panzer Army.

The forces on the external flanks of Army Group South's two attack groups—Fourth Panzer Army and *Armeeabteilung* Kempf—lacked sufficient strength. *Armeeabteilung* Kempf did not manage to topple the pillar of the Russian defenses northeast of Belgorod until 11 July. Due to the *Armeeabteilung*'s failure, Fourth Panzer Army had to shield its right flank with units of its own, diminishing the force of its push to the north and northeast. Likewise, the units of Second Panzer Army, which were to secure Ninth Army's flank in the north, were unable to stand their ground.

The repeated postponement of the attack, and the lengthy period during which we held the assault divisions in readiness directly behind the front, combined to deprive us of the element of tactical surprise. Two factors caused OKH and Army Group South to hold these divisions in a prolonged state of readiness so close to the front. First, the Red Army at any moment was poised to overrun the thinly held German lines west of Belgorod, roll up the Donets sector, and recapture Kharkov. Precautionary measures against such an occurrence were deemed essential. Second, the period of time between the attack order and the start of the offensive was intended to be as brief as possible, with the strategic concentration and movement into assembly areas consuming no more than two brief summer nights. This requirement to a large extent dictated the distance between the billets of the panzer units and the outpost line near Belgorod.

Judging from the situation along and behind our lines in the Kursk salient, the Red Army had been well prepared for a two-pronged attack from north and south; the STAVKA had certainly been granted enough time to make such preparations. The Russians concentrated powerful artillery units near Belgorod and in front of Ninth Army. From the very beginning, the Soviet command intended not only to defend its positions in the north but also to repulse Ninth Army's attack. By contrast, the Russians seem to have wanted merely to wear down Fourth Panzer Army; defenses in the south concentrated on strong antitank obstacles. The Soviets moved their main forces out of range of our initial artillery preparation by establishing a deep and heavily mined outpost area.

In addition, Russian forces in the Kursk salient had been kept as low as possible. For example, no airfields had been constructed in this area, with the exception of the one at Kursk. In Fourth Panzer Army's front, only the

X Tank Corps had been held in readiness near Oboyan for participation in the early stages of the battle. Instead, the Soviet strategic tank reserves were to be committed at the moment when our panzers had become weakened by slugging their way through the Russian defensive system. These reserves, therefore, could be maintained outside the Kursk salient.

Red Army officers and noncommissioned officers had been briefed in detail on Russian responses in case of a German attack. This conclusion is supported by the fact that a sand table was discovered in the woods where the headquarters of a major Russian unit had placed its command post. Besides, we could easily tell that Soviet operations had been meticulously prepared by the absence of any sign of disorder and no indications of hasty or panicked retreat by the units in the defensive system. There were no radioed "SOS" calls, which had been so frequently intercepted in the past. These procedures had obviously been copied from the Germans, with excellent effect. The enemy, like us, felt confident in the first few days of the battle that everything was unfolding according to plan.

The objective of Operation Citadel had been to shorten the line of defense between Belgorod and Orel; this was not accomplished. Yet the fact that the offensive had to be discontinued prematurely does not imply that the operation ended in defeat. Fourth Panzer Army certainly came through the fighting undefeated. The troops expressed bitter disappointment when the attack was called off, for they had retained their aggressiveness, their steadfastness when on the defensive, and their will to make necessary sacrifices in spite of the disasters during the winter of 1942–1943. All levels of German leadership had again proven themselves skillful and equal to any and all situations.

The final German strategic offensive of this war on Russian soil had to be discontinued after a duration of twelve days. The initiative irrevocably passed to the Red Army. German forces on the Russian front had extremely heavy fighting ahead of them, which was bound to place an unusually heavy strain on the troops.

Order of Battle: Fourth Panzer Army, 12 March 1943[5]

Colonel General Hermann Hoth

SS Panzer Corps
Obergruppenfuehrer Paul Hausser

Liebstandarte Adolph Hitler *SS Panzergrenadier Division*
Gruppenfuehrer *Sepp Dietrich*
  SS Panzer Regiment 1 *LAH*
  SS Panzergrenadier Regiments 1, 2 *LAH*
  SS Panzer Reconnaissance Battalion 1 *LAH*
  SS Panzer Artillery Regiment 1 *LAH*
  SS Assault Gun Battalion 1 *LAH*
  SS Flak Battalion 1 *LAH*
  SS Mortar Battalion 1 *LAH*
  SS Panzerjaeger Battalion 1 *LAH*
  SS Engineer Battalion 1 *LAH*

Das Reich *SS Panzergrenadier Division*
Brigadefuehrer *Willi Bittrich*
  SS Panzer Regiment 2
  SS Panzergrenadier Regiment 3 *Deutschland*
  SS Panzergrenadier Regiment 4 *Der Fuehrer*
  SS Panzer Reconnaissance Battalion 2
  SS Panzer Artillery Regiment 2
  SS Flak Battalion 2
  SS Mortar Battalion 2
  SS Panzerjaeger Battalion 2
  SS Engineer Battalion 2

Totenkopf *SS Panzergrenadier Division (minus detachments)*
Gruppenfuehrer *Theodor Eicke*
  SS Panzer Regiment 3 *Danmark*

SS Panzergrenadier Regiment 6 (*Totenkopf*)
SS Panzer Reconnaissance Battalion 3
SS Panzer Artillery Regiment 3
SS Assault Gun Battery 3
SS Flak Battalion 3
SS Mortar Battalion 3
SS Panzerjaeger Battalion 3
SS Engineer Battalion 3

Detached
SS Panzergrenadier Regiment 5 *Thule* (attached to 320th Infantry Division)

Artillery Commander 122

Engineer Battalion (Motorized) 127

XLVIII Panzer Corps
General of Panzer Troops Otto von Knobelsdorff

11th Panzer Division
Major General Johann Mickl

Panzer Regiment 15
Panzergrenadier Regiments 110, 111
Panzer Reconnaissance Battalion 231
Panzer Artillery Regiment 119
Panzerjaeger Battalion 231
Panzer Engineer Battalion 231
Flak Battalion 277

106th Infantry Division (minus detachments)
Lieutenant General Werner Forst

Grenadier Regiments 239, 240, 241
Reconnaissance Battalion 106
Artillery Regiment 106
Panzerjaeger Battalion 106 (one company detached to
    168th Infantry Division)
Engineer Battalion 106

6th Panzer Division
Colonel Walther von Huenersdorff

Panzer Regiment 11
Panzergrenadier Regiments 4, 114
Panzer Reconnaissance Battalion 6
Panzer Artillery Regiment 76
Panzerjaeger Battalion 41
Panzer Engineer Battalion 57
Panzer Engineer Battalion 52
Bridge Column 16

LVII Panzer Corps
General of Panzer Troops Friedrich Kirchner

17th Panzer Division
Lieutenant General Fridolin von Senger und Etterlin

II Battalion, Panzer Regiment 39
Panzergrenadier Regiments 40, 63
Panzer Reconnaissance Battalion 27
Panzer Artillery Regiment 27
Panzerjaeger Battalion 27
Panzer Engineer Battalion 27

15th Infantry Division
Major General Erich Buschenhagen

Grenadier Regiments 81, 88, 106
Reconnaissance Battalion 15
Artillery Regiment 15
Panzerjaeger Battalion 15
Engineer Battalion 15

Artillery Commander 121

Assault Gun Battalion 203
One battery/Artillery Battalion 732

Army Troops

Engineer Training Battalion 1
Construction Battalion 507
Bridge Construction Battalion 21

Korueck 312

Field Training Regiment 257
Armored Train 7
One company/Military Police Battalion 521

Commandant, Dnepropetrovsk

Light Infantry-gun Battalions 742, 899, 943
1 and 2/Guard Battalion 17
Bridge Construction Battalion 624
Alarmeinheiten Dnepr (Total: 3,000 men)
Armored Train 28

This order of battle clearly reveals that von Manstein's counterstroke—at least insofar as Fourth Panzer Army was concerned—relied on maneuver rather than firepower. The entire army boasted only one artillery and one assault gun battalion outside the organic strength of its eight divisions. Compare that with the order of battle for Operation Citadel below, in which at least sixteen artillery, assault gun, mortar, and flak battalions supported ten divisions.

APPENDIX 3B

Order of Battle: Fourth Panzer Army, 5–6 July 1943[6]

Colonel General Hermann Hoth
LII Corps
General of Infantry Eugen Ott

57th Infantry Division
Major General Maximilian Fretter-Pico

Grenadier Regiments 179, 199, 217
Reconnaissance Battalion 57
Artillery Regiment 157
Panzerjaeger Battalion 157
Engineer Battalion 157

255th Infantry Division
Lieutenant General Walter Poppe

Grenadier Regiments 455, 465, 475
Reconnaissance Battalion 255
Artillery Regiment 255
Panzerjaeger Battalion 255
Engineer Battalion 255

332nd Infantry Division
Lieutenant General Hans Schaefer

Grenadier Regiments 676, 677, 678
Reconnaissance Battalion 332
Artillery Regiment 332
Panzerjaeger Battalion 332
Engineer Battalion 332

Artillery Commander 137

Artillery Battalion I/108
Artillery Battery 3/731
Heavy Mortar Regiment 1

Engineer Regimental Staff 677 (Special Employment)

Engineer Battalion 74
Bridge Columns 23, 80
Construction Battalion 217

Bicycle Security Battalion 226 (minus one company)

XLVIII Panzer Corps
General of Panzer Troops Otto von Knobelsdorff

167th Infantry Division (minus detachment)
Lieutenant General Wolf Trierenberg

Grenadier Regiments 331, 339
Reconnaissance Battalion 167
Headquarters, I, III, Artillery Regiment 167
Panzerjaeger Battalion 167 (minus one company)
Engineer Battalion 167

Grossdeutschland *Panzergrenadier Division*
Lieutenant General Walter Hoernlein

Panzer Regiment *Grossdeutschland*
Panzergrenadier Regiment *Grossdeutschland*
Fusilier Regiment *Grossdeutschland*
Reconnaissance Battalion *Grossdeutschland*
Panzer Artillery Regiment *Grossdeutschland*
Assault Gun Battalion *Grossdeutschland*
Panzerjaeger Battalion *Grossdeutschland*
Panzer Engineer Battalion *Grossdeutschland*
Flak Battalion *Grossdeutschland*

3rd Panzer Division
Lieutenant General Franz Westhoven

Panzer Regiment 6 (one battalion only)
Panzergrenadier Regiments 3, 394
Panzer Reconnaissance Battalion 3
Panzer Artillery Regiment 75
Panzerjaeger Battalion 543
Panzer Engineer Battalion 39
Flak Battalion 314

11th Panzer Division
Major General Johann Mickl

Panzer Regiment 15
Panzergrenadier Regiments 110, 111
Panzer Reconnaissance Battalion 231

Panzer Artillery Regiment 119
Panzerjaeger Battalion 231
Panzer Engineer Battalion 231
Flak Battalion 277

10th Panzer Brigade
Colonel Karl Decker

Panzer Regimental Staff 39
Panzer Battalions 51, 52

Artillery Commanders 132, 144

Artillery Regimental Staff 70 (Special Employment)
Artillery Battalions III/109, 101, 842
Assault Gun Battalion 911
Light Observation Battalion 19

Engineer Regimental Staff 515 (Special Employment)

Engineer Battalion (Motorized) 48
Engineer Training Battalion (Motorized) 1
Bridge Column Section Staff 938
Bridge Columns 22, 609, 639, 649, 676, 841
Bridge Construction Battalion 37
Light Bicycle Road Construction Battalion 507
Construction Battalion 84 (minus one company)

Army Flak Battalion 616

II SS Panzer Corps
Obergruppenfuehrer **Paul Hausser**

Liebstandarte Adolph Hitler *SS Panzergrenadier Division*
Brigadefuehrer *Theodor Wisch*

SS Panzer Regiment 1 *LAH*
SS Panzergrenadier Regiments 1 *LAH*, 2 *LAH*
SS Panzer Reconnaissance Battalion 1 *LAH*
SS Panzer Artillery Regiment 1 *LAH*
SS Assault Gun Battalion 1 *LAH*
SS Flak Battalion 1 *LAH*
SS Mortar Battalion 1 *LAH*
SS Panzerjaeger Battalion 1 *LAH*
SS Engineer Battalion 1 *LAH*

Attached

Regimentsgruppe, 167th Infantry Division
(Grenadier Regiment 315)
(II Battalion, Artillery Regiment 238)
(1st Company, Engineer Battalion 238)

Das Reich *SS Panzergrenadier Division*
Brigadefuehrer *Willi Bittrich*

SS Panzer Regiment 2
SS Panzergrenadier Regiment 3 *Deutschland*
SS Panzergrenadier Regiment 4 *Der Fuehrer*
SS Panzer Reconnaissance Battalion 2
SS Panzer Artillery Regiment 2
SS Flak Battalion 2
SS Mortar Battalion 2
SS Panzerjaeger Battalion 2
SS Engineer Battalion 2

Totenkopf *SS Panzergrenadier Division*
Brigadefuehrer *Hermann Preiss*

SS Panzer Regiment 3 *Danmark*
SS Panzergrenadier Regiment 5 *Thule*
SS Panzergrenadier Regiment 6 *Theodor Eicke*
SS Panzer Reconnaissance Battalion 3
SS Panzer Artillery Regiment 3
SS Assault Gun Battery 3
SS Flak Battalion 3
SS Mortar Battalion 3
SS Panzerjaeger Battalion 3
SS Engineer Battalion 3

Artillery Commander 122

Artillery Battalions 861, III/818

Mortar Commander 3

Mortar Regiment 55
Mortar Training Regiment 1

Engineer Regimental Staff 680 (Special Purpose)

Engineer Battalions (Motorized) 627, 666
Bridge Column Sector Staff (Motorized) 929
Bridge Columns 2/41, 11, 21, 31, 537, 840
Commander of Construction Troops 8
Bridge Construction Battalion 26
Light Bicycle Road Construction Battalion 508
Construction Battalion 410
Bridging Supply Unit 812

Army Troops
Senior Artillery Commander 312

Senior Construction Staff 14
Commander of Construction Troops 35

Construction Battalions (POWs) 155, 305
Bridge Column Sector Staff 922
Bridge Columns 671, 2/413
Organization *Todt* Operational Staff Kretzer
Organization *Todt* Units 71, 73

Panzer Army Signal Regiment 4

Panzer Propaganda Company 694

Military Intelligence Troops 323, 206, 104

Military Police Companies 34, 37

4

Ninth Army and
Second Panzer Army

by Major General Peter von der Groeben
Operations Officer, Second Army, then Army Group Center

Editor's Introduction

Even today far less is known about Ninth Army's attack and the subsequent battle for the Orel salient than the pseudoclimactic tank battle at Prokhorovka and the battles for Belgorod, Kharkov, and the Mius River that followed. Part of this gap can be attributed to the nature of operations on the northern face of the Kursk salient. Because Ninth Army never achieved a breakthrough of the final Soviet defensive belt, the week of hellish fighting that reached its height at Olkhovatka and Ponyriy is difficult to portray as anything other than a repeat of the battle of Verdun, with tanks added to increase the noise level. Reading the reports and accounts of the officers involved, few of them ever really knew just where they were or what the assault on any given hill or nameless village had to do with the grand strategy of the battle.

The three-week fight for the Orel salient that followed involved far more room for maneuver and included actions and incidents that appear tailor-made for high dramatic narratives. During this battle, for example, the Luftwaffe claimed to have saved two armies from destruction by destroying several Russian tank brigades without the assistance of ground troops. Four understrength German infantry divisions east of Orel somehow managed to withstand massive Red Army tank attacks for several days, holding their ground long enough to allow both Ninth and Second Panzer Armies to retreat to the Hagen position, bloodied but still fighting. Yet again, narratives of this critical battle are almost always cursory and lacking any sense of the moment-to-moment tension that hung over the battlefield.

A major reason for this silence was the subsequent fate of the two armies involved. Second Panzer Army headquarters had to be yanked out of the line and transferred to the Balkans in August, and it is obvious in examining the surviving records that the staff did not have a lot of time to spare for organizing and preserving their records of the fight for Orel. The following June, in the offensive that ripped the heart out of Army Group Center, Ninth Army virtually ceased to exist, and the Soviets captured its headquarters and most of its operational records. Though significant material survived, it did so in disorganized form, often under misleading titles, and it has thus far resisted the serious attention of military historians. Worse still, nearly all the officers of Ninth Army's headquarters staff—the men who might have filled in this gap with personal knowledge—either died or marched into Soviet captivity. Thus when Theodor Busse set out to organize his Kursk study, he could not find an officer in U.S. hands with the type of firsthand experience at Ninth or Second Panzer Armies that Raus and Fangohr brought to their chapters on Army Group South.

Fortunately for Busse, Major General Peter von der Groeben happened to be available, and he turned out to be the best possible replacement. Born on 12 December 1903 in Langheim, East Prussia, von der Groeben entered the Reichswehr as an officer candidate on 1 March 1924, receiving his commission and a posting to Cavalry Regiment 9 on 1 December 1927. When war began, the young major was serving as a staff officer for Army Group North, under the command of then–Colonel General Fedor von Bock. He held this position under von Bock through the Polish and French campaigns, as well as through the initial planning for the invasion of the Soviet Union. Upon hearing that he would be losing the young officer in May 1941, von Bock characterized von der Groeben in his diary as "fabulous." Writing forty years later, von der Groeben obviously retained fond feelings for his old boss: "I admired him very much; he was a fascinating person, a gentleman in the best sense of the word and a great expert in the field." With the keen analytical eye that reveals itself in the essay to follow, von der Groeben also candidly admitted that "very self-assured, he [Bock] was definitely neither a 'comfortable' subordinate nor a superior."

After spending more than eighteen months in the field as operations officer of the 86th Infantry Division, von der Groeben (a lieutenant colonel since 1 April 1942) became the operations officer for Second Army on 25 November 1942.[1] More than likely the army's commander, General of Infantry Hans von Salmuth (von Bock's old chief of staff), specifically requested his appointment. Promoted to colonel on 1 March 1943, von der Groeben held his post during the disastrous days of the Russian attacks along the Don River and the retreat into the Ukraine around Kharkov. He remained at Second Army, which had the mission of securing the western face of the Kursk bulge while the main attacks hit the northern and southern fronts, until 25 July 1943. Then, at the height of the battle for the Orel salient and the beginning of the withdrawal toward the Hagen position, von der Groeben was transferred to become the operations officer for Army Group Center.

From this position von der Groeben had full view of all operations conducted by Ninth and Second Panzer Armies, as well as access to information that staff officers within those armies may have lacked. He was therefore able to write authoritatively about all aspects of the battle, and his general perspective more than compensated for any lack of direct personal involvement.

Peter von der Groeben remained as army group operations officer for eighteen months, through four commanders (Gunther von Kluge, Ernst Busch, Walter Model, and Hans-Georg Reinhardt) and the virtual destruction of the command in the Red Army's Bagration offensive in June–July 1944. When von der Groeben had been appointed, Army Group Center still threatened Moscow from positions as far forward as Bryansk and Orel; when he left in December 1944 to take command of the 3rd Cavalry Brigade, the Russians stood on the Vistula in central Poland and had already entered East Prussia.

The 3rd Cavalry Brigade grew (at least nominally) into the 3rd Cavalry Division in January 1945, with von der Groeben as its commander; he received promotion to major general on 1 March 1945. Following the war, von der Groeben worked with the U.S. Army Historical Program for several years and eventually became involved in the organization of the Bundeswehr (West Germany's postwar army), reaching the rank of Lieutenant General before his retirement.

For the historical program von der Groeben wrote three brief manuscripts covering tactical air support (C-21), weather in combat (Supporting Study No. 9 to P-211), and General Staff training (P-031b/IX), but his recognized magnum opus was an extended study (T-31, "Collapse of Army Group Center, 1944"), which has been used by historians as a basic source for decades. In addition, and unrealized until now, von der Groeben also contributed the following text on Operation Citadel. The evidence regarding his authorship of the work is exceptionally strong when his writing style, organization, and approach are compared to the other monograph. Moreover, it is already established that von der Groeben had been collaborating the same year with another study author, Friedrich Kless, to produce Manuscript C-21.

The study produced by von der Groeben is comprehensive and serves as a basic narrative framework for the fighting in the Orel salient. It is interesting to note that the author places far more emphasis on the defensive fighting than the actual assault toward Kursk. He also reaches a provocative conclusion about the success or failure of the Citadel offensive, crediting Ninth Army's attack with causing enough damage to the Red Army to prevent it from overrunning the Orel salient in one rush. The result, von der Groeben points out at the end, was that upon occupying the Hagen position Army Group Center freed nineteen divisions for transfer to other threatened sectors of the front.

His perspectives on the views—often conflicting—of von Kluge and Model regarding Operation Citadel and the conduct of the Orel battle are also enlightening. Much is to be said about the nature of the relationship between army and army group commander, as well as Hitler's impact on such relationships, by the fact that Model's views prevailed over those of his boss on almost every occasion. The reader is left wishing von der Groeben had provided even more detail.

Ninth Army and Second Panzer Army
by Major General Peter von der Groeben
Operations Officer, Second Army, then Army Group Center

Introduction

This narrative of the battle in the Orel salient has been written from memory. Available reference material consisted of several rough sketches, complete with dates and legend, on the German and Russian situation in the Orel sector during the summer of 1943. I have reconstructed estimates of the situation in the various sectors in the course of the battle in conference with other available officers. Errors in the chronology of the battle are unlikely in view of the fact that such reference materials and aids mentioned above were available to me.

Near the end of 1942, the Red Army staged a large-scale offensive against the Don River front, which was held by satellite armies. In the course of this offensive, the Russians broke through the lines of Army Group B, which held the sector between Army Group South and Army Group Center. Surviving forces of Army Group B had to split into corps and division-size *Kampfgruppen* to fight their way back to the stationary interior wings of Army Groups South and Center. By the beginning of February 1943, the situation had developed to the point where Soviet forces in the Kursk area had fanned out. One grouping attacked Army Group South via Sumy and Kremenchuk; the other penetrated to the line Novgorod-Seversky. The STAVKA appears to have been trying to unhinge the German defenses in the Orel salient, possibly with the assistance of Russian units on the offensive near Sukhinichi.

By the time the "muddy season" set in, improvised German counterattacks had recast the front line into the shape it would retain for several months. The Russian advance ground to a halt in the great salient west of Kursk, and the enemy began to concentrate his defenses along his extended flanks.

OKH had originally intended to rout the Soviet forces in the area west of Kursk by having the Second Army and—adjoining it to the south—the Fourth Panzer Army stage a frontal assault. Two decisive factors caused this plan to be discarded. The shortage of rail transportation facilities [in addition to] partisan attacks made it impossible to accomplish the strategic concentration of forces earmarked for such a large-scale offensive in the time allotted. In addition, the onset of the muddy season arrived in late February, earlier than expected, rendering mobile warfare impossible.

Subsequent planning aimed at staging a pincer movement from the shoulders of the base of the salient, where the lines of Army Group South and Army Group Center (the arc of the Orel salient) had stood fast. The two attack forces would form narrow wedges and crash through to Kursk. A line of defenses facing east was to be established east of the line Belgorod-Kursk-Orel. Enemy forces west of this line would be annihilated. OKH repeatedly demanded that this operation commence as early as possible (or in mid-May at the latest) because the Soviets had continuously reinforced their positions facing the sector in which the Germans intended to stage their breakthrough. Concurrently, a steady stream of intercepted messages indicated Russians preparing a summer offensive of their own. Necessity, it was thought, required us to strike first.

During mid-May, therefore, this was the situation in the Orel salient. The Red Army facing the entire southern sector of the salient (held by our Ninth Army) was preparing strong forces for a delaying defense. Radio interceptions identified nine rifle divisions in the Dmitriyev–Lgovskiy–Malo-arkhangel'sk sector alone. Russian troops occupying the front-line trenches appeared especially alert and watchful. German assault detachments reported extensive wire obstacles and minelaying in the outpost area. Luftwaffe aerial photoreconnaissance identified a prepared defensive system consisting of about seven successive defensive positions spaced over a depth of eight to ten kilometers. It was unlikely that the Russians knew of German intentions at this time; these preparations represented a common-sense effort to be ready in the eventuality of a German attack. Moreover, if the Soviets ultimately desired to attack the Orel salient from the north, they first had to provide strong screen forces along its southern face.

Opposite the eastern and northern sectors of the Orel salient (held by Second Panzer Army) the Russians busily assembled strategic reserves at the same time that the strength of the Second Panzer Army had been greatly reduced in favor of reinforcing the Ninth Army for the main effort toward Kursk. The width of division sectors on the eastern and northern faces of the salient averaged between thirty and thirty-five kilometers. General reserves available to buttress this 260-kilometer-long front consisted only of one weak infantry division and one panzer division.[2]

The southern face of the Orel salient by no means remained quiet. German and Russian troops occupying the front-line trenches, both supported by general reserves, stayed constantly locked in battle, even as Colonel General Walter Model's Ninth Army prepared for the Citadel attack. (Ninth Army at this juncture had been assigned the deception code name "*Gruppe* Weiss." The army had just completed Operation Buffalo, the planned withdrawal of German positions from the Vyazma-Rzhev-Yartsevo salient to a cord position east of Smolensk. In mid-April 1943 Ninth Army headquarters took control of operations in the southern half of the Orel salient.) The panzer divisions earmarked for this offensive completed their strategic concentration by mid-May. Important army troop units, particularly those equipped with new weapons, such as Panther tanks (Pzkw V), Tiger tanks (Pzkw VI), and eighty-ton Ferdinand tanks were en route to the front during early May.[3] Two or three infantry divisions had not arrived by that time, but Army Group Center planned to utilize them as a general reserve and commit them in the wake of the attacking divisions.

Seasoned veterans who had been tried and proven in many a critical battle since the very start of the Russian campaign composed the divisions earmarked to spearhead the offensive. These divisions reorganized in rear areas in early spring, filling their ranks with new soldiers and—to some extent—receiving new weapons and equipment. Thus, despite a cadre of experienced troops, in their new organization and composition these divisions completely lacked combat experience and—to be more specific—experience in staging attacks through heavily fortified defenses. It was absolutely necessary that these divisions receive this kind of training prior to the large-scale offensive envisioned by OKH. Carefully planned, well-disciplined and -controlled training was indispensable and would require at least four weeks.[4]

At the same time, Army Group South calculated that the supply phase prior to the offensive was not going to be completed before the end of June.

The woods east of the Desna River in the rear area of the two Orel armies had been contaminated by Russian partisans. The Bryansk-Konotop and Bryansk-Shirekina rail lines, as well as all roads leading south from

Bryansk, had to be closed to traffic. The main supply route leading from Bryansk to Orel could be traveled intermittently and in convoys only.

The extensive and heavily wooded terrain west of the Desna served as an excellent hideout for the partisans. These bands had been holding out in this area for over a year, receiving supplies and reinforcements from the air. During March–April, Second Panzer Army directed Operation *Fruelingesturm* to smash this partisan force. Several spearhead divisions participated in this maneuver.

It had been absolutely necessary to clear our rear areas of the enemy as a prerequisite for future offensive operations in the Orel salient. Unfortunately, the antipartisan operation consumed time and resulted in considerable losses, especially in motor vehicles. Although it can be argued that the spearhead divisions participating in this operation did receive valuable training while engaging in "brush warfare," this experience could by no means be considered sufficient to prepare them for the kind of fighting they would have to do in open terrain, assaulting prepared Soviet positions.

The road net in the Orel salient existed in an almost primeval condition as roads go. The Bryansk-Orel *Rollbahn*[5] served as the main supply artery for both armies. Several stretches of this *Rollbahn* consisted of gravel road, but most of it was not reinforced in any way except by a one-lane corduroy road that had been completed by German construction troops in 1942. Ninth Army's strategic concentration and its supply phase required at least two north-south traffic arteries of the *Rollbahn* type, which required existing roads to be transformed into corduroy roads. Distribution of supplies to dumps and depots, and the maintenance of a smooth uninterrupted flow of supplies once the offensive opened, rendered this an absolute necessity. Likewise, all bridges in the Ninth Army area had to be reinforced so that they would support the new superheavy eighty-ton Ferdinands; this also required several raids to be staged into enemy-held territory to deprive the Russians temporarily of commanding terrain. Unfortunately, these measures likewise consumed time we could not afford to waste.

Field Marshal Gunther von Kluge, commanding Army Group Center; Colonel General Rudolf Schmidt, commanding Second Panzer Army; and Colonel General Model all agreed that the Citadel offensive constituted a definite risk in view of powerful Russian concentrations opposite the northern face of the Orel salient. They shared the view that accepting this risk with the full knowledge of the inadequate German strength available for the offensive represented nothing less than a case of lightheadedly taking chances. The fact that Soviet defenses had been concentrated precisely in the area where Ninth Army's main effort was to be staged was an additional factor contributing to their doubts about the ultimate success of the Kursk operation (see Map 4.1).

It would have been possible to regroup the spearhead divisions and stage a more limited attack, issuing from the sector on both sides of the boundary line between Ninth Army and Second Army (west of the Kursk bulge and not to be confused with Second Panzer Army). This attack, aimed east toward Kursk across the Sev River, however, even if successful would not have resulted in the annihilation of significant Red Army forces, would not noticeably have relieved overall Soviet pressure along the entire Eastern front, and—above all—would have increased the threat to the forces in the northern half of the Orel salient.

On the basis of these deliberations, General Model arrived at the following conclusions. Army Group Center could move two panzer divisions and four full-strength infantry divisions—reinforced by a number of army troops, including assault gun, tank, and antitank outfits—into the Orel-Karachev area. These reserves would stand by either to be employed on the northern sector if the situation required or to follow behind the spearhead divisions in the depth of the attack zone in case the enemy should regroup his own strategic reserves in that direction.

Model's second alternative was to discard the plans for the Citadel operation altogether. In such a case, the spearhead divisions would be held in the center of the Orel salient as a strong strategic reserve. Army Group Center would wait for the Russians to make their main thrust from the east or north, then counterpunch in major strength wherever the opportunity arose. Previous experience strongly suggested that the Soviets would stake everything on a single blow; one could consequently expect Red Army strategic reserves to be exhausted at an early stage.

If, on the other hand, in giving up on the idea of staging the Citadel offensive OKH contemplated the withdrawal of Army Group Center's spearhead divisions for employment elsewhere, then it was high time to prepare for the orderly evacuation of the entire Orel salient. Second Panzer and Ninth Armies would therefore have taken new positions behind the line Desna River–Bryansk–Kirov. Such a maneuver would have required the completion of prepared defenses on both sides of Karachev, along the eastern edge of the woods east of the Desna (later called the Hagen line) and along the Desna to the north.

General Model submitted these suggestions through official reports and ably supported his contentions through a detailed presentation of facts and reasons. Hitler vetoed these propositions, giving as his reason the necessity of completing the preparations for Citadel as quickly as possible and thus striking the first blow. Hitler argued that this offensive would force the Soviets to abandon their own attack plans and regroup; that our armies would be unable to employ their spearhead divisions until after the Russian defensive system had been breached; and furthermore that the German soldier was far superior to his Russian counterpart when it came to slugging it out in open battle. The additional infantry divisions and about 180 Panthers would be committed to reinforce the main attack force. (The Panthers, however, were routed to Army Group South instead of the Orel salient.)

This being the situation, General Model ordered that the reserve battle positions mentioned above be completed immediately. This action was taken in defiance of Hitler's orders but with the approval of Field Marshal von Kluge. In addition, General Model untiringly pushed troop training prior to the offensive, so that Ninth Army would have an effective striking force at its disposal when the offensive commenced. This mobile, spirited, and thoroughly trained force, though small, constituted a critical factor in the subsequent fighting. General Model placed his full confidence in this force: Even in situations that appeared utterly hopeless, his spearhead troops won out in the end.

The Battle in the Orel Salient, 5–30 July

Ninth Army accomplished the strategic concentration for the offensive in two successive nights. Artillery fire and overflights by Ju 52 transport aircraft drowned out the clatter of the Ferdinands and Tigers moving into the assembly areas. The enemy apparently did not detect the relief of the units holding the front line or the arrival of the assault troops.

Ninth Army launched Operation Citadel on 5 July, a clear summer day. The army was on the march to Kursk: The troops intended to smash the powerful Red Army concentration in the salient and, if possible, to encircle and annihilate them in a combined operation with attacking forces of Army Group South.

The individual corps of Ninth Army received the following missions within the context of the overall operation (note: these orders are presented in their general context; the exact wording was not available to the author):

The XLVII Panzer Corps (commanded by General of Panzer Troops Joachim Lemelsen and consisting of the 2nd, 9th, and 20th Panzer Divisions and 6th Infantry Division) will deploy along a narrow sector, break through the enemy defensive system between the highway and railway Orel-Kursk, exploit the speed of its panzer formations to the fullest, and gain the high ground in the vicinity, and north, of Kursk. There the corps will establish contact with lead units of Army Group Center that will be approaching from the south. The corps will maintain close contact with the corps on each of its flanks and hold the corridor thus carved out against enemy attacks that can be expected from both east and west. The initial breakthrough will be accomplished by infantry divisions that will be supported by the Luftwaffe, by the entire artillery, and by army panzer units, which in turn will be closely followed by the panzer divisions.

Strong units of the left wing of the XLVI Panzer Corps (commanded by General of Infantry Hans Zorn and consisting of the 7th, 31st, 102nd, and 258th Infantry Divisions) will break through the enemy defensive system. The corps spearheads will maintain close contact with the XLVII Panzer Corps, which is attacking in the zone of the main effort. The XLVI Panzer Corps will screen the right flank of the XLVII Panzer Corps against the west and southwest along the general line Smitrovsk–Orlovskiy–Chern Creek–Tysnokoye–Fatesh. As soon as it has been noticed that the enemy is withdrawing forces from his sector opposite the right wing of the XLVI Panzer Corps, the corps will likewise attack on its right wing, this time in close contact with XX Corps. The corps will place its main priority on immediately gaining the Svapa Creek line.

It is planned to move the 12th Panzer Division from army group reserve to the left wing of XLVI Panzer Corps. Maintaining contact with the XLVII Panzer Corps will assist in completing the breakthrough to Fatesh.

The XLI Panzer Corps (commanded by General of Panzer Troops Joseph Harpe and consisting of the 18th Panzer Division and 86th and 292nd Infantry Divisions), with its main attack effort launched on both sides of the Orel-Kursk highway, will break through the enemy defensive system along the entire width of its sector, maintaining close contact with the spearheads of XLVII Panzer Corps. Upon reaching Brusovoye, the XLI Panzer Corps will wheel hard east, gaining and holding the high ground east of Snova Creek. It is of vital importance for the corps quickly to defeat the strong enemy force identified in Ponyriy and clear the rail line of the enemy. The corps must be prepared for powerful enemy counterattacks against the newly established corps sector.

The XXIII Corps (commanded by General of Infantry Johannes Friessner and consisting of the 78th Assault Division and 216th and 383rd Infantry Divisions) will storm the firmly held enemy strongpoint at Malo-arkhangel'sk. The corps will ensure the maximum utilization of special support, such as remote-controlled guided tanks and mobile engineer demolition equipment. The corps will likewise see to it that the heavily armed 78th Assault Division is properly employed in this operation. The corps will make it a priority to establish contact with the XLI Panzer Corps east of Ponyriy and participate in the defense of the new sector.

The XX Corps (commanded by General of Artillery Freiherr Rudolf von Roman and consisting of the 45th, 72nd, 137th, and 251st Infantry Divisions) will defend the positions it is holding as of now. From the very first day of the attack the corps will exploit every opportunity to push its lines east, maintaining close contact with the XLVI Panzer Corps.

Starting on the third day of the offensive and depending on the general progress of the Kursk breakthrough, the corps will be ready quickly to assemble three attack groups, each approximately of division size, and execute the following mission:

One attack group will debouch from the Sevsk area and advance toward the line Dmitryev-Lgovsky. The second attack group will assemble in the Kamarichi area for an advance on Deryugino. The third attack group will assemble in the Dmitrovsk-Orlovskiy area and crash through toward Mikailovka in order first of all to gain the Svapa Creek line. Close contact will be continuously maintained with the corps on the left wing of Second Army, which has orders to proceed in the same direction.

Supported by strong aerial attacks, the panzer wedge of XLVII Panzer Corps knocked a fourteen-kilometer-deep breach into the Russian fortifications during the initial assault. The corps wedge struck in a powerful, concentrated attack, with its right flank covered by XLVI Panzer Corps and its left by XLI Panzer Corps. The Soviet lines had been ripped open along a width of thirty kilometers (see Map 4.2). Starting on the second day, however, enemy resistance rapidly stiffened, with the Russians quickly throwing both tactical and strategic reserves into the breach in a desperate attempt to keep the German panzers from breaking through and spilling out into open terrain. One tank corps—hastily moved forward—and three Guards rifle divisions were thrown into XLVII Panzer Corps's path as early as the second day of the attack. Simultaneously, several hundred Russian tanks moved from rear areas to the critical point on the battlefield. A giant tank battle ensued, lasting for days. Here German panzers demonstrated their superiority, slowly inching forward in a spirited attack against new Soviet strongpoints crystallizing near Nikolskoye, Olkhovatka, and Ponyriy. These defenses received a steady stream of reinforcements from the rear.

Beginning on 7 July the Russians debouched from these strongpoints to strike with heavy, concerted counterstrokes. In the beginning, Ninth Army repulsed these attacks and the enemy lost heavily. Our panzer spearheads were regrouped and reinforced, whereupon the attack rolled toward the line Teploye-Plkhovatka-Ponyriy across a width of ten kilometers. Upon reaching this line, however, the German attack again struck an especially strongly fortified and heavily mined position that had been established on high ground. This position, garnished and honeycombed with dug-in tanks and other antitank weapons, withstood the impetus of the German frontal assault for days. At this moment—shortly before our troops had broken through the final Russian position—we had reached the climax of the battle, and Field Marshal von Kluge acceded to Colonel General Model's urgent requests to release the 12th Panzer Division and 36th Infantry Division to reinforce the attack. The entire assault force was to regroup, integrating these additional divisions, and the attack continued in an attempt to exploit the breakthrough. Upon its resumption, the attack would be directed southwest with XLVI Panzer Corps constituting the main effort.

It was precisely at this moment, on 11 July, that certain events occurred in the eastern and northern sectors of the Orel salient, which forced OKH and Army Group Center to discontinue Ninth Army's attack. The Red Army commenced a large-scale offensive against Second Panzer Army across a broad front. Such an attack had obviously been in the works for quite some time. Influenced by the Citadel offensive, the STAVKA probably elected to launch this offensive considerably earlier than originally planned. Thus greatly superior enemy forces struck Second Panzer Army west of Novosil, east of Bolkhov, and northwest of Ulyanovo. Second Panzer Army's entire sector was thinly held by a total of fourteen infantry and one panzer division. Within forty-eight hours the Red Army effected broad penetrations, some up to ten kilometers deep. Field Marshal von Kluge immediately faced the necessity of drawing upon Colonel General Model's attack force with delay for units to prevent an enemy breakthrough into the Orel salient. Such a redeployment was imperative, for the loss of Orel—coupled with the blocking of railways and roads emanating from this key traffic center—threatened to paralyze Ninth Army supply. With the bulk of Ninth Army's strength embroiled in the offensive toward Kursk, the loss of Orel would not only compel us to discontinue the Citadel operation but also threaten large elements of two armies with encirclement.

On 12 July Field Marshal von Kluge therefore ordered the 12th, 18th, and 20th Panzer Divisions, as well as the 36th Infantry Division and detachments of Ferdinands and heavy artillery, to be made available and rushed to Second Panzer Army. At first the field marshal hoped that the critical situation along Second Panzer Army's front might be eased as the result of the lightning-fast intervention of these reinforcements. Such hopes had to be abandoned for good on 13 July, as the sheer scope of the Soviet offensive against the Orel salient gave us a clear indication of the enemy's strategic objective (see Map 4.3). It appeared that the Russians contemplated nothing less than a large-scale offensive that had the goal of crushing all German forces in the Orel salient.

In this hour of supreme tension, Field Marshal von Kluge gave Colonel General Model command of Second Panzer Army in addition to his own, pursuant to plans made earlier. Though both army headquarters remained as they were, this measure ensured a unified command in the Orel salient. General Model decided to wait until the dust settled in Second Panzer Army's sector and Russian tactical intentions were revealed more clearly before undertaking a comprehensive regrouping of our forces in the salient. He dispatched orders through Ninth Army headquarters that, post haste, the 2nd Panzer Division, two assault-gun battalions, two battalions of heavy artillery, and one *Nebelwerfer* battalion be transferred to Second Panzer Army. In this manner a wide sector of the eastern face of the Orel salient had its appearance radically changed in just forty-eight hours, and with practically the flick of a wrist the main action shifted to Second Panzer Army.

The crisis intensified with the speed of an avalanche, and the only hope of saving the day was to implement all possible emergency measures at the utmost speed. Colonel General Model therefore demanded that the fighting troops give their all and that units en route be on the move day and night, putting forth a supreme effort. By road and rail the reinforcements so urgently needed flowed to the critical sector in express transports. Many officers, including general staff officers from both headquarters, flew back and forth in Fiesler "Storch" liaison planes to control traffic and keep it moving in a steady stream along jam-packed roads. In this manner the 12th and 18th Panzer Divisions became available for employment against the Soviet penetration northwest of Bolkhov and north of Ulyanovo almost immediately after our general and tactical reserves had been committed. Meanwhile the 8th Panzer Division and the 36th Infantry Division (loaded on vehicles) moved toward the sector east of Orel, followed on 15 July by 2nd Panzer Division.

On 13 July Colonel General Model succeeded in establishing a continuous emergency line east of Arkhangelskoye, Kichety, Baranovo, and Medyn. The Russian force advancing southwest, heading straight for Bolkhov, was stopped northwest of the city, though it remained as yet impossible to throw adequate forces in the path of the enemy tank forces pushing due south. North of Ulyanovo, the Soviets were preparing to push both southeast and southwest in order to widen their penetration of our lines. This resulted in increased pressure against the 293rd Infantry Division and the 5th Panzer Division along the Vytebet and Resseta Rivers. By 15 July the Russians had fought their way across both rivers, though elements of 5th Panzer retained a strategic bridgehead east of Ktsyn. *Gruppe* Esebeck (consisting of elements of the 18th and 20th Panzer Divisions) in the meantime managed provisionally to seal off this penetration.

When the Russian offensive had begun, we had believed the main strategic threat to lie in the area north of Ulyanovo, but as the operation progressed it gradually became clear that the Red Army intended to effect a decisive breakthrough to Orel by releasing a deluge of tanks against the eastern face of the salient. The force of the drive toward Bolkhov had diminished substantially, probably due to heavy tank losses inflicted by German troops.

As the Orel offensive unfolded, it also became clear that the Russians were hurriedly pushing preparations for a counteroffensive against Ninth Army in the Kursk salient. Ninth Army, having already dispatched significant strength to Second Panzer Army, regrouped its own forces for defensive action with equal speed. On 15 July the Soviets, powerfully supported by artillery, tanks, and planes, launched their counteroffensive against Ninth Army along a broad front. Already numerically superior, the Russians had reinforced this attack with two additional rifle divisions, one tank corps, four independent tank brigades, and one Guards mortar regiment, all of which had been moved up from the western part of the Kursk salient. The main attack struck XLI Panzer Corps and the interior wings of XLVII Panzer Corps and XXIII Corps. Ninth Army repulsed the enemy along the line after a day of hard fighting, knocking out 250 Soviet tanks. Yet it remained clear that more attacks and additional heavy fighting lay in store for our troops in both army sectors. Realizing that his forces needed a shorter, more defensible position if they were not ultimately to be overrun, Colonel General Model requested and received permission to retire Ninth Army to its original line. Model expected to free four additional divisions in this manner to use as a reserve while he also exploited the defensive advantages of the old line. Our retirement, which the troops executed in three successive nights, baffled the Russians. Caught off-balance, they eventually sent out strong forces to maintain direct pressure in order to prevent Ninth Army from establishing a new defensive line. Though every available tank and combat aircraft appears to have been employed in this effort, the enemy failed in this undertaking.

On 16–17 July the Russians attempted to crack open Ninth Army's defenses, smashing against our lines with terrific impact, particularly east of the railway, but these attacks crumbled against solid German defenses. Between 15 and 17 July, Ninth Army antitank gunners littered the battlefield with 530 enemy tanks. By the morning of 18 July, our troops again held their original positions, ready for more defensive fighting.

The situation of Second Panzer Army reached its strategic climax on 19 July. Newly arrived, the Third Tank Army crashed into General of Infantry Dr. Lothar Rendulic's XXXV Corps with terrific force. The gallant divisions of this corps (34th, 56th, 262nd, and 299th Infantry) had so far been holding their own against heavy Soviet pressure, but now, with these reinforcements, the Russians attempted to pry open the Ulyanovo sector at its shoulders. Colonel General Model scraped together whatever happened to be available and met the crisis in Rendulic's sector just in time. The 2nd and 8th Panzer Divisions rushed toward the XXXV Corps, as well as the 36th Infantry Division, which had been previously dispatched. Elements of the 9th Panzer Division raced toward the sector from the southeast. These forces combined to check the Soviet tank attack. At the same time, the 183rd, 253rd, and 707th Infantry Divisions had been moved toward the salient from the southwest. In the meantime, however, a Russian tank brigade had cut the rail line and highway connecting Orel to Karachev near Ilinskoye, but the direct threat to our communications was removed by the Luftwaffe. Twin-engine fighters and fighter-bombers made a spirited and dashing attack against the tank brigade and wiped it out. The 253rd Infantry Division, which had received orders to change its original direction of march to deal with this threat, now approached Ilinskoye from the south, taking firm possession of the town on 21 July (see Map 4.4). By 23 July the greatest danger could be considered as having passed.

Even as these operations unfolded, the gap east of Orel assumed precarious proportions. German troops along the flanks of the Soviet penetration withdrew in an orderly fashion to shorten their lines and make some elements available as tactical reserves, while the 12th Panzer Division moved rapidly into the area from the vicinity of Bolkhov; likewise, the 78th Assault Division, transferred from Ninth Army, arrived with the utmost speed and dispatch. Though several ticklish tactical situations occurred, the immediate strategic threat to Orel was averted at the last moment. By 23 July, therefore, the situation along Second Panzer Army's entire front could be considered as once again having been consolidated. Colonel General Model had mastered these crises by a combination of fast movements and regrouping of compact units, supported by outstanding achievements of our mobile antitank weapons (assault guns and self-propelled guns).

The Red Army had in the meantime effected deep penetrations, and it had become necessary to shorten our lines in the areas east and northeast of Orel to reconcile the situation. These moves resulted in the following picture: A bulging salient had taken shape in the Bolkhov area. The Russians were not attacking the salient from the north, but the bulge was threatened with strangulation from two sides just the same. Before the enemy could take advantage of this opportunity, General Rendulic shortened his lines, withdrawing to a position whose front line just shaved past the southern edge of Bolkhov. In the nick of time to foil a Soviet attempt to envelope Bolkhov from the south by staging a mass tank thrust from Krasnikovo, the 10th Panzergrenadier Division arrived from Ninth Army. This serious threat could be removed only by a supreme physical effort and through operations conducted in keeping with the fundamental principles of mobile warfare on both the strategic and tactical levels. Stiff defense and jabbing counterblows visibly whittled down the fury of the Russian drive, which foundered in front of the shortened Orel switch positions.

Events in Ninth Army's sector from 18 July confirmed the suspicion that the Russians were pursuing a unified strategy against both armies in the Orel salient and that Colonel General Model was fighting one giant battle along a front nearly 400 kilometers in length. Because Soviet forces attacking out of the Kursk salient had so far failed to crack Ninth Army lines by frontal assaults, their attack forces hurriedly regrouped and shifted west to the Trosna-Fatesh road and the Chern River bend in order to thrust into the army's extended southern flank. Alert German reconnaissance units detected this movement, and fortunately, on that same day—18 July—two divisions that had just become available, plus some Army troops, could be dispatched immediately to counter the threat. When the Russians attacked with three rifle divisions and sixty tanks along both sides of the Trosna-Fatesh road on 19 July, they encountered prepared and reinforced defenses. This attack achieved nothing beyond local tactical penetrations. Simultaneously, however, enemy tanks broke through to the Karachev-Bryansk road in Second Panzer Army's sector, clearly revealing the sweeping Soviet pincer movement aimed at the entire Orel salient. Second Panzer Army withdrew its lines again, which in turn necessitated Ninth Army pulling back to a corresponding switch position. These moves had to be accomplished under the most adverse weather and road conditions, and while the maneuver was in progress a concentric tank attack against Smiyevka ripped through the boundary between the two armies. Colonel General Model committed his very last reserves, which managed to only partly seal the breach on 24 July.

In view of the overall strained situation on the Eastern Front, on 26 July OKH finally issued orders to the field armies to prepare for the evacuation of the entire Orel salient. This retrograde movement, which was to be effected very soon, involved retirement to a cord position along the base of the salient, the so-called Hagen line. Construction of this position had been rushed forward for some time. OKH gave the execution order on 28 July, anticipating that the withdrawal would make twenty divisions available for employment in other sectors. Divided into four phases, with the temporary occupation of interim lines and switch positions, the retirement had been projected to be accomplished between 31 July and 17 August (see Map 4.5).

For the troops in the Orel salient this decision came none too soon. The Russian onslaught had been stopped at all points, with heavy losses. Nevertheless, in the face of massed Soviet strength (which was being constantly reinforced), our lines could not be expected to hold unless additional units could be extracted from the front line and pooled as reserves; this was especially true in light of the fact that the enemy was winding up for another punch. When the expected victory east of Orel failed to materialize, by about 22 July the STAVKA began to shift the main effort away from this area. The Third Tank Army moved south to the vicinity of the boundary between Second Panzer and Ninth Armies while additional tank forces concentrated in the north, indicative of a renewed attempt to envelop Orel in a pincer attack. At the same time, the Soviets committed the Fourth Tank Army in the Bolkhov area for another try at snipping off the German-held salient; in the following days there would be fierce battles as the Russians rammed up against Bolkhov's defenders. The situation in the enemy-held penetration area south of Ulyanovo remained precarious but had been consolidated somewhat by the arrival of the 95th Infantry Division to take a position on the right flank of General of Infantry Erich Jaschke's LV Corps at the same time that the *Grossdeutschland* Panzergrenadier Division (transferred from Fourth Panzer Army), the 293rd Infantry Division (from LIII Corps), and the 129th Infantry Division (released by Fourth Army's XXVII Corps) launched a timely counterattack. These divisions jabbed directly into Russian assembly areas, denying the Red Army any chance to spring their own assault against the Khotynets-Karachev railway and the *Rollbahn*—the twin communications and transportation lifelines for the entire Orel salient.

The Soviets also attempted to break through toward Bryansk along the Tereben-Bryansk railway but were effectively delayed by stiff resistance from *Gruppe* Boselager (based on Cavalry Regiment *Mitte*) and *Gruppe* Busich (elements of the 707th Infantry Division), both of which had been moved up between 15 and 17 July.

By July's end the fighting centered chiefly around the Bolkhov salient. There the Russians repeatedly attempted to break through at various points northeast and southwest of Bolkhov. Each of these attacks crumbled under the fire of the German defenders. *Gruppe* Harpe, based on XLI Panzer Corps headquarters (transferred from Ninth Army), consisted of General of Infantry Heinrich Cloessner's LIII Corps with the 208th, 211th, and 293rd Infantry Divisions and the 25th Panzergrenadier Division, augmented by the 10th Panzergrenadier Division and the 18th and 20th Panzer Divisions. This command destroyed over 200 Russian tanks each individual day of the action. On 31 July, having completed [its] strategic redeployments, the Soviet Third Tank Army opened a new large-scale offensive against Ninth Army's Nikolskoye-Filosopov sector.

In the middle of these great battles, OKH pressured both Second Panzer and Ninth Armies into preparations for Operation Hagen, which had been ordered on 26 July. This required the army staffs to shoulder additional tactical and organizational missions of monumental proportions. An area 100 kilometers deep had to be evacuated within three weeks—fighting every inch of the way. Tactical reshuffling of troops without regard for their formal organization became commonplace, while commanders and their staffs paid particular attention to those aspects of a retrograde movement that included tactics, transportation, and morale. We hastily reconnoitered successive lines of resistance, preparing them for at least a few days of defensive fighting. All available labor—engineers (including the combat engineer battalions from the fighting divisions), construction troops, and supply train soldiers—had to be marshaled for this work. The entire supply system, particularly that part of it serving with Ninth Army, to this point remained geared to the requirements of a sweeping offensive. Accordingly, supplies and equipment lay stockpiled very close to the front, and with literally a flick of the wrist the entire distribution system had to be reorganized to support a retrograde operation. Signal communications presented similar difficulties, and the huge ammunition dumps east of Kromy had to be evacuated in the first few days. Despite the fact that the roads remained in pitifully poor condition, every last available vehicle was corralled and the task accomplished despite the worst hardships imaginable.

Withdrawal to the Hagen Line, 31 July–18 August

Operation Hagen commenced in the evening of 31 July. Several days of continuous rain had transformed nearly all roads and trails in the Orel salient into a state reminiscent of the muddy season, but the basic objectives of the operation permitted no further delay or hesitation. The first planned retrograde movement resulted in an easing of the situation along all sectors of the Orel salient, even though the Red Army attempted to maintain pressure in pursuit from the east and continually tried to outflank our withdrawing armies. For Colonel General Model, this made the withdrawal that much more perilous during the initial stages, at least until both extended German flanks had contracted as a natural result of the withdrawal.

The Russians increased their pressure against Ninth Army's southern flank the moment our retirement began. Not content to follow the withdrawal, the Soviets aimed to break through our lines and cut off large

German forces before our defenses consolidated at the next switch line. Thus on 1 August heavy attacks—consisting of at least four rifle divisions and 120 tanks, supported by waves of aircraft—hit the 7th, 31st, and 258th Infantry Divisions in the Shepelovo-Gomel sector. Heroic resistance on the part of already exhausted troops stopped the Russians in their tracks with the loss of seventy-seven tanks, and on 4 August Ninth Army reached the Kromy area. Because the Soviets continued to maintain heavy pressure, especially from the Chern River bend, Colonel General Model found himself forced to order a temporary shift in the Luftwaffe's air support priorities from Second Panzer to Ninth Army.

The Kromy sector constituted a substantial antitank obstacle; nonetheless, by 5 August Red Army concentrations in this area had progressed sufficiently for the enemy to launch a powerful thrust southwest of Kromy. This attack employed over 200 tanks, large infantry units, and strong aerial formations, with which the Russians planned to pierce the retiring German lines and seize the traffic center at Kromy as rapidly as possible. Fifteen times on that one day—5 August—the flood of Soviet manpower, accompanied by countless tanks, surged against the 258th Infantry Division of the XLVI Panzer Corps. Wire connections between division and regimental headquarters and their constituent units were constantly cut by Russian bombing, and practically overnight guerrillas stepped up their activities against our rail communications, causing a critical ammunition and fuel shortage. Despite these disadvantages, every Soviet attack was met and repulsed in bitter fighting. Still the battle approached a new climax, and Colonel General Model understood clearly that the focal point of operations in the Orel salient had almost completely shifted back to Ninth Army. He therefore ordered the following measures to be executed: strictest concentration of antitank weapons and ammunition only at points of main effort; increased employment of mines and Falk combat squads; transfer of 12th Panzer Division to the area east of Smablykin. Second Panzer Army had just made 12th Panzer available to relieve the battered 292nd and 383rd Infantry Divisions. The Luftwaffe also received orders to continue its concentration of effort on Ninth Army's front. In this manner we weathered the storm, holding the Kromy sector for two days as planned. Colonel General Model had recognized Soviet intentions and foiled their plan to envelop large German forces by attacking Kromy on one side and Khotynets (in Second Panzer Army sector) on the other.

In the meantime, on 5 August Second Panzer Army accomplished the evacuation of Orel. Retiring, the army destroyed all bridges and other installations important to the war effort while evacuating 53,000 tons of equipment and 20,000 wounded. Intelligence now noted a gradual Soviet

reorganization of forces in the area, especially Fourth Tank Army. Consequently, just as Ninth Army finished its successful defensive stand at
Kromy, a tactical crisis developed along Second Panzer Army's front
from 6 to 8 August. Heavily supported by tanks, the Russians debouched
from the area west of Uskoye and attempted to break through the northern salient of *Gruppe* Harpe. General of Panzer Troops Harpe had to undertake several improvised changes in his phase-line withdrawals,
which he accomplished on 7 August. His new line along the Moshchenka
River, though necessitated by enemy attacks, provided the Soviets with
the opportunity to renew their flanking thrust toward Khotynets; these
attacks continued without success through 10 August.

Withdrawal from the Kromy sector gave Ninth Army a greater degree
of maneuverability, primarily because the next set of phase-lines veered
sharply to the north and deprived the Russians of the effectiveness they
had heretofore enjoyed. On the other hand, such a deployment positively
invited the enemy to strike Second Panzer Army's now exposed southern
flank below Smitrovsk. As early as 1 August our intelligence identified a
major Soviet concentration there, which finally attacked on 8 August. A
large-scale attack from the Bryantsovo area struck Dmitrovsk, held by
72nd Infantry Division; aided by a thunderstorm, the Russians penetrated deeply into the division's attenuated line. But even though the Soviets committed an additional three rifle divisions and more tanks on
9–10 August, they did not succeed in breaking through—72nd Infantry
resolutely stood its ground. Colonel General Model committed 31st Infantry behind the 72nd as a general reserve; this division had been freed
by the arrival of the 20th Panzergrenadier Division from Second Panzer
Army. The planned retirement of both armies continued on 9–10 August,
and the situation eased, primarily because Colonel General Model insisted that Dmitrovsk be held as a breakwater for as long as possible. He
realized that Dmitrovsk's premature loss would jeopardize the orderly
continuation of Operation Hagen and the maintenance of contact between the two armies. On 10 August the Fourth Tank Army, employing
waves of infantry and sixty tanks massed along a narrow sector, made
one final attempt to batter its way into the town; the collapse of this assault closed the book on the Dmitrovsk battles. German troops evacuated
the town on the night of 11 August, according to Colonel General
Model's timetable, not that of the enemy.

Notwithstanding the successful defense of Dmitrovsk, tremendous
tension still hovered over the entire Orel salient. The Red Army had
opened new offensives—to the north an attack against the Fourth Army
and in the south against Field Marshal von Manstein's army group. OKH
therefore increased its pressure for Second Panzer and Ninth Armies to

accelerate Operation Hagen in order to free vitally needed front-line divisions for use as reserves all along the Eastern front.

It had been previously established that the headquarters of the Second Panzer Army would be pulled out of the front for employment elsewhere, with Ninth Army taking over full control of all troops retiring from the Orel salient. This occurred sooner than we expected; on 13 August Colonel General Model's Ninth Army headquarters assumed control of both sectors, inaugurating the final phase of the Hagen withdrawal. This portion of the operation took its peculiar character from the ferocity of the defensive battles fought by the enlarged Ninth Army near Karachev. Vast bodies of Russian troops—maintaining pressure and grouping more and more densely as the front contracted—had congealed to form a powerful main effort in the Karachev area. That the Soviets intended a direct frontal assault became evident, and, anticipating this move, Colonel General Model concentrated his own reserves at the point of attack—especially all available engineer troops. These measures robbed the concentric Russian breakthrough attack of its momentum from the outset. The enemy attacked on 13 August along a broad front on both sides of Karachev, employing infantry, tanks, artillery, rocket launchers, and aerial formations in steadily increasing numbers. The German defenders—particularly the 8th and 18th Panzer Divisions—resisted tenaciously, confining Russian success on 13–14 August to tactical penetrations. The Luftwaffe participated with particular success in this action. The Soviet assault completely fizzled as Ninth Army retired into the Hagen line proper, its lead elements taking up positions in the evening of 14 August, the rear guards arriving by the evening of 18 August.

The Soviets did not immediately realize that the Hagen line represented the final German defensive position. Beginning on 16 August the Russians crashed unawares into our strongly prepared defensive system, suffering heavy losses. Undaunted, the Soviets regrouped their forces for main-effort attacks at the following points: southwest of Shablykino; southwest of Karachev; and northwest of Kirov. Meanwhile, Ninth Army improved its defensive line with all possible speed and thoroughness, ensuring that the distribution of forces (especially antitank weapons) corresponded to enemy main-effort concentrations. Engineers and construction troops worked feverishly to complete the roads and trails immediately behind the Hagen line to allow for the lateral movement of reserves; alternate artillery emplacements, switch positions, and straggler lines were designated. Unfortunately, even though Ninth Army had been heavily decimated during the battle for the Orel salient, OKH found it necessary to order the immediate transfer of the 1st, 102nd, 183rd, 258th, and 293rd Infantry Divisions; the 4th, 9th, and 12th Panzer Divisions; and numerous army troops. The fact that Ninth Army also received orders to incorporate the weakly held sectors of the LVI Panzer Corps and XII Corps (both from Fourth Army) into its own sector constituted an additional and by no means inconsiderable burden.

On 19 August the Red Army launched an offensive against XXIII Corps, expanding the attack on 26 August to include XLVI Panzer Corps and striking *Gruppe* Harpe on 28 August. This fighting ushered in a new phase in the combat history of Ninth Army: the battle for the Hagen line. With the opening of this new fight, Ninth Army—after having closed out the battle in the Orel salient—again found itself embroiled in the great defensive battle that had been raging ever since 5 July along practically the entire Eastern Front from the Kuban bridgehead to Lake Ladoga.

Conclusion

Ninth Army's Citadel offensive hit the Russian armies about to launch their own offensive out of the Kursk salient with such impact and weakened them to such an extent that these enemy armies no longer were strong enough to carry out the mission assigned to them within the scope of the concentric offensive against the Orel salient (the breakthrough to the line Khotynets-Karachev from the south). Operation Hagen, executed almost exactly according to plan by the two armies under Colonel General Model's command, served to wear down a large part of the Russian strategic reserve and freed a large number of German divisions and army units for employment elsewhere. By the end of August, nineteen divisions had been made available in this manner:

Five panzer divisions
Three panzergrenadier divisions
Eleven infantry divisions
Numerous Army units

From the war diary of Ninth Army we learn that for almost seven weeks the German divisions were engaged in large-scale fighting without rest or reprieve, standing their ground despite crushing enemy numerical superiority. We identified the following enemy units employed against Second Panzer and Ninth Armies:

Eighty-five rifle divisions
Three rifle brigades
Thirteen tank corps (i.e., thirty-nine tank brigades and thirteen motorized rifle brigades)

Two mechanized corps
Thirty-three independent tank regiments
One cavalry corps

The tactical successes of the German fighting troops can be measured by the following figures of men and equipment captured or destroyed:

11,772 prisoners of war
2,007 deserters
203 artillery pieces
362 anti-tank guns
32 anti-aircraft guns
206 mortars
827 machine guns
799 sub-machine guns
32 rocket projectors
34 Russian aircraft shot down by group troops

The 1st Fleiger Division flew 37,421 sorties, with each serviceable aircraft averaging five or six sorties per day. This division supported the two armies in the Orel salient and often brought about a decision at the most critical moment. Luftwaffe pilots chalked up 1,733 aerial victories, as compared to sixty-four of its own losses. In addition, 1st Fleiger Division accounted for numerous enemy tanks, artillery pieces, and vehicles put out of action. The 12th Flak Division downed a total of 383 aircraft and two observation balloons.

This battle consumed roughly 120,000 tons of ammunition, including almost 2 million rounds of light field howitzer ammunition, plus 40,000 cubic meters of fuel. Combat engineers laid approximately 250,000 mines of all types during the battle. The signal troops (in this case the 511th Signal Communications Regiment of Ninth Army) installed 1,460 kilometers of spiral-four cables and 622 kilometers of open wire. They recovered 1,480 kilometers of spiral-four cables and 1,130 kilometers of open wire. The central switchboard handled 10,500 telephone calls, while the teletype section handled 20,500 messages. The railroads dispatched 200 trains carrying ammunition and 400 troop trains. These figures have to be considered in addition to the extremely large number of trains dispatched in connection with supply and maintenance traffic. (It must be remembered that repairs were necessary in numerous instances where the tracks had been dynamited by partisans.)

APPENDIX 4A

Order of Battle: Ninth Army, 5 July 1943

Colonel General Walter Model

XX Corps
General of Artillery Rudolf Freiherr von Roman
45th Infantry Division
Major General Hans Freiherr von Falkenstein

 Grenadier Regiments 130, 133, 135
 Artillery Regiment 98
 Reconnaissance Battalion 45
 Panzerjaeger Battalion 45
 Engineer Battalion 81

72nd Infantry Division
Lieutenant General Albert Mueller-Gebhard

 Grenadier Regiments 105, 124, 266
 Artillery Regiment 172
 Reconnaissance Battalion 172
 Panzerjaeger Battalion 172
 Engineer Battalion 172

137th Infantry Division
Lieutenant General Hans Kamecke

 Grenadier Regiments 447, 448, 449
 Artillery Regiment 137
 Reconnaissance Battalion 137
 Panzerjaeger Battalion 137
 Engineer Battalion 137

251st Infantry Division
Major General Maximilian Felzmann

 Grenadier Regiments 451, 459, 471
 Artillery Regiment 251

Reconnaissance Battalion 251
Panzerjaeger Battalion 251
Engineer Battalion 251

Artillery Commander 129

Artillery Battalion 860
Light Observation Battalion 15

Engineer Regimental Staffs 4 (Special Employment), 512

Engineer Battalion 750
Bridge Column 626
Construction Battalions 49, 80, 418
Construction Battalions (POWs) 244

XLVI Panzer Corps
General of Infantry Hans Zorn

7th Infantry Division
Lieutenant General Fritz-Georg von Rappard

Grenadier Regiments 19, 61, 62
Artillery Regiment 7
Reconnaissance Battalion 7
Panzerjaeger Battalion 7
Engineer Battalion 7

31st Infantry Division
Lieutenant General Friedrich Hossbach

Grenadier Regiments 12, 17, 82
Artillery Regiment 31
Reconnaissance Battalion 31
Panzerjaeger Battalion 31
Engineer Battalion 31

102nd Infantry Division
Major General Otto Hitzfeld

Grenadier Regiments 232, 233, 235
Artillery Regiment 102
Reconnaissance Battalion 102
Panzerjaeger Battalion 102
Engineer Battalion 102

258th Infantry Division
Lieutenant General Hans-Kurt Hocker

Grenadier Regiments 458, 478, 479
Artillery Regiment 258

Reconnaissance Battalion 258
Panzerjaeger Battalion 258
Engineer Battalion 258

Gruppe *von Manteuffel*
Colonel Guentherr von Manteuffel

Jaeger Battalions 9, 10, 11
Light Infantry Gun Battalion 1
(Light Infantry Gun Batteries 423, 433, 443)

Artillery Commander 101

Artillery Regimental Staff 609 (Special Employment)
Artillery Battalions II/47, 430, 611
Heavy Mortar Battalion 18
Heavy Flak Battery 3/620
Assault Gun Battalion 909
Light Observation Battalion 6

Engineer Battalion 752

Bridge Column Sector Staff 930

Bridge Columns 12, 29

Commander of Construction Troops 33

Road Construction Battalion 584

XLVII Panzer Corps
General of Panzer Troops Jaochim Lemelsen
6th Infantry Division
Lieutenant General Horst Grossmann

Grenadier Regiments 18, 37, 58
Artillery Regiment 6
Reconnaissance Battalion 6
Panzerjaeger Battalion 6
Engineer Battalion 6

2nd Panzer Division
Lieutenant General Vollrath Luebbe

Panzer Regiment 3 (one battalion only)
Panzergrenadier Regiments 2, 304
Panzer Artillery Regiment 74
Panzer Reconnaissance Battalion 5

Panzerjaeger Battalion 38
Panzer Engineer Battalion 38

9th Panzer Division
Lieutenant General Walter Scheller

II Battalion, Panzer Regiment 33
Panzergrenadier Regiments 10, 11
Panzer Artillery Regiment 102
Panzer Reconnaissance Battalion 9
Panzerjaeger Battalion 50
Panzer Engineer Battalion 86

20th Panzer Division
Major General Mortimer von Kessel

Panzer Battalion 21
Panzergrenadier Regiments 59, 112
Panzer Artillery Regiment 92
Panzer Reconnaissance Battalion 92
Panzerjaeger Battalion 92
Panzer Engineer Battalion 92

Panzer Brigade Staff 21

Tiger Battalion 505

Panzer Company 312 (Flammpanzer [flame-throwing tanks])

Senior Artillery Commander 130

Artillery Battalions II/63, II/67, 637
Artillery Battery 1/620
Heavy Mortar Regiment 2
Assault Gun Battalions 245, 904

Engineer Regimental Staff 678

Engineer Training Battalion 2

Engineer Battalion (Motorized) 47

Bridge Construction Battalion 145

Bridge Column Sector Staff 928

Bridge Columns 47, 2/402, 845

XLI Panzer Corps
General of Panzer Troops Josef Harpe

86th Infantry Division

Lieutenant General Hellmuth Weidling

Grenadier Regiments 167, 184, 216
Artillery Regiment 186
Reconnaissance Battalion 186
Panzerjaeger Battalion 186
Engineer Battalion 186

292nd Infantry Division

Lieutenant General Guenther von Kluge

Grenadier Regiments 507, 508, 509
Artillery Regiment 292
Reconnaissance Battalion 292
Panzerjaeger Battalion 292
Engineer Battalion 292

18th Panzer Division

Major General Karl-Wilhelm von Schlieben

Panzer Battalion 18
Panzergrenadier Regiments 52, 101
Panzer Artillery Regiment 88
Panzer Reconnaissance Battalion 88
Panzerjaeger Battalion 88
Panzer Engineer Battalion 209

Panzerjaeger Regimental Staff 656

Panzerjaeger Battalions 653, 654

Sturmpanzer Battalion 216

Panzer Companies 313, 314 (Flammpanzer)

Heavy Mortar Battalion 19

Artillery Commander 35

Artillery Regimental Staff 69
Artillery Battalions II/61, II/64, 425, 427, 604, 616
Artillery Battery 2/620
Mortar Regiment 53
Assault Gun Battalions 177, 244

Engineer Regimental Staff 104 (Special Employment)

Engineer Battalion (Motorized) 42

Construction Battalion 417

Bridge Column Sector Staff 932

Bridge Columns 2/409, 606

XXIII Corps
General of Infantry Johannes Friessner
78th Sturm *Division*

Lieutenant General Hans Traut

Grenadier Regiments 195, 215
Artillery Regiment 178
Reconnaissance Battalion 78
Panzerjaeger Battalion 178
Engineer Battalion 178

Attached

Assault Gun Battalion 189

216th Infantry Division

Major General Friedrich-August Schack

Grenadier Regiments 348, 396, 398
Artillery Regiment 216
Reconnaissance Battalion 216
Panzerjaeger Battalion 216
Engineer Battalion 216

383rd Infantry Division

Major General Edmund Hoffmeister

Grenadier Regiments 531, 532, 533
Artillery Regiment 383
Reconnaissance Battalion 383
Panzerjaeger Battalion 383
Engineer Battalion 383

Attached

Infantry Regiment 87 (36th Infantry Division)
Artillery Commander 112
Artillery Regimental Staffs 109 (Special Employment), 41, 775
Artillery Battalions II/59, II/66, 422, 426, 709, 848, 859
Artillery Batteries 4/69, 1 and 2/635, 1/817
Assault Gun Battalion 185
Mortar Regiment 51
Light Observation Battalion 22

Engineer Regimental Staff 623

Engineer Battalion 746

Mountain Engineer Battalion 85

Construction Battalion 78

Bridge Column 88

Panzer Engineer Companies 811, 813

Jaeger Battalions 8, 13

Army Troops:
203rd Security Division
Lieutenant General Rudolf Pilz
   Security Regiments 608, 613
   Artillery Battalion 507
   Fusilier Company 203
   Panzerjaeger Company 203
   Engineer Company 203

221st Security Division (minus detachments)
Lieutenant General Hubert Lendle
   Security Regiment 45
   Artillery Battalion 701
   Fusilier Battalion 221
   Panzerjaeger Company 221
   Engineer Company 221

Division Staff 442 (Special Employment—Gruppe Bornemann)
Lieutenant General (Special Employment) Karl Bornemann
Commander of Mortar Troops 4
   Engineer Battalions 654, 751
   Bridge Columns 1/430, 535
   Commander of Construction Troops 42
   Senior Construction Staff 10
   Bridge Construction Battalions 42, 593
   Road Construction Battalions 544, 576, 580

Army Group Center reserve
(for commitment to Ninth Army)
10th Panzergrenadier Division
Lieutenant General August Schmidt
   Panzer Battalion 7
   Panzergrenadier Regiments 20, 41

Panzer Artillery Regiment 10
Panzer Reconnaissance Battalion 110
Panzerjaeger Battalion 10
Panzer Engineer Battalion 10

Gruppe *Esebeck*
Lieutenant General Hans-Karl Freiherr von Esebeck
4th Panzer Division
Lieutenant General Dietrich von Saucken

I Battalion, Panzer Regiment 35
Panzergrenadier Regiments 12, 33
Panzer Artillery Regiment 103
Panzer Reconnaissance Battalion 7
Panzerjaeger Battalion 49
Panzer Engineer Battalion 79

12th Panzer Division
Major General Erpo Frieherr von Bodenhausen

II Battalion and 8th Company, Panzer Regiment 29
Panzergrenadier Regiments 5, 25
Panzer Artillery Regiment 2
Panzer Reconnaissance Battalion 2
Panzerjaeger Battalion 2
Panzer Engineer Battalion 32

APPENDIX 4B

Order of Battle: Second Panzer Army, 5 July 1943

LV Corps

General of Infantry Erich Jaeschke

110th Infantry Division

Lieutenant General Eberhard von Kurowski

Grenadier Regiments 252, 254, 255
Artillery Regiment 120
Reconnaissance Battalion 110
Panzerjaeger Battalion 110
Engineer Battalion 110
Ost Company 110

134th Infantry Division

Lieutenant General Hans Schlemmer

Grenadier Regiments 439, 445, 446
Artillery Regiment 134
Reconnaissance Battalion 134
Panzerjaeger Battalion 134
Engineer Battalion 134

296th Infantry Division

Major General Arthur Kullmer

Grenadier Regiments 519, 520, 521
Artillery Regiment 296
Reconnaissance Battalion 296
Panzerjaeger Battalion 296
Engineer Battalion 296

321st Infantry Division

Lieutenant General Wilhelm Thomas

Grenadier Regiments 588, 589, 590
Artillery Regiment 321

Reconnaissance Battalion 321
Panzerjaeger Battalion 321
Engineer Battalion 321

339th Infantry Division

Major General Martin Ronicke

Grenadier Regiments 691, 692, 693
Artillery Regiment 339
Reconnaissance Battalion 339
Panzerjaeger Battalion 339
Engineer Battalion 339
Ost Battalion 339

Artillery Commander 146

Artillery Regimental Staff 786 (Special Employment)
Artillery Battalion 841

Ost *Staff 455 (Special Employment)*

Ost Battalion 447
Ost Company 455
1. and 2./*Ost* Cavalry Squadron 447

LIII Corps

General of Infantry Erich Cloessner

112th Infantry Division
Lieutenant General Theobald Lieb

Grenadier Regiments 110, 256, 258
Artillery Regiment 86
Reconnaissance Battalion 120
Panzerjaeger Battalion 112
Engineer Battalion 112

208th Infantry Division

Colonel Hans Piekenbrock

Grenadier Regiments 309, 337, 338
Artillery Regiment 208
Reconnaissance Company 208
Panzerjaeger Battalion 208
Engineer Battalion 208

211th Infantry Division

Lieutenant General Richard Mueller

Grenadier Regiments 306, 317, 365
Artillery Regiment 211

Reconnaissance Battalion 211
Panzerjaeger Battalion 211
Engineer Battalion 211

293rd Infantry Division

Major General Karl Arndt

Grenadier Regiments 510, 511, 512
Artillery Regiment 293
Reconnaissance Battalion 293
Panzerjaeger Battalion 293
Engineer Battalion 293

25th Panzergrenadier Division

Lieutenant General Anton Grasser

Panzer Battalion 125
Panzergrenadier Regiments 35, 119
Panzer Artillery Regiment 25
Panzer Reconnaissance Battalion 25
Panzerjaeger Battalion 25
Panzer Engineer Battalion 25
Ost Company 25

Security Regiment 350 (221st Security Division)

Artillery Commander 148

Artillery Battalion II/41
Artillery Battery 2/635
Panzerjaeger Battalion 270
Ost Battalion 441
Ost Company 453

XXXV Corps

General of Infantry Lothar Dr. Rendulic

34th Infantry Division

Lieutenant General Friedrich Hochbaum

Grenadier Regiments 80, 107, 253
Artillery Regiment 34
Reconnaissance Battalion 34
Panzerjaeger Battalion 34
Engineer Battalion 34

Attached

Artillery Battalion I/70
36th Infantry Division (minus detachments)
Lieutenant General Hans Gollnick

Grenadier Regiments 118, 165
Artillery Regiment 268
Reconnaissance Battalion 36
Panzerjaeger Battalion 36
Engineer Battalion 36

56th Infantry Division
Major General Otto Luedecke

Grenadier Regiments 171, 192, 234
Artillery Regiment 156
Reconnaissance Battalion 156
Panzerjaeger Battalion 156
Engineer Battalion 156
Ost Guard Company 156

262nd Infantry Division
Lieutenant General Friedrich Karst

Grenadier Regiments 467, 487, 497
Artillery Regiment 267
Reconnaissance Battalion 267
Panzerjaeger Battalion 267
Engineer Battalion 267

299th Infantry Division
Major General Ralph Graf von Oriola

Grenadier Regiments 528, 529, 530
Artillery Regiment 299
Reconnaissance Battalion 299
Panzerjaeger Battalion 299
Engineer Battalion 299
1./*Ost* Cavalry Squadron 299

Artillery Commander 136

Artillery Battalions II/69
Artillery Batteries 1/635, 3/817
Observation Battalions 37, 45, 46, 49, 54, 59, 61
Nebelwerfer Regiment 2

Army Troops
5th Panzer Division (behind LV Corps sector)
Major General Eduard Metz

Panzer Regiment 31 (one battalion only)
Panzergrenadier Regiments 13, 14
Panzer Artillery Regiment 116

Panzer Reconnaissance Battalion 8
Panzerjaeger Battalion 53
Panzer Engineer Battalion 89
Ost Company 85

8th Panzer Division (OKH Reserve; arrives 12 July)
Major General Sebastian Fichtner

I Battalion, Panzer Regiment 10
Panzergrenadier Regiments 8, 28
Panzer Artillery Regiment 80
Panzer Reconnaissance Battalion 59
Panzerjaeger Battalion 43
Panzer Engineer Battalion 59

305th Infantry Division
Major General Friedrich-Wilhelm Hauck

Grenadier Regiments 576, 577, 578
Artillery Regiment 305
Reconnaissance Battalion 305
Panzerjaeger Battalion 305
Engineer Battalion 305

707th Infantry Division (Static; subordinated to Korueck 532)
Major General Rudolf Busich

Grenadier Regiments 727, 747
Artillery Battalion 657
Reconnaissance Company 707
Panzerjaeger Company 707
Engineer Company 707
Staff, II./Railroad Engineer Regiment 5

Propaganda Company 693

Army Weapons School (becomes Brigade Staff 4—Special Employment)

Training Detachment (later Sturm Battalion 2)

Artillery Training Battalion
Senior Artillery Commander 305

Artillery Battalions 709, 2 and 3/817, 849
Assault Gun Battalions 190, 1./202, 270, 600
Panzerjaeger Battalion 2 (Special Employment)
Heavy Panzerjaeger Battalions 561, 655
Army Flak Battalions 273, 284, 288, 293, 290

Senior Army Engineer, Second Panzer Army

Engineer Regimental Staffs 507, 518
Engineer Battalions 50, 236, 630, 745
Engineer Training Battalion
Engineer Company "Orel"
Engineer Listening Post (Motorized) 5
Special Staffs Panther, Hagen, Himmler
Organization Todt Regiments "Zinth," "Wederkind"
Organization Todt Battalions 29, 37
Senior Construction Staffs 17, 18
Commander of Construction Troops 15, 35, 106
Construction Battalions 9, 11, 44, 46, 3/63, 103, 125, 136, 213, 222, 248, 320, 420, 421
Road Construction Battalions 11, 46, 137, 213, 420, 679
Ost Construction Battalion "Bryansk"
Bridge Construction Battalions 3/4, 84, 159

Korueck 532

Regimental Staff "Desna"
Panzergrenadier Brigade Staff 21 (Special Employment)
Brigade Staff 17 (Special Employment)
Kaminski Brigade
Brigade Staff 18 (Special Employment)
Commander of *Ostruppen* 702 (Special Employment)
Commander of *Ostruppen* 709
Ost Battalions 582, 615, 616, 617, 618, 619, 620
Armenian Field Replacement Battalion II./9
Azerbaijani Infantry Battalion 807
Armenian Infantry Battalion I/125
Ost Artillery Battalion 621
Security Regiment 57
Security Battalions 304, 313, 350, 587, 738, 791, 793, 862
Bicycle Security Battalion 757
Jaeger Battalion 14
Cossack Artillery Battery 553
Cavalry Detachment *Trubschewek*
Commandant, Karachev
Armored Train 2
Armored Train 4
Army Installation Guard 12 (Special Employment)
Field Disciplinary Battalions 1, 2, 13

APPENDIX 4C

Deception Designations Used by Ninth Army Prior to Operation Citadel

In a concerted effort to confuse the Soviets with regard to precisely what happened to Ninth Army and its constituent units after the withdrawal from the Rzhev salient, the Germans employed a number of deception designations (*Tarnbezeichnungen*) throughout the spring and early summer of 1943. Army Group Center appears to have been particularly concerned with obscuring the location of Ninth Army and XLVII Panzer Corps headquarters, the two commands tasked with the primary assault missions in Operation Citadel. Just how successful these cover names were in deceiving the Russians is still an open question, though they have certainly befuddled more than a few historians. The list below is admittedly partial and, in two cases, conjectural.

Deception designation	Actual unit designation
Fortress Staff 11	Ninth Army
Gruppe Weiss	Ninth Army
Staff Breitenbuch	XLVII Panzer Corps
Rear Area Staff 3	XLVII Panzer Corps
XXXI *Ost* Corps	XXIII Corps
407th Infantry Division	7th Infantry Division
410th Infantry Division	10th Panzergrenadier Division
419th Infantry Division	18th Panzer Division (?)
467th Infantry Division	4th Panzer Division (?)
492nd Infantry Division	292nd Infantry Division

Tactical Group Designations: Second Panzer and Ninth Armies, 13 July–13 August 1943

Though not utilized for deception purposes as were the designations in the preceding appendix, the German practice of naming provisional tactical groups (*gruppen*) after their commander, even if such groups existed for a few days, can make following a battle narrative almost impossible. That the Germans themselves had this problem is indicated by the fact that their armies routinely churned out lists of such designations, their composition, and the dates of their employment. The following is—hopefully—a complete list of such designations utilized during the confusing battle for the Orel salient.[6] As can be quickly observed, such informal groups routinely found employment controlling as much as several army corps or as little as a few battalions.

1. Corps-level *Gruppen*

A. Gruppe *Harpe*

Built around the staff of the XLI Panzer Corps, this *Gruppe* (confusingly often commanded not by General Harpe but by General Friessner) was subordinated to Second Panzer Army from 16 July to 10 August. From 16 to 20 July it controlled XLI Panzer Corps, LIII Corps, and *Gruppe* Esebeck (see below), with XXIII Corps added to its organization on 23 July, making this improvised structure essentially the equivalent of an army command. At its largest, around 23 July, *Gruppe* Harpe controlled the following:

XLI Panzer Corps
2nd Panzer Division
8th Panzer Division
9th Panzer Division
Grossdeutschland Panzergrenadier Division
LIII Corps
25th Panzergrenadier Division
26th Infantry Division

34th Infantry Division
253rd Infantry Division
Security Regiment 350 (221st Security Division)
Gruppe Wuethmann (subordinate to LIII Corps)
208th Infantry Division
112th Infantry Division
12th Panzer Division
Assault Gun Battalion 270
XXIII Corps
10th Panzergrenadier Division
129th Infantry Division
134th Infantry Division
183rd Infantry Division
Gruppe Esebeck (subordinate to XXIII Corps)
18th Panzer Division
20th Panzer Division

B. Gruppe *Esebeck*

This group, containing the 4th and 12th Panzer Divisions, had been created prior to Operation Citadel as an improvised headquarters to control the two panzer divisions held in Army Group Center's reserves to support Ninth Army's offensive. Its commander, Lieutenant General Hans-Karl Freiherr von Esebeck, had led the 2nd Panzer Division until October 1942 and then drew an assignment as deputy commander of the XLVI Panzer Corps. His staff appears to have been cobbled together from whatever was available. The staff does not appear to have been utilized operationally by Ninth Army, as the two panzer divisions were committed in two different corps sectors. On 13 July this staff, then controlling the 18th and 20th Panzer Divisions, was transferred to Second Panzer Army and subordinated first to LIII Corps (13–15 July), then to Group Harpe (16 July). The group was disbanded and both divisions assigned directly to XLI Panzer Corps on 18 July.

C. Gruppe *Gollnick/Luebbe*

This confusing *Gruppe* had two commanders and interchangeable names throughout its brief existence. Originally led by the 2nd Panzer Division's Lieutenant General Vollrath Luebbe, at some point (either 24 or 26 July would be the best guess), Lieutenant General Hans Gollnick of the 36th Infantry Division took over command. Whether or not Luebbe ever returned to command of the ad hoc unit is questionable, as the war diary and morning reports of Second Panzer Army are extremely contradictory on this point. At any rate, the *Gruppe* composition remained constant: the main body of the 2nd Panzer Division, 8th Panzer Division, and 56th Infantry Division. From 21 to 25 July this *Gruppe* fought under XXXV Corps and, from 26 to 29 July, directly under Second Panzer Army headquarters before being disbanded on 29 July.

D. Gruppe *Grasser*

Under the command of Lieutenant General Anton Grasser (25th Panzergrenadier Division), this *Gruppe* consisted of his own division and elements of the 293rd Infantry Division. The *Gruppe* existed only from 14–19 July and fought under LIII Corps.

E. Gruppe *Mueller*

Commanded by Lieutenant General Richard Mueller, this *Gruppe* consisted of his own 211th Infantry Division and the 5th Panzer Division. It existed from 13 July to 8 August under control of the LV Corps.

F. Gruppe *Praun*

Lieutenant General Albert Praun controlled his own 129th Infantry Division, plus the 8th Panzer Division, 10th Panzergrenadier Division, and 293rd Infantry Division. From 11 to 12 August this *Gruppe* served directly under Second Panzer Army headquarters, transferring to Ninth Army when the former army headquarters was removed to the Balkans. Precisely how long *Gruppe* Praun continued to exist thereafter is unclear.

G. Gruppe *Roehricht*

Commanded by Lieutenant General Edgar Roehricht, who does not appear to have held a permanent command during the period, this *Gruppe* fought from 9 to 12 August under Second Panzer Army; briefly on 12 August under XXIII Corps; and then passed under Ninth Army control on 13 August for an undetermined period. This *Gruppe* consisted of:

95th Infantry Division
707th Infantry Division (Static)
Assault Gun Battalion 190 (minus Company 2)
Light Artillery Battalion 849
I/Panzergrenadier Regiment 14 (5th Panzer Division)
Heavy infantry-gun Company 704 (5th Panzer Division)
Panzerjaeger Battalion 53 (minus Company 3) (5th Panzer Division)
Company 1, Panzer Engineer Battalion 89 (5th Panzer Division)

H. Gruppe *Traut*

Lieutenant General Hans Traut commanded his own 78th *Sturm* Division, 36th Infantry Division, and 262nd Infantry Division as a *Gruppe* under XXXV Corps (23 July–8 August) and then under *Gruppe* Harpe (8 August–12 August) before being disbanded.

I. Gruppe *Wuthmann*

Lieutenant General Rolf Wuthmann briefly commanded his own 112th Infantry Division, 208th Infantry Division, 12th Panzer Division, and Assault Gun Battalion 270 as a *Gruppe* under LIII Corps from about 19 July to 23 July before being disbanded.

2. Division- or regimental-level *Gruppen*

A. Gruppe *Boeselager*

Formed under the commander of Cavalry Regiment Center, Lieutenant Colonel Georg Freiherr von Boeselager, this *Gruppe* existed from 18 to 26 July under LV Corps; 27 July to 9 August under *Grossdeutschland* Panzergrenadier Division; and from 10 August through an indeterminate date under Ninth Army. Its constituent units were:

> II/Grenadier Regiment 727 (707th Infantry Division)
> II/Grenadier Regiment 747 (707th Infantry Division)
> Engineer Company 707 (707th Infantry Division)
> Jaeger Battalion 14
> 2/Construction Battalion 421
> I/Cavalry Regiment "Center"

B. Gruppe *Hamann*

Formed under Major General Adolf Hamann (commandant of Orel) this *Gruppe* consisted of III/Brandenburg Regiment and various alarm units (*Alarmeinheiten*). It served from 20 July to 1 August under XXXV Corps.

C. Gruppe *Wuestmann*

Major Wuestmann, commandant of Karachev, commanded this *Gruppe* from 15 to 26 July under Korueck 532, then from 27 July to 20 August under *Gruppe* Harpe. It consisted of:

> Panzergrenadier Brigade Staff 4 (Special Employment)
> One armored car company (4th Panzer Division)
> One Infantry-gun company (4th Panzer Division)
> Panzer Training Battalion 9 (Ninth Army)

D. Gruppe *Schaal*

This *Gruppe* controlled Panzer Reconnaissance Battalions 4 (4th Panzer Division) and 9 (9th Panzer Division) on 26 July under *Gruppe* Harpe and from 27 July to 5 August under *Grossdeutschland* Panzergrenadier Division

E. Gruppe *Wenninger*

Colonel Gustav Wenninger, commander of Second Panzer Army Weapons School, commanded this *Gruppe*, composed of the exact same units as *Gruppe* Boeselager (see above) with the exception of the cavalry battalion, under LV Corps from 17 to 18 July. With the addition of the cavalry, Boeselager apparently superceded Wenninger, and the *Gruppe* continued under his name.

F. Grossdeutschland *Panzergrenadier Division*

This entry represents something of a special case. When *Grossdeutschland* was committed around Karachev between 24 July and 3 August it was not ever referred by a *Gruppe* designator, a fact that may be explained by the division's elite status. Nonetheless, Lieutenant General Walter Hoernlein controlled significant nondivisional assets on a par with the other *Gruppen* detailed above. During this period, while first subordinated to XLI Panzer Corps (24–27 July) and then XXIII Corps (28 July–3 August), *Grossdeutschland* exercised authority over the following assets:

Gruppe Boeselager (see composition above)
Gruppe Schaal (see composition above)
Security Regiment 45
Panzerjaeger Battalion 104
Engineer Battalion (Motorized) 42

3. *Gruppen* formed from security troops under Korueck 532

Note: The *Gruppen* listed below represented even more ephemeral tactical conglomerations than those employed by the field units. Korueck 532, the rear area command for Second Panzer Army, conducted numerous antipartisan sweeps on a monthly or even weekly basis, even when the front was quiet. Once the Soviet offensive against Orel started, rear-area activity increased. About the groups below it has been impossible to determine more than the surname of the leader (none of whom were general officers), the period of its existence, and—in some cases—partial listings of the units involved. All of these *Gruppen* should be assumed to have been subordinated to Korueck 532 unless otherwise specified:

Gruppe *Ruebenau*

(Brigade Staff 17 [Special Employment])
In continuous existence
Subordinated to Ninth Army on 13 August
People's Defense Brigade Kaminski

Gruppe *Jolasse*

(Brigade Staff 18 [Special Employment])
In continuous existence to 12 August

Gruppe *Kietz*

In continuous existence
Remained under Korueck 532 after 13 August

Gruppe *Metterhausen*

In continuous existence
Subordinated to Ninth Army on 13 August
Armenian Infantry Battalion II/9

APPENDIX 4E

Artillery Strength: Second Panzer and Ninth Armies, 5 July 1943

Both Second Panzer Army and Ninth Army filed detailed reports on 2 July and 27 June 1943 regarding the field artillery assigned to corps and divisions. The reports, unfortunately, followed extremely different formats and are therefore difficult to reconcile concisely. Second Army, for example, broke down its artillery strength by division but did not reliably differentiate between heavy and light guns, nor did the report detail intelligence estimates of enemy artillery in directly opposing sectors. Ninth Army *did* break down the types of guns and provide intelligence estimates but *did not* detail the report below corps level. In other documents, Ninth Army listed guns, division by division, but these papers contain so many cross-attachments and caveats as to be nearly useless for developing divisional averages. Nonetheless, from these reports it is possible to draw some interesting conclusions about the relative artillery strengths of the two armies.

Second Panzer Army[7]
Artillery Strength
2 July 1943
LV Corps

134th Infantry Division	4 battalions	42 guns
296th Infantry Division	4 battalions	36 guns
110th Infantry Division	3 battalions	41 guns
339th Infantry Division	2 battalions	22 guns
5th Panzer Division	3 battalions	38 guns
Corps artillery	1 battalion	12 guns
Total	17 battalions	191 guns
Division average		38 guns

LIII Corps

208th Infantry Division	3 battalions	46 guns
112th Infantry Division	4 battalions	36 guns
25th Panzergren. Division	3 battalions	51 guns
293rd Infantry Division	4 battalions	35 guns

211th Infantry Division	4 battalions	37 guns
Corps artillery	1 battalion	12 guns
Total	19 battalions	217 guns
Division average		43 guns

XXXV Corps

299th Infantry Division	4 battalions	37 guns
262nd Infantry Division	4 battalions	43 guns
56th Infantry Division	4 battalions	38 guns
34th Infantry Division	4 battalions	45 guns
Corps Artillery	2.5 battalions	29 guns
Total	18.5 battalions	192 guns
Division average		48 guns

Second Panzer Army totals

(Note: Army artillery was not included in the original report; for the sake of completeness, other fragmentary sources and armywide averages have been used to determine an estimate.)

LV Corps	17 battalions	191 guns
LIII Corps	19 battalions	217 guns
XXXV Corps	18.5 battalions	192 guns
Army artillery	3 battalions	33 guns
Total	55.5 battalions	633 guns

Ninth Army[8]
Artillery Strength
27 June 1943

	German artillery			Soviet artillery		
Corps	Lt.	Hvy.	Total	Lt.	Hvy.	Total
XX	120	41	161	220	12	232
XLVI Pz.	147	66	213	280	105	385
XLVII Pz.	115	123	238	64	30	94
XLI Pz.	127	109	236	108	48	156
XXIII	111	138	249	232	66	298
Total	620	477	1,097	904	261	1,165

(Note: All artillery assets in Ninth Army had by this time been deployed forward with the corps headquarters. The totals actually account for the organic artillery of the 4th and 12th Panzer Divisions and 10th Panzergrenadier Division, in army group reserve, close to the front, with the exception of ten heavy pieces assigned to the 10th Panzergrenadier Division.)

Divisional estimates

XX Corps	4 divisions	161 guns	40 guns/division

XLVI Panzer Corps	4 divisions	213 guns	53 guns/division
XLVII Panzer Corps	4 divisions	238 guns	60 guns/division
XLI Panzer Corps	3 divisions	236 guns	79 guns/division
XXIII Corps	3 divisions	249 guns	83 guns/division

These figures stimulate a number of insights regarding the preparations and assumptions made by Army Group Center for Operation Citadel. First, and perhaps most critical, is the fact that the Germans badly underestimated Soviet artillery strength along Ninth Army's assault front. Figures normally cited for the Red Army are difficult to compare to those used by the Germans, because the Germans habitually differentiated between field artillery, antitank guns, flak, and mortars, whereas the numbers usually cited for the Russians are simply listed as "guns and mortars." Nonetheless, some rough comparisons can be made. The two armies opposite Ninth Army—the Soviet Thirteenth and Seventieth—reported between them 4,592 guns and mortars on 1 July. Even if the extreme assumption is made that 60 percent of this figure represents other than field artillery, comparable Russian artillery strength would have exceeded 1,800 guns in the assault zone—650 more than the Germans estimated. This figure takes no account of the artillery reserves available from Central Front reserves, which were considerable (1,128 guns and mortars), whereas Ninth Army had committed every weapon it possessed at the outset. Plainly the Germans, who knew that they would be outnumbered by Soviet armor, had mistakenly convinced themselves that they had attained at least parity in terms of artillery.[9]

The second startling fact to emerge from these figures is that in terms of offensive concentration for a major assault the Germans did worse in terms of artillery than they managed with respect to men, tanks, or planes. In fourteen infantry divisions and four panzer divisions, at full strength the divisional artillery establishment alone should have totaled 964 guns, and roughly twenty-three corps artillery battalions (excluding mortar, assault gun, and flak units) should have added an additional 276, for a grand total of 1,240 guns. Ninth Army, with 1,097 guns, came up 143 guns short of establishment (11.5 percent), and even that figure could be achieved only by stripping Second Panzer Army of essential artillery support (more on that subject below).

Third, Ninth Army chose a peculiar distribution for its field artillery, concentrating the bulk of its artillery (485 guns) in the six divisions of the two corps on the left flank of the assault (XX and XLVI Panzer Corps) while leaving its main effort—XLVII Panzer Corps—with only 238 guns to support the four divisions making the main effort. Ostensibly, General Model and his staff were depending upon the weight of armor employed on XLVII Panzer Corps front to make up for the lack of artillery, but this was a strange decision that has been rarely if ever commented upon by participants or historians.

Finally, these artillery figures make explicitly clear the dangerous position in which Operation Citadel left Second Panzer Army. The thirteen divisions in this army should have had, on establishment, 748 guns, plus at least another ninety in the corps and army artillery battalions, for a grand total of 838 guns. Instead, Second Panzer Army had a shortfall of 205 guns (24 percent). When the length of the army's front is considered, along with parallel weaknesses in infantry and armor, the only wonder remaining is that the Soviet counteroffensive did not break through more rapidly and more completely. These figures also, however, partly explain how XXXV Corps put up such a tenacious defense immediately east of Orel, whereas LV Corps collapsed very quickly to the north; divisions in LV Corps were roughly sixteen guns (or four batteries) short of establishment, and the divisions in XXXV Corps had been sufficiently reinforced by army artillery assets that they were each only six guns shy of their complete organization.

APPENDIX 4F

Replacements Available, Ninth Army, 5 July 1943

The extent to which the Germans committed their full resources to a single throw of the dice at Kursk is also highlighted in the replacement situation for Ninth Army at the beginning of the offensive. On 2 July 1943 Ninth Army filed a partial report of the field replacements actually available to six divisions and the general pool of replacements for the panzergrenadier regiments in its panzer divisions.[10] The *Feldersatz* battalions for these divisions contained the following:

137th Infantry Division	450 men
251st Infantry Division	450 men
6th Infantry Division	600 men
10th Panzergrenadier Division	300 men
258th Infantry Division	300 men
292nd Infantry Division	300 men

These figures suggest, by extension, a divisional average among Ninth Army's eighteen divisions of 355 men, or a total of 4,970 replacements for an army with a total strength of 355,000 men. To this should be added one and one-half march battalions at the Army Weapons School, one XX Corps training battalion at Lokot, one panzergrenadier march battalion at the Bryansk Weapons School, and two panzergrenadier march battalions from the training staff near Kromy—about 1,950 more men, bringing the grand total available to Ninth Army to about 6,920. Against combat losses that quickly mounted above 20,000, this was clearly inadequate. As with artillery, Army Group Center and Ninth Army had placed nearly all their assets in the front line on the first day of the assault.

5

Luftflotte Six

by General of Fliers Friedrich Kless
Chief of Staff, Luftflotte Six

Editor's Introduction

Compared to the question of who wrote the other manuscripts in the Operational Citadel study, the men behind two Luftwaffe studies were easy to find, because both documents reappeared in other venues with full authorial attribution. A somewhat revised and polished version of this chapter appeared as *Bericht ueber de Einsatz der Luftflotte 6. waehrend 'Zitadelle' und in der Schlacht im Orelbogen* (G/VI/5a, Karlsruhe Document Collection, U.S. Air Force); that of the following text appeared as *Das VIII. Flieger-Korps im Einsatz waehrend der Operation 'Zitadelle'* (G/VI/5a, Karlsruhe Document Collection, U.S. Air Force). Taken together, these documents became the main sources underlying the chapter on Kursk in the often-cited narrative by Herman Plocher, *The German Air Force Versus Russia, 1943*. Thus the accounts that appear here will, in many respects, be familiar to many readers, raising the question of why it would be necessary to retranslate and republish well-known materials.

There are several reasons to provide these original documents to a wider audience, not the least of which is to set the record straight and credit the original authors. Plocher's introduction to his synthesis suggests that his narrative was "submitted whenever possible in preliminary draft form to actual participants in the particular actions described for their comments, criticisms, and additions," though "the author has not hesitated to express his own opinions." This is both disingenuous and misleading, as even a cursory reading of Chapters 5 and 6 will reveal. Plocher thoroughly mined the studies by Friedrich Kless and Hans Seidemann, limiting himself almost exclusively to the material they first presented and rarely, if ever, changing an interpretation or conclusion. At most, Plocher condensed the accounts by Kless and Seidemann, omitting a wealth of specific supporting details.[1]

Those details constitute the second major reason for examining the original manuscripts. Kless, for example, goes into depth regarding the difficulties of the pre-Citadel logistical buildup, which raises an interesting question. In his introduction to the study, Kless admits that he had retained "no original reference material" and "was thus forced to write this study from memory." This is peculiar when compared to the precise numerical information presented on fuel stocks and consumption; ammunition supplies; and claims of enemy material destroyed. If Kless in fact lacked contemporary documentation, how could he possibly have presented such detailed statistics? If these numbers were, as admitted, generated completely from memory, this would call into question the many subsequent works that have—through Plocher—simply accepted and reprinted those statistics. How many interpretations have been based on numbers that may not be verifiable from original sources?

Finally, there are several key interpretive points in the longer original manuscripts that should not be lost. Kless, a longtime staff officer who was then aspiring to an operational command of his own, pays particular attention to the thinking, analysis, and strategy of Luftflotte Six's commander, Field Marshal Robert Ritter von Greim. These insights, by and large, did not surface in Plocher's book. Given the new arguments about the Luftwaffe in Russia that have recently been advanced by scholars like James Corum, E. R. Hooten, Richard Muller, Williamson Murray, and Joel S. A. Hayward following extensive archival research, taking a fresh look at the Kless and Seidemann narratives becomes even more critical.[2]

Luftflotte Six
by General of Fliers Friedrich Kless
Chief of Staff, Luftflotte Six

Introduction

In writing this description of the activities of Luftflotte Six, no original reference material dating back to the period involved was available to me. This applies to all but a few instances. I was thus forced to write this study from memory and in most cases have had to omit the description of details. The only thing I could do was to record events in broad outline and extract for presentation the most important aspects of the period involved. Individual units are listed and individual combat phases described only to the extent I could do so while still preserving the historical accuracy of the story told. The description of the enemy situation and other statistical figures for the month of July 1943 are as authentic as possible considering the limited reference material available to me.

Air Situation, Mid-April 1943

Luftwaffe formation in the area of Army Group Center had been under the direction of *Luftwaffenkommando Ost* since 10 April 1942; on 1 May 1943 this headquarters became Luftflotte Six. Army Group Center and the Luftflotte were instructed to work together.

Luftflotte Six, commanded by Field Marshal Robert Ritter von Greim, shared a boundary with Luftflotte Four to the south along the line Chernigov-Rylsk-Kursk-Svoboda (these towns located in the area of Luftflotte Six), and with Luftflotte One to the north along the line Polotsk–Velikiye Luki–Bologoye–Rybinsk (these towns located in the area of Luftflotte Six). Luftflotte Six's headquarters was located in Smolensk.

In mid-April Luftflotte Six deployed the following formations in support of the southern half of Army Group Center:

1st Fleiger Division: Assigned to Second Army/Second Panzer Army sector; headquarters at Orel; commanded by Lieutenant General Paul Deichmann; including the following elements:
  Two close-range reconnaissance groups (He 123s); one each supporting Second Army and Second Panzer Army;
  51st Fighter Wing (FW 190s), composed of an operations substaff, 1st and 3rd Fighter Groups, and the Spanish 13th Fighter Squadron;
  1st Ground Attack Wing (Ju 87s), consisting of the wing headquarters, 2nd and 3rd Groups;
  14th Squadron, 1st Ground Attack Wing (fighter-bombers);
  1st and 3rd Groups, 3rd Bombardment Wing;
  One or two harassing squadrons.
12th Flak Division: Assigned to Second Panzer Army/Fourth Army sector (Fourth Army area was in the process of being assigned coverage by the 18th Flak Division); headquarters at Orel; commanded by Lieutenant General Ernst Buffa; including the following elements:
  21st, 34th, 101st Flak Regiments;
  One flak regiment headquarters staff (a railway defense unit in the process of organizing, which included approximately twelve mixed flak battalions, along with elements of three heavy and two light flak battalions);

Two railway flak battalions;

Two searchlight battalions.

10th Flak Brigade: Assigned to Second Army area; headquarters at Konotop; commanded by Major General Paul Pawel; including the following elements:

One flak regiment headquarters staff;

Two motorized flak battalions;

Two or three mixed flak battalions;

One light flak battalion;

One provisional railway flak battalion;

Two searchlight batteries.

The winter fighting had worn down some units considerably and others to an even greater degree; this was particularly true of flak units in
the Orel-Konotop area. Units of the 10th Flak Brigade had lost, on the average, 50–70 percent of their equipment, though most of their personnel
remained present. A thorough reorganization started as the muddy season set in, pursued with great energy. In this manner we substantially restored the combat readiness of the brigade, even though the entire
process had to be conducted on the front lines. Lack of sufficient forces
rendered it impossible to pull units back to the rear.

Replacing equipment, except for motor vehicles, did not present a serious problem. Complete motorization of flak units—at the best of times—
presented serious difficulties. At this time, no matter what we tried, we
did not succeed in motorizing our reserve flak battalions; the best we
could do was to make them "transportable" by truck companies. Personnel replacements, particularly specialists, were frequently hard or impossible to find. Fuel remained in very short supply. Luftflotte Six normally
retained on hand only a few units of daily consumption. Other supplies
were available in adequate quantities.

The front lines had congealed at the end of the winter battles, leaving behind in Second Army's area the sharply protruding Russian
salient at Kursk. This salient clearly suggested the possibility of a Soviet pincer movement against Bryansk, issuing from Kursk and
Sukhinichi, though it also presented OKH with the possibility of staging a two-pronged offensive along the boundary between Army
Groups Center and South, with the objective of isolating and annihilating enemy forces around Kursk. Continuous and thorough coverage of
the entire Kursk-Kirov sector by Luftwaffe aerial reconnaissance,
though hampered temporarily by unfavorable weather during the
brief muddy season, produced the following accurate picture of the
Red Army's situation.

Strong ground forces had been moved into the Kursk salient, deployed in defensive lines that were unusually strong and uncommonly far echeloned in depth. Beginning in April, these forces received a steadily swelling stream of equipment and personnel reinforcements that gradually exceeded the size of anything required by a purely defensive deployment. The only rail line feeding the Kursk area (which ran Voronezh-Kastornaya-Kursk) was carrying trains in uninterrupted succession while reconnaissance flights frequently discerned major nighttime movements approaching and/or starting for Kursk on the highways. The same was partially true of daytime movements on the highways. Aerial photographs also revealed an extraordinary increase in the number of still-unoccupied but completely constructed artillery emplacements. We likewise identified a strong Soviet buildup in the Sukhinichi-Kozelsk-Belev area, which was watched closely for strategic reasons. Between these two concentrations, reconnaissance identified tactical points of potential enemy main effort near Novosil and southwest of Bolkhov. [Details regarding these Russian concentrations have already been presented in preceding chapters.]

It must be recorded as a matter of fact that the Luftwaffe identified the Soviet buildup as it shaped up at the start of the offensive in its most important details at a very early date. In full agreement with the ground forces, the Luftwaffe repeatedly emphasized the danger of a Russian thrust from Sukhinichi aimed south.

The strategic concentration of the Soviet air force (VVS) fit perfectly into this picture. Since May we had established Russian reinforcement of their aerial formations east of Kursk and along the entire eastern front of Second Panzer Army. The Second Air Army (headquarters at Oboyan) had been assigned to the area opposite the boundary between Luftflottes Four and Six and stood prepared to send approximately 200 combat aircraft over the Kursk salient at any time.

The Fifteenth and Sixteenth Air Armies' operational areas were presumably separated along the line Novosil-Yefremov. We estimated the Sixteenth Air Army at six fighter divisions, two ground attack divisions, and one bombardment division. A noteworthy feature of the Sixteenth Air Army was the presence of additional fighter formations attached from the Soviet Home Air Defense Command (PVO), which had been specifically based in the Kursk area to prevent air raids on supply dumps and transportation lines during the enemy buildup. On the basis of its composition (three bombardment divisions and three fighter divisions) we guessed that Fifteenth Air Army had been earmarked for offensive operations. Two of its fighter divisions had been grouped under a corps headquarters, which further emphasized its potential for offensive missions. Aerial photographs of Russian airfields yielded an estimate of the total strength of Fifteenth and Sixteenth Air Armies at 900 aircraft, though previous experience suggested that the actual total could be twice as high.

Long-range bombardment divisions had been based in the Serpukhov region, primarily in the Yuhnov-Kaluga-Sukhinichi area. We placed their strength at eight air divisions, among them the 7th Guards Fighter Division, which had just been flown in. Photographic reconnaissance reported a strength of approximately 460 aircraft. In addition, aerodromes in the Svoboda-Tambov-Ryazan-Yelets area, as well as within the vicinity of Moscow, served as bases for medium-sized and large formations of twin-engine aircraft, indicating the impending commitment of Soviet long-range weapons and the assembly of extensive combat aircraft reserves. Numerous newly constructed airfields, which had been completed with unusual speed, appeared along the entire Kursk-Sukhinichi sector, with Kursk in this instance representing the point of main effort. Aerial reconnaissance also reported numerous VVS ground organizations moving into these facilities.

Taken together, these facts indicated that the expected Soviet air effort in the coming offensive would be the most powerful to date, far exceeding anything previously attempted by our opponents. It was also especially disquieting to note that this concentration of forces had occurred during the first period of the war in which the VVS had access to significant quantities of American equipment. We even considered the possibility that American aerial formations, based on Russian airfields, might be employed against us, though that eventuality was judged unlikely.

The VVS countered Luftwaffe bombing raids in the Kursk region with steadily increasing fighter activity, to such an extent that our air reconnaissance flights became increasing difficult. Soon we found ourselves compelled to jam through these flights on an almost regular basis with the assistance of concurrent fighter attacks. This tactic frequently led to major air battles because the Russians needed to conceal the extent of their buildup on the ground, especially in the Kursk area. This required them to challenge German aerial reconnaissance at every possible opportunity, which they did, though judging by the tactics employed we concluded that only a portion of the enemy's available air strength had been committed. The full strength of the VVS would apparently be employed when the main battle had been joined and not sooner.

The VVS also took active countermeasures to interfere with the German strategic buildup on the ground, although these operations remained confined within fairly modest limits. Russian fighters flew the customary close support sorties, and ground attack activity (especially between Novosil and Bolkhov) frequently became intense. Soviet air re-connaissance activities also picked up. Major bombing raids occurred several nights in succession, usually carried out with twenty-plane formations, though in some instances the numbers rose as high as fifty. These raids chiefly targeted railway installations around Bryansk and—in a few cases—Karachev. The results of such raids were rarely noteworthy: one of the three switching yards at Bryansk was knocked out of commission several times for periods never exceeding twenty-four hours, and the German strategic concentration continued unabated.

The Luftwaffe began raiding Russian armament industries at Gorkiy and Yaroslavl. Our bomber formations took off—among others—from bases in the Orel-Bryansk area and farther west. Following the first three German raids, the VVS made unsuccessful attacks on Luftwaffe aerodromes around Orel and Bryansk. In this connection, the Soviets carried out rolling night raids, a few of which started at dusk and continued throughout the hours of darkness. Luftflotte Six fighters intercepted and smashed four such concentrations, inflicting heavy Russian losses. On 8 June, for example, the Soviets lost sixty-seven aircraft and another sixty-five two nights later. Because the weather during the first half of June remained favorable, the VVS made an estimated 4,000 penetration flights into the Orel-Bryansk area, a number that dropped to 3,000 during the last two weeks of the month. Enemy nighttime penetration raids generally targeted our rear areas (over 800 sorties) and were made for the purpose of supplying Russian partisans.

The Soviets also began to increase the concentration of medium and large antiaircraft units in the Kursk region, especially along the Kursk-Voronezh highway and in tactically important sectors of the front lines. Under the cover of these guns, the Russians repaired even heavily damaged railway installations, placing them back in service within an amazingly short time after Luftwaffe bombing raids had taken place.

Air Situation Through the Beginning of Operation Citadel

From the end of the winter battle, Field Marshal von Greim realized the critical importance of using our airpower to hinder the movement of Red Army units into the Kursk region, regardless of the strategic decisions that might later be made by Adolf Hitler and OKH. To this end, our bombers and ground attack aircraft struck rail traffic, railway installations, and bridges along the Kastornaya-Kursk railway, beginning in mid-April. These attacks created interruptions of rail traffic that allowed our pilots to follow up with especially effective raids against the resulting rail congestions. We also hit railway installations at Kursk, Shchigri,

Kastornaya, and—at times—Voronezh. Field Marshal von Greim ordered these raids to be carried out day and night whenever the weather was favorable.

Several large-scale raids on the Kursk railway station caused heavy damage. One raid, conducted on 2 June with all available bombardment, dive-bomber, destroyer, and fighter formations in several waves was particularly successful, as was the repeat performance on 5 July. In the course of this second raid, our fighter escort bagged forty Russian fighters, suffering almost no casualties in the process. Thereafter the Soviets proceeded to protect the Kursk station and other key installations with uncommonly strong antiaircraft defenses, and subsequently maintained powerful fighter forces in the air above them as well, almost around the clock. Throughout June these measures resulted in bitter air battles whenever Luftflotte Six flew sorties into such protected areas.

Because VVS night-fighter activity manifested itself in its most primitive initial stages, and was unable to register any victories, Field Marshal von Greim shifted to raiding major targets by night. For example, two major night raids hit the Kochetovka switching yard; two night raids struck the Yelets station; and one night raid targeted the South Kastornaya station. Simultaneously, our ground attack formations increasingly concentrated their daylight activities on minor railway stations, on train and locomotive hunting, and on quick attacks against the resulting rail congestions. The Russians, however, exhibited noteworthy skill in quickly improvising antiaircraft protection for such rail congestions.

In the meantime, our dive-bomber formations attacked Russian targets in forward areas in direct support of our front-line ground troops. Destroyer aircraft hit Soviet aerodromes, and Luftflotte Six's antitank squadron experimented with hunting enemy locomotives in the forward area. We also conducted harassment raids at night against Russian movements and their assembly positions in forward areas.

By June almost the entire length of the Kastonaya-Kursk railway and the rail spur branching off twenty kilometers west of Shchigri toward Kolpa had been protected by antiaircraft guns and fighters to the point where raiding them became an increasingly difficult proposition. Field Marshal von Greim, however, continued to interfere with the Russian buildup by exploiting such surprise factors as weather and time, by greatly varying the selection of targets, and by carrying out combined low-level and high-level attacks under fighter protection. The Soviets saw themselves forced to unload most of their trains at points farther to the east, in the Kastornaya-Livny-Shchigri area. In several instances, Red Army motorized columns rolling west from this zone into the Kursk salient suffered continuous air attacks until they arrived at their destinations. At the same time, the Luftwaffe responded to increased Soviet protection of the railways near the front by carrying its raids deeper into enemy territory, hitting railway stations at Yelets, Livny, and Verkhovye.

In summary, the following can be said about Luftflotte Six's conduct of air raids in the Kursk region: The Red Army buildup was disturbed quite substantially. Numerous strike photographs and prisoner-of-war statements attested to the many time- and strength-consuming emergency measures that the Russians had to implement. Field Marshal von Greim, however, found himself unable to exploit one particular opportunity that presented itself. The nature of the Soviet line-of-communications net presented the possibility of completely blocking the enemy railroad net. Once this step had been accomplished, powerful Russian concentrations could have been prevented, and Russian strategy in the Kursk region would have been hamstrung. Unfortunately, such an operation would have required considerably larger aerial strength than we possessed. Field Marshal von Greim frequently submitted requisitions for additional forces, pointing out the extraordinary chances of success slipping through our fingers, but the Luftwaffe High Command (OKL—*Oberkommando der Luftwaffe*) could not furnish Luftflotte Six with any additional aircraft. Already engaged in too many theaters of war, the Luftwaffe lacked the strength to achieve decisive results.

OKL did, however, attach the entire bomber force it had on the Eastern Front to Luftflotte Six on several occasions during June. The upshot of this move was a series of very effective raids on the Soviet armaments industry. The Gorkiy tank factory was bombed seven times and the Yaroslavl rubber factory raided twice. Despite the positive results of these raids, their conduct meant that the German bomber fleet could not be employed to smash the Soviet ground buildup during its most critical stage. It appears that Hitler and OKH mistook Soviet offensive preparations in progress in the Kursk-Sukhinichi area for a Russian deception and thus gave precedence to warfare against the enemy's armaments industry.

Similar conditions existed on the northern sector of Second Panzer Army, though less buzzing activity marked the enemy concentration there. As the Russians moved troops into the area south of Sukhinichi, the Luftwaffe tore into these preparations, bombing the Sukhinichi railway installations (including the yards south and west of the town); striking Kozelsk; hitting the Oka River bridge at Belev (though without success); targeting Kaulga and Dibrachevo; and attacking the railroad between Gorsachevo and Mzensk. Unfortunately, the heavily wooded nature of the terrain in these areas allowed the Red Army to do a much better job of camouflaging its assembly areas than was possible farther south. Nonetheless, Luftflotte Six gathered sufficient information through tactical reconnaissance flights to warn of the possibility of a large-scale Soviet offensive driving south out of Sukhinichi. In particular, large troop concentrations around Novosil and south of Belev had been—quite accurately—interpreted as precursors for a major strategic offensive.

By early June Field Marshal von Greim could already present to OKL an accurate (if approximate) appreciation of the overall Soviet strategy for the upcoming summer battles; by mid-June his working assumptions approached a degree of certainty. No one could claim, therefore, that enemy actions in July came as any sort of strategic surprise. In covering our own buildup of forces, von Greim placed a provisional night-fighter umbrella over Orel and Bryansk, directed by rail-mounted radar equipment; approximately thirty VVS aircraft were shot down between April and June in this area.

During the spring and early summer, Field Marshal von Greim ordered the disposition of flak units to be coordinated with the degree and placement of Soviet air threats, as well as the relative importance of German objectives that required protection from air attacks. Luftflotte Six concentrated its flak assets to protect airfields and supply centers at Orel, Bryansk (12th Flak Division), and Konotop (10th Flak Brigade). Flak strength at any given location varied according to local requirements and the degree to which the ground troops needed the indispensable support of our flak *Kampfgruppen*. In Orel, for example, the smallest amount of flak committed at any given moment was seven batteries of 88mm guns; at some points sixteen batteries of 88mm guns defended the city. The following figures constitute an overall order of battle for the 12th Flak Division:

21st Flak Regiment (Bryansk *Flakgruppe*), consisting of about:
    Three mixed flak battalions;
    One light flak battalion;
    One searchlight battalion;
    One mixed flak battalion detached in Karachev.
101st Flak Regiment (Orel *Flakgruppe*), consisting of about:
    Four or five mixed flak battalions;
    One searchlight battalion;
    Light flak batteries in Mzensk, Bolkhov, Kromy, and Semyevka.
152nd Flak Regiment, whose composition and commitment varied.

Soviet air tactics during June did not require any radical regrouping of these assets, except for an increase in the forces protecting Orel and

Bryansk. We continued to pursue absolutely necessary improvements, especially in our motor vehicle situation, under a priority system that continued even during active combat.

After the formal orders for Operation Citadel had been issued, Field Marshal von Greim immediately requested an increase in Luftflotte Six's aircraft and flak strength, pointing out several critical factors. The unusual strength already witnessed in VVS formations in comparison to their past performance indicated better training, improved equipment, and increased aggressiveness, all of which pointed to an extremely powerful enemy air assault once our offensive opened. Luftflotte Six had been tasked with a dual mission: The anticipated large-scale offensive against Second Panzer Army had to be met immediately by a powerful Luftwaffe response without diminishing the strength of the formations already supporting Ninth Army's attack toward Kursk. The difficulty of this situation was exacerbated by the fact that Ninth Army did not possess enough attack divisions (particularly panzer divisions) and was insufficiently equipped with artillery. It therefore appeared absolutely necessary for the Luftwaffe to furnish Ninth Army with especially effective air support.

Supply problems further complicated the picture. The attacking divisions depended entirely on the Bryansk-Orel railway (the only line available to them) and the very poor road net, which was greatly affected by the weather. As the offensive progressed, therefore, Luftflotte Six had to be prepared to undertake—on a large scale—additional tasks that were more in the nature of pure artillery firing missions than ground support because we could expect an ammunition shortage. One would also have to calculate that the panzer divisions, as they advanced, would at some point require aerial resupply to press their operations.

The OKL did not reject these ideas outright, yet it was not in a position to translate these ideas into action within the context of the actual execution of the offensive. General of Flyers Hans Jeschonnek, chief of the Luftwaffe General Staff, admitted to me that our available force was not sufficient to guarantee victory. Thus the Luftwaffe participated in the last great German strategic offensive on the Eastern Front with inadequate strength and insufficient supplies while facing a Russian enemy who enjoyed a four- or fivefold superiority in the air, which was backed up by mountains of supplies on the ground.

During the planning phase prior to the offensive, OKL did—albeit briefly—contemplate the question of rushing nearly all available forces into the Bryansk-Orel area in the event of a Soviet offensive against the northern flank of Second Panzer Army. It was clearly realized that only maximum Luftwaffe support would allow the German ground forces in the Orel salient to neutralize the thrust of superior Red Army forces. But with the imposed constraint that Ninth Army's attack must continue with undiminished vigor and the limitations placed on our operations by the availability of supplies (particularly fuel), this plan had to be dropped.

Supply remained the key problem throughout. Prevailing shortages prevented supplies from being stockpiled in sufficient quantities to satisfy all our operational requirements and to ensure even distribution. The traffic bottleneck leading into the Orel salient by itself almost ensured that an adequate flow of supplies for flexible operations would arrive too late. Besides, even if the supply problem could be resolved and OKL found significant reinforcements for Luftflotte Six, it would have been impossible to increase the number of airfields available with sufficient speed to assemble these formations if and when they arrived.

Starting on 3 July, Luftflotte Six began directing the overall air effort in its zone from a forward headquarters at Kamenets, fifteen kilometers northeast of Kromy. Direction of aerial operations fell to 1st Fleiger Division, while the 12th Flak Division directed antiaircraft protection for Ninth Army and the 10th Flak Brigade did the same for Second Panzer Army. Field Marshal von Greim had been able to reinforce these units in the following manner:

1st Flieger Division

> One close-range reconnaissance group (single-seat Bf 109s, from OKL);
> Headquarters, 51st Fighter Wing (from Smolensk);
> 1st and 3rd Groups, 51st Fighter Wing (transferred from Luftflotte One on orders from OKL);
> Two or three groups, 2nd Ground Attack Wing (from Smolensk);
> One or two groups, 3rd Ground Attack Wing (one from OKL; one from Africa);
> One or two antitank (14th) squadrons (from OKL);
> Two special fighter squadrons (antitank; from OKL);
> 1st and 3rd Groups, 1st Destroyer Wing (from OKL);
> 1st and 2nd (and perhaps 3rd) Groups, 4th Bombardment Wing (from northern sector, Luftflotte Six);
> 1st and 3rd Groups, 53 Bombardment Wing (from OKL).

In this manner Luftflotte Six had bared its entire northern sector of all aerial formations with the exception of reconnaissance units and the 4th Group, 51st Fighter Wing, based in Smolensk, in order to concentrate the maximum available strength in the Orel area.

12th Flak Division (reinforced exclusively with units already in the Luftflotte Six area)

One flak regimental headquarters;

Four mixed flak battalions (at least three were motorized; one may only have been "transportable");

Three light flak battalions (motorized);

One railroad flak battalion;

One searchlight battalion.

Several poorly motorized or nonmotorized units of the 12th Flak Division were exchanged for better-equipped units from the 18th Flak Division and Feldluftgau Kommando XXVII. In this manner most of the motorized units (as well as those with the most combat experience) were concentrated in 12th Flak Division. Flak protection in Luftflotte Six's northern sector (18th Flak Division) therefore had been reduced to the bare minimum.

It proved impossible, however, to reinforce the 10th Flak Brigade.

The order of battle for Luftflotte Six on 5 July 1943 therefore consisted of:

1st Flieger Division

Three close-range reconnaissance groups, one each with Second and Ninth Army (one group of single-seat Bf 110s) and one with Second Panzer Army;

1st, 3rd, 4th Groups, 13th Spanish Squadron, and Headquarters, 51st Fighter Wing (Commodore Lieutenant Colonel Nordmann commanding);

1st, 2nd, 3rd Groups and Headquarters, 54th Fighter Wing;

2nd, 3rd Groups and Headquarters, 1st Ground Attack Wing;

Two or three groups, 2nd Ground Attack Wing (Commodore Lieutenant Colonel Friessler commanding);

One or two groups, 3rd Ground Attack Wing (Captain Jacob commanding one of the groups);

Antitank aircraft: 14th Squadron, 1st Ground Attack Wing plus one or two additional 14th [antitank] squadrons;

Two special antitank squadrons, including one experimental squadron from Rechlin (4th, Group, 9th Ground Attack Wing?) [both of these squadrons arrived on 5 July];

1st, 2nd, 3rd Groups and Headquarters, 1st Destroyer Wing (Bf. 110's);

1st, 2nd, 3rd Groups and Headquarters, 3rd Bombardment Wing (Ju 88's);

1st, 2nd, 3rd (?) Groups and Headquarters, 4th Bombardment Wing (He 111s);

1st, 2nd, 3rd Groups and Headquarters, 54th Bombardment Wing (He 111's) [may have been attached after the start of the offensive];

One or two harassing squadrons.

12th Flak Division (total strength):

Four flak regimental headquarters;

One railroad flak regimental headquarters;

Approximately sixteen mixed flak battalions (twelve motorized and four "transportable"; there were three heavy and two mixed batteries in each battalion);

Seven light flak battalions (five motorized and two "transportable"; there were two batteries in each battalion);

Three railroad flak battalions (three batteries each);

Two or three searchlight battalions (three batteries each).

Among these were the following units:

21st Flak Regiment (Colonel Vorbrugg commanding): four or five mixed flak battalions (motorized) plus two light flak battalions (motorized);

101st Flak Regiment (Lieutenant Colonel Müller commanding):

76th Light Flak Battalion (motorized);

83rd Light Flak Battalion (motorized);

783rd Light Flak Battalion (motorized);

853rd Light Flak Battalion ("transportable");

802nd Mixed Flak Battalion ("transportable");

115th Heavy Railroad Flak Battalion;

395th Heavy Railroad Flak Battalion;

872nd Heavy Railroad Flak Battalion.

10th Flak Brigade:

One flak regimental headquarters;

Two mixed flak battalions (motorized; included 54th Mixed Flak Battalion);

Two or three mixed flak battalions ("transportable"; included 235th and 713th Mixed Flak Battalions);

One provisional railroad flak battery;

Two searchlight batteries.

(In summary, it should be noted that this organization had not substantially changed since mid-April.)

Formations and units directly under Luftflotte Six control:

One night fighter group;

One long-range reconnaissance group of two or three squadrons (based in Orel);

Approximately two signal communications regiments (including about five telephone construction and radio battalions);

One operational staff (temporarily attached), provisionally (and almost presciently) established at Bryansk to control the area northwest of the city (*Luftwaffenkampfgruppe* 3), which did not have to be employed as events unfolded;
One well-functioning radio-intercept unit.

Ground organizations fell under control of Feldluftgau Kommando (which had formerly been Luftgau Kommando Moskau). All airfields used during Operation Citadel (except rear-area bomber bases) were organized under Luftdienst Kommando Orel. The number of airfields increased from three to fifteen. Two additional airfield commands plus supply columns were made available for use on airfields to be established around Kursk in the future. Four or five field repair shops (motorized), each consisting of three platoons, had been concentrated under Luftdienst Kommando Orel to handle technical servicing. This force constituted the entire motorized technical services available in the Luftflotte Six area. Approximately three Luftwaffe construction battalions were standing by for use in the establishment of new airfields around Kursk and Orel. One night-fighter guide base unit had also been made available for future use at Kursk.

The bottleneck hampering the entire operation was to be found in the fuel department. The same bottleneck had gravely hindered the execution of intended operations in the past. Toward the end of June, the total stocks of B4 (89-octane aviation fuel) dropped to 4,886 tons; daily consumption throughout June had averaged 287 tons. Most of the B4 stockpiles existed in the area affected by Operation Citadel. During June, against a total consumption of 8,634 tons of B4, only 5,722 tons had been delivered. During the same month, the total consumption of C3 (94-octane aviation fuel) used by our FW 190s had been 1,079 tons, as compared to 441 tons delivered. The resultant difficulties created by these shortfalls began to crop up throughout June, especially when consumption climbed beyond our capacity to store fuel at or near the operational airfields. This situation could only be partially remedied through the unsatisfactory expedient of changing storage arrangements while uneconomically delivering fuel by air and truck as well.

Thus only with great difficulty was Luftflotte Six able to meet its mission requirements for the preparatory sorties prior to the start of the offensive with such inadequate quantities of fuel. Nor was it at all easy to hoard sufficient fuel to support five days of intensive action at the various airfields. (Field Marshal von Greim's mission tasking required at least two sorties per day for bombers; three or four for ground attack aircraft; and five or six sorties by fighters.) Existing quantities of fuel on hand were backed up by two or three fuel trains held as OKL reserves. In view of the abominable transportation situation in central Russia, any deliveries of fuel after the start of the offensive could be expected to require at least two—but more often four to eight—days from the time they left the German borders until they arrived at the forward airfields. To state the matter in a different fashion: fuel arrived ten days to two weeks after the fuel allotment was made. Railroad transportation, of course, had been considerably encumbered by the numerous partisan attacks against rail lines. These attacks peaked in Army Group Center's rear areas during June, when partisans conducted 841 attacks that damaged 298 locomotives, 1,222 railroad cars, and forty-four bridges. On any given day, partisan attacks in this sector damaged the tracks themselves in about eighty-four distinct locations.

These factors combined to place extraordinary constraints on planning, as fuel came to dictate the pace of operations. Literally speaking, we had to introduce "fuel tactics." Any given main-effort operation found its strength influenced more by the quantity of fuel required than by the number of flying formations assigned. We consciously denied air support to ground units in many instances where the situation would normally have been characterized as tense. Only through such harsh measures could Luftflotte Six provide fully sufficient force whenever the situation became critical and the battle rose to a climax. The staff examined every sortie to determine whether it was truly worth the fuel expenditure. When it came to selecting the formations to fly a particular mission, the following question frequently became decisive: "Can a few cubic meters of aviation fuel be saved by accepting certain other disadvantages?"

In spite of these major difficulties, careful planning and the understanding attitude of our flight personnel allowed us to fly the most important sorties.

Aircraft allotments were generally sufficient to make up for losses, with the exception of FW 190s, Ju 88s, and Bf 110 G-2s, but engine replacements were inadequate, and no aircraft reserve could be amassed prior to the beginning of the offensive. Thus our formations—especially those of FW 190s—were bound to lose strength rapidly due to major losses and mechanical attrition whenever involved in periods of intensive combat.

A two-week battle supply of the following types of bombs was assured: SD1, SD2, fifty-kilogram, 250-kilogram, and 500-kilogram. All other types of bombs were on hand in sufficient quantities. The ammunition supply for onboard armament could be considered adequate. Considering the rates of consumption (which were often quite high), insufficient quantities of flak ammunition had been delivered—fewer than four issues per gun. We suffered from particular shortages of 88mm high-explosive shells (Type ZZ, or timed fuse) and 20mm flak ammunition. Concentration of flak ammunition for the offensive could be achieved only by depleting all reserves in the Luftflotte Six area.

With respect to motor vehicles, the quantity available was sufficient, but as far as quality was concerned the equipment was overage and our vehicles types varied too greatly. Luftflotte Six disposed over 21,779 motor vehicles, 84 percent of which were in operable condition, but no reserve existed to make up for losses.

Luftflotte Six assigned missions to its major formations in approximately the following language:

The 1st Flieger Division will launch its initial sortie as early as possible on 5 July, attacking the heavy concentrations of Russian aircraft on airfields in the Kursk area. Elements of the division will attack strong enemy artillery groups around Malo-arkhangel'sk in coordination with Ninth Army's artillery fire plan.

Thereafter the division, making a continuous and supreme effort, will concentrate its formations and support the swift breakthrough of the XLVII Panzer Corps through the enemy defenses and its subsequent swift thrust toward Kursk. The most important priority is to drive the points of the attacking force forward relentlessly with the help of ever-present ground attack formations and to maintain the momentum of the attack force after the breakthrough.

Elements of the division must support and ensure the advance of XLVI Panzer Corps, preventing the danger of enemy flanking thrusts from the west against XLVII Panzer Corps.

In a similar manner it may become important to neutralize enemy forces along the flank in the Malo-arkhangel'sk area (specifically, Soviet artillery groups) and at a later date to combat enemy reserves advancing west from the Kolpa-Shchigri area. The XLVI Panzer Corps must be in a position to shift its main effort quickly.

Any sorties in the Second Panzer Army area require the approval of Luftflotte headquarters.

Reconnaissance sorties are to be flown continuously and with complete coverage. Aerial reconnaissance will pay particular attention to identifying, in the earliest possible stage, enemy assembly positions and the concentration of reserves (especially tanks) on the flanks and all advances toward our attack wedge.

In addition, it is of vital importance that the enemy main effort opposite the northern sector of Second Panzer Army be observed constantly in a manner that will permit the discovery of major enemy attack preparations in time.

[Long-range reconnaissance received similar missions, concentrating on the Voronezh-Yelets-Verkhovye-Kursk area and the Volovo-Sukhinichi-Kaluga-Stalinogrosk area, as well as on troops and material being transported from the Moscow area and along the line Ryazesk-Svoboda.]

[Operational details for individual formations were disseminated in daily orders.]

The 12th Flak Division will reliably protect the Orel supply areas (main priority) and Bryansk, as well as airfields in use but will employ the minimum forces to accomplish these missions. The primary mission of the division is to protect the advancing attack wedges and the most important supply roads of the attack divisions from enemy air raids. The main strength of the division will be concentrated in the sector of XLVII Panzer Corps.

Strong flak elements are to be committed directly behind the most advanced panzer elements. Flak will be committed against enemy tanks only temporarily and whenever such action is unavoidable. Individual flak *Kampfgruppen* must not be used for antitank action; the minimum flak force committed in action will be of battalion strength.

Certain flak elements will, by way of exception to the foregoing, be moved up to participate in the preparatory artillery fire within the scope of Ninth Army's artillery fire plan for the first attack on the morning of 5 July. These flak elements will destroy particularly strong enemy centers of resistance and in this manner facilitate the initial penetration.

The 10th Flak Brigade will for the moment continue to protect the important objectives already assigned, concentrating its forces at Konotop. The brigade will move up all motorized flak elements in time before the attack elements of Second Army jump off and furnish the troops with antiaircraft protection at the two points of main effort.

The Kursk Attack, 5–11 July

As the offensive opened, at 0330 on 5 July, commanders and troops all shared complete awareness of the importance of the operation and the critical difficulties associated with it. Ninth Army's ground attack force and Luftflotte Six's aerial formations were both too small. We possessed no healthy surplus strength in the form of troops or equipment reserves available to meet and overcome unexpected developments during the battle. Luftflotte Six, in particular, could not hold even a single formation in reserve; there would be no fresh pilots or machines to throw into the fray as the battle reached its climax.

Everyone involved clearly recognized that the attack division would encounter unusual difficulties in breaking through the deep Soviet defenses before the well-proven talent of the German soldiers for doing battle in the open field would come into play in the Russian rear areas. The skill of the Red Army in constructing earthworks and the tenacious stubbornness of Russian troops on the defensive were only too well known, while the exceptional strength of the artillery in the Kursk salient (especially around Malo-arkhangel'sk) caused the German command serious concern from the first moment it began planning the offensive. Moreover, the concentration of Soviet forces opposite the northern sector of Second Panzer Army, which we could not afford to match, made the German command feel as if it constantly had the sword of Damocles hanging above its head. Thus as the battle commenced, seasoned troops prepared to give their all, but their senior field commanders could not as yet be sure that Operation Citadel would be successful. The concerns and worries they had so often communicated to Hitler and OKH had apparently received no consideration at all. For Field Marshal von Greim and the other senior commanders the only option remaining was to accept the existing conditions and do the best with the forces and supplies available.

The final elements of the flying formations arrived at their respective operational airfields in the evening of 4 July, adhering carefully to secrecy regulations. At about 0300, 5 July, the first sorties flew over the front line and successfully attacked a series of heavily occupied Soviet airfields around and west of Kursk. At the same time, other large formations participated in smashing enemy artillery concentrations around Malo-arkhangel'sk in Ninth Army's front.

Thereafter (still on the first day of the offensive), Luftflotte Six effectively neutralized many powerful Red Army artillery concentrations. In this connection the Malo-arkhangel'sk area soon proved to be the greatest threat to a complete breakthrough. To combat this menace, our formations were committed one after the other, with each succeeding formation to circle over the Russian artillery positions for ten to twenty minutes, attacking repeatedly in the process. Experience had shown that the mere appearance of our aircraft would very often silence Soviet artillery. On the other hand, complete destruction of pinpoint targets such as gun positions could not be expected, even though the new small-caliber bombs of the SD1 and SD2 types had been employed en masse for the first time. The increased accuracy possible with these munitions certainly increased the chances for bombing success. Normally the Luftwaffe committed its main effort in concentrated blows; here we attempted to smother the enemy fire with continuous waves. This manner of employment of our larger flying formations was somewhat unorthodox but corresponded to the express desires of Ninth Army headquarters. It may, in this particular situation, have been the best tactic for supporting the attacking divisions on the ground. A few sorties on that first day, however, were reserved to be directed against Soviet antitank gun switch positions and tank elements in their previously identified assembly areas.

Luftflotte Six flew an exceptional number of sorties that day, as it did on all other critical days during the operation. In the beginning, six or even seven sorties per formation per day would have been the average, an operational tempo that would recur several times. Flying missions at this pace meant that often an interval of less than an hour separated the time formations landed from they moment they took off again. The wonderful summer weather prevailing at the start of the offensive made it possible to fly an unusually great number of sorties and thus fulfill all of Ninth Army's requests for air support.

The Soviets ventured their first countersorties—rather late, by the way—about 1000, 5 July. These sorties were at first unimpressive, which indicated that at least tactical surprise had been achieved in the timing of the attack. For the most part the VVS committed fighter formations to protect Russian ground troops. Our fighters intercepted these missions, and intense air battles followed; by the end of the day, about 110 enemy aircraft had been shot down, whereas German losses were small. Soviet ground attack planes made their initial appearance on the battlefield around noon but did not manage to hamper the operations of our ground troops in any serious manner. Enemy bomber formations entered the fray on 5 July in a few rare instances only.

Without doubt the Luftwaffe ruled over the field of battle on 5 July. The breakthrough attack had gotten under way without noteworthy interference from the VVS.

All movements by flak units prior to the beginning of the offensive had taken place at night, under the strictest measures to ensure secrecy. We worked extremely hard to prevent the enemy from discovering the changes in our flak groupings from which certain conclusions would have followed regarding the time and place of the main attack, even though the assumption must be made that the Russians were already expecting an attack against the Kursk salient. Flak units had orders forbidding them to fire before the opening of the battle, and each battery moved into the positions from which it would execute its battle firing missions during the very last night preceding the attack. The detailed preparations for such a movement required many days, especially for those batteries assigned to combat particularly tough Soviet objectives or that had received direct-fire missions; for these units the proposition of moving forward in the darkness was especially difficult.

The 21st Flak Division attached to XLVII Panzer Corps (executing the main effort attack) the 21st Flak Regiment, which controlled five mixed flak battalions (motorized) and two light flak battalions (motorized). XLI Panzer Corps (with its flank protection mission) received the 162nd Flak Regiment, which controlled four mixed flak battalions (motorized) and two light flak battalions (motorized). The 101st Flak Regiment was committed to the defense of Orel, and the new regimental headquarters staff controlled the defenses at Bryansk. Thus on the morning of 5 July the flak batteries had about 100 88mm guns assigned to fire within Ninth Army's initial artillery preparation. Flak elements behind the assault lines were partly employed in plotted fire against enemy assembly areas. Each participating battery expended between 200 and 500 rounds. (Most of the flak units reserved for antiaircraft defense did little or no firing on 5 July; light flak batteries combated a few attacks by VVS ground support formations against the German spearhead elements.)

Subsequent days of the attack toward Kursk (which was suspended on 11 July) were characterized by bitter Soviet resistance and—from 7 July onward—continued enemy counterthrusts and counteroffensives. The intensity of the Russian air effort increased day by day. On 6 July the Soviets began committing bombers in large numbers, including a major formation of Bristol bombers that—considering all that we had seen of previous VVS operations—exhibited particularly good flying discipline and exceptional aggressiveness. Great air battles raged daily over the focal points of the ground fighting and over the immediate rear areas behind the Russian lines because almost every Luftwaffe air attack met with considerable enemy air defenses. Throughout these battles the Soviets always lost a substantial number of aircraft while our losses stayed within moderate limits—almost without exception. The loss ratio hardly ever dipped below six-to-one, and more often the VVS lost at least twelve planes for every Luftwaffe aircraft shot down. Despite such losses, however, the Russians maintained their numerical air strength by continually committing fresh formations. By 7–8 July the Soviets were able to keep strong formations in the air around the clock. Even so, Luftflotte Six fighters rarely had difficulty attaining air superiority, even in cases of extreme numerical inferiority, but everyone recognized that this could not continue indefinitely. Unremitting air actions of extended duration necessarily caused the technical serviceability of our formations to decrease, therefore making it unavoidable that the quantitative Soviet superiority should temporarily be in a position to act directly against German troops during temporal and spatial gaps in Luftwaffe fighter coverage. Since Ninth Army's ground troops remained engaged in an extremely important offensive, the unavoidable Soviet tactical air breakthroughs were at all times very unpleasant.

Russian air attacks began to hit the important supply roads of our spearhead divisions to an increasing extent, with raids striking points as far as twenty-five kilometers behind German lines. Fortunately, as yet the VVS had little experience or skill in such operations, and these attacks never constituted a serious threat to our supply lifelines. In isolated areas Soviet aircraft attacked heavily occupied German airfields, particularly the complex around Orel. Here again the results achieved by the enemy were consistently poor. A large measure of the credit could be ascribed to the superior accomplishments of the German radio intercept service. Our operators frequently picked up the takeoff messages of Russian formations, allowing those formations to be intercepted as they approached and defeated with heavy losses.

The Soviets also increased their nighttime bomber sorties, especially targeting railway installations and the city of Orel and often against Bryansk as well. These night raids became more frequent—often lasting all night—but did not appear to be part of any coordinated effort and did not evidence any ability to strike concentrated blows. Soviet flight training had obviously not yet graduated to missions of that kind. The presence of German night-fighter formations over Orel and the fire of powerful flak concentrations (especially our searchlight beams lancing into the sky) had a disproportionately greater dampening effect on Russian air aggressiveness.

In the narrow corridor where the two opposing air forces clashed, there was no room for evasion, and our original estimate of the VVS was put to the test. Our early projections were, in the main, borne out. Soviet air appeared strong in numbers, average in quality, and not yet sufficiently well trained. Even so, it had to be admitted that the Russians had learned a lot during the war years, making great progress compared to their primitive 1941 standards. The performance of certain individual formations and particularly that of ground attack formations was worthy of acknowledgment.

Soviet antiaircraft proved to be a very formidable adversary, both with respect to numbers and quality. Enemy antiaircraft fire became, without exception, unusually heavy whenever German planes flew over the front lines, with the accuracy of light Russian antiaircraft guns in particular being great. By contrast, Russian heavy antiaircraft guns obviously remained hampered by defects in their fire direction equipment. Against our low-level attacks, Red Army infantry weapons strongly supplemented the antiaircraft systems, often scoring heavy damage to our formations. On the whole, German pilots considered Russian antiaircraft artillery a much more formidable enemy than the enemy fighter arm.

It is impossible to present a detailed reconstruction of the Luftwaffe air effort during this phase of the offensive because reference materials are lacking, but its relentless, powerful attack waves were repeatedly directed against enemy artillery concentrations, antitank gun switch positions, assembly areas of all kinds, counterattacks, and tank formations. On occasion Luftflotte Six also struck particularly heavily occupied airfields and Russian reserves en route to the battlefield. The flying formations remained in action from dawn to dusk, and their operational capacities were pushed to the absolute limit. In the final analysis the Luftwaffe's limited strength dictated at all times that main effort concentrations and coordinated counterattacks be restricted to the currently decisive point of battle. With the exception of free-range fighter patrols, it was often impossible to fly significant sorties over the remainder of the front. In no other fashion could we marshal sufficient air strength for really lasting and powerful attacks in at least one locality. Available fighter strength consistently dropped after the first day of the offensive until it reached a point at which it only sufficed for escort duty. This decline resulted from the strain of continual combat on our pilots and the unremitting attrition of our equipment. Freelance fighter sorties that the Luftwaffe always attempted to maintain often could not be flown due to numerical inadequacies. The very thing Field Marshal von Greim had most feared began to occur after the first week of the fighting: Our aircraft replacements could no long keep pace with attrition. That fact, combined with the apparently endless supply of Russian aircraft replacements, resulted in an increasingly disproportionate numerical relationship between the two adversaries, which became unbearable over time.

Limited initial strength and the ravages of attrition also explained why it proved impossible to exploit the still-existing opportunity for staging heavy, effective air attacks against the Soviet rail system. Available air assets barely sufficed to satisfy the clamor of the front-line ground troops for air support, and ground commanders at all levels admitted that only Luftwaffe support brought about a decision in many combat situations during the first days of the offensive. No matter how clearly Field Marshal von Greim recognized the opportunity and need for strategic attacks against Soviet rear areas, the unavoidable pressing necessity of tactical air support for the outnumbered and heavily engaged ground troops was greater. We simply did not possess the resources for liberal target planning.

Even so, air support during the first phase of the offensive on the whole fulfilled its requirements. In those situations where target designations were more ambitious than they normally should have been in view of our limited assets, the targets involved were, almost without exception, those that the Luftwaffe had to attack because Ninth Army's artillery strength was inadequate. Such targets included antitank gun switch positions, individual strongpoints, artillery positions, and others that could be observed from the ground. Striking these targets was the reason why Luftflotte Six's bomber formations had to be committed over the tactical and combat zone. Our formations, however, were always strong enough to gain air superiority at will over all points in the zone of main effort.

With the exception of those units defending critical fixed installation, our flak machine-gun units remained close to the front lines. Certain elements were committed at bottlenecks on the most important supply roads, but it was chiefly our batteries at the front that were continually engaged in heavy firing, bagging a large number of Russian aircraft. The Soviets did not hesitate to send their ground attack formations again and again against important sectors of the front, even though the VVS certainly recognized that these points were strongly protected by our flak, and as a result there were days in which the light flak units shot down an exceptionally large number of enemy aircraft. Soviet counterattacks and the unavoidable tank breakthroughs led to our heavy flak batteries becoming embroiled in ground fighting along with their air defense mission. When from necessity employed against Russian armor, our 88mm flak guns demonstrated their exceptional penetration power by knocking out large numbers of enemy tanks. Because these heavy flak batteries often constituted the strongest antitank defenses available to our infantry, their presence gave the troops a wonderful feeling of security and constantly jacked up troop morale. Senior commanders therefore found it difficult if not impossible to extract flak from ground fighting once it had become involved and return it to its air defense mission.

The Defense of the Orel Salient, 11–30 July

The turning point of Operation Citadel occurred on 11 July, when the Red Army attacked south of Sukhinichi. Because the Second Panzer Army held its northern sector only weakly and the heavily wooded terrain afforded poor observation of the assembling assault forces, the Russians quickly gained ground. The Soviets clearly aimed at strangling and then encircling the Orel region, and it became obvious by 13 July that Ninth Army could no longer continue its offensive mission.

On 11 July Luftflotte Six diverted all available elements from Ninth Army to support Second Panzer Army ground troops east of Zhizdra. The advancing Soviet armies had to be delayed long enough to allow the

German reserves being shifted by Army Group Center to arrive in time. This was an especially difficult proposition where wooded areas afforded the Russians excellent opportunities for concealment, which meant that the Luftwaffe could do little more than prevent Soviet troop movements—especially those of tank units—on the very few existing highways and roads. Off the roads it proved nearly impossible to discover, let alone attack, enemy units moving through the woods. Luftflotte Six did make several raids on Soviet railheads around Sukhinichi, attempting to hamper front-line supplies and the arrival of reinforcements. Attacks against rail facilities and moving trains in the Kozelsk and Kaluga areas served the same purpose. These measures, however, produced no visible results, as the available bomber force was too weak and the weather hindered operations.

The Luftwaffe's shining hour came when the Russians, with surprising speed, emerged from the southern edge of the great tree belt, charging across open ground and heading for Khotynets on the critical Bryansk-Orel highway. There were no ground troops to speak of in the Khotynets area that could protect the railroad against the daring thrust of a Soviet tank corps. Thus from 14 to 17 July every last available antitank aircraft of any type or make, as well as fast ground support planes, delivered unremitting low-level attacks from morning to night against the advancing Russians—especially targeting tanks. German pilots knocked out hundreds of tanks in a confined area, annihilating the mass of Soviet armor that had rushed forward. By the time the battered Russians organized themselves to seize Khotynets at night by coup de main, the flak battalion from Karachev had arrived and repulsed the attack. Luftflotte Six—all by itself—had for two whole days prevented a powerful Russian tank formation from reaching the railway. This amazing action secured possession of that vital line until the first reinforcements—*Grossdeutschland* Panzergrenadier Division—arrived. Holding the Bryansk-Orel railway was an essential prerequisite for our eventual withdrawal from the Orel salient.

Starting on 12 July the formations still supporting Ninth Army had the difficult task of assisting the army as it changed over to defensive action. Adequate air strength could be made available for employment against Russian tanks, assembly positions, reserves, and artillery positions in the Ponyriy–Malo-arkhangel'sk area as long as Luftflotte Six could not find any worthwhile targets in the woods south of Sukhinichi during the initial stages of the Soviet counteroffensive. When, however, the fighting spread to the Khotynets area—as just described—our ability to support Ninth Army threatened to become inadequate. This situation was exacerbated by the fact that the VVS at first maintained the bulk of its strength south of Orel though later shifted somewhat into the area east of the city.

Army Group South's attack from Belgorod against the southern face of the Kursk salient had in the meantime been discontinued. OKL therefore decided to weaken the aerial strength of Luftflotte Four in the Belgorod-Kharkov sector and attach significant forces to Luftflotte Six for use in the Bryansk-Orel area. These elements arrived in time to participate in the battle at its most critical moment and included the following formations:

One or two fighter groups;

Three groups of 77th Ground Attack Wing;

Antitank group, 2nd Ground Attack Wing (Lieutenant Colonel Hans Ulrich Rudel, commanding);

Several bombardment groups of the 27th and 55th Bombardment Wings.

Even if additional elements had been transferred, Luftflotte Six could neither have accommodated them on existing airfields nor provided servicing.

On 15 July the Russians facing Ninth Army launched a systematic counterattack, committing tanks, artillery, and combat aircraft along a broad front. The gigantic struggle that ensued was fought continuously on land and in the air, where time and again our pilots had to attack Soviet assembly areas, artillery emplacements, attack preparations, and—to an ever-increasing extent—enemy tank formations that had broken through German lines. Soviet air remained very active, particularly with regard to its ground attack planes and fighters.

By 20 July the situation north and northeast of Orel had begun to approach a critical stage as well, increasing the demands on our formations and the strain on our pilots. Since the fighting was now separated into four distinct combat areas, Luftflotte Six could provide air support to the ground forces only in the most urgent situations. We could only avoid the constant danger of our aerial assets being split into small, ineffective pieces by massing our strength for main-effort operations. This necessarily meant that many justified army requests for air support went unfulfilled during these crisis-studded weeks. In particular, heavy losses in artillery and antitank guns prompted Second Panzer and Ninth Army to keep asking for Luftwaffe support with an increasing sense of urgency. Meanwhile, the supply situation—especially fuel—had become so difficult that it was actually necessary to ground some of our formations temporarily at the height of the battle. The situation that Field Marshal von Greim had feared from the outset began to manifest itself. The main supply volume had to be shifted to airfields west of the Desna River as the Orel salient ever more clearly became untenable. This occurred at the same moment we were forced to begin evacuating several advanced airfields north and south of Orel that had become too exposed to continue operations while simultaneously a new group of fields had to be installed around Karachev. These fields had to be selected with a view toward facilitating sorties against Russian forces threatening from Sukhinichi as well as the ability to support the fighting in the immediate vicinity of Orel. Headquarters, Luftflotte Six, moved to Suponevo (just south of Bryansk) on 12 July.

The difficult and—it must be admitted—sacrificial dual mission of 12th Flak Division characterized its operations during the second half of July. The division had to protect the ground troops against the unending onslaught of Soviet air attacks while also participating in sealing off numerous Russian tank breakthroughs. As the battle progressed, this second (and originally secondary) mission gradually gained in importance and scope because the army's antitank units suffered both from heavy combat losses and ammunition shortages. The vehemence and sheer numbers of Soviet tank attacks launched against tattered German lines finally forced Colonel General Model to demand frequently that more than half of the motorized flak units be employed in antitank gun switch positions or for rear-area security. Thus our 88mm guns became the "backbone of the defense," the unshakable nucleus around which those infantry units that could still fight would crystallize as the great tank battles raged.

As flak units became unavoidably involved in ground combat, their losses—particularly in equipment—became heavy, with the inevitable consequence that they were not available when it came to firing their basic antiaircraft missions. This state of affairs made things easier for Soviet fighters and in turn resulted in the ground troops clamoring for increased fighter support. Unfortunately, as a result of the logistical considerations already explained, our fighters could not be committed in the numbers required. It nonetheless remained nearly impossible to pull the flak battalions out of the line to resume their antiaircraft mission. Worse still, in ground combat the high silhouette of the 88mm guns made them excellent targets, and almost every ground combat mission seemed to result in considerable losses. The need of the hour in many instances caused local army commanders to commandeer remaining flak personnel (minus guns, which had been knocked out unceremoniously) for commitment in combat as infantrymen despite their inadequate training and armaments. The steady decline in the strength of 12th Flak Division in the Orel area is best exemplified by a screw or an endless merry-go-round of hazardous antiaircraft missions, emergency antitank missions, declining combat strength, and a steadily increasing Soviet air onslaught.

On the whole it must be established that 12th Flak Division did justice to its critical dual mission despite all limitations. Though inadequately equipped, the division learned how to steer past every crisis arising throughout many weeks of large-scale fighting. Beyond that, 12th Flak managed repeatedly to give such strong support to our hard-pressed ground troops that it frequently became the last rallying point in case of Russian tank breakthroughs. In terms of the shining courage and gallant abandon of the flak crews, it will be difficult to find similar episodes in military history, wherein such a supporting arm so frequently became the last decisive bulwark of the defense.

Withdrawal to the Hagen Line, 31 July–26 August

Orders for the execution of Operation Hagen were issued on 26 July, and the retirement had to begin on 31 July, much earlier than originally planned. The brief interval between the dissemination of these orders and the actual evacuation created a crisis of its own. However, as early as 18 July, taking the entire tactical situation into account, Field Marshal von Greim had ordered Luftflotte Six to begin the surreptitious withdrawal of nonessential equipment and supplies behind the Desna River. Now our insistence on committing primarily motorized units to support the offensive turned out to be a major advantage, for with a supreme effort it was possible to save all equipment and critical supplies even though we had little time in which to do so. Large stockpiles of aerial bombs constituted the only major exception to this case, and they were employed efficiently in the destruction of our abandoned forward airfields. As a result, no critical equipment or usable Luftwaffe installations fell into Russian hands (we destroyed the great complex around Orel with particular thoroughness). The large number of bombs that still remained was given to the army to use in dynamiting railways and bridges. Simultaneously, our Ju 52 transport aircraft flew around the clock to evacuate the wounded.

As the ground troops withdrew from phase line to phase line, our flying formations and flak units continued to provide support, though the retirement went off without many of the critical moments that had been so numerous throughout July. Luftflotte Six concerned itself primarily with the following missions: delaying enemy pressure in direct pursuit; combating occasional incipient encircling attempts by the pursuing Soviet armies; preventing the VVS from interfering with the movements of our withdrawing columns; and delaying the forward movement of Russian air assets to occupy our evacuated airfields.

Enemy flanking pressure from the area northeast of Karachev remained weak and required no substantial countermeasures by Luftflotte Six. The chief missions were flown directly over the main route of the retreat along the Bryansk-Orel highway. Later we concentrated against Soviet attempts to effect an encirclement during pursuit south of that highway and south of Navlya. During this period, Field Marshal von Greim directed his attention to the withdrawal of our flying formations behind the Desna River in an orderly fashion and to the preparations for a possible defensive battle along the river line. All measures necessary to these tasks were carried out without friction and without Russian interference.

The ability of Soviet aerial formations to interfere with the withdrawing troops—even in the critical traffic center at Bryansk—was minimal, and Russian planes had virtually no effect west of the Desna. The VVS failed to exploit a rare opportunity for a strategic air effort that could conceivably have gravely hindered our retirement.

Headquarters, 1st Flieger Division, had been located in Bryansk since about 30 July. Thereafter, when the Russians threatened to expand the scope of their encirclement pursuit to the south, the command post successively relocated at Novgorod Severski, Gomel, Stary Bykhov, and finally at Bobriusk.

Operation Hagen terminated on 26 August. On this date we find Luftflotte Six weakened by losses but nevertheless intact, in order, and ready to do battle. Field Marshal von Greim's command remained fully able to execute future defensive missions against coming Soviet attacks. After a brief period of reorganization the flying formations again became available for unrestricted employment, though the replacement of flak equipment losses (especially motor vehicles) took another month or two. Even so, all gaps had been filled by the time the winter fighting started.

In the course of the battles herein described, 1st Flieger Division flew 37,421 sorties, shooting down 1,733 enemy aircraft, 1,671 of which were accounted for by German fighters. German losses totaled sixty-four aircraft. The division put out of action somewhere in excess of 1,100 tanks and 1,300 tracked vehicles or trucks while also inflicting severe losses on enemy artillery batteries, rolling stock, supplies of all kinds, and personnel. At the same time, 12th Flak Division downed 383 aircraft and two captive observation balloons, knocked out 225 tanks, destroyed a large number of fortified positions, silenced many large-caliber guns, and accounted for a tremendous number of dead Russians.

German losses cannot be reconstructed in detail, but it must be said that they were moderate all around, including those incurred by the motorized flak battalions.

Order of Battle: Luftflotte Six, 1 July 1943

Colonel General Robert Ritter von Greim

1st Flieger Division
Major General Paul Deichmann
Operations Officer: Major Sigismund Freiherr von Rotberg
Attached to Ninth Army:
Nahaufklarungsgruppe 4
Major Toni Vinek

Attached to XLVI Panzer/XLVII Panzer Corps:
1./NAGr 4 (Bf 109G)

Attached to XLI Panzer/XXIII Corps:
2./NAGr 4 (Bf 109G)

Attached to XX Corps:
3./NAGr 4—6.(H)/21 (Bf 110 G)

Attached to Second Army:
Nahaufklarungsgruppe 10
Captain Kurt Weidtke
1./NAGr 10—3.(H)/21 (Hs 126)
2./NAGr 10—2.(H)/31 (Fw 189A)

Attached to Second Panzer Army:
Nahaufklarungsgruppe 15
Major Hubert Correns
1.(H)/11 (Fw 189A)
11.(H)/12 (Fw 189A)
12.(H)/13 (Fw 189A)

III. Sturzkampfgeschwader 3 (Ju 87D) (organizing)
Captain Eberhard Jacob

Zerstoerergeschwader *1 (Bf 110G)*
Lieutenant Colonel Joachim Blechschmidt

  I./ZG 1(Bf 110E/F/G)
  Captain Wilifried Hermann
  Panzerjagdstaffel/ZG 1 (Bf 110F/G)
  (*Panzerjagdstaffel* 110)

Sturzkampfgeschwader *1*
Lieutenant Colonel Gustav Pressler

  Stabstaffel/StG 1 (Ju 87D; Bf 110 E/G)
  I./StG 1 (Ju 87D)
  Captain Helmut Krebs
  II./StG 1 (Ju 87D)
  Captain Frank Neubert
  III./StG 1 (Ju 87D)
  Major Friedrich Lang

Kampfgeschwader *51 "Edelweiss"*
Major Heinrich Conrady

  Stabstaffel/KG 51 (Ju 88A)
  II./KG 51 (Ju 88A)
  Major Herbert Voss
  III./KG 51 (Ju 88A/C)
  Captain Wilhelm Rath

Kampfgeschwader *3 "Blitz"*
Lieutenant Colonel Walter Lehwess-Litzmann

  III./KG 1(Ju 88A/C)
  Captain Werner Kanther
  I./KG 3 (Ju 88A)
  Major Joachim Joedicke
  II./KG 3 (Ju 88A)
  Major Horst Bengsch

Kampfgeschwader *4 "General Wever"*
Lieutenant Colonel Werner Klosinski

  Stabstaffel/KG 4 (He 116H)
  II./KG 4 (He 111H)
  Major Reinhard Graubner
  III./KG 4 (He 111H)
  Major Kurt Neumann

Kampfgeschwader *53 "Legion Condor"*
Lieutenant Colonel Fritz O. Pockrandt

  I./KG 53 (He 111H)

Major Karl Rauer
II./KG 53 (He 111H)
Major Herbert Wittmann
III./KG 53 (He 111H)
Major Emil Allmendinger

Jagdgeschwader *54*

Major Hubertus von Bonin

Detachment, II./JG 54 (Fw 190A)
Major Erich Rudorffer

Jagdgeschwader *51 "Moelders"*

Lieutenant Colonel Karl-Gottfried Nordmann

Stabstaffel/JG 51 (Fw 190A)
Lieutenant von Eichel-Streiber
I./JG 51 (Fw 190A)
Major Erich Leie
III./JG 51 (Fw 190A)
Captain Fritz Losigkeit
IV./JG 51 (Fw 190A; Bf 109G)
Major Rudolf Resch
15. (Spanish)/JG 51 (Fw 190A)
Major Mariano Cuadra

Under direct Luftflotte control:
Feldluftgau *XXVII*

Lieutenant General Veit Fischer

Chief of Staff: General Georg Neuffer

Luftwaffe Signal Regiment 27

Transportstaffel *1 (Ju 52)*

Flugbereitschaft Lfl. *6 (Fi 156)*

San.Flugberichtschaft *4 (Fi 156; Ju 52)*

Fernaufklarungsgruppe *2*
Major Oskar Otolsky

2.(F)/*Nacht* (Do 217K)
4.(F)/11 (Ju 88)
4.(F)/14 (Ju 88D)
1.(F)/100 (Ju 88A/D)
4.(F)/121 (Ju 88D)

Storkampfgruppe Lfl. *6*

Captain Heinz Mueller

1. *Storkampfstaffel* (He 46; Ar 66)
2. *Storkampfstaffel* (Go 145)
3. *Storkampfstaffel* (Ar 66; Fw 58)

IV. Nachtjagdgeschwader *5 (Ju 88C; Do 217J/N)*

Captain Heinrich Prinz zu Sayn Wittgenstein

Transportgeschwader 3

Lieutenant Colonel Theodore Beckmann

I./TG 3 (Ju 52)
Captain Hans-Hermann Ellerbrock
II./TG 3 (Ju 52)
Major Otto Baumann

Transportgeschwader 4

Lieutenant Colonel Richard Kupschus

II./TG 4 (Ju 52)
Lieutenant Colonel Werner Hoffmann

Verbindungskommando *5 (He 111; Do 17; Hs 126; DFS 230)*

10th Flak Brigade
Major General Karl Schuchardt
(composition uncertain; see text)

12th Flak Division

Lieutenant General Ernst Buffa

Flak Regiments 21, 101, 152
Luftwaffe Signal Battalion 132

18th Flak Division

Lieutenant General Heinrich Reuss

Flak Regiments 6, 10, 34, 35, 125, 133
Luftwaffe Signal Battalion 138

Luftwaffe Signal Regiment 22

6

Luftflotte Four

by General of Fliers Hans Seidemann
Commander, VIII Flieger Corps

Editor's Introduction

Had Adolf Hitler not postponed Operation Citadel several times, Hans Seidemann probably would not have been a participant. Until 15 May 1943 Seidemann had been the commander of Flieger Command Tunis, overseeing Luftwaffe operations in Germany's ill-fated attempt to retain a bridgehead in North Africa. Once his planes, pilots, and ground installations had been safely returned to Europe (avoiding the fate of the unfortunate ground troops left behind), Seidemann received a promotion to lieutenant general and command of VIII Flieger Corps, arriving none too soon to assume the primary responsibility for tactical air support in the Army Group South assault sector.

Hans von Seidemann was born in Prussia in 1901, attended cadet academies at Potsdam and Lichterfelde, and barely missed his opportunity to fight in World War I. Frustrated by the Armistice, which occurred when he was only seventeen, von Seidemann enlisted in *Freikorps* Maercker in 1919, getting the opportunity to take part in the bloody suppression of the Spartacist revolt. The young officer followed the bulk of his unit directly into the Reichswehr, earning a lieutenant's commission in the prestigious Infantry Regiment 9 (headquartered at Potsdam and known throughout the service as "I.R. von 9" for its elite social and military status). Trained as a General Staff officer, then-Captain von Seidemann transferred to the Luftwaffe in 1935. He served as Wolfram von Richthofen's chief of staff for the Condor Legion during the Spanish civil war, then remained with von Richthofen through mid-1940 as operations officer and then chief of staff to VIII Flieger Corps, the Luftwaffe's premier ground support organization. In August 1940 von Seidemann became Albert Kesselring's chief of staff at Luftflotte Two, serving there throughout the initial drive into Russia and then following his chief to the Mediterranean theater.[1]

As pleased as he may have been to take command of VIII Flieger Corps, von Seidemann would certainly have been dismayed by the concurrent transfer of Field Marshal von Richthofen from command of Luftflotte Four to the Mediterranean. Not only did this move deprive von Seidemann of the chance to work again with his old boss; it also cost Luftflotte Four the presence of one of the Luftwaffe's strongest and most successful advocates of close support operations. Considerable wrangling ensued over who would become von Richthofen's successor, with Hans von Jeschonnek, chief of the Luftwaffe General Staff, lobbying hard for the post. In the end, however, command went to General of Flak Artillery Otto Dessloch, a fifty-four-year-old former aviator from World War I who possessed significant helpings of personal courage and tenacity and considerably more modest portions of intelligence and doctrinal understanding. As historian Richard Muller diplomatically observes, Dessloch "seems to have left most of the operational planning to the staff he inherited from Richthofen."[2]

Von Seidemann chafed under the new regime, which becomes obvious throughout this manuscript, nowhere more so than during his description of the limitations placed on his operations at the outset of the offensive. He obviously felt that Dessloch and/or his staff had invaded his legitimate prerogatives as VIII Flieger Corps commander by placing specific restrictions on the kinds of missions he could accept. Again, this irritation is an important point, especially considering that Hermann Plocher later edited it out of his own study on the attack.

This manuscript also makes the point, with exceptional clarity, concerning the negative impact of the 7 July decision to transfer nearly 40 percent of VIII Flieger Corps's assets to Army Group Center, even as the attack in the south had entered a critical phase. The significance of this decision is rarely addressed in histories of the battle of Kursk, but as the charts illustrating day-by-day sortie rates that accompany this chapter prove, a very real chance for Fourth Panzer Army to achieve a breakthrough may have been squandered through high-level vacillation over air support.

Finally, von Seidemann's study provides important nuts-and-bolts insight into just how air-ground coordination worked between the German army and the Luftwaffe. The space he devotes to signal networks and ground-force liaison teams represents one of the best accounts of this critical process to be found anywhere.

Luftflotte Four
by General of Fliers Hans Seidemann
Commander, VIII Flieger Corps

Situation, Mid–April 1943

Luftflotte Four (Field Marshal Wolfram von Richthofen, commanding) directed all Luftwaffe formations—including flak units—in the Ukraine and the Crimea. From its command post in Kamenskoye near Dnepropetrovsk, Luftflotte Four cooperated with and supported Army Groups South and A. At that time the following commands had been subordinated to Luftflotte Four:

I Flieger Corps: (Crimea and Kuban bridgehead; headquarters at Simferopol) operating with Army Group A and Seventeenth Army.

IV Flieger Corps: (Mius and Donets River sectors up to Liman, which was fifty kilometers southeast of Kharkov; headquarters at Stalino) operating with Sixth Army and First Panzer Army.

Romanian Air Corps: (Mius River sector) committed with IV Flieger Corps.

VIII Flieger Corps: (Kharkov area due north to the army group boundary; headquarters initially at Poltava but moved in mid-April to Kharkov) operating with *Armeeabteilung* Kempf and Fourth Panzer Army. The Royal Hungarian Air Division fell under the operational control of VIII Flieger Corps.

I Flak Corps: consisting of the 10th, 15th, and 17th Flak divisions distributed over forward and rear areas of the field armies.

The winter fighting had greatly weakened all these formations. The vicissitudes of combat in a wide variety of places along the far-flung front, combined with numerous unit transfers and shifts, necessarily resulted in increasingly lowered technical and personnel serviceability. The physical strength of all our troops had likewise been overtaxed.

The I Flieger Corps had been initially committed in the Kharkov region, then transferred to the Crimea late in March. The IV Flieger Corps and the Romanian Air Force Corps remained in the Mius River sector while VIII Flieger Corps operated the airlift supplying the Kuban bridgehead. This command had been pulled out toward the end of March and redeployed near Kharkov in place of I Flieger Corps.

The units of the I Flak Corps, as far as they were not constantly employed in the protection of our rear areas, had likewise suffered heavy losses as the result of the winter campaign. Losses incurred by our flak battalions in ground fighting were particularly severe because when committed to such combat situations our flak crews were invariably employed as antitank artillery in the front lines at the focal points of the most critical actions.

Both the flying formations and flak units had been committed without a break and without regard for existing weather conditions. Executing primarily missions in direct ground support, Luftflotte Four's elements (including our ground installations) were in urgent need of reorganization, to say nothing of personnel and equipment replacements. The only way to accomplish this absolutely necessary reorganization was for Field Marshal von Richthofen to ignore the many tactical opportunities the Russians presented at this time and to turn a deaf ear to the army's many requests for Luftwaffe and flak missions the moment the great land battles had ceased. This occurred about the time that the spring thaw set in and allowed him to establish Luftflotte Four's priorities as the conservation of men and equipment, rest, and reorganization.

The troops badly needed the rest. Accurate strength figures for this period are not currently available. It is, however, fair to assume that the strength of our flying formations had fallen to about 30 percent of authorization while the flak units (here referring to those directly committed to ground combat) mustered only 20–25 percent of their authorized strength. Fuel was extremely low in all quarters, and there were no reserves available. In terms of ammunition, we had plenty of aerial bombs available, but a chronic shortage of flak ammunition, chiefly attributable to ground combat, had developed. This shortage was partly due to transportation problems. By mid-April Luftflotte Four could be credited with:

Three bombardment wings (eight bombardment groups; twenty aircraft each)	160 aircraft
Two fighter wings (six fighter groups, twenty aircraft each)	120 aircraft
Two dive bomber wings (seven groups, twenty aircraft each)	140 aircraft
One anti-tank ground attack group	40 aircraft
Three harassing groups (thirty aircraft each)	90 aircraft
Two long-range reconnaissance groups	50 aircraft
Three close-range reconnaissance groups	90 aircraft
Two air transport groups	30 aircraft
Romanian Air Force Corps	approximately 100 aircraft
Hungarian Air Division	approximately 50 aircraft
Total	870 aircraft

Serviceability rates, having declined, can be placed at 75 percent, yielding a total of 600 operational aircraft.

Gun, vehicle, and personnel losses within I Flak Corps had been so high that some units had to be pulled out of the front completely before they could be restored to full strength. Almost all our motorized flak units had been drawn into the ground fighting, losing most of their equipment and many personnel to enemy action and terrain difficulties. The entire 9th Flak Division had remained in Stalingrad and been destroyed along with Sixth Army; it was beginning the process of reconstitution in the Crimea. Our "fixed" or "transportable" units—those assigned to static protection of our line-of-communications installations—likewise lost significant amounts of materiel during repeated withdrawals. Guns could be replaced quickly, but the repair and replacement of motor vehicles was another story.

Situation, Early July 1943

Between April and the end of June, Luftflotte Four had essentially grounded itself while it filled the ranks of its flying formations, flak units, and ground elements, restoring them to an operational status for new missions. Only through this expedient could reserves of fuel, ammunition, aircraft, and flying equipment be amassed. The formations that required the heaviest personnel replacements underwent training to prepare them for combat. Most of our flying formation were billeted during this period in the I and IV Flieger Corps areas.

Meanwhile Field Marshal von Richthofen and the headquarters staff began planning to support Operation Citadel with the maximum possible air strength. This would require depleting Luftwaffe formations along our entire southern wing and in the Mius River sector. Headquarters, I and IV Flieger Corps, as well as their reconnaissance formations and harassing squadrons, remained in their old operational areas; the Romanian Air Force Corps also stayed in the Mius River sector. Most of the flying formations earmarked for the offensive were attached to VIII Flieger Corps, whose command post had located in Kharkov. As the attack got under way, this headquarters relocated to Mikoyanovksa, south of Belgorod. For reasons of security and deception, the flying formations themselves deployed to their forward airfields only during the evening preceding the attack.

Preparations for this concentration had begun in early May. Because the Kharkov airfield was not large enough to accommodate most of our formations, it became necessary to construct a series of advanced airfields north of the city, immediately behind the point of main effort for the ground attack. Assembling and storing the required stocks of ammunition and fuel necessitated the establishment of new supply dumps. Likewise, VIII Flieger Corps operations would need a well-functioning communications net for the transmission of orders, direction of fighters and dive-bombers, operation of the aircraft reporting service, and liaison with army ground units. This network had been established by the end of May.

At the beginning of Operation Citadel in early July, therefore, Luftflotte Four was deployed in strength as follows:

Luftflotte Four (commanded by General of Flak Artillery Otto Dessloch following Field Marshal von Richthofen's transfer to the Mediterranean theater) had its headquarters at Murafa, twenty kilometers southwest of Bogodukhov. The only formation directly attached to the headquarters was one long-range reconnaissance group of twenty-four aircraft.

I Flieger Corps (headquarters at Simferopol) had the mission of cooperating with Seventeenth Army in the defense of the Kuban bridgehead and the Crimea. This headquarters controlled:

One close-range reconnaissance group	35 aircraft
One long-range reconnaissance squadron	9 aircraft
One harassing group	40 aircraft
One Slovak fighter squadron	12 aircraft
One naval patrol squadron	10 aircraft
Total	106 aircraft

With a serviceability rate of 75 percent, this meant that I Flieger Corps possessed eighty operational aircraft. In addition, in the Crimea there was also one mixed Romanian formation, consisting of reconnaissance aircraft and fighters. Its mission was to reconnoiter and patrol the Black Sea between the Crimea and Romania. This formation numbered about eight aircraft.

IV Flieger Corps (headquarters at Stalino) had the mission of supporting the Sixth Army and First Panzer Army near Izyum and along the Mius River line. This headquarters controlled:

Romanian Air Force Corps	150 aircraft
One close-range reconnaissance group	35 aircraft
One long-range reconnaissance squadron	9 aircraft
One harassing group	40 aircraft
Total	234 aircraft

With a serviceability rate of 75 percent, this meant that IV Flieger Corps possessed 180 operational aircraft.

VIII Flieger Corps (headquarters at Mikoyanovka) had the mission of supporting Fourth Panzer Army and *Armeeabteilung* Kempf in Operation Citadel. This headquarters controlled:

Bombardment formations:	
Two groups, 3rd Bombardment Wing	70 aircraft
Three groups, 27th Bombardment Wing	100 aircraft
Three groups, 55th Bombardment Wing	100 aircraft
Fighter formations:	
Three groups, 3rd Fighter Wing	120 aircraft
Three groups, 52nd Fighter Wing	120 aircraft
Ground Attack formations:	
Two groups, 1st Ground Attack Wing	80 aircraft
Three groups, 2nd Ground Attack Wing	130 aircraft
(also included one anti-tank squadron)	
Three groups, 77th Ground Attack Wing	120 aircraft
Reconnaissance formations:	
One close-range reconnaissance group	40 aircraft
One long-range reconnaissance squadron	10 aircraft
One ground attack aircraft group	60 aircraft
(4th Anti-tank Group, 5th Ground	
Attack Wing)	
One harassing group	60 aircraft
One air transport squadron (Ju 52s)	12 aircraft
Hungarian Air Division:	
One fighter group	30 aircraft
One dive bomber group	30 aircraft
One ground attack squadron	12 aircraft
One close-range reconnaissance squadron	9 aircraft
One long-range reconnaissance squadron	9 aircraft
Total	1,112 aircraft

With a serviceability rate of seventy-five percent, this meant that VIII Flieger Corps possessed 900 operational aircraft.

At the beginning of July, therefore, Luftflotte Four had 1,556 aircraft available of which about 1,200 were operational.

I Flak Corps had seen its three divisions brought up to strength and made ready for active service. Ammunition and traction equipment in sufficient quantities were both on hand. All mobile flak units, except those committed in the Crimea, had been pulled out of the Mius and Donets sectors, and by this extensive depletion we managed a powerful flak concentration in the projected zone of attack. The flak main effort consisted of three mixed regiments (two heavy and one light battalion each) supporting *Armeeabteilung* Kempf. Another flak regiment had been attached to Fourth Panzer Army for direct support of the ground troops. In addition, our forward airfields had been provided with protection by motorized flak units so that they could follow immediately if the flying formations subsequently moved up to new bases as planned.

Luftwaffe Participation in Operation Citadel

General Dessloch assigned VIII Flieger Corps the mission of direct support for Fourth Panzer Army and *Armeeabteilung* Kempf. I had instructions to concentrate my elements only at the points of main effort, which meant supporting ground troops in other sectors on an emergency basis only. The flying formations—including the bomber formations—I was to employ over the battlefield in purely tactical missions. Strategic targets in Russian rear areas could be attacked only in cases involving troop movements in the Oboyan-Kursk area and the railway targets at Stariy Oskol or Valuiki.

General Dessloch also prohibited me from making the customary strikes against Soviet airfields at the outset of the offensive. My aircraft were to appear over the battlefield as soon as the attack commenced and not sooner. There were two reasons for this decision, the first of which was the hope that such a tactic might allow us to achieve tactical surprise. Additionally, however, General Dessloch realized that attacks against Russian airfields, though certainly damaging, would have no long-term effect on the offensive in view of the steady stream of Soviet aircraft replacements, which would soon make up for any losses VIII Flieger Corps might initially inflict. Our own forward bases had been located directly behind the attacking ground troops, and the necessary measures had been taken to make their ground elements mobile. Once Army Group South had broken through the Russian defenses and driven toward Kursk, we anticipated the necessity of quickly moving these base formations up to new positions.

Providing quick and effective ground support necessitated smoothly functioning communications between the attacking armies, corps, and divisions and headquarters, VIII Flieger Corps. The Luftwaffe had maintained a corps of liaison officers since the beginning of the war, composed of men who had strong experience in ground support operations. As usual during an offensive, we attached these teams directly to Army Group South's corps and division headquarters, and they accompanied their units directly onto the field of battle. There the Luftwaffe officers also acted as dive-bomber and fighter guides, using their radios to direct approaching formations to the targets indicated by the ground commander, correct their fire, and provide updates on the current tactical air situation in the local area. These liaison teams also reported the ground situation, air situation, and any unusual information directly to VIII Flieger Corps every two hours. This procedure kept both the controlling headquarters and the flying formations constantly informed as to the progress of the attack. Two Luftwaffe signal communications regiments had installed VIII Flieger Corps's signal network in a manner that permitted airfields to be contacted on two different telephone lines, as well as by telegraph and radio. Thus our available signal equipment was employed to facilitate the mass employment of our flying formations.

Ground elements at the forward airfields had been reinforced. In addition to airfield maintenance crews (who were responsible for servicing the flying formations), our airfield commanders had also been assigned additional labor forces, including Luftwaffe construction battalions and Reich Labor Service units. Maintenance platoons and workshops had been reorganized at full strength and were ready to go to work as the offensive opened.

Luftflotte Four had massed adequate stocks of bombs, ammunition for onboard armaments, and flak ammunition for the attack, and throughout the offensive none of these items was found to be in short supply. Fuel sufficient for about ten sorties per plane had been stored at the forward airfields, with fuel trains held in readiness to the rear for dispatch to the front with replenishment supplies. We had also managed to solve the problem of replacement parts and aircraft replacements. Even though attrition and losses throughout the offensive were heavy, Luftflotte Four maintained the serviceability of its flying formations at a consistent 60 percent. It might be worth mentioning at this point that the small, one-kilogram fragmentation bomb was dropped in large quantities for the first time during Operation Citadel. Our bombardment aircraft dropped this armament in bomb-shaped 250- and 500-kilogram canisters (Models AB250 and AB500). These fragmentation bombs proved to be extremely effective against live targets when discharged by a scatter drop (an adaptation of the Molotov "bread basket").

VIII Flieger Corps's ground attack formations flew five to six sorties daily per crew. The bombardment formations flew three to four sorties, and the fighters averaged five sorties each day. These figures, extended over a period of several days, signified an extraordinary achievement by both flight and ground personnel. Although our actual losses remained within conservative limits, it was really the knowledge that they were in

position to do their part again and again at the decisive points in a critical battle that spurred our pilots to do their very best. Morale—already
high at the beginning of the attack—remained good.

The flak units that had been directly attached to the ground forces
were not under the operational control of VIII Flieger Corps, and the lack
of available reference material at the time this report is being prepared
makes it impossible to cite accurate figures regarding their strength.
These units often found employment against Russian tanks as well as
enemy aircraft. Cooperation between the flying formations of VIII Flieger
Corps and these flak regiments was secured by informing the flak commanders about approaching Soviet formations through the air-raid
warning service.

During the continuous fighting in the winter of 1942–1943 the VVS had
been primarily employed on purely tactical missions. When the spring
thaw halted ground operations, Russian flying formations—like our
own—needed an extended rest period to replenish their ranks, reorganize,
and restore their technical serviceability. Thus, with the exception of a few
raids on targets in the immediate vicinity of the front lines, Soviet air activity throughout the spring remained relatively weak. Enemy air operations (including nighttime nuisance raids) increased as indications of an
impending German offensive became evident. Russian ground elements in
the Valuiki–Stariy Oskol–Kursk areas underwent expansion, new airfields
being constructed at great speed and then filling gradually with aircraft.
The Soviet Second Air Army took over responsibility for the Belgorod sector in mid-June, with the Fifth and Seventeenth Air Armies soon identified
in adjoining sectors. The main body of the Soviet air concentration was located around Korocha, Tim, and Kursk, with the bombardment formations
mostly deployed along the Valuiki-Stariy-Oskol railroad and a secondary
concentration identified near Kupyansk. Although it is impossible at this
time to cite accurate strength figures, the Soviets enjoyed at least a two-to-
one and possibly a three-to-one air superiority. Significant increases in
Russian fighter strength came to our attention, as did the appearance of Il2
ground attack aircraft in large numbers. Bomber formations, on the other
hand, were identified only in moderate numbers.

On the whole, both the quality and numbers of the VVS had improved
considerably, and Russian pilots now represented serious adversaries.
Soviet fighter pilots in particular had improved as far as their level of
training, though they remained handicapped by the fact that their aircraft were not technically superior to their Luftwaffe counterparts. A few
squadrons, however, were very well led and could be classified as formidable opponents. Russian ground attack formations were mainly
equipped with the cumbersome but heavily armed Il2s. These aircraft

frequently fell victim to our Me109s. A few Lend-Lease U.S. P-39 "Aira-
cobras" appeared in the sky here and there, distinguishing themselves by
their maneuverability and speed, which greatly outclassed the Il2s. VVS
bombardment formations remained numerically weak, and their generally ineffective attacks were confined to the front lines and forward airfields. In general, Russian pilots had proven themselves to be brave but
orthodox in their tactics and not sufficiently skilled to face our pilots on
equal terms. One gained the impression also that the Soviet ground
crews had not been adequately trained and lacked familiarity with the
technical aspects of their jobs.

On the afternoon of 4 July (the day before the offensive started), VIII
Flieger Corps supported the diversionary attack by the western wing of
XLVIII Panzer Corps with a few dive-bomber and bomber raids. During
the evening our formations moved forward to their operational airfields.

As the offensive opened on 5 July, VIII Flieger Corps placed its main
air effort in front of II SS Panzer Corps and XLVIII Panzer Corps with all
dive-bomber and bomber formations to strike at daybreak, in coordination with Fourth Panzer Army's artillery fire plan. Most of our flak had
been committed in the XI Corps sector of *Armeeabteilung* Kempf in a
ground support role. The Russians attempted a preemptive strike early
that morning, committing powerful bomber and ground attack formations to raid the densely occupied Luftwaffe airfields around Kharkov.
Fortunately, our fighter formations were alerted in time and attacked the
Soviet formations continuously as they made their approach run, as well
as pursuing them aggressively on their return flight. At the same time,
concentrated flak fire likewise inflicted heavy Russian losses. Approximately 120 Soviet aircraft were shot down in the course of this first raid,
and the Russian attack really had little discernable effect on VIII Flieger
Corps formations, as our losses were very small.

Throughout the remainder of the day, VIII Flieger Corps's sorties were
mainly flown forward of the interior wings of the two attacking panzer
corps. Our primary targets consisted of enemy pockets of resistance, antitank gun switch positions, and concentrations of Russian artillery.
These air attacks continued without interruption from morning till night.

Our fighters enjoyed tremendous success against their opponents,
shooting down 200 Soviet planes that day alone. This great bloodletting
seemed to diminish the aggressive impetus of the Russian pilots somewhat; at any rate, Soviet aerial formations were observed to become
rather reluctant to engage us. They frequently discontinued their raids
when Luftwaffe fighters appeared. Intercepted radio traffic indicated
that Russian formations at times received specific instructions not to
fight, which may have conserved their forces but allowed us to gain air

superiority on the first day of the attack. This state of affairs changed but little during the entire Citadel offensive.

On 6 July VIII Flieger Corps flew its sorties over the same sectors as the previous day, continually attacking the second Russian defensive line, which contained numerous antitank guns and artillery positions. Once again both our fighters and flak formations proved extremely successful, chalking up a score of 120 Soviet planes downed between them. That night the Luftwaffe made nuisance raids on Russian reserves in their assembly areas and as they moved on the roads. Our reconnaissance units confirmed active convoy traffic carrying reserve units toward the battle.

Because of the bitter fighting in progress east of Belgorod, certain ground attack formations had to be diverted on 7 July to support *Armeeabteilung* Kempf's III Panzer Corps. That afternoon our reconnaissance aircraft identified extensive Soviet movements along the Belgorod-Kursk railway and in the woods and localities east of it. A Russian armored train was destroyed in Teterevino. Night reconnaissance revealed even more extensive enemy movements in the area around Korocha, as well as north and northeast of Prokhorovka. We flew nighttime nuisance raids over these areas. The number of Soviet aircraft shot down on 7 July was smaller than the totals scored on the two previous days, probably because of the heavy losses inflicted on the VVS during the first forty-eight hours of the offensive.

As a result of the failure of Ninth Army's attack in the Orel area to push forward as expected, orders were issued to VIII Flieger Corps on the evening of 7 July that transferred the following formations to 1st Flieger Division, Luftflotte Six, supporting Ninth Army:

Two groups, 3rd Fighter Wing
Three groups, 2nd Ground Attack Wing
Two Groups, 3rd Bombardment Wing

This transfer represented a 40 percent reduction in fighter strength, a 50 percent decrease in ground attack formations, and a 30 percent reduction in VIII Flieger Corps bomber strength.

By 8 July our night reconnaissance flights had again reported extremely heavy enemy traffic headed for the Russian front lines. Major Soviet counterattacks also became noticeable that day. Daytime reconnaissance revealed the presence of major Russian tank assembly areas around Prokhorovka. This appeared to us the result of Ninth Army's failure to crash through the Soviet defenses in the north, which had allowed the Russians to transfer tank and motorized units south to operate in the Belgorod sector.

Though a number of our formations had been transferred elsewhere, VIII Flieger Corps continued to be active. Our ground attack formations concentrated on Russian tanks in the sectors of III Panzer Corps (northeast of Belgorod) and II SS Panzer Corps (south of Prokhorovka). Soviet air formations became more active, but air superiority remained in our hands. That afternoon our antitank ground attack aircraft scored a particularly notable success. When reconnaissance identified a powerful Russian tank thrust issuing out of the woods east of Gostchevo station aimed at II SS Panzer Corps's extended flank, the 4th Group, 9th Ground Attack Wing, took charge of the situation. Scrambling to meet this threat, the group destroyed a large number of Russian tanks, halting the attack in its tracks. After an hour the remnants of this force discontinued their approach and withdrew. Approximately forty Soviet tanks had been dispatched.

Night reconnaissance again reported additional enemy motorized units being moved to the front from the Kursk area. In view of the continued deterioration of Ninth Army's situation south of Orel, we received orders that night to transfer the antitank ground attack group to 1st Flieger Division the next morning.

Throughout 9 July stubborn enemy resistance opposite III Panzer Corps and II SS Panzer Corps continued. Our remaining dive-bombers and bombers were continuously employed in support of the ground troops.

By 10 July not only had a considerable number of VIII Flieger Corps formations been transferred to the Orel area, but we lost several bombardment units as well. Red Army concentrations identified in the Mius River area, as well as increasing enemy attacks there, made it necessary to commit those formations (and additional fighter groups) in support of Sixth Army. Through these orders, VIII Flieger Corps had now waned to about one-third of its original strength.

Nevertheless, we provided continual air support to the army throughout the day. This was the first day the XLVIII Panzer Corps finally received most of the air support mission flown. This corps was under attack from Russian tank formations driving south along the Oboyan-Belgorod highway and east from the Bogaty area. Air reconnaissance identified large Soviet motorized and tank units moving toward XLVIII Panzer Corps's front. In addition, III Panzer Corps and II SS Panzer Corps still needed our support. Attempting so many missions with such reduced strength inevitably resulted in the dissipation of our air strength at the very moment the Russians had thrown increasing numbers of their strategic reserves into the battle. Throughout the day, the Red Army hit Army Group South's attacking panzer wedges with full force, including ground attack aircraft.

On 11–12 July, encumbered by powerful Russian counterattacks and stubborn resistance, the German attack wedges made only slow progress. The Soviet divisions facing III Panzer Corps had been offering stiff resistance from the very beginning. The II SS Panzer Corps was now locked in a bitter tank battle south and southwest of Prokhorovka. Simultaneously, XLVIII Panzer Corps weathered heavy attacks from the west but succeeded in pushing toward Oboyan despite obstinate resistance. Some XLVIII Panzer Corps units managed to cross the Psel River, though the enemy defenses continued to stiffen.

Russian airpower began to take an increasing role in the fighting. Our advance had considerably shortened the length of the approach runs that Soviet formations had to make in order to reach the front lines, which meant that German fighters could no longer sweep the skies of enemy aircraft at all times. To counter this situation, VIII Flieger Corps began moving its own fighter and ground attack formations forward into the area southwest of Prokhorovka. Two airfields were also prepared north of Luchki, though there was never an opportunity to utilize them.

Before daybreak on 13 July night reconnaissance again reported heavy Russian traffic on the roads leading into the battle area from Kursk and Stariy Oskol. VIII Flieger Corps continued to fly ground support missions. As III Panzer Corps reached the wooded area fifteen kilometers northeast of Belgorod, our formations now hit an area that previously had not been touched. The Soviets, however, had been using it as a staging area for continuous counterattacks against II SS Panzer Corps's eastern flank. Heavy fighting continued to rage in the II SS Panzer Corps sector around Prokhorovka and along the Psel; Russian tank losses kept mounting. Northeast of Bogaty the XLVIII Panzer Corps finally defeated the enemy force directly in its front and regained freedom of movement to face the powerful Soviet reserves blocking the main highway leading into Oboyan.

VIII Flieger Corps extensively participated in all of these battles and also raided Soviet assembly areas. The necessity of keeping enemy assembly areas under observation had once again been demonstrated. Dive-bomber attacks, launched as soon as new Russian concentrations were reported, often smashed an incipient attack while it was still being organized. Such instances demonstrated the true value of our Luftwaffe liaison teams attached directly to the panzer divisions. When the liaison officer rode into combat in the command tank with the division commander, it was possible to direct our air attacks almost instantaneously against dangerous enemy targets as required. Unfortunately, it had been impossible to provide such liaisons to all divisions or to mount all of our teams in tanks or half-tracks. The cumbersome half-track SdKfz 305s that many teams were forced to employ frequently could not follow the attacking units closely enough over rough terrain.

Although advancing but slowly and suffering by no means inconsiderable casualties, German ground troops nevertheless moved forward gradually on 14 July. The weather had been favorable, and the operational strength of VIII Flieger Corps's remaining flying formations had remained at about two-thirds of the morning report strength. Cooperation between our headquarters and the ground force units continued to be smooth. Again our aircraft flew continuous sorties, targeting Prokhorovka and the area south of Oboyan for our main effort.

This was the day that orders arrived discontinuing the Citadel offensive, although that did not mean the Luftwaffe formations were excused from further activity in the battle zone. Ground attack sorties now had to be directed against increasingly powerful enemy attacks, attack preparations, and artillery concentrations. As always, reconnaissance retained its prime importance; now more than ever it was critical to discover Russian intentions in a timely manner.

Conclusions

The massed Luftwaffe effort at the start of the Citadel offensive was the last gigantic German air effort staged over a comparatively narrow assault sector. This air effort wrested air superiority from the Soviets in the skies over the battle area and in this manner made it possible to give Army Group South the kind of air support it needed.

As mentioned previously, excellent signal communications made it possible to employ our flying formations with great flexibility. The telephone lines, frequently superimposed on those of the army, had been laid in a manner permitting their simultaneous use by the army and the Luftwaffe. This often occurred when important and urgent messages had to be channeled through to a certain headquarters.

Air transport planes ferried equipment and critical supplies to the operational airfields and evacuated the wounded on their return flights. Medical corps aircraft were employed in cooperation with the Army Medical Corps. In this manner a large number of wounded personnel could be treated and evacuated very quickly. Replacement parts and other special items for the panzer divisions also had to be airlifted in many instances.

Liaison squadrons transmitted orders and delivered maps, messages, and aerial photographs. On numerous occasions these liaison aircraft voluntarily evacuated wounded soldiers on their return trips.

The lack of reference material available to the author makes it impossible to deal with the performance of our flak units in the detail that they deserve. It was a matter of common knowledge, however, that those flak regiments attached to the army not only furnished antiaircraft protection but distinguished themselves in ground action whenever it became necessary.

The Citadel offensive failed because the German units attacking north of Belgorod and in the vicinity of Orel met a powerful and prepared Red Army, backed by strong strategic reserves of infantry and tanks that had previously been positioned in favorable locations. It appeared to us that the Soviets had been informed with reasonable accuracy not only as to the timing of the offensive but also the direction of the attack and the location of our points of main effort as well.

Although the attack of Army Group South progressed slowly but steadily, it must be said that the available German infantry reserves were inadequate in view of the heavy losses incurred.

Finally, Ninth Army's failure at Orel in the initial stage of the offensive made it necessary to withdraw elements from Army Group South, which in turn weakened the assault from Belgorod. VIII Flieger Corps likewise had to transfer half of its formations away from the Kharkov area, and subsequently lost additional formations to support our defense of the Mius River line.

APPENDIX 6A

Order of Battle: Luftflotte Four, 1 July 1943

General of Flak Artillery Otto Dessloch
Chief of Staff: Major General Karl-Heinrich Schulz

I Flieger Corps (Simferopol)
Lieutenant General Kurt Angerstein
Chief of Staff: Colonel Klaus Uebe
   13. (Slovakian)/JG 52 (Bf 109G)
   15. (Croatian)/JG 52 (Bf 109G)
   10./ZG 1 (Bf 110)

Seelfiegerfuehrer "Schwarzes Meer"
Lieutenant Colonel Joachim Bauer

SeeAufklarungsgruppe 125
Lieutenant Colonel Helmut Schalke

Stabstaffel *SAGr 125 (Bv 138)*
   1./SAGr 125 (Bv 138)
   2./SAGr 125 (AR 196)
   3./SAGr 125 (Bv 138)

Romanian air force units subordinate to I Flieger Corps:
   20th Army Cooperation Squadron (IAR 39)
   22nd Army Cooperation Squadron (IAR 39)
   102nd Seaplane Squadron (He 114)
   1./3rd Long-range Recon. Squadron (Blenheim)
   49th Attack Squadron (IAR 80C)
   78th Bomber Squadron (He 111H)
   2nd Bomber Group
   82nd Bomber Squadron (JRS 79B1)
   83rd Bomber Squadron (JRS 79B1)

Luftwaffe Signal Regiment 31
Colonel Alfred Eckholdt

IV Flieger Corps (Ssalsk)
Lieutenant General Kurt Pflugbeil
Chief of Staff: Lieutenant Colonel Anselm Brasser

Reconnaissance squadrons:

2.(F)/22 (Ju 88A)
2.(F)/100 (Ju 88; Do 215)

I Romanian Air Corps (Mariupol)

115th Light Reconnaissance Squadron (Fleet 10G)
116th Light Reconnaissance Squadron (Fleet 10G)
105th Transport Squadron (Ju 52)
2nd Long-range Reconnaissance Squadron (Ju 88D)
Anti-aircraft Regiment 5

1st Fighter Flotilla

7th Fighter Group
56th Fighter Squadron (Bf 109G)
57th Fighter Squadron (Bf 109G)
58th Fighter Squadron (Bf 109G)

8th Attack Group
41st Attack Squadron (Hs 129B)
42nd Attack Squadron (Hs 129B)
60th Attack Squadron (Hs 129B)

9th Fighter Group
43rd Fighter Squadron (IAR 80A)
47th Fighter Squadron (IAR 80A)
48th Fighter Squadron (IAR 80A)

3rd Bomber Flotilla

3rd Dive-bomber Group
73rd Dive-bomber Squadron (Ju 87D)
81st Dive-bomber Squadron (Ju 87D)
85th Dive-bomber Squadron (Ju 87D)

5th Bomber Group
77th Bomber Squadron (Ju 88A)
79th Bomber Squadron (Ju 88A)
80th Bomber Squadron (Ju 88A)

6th Bomber Group
74th Bomber Squadron (Ju 88A)
86th Bomber Squadron (Ju 88A)
87th Bomber Squadron (Ju 88A)

Luftwaffe Signal Regiment 34
Lieutenant Colonel Ulrich Schroth

VIII Flieger Corps (Mikojanovka: Supporting Operation "Citadel")
Major General Hans Seidemann
Chief of Staff: Colonel Thorsten Christ
Korpstransportstaffel *(Ju 52)*
Flugbereitschaft *VIII Flieger Corps (Fi156)*
San.Flugbereitschaft *3 (Fi 156; Ju 52)*
Nahaufklarungsgruppe *6 (North of Kharkov)*
Major Herbert Rinke

> 1./NAGr 6—1.(H)/21 (Fw 189A)
> 2./NAGr 16 (Fw 189A)
> 1./NAGr 2—4.(H)/10 (Bf 109G)
> 5.(H)/32 (Hs 126B)
> 2.(H)/33 (Bf 110G)

Kampfgreschwader *100 (He 111H) (Poltava/Stalino)*
Major Hans-Georg Baetcher

Jagdgeschwader *52 (Besonovka/Kharkov)*
Lieutenant Colonel Dietrich Hrabak

> *Stabstaffel*/JG 52 (Bf 109G)
> I./JG 52 (Bf 109G)
> Captain Helmut Bennemann
> II./JG 52 (Bf 109G)
> Captain Helmut Kuehle
> III./JG 52 (Bf 109G)
> Captain Guenther Rall

Jagdgeschwader *3 "Udet"*
Major Friedrich-Karl Mueller

> II./*Jagdgeschwader* 3 (Bf 109G) (Varvarovka)
> Major Kurt Braendle
> III./*Jagdgeschwader* 3 (Bf 109G)
> Major Wolfgang Ewald

Kampfgeschwader 27 "Boelcke"
Lieutenant Colonel Freiherr von Beust

> I./KG 27 (He 111H)
> Captain Joachim Petzold
> II./KG 27 (He 111H)
> Major Karl-August Petersen
> III./KG 27 (He 111H)
> Captain Karl Mayer
> 14.(*Panzerjagd*)/KG 27 (He 111H)

Kampfgeschwader *55*

Lieutenant Colonel Dr. Ernst Kuehl

II./KG 55 (He 111H)
Major Heinz Hoefer
III./KG 55 (He 111H)
Major Wilhelm Antrup
14.(*Panzeerjagd*)/KG 55 (He 111H)
Lieutenant Mathias Bermadinger

Sturzkampfgeschwader 2

Major Dr. Ernst Kupfer

Stabstaffel/StG 2 (Ju 87D)
I./StG 2 (Ju 87D)
Captain Wilhelm Hobein
II./StG 2 (Ju 87D/G)
Captain Hans-Karl Stepp
III./StG 2 (Ju 87D)
Captain Walter Krauss
Panzerjaegerstaffel/StG 2 (Ju 87D)
Lieutenant Helmut Schuebe

Sturzkampfgeschwader 77

Major Helmut Bruck

Stabstaffel/StG 77 (Ju 87D)
I./StG 77 (Ju 87D)
Major Werner Roell
II./StG 77 (Ju 87D)
Captain Helmut Leichte
III./StG 77 (Ju 87D)
Captain Franz Kieslich

Schlachtgeschwader *1*

Lieutenant Colonel Alfred Druschel

Stabsschwarm/SchG 1 (Fw 190A/F)
I./SchG 1 (Fw 190A/F)
Captain Georg Doerffel
II./Schg 1 (Fw 190A/F)
Captain Helmut Leichte

Fueher der Panzerjaegerstaffeln

Captain Bruno Meyer

Panzerjaeger-Kommando/SchG 1
4.(*PzJgr*)/SchG 1 (Hs 129B)
Lieutenant Georg Dornemann
8.(*PzJgr*)/SchG 1 (Hs 129B)

Captain Rudolf-Heinz Rugger
4.(*PzJgr*)/SchG 2 (Hs 129B)
Lieutenant Frank Oswald
Panzerjagd-Staffel/JG 51 (Hs 129B)
Lieutenant Hans Jentsch

Hungarian air force units subordinated to VIII Flieger Corps:

2nd Air Brigade (Kharkov area)
5./I Fighter Group
Major Aladár Heppes
1./5 (Bf 109F/G)
Captain Gvörgy Ujszászy
2./5 (Bf 109F/G)
Captain Gvula Horváth
1./1st Long-range Recon. Squadron (Ju 88D)
Captain Adorján Mersich
1./3rd Short-range Recon. Squadron (Fw 189A)
Captain Loránt Telbisz
1./4th Bomber Squadron (Ju 88A/C)
2./2nd Dive-Bomber Squadron (Ju 87D)
Captain Jenö Korosy

I Flak Corps
Lieutenant General Richard Reimann
Chief of Staff: Colonel Erich Groepler
9th Flak Division
Lieutenant General Wolfgang Pickert
Operations Officer: Major Franz Kaiser

Flak Regiment 27
Flak Battalions 137, 181, 191, 257, 293, 505
Flak Regiment 42
Flak Battalions I./4, 164, L86, L89
Army Flak Battalions 275, 279
Flak Batteries 3./735, 12./LW Jaeger Regiment 3
Flak Regiment 77
Flak Battalions 251, 541, 702, 739
Flak Battalions III./8, III./43, I./Lehr-Versuch. FAS
Flak Batteries 3./321, 4./850, 2./728
Luftwaffe Signal Battalion 129

10th Flak Division
(*most units detached to* Armeeabteilung *Kempf*)
Major General Franz Engel
Operations Officer: Captain Kurt Gerhardt

Flak Regiment 124
Flak Battalion I./19
Luftwaffe Signal Battalion 130

15th Flak Division
(most units detached to Armeeabteilung *Kempf)*
Lieutenant General Eduard Muehr
Operations Officer: Major Karl Bundt

Flak Regiment 104
Luftwaffe Signal Battalion

17th Flak Division
(several units detached to Armeeabteilung *Kempf)*
Lieutenant General Karl Veith
Operations Officer: Major Ernst Bodensteiner

Flak Regiments 12, 17
Luftwaffe Signal Battalion 132

Under direct Luftflotte control:
Feldluftgau *XXV*
General of Fliers Albert Vierling

Luftwaffe Signal Regiment 25
I. and II./Luftwaffe Training Battalion (*Hiwi*)

Fernaufklarungsgruppe 4 *(Zaporozhe/Stalino/Kharkov)*
Major Hans-Dietrich Klette

1.(F)/*Nacht* (Do 217M; He 111H)
2.(F)/22 (Ju 88D) (Attached to IV Flieger Corps)
2.(F)/100 (Ju 88D)
2.(F)/11 (Ju 88D) (Attached to VIII Flieger Corps)
3.(F)/121 (Ju 88D)
Wekusta 76 (Ju 88D)

Verbindungskommando *(S) 4*
(He 111H; Ju 87R; DFS 230; Go 242)
Captain [——] Landwehr
Storkampfgruppe der Luftflotte 4

1. *Storkampfstaffel* (He 46; Do 17; Hs 126)
2. *Storkampfstaffel* (Ar 66; Fw 189; Ju W34)
3. *Storkampfstaffel* (Go 145)
4. *Storkampfstaffel* (Ar 66; Fw 58; Ju 87B/R/D)
5. *Storkampfstaffel* (He 46; Hs 126; Ar 66)
6. *Storkampfstaffel* (Go 145)

7

Railroad Transportation

by Colonel Hermann Teske

Chief of Transportation, Army Group Center

Editor's Introduction

The extent to which the German army depended upon railroad transportation to support operations in the Soviet Union has rarely been emphasized in campaign histories and narratives. Constantly lacking the motor vehicles to provide tactical mobility to front-line combat units, the Germans literally stripped their rear areas of everything with an internal combustion engine that would roll. All categories of supplies, soldiers departing for and returning from furloughs, and the wounded all overwhelmingly moved by rail or horse-drawn vehicle. Often the combat soldiers themselves simply walked. Bernard Averback, an antitank gunner in the 95th Infantry Division, recalled that the troops rarely expected any transport to meet them at the railhead. Deployed to Russia for the first time in February 1942, when his replacement detachment detrained at Orel, "neither our guns nor our truck were at hand so we set off on foot to Kolpny, 60 miles to the south." Earning a furlough the next winter, Averback "had to walk 10 miles to the railroad station" on "a clear night with a full moon and minus 48 degrees."[1]

By late 1942–early 1943 an additional burden had been placed on the railroads: strategic transfer of forces. Nearly two dozen divisions had to move by rail from France to Russia during the aftermath of Stalingrad, and another half-dozen transited laterally across the front from Army Groups Center and North. In the beginning this was an emergency measure, but as 1943 progressed it became increasingly obvious that the Germans no longer possessed the transportation resources to shift divisions from place to place (even within the same army group)

201

without recourse to the rails. The nonmotorized infantry divisions had never, of course, possessed enough organic motor transport to lift more than a fraction of their troops; the army relied instead on a small number of motor transport columns (those organized both by the army and by the National Socialist Motor Transport Corps) to move these divisions. Unfortunately, these rear-area transport assets were hit time and again by the front-line units, desperate for additional manpower and vehicles.[2] The result was an increased burden on the railroads and commanders, who sometimes faced the choice between moving up reinforcements or supplying ammunition to the troops already holding the line.

At the same time, partisan attacks on the railroads intensified, especially through Belorussia and the Bryansk-Moscow axis. Exactly when the officers responsible for transport found themselves forced to give up their admittedly second-rate security forces, they faced daily attempts to sabotage critical rails and bridges. Increased reliance on foreign troops (*Ostruppen*) became more of a problem than a solution; by 1943 it was not unheard of for entire companies or battalions of these troops to massacre their handful of German officers and desert en masse, often first destroying the very installations they had been charged to protect.

Colonel Hermann Teske's brief narrative about railroad transportation for Army Group Center before, during, and immediately after Operation Citadel is significant for three main reasons. Unlike many other officers working in the U.S. Army historical program, Teske retained a considerable portion of his contemporary records; his account is thus packed with valuable statistical information. The Teske study is also a rarity in the sense that very little material outside archival sources exists to document this critical facet of the war. Finally, it is important to read Teske's original manuscript to discover how heavily most historians have relied upon it for almost all their generalizations on railroad supply and the effectiveness (or lack thereof) of the partisans operating behind Army Group Center.[3]

Teske's work did not formally constitute a part of the Busse staff study on the battle of Kursk (it was apparently written six months or a year later), but it is such a natural extension that it is not difficult to suspect that it may have been commissioned as a result of the larger study. Whether or not there was any direct relation, this essay on railroad transportation deserves to be considered along with the operational narratives of the army and Luftwaffe. Without the trains, there would have been no chance for victory at all.

Railroad Transportation
by Colonel Hermann Teske
Chief of Transportation, Army Group Center

Introduction

As chief of transportation for Army Group Center during the period herein described, I have had at my disposal a variety of memoranda, orders, status reports, and other pertinent documents for the completion of this study. For this reason I have chosen to focus on chronological accounts that will throw the greatest light on the subject rather than to record general observations. This study focuses exclusively on the events surrounding Operation Citadel and that operation's consequences from the perspective of Army Group North, that is, the northern attacking wing in the offensive.

Broad Outline of the Course of Operations

Three factors led to the creation of the deep salient in the German front west of Kursk: Army Group Don's withdrawal of its northern wing from the Donets River; the insistence of OKH that Second Panzer Army hold its position around Orel; and the subsequent recapture of Kharkov by Army Group Don. Contrary to the proposal by Field Marshal Gunther von Kluge, commander of Army Group Center, that he be allowed to retire his front (especially those units around Orel) to the Dnepr-Soj River line (Kiev-Gomel-Orsha-Nevel), Hitler at the beginning of March ordered that the interior wings of Army Groups Center and South prepare for an attack on the Kursk salient.

The staff of Army Group Center began preparations pursuant to these orders on 7 March 1943. The first order of business entailed the transport from the Smolensk-Yelnya-Yartsevo area to the area south and east of Bryansk of the ten divisions of Colonel General Walter Model's Ninth Army that had been freed for redeployment after completing its withdrawal from the Rzhev salient. According to the capacity of the route, as well as that of the loading and unloading stations, we estimated that this movement could have been carried out in eighteen days. The actual movement took longer, as no specific time had yet been fixed for the beginning of the Citadel offensive.

Ninth Army launched its attack toward Kursk on 5 July after having it postponed several times for the necessary rehabilitation of its divisions and for the thorough preparation of personnel and equipment. Shortly before the offensive actually opened, OKH asked me about the feasibility of rapidly regrouping the attack units from the area south of Orel into that of Voroshba. Apparently, concerns had been raised regarding the concentration of strong Russian strategic reserves northeast of Kursk, and this led to consideration of a shift in the main effort of the attack from the salient's flank to its western edge. I confirmed that such a deviation in transportation was possible, but it was never ordered.

By 7 July Ninth Army's attack had already encountered considerable Soviet resistance north of Kursk, and on 11 July a strong Russian counteroffensive opened against Second Panzer Army on the northern and eastern faces of the Orel salient. This offensive brought Operation Citadel to a halt and required a rapid regrouping of forces and the establishment of a uniform command over the entire Orel salient (General Model was given command of both armies). Ironically, out of the planned German pincer movement against Kursk a much stronger Red Army pincer movement against Orel had developed.

Following the temporary break in the Orel-Bryansk railroad made by Russian tank units on 18 July, and increasingly heavy enemy attacks on the salient's southern front during the following days, OKH issued to Army Group Center the order to prepare for a systematic evacuation of the Orel salient on 26 July. The army group executed this retirement in four phases during the period 31 July–7 August, taking up new positions in the Hagen line east of the Desna River; during the movement we suffered relatively insignificant losses but inflicted heavy losses on the Red Army.

During this movement the scope of the Soviet counteroffensive expanded, exploding with unrestrained violence against both the northern wing of Army Group South and our own Fourth Army, which had been fighting north of the Hagen line. The balance of forces had irrevocably tipped against us, and new withdrawal movements became necessary— this time Field Marshal von Kluge had to pull back the entire army group front. These retrograde operations were carried out systematically, again in separate phases; the rivers flowing north to south throughout our sector he utilized as intermediate positions. This series of withdrawals ended on 1 October in the Panther position.

Organization of the Railroad Transportation System

The transportation system, which acted as the agent for the demands of the troops and as consultant for the headquarters and railroads that carried out their requests, repeatedly faced a wide variety of challenges throughout these operations. Railroad transportation in Russia had always been the indispensable means for OKH to move troops, equipment, and supplies, not only due to the great distance between the front and the Zone of the Interior but also because of the relative intricacy of the Soviet railroad net as compared to the absence of all-weather roads and our ever-increasing shortage of motor vehicles.

To oversee railroad transportation, therefore, our organization was established as follows: At the head of Army Group Center's transportation system (basically operating under the direction of the chief for transportation at OKH) stood the chief of transportation and a staff of professionally trained assistants. I was responsible both to OKH, on the one hand, and to Army Group Center, on the other, regardless of whether the question concerned efficiency of operation, utilization of every possible means, or the demolition of facilities.

For implementing and transmitting orders, the following units and administrative centers fell under my jurisdiction:

Plenipotentiary officers of the army headquarters at Third Panzer, Fourth, Second Panzer, and Ninth Armies; these officers served as liaison agents and also as consultants and directors of transport operations in their own districts.

Transportation Headquarters Minsk; this office served as liaison with the civilian Reich Traffic Administration Minsk.

Transport Groups of Field Railroad Commands 2 (North) and 3 (South); these headquarters served as liaison agencies to the military field railroad authorities and military specialists in transportation in their districts. Under their jurisdiction fell the outlying posts of the unloading commissars and of the railroad station headquarters in important unloading areas.

If local or traffic conditions warranted, special provisional administrative centers could be established, such as:

The outlying post of Field Railroad Command 2 in Bryansk, which controlled all incoming and outgoing transportation in the Orel salient.

Plenipotentiary Commissar for Transportation Orel, who assumed responsibility for evacuation of that area.

The manpower assigned to the transportation could be broken down as follows: Within the individual army sectors Field Railroad Command 2 and 3, each consisted of 22,000 men. In the rear area of Army Group

Center (extending to our boundary with the *Riechkommissariat*), the civilian Reich Traffic Administration Minsk had a strength of 7,000 civil officials, 14,000 German, and 65,000 native railroad workers. Construction and demolition tasks devolved on the 14,858-man-strong 2nd Railroad Engineer Brigade, which attached a railroad engineer commander at each army headquarters to work in accordance with orders from that army's plenipotentiary officer for transportation.

Security for railroad signal communications in the theater of communications was provided by a railroad signal regiment of two battalions—about 1,200 men. Security of the roads themselves and the installations along them rested with the armies or the army group responsible for a particular area, but that of the transportation system proper fell to me. To accomplish this task I had the Transport Security Regiment Ostland (8,617 men) and the Railroad Transport Flak Detachment (600 men) at my disposal.

Only a close and unified cooperation between all of these agents serving the transportation system made it possible to fulfill the high demands placed upon us by Hitler and OKH. In addition, cooperation with the administrative centers of the supply system; officers in charge of loading and unloading troops; the Luftwaffe; the construction troops; and a variety of other entities was absolutely essential to our operations.

Support for Operation Citadel, 8 March–11 July

As noted above, I received my first orders in connection with Operation Citadel, which required the redeployment of ten divisions of the Ninth Army, on 7 March. As no jump-off date had been specified, these transport operations were executed in a routine manner and lasted through May. Simultaneously, a number of special attack and Luftwaffe units had to be transported—some from the Zone of the Interior and others from different army groups or even other theaters of war. In addition to the regular constant forward movement of supplies, considerable amounts of equipment, ammunition, and fuel had to be moved in anticipation of the offensive and stockpiled in dumps between Bryansk and Orel. Generally speaking, the internal troop transport within Army Group Center proceeded along the single-track railroad line via Smolensk-Roslavl while all outside transport (especially supply trains) moved via Gomel-Bryansk.

In mid-March Soviet partisans blew up both Desna River bridges southwest of Bryansk near Vigonichi. Approximately 100 men of a partisan band inhabiting the Bryansk woods, led by a Red Army officer, carried out this work of destruction. They blew the bridges only after a heavy and costly combat that annihilated the regional defense company assigned as bridge guards. This attack temporarily eliminated the important double-track stretch between Gomel-Bryansk. At the time, the situation this interruption created appeared quite serious, especially because we all believed the Kursk attack was imminent, and the Desna constituted a serious strategic obstacle. Repairs were complicated by the fact that both bridges (respectively 8,640 meters and 9,620 meters long) rose to a height of 1,050 meters. In spite of this difficulty our railroad engineers succeeded in restoring the southern bridge in five days by refilling the blown-up field with a log crib, and the northern bridge in twelve days through the use of emergency bridging equipment. This occurrence represented only a single instance of a premeditated Soviet plan for constructing obstacles along our railroads in accordance with greater strategic objectives; the following months provided numerous additional examples.

April, like March, was marked by heavy troop transport requirements within the army group. Accordingly, Soviet air assets attempted to interfere primarily at points of approach and intervehicular communications near the front-line area, as well as at unloading stations. The increasingly frequent partisan raids, by contrast, aimed at our communications lines in the rear, upon which we depended for supply and individual troop transports. Nevertheless, Field Railroad Headquarters 2 achieved maximum efficiency along the Smolensk-Bryansk-Orel line, which was critical to the strategic buildup.

During May the number of troop and supply transports decreased, as the strategic concentration for Operation Citadel had been, in general, completed. On the other hand, the number of troop transports moving through our area to Army Group South, and intended for the southern attack wing out of the Kharkov-Belgorod area, increased. Accordingly, the Soviets aimed their air and partisan attacks at the points of main effort, which in this case meant the important railroad stations at Gomel, Orsha, and Minsk, as well as the critical short stretch of track between Zhlobin-Gomel. In May alone that section of railroad came under attack sixty-nine times, resulting in 156 hours of blockage on the single-track line and 222 hours along the double-track line. We also lost thirty-five locomotives and 106 cars.

In June, the last month of the strategic concentration, we saw another increase in troop movements for attack units. Simultaneously, the number of interruptions in traffic and partisan raids increased to an average of twenty-four per day, culminating in a loss of 298 locomotives, 1,222 cars, and forty-four bridges throughout Army Group Center's area. Soviet air raids were limited to the immediate area of the strategic buildup

and struck the railroad stations at Bryansk, Orel, and Karachev. A coun-
teraction against the partisans in the badly infested woods south of
Bryansk—Operation Gypsy Baron—involved eleven front-line divisions
and brought only temporary relief.

The opening of the Citadel offensive consumed the first third of July.
On 6 July I ordered a priority placed on the restoration of the Orel-Kursk
stretch of railroad, and the construction engineers closely followed the attacking divisions, working part of the time under enemy fire. When the
turning point of the battle arrived on 11 July, it also placed before the
transportation system a set of new and extremely difficult tasks.

Defense, 12–30 July

Heavy defensive fighting along the entire front of the Orel salient during
the second half of July necessarily resulted in a considerable increase of
troop movements of all kinds throughout the army group area. Such
movements included internal transports within the army group, as well
as from the adjacent sectors of the front and the Zone of the Interior. All
these movements to support the front-line fighting positions also entailed an increase in the number of supply trains to be handled. Facing
further withdrawals toward the end of the month, we began to throttle
all supply from the Zone of the Interior in order to use up the accumulated stocks in our rear supply dumps.

Assisted by their partisans, the Russians attempted in every way possible to block our movements. The number of raids increased 30 percent
as compared to June, averaging thirty-six per day throughout the entire
month. Mass blastings with a new type of mine occurred for the first time
on 22 July; these interrupted troop movements between Army Groups
Center and South along the crowded Khutor-Mikhailovsky-Bryansk line
430 times, crippling such movements for two entire days. A gigantic
mine attached to a tank truck in the Osipovichi station destroyed one fuel
train, two ammunition trains, and one loaded with Pzkw VI Tigers.

The appearance of Russian tanks along the Bryansk-Orel railroad on 18
July could have had the most disastrous results, especially for the evacuation of the wounded from Orel, had it not been for the immediate commitment into ground combat of the rear flak units, which then completed
the evacuation.

On 22 July, immediately following the decision to evacuate the Orel
salient, I ordered the establishment of an administrative center for the
plenipotentiary commissar for transportation. This commissar received
responsibility for the execution of all official incoming and outgoing
transport missions in the area east of Bryansk. These duties included

nearly everything connected to the general evacuation and especially the dismantling, demolition, and/or withdrawal of transportation equipment and installations by the field railroad engineers, who maintained traffic operations to the very last moment.

Withdrawal, 31 July–30 September

During August the Russian attacks that continued to spread across the entire eastern front and to increase in violence forced us—in order to balance our lack of troops—into a continuous series of shuttle movements. This circumstance explains the exceptionally high number of internal troop transports within the army group area (835 trains). Parallel to their efforts at the front, the Soviets stepped up their attempts (and refined their methods) of blocking our railroad communication, as usual with the help of partisans. The new method of series blasting (which had appeared sporadically in July) now began to spring up everywhere. In this month we experienced 364 cases of series blasting, in addition to ten demolition sites uncovered before they could be detonated. In all our security troops counted 20,505 mines and removed 1,528. The month averaged forty-five raids per day.

On the night of 2–3 August the partisans launched a large-scale attack, undoubtedly prompted by Operation Hagen and the urgings of the STAVKA. During that single night, 8,422 demolition sites were identified and 2,478 mines removed—a total of 10,900 destruction attempts. This increase in mine attacks was accompanied by a similar increase in acts of sabotage. Most of these acts were carried out by hitherto trusted native railroad workers. Moreover, the *Ostruppen* that had been routinely employed as railroad guards showed a definite tendency to go over to the partisans, sometimes as complete units. On the other hand, enemy air attacks were generally confined to junctions and unloading stations. The consequences of all these obstructions were considerable: For security reasons it became necessary to slow down transport speeds, to travel only by day and only in groups, to detour, and to decrease the total number of trains (usually supply trains). Losses in personnel and equipment increased, lowering our efficiency significantly.

On 17 August Operation Hagen and the evacuation of the Orel salient ended. Despite all difficulties, we managed through well-established improvisations to execute all orders received from Army Group Center with regard to transfer of tactical units and supply while simultaneously evacuating all equipment and wounded. The administrative center for the plenipotentiary commissar for transportation for the Orel salient was dissolved on 11 August.

Arrival in the Hagen line, however, did not lead to a decrease in the tension in the transport situation. Quite the contrary; withdrawal movements continued along the entire army group front—still the immediate effect of the failure of Operation Citadel. Admittedly, as the withdrawal progressed, the distance to the front grew shorter, resulting in a decrease in troop and supply transports from the Zone of the Interior (with the exception of small traffic, primarily replacements). On the other hand, there was an offsetting increase in the number of supply trains from the rear depots (refittings), and especially of ammunition trains, which had not been registered up to then because they had been improvised. Thus between 1 and 30 September we handled 713 evacuation trains (a daily average of twenty-six trains), which—in view of all other capacity limitations—represented an indication of the general high efficiency of our railroad personnel.

During the middle of September the traffic situation became quite critical behind the southern wing of the army group in the Gomel area and immediately east thereof. At one point we had 130 evacuation trains waiting for departure while just a few kilometers from the town our troops and the Russians were locked in battle. The trains sat immobile and unable to depart because the rail lines and stations in the rear areas were blocked and obstructed due to partisan or air attacks, on the one hand, and the immense traffic demands on the other. Fortunately, we finally succeeded in dispatching them without a single train falling into enemy hands.

Partisan activity continually increased, with an obvious Soviet concentration on the Minsk-Gomel-Mogilev lines, which were attacked between five and thirty-five times per day. Even the additional security forces along the lines, increased by alert units and replacement transports from the Zone of the Interior, could no longer cope with this threat. During the nights of 18–19 and 25–26 September the partisans passed over to large-scale action and attempted to blow up the lines at 3,250–4,240 distinct points. The native railroad men and *Ostruppen* assigned to protect the lines continued to desert.

Meanwhile, on 1 October our withdrawal reached the Dnepr River line and the Panther position. There the retirement came to a halt, and the Russians themselves found it necessary to take a breathing spell. The transportation system began a rapid preparation of the areas behind the new German front that lacked transportation facilities: constructing unloading stations and yards for making up trains. Such steps were necessary so that the front line could be adequately equipped for the heavy defensive combats that were certain to break out soon.

Through their untiring efforts in building obstructions of every type and demolishing our own facilities, our railroad engineers prevented the Soviets from too rapidly pursuing our evacuations and thus avoided many potential casualties. Whenever the evacuations proceeded systematically, the necessary interruptions and demolitions could be carried out carefully and thoroughly, but they could not be executed with the required thoroughness at those points where the Red Army exercised great pressure in its pursuit. Often the problem lay with our own front-line troops, who naturally wanted to use the railroad bridges and lines up to the last possible moment, thus hindering the blastings or the preparations for them.

Summary and Comparisons

The following tables make comparisons possible and illustrate the development of operations, as well as the delays caused by the enemy. Specific explanation of cases is to be found in the preceding month-by-month narrative. Army Group Center, during August, consisted of 1,665,800 troops and 374,650 horses. The railroad network comprised 12,909 kilometers at the beginning of the movements described.

A. OPERATIONAL PERFORMANCE

1. Total numbers (trains)

Month	Troop Transports	Supply Transports
April	885	1,731
May	752	1,568
June	867	1,555
July	1,169	1,763
August	1,324	1,627
September	1,107	922

2. Details (trains)

2a. Unit movements

Month	Within the Army Group	Outside	Through Trains
April	373	—	85
May	200	—	153
June	371	83	18
July	461	159	11
August	652	19	34
September	312	—	98

2b. *Individual trains*

Month	Within the Army Group	Outside	Through Trains
April	339	88	—
May	307	92	—
June	222	92	81
July	410	121	7
August	183	280	156
September	507	190	—

2c. *Supply (trains)*

	Supply trains (1)		Other military Traffic (2)	Civilian Traffic (3)
	From Zone of Interior	From rear depots		
April	918	—	312	501
May	851	—	396	321
June	852	—	382	321
July	752	251	403	357
August	668	288	323	348
Sept.	414	540	173	209

Notes:

(1) Ammunition, fuel, rations, hospital trains, etc.

(2) Luftwaffe, railroad engineers, salvage platoons, furlough traffic.

(3) *Reichsbahn* (German Railroad System), Economy, etc.

B. ENEMY INTERFERENCE

Month	Partisan Raids	Air Raids	
February	393	??	
March	404	??	
April	626	94	
May	765	159	
June	841	123	
July	1,114	115	
August		1,392	152
September		1,256	64

(Note: September figures cover a much smaller area)

C. IMPORTANT EVENTS IN BRIEF

April: Strategic concentration of units within the army group from Smolensk to Bryansk-Orel. Supplies for offensive from Zone of the Interior. Increased partisan activity.

May: Strategic concentration within the army group, weaker, hence through traffic to Army Group South. Increasing partisan attacks; air raids at their height. (Russians expect an attack this month?)

June: Renewed increase in assembly of troop transports within the army group. Increased partisan activity.

July: Considerable increase in troop transports within the army group and especially from the outside (reinforcements for front-line units under attack). Sporadic increases in partisan activity.

August: Continuous shuttle transports to balance the lack of reserves. Replacement transports to Army Group South (through-traffic). Partisan activity at height; heavy air activity.

September: Transports to balance the reorganization of the Panther position; continuing priority on small, specialized units. New supply and refitting. Partisan attacks persist.

Conclusions

The commitment of field railroad commands, trained and organized on a military basis, proved its worth even more so during withdrawal operations than during our advances. This manifested itself especially when the Red Army penetrated into the railroad areas of operation and civilian railroad men were forced to take over transport operations. Often this occurred under enemy action, or at least in the proximity of the enemy, and without military training or weapons these civilians lacked the necessary confidence and attitude to accomplish their mission. Such situations inevitably resulted in significant decreases in efficiency. From time to time we made efforts to have echelons of the military field railroad commands take over the front-line traffic, but higher headquarters consistently rejected the idea, fearing that unfamiliarity with the lines would result in even greater inefficiency.

The development of an improvised administrative center for the plenipotentiary commissar for transportation for the evacuation of Orel did not prove its worth. Ignorance of local conditions and personnel, lack of time for indoctrination, and lack of the necessary communications that could only have developed through long-term cooperation were factors that worked against this concept. Later experiences proved that it would have been more expedient to strengthen the existing administrative centers (in this case the plenipotentiaries for transportation at Second Panzer and Ninth Armies) with personnel and equipment (especially signal communications, motor vehicles, etc.) and to extend their authority to subordinate officials who had previously acted only as assistants.

The evacuation operation suffered greatly from arbitrary troop shiftings and the lack of cooperation between the quartermaster and transport administration centers, which resulted—for example—in multiple cases when important equipment was left behind while unimportant goods were transported. According the availability of empty trains (not troop transport trains on return trips, which were immediately needed in their intended capacity), the army supply and administration officers had to fix priorities with which all points had to comply. At times this process became so contentious that an army chief of staff or even a commander would have to step in.

Evacuation trains must have objectives that are clearly stipulated and are situated far away in the rear. Switching and unloading near the front blocks lines and stations, hindering the flow of all traffic, but most especially of critical troop transports and supplies.

Our front-line troops appeared consistently determined to use railroad bridges as long as possible during the withdrawals—especially those that were well constructed and required longer and more careful preparation for demolition or obstruction. As a result, important river bridges frequently fell undestroyed into Russian hands, becoming immediately available to their pursuit forces. The blame for this situation lay in the fact that even the panzer platoons covering the last withdrawals insisted on using these bridges, which necessarily delayed their demolition. In addition, such demolitions had to be specifically approved on a case-by-case basis by army headquarters before they could be executed.

Despite all our efforts, the system of track security, as organized, did not prove its worth, as the continually rising figures on partisan attacks and blockages testify. In retrospect, I believe that—in the vast Russian theater—organized and well-equipped security forces are a necessity.

That Soviet partisan activity never managed to have a decisive impact on operations was solely due to the untiring assistance rendered by all transport and railroad administration centers, consisting primarily of preliminary traffic arrangements (rerouting, group travel, slow speeds through dangerous stretches, daytime-only traffic, bulletproof vehicles, etc.) and an indispensable loyal, fighting spirit that infused all of our civilian and military personnel. This was particularly true in regard to our locomotive engineers, as well as the train and line servicemen.

PART 2

Tactical Aspects of Operation Citadel

Eyewitness Accounts by German Commanders

8

XXXV Corps, East of Orel

by Colonel General Lothar Rendulic
Commander, XXXV Corps

Editor's Introduction

When the Red Army opened Operation Kutuzov against the Orel salient
on 12 July 1943, the STAVKA aimed at nothing less than crashing into the
German front so rapidly that Second Panzer Army would be dismem-
bered before reserves could be pulled away from Ninth Army's assault
toward Kursk. With luck, Second Panzer Army's collapse would allow
the Western and Bryansk Fronts to roll up Ninth Army's left flank while
simultaneously penetrating its communications. The resulting hole torn
out of the middle of Army Group Center would then have opened the
possibility of immediate pursuit to the Dnepr River and even beyond.

Several factors combined to stall the Soviets short of their objectives.
First and foremost, von Kluge and Model recognized the enormity of the
threat immediately and took appropriate action. Army Group Center
handed over control of both armies to Model, by then recognized as the
German army's foremost specialist in positional defense. Model had already ordered preliminary work on phased defensive lines (in direct violation of orders from Hitler and OKH), and now he called off his attack
to the south and transferred half a dozen battered but still powerful divisions into the breakthrough sectors much faster than the Russians had
believed possible. At the same time, what had been an unfortunate decision for Operation Citadel—the transfer of significant Luftwaffe assets
from Army Group South to Army Group Center—ironically provided the
Germans in the Orel salient with a greater strength in combat aircraft
than they had possessed at the start of the offensive.

Even so, the Soviets' Eleventh Guards and Fourth Tank Armies tore
open the German lines northwest of Bolkhov and instantly created a situation wherein any other rupture in Second Panzer Army's front, no

matter how minor, would have proven fatal. Specifically, the Soviets concentrated 170,000 men, roughly 1,500 guns and mortars, and more than 350 armored fighting vehicles of the Third and Sixty-third Armies (with more than 700 AFVs [armored fighting vehicles] in reserve under the Third Tank Army) for an attack due west from Novosil toward Orel.[1]

The only obstacle between these armies and Orel was General of Infantry Lothar Rendulic's XXXV Corps, with four understrength infantry divisions, deploying fewer than 40,000 combat troops, fewer than 200 guns, and no tanks. In one of the classic defensive stands of the war, Rendulic correctly anticipated Soviet intentions, gambled on his enemy's lack of tactical flexibility, and concentrated nearly all of his defensive assets on the probable main axis of attack. Heavily outnumbered, his troops gave ground only grudgingly and managed to stave off a breakthrough for forty-eight hours—enough time for panzer divisions transferred from Ninth Army to roll in and seal off the penetration.

Rendulic wrote two accounts of this action, the initial narrative being embedded in U.S. Army Historical Program Manuscript P-079 ("The Russian Command in World War II; Possible Development Since World War II") and the second included in his memoirs.[2] Both accounts are generally accurate, for despite being a committed Nazi and a virulent anticommunist, Rendulic possessed a keen tactical mind and generally avoided the impulse to improve his own performance in hindsight. The first study, however, is useful because it was undertaken not specifically to concentrate on what the Germans did but to explain how they took advantage of Russian tactical predictability and operational rigidity. From a perspective more than fifty years later it is easy enough to dismiss Rendulic's racial-political theories about the intellectual capacity of the Russians, but the fact remains that even by mid-1943 German infantry divisions in their increasingly weakened condition could often frustrate Soviet intentions against huge odds.

XXXV Corps, East of Orel
by Colonel General Lothar Rendulic
Commander, XXXV Corps

The battle of Orel in July 1943 furnished an excellent example of the capabilities and limitations of Russian command at the army level. I was then commanding XXXV Corps, Second Panzer Army, which was located about fifty kilometers east of Orel. My four divisions had been deployed over the extraordinary distance of 140 kilometers. From north to south, the 34th Infantry Division covered thirty kilometers, the 56th Infantry Division forty kilometers, the 262nd Infantry Division thirty kilometers, and the 299th Infantry Division forty kilometers. No reserves could be made available at the corps, army, or army group levels. In order to create a tactical reserve, I risked the assumption that the Soviets would hardly attack along the entire front at once. I therefore ordered each division to prepare one infantry battalion and one light artillery battery to be put at the disposal of the corps.

The Russians facing us had six rifle divisions in the line and strong reserves in their rear. Starting in early July, they concentrated considerable forces in the Novosil area. We observed much of this buildup, but the complete picture emerged only during the actual battle. On 11 July the Soviets disposed over sixteen rifle divisions and one tank army (composed of three corps), further reinforced by an additional tank corps and six independent heavy tank brigades. A Russian tank corps at that time had 245 heavy tanks (T-34s and KV-1s), while a tank brigade controlled sixty tanks. In addition, the Russians had brought up a so-called motomechanized corps, which consisted of one tank and one motorized division. All together the enemy had concentrated 1,400 heavy tanks in the area. His artillery buildup consisted of more than 100 new batteries, and radio intercepts indicated that the Soviet main-effort attack was to be directed against the 431st Infantry Regiment on the left wing of Lieutenant General Friedrich Karst's 262nd Infantry Division. If the Russians succeeded in breaking through there, they would find the terrain quite favorable for the mass employment of their tanks. It became evident on the first day of the battle that the Soviet main effort had come exactly in the area in which we had anticipated it.

The defensive positions of the 431st Infantry Regiment (and almost the entire corps front) ran behind a thirty-meter-wide stream. The river had cut deeply into the terrain, making it impossible for tanks to ford it. The regimental position was ten kilometers wide and consisted of a continuous trench. A second trench, as yet incomplete, ran 150–200 meters behind the first. Strongpoints for heavy machine guns, mortars, and heavy antitank guns had been echeloned in depth. Artillery positions had also been built up into strongpoints. One or two belts of barbed wire entanglements had been strung in front of the position. The strongpoints were protected by barbed wire, while minefields had been laid in front of, and between, the wire obstacles.

I formed a defensive main effort opposite the Russian attack main effort. This was only possible by stripping other positions of most of their personnel, leaving behind a skeleton defense force. Our main effort consisted of six battalions, with two battalions in line and four battalions in reserve; one battalion belonged to the 262nd Infantry Division reserve.

Our artillery strength was eighteen field batteries and twenty-six anti-tank guns. These units constituted only a minor force compared to that possessed by the Soviets, but they represented all that could be mustered. The great danger existed that the rest of the front had been left so weak that it could not even have resisted even small-scale operations. I had to take this calculated risk, however, if the enemy was to be engaged at all in the main-effort zone. Had the Russians acted in accordance with our tactical and operational principles, they would have advanced with their infantry spearheaded by their tanks toward Orel after overrunning our main defenses. The Red Army would have reached Orel that very night, because it would have encountered only our supply troops. On the basis of my previous experiences, I knew that the Russians were more likely to act methodically and often did not make decisions involving long-range objectives. On the other hand, one could never be sure that the experience of previous battles would still hold true.

In the early morning hours of 12 July the Russians laid down a heavy barrage from more than 100 batteries on the positions of the 431st Infantry Regiment. Despite the great tension, a certain calm prevailed because the estimate of the Soviet main effort had been substantiated. Five rifle divisions launched an attack against the regiment. After heroic fighting, the first trench was lost at noon. Russian infantry, however, did not continue their advance, and the regiment established itself in the second line of resistance; General Karst committed his reserve battalion. As soon as the attack had begun, the Russians started to construct numerous bridges across the stream, taking advantage of the fact that the river was not subject to observation from our positions. Whenever possible, however, our batteries fired on the stream. Because the Russians were very densely concentrated, even area fire by our artillery inflicted heavy casualties.

In the afternoon 200 tanks rolled over our second line of resistance and advanced into the interior, where they were engaged by our antitank guns and a number of artillery batteries. The tanks overran several antitank gun positions. Three tanks attempted to destroy one of our batteries, but two of them ran over mines in the barbed-wire entanglements and exploded. From then on, Russian tanks no loner tried to overrun batteries protected by wire obstacles. We destroyed sixty tanks during this engagement. Two hours later the surviving tanks withdrew behind their infantry. Captured officers disclosed the fact that the tanks had the mission of eliminating the antitank guns in our rear.

The Soviet infantry had also resumed its attack in conjunction with the tank attack. Due to the close quarters of the battle, our artillery concentrated on the enemy reserves. An unparalleled battle developed, with the result that most of the position was finally held due to the timely commitment of a reserve battalion. Individual strongpoints were established opposite lost positions. I rejected the idea of launching a counterattack with the two battalions still available because offensive action could not be justified in this situation. Even if enemy superiority had not been so tremendous, the day would have been considered a great success. Nonetheless, everyone remained concerned about the next day.

The battle resumed on 13 July. Russian artillery could not fire on the German forward trench because it was too close to its own infantry positions. By the same token, our own artillery had to remain idle against the Russian forward positions. On the other hand, German artillery fired with devastating effect on the enemy reserves. Five rifle divisions again attacked the 431st Infantry Regiment. Due to the fire of our infantry and heavy weapons, the Russians proved unable to leave their trenches for some time, or could only do so in small groups, but shortly thereafter about 100 tanks overran the German position. Some of these tanks participated in the battle for our forward position and gained local successes because the *Panzerfaust* [antitank rockets; German equivalent of the bazooka] was not yet available to our infantry. Heavy antitank guns in our rear were effective against Russian armor but could only fire when not under attack themselves. Thus the enemy tanks managed to contribute to the loss of several sections of the trench. The most threatened areas were protected by committing one of the two remaining reserve battalions. At noon the Russian tanks again withdrew behind their infantry after having destroyed some heavy antitank guns, one artillery battery, and several machine-gun nests at the cost to themselves of twenty tanks. In the afternoon the Soviets launched an isolated attack with about fifty tanks, deep into the right wing of our defense line. They lost another twenty tanks within a short time, raising their losses for the day to forty machines. Although our infantry positions had been reinforced in a makeshift manner by weak strongpoints, the Russians failed to penetrate them.

The first support elements arrived in the corps area in the later afternoon and consisted of two assault gun battalions with a total of thirty StG III assault guns and one antitank company containing eight 75mm self-propelled antitank guns. These units arrived directly from the fighting near Kursk. They had lost many guns but were experienced in armored warfare. Despite their great weight, the StG IIIs were very maneuverable and well-suited for antitank defense. The self-propelled antitank guns were of different and smaller construction. They also mounted a 75mm gun, but their weight was not as effectively balanced, which made them less maneuverable.

On 14 July the battle resumed with greater intensity. Eight rifle divisions and one tank corps with about 250 tanks attacked in the same sector. Both sides' artillery was again unable to fire on the front lines because the fighting was too close. German artillery once again concentrated its fire against Soviet reserves. Russian tanks launched repeated and strong thrusts against our position but failed to break through. The antitank guns, as well as the StG IIIs and the self-propelled antitank guns, waged a furious defensive battle. Considerable portions of the front line were nonetheless lost during the day. However, a number of new strongpoints were created by committing the last reserve battalion. The line held, and the Russian infantry did not achieve a breakthrough. A total of 120 Soviet tanks were destroyed that day. Even so, it was doubtful that we would be able to withstand renewed large-scale attacks on the following day. Reserves were no longer available. Reinforcement by an infantry division and more assault guns had been promised by army headquarters, but they could not be expected to arrive in the XXXV Corps area before the afternoon of 15 July.

On the following day, 15 July, the Russians failed to attack.

On 16 July the Soviets resumed the attack in the same area, but we had committed Lieutenant General Hans Gollnick's newly arrived 36th Infantry Division there. During the morning the Russian attacks were also directed against the southern regiment of the 262nd Infantry Division. This regiment held a front of ten kilometers and was pushed back about two kilometers. The Russians merely followed up with patrols and did not exploit their gains. Of 300 tanks the enemy committed to his main attack, more than 150 were destroyed. In the afternoon, the Russians extended their attack against elements of Major General Albert Newiger's 52nd Infantry Division north of our main defenses and gained some ground. Major General Sebastian Fichtner's 8th Panzer Division, which had just arrived from the fighting at Kursk, was committed there, even though its panzergrenadier regiments were understrength and the unit had only eight tanks remaining to it.

On 17 July the Russians attacked with ten rifle divisions and 400 tanks. The 36th Infantry Division was driven back a few kilometers, but the continuity of the front maintained. Two hundred enemy tanks were destroyed. Fifty tanks broke through Lieutenant General Otto Lüdecke's 56th Infantry Division and halted fifteen kilometers behind the front. They remained in that area all night and were finally destroyed by thirty StG III assault guns.

Lieutenant General Friedrich Höchbaum's 34th Infantry Division on our extreme left wing had to be withdrawn during the day because the adjacent LIII Corps lost Bolkhov. This also made the withdrawal of the left wing of the 56th Infantry Division necessary. Only weak Russian elements pursued the retiring divisions while the enemy renewed his attack in the main effort area. Here [the enemy] committed 600 tanks—the largest number thus far employed—but our positions still held. Roughly 300 tanks were destroyed during the day, a total that included the fifty tanks accounted for by the 56th Infantry Division.

In the meantime, Lieutenant General Vollrath Lubbe's 2nd and Major General Erpo Freiherr von Bodenhausen's 12th Panzer Divisions also arrived from the fighting at Kursk. These divisions had been considerably battered and had only forty tanks between them, half of which were in no condition to be committed.

On 18 July the Russians attacked along the entire XXXV Corps front and forced us to withdraw at various points. The enemy still could not achieve a breakthrough.

Major engagements continued until 21 July, after which the Russians launched only small-scale attacks. The Soviets in our front were exhausted; they had lost 900 of 1,400 tanks.

This narrative has been written on the basis of sketchy notes and from memory. The description possibly differs from the actual facts with regard to the sequence of certain events; its essence, however, especially where it concerns the characteristics of the Russian command, is absolutely correct. The Russian command and the lack of initiative of enemy infantry and tanks were responsible for the Russian defeat. My opponent in this battle was Marshal Konstantin K. Rokossovski, who now commands the Polish Army.

APPENDIX 8A

Order of Battle: XXXV Corps, 12 July 1943

General of Infantry Lothar Dr. Rendulic

34th Infantry Division

Lieutenant General Friedrich Hochbaum

> Grenadier Regiments 80, 107, 253
> Artillery Regiment 34
> Reconnaissance Battalion 34
> Panzerjaeger Battalion 34
> Engineer Battalion 34

Attached:

> Artillery Battalion I/70

Total Field Artillery (105mm or larger): 49 guns

56th Infantry Division

Major General Otto Luedecke

> Grenadier Regiments 171, 192, 234
> Artillery Regiment 156
> Reconnaissance Battalion 156
> Panzerjaeger Battalion 156
> Engineer Battalion 156
> *Ost* Guard Company 156

Total Field Artillery (105mm or larger): 38 guns

262nd Infantry Division

Lieutenant General Friedrich Karst

> Grenadier Regiments 467, 487, 497
> Artillery Regiment 267
> Reconnaissance Battalion 267
> Panzerjaeger Battalion 267
> Engineer Battalion 267

Total Field Artillery (105mm or larger): 43 guns

299th Infantry Division
Major General Ralph Graf von Oriola

Grenadier Regiments 528, 529, 530
Artillery Regiment 299
Reconnaissance Battalion 299
Panzerjaeger Battalion 299
Engineer Battalion 299
1./Ost Cavalry Squadron 299

Total Field Artillery (105mm or larger): 37 guns

Artillery Commander 136

Artillery Batteries 1./635, 3./817
Artillery Battalions II/69, 422

Total Field Artillery (105mm or larger): 29 guns
Panzerjaeger Battalion 290

9

XX Corps in Defensive Fighting, August–October 1943

by General of Artillery Rudolf Freiherr von Roman
Commander, XX Corps

Editor's Introduction

Rudolf Freiherr von Roman's manuscript fits in no particular place within the general scheme of the U.S. Army Historical Program. The narrative does not appear to have been commissioned either as part of a larger general study or as an adjunct to one. Neither did the officers editing the various publications on Russian front tactics during the 1950s mine it for illustrative situations. The study therefore sits isolated as one of the few corps-level accounts of extended infantry fighting against the Red Army. As such it would have tremendous apparent value, if it were not marred by several complicating problems.

The draft translation of the work was poor, even by the U.S. Army's somewhat lax standards. Sentences—even entire paragraphs—become too convoluted even to understand in a literal sense. Much of this awkwardness, however, should be attributed to the original author, who wrote casually and without notes, adding suddenly remembered interjections about events already covered into the middle of paragraphs concerning something else entirely. General Roman's internal chronology, grasp of geography, and accuracy in terms of place names are all poor, and the young officers assigned to deal with the manuscript made no attempt to improve them. All in all, this study of XX Corps operations following the evacuation of the Orel salient represents a daunting challenge to the translator and editor who would attempt to prepare it for publication.

Yet ultimately Roman's narrative repays the labor necessary to present it. The underlying challenge of corps command is that Roman could never assume, from day to day, to which section of the front he might find himself assigned and what divisions he would have available for the task. The reader is given the opportunity to peer over the shoulder of an officer and his staff as they repeatedly solve difficult tactical problems. Considerable detail on German infantry doctrine also emerges, as well as the methodology of blunting enemy attacks, launching tactical counterpunches, and sealing off penetrations before they evolved into breakthroughs.

Roman candidly admits that as exhaustion set in and morale declined so, too, did the combat value of his infantry regiments diminish. With a lack of perspective that is none too unusual, the author fails to make the connection that the only reason why the Red Army never managed to rupture his lines completely is that the Soviet units opposite his divisions were almost as exhausted and depleted. Instead, as was the usual practice among German officers, he pictured an ever thinner gray line of troops warding off endless human waves of Russian infantry and tanks.

Roman himself is an interesting case study, representative of the anonymous majority of German field commanders whose competence (albeit not brilliance) kept their divisions from disintegrating in the long retreat from the interior of the Soviet Union. A Bavarian born in 1893, Roman began World War II as a colonel commanding Artillery Regiment 10 and then 17 before advancing to become Arko (Artillery Commander) 3. He took command of the 35th Infantry outside Moscow in December 1941, just as the Soviet counteroffensive opened. Having already established something of a reputation for battlefield leadership, von Roman won the Knight's Cross on 19 February 1942. Then he was appointed commander of XX Corps, a position he held until the end of the war. For the period covered in this chapter, von Roman received the Oak Leaves to his Knight's Cross on 28 October, though one would never guess it from his laconic presentation.[1]

XX Corps in Defensive Fighting, August–October 1943
by General of Artillery Rudolf Freiherr von Roman
Commander, XX Corps

Fighting During the Summer of 1943, April–August

At the beginning of April XX Corps headquarters assumed command over the divisions that had checked the Red Army's drive westward from Kursk near Sevsk. The corps front began—roughly—at Pogreby (south of Sevsk), ran along the eastern edge of Sevsk, crossed the Sevsk River at

Krivtsovo, and extended northeast across the Lokot-Dmitriev railroad near Cheblovo toward the area southeast of Dmitrovsk. General of Infantry Erich Straube's XIII Corps stood on our right, General of Infantry Hans Zorn's XLVI Panzer Corps on our left. From spring to summer the following divisions were committed in this sector: 251st, 137th, 45th, and 72nd Infantry Divisions.

Operation Citadel began on 6 July. The objective of the operation was to launch simultaneous attacks from the north and south in order to cut off and destroy the strong Red Army forces in the Kursk salient, which protruded as far west as Sevsk. One assault force (Ninth Army) was to advance from Orel, the other (Fourth Panzer Army and *Armeeabteilung Kempf*) from Kharkov. Due to the superiority of the Soviet forces, the attack—which at first progressed according to plan—soon slowed down and finally ground to a halt before the pincers could meet. Almost immediately, the Russians launched a well-prepared counteroffensive, which began to gain ground in mid-July. They proved powerful enough to push back our front line south of Orel and push toward the northwest. Eventually the order was given to abandon Orel. As the Soviets continued to attack, XX Corps lost direct contact with XLVI Panzer Corps on the left and even the left wing of our own 72nd Infantry Division. In order to assure a functioning line of communications and chain of command, Colonel General Walter Model (commanding Ninth Army) decided to attach the 72nd Infantry to the XLVI Panzer Corps.

The situation on 20 August therefore stood as follows: We had known for some time that XX Corps would soon be drawn into the fighting. Russian preparations along the corps front indicated an impending attack. Our reconnaissance patrols and prisoner interrogations had identified new enemy units entering the area. Luftwaffe reconnaissance confirmed the massing of Soviet artillery batteries in the Sevsk salient, with the majority of the guns facing west, northwest, and north. Both aerial and ground reconnaissance established the passage of large motor convoys along the roads leading from Dmitriev to the front. Presumably, these convoys transported troops and ammunition.

I ordered the corps to take every possible defensive measure, including the following:

1: Defensive positions were to be improved by all available means. Well-protected dugouts and foxholes that were recessed into the trench walls would give adequate protection against the expected artillery preparation.

2: In order to facilitate the elimination of enemy penetrations and the launching of prompt counterattacks, I ordered construction of switch lines and chord positions throughout the depth of the corps sector. By the time the attack opened, we had completed (or had almost done so) a second line of defensive and antitank positions behind the front line.

3: Our reserves had not only been designated and prelocated but also thoroughly familiarized with their future mission.

4: Artillery units registered for both concentrations and barrage fires and prepared to fire concentrations of any type upon demand. A network of observers, many of them forward with the first lines of the infantry, guaranteed observation of the battlefield and the ability to direct appropriate defensive fires accurately. Alternate firing positions had been reconnoitered; they could be rapidly occupied, with the batteries prepared to open fire on the most important targets almost immediately. We designated a number of batteries in each division sector as roving batteries; these had to be able to change position in the briefest possible time and move to any threatened sector in the corps area.

5: I ordered our antitank defenses to be thoroughly tested, and commanders of assault gun batteries had to reconnoiter possible avenues of commitment. So that assault guns and tanks could move freely behind the main battle line, our engineers reinforced bridges and repaired roads.

6: My corps headquarters, which had been stationed in Radogoshchi since May, moved to Sharovo in order to be closer to the front and because Sharovo was located more favorably with regard to communications. From there XX Corps could more effectively direct the defensive battle against the expected Russian threat to the Sevsk sector. At the same time, Army Group Center transferred XX Corps from General Model's Ninth Army to General of Infantry Walter Weiss's Second Army. General Weiss, recognizing the seriousness of the tactical situation, reassigned the 86th Infantry Division to XX Corps. I decided to commit this division between the 251st and 137th Infantry Divisions in order to reduce considerably the lines held by those units.

With four divisions now in line, we awaited the opening of the Soviet attack.

The Russians opened their attack on 26 August with an artillery preparation along the entire length of XX Corps's front, concentrating particularly on Major General Maximilian Felzmann's 251st and Lieutenant General Helmuth Weidling's 86th Infantry Divisions. We quickly established that the enemy attacks against Major General Freiherr Hans von Falkenstein's 45th and Lieutenant General Hans Kamecke's 137th Infantry Division were weak and only intended to be containing attacks. These diversionary attacks our troops repelled, but heavy fighting—lasting several days—developed along the fronts of the 251st and 86th Infantry Divisions. Red Army infantry and artillery forces in these attacks outnumbered our own by at least three to one and sometimes five to one. In seesaw battles, the Soviets penetrated the lines of the 251st Infantry Division on both sides of Sevsk, often supported by tanks and fighter aircraft. Northwest of the town, enemy forces broke through on a narrow sector on an axis directed toward Seredina Buda (about twenty kilometers to the west), driving to a point halfway between the two towns. South of Sevsk, especially in the densely wooded area on the boundary between XX and XIII Corps, the situation was completely obscured. We remained unsure precisely how far the Soviets had managed to penetrate our lines there. General Weiss ordered Lieutenant General Fritz-Georg von Rappard's 7th Infantry Division up to support our lines, but this did not materially improve matters. The 7th Infantry had been so greatly exhausted in earlier fighting west of Dmitriev that it could not be committed as a whole. Instead, General von Rappard found himself forced to throw his battalions into the fight piecemeal as each arrived.[2] The operation was unsuccessful.

On 27 August the Russians mounted as many as twenty-five attacks (ranging from battalion to division strength) against the left wing of the 251st Infantry Division northwest of the Sevsk River and also the right flank of the 86th Infantry Division. We repulsed all these attacks, inflicting heavy Soviet losses. That this could be accomplished was due greatly to the timely but unexpected arrival of Lieutenant General Sebastian Fichtner's 8th Panzer Division, which prevented a Russian breakthrough in the Novo Yamskoye area (on the boundary between the 251st and 86th Infantry Divisions).

Unfortunately, the situation southwest of Sevsk in the wooded area had reached such a critical point that on 28 August General Weiss ordered the 8th Panzer Division pulled out of the Novo Yamskoye area and transferred to the threatened sector. Thus in the wake of a successful counterattack, lead elements of the division departed immediately, with the main body following on 29 August. Second Army intended to replace the 8th Panzer at Novo Yamskoye with Lieutenant General Horst Grossmann's 6th Infantry Division from army group reserves, but as the main body of the panzer troops withdrew, only motorized elements of the 6th Engineer Battalion and other components of the division's advance detachment had arrived. This weak force proved unable to prevent the Russians from gaining additional ground near and southwest of Novo-Yamskoye before the motor columns transporting the main body of the 6th Infantry Division arrived later on 29 August. Again, individual regiments and battalions had to be committed to fierce fighting immediately upon their arrival. Despite this handicap, the 6th and 86th Infantry Divisions between them managed to hold our second line of defenses, running from the southern edge of Novo-Yamskoye via Shvestshikovy along the road to Glebovo.

General Weiss, in the meantime, redefined the boundary between the XX and XIII Corps, dividing responsibility along the line of the Sevsk River. General Felzmann's 251st Infantry Division, having been committed south of the Sevsk, became assigned to XIII Corps. Elements of the division still north of the river received orders to rejoin the main body.

Our supply situation by this point had grown very tense due to the fact that XX Corps's main supply road (which ran south-southwest from Lokot) had been temporarily commandeered for use by the 4th and 12th Panzer Divisions. Field Marshal Gunther von Kluge, commanding Army Group Center, had ordered these two divisions transferred from Ninth Army to Second Army in order to alleviate the critical situation southwest of Sevsk. Only that supply road had the capacity for the swift transfer of two panzer divisions, and a heavy rainstorm on the evening of 29 August rendered even it impassable in many places. Many of the rivers and marshes in the area flooded, and on potential bypass routes few of the bridges had been reinforced to make them capable of supporting tanks. The unfavorable effect of this situation on XX Corps supply was exacerbated by the fact that our main supply base had been located a full forty-five kilometers behind the front for reasons of traffic control. This was simply too great a distance for horsedrawn columns to keep our divisions in supply. This experience clearly demonstrates that every possible effort must be made to reinforce bridges and establish forward supply bases, regardless of the difficulties inherent in such operations.

Further complicating our situation, we received orders on 31 August that General Weidling's 86th Infantry Division was to be relieved the following evening for service elsewhere. The division's sector would be covered by extending the lines of the 6th and 137th Infantry Divisions. This extension was particularly unwelcome because the 86th Infantry Division had been opposed by at least six Soviet rifle divisions, which had received up to 2,000 fresh replacements during the past few days. Admittedly the Russian replacements consisted mostly of young men between seventeen and nineteen years old or older men from forty-five to fifty, but the influx of numbers brought the enemy divisions back up to the strength necessary to resume the attack. This opinion would be confirmed by the continuous heavy fighting that developed in this sector.

Withdrawal to the Desna River, 1–17 September

I also learned on 31 August of Field Marshal von Kluge's intention to withdraw the front behind the Desna River. This decision had been prompted by the fact that the Russian breakthrough south of Sevsk had achieved a penetration of forty to sixty kilometers. Red Army units had already begun to turn north, with the obvious intent of cutting off all German divisions east of the Desna, a development that rendered such a retirement even more imperative. As an initial precaution, all available motorized and horsedrawn supply trains received immediate orders to proceed westward. These elements reached the western banks of the Desna only after a three-day march. Simultaneously with this movement of the support troops, I ordered the organization of a corps reconnaissance party and dispatched it into the Desna area. This group had as its mission the reconnaissance of a new main battle line, planning of sector assignments, guiding troop and supply units upon their arrival to the appropriate sectors, and the immediate employment of all available service troops for the construction of defensive positions.

Heavy fighting continued on 1 September as the 6th and 137th Infantry Divisions relieved the 86th Infantry Division. Only their courageous efforts and unbroken will allowed them to repel a numerically superior enemy and hold their positions. Meanwhile the 45th Infantry Division sector remained quiet, except for several reconnaissance patrols.

Withdrawal behind the Desna began during the night of 1–2 September, caused primarily by the actions of Colonel Wilhelm Ochsner's 31st Infantry Division. This division, which belonged to XIII Corps and was stationed on the immediate right of the 251st Infantry Division, had been forced to fall back due to the depth of the Russian penetration. This movement exposed the right wing of XX Corps, and, having lost signal communications with Second Army headquarters, I decided to order a general withdrawal of the front at 2300 hours. This retirement of six to eight kilometers along the entire corps front represented an almost insoluble problem. Nevertheless our troops successfully disengaged from enemy contact (albeit under extremely heavy pressure on our left) and managed to establish the new position in the morning of 2 September.

During the following days, XX Corps continued a systematic withdrawal behind the Desna, again hampered by the lack of reinforced bridges across the Sevsk River. The few existing crossing sites became rapidly overcrowded with our own troops and trains, as well as units of other divisions (most notably the 86th Infantry Divisions, which had also been withdrawn). Horrendous traffic jams resulted, and the difficulties only increased when virtually the entire corps had to be routed directly through Seredina Buda due to Soviet penetrations and poor road conditions. From that bottleneck several routes of march existed, though the roads that traversed the southern part of the Bryansk forest proved inadequate for large-scale troop movements. Within the woods, partisans had prepared many roadblocks, which could be eliminated only by fighting and driving off each band, one by one.

At the beginning of the withdrawal, we released the 45th Infantry Division to the XLVI Panzer Corps on our right. This obliged General von Falkenstein's regiments to work their way through the northern part of the Bryansk forest under the direction of its new headquarters. At the same time, due to shifting divisional sectors in XIII Corps to our right, XX Corps received Major General Otto Hitzfeld's 102nd Infantry Division. This division experienced some critical moments attempting to disengage but successfully navigated the Seredina Buda bottleneck and continued its march to the Desna. The 102nd Infantry Division's route of march followed the Seredina Buda-Chernatskoye-Urakovo-Rogovka highway, the Chernatskoye–Lesnoye–Snop Trubchevskaya–Unitsi–Vitemlya road, and the Seredina Buda–Novaya Guda–Staraya Guta–Ulitsa–Unichi–Vitemlya road. Repeatedly our rear-guard elements prepared and held delaying positions to retard the enemy's pursuit. XX Corps crossed the Desna over the highway bridge at Rogovka (102nd Infantry) and the railroad bridge near Vitemlya (6th and 137th Infantry, plus all corps troops).

The corps and divisional reconnaissance parties previously dispatched to the new position had not been idle. The new main battle line had been fully reconnoitered and a continuous trench with machine-gun pits and chord positions constructed by the service troops. A series of artillery observation posts had also been completed. All obstacles which might have interfered with our crossing of the Desna had been eliminated. In these efforts the cooperation of Organization Todt had proven extraordinarily valuable. Thus in the early morning hours of 6 September one unit after another proceeded across the Desna bridges, the flow of troops and vehicles regulated by a strict traffic-control system in which all control points had been connected by telephone. The assistance provided by this system was particularly critical at the Vitemlya bridge, where two divisions and all corps troops had to cross. By the morning of 7 September the last of our troops marched across the bridges. Our engineers blew up the Vitemlya bridge at noon. Shortly thereafter, the Russians appeared on the eastern bank of the river and began to shell our work details.

In the meantime, our divisions and regiments had occupied their assigned sectors. A sufficient number of construction troops were available to continue improving the defensive positions. XX Corps sector covered a front approximately sixty kilometers wide, extending from Leskonogi (about fifteen kilometers north of Novogord Severski), via Rogovka-Kamenskaya Sloboda-Vitemlya, to Sagutyevo. General Hitzfeld's 102nd Infantry Division occupied the right flank, General Kamecke's 137th Infantry Division the center, and General Grossmann's 6th Infantry

Division the left flank. Unfortunately, the combat strength of these divisions had been greatly diminished during the fighting around Sevsk and the withdrawal; our infantry battalions fielded only about forty-five to seventy men each. Considering the width of the corps sector, double sentries in three shifts had to be posted every 250 meters.

Given how widely we had to disperse our troops, it came as no surprise that a group of thirty Russians successfully crossed the river in the sector of the 37th Grenadier Regiment (6th Infantry Division) on the very same day XX Corps took up its new position. The main reason for this immediate enemy crossing, however, lay not so much in our weakness but in the nature of the river itself. The Desna had many bends and arms and frequently flowed through marshy terrain that could not be incorporated into the main battle line. To create a continuous defensive position, therefore, required chord positions—often at some distance from the river—to be prepared. This shortening of the main battle line also had the secondary objective of concentrating our depleted combat strength. Inevitably, however, this meant that the river lost much of its value as a defensive obstacle. On the contrary, due to the dense growth on the riverbanks, the Soviets might well have enjoyed the tactical advantage because they could approach very close to our positions without being detected. Such a condition meant that the construction of positions behind the main battle line had to begin immediately, and it was here that the presence of construction troops proved especially invaluable.

In the meantime the Russians moved up to the Desna along our entire front and began conducting raids across the river against all three divisions. Once the Soviets had gained a foothold on the western bank of the river, successful counterattacks against the penetration from both flanks found themselves hampered by accurate fire from well-camouflaged machine guns and snipers on the opposite bank. By 13 September the Red Army had succeeded in establishing several small infantry bridgeheads on the western bank of the river. In some places Russian engineers had begun to build bridges. Lacking the strength to eliminate these bridgeheads, our divisions withdrew—first to the chord positions, and then to the second defensive line along the heights west of the Desna. Soviet reinforcements and the appearance of considerable artillery suggested that the main enemy attack would be made against the 102nd Infantry Division; I ordered corps headquarters moved to Kostobobr in order to cope with this situation. A breakthrough in this sector would have been fatal to the adjoining Ninth Army, which still had its divisions echeloned well forward of the river. Realizing that no reserves were available, I issued orders to make the conduct of the battle more flexible, the first of which was to send trains and noncombat units to the rear.

The next several days constituted a crisis for the right wing of Second Army, especially in light of developments in the sector of Army Group South. As part of their breakthrough operation from Konotop to Kiev, the Russians now attacked toward Chernigov. This movement left the deep right flank of Second Army open as far as the Dnepr River. Worse still, the Red Army managed to occupy a wide sector of the Desna bank near and southwest of Novgorod Severski, where it continued to gain ground toward the west. These changes meant that the withdrawal of Second Army's left and center wings behind the Sozh River, and of the right wing behind the Dnepr, had become unavoidable.

Withdrawal to the Dnepr, 17 September–15 October

XX Corps began its withdrawal during the night of 17–18 September. The critical situation on Second Army's right flank (the Russian penetrations referred to above) necessitated an oblique withdrawal. Our right wing had to pull back rapidly, but the left wing had to be withdrawn more slowly, so that Second Army would not lose contact with the divisions of Ninth Army, which were still echeloned far to the front. These two competing requirements temporarily stretched our front from sixty kilometers to nearly 100 kilometers, running from northeast to southwest. Our difficulties increased when General Weiss decided to take the 137th Infantry Division away from XX Corps and transfer it to the far right wing of Second Army to act as a flank protection reserve, leaving the entire defensive burden to the weakened 6th and 102nd Infantry Divisions. Not only had we been left with an inadequate number of troops to man an extended line, but the oblique nature of the front created great difficulties in retiring from one line to the next. That XX Corps nevertheless conducted this withdrawal successfully owed much to the fact that the Russians desisted from any large-scale attacks, though they did pursue us closely.

The complexity of the operation created a great strain on the workload of staffs at all levels and required the complete devotion of the troops. In order to prevent the Russians from following our withdrawal too rapidly, their progress had to be arrested at successive holding positions. Each of these positions had to be reconnoitered, first occupied by advance detachments, and then by the main body of our rear guards. Support from artillery and other heavy weapons had to be coordinated at each line while the engineers constructed obstacles to hinder the enemy's pursuit. For the troops this period represented a series of night marches and frantic efforts to prepare new defensive positions. Continued fair weather favored our withdrawal, but conversely we soon discovered the entire area to be infested with partisans. These bands mined roads and conducted ambushes, making it necessary to take increased security measures.

By 19 September it became clear that the pace of the withdrawal would have to be accelerated. In the south the Russians had seized Chernigov and thrust northwest from the city. Our intermediate positions, therefore, could not be held for more than twenty-four hours. Our advance detachments reconnoitering and preparing the Sozh River position found themselves forced to work under severe time constraints but nonetheless could be counted upon to complete their missions.

XX Corps once again occupied a straight-line defensive position on both sides of Semenovka on 20 September; corps headquarters was established at Chelhov. The 102nd Infantry Division held the right wing, a *regimentsgruppe* of the 137th Infantry Division (which we had found it impossible to relieve when the main body of the division had been transferred) occupied the center, and the 6th Infantry Division was posted on the left. General Hitzfeld personally directed the repulse of a Russian attack on Semenovka that morning. In the afternoon, however, the Soviets advanced south and southwest of the city, penetrating our main battle line and exerting heavy pressure on our right wing and deep flank. This created a particularly dangerous situation because the LVI Panzer Corps on our right flank had already withdrawn in the face of heavy pressure from the Russian drive out of Chernigov. At 1500 hours I decided to withdraw our right wing to a new defensive line at the Snov River while extending the 6th Infantry Division's left wing to make contact with the 45th Infantry Division of the adjoining XXXV Corps (this was considered necessary to hold the Semenovka line). Marching at top speed, our troops reached the Semenovka line on 20 September but did not manage to cross the Snov that day. The withdrawal of the right wing over the Snov during the night of 20–21 September allowed the relief and release of the *regimentsgruppe* of the 137th Infantry Division, even though the Russians closely pursued the 102nd Infantry Division as it pulled back. Even under these conditions, however, our troops successfully occupied the new main battle line.

Fuel and ammunition had meanwhile become dangerously scarce. This supply crisis stemmed from the disruption of the railroad lines by partisans, especially in the Gomel area. Contributing to this problem also was the chronic shortage of bridging equipment. Only one bridge across the Dnepr between Kiev and Gomel had been completed. Because of the absolute necessity of gaining time for additional bridge construction, General Weiss ordered that the Snov positions would be held as long as possible.

The seven Soviet rifle divisions we had identified opposite XX Corps attacked on 22 September. After heavy fighting in the 102nd Infantry Division sector, General Hitzfeld managed to seal off an enemy penetration in the vicinity of Uborki and Kamenskiy. Troops from General Grossmann's 6th Infantry Division, as well as the 133rd Grenadier Regiment of the 45th Infantry Division (attached to XX Corps for this purpose), had to be committed in order to master the situation. By nightfall a breakthrough had been averted, and despite heavy fighting and determined Russian pursuit all units of XX Corps had successfully withdrawn behind the Snov. Even as this occurred, however, the Soviets launched another attack from Kamenskiy, pushing weak delaying forces of the 102nd Infantry Division beyond Solovyevka. Only a resolute counterattack by a battalion of the 58th Grenadier Regiment of the 6th Infantry Division managed to eject the Russians from the village. During the night all elements of the corps extended to make direct contact with units on their left and right flanks; by the morning of 23 September a continuous—if dangerously thin—line had been established.

The main body of General von Falkenstein's 45th Infantry Division arrived in the Novo-Ropski assembly area during the night of 22–23 September, its men and horses completely exhausted by a ninety-kilometer forced march. That this division was in no condition to be committed until the following night placed extra pressure on the weary soldiers at the front to hold their lines.

In the rainy morning of 23 September, the Russians seized Malinovka in the 6th Infantry Division area. General Grossmann frustrated the Soviet intention to use this penetration as the springboard to cut off XX Corps's left wing and roll up the flank of General of Infantry Friedrich Wiese's XXXV Corps to the north. His prompt counterattack, supported by assault guns, recovered the village. Simultaneously, however, the Soviets hit the 102nd Infantry Division on the extreme right flank of the corps position at Gorsk. This attack, coordinated with the partisans operating in the area, succeeded in encircling several companies. Breaking out of the trap through the dense woods cost these companies heavy casualties and forced the abandonment of their heavy weapons, but General Hitzfeld's ensuing counterattack recaptured the village.

During the afternoon the northern units on the left wing of the LVI Panzer Corps (Lieutenant General Dietrich von Saucken's 4th Panzer Division and Colonel Ochsner's 31st Infantry Division) received orders assigning them to XX Corps. Lieutenant General Friedrich Hossbach's LVI Panzer Corps had been relieved of its front-line sector and sent to the rear with the task of preparing the defensive line along the Dnepr River.

During the night of 23–24 September XX Corps withdrew behind the Tribush River and on the following night fell back to a main battle line extending from Andreyevka via Usoj to Lenino and Asarichi. The retreat continued on 26 September to an expanded bridgehead position east of the Sozh River, which ran approximately from Glinyanka via Dobryanka to Grabovka and Teryusha. Seventy-two hours of continuous withdrawals demanded great marching efforts from the soldiers of XX Corps, especially from the divisions on the left wing. Moreover, time worked against us, because the Russians to the south had already breached the Dnepr in unknown strength along the Chernigov-Chernobye highway. This development meant that in order to hold the Sozh River line—the so-called Panther position—we would have to drive the enemy from the Dnepr's western bank.

We learned from the statements of prisoners of war that the Red Army had suffered heavy casualties in the fighting along the Desna. The fact that during the past several days they had pursued the left and center of the corps without launching any major attacks tended to confirm this view. Along the right wing, however, the 4th Panzer Division became embroiled in some heavy fighting with partisan bands, during which the Soviets made several penetrations of the front. General von Saucken's division sealed off these penetrations with immediate counterattacks, capturing many prisoners and considerable amounts of equipment in the process.

The Sozh River bridge at Sharpilovka, which had in the meantime been completed by the engineers, was designated on 25 September as the corps crossing site. All division trains, supply columns, and noncombat elements that could be spared crossed the river immediately. We were also authorized to use the Gomel highway, east of the Sozh, and the bridge at Gomel in order to relieve traffic over the Sharpilovka bridge. Numerous motor vehicles of all XX Corps divisions used this bridge, as well as most units of the 6th Infantry Division that were not needed at the Dobryank bridgehead position.

During 26 September the Russians remained inactive. During the night of 26–27 September, however, the situation demanded a withdrawal to the second bridgehead position, which formed a semicircle around the bridge over the Kravtsovka. I ordered corps headquarters to be relocated to Sharpilovka, where it remained.

On 27 September our columns continued crossing the Sharpilovka bridge without interruption and according to plan. Soviet air attacks on the crossing site failed to cause any appreciable damage or losses in men or equipment. The Russians continued to exert strong pressure against our right wing—fierce fighting erupted everywhere along that line and some critical situations arose, but we prevented any major penetrations. Even so, the overall tactical situation had deteriorated to such a point that I ordered the withdrawal of the second Sozh River bridgehead position on the morning of 28 September. In the meantime all divisions sent their nonessential staffs and elements to the rear, assigning them to security missions and to construction of the new defensive Sozh line.

Evacuation of the bridgehead began at 1400 hours, 28 September, in a rainstorm. The strong rear-guard forces left in the bridgehead had orders to disengage and cross at 2200 hours. To protect the bridge itself, elements of the 17th Grenadier Regiment of the 31st Infantry Division moved into a prepared defensive position in a close semicircle around the bridge. After all the troops from the front, including the rear guard, had passed and the bridge had been blown, these companies were to cross the river on pneumatic floats. Unfortunately, in the early morning the Russians (guided by partisans) had succeeded in infiltrating in battalion strength through a gap in the front line near Markovichi, from which they advanced to the banks of the Sozh. This battalion then turned south along the eastern bank of the river, launching an attack toward the bridge. Supported by heavy antitank and machine-gun fire, the Russians managed to capture the bridge, both riverbanks, and the village of Sharpilovka.

This rapid advance not only thwarted our attempts to withdraw across the bridge but also threatened to cut off elements of the 4th Panzer Division and the 31st and 102nd Infantry Divisions before they could evacuate the second bridgehead position. At this critical moment, the 232nd Grenadier Regiment of the 102nd Infantry Division arrived at the crossing site. The regiment immediately threw itself into a magnificent counterattack, forcing the enemy to withdraw with the loss of many weapons, including six antitank guns and three mortars. Traffic across the bridge resumed, despite heavy artillery, antitank, and mortar fire falling on the area around the bridge. To ensure the security of the narrow bridgehead defenses, arriving elements of the 4th Panzer Division were also committed. By about 1300 hours all units, including rear guards, completed the crossing. We blew the bridge at 1315 hours, and the last rear guards crossed the river in their pneumatic floats.

In the new XX Corps main battle line along the Sozh, the 102nd Infantry Division held the right wing, the 31st Infantry Division took the center, and the 6th Infantry Division occupied the left; the 4th Panzer Division was detached from the corps. XXXV Corps in the Gomel bridgehead remained the adjoining unit to the north, XLVI Panzer Corps to the south. The situation along Second Army's far right wing was still critical. The Russians continued to press their advance to the west, and an anticipated counterattack by several panzer divisions had not as yet begun.

The troops of XX Corps had become greatly exhausted from the uninterrupted series of marches and battles of the previous weeks. The combat strength of each of the divisions had declined to about twenty to twenty-five officers, ninety to 100 noncommissioned officers, and 600 men.[3] At the same time, the average width of the divisional sectors amounted to fifteen kilometers. Replacements were urgently needed, and we attempted every expedient to find troops for the battle line. Commanders once more combed out their trains and support units as thoroughly as possible while convalescents and furlough personnel quickly received assignments to each division.

From 29 September to 5 October the Russians repeatedly attempted to cross the river in force. Again, due to numerous bends in the course of the river—especially in the area of the 6th and 31st Infantry Divisions—they succeeded in gaining footholds in a number of locations along the western bank and even began constructing bridges. A meandering river, the swampy nature of its banks, and the weakness of our forces had prevented the Sozh—like the Desna before it—from representing a viable defensive obstacle. The 6th and 31st Infantry Divisions suffered ongoing attacks from every Soviet company and battalion that could keep a grip on the riverbank, sometimes supported by tanks. The counterattacks inevitably necessary to neutralize these penetrations forced these divisions into continuous battles with attendant heavy losses. This situation occurred at a time when XX Corps sector had become increasingly important both to Second Army and Army Group Center: Should the Red Army break through our weakly manned position on the Sozh, it would be able to take Gomel from the rear.

Commencing early on the morning of 6 October the Russians launched a major effort to extend their penetration in General Grossmann's 6th Infantry Division's sector. They captured the villages of Staro-Dyatkovichi, Kovo-Dyatkovichi, and Krasnaya Dolina, fed new reinforcements into the gap, and attempted to break through toward the northwest. After the division made an unsuccessful counterattack, General Grossmann had to resort to sealing off the penetration area—in which two rifle divisions had been identified—with a weak security line. General Weiss attached Major General Friedrich-August Schack's 216th Infantry Division from XXXV Corps and an assault gun battalion from Second Army reserves to XX Corps. The reinforced division proceeded immediately against the penetration, recapturing Krasnaya Dolina on 7 October. Despite our best efforts, however, the Soviets denied us any further success, even though heavy fighting continued through the next day.

Fierce fighting continued on 9 October: At 0900 hours strong Russian forces attacked out of the penetration area, broke through to the north along the western shore of the Sozh Lake, drove beyond Sherebkaya, and captured the small forest west and southwest of the village. Our troops managed to retake the woods, and our artillery personnel also retook several gun positions that had been lost there, but Sherebkaya could not be recovered. As a result of this reverse, General Weiss had to order XXXV Corps to abandon the Gomel bridgehead to the north; the main battle line withdrew entirely to the Sozh in order to concentrate the resources of both the XX and XXXV Corps to annihilate the enemy at Sherebkaya.

Even through this expedient we could not muster the strength to achieve more than limited success. The 45th Infantry Division spent 10–13 October trying to recapture Sherebkaya from the north while the 216th Infantry Division, supported by reserve elements of the 102nd Infantry Division, attacked from the south. General Falkenstein's 45th Infantry reached Babovichi and the area south of it; General Schack's 216th Infantry reestablished contact with the 45th Infantry; and General Grossmann's 6th Infantry closed the gap in the 216th Infantry sector by retaking Krasnaya Dolina. Though capture of Sherebkaya eluded us, we managed to restore a continuous though weakly manned front, and the next few days passed quietly.

During the night of 14 October we unfortunately received orders that the 216th Infantry Division was to be relieved and attached to General of Infantry Hans Gollnick's XLVI Panzer Corps. The XLVI Panzer Corps's 137th Infantry Division had lost Loyev, and the Soviets had penetrated north of the village. Meanwhile, on our own front, the Russians attacked on 15 October after an extensive artillery preparation, just in time to interfere with the process of the 6th Infantry Division taking over the 216th Infantry's sector on the night of 15–16 October. This operation became even more complicated because all the regimental boundaries had to be changed to enlarge the divisional sector. Following its relief, the 216th Infantry Division proceeded by a forced march along the Dnepr highway in the direction of the 137th Infantry but had its approach impeded by Soviet air attacks. Meanwhile, with the forces remaining to us, the most urgent task for XX Corps revolved around the establishment of flank protection for the southern flank at the right corps boundary. No other units were available for this mission except the corps engineer battalion and some *Alarmeinheiten* [emergency response units] from the 102nd Infantry Division (whose main body was engaged in continuous fighting to hold the Sozh position). These battles successfully mastered the immediate crisis, but only at the cost of additional heavy casualties.

Withdrawal to the Panther Position, 16 October–9 November

During the night of 16–17 October XX Corps withdrew to the Panther position. The right wing of the 102nd Infantry Division held the Dnepr main battle line in the Kasarogi area. Adjacent to this division we positioned the 31st Infantry Division, with its right wing located along the Chaplin heights. The division's left wing held a chord position, which ran approximately from Chaplin to Karimonova, diagonally through the area between the Dnepr and the Sozh, making contact with the 45th Infantry Division near Mikhalki. The 6th Infantry Division occupied the chord position in the Marinonova-Mikhalki area. This entire defensive line lacked natural obstacles and needed considerable improvement.

The Soviets failed to extend their penetration in the XLVI Panzer Corps sector to the north but succeeded in gaining ground toward the west, which required the 216th Infantry Division to be committed on the XLVI Panzer Corps's left flank. On 17 October, after the Dnepr position had been occupied, General Weiss assigned the 102nd Infantry Division to XLVI Panzer Corps as well in order to bring the Loyev area under a unified command. The Russians launched weak attacks against the 6th and 31st Infantry Divisions on 18–19 October but managed to take Kasarogi from the 102nd Infantry. As a result of this reverse, plans to eliminate the Loyev penetration had to be dropped for want of personnel. Meanwhile, in the 45th Infantry Division's sector, the Soviets threw strong attacks around Sherebkaya. XX Corps headquarters moved to Yanovka.

Strong Russian tank forces, supported by motorized infantry, pierced the northern front of the Loyev penetration area near Kasarogi, advancing via Progres to Niva; simultaneous enemy attacks broke into Mokhovo. General Hitzfeld's 102nd Infantry bore the brunt of this onslaught and was thrown into such confusion that the division, at least for the time being, could not be counted upon for any offensive tasks whatsoever. Because General Gollnick's XLVI Panzer Corps could not maintain communications and control over this sector, XX Corps assumed jurisdiction there, including command of the much-disrupted 102nd Infantry Division. Despite heavy pressure along the entire line, I ordered the formation of a *regimentsgruppe* to deal with the emergency. From its relatively quiet sector on the Dnepr, the 31st Infantry Division was able to release several companies to act as the nucleus. By evening these companies, augmented by *Alarmeinheiten* of all descriptions, had established a new defensive line running from Stradubek (at the Dnepr) via Rekord and north of Niva to Smely (though we voluntarily relinquished Smely during the night to shorten the front).

This day constituted the worst crisis for XX Corps during the entire period. If the Soviet attacks continued to be successful, the entire Dnepr front could be split wide open; both Second and Ninth Armies would suffer possibly fatal damage. No substantial reserves remained uncommitted; we could organize them only by further denuding the front line, a process that courted even greater disaster. Nonetheless, I ordered an infantry battalion from the 57th Grenadier Regiment on the left wing of the 6th Infantry Division pulled out of the line; its sector was covered by an extension of the neighboring 45th Infantry Division. At the same time, General Wiese agreed to transfer his only reserve—the 904th Assault Gun Battalion—from XXXV Corps to XX Corps.

Despite these moves, I faced 21 October with great apprehension. The Russians launched their attack at 1000 hours, and savage battles raged back and forth all day. Ultimately we managed to seal off all enemy penetrations and thwart the Soviet breakthrough attempt. General Weiss stripped Second Army's own limited pool of reserves to give us the greatest possible support, committing the 2nd *Sturm* [Attack] Battalion and the 244th Assault Gun Battalion, as well as one light and two heavy flak battalions. I committed these flak units, as well as every battery that had been assigned to XX Corps, to form an antitank defense line in the most critical sectors. Red Army tanks would have to be stopped there, at the latest, if we were to avert disaster. The antiaircraft mission of the flak units had to assume only secondary importance.

Later in the day General Weiss gave XX Corps control of the northern group of General Gollnick's XLVI Panzer Corps, consisting of Lieutenant General Vollrath Lubbe's 2nd Panzer Division and the 102nd and 216th Infantry Divisions (which had been traded back and forth between these corps for several days). Unfortunately, control over the 2nd Panzer and 216th Infantry Divisions could not be immediately exercised until effective signal communications had been established. The Luftwaffe also contributed to our ability to hold the front: Effective air attacks by two dive-bomber and four bombardment wings against the leading edge of the Russian penetration brought critical relief to our outnumbered and hard-fighting grenadiers.

Despite our best efforts, the situation at the boundary between XX and XLVI Panzer Corps continued to deteriorate throughout the day. Successful enemy attacks against General Gollnick's northern sector forced him to order XLVI Panzer Corps to withdraw to a second defensive line. This retirement opened a large gap west of the wooded area between the northern boundary of his corps and the southern boundary of mine. As a consequence of this event, the Soviets now had the ability to feed reinforcements into the woods without interference.

By 22 October, therefore, the situation in XX Corps sector stood as follows: The 6th Infantry Division held the left wing of the corps defensive line, making contact with the adjoining XXXV Corps near Machalki. The 31st Infantry Division sector began at Dubrovka; Colonel Ochsner's primary responsibility was to prevent a Soviet breakthrough to the north. In addition, this division also had a *regimentsgruppe* beyond the Dnepr toward Marimonovo. On the right wing a group consisting of the 2nd Panzer Division, as well as the 216th and 102nd Infantry Divisions, had been placed under the command of General Luebbe of the 2nd Panzer Division. The 102nd Infantry Division's main battle line ran one to two kilometers from the western outskirts of Dubrovka to the fringes of the large forest. This greatly weakened division had been reinforced by elements of the 2nd Panzer Division while General Luebbe held the main body of his own division in reserve. The 216th Infantry Division, in the Ostrovy-Chanez area, was the southern-most element of this group, and made contact with the 137th Infantry Division of XLVI Panzer Corps near Ostrovy.

The Russians launched an attack that primarily targeted the 31st Infantry Division at 1030 hours on 22 October. Supported by the flak battalions in an antitank role, Colonel Ochsner managed to repel all attacks and seal off all penetrations. The Soviets then carried out weak—and unprofitable—attacks against those units of 2nd Panzer Division in the main battle line. That evening, however, the Russians penetrated at the corps boundary between the 216th and 137th Infantry Divisions. Although we managed to seal off the penetration, the situation remained critical, as Luftwaffe reconnaissance flights reported that the Soviets continued to feed infantry reinforcements into the gap in the forest. Heavy fighting continued all day.

Confronted by an increasing number of salients caused by enemy penetration of the main defensive line, coupled with heavy combat losses, XX Corps became progressively weaker. The reinforcements available did not suffice to make up the difference. Our grenadiers had reached an all-time low in terms of both physical strength and morale, yet day after day they somehow rallied to give their all in continuous attacks and counterattacks. Still, it remained highly questionable just how long we could delay a Russian breakthrough toward Rechitsa.

From 23 to 27 October combat action briefly subsided, though the Soviets continued to make small-scale attacks (usually one or two rifle regiments supported by tanks), especially against the 102nd Infantry Division in the Uborok-Yatrebka area. We stopped or repelled these attacks with rapid counterattacks by strong assault detachments with plentiful artillery support. It was clear, however, that these actions were merely preparatory in nature while all other signs pointed to the imminent resumption of the large-scale offensive. We specifically noted systematic registration by the Russian artillery and a significant increase in reconnaissance activity in the air and on the ground. Unfortunately, the lack of a corps observation battalion and the foggy weather that prevailed during the period rendered us unable to identify precisely the Soviet artillery buildup or to locate the assembly of their infantry and tank reinforcements.

The anticipated offensive began on 28 October, and heavy fighting continued through 30 October. Supported by multibarrel rocket launchers (*Stalinorgeln*), the Soviet artillery preparation commenced at 0815 hours and quickly engulfed the entire Dnepr front. Judging by the intensity of the fire, I expected the main effort of the Russian attack to be directed against the 102nd Infantry Division in the Lypnyaki area, and at 0915 hours the enemy confirmed this conclusion. Through 1400 hours, General Hitzfeld's division managed to repel most of the attacks between Uborok and Lypnyaki, though the Soviets had captured Lypnyaki itself and opened a four-kilometer gap extending on both sides of the village. Strong Soviet air activity impeded all movement on the battlefield. Even so, at 1500 hours Major General Erpo Freiherr von Bodenhausen's 12th Panzer Division (which had just been assigned to XX Corps) succeeded in organizing a counterattack against Lypnyaki. The Russian, however, constantly fed reinforcements into the fight across the Peredelk bridge and remained victorious throughout the next day. I had to abandon plans to recapture Lypnyaki. By 30 October our fortunes took a turn for the better, and employing concentrated, well-directed artillery fire we managed to squash a major Russian attack supported by thirty tanks before it even got rolling. This action eased the pressure against the front sufficiently to allow us to seal off the penetration between Lypnyaki and Volkoshanka immediately, and the one between Lypnyaki and Smely by midnight, restoring a continuous front in the 102nd Infantry Division's sector. Specific recognition should be accorded to the conduct of the troops, especially the 232nd Grenadier Regiment (102nd Infantry Division) and all elements of the 12th Panzer Division that participated in the action. Casualties ran high, particularly among the officers, though on the positive side we captured 200 prisoners and destroyed sixty Soviet tanks and thirteen aircraft.

This attack represented the last gasp of an enemy as exhausted as we were. My corps front remained quiet between 31 October and 9 November, except for a few Russian patrols sent out to draw fire in order to identify our artillery firing positions. Unfortunately, heavy fog again obstructed our own reconnaissance and observation, rendering an accurate enemy situation estimate difficult. Luftwaffe reconnaissance flights did report about 2,000 armored vehicles moving toward the front, which indicated the arrival of fresh Soviet reinforcements, while prisoner statements confirmed the belief that the Red Army would be prepared to launch a new offensive as early as 8 November. On 6 November the skies cleared and temperatures dropped, facilitating observation again and allowing us to ascertain that the Soviets had spent considerable effort to improve their own front-line positions. We later established that most of these improved positions represented newly construction forward command posts to be occupied during the onset of the new offensive. Daylight aerial reconnaissance spotted about 200 Russian batteries, mostly aimed north and northwest. Our ground reconnaissance patrols began taking prisoners from rifle divisions that had been mauled in the past to such an extent that they had been removed from the line; now, apparently, these divisions had been reconstituted. Taking all of these factors together, I believed by 8 November that the Russians would open a major offensive within a matter of days.

Withdrawal Toward the Pripet Marshes, 10–25 November

The Soviets attacked on 10 November following a one-hour artillery concentration. Strong tank forces appeared opposite the 102nd Infantry Division and the 12th Panzer Division (which had taken over the Uborok-Smely area). Fierce tank battles erupted on 11 November, in which the Russians broke through to Nadvin. That day the Red Army also penetrated the front line of the 31st Infantry Division in several places.

The situation demanded a withdrawal, and during the night of 11–12 November the 102nd and 216th Infantry Divisions, as well as the 12th Panzer Division, retired into to a line running from Rudnaya Udalevka to Nadvin. There contact was regained with the 31st Infantry Division, which had changed front to face south along the flank of the enemy penetration. The 6th Infantry Division, which in the meantime had suffered heavy attacks in its bridgehead position east of the Dnepr, was attached to XXXV Corps. That division withdrew across the river during the night, establishing a new defensive line on the eastern bank and linking up with the 31st Infantry Division.

On 12 November, in the morning, the withdrawal of the 12th Panzer and 31st Infantry Divisions into the so-called Bear position near Nadvin had just gotten under way. An early morning counterattack, planned against Nadvin to establish that village in the main defensive line, could not be carried out, although the 508th Grenadier Regiment of the 292nd Infantry Division (XXV Corps) had been attached to the 31st Infantry Division for this purpose the previous afternoon. The Russians had so strengthened their forces in Nadvin by shuttling reinforcements across the river that they became able to launch an attack north along the western bank of the Dnepr. This attack, supported by tanks, gained ground quickly because our flak battalions had not completed their redeployment into the new defensive position. This created a serious threat to the flank of the 31st Infantry Division, which was still being attacked all along the front. Colonel Ochsner had to pivot the division's left wing and fall back into positions facing south and southwest on the approximate line Vechin-Chomedh. To the west, leading Soviet units attacked the Bear position, but our troops held.

During the morning of 13 November the Russians enlarged their penetration between Trud and Artuki into a breakthrough, because our defensive line was so inadequately manned. They seized Yanovka, then advanced tank spearheads into a blocking position on the Rechitsa-Khoiniki road. Strong forces—mainly cavalry—poured into the gap between the 12th Panzer and 31st Infantry Divisions. Having moved corps headquarters from Yanovka via Berezovka to Perevoloka, I was no longer in a position to exercise effective command over the 31st Infantry Division; General Weiss therefore transferred the division to XXXV Corps. At noon on 12 November Lieutenant General Richard John's 292nd Infantry Division was attached to XX Corps, after having moved from the Rechitsa area (XXXV Corps) to XLVI Panzer Corps, on whose southern wing it had been partly committed. Due to the breakthrough in my sector, those elements already placed in the XLVI Panzer Corps line were immediately relieved, and those units still en route were immediately diverted to XX Corps. This precarious situation accounted for the fact that as each battalion of the 292nd Infantry Division arrived in our sector it was committed piecemeal. The advance elements arrived along the highway in the Andreyevka-Berezovka area during the afternoon of 13 November, in time to defend those towns against a Soviet attack out of Yanovka. The Russians countered by flowing south of the villages to seize the small forest on both sides of the main highway northeast of Malodush. The next-arriving units of the 292nd Infantry, arriving from the southwest, proved unable to eject the Soviets that evening or to make contact with our troops near Berezovka. These units therefore moved into a blocking position that followed the west edge of Malodush to the eastern outskirts of Staro-Barsuk. During this movement contact with the 12th Panzer Division was regained. General Freiherr von Bodenhausen's division had been forced to withdraw its front along with the adjacent divisions to the south only after repelling many Soviet attacks with heavy losses. Following the completion of the 12th Panzer's withdrawal, the line ran approximately from Rudnaya Udalevka via Litishiny, Dukhanovka, and Novy Barsuk to Stary Barsuk.

The early part of 14 November brought no appreciable change in our position, although Russian tanks probed the Rechitsa-Kalinovichi highway as far as Korovachi. Enemy activity almost completely ceased during the afternoon. Turning west, XX Corps moved its headquarters to Khoiniki.

Between 15 and 19 November the Russians attacked our positions around Malodush, and we attempted to close the wide gap between Malodush and the road junction about ten kilometers south of Rechitsa. General Hossbach's LVI Panzer Corps, with General von Saucken's 4th and Colonel Karl Decker's 5th Panzer Divisions, supported by units of the XXXV Corps (particularly the 45th Infantry Division), attempted to attack the salient from both flanks. LVI Panzer Corps's attack from the south, launched from the east of Malodush through the 292nd Infantry Division sector, failed. After an initial success, the 45th Infantry Division's attack from the north also bogged down. Thus Second Army's plan to close the gap had to be abandoned because the Russians continued to gain ground along the road to Kalinovichi. The 4th and 5th Panzer Divisions had to be relieved immediately in order to protect this road, thus leaving XX Corps's area almost as soon as they arrived.

Second Army's general situation demanded that the withdrawal continue to the eastern edge of the Pripet Marshes in the Kalinovichi area. Difficulties arose, however, when both the 102nd and 216th Infantry Divisions reported the large forest around Omelkovchina to be marshy and strongly infested with partisans. Both Generals Hitzfeld and Schack considered a movement through this area impossible, even for infantry. The sole available alternative involved requiring the 102nd and 216th Infantry Divisions and the 12th and 2nd Panzer Divisions (the 2nd Panzer having been reduced to a weak *kampfgruppe* and attached to the 12th) to bypass the woods in the northeast and proceed directly along the road to Khoiniki. With the exception of divisional rear guards, security for this withdrawal fell almost entirely to General Schack's 216th Infantry Division. Accomplishing this mission required the division to hold its current positions at Stary Barsuk and Malodush at all hazards until the other units had completed their movement. This the division did, and the withdrawal of two panzer and two infantry divisions progressed toward Khoiniki during 20–21 November without delay.

By contrast, the situation in the 292nd Infantry Division sector deteriorated hourly. Besides attacking toward Malodush, the Soviets made repeated attempts to outflank the division to the west. General John therefore found himself forced to extend his defensive line again and again as heavy casualties made holding a continuous front exceedingly difficult. But the grenadiers of this division, too, were well aware of their responsibility and held their precarious position until 22 November, at which time the withdrawal of the other four divisions had been completed. In doing so, the division repulsed many Soviet flank attacks and found itself in an increasingly dangerous position. The climax occurred when the Russians unexpectedly advanced from the east, blocked· the road in the Dubrovitsa area, and cut off a large part of the division. In a dashing counterattack, led personally by General Schack, the division cleared the road again, then withdrew in the face of the enemy to the Khoiniki area, where it moved into new positions north of the village, still covering the movement of the other divisions.

By 25 November all six divisions of XX Corps had arrived via Yurevichi in the Kalinovichi area without significant pressure from a badly mauled Red Army. While both panzer divisions received orders transferring them elsewhere, the 216th Infantry Division (now very weak) and the 102nd Infantry Division were combined, with the augmented 102nd and the 292nd Infantry Divisions now composing XX Corps. The 292nd Infantry Division occupied positions directly south of the railroad, and the 102nd Infantry Division extended this line farther to the south. XLVI Panzer Corps was the adjacent unit on the right, LVI Panzer Corps on the left. We occupied these positions for the next few weeks.

Conclusions

The difficulties that had to be overcome during the long withdrawal from the Sevsk River to the Pripet Marshes can be summarized as follows:

1. Lack of improved positions on the Desna, Sozh, and Dnepr Rivers (such preparations had been prohibited);
2. Inadequate roads and bridges (their timely improvement had not been possible due to lack of personnel);
3. Russian superiority in men and equipment (especially tanks and aircraft);
4. Uninterrupted commitment, daily fighting, defense of positions, and night marches exhausted our troops;
5. The small number of replacements received were no compensation for our heavy casualties;
6. Lack of general reserves that might have neutralized some reverses;
7. Supply difficulties (especially shortages of ammunition and fuel), caused chiefly by partisans in the rear areas.

APPENDIX 9A

Order of Battle: XX Corps,
8–9 August 1943[4]

General of Artillery Rudolf Freiherr von Roman

45th Infantry Division

Major General Hans Freiherr von Falkenstein

Grenadier Regiments 133, 135 (three battalions each)
Fusilier Battalion 45
Engineer Battalion 81
Artillery Regiment 98
I/98 (fifteen 105mm; six 150mm)
II/98 (fourteen 105mm; twelve 150mm)
III/98 (HQ only; guns detached to other battalions)

Attached:

I/99 (HQ only)
one battery of heavy mortars
one battery, Assault Gun Battalion 904
Artillery Battalion (Motorized) 430 (ten 105mm)

Attached:

Ost Company, 45th Infantry Division

137th Infantry Division

Lieutenant General Hans Kamecke

Grenadier Regiments 447, 448 (two battalions each)
Fusilier Battalion 137
Panzerjaeger Battalion 137
Engineer Battalion 137
Feldersatz Battalion 137
Artillery Regiment 137
I/137 (nine 105mm)
II/137 (nine 105mm)
III/137 (nine 105mm)
IV/137 (nine 150mm)

Attached:
 II/61 (thirteen 150mm)
 Light Artillery Observation Battalion 15 (minus one battery)

Attached:
 Cossack Cavalry Battalion 137

86th Infantry Division
Lieutenant General Hellmuth Weidling

 Grenadier Regiments 167, 184, 216 (two battalions each)
 Sturm Battalion 186
 Panzerjaeger Battalion 186
 Feldersatz Battalion 86
 Artillery Regiment 186
 Gruppe Henkel
 I/186 (seven 105mm)
 III/186 (six 105mm)
 II/186 (eight 105mm)
 IV/186 (eight 150mm)

Attached:
 Artillery Battalion 860 (twelve 105mm)

251st Infantry Division
Major General Maximilian Felzmann

Grenadier Regiments 451, 459, 471 (two battalions each)

 Schnelle Battalion 251
 Feldersatz Battalion 251
 (All divisional and attached artillery under the control of Artillery
   Commander 129)
 Artillery Regiment 251 (minus I and IV)
 II/251 (nine 105mm; two 150mm)
 III/251 (nine 105mm)
 Artillery Regimental Headquarters 41 (Special Employment)
 I/251 (six 105mm; two 150mm)
 IV/251 (three 105mm; two 150mm)
 Artillery Battalion 604 (six 210mm)
 1 battery, Light Artillery Observation Battalion 15

Corps troops

 Assault Gun Battalion 904 (minus one battery)
 XX Corps Assault Battalion (two companies plus one *Ost* co.)
 Artillery battery 1./620 (three 150mm)

Engineer Commander 152

Engineer Regimental Staff 512 (Special Employment)

Engineer Battalion (Motorized) 750

Construction Battalions 44, 80

Construction Battalion (POW) 244

Bridge Column 628

Machine-gun Battalion 273

A comparison between the organizations of these infantry divisions in early August and the same units in early July (see Chapter 4) reveals the extent to which the hard-fought *landsers* [soldiers] of the German army had been ground down in six weeks of fighting. Virtually all of these divisions in July had possessed the full complement of reconnaissance, panzerjaeger, and engineer battalions, however small they may have been. By mid-August most infantry-capable units had been consolidated into Fusilier, *Sturm*, or *Schnelle* battalions, organized around whatever remained of those earlier organizations.

10

XI Corps in the Battles for Belgorod and Kharkov

by Colonel General Erhard Raus

Commander, XI Corps

Editor's Introduction

This second excerpt from the reconstructed Raus memoir recounts at great length the critical defensive fighting following the termination of Operation Citadel through the withdrawal from Kharkov roughly one month later. In it, Raus dropped all pretense of narrating the larger operations of *Armeeabteilung* Kempf/Eighth Army and concentrated entirely on the operations of his own XI Corps. As a result, we are left with a narrative rich in tactical detail but often devoid of any feel for what was happening along the XI Corps's long, open left flank. This lack is complicated by the fact that there is no solid, comprehensive narrative of this segment of the war readily available; the best that can be done is to refer the interested reader to several monographs, each of which presents in detail a specific part of the picture.[1]

Once the inherent limitation of the Raus narrative is understood, however, a first-rate historical source emerges that captures the German perspective on heavy defensive fighting. Raus begins by narrating the critical position in which his own corps was placed by the collapse of the front on his immediate left. He takes the reader through the internal deliberations of a corps commander, responsible for thousands of troops, left suddenly to cope with only his own, inadequate resources in the face of immense enemy superiority.

There follows a lengthy segment on the defensive battles along the Donets River, the critical right flank that XI Corps had to hold in order to have any chance of conducting a fighting retreat. Concentrating exclusively on the operations of the 320th Infantry Division, Raus manages to keep readers on the edge of their seats while simultaneously instructing them about the differences between German and Soviet tactical methods. As with the earlier account of Operation Citadel, there are elements of a Cold War morality play in which the perfidious Russians disregard the rules of war and disguise themselves in German uniforms and engage in "an inhumane form of kidnapping" against presumably innocent German sentries during the middle of the night. The careful reader will not disregard these sections as fictional but will realize that Raus cannot be expected to spend equal time detailing German ruses and/or violations of the laws of war. Here again, Raus is consistent in approach with his contemporaries writing in the mid-1950s.

Returning to the final retreat toward Kharkov, Raus presents the perspective of a senior officer who has to convince his own division commanders that the day isn't lost so long as they do not give up. His task is complicated by the virtual disappearance of an entire division, later found skulking in the woods in one of the more bizarre (but well-documented) incidents in the war.

Finally, Raus describes the climactic fourth battle of Kharkov in considerable detail. Many readers will recognize much of what is presented here, for Paul Carell leaned heavily on an article adaptation of the material Raus first wrote for the U.S. Army. Contrary to some recent criticisms, the details cited by Raus hold up remarkably well when compared to contemporary documents.

The entire Raus memoir covers the Russian campaign from the first day of the war to his relief from command in Pomerania at Hitler's order in the spring of 1945. It includes a detailed examination of the 6th Panzer Division's drive to Leningrad, Raus's own experiences in the Soviet winter counteroffensive around Moscow, and the unsuccessful attempt to relieve Stalingrad before the two excerpts presented here. Following the evacuation of Kharkov, Raus discusses the withdrawal across the Dnepr at Kremenchug, fighting around Kovel, and the final desperate battles inside Germany.

XI Corps in the Battles for Belgorod and Kharkov
by Colonel General Erhard Raus
Commander, XI Corps

The Soviet Breakthrough at Belgorod, 23 July–8 August

The heat of summer still parched the blood-drenched fields along the banks of the upper Donets River when the four exhausted divisions of XI

Corps (106th, 168th, 198th, and 320th Infantry Divisions) returned on 22 July to their old, well-fortified positions on both sides of Belgorod. During the Citadel offensive these divisions had all seen heavy fighting, which continued for the better part of a month and in which they had taken heavy losses. Combat strengths had declined to 40–50 percent of that prescribed in the tables of organization, and in the case of some infantry regiments conditions were even worse. Nor could these divisions expect to receive any replacements for a long time to come.

On the other hand, our disengagement from the Russians had proceeded smoothly. Even the bridgehead at Belgorod, which XI Corps held as the last German unit to fight east of the Donets River, was evacuated with ease. The Red Army rifle divisions, which had been beaten shortly before, did not understand why the Germans were withdrawing voluntarily, and therefore remained suspicious. These suspicions were not unjustified, because many a German retirement had been followed by a surprise attack, which had wrought havoc on Soviet forces. This time, however, the withdrawal was genuine, with no trickery intended, having been solely dictated by the desire to intercept the counterattack of the still-intact Russian strategic reserves on a shorter, fortified line.

On 5 August 1943, after Soviet artillery had fired heavily for one hour, the enemy offensive began along the Belgorod-Kursk highway, with the unmistakable aim of pushing through the salient around Belgorod where the boundary between the Fourth Panzer Army and *Armeeabteilung* Kempf was situated and thereby dislocating the entire defensive line. In this the Russians succeeded completely. Their heavy barrage hit the 167th Infantry Division, which had taken up positions in a former Soviet antitank ditch, located a few kilometers in front of the well-fortified line. Within a short time massed Red Army tanks had crossed this ditch; by noon they passed the corps command post and poured into the depth of the German positions, all the while firing on our fleeing trains.

The attempt made by Fourth Panzer Army to close the gap in its flank by a frontal counterattack on the part of the 6th Panzer Division was as little successful as that made on 6 August by a pincer attack of the battleworn 6th and 19th Panzer Divisions between Belgorod and Tomarovka. Their panzer regiments barely contained a dozen tanks each and were not nearly adequate for that difficult task. In this connection the 19th Panzer Division became encircled by the Russians, and the 6th Panzer deflected into the region under XI Corps command and was placed under my orders. On 6 August, after a nighttime forced march, Russian spearheads had reached the surprised headquarters of the Fourth Panzer Army at Bogudukhov, forcing it to make a hasty withdrawal. Because Fourth Panzer Army had no other reserves available to stop the flood of enemy tanks that had already broken through to a depth of 100 kilometers, Russian spearheads reached the area northeast of Poltava and Akhtyrka on 7 August. Our situation maps illustrate more clearly than words the dangerous situation into which this development thrust XI Corps, which had been fighting with its front to the east.

On the very first day of the Soviet offensive, XI Corps had been attacked in the rear by enemy tank forces situated thirty kilometers in the depth of our positions. These tank forces simultaneously exerted crushing pressure on our unprotected left flank. At this critical moment, XI Corps not only had been left to its own devices but also had been handicapped by a direct Fuehrer Order, which had arrived at the last minute and insisted that Belgorod was to be held under all circumstances.

The corps front now formed a deep salient into enemy territory, like the pillar of a ruined bridge, which might have disintegrated with complete encirclement as its final destiny. This would have meant a widening of the existing Belgorod-Tomarovka gap from twenty-five to eighty kilometers and the immediate loss of several divisions. In view of XI Corps's limited strength, it would have been a mistake to attempt to close the gap by widening the corps sector—nor was any such plan feasible, because the Russians had kept up their pressure along the entire front. On the contrary, we had to keep our forces together and form a solid breakwater against numerically superior Soviet forces. The XI Corps could not, therefore, try to fight the Russians to a halt at Belgorod nor continuously avoid contact in order to extricate itself from the noose.

With these considerations determining the conduct of operations, I decided—Hitler's order notwithstanding—to fight a delaying action in successive positions until the withdrawal reached Kharkov, and then to hold the city. XI Corps therefore had to build up a front facing north and protect its left flank against an enemy envelopment while the right flank remained anchored on the Donets. We had to resist the immediate temptation to take forces out of XI Corps's eastern front along the Donets River in order to employ them (with their front reversed) along the Lopan River to protect our rear. The Donets front was not only very long, it was thinly held; removing any forces from it would expose this sector to disaster even if the Russians restricted themselves to conducting feints and relief attacks. Because such a weakening would have spelled doom for XI Corps, other measures had to be attempted.

The only units immediately available to me were the remnants of the 167th Infantry Division that had become separated from Fourth Panzer Army during the breakthrough (about 500 battle-weary soldiers without artillery or heavy weapons) and the weak 6th Panzer Division, whose men—although they only had ten tanks—possessed good morale. As both divisions had been cut off from their own command, I immediately assumed command over them and utilized them to build a defensive screen along the Lopan River. During the night of 5–6 August I ordered the 168th and 198th Infantry Divisions (on the corps's left and resisting heavy pressure north of Belgorod) to pivot 180 degrees around Belgorod. We evacuated the city after heavy street-fighting and occupied a new defensive line (prepared on the high ground immediately south of Belgorod). This positioned the divisions to join those elements mentioned above in protecting our rear; I also reinforced them with an antitank battalion, one company of Pzkw VI Tigers, and another of StG III assault guns—together composing a total of twenty-five armored vehicles. Sustained by their antitank guns and this handful of tanks, the two weak divisions withstood all attacks by Russian infantry, which were supported by large numbers of ground attack aircraft and at least 150 tanks. The weakened 6th Panzer Division and the battered remnants of the 167th Infantry Division took responsibility for ensuring the Belgorod was not enveloped from the south while we were conducting these moves.

In the long, threatened sector south along the Lopan River, XI Corps rapidly had to improvise combat forces from Luftwaffe ground installations, as well as the corps combat trains and supply services. With the aid of the Luftwaffe's 88mm flak batteries in Flak Regiments 7 and 48, which we employed solely against Russian tanks despite the enemy's continuous air raids, these makeshift units managed to prevent the Soviets from pivoting their troops against the Kharkov-Belgorod *rollbahn* and slicing into the rear of our Donets River front. On the morning of 8 August, however, Red Army tanks succeeded in breaking through the 168th Infantry Division and gaining an immediate foothold on the eastern bank of the Lopan River. Only an immediate counterattack by the 6th Panzer Division threw the enemy back and eliminated the threat. This time, by the narrowest of margins, events had played out in our favor.

Meanwhile Soviet tank forces lunging farther south had managed to force the Lopan River at another location, from which they pushed immediately toward the critical Belgorod-Kharkov *rollbahn*. By a fortunate coincidence, Assault Gun Battalion 905 had been rushed up from the Kharkov area, and its forty-two StG IIIs hit the enemy tank groups that had crossed the river, destroying them one by one. After this victory, Assault Gun Battalion 905 became XI Corps's only mobile tactical reserve.

Battles Along the Donets River, 31 July–9 August

The regiments of Major General Georg Postel's 320th Infantry Division were situated approximately thirty kilometers south of Belgorod on the hills on both sides of A[——] Brook valley, through which a highway ran westward of the big Belgorod-Kharkov *rollbahn*, and those of Lieutenant General Werner Forst's 106th Infantry Division held a position directly north of them.[2] Any Russian advance through this valley would quickly interrupt this vital line of communications, which placed a heavy responsibility on the battalions stationed on both sides of the valley to prevent such incursions.

Our tactical withdrawal to the eastern bank of the Donets on 22 July had so surprised the Soviets in this sector that they only cautiously and hesitantly felt their way forward to the river on 23 July. In the 320th Infantry Division's sector the western bank of the Donets was much higher than the eastern, and—particularly at the junction of A[——] Brook with the river—the terrain was swampy and covered with reeds. The Donets was not fordable at any point, and it seemed obvious that the Russians would have a difficult time forcing a breakthrough in this locality. During the day they would probably be able to hide along the eastern bank in the maze of trenches remaining from their battered former positions and in the innumerable shell craters, but they would be unable to move into the open without being identified and brought under fire by the German defenders.

The weapons of the 320th Infantry, from their well-concealed bunker positions, controlled the Donets River valley (which was very level along its entire extent of three to four kilometers) so effectively that it was impossible for the enemy to prepare a daylight attack. Our artillery and heavy weapons we positioned in the hills southwest of village B[——], zeroing them in on a former bridge site and preparing them for night-firing. Ridge 675, which afforded excellent visibility to the east, had been transformed into a virtually impregnable bastion. Shell-proof dugouts, deep shelters, and communications tunnels protected the gun crews there from Russian counterbattery fire. Exits from the tunnels that faced the river had been expertly camouflaged, with machine guns emplaced in these exits to command the river in case the enemy attempted a night crossing. Their fields of fire covered not only the potential bridge site but also concentration areas and approach routes on both banks of the Donets. Firing data for these weapons had been computed and carefully rechecked, while searchlights had been emplaced along the ridge to illuminate the immediate outpost area. The Russians lacked specific knowledge of these meticulous preparations but were fully aware that our troops had enjoyed ample opportunity to improve their defenses. As a result, a dead silence prevailed in the sun-drenched, glittering sand desert on the eastern bank of the Donets throughout the long summer days of late July.

During the brief nights, however, there was lively activity. First, Russian scouts looked for convenient crossing sites along the riverbank. Later, small groups of enemy soldiers appeared on the western bank to reconnoiter our defenses and take prisoners. To this end they applied a method that they had already frequently used with success on previous occasions. In the darkness Russian scouts crept up to a German sentry standing in a trench and waited—often for hours at a time—for a suitable moment to overpower him. When they had succeeded in doing so, they immediately gagged the surprised victim, tied his arms and legs with ropes, and made a loop around his ankles, by which he was often dragged over distances of several hundred meters to the nearest Soviet trench. Such abductions were accomplished in complete silence. Only the tracks discovered the following morning indicated the direction in which the victims had been taken.

The only possible method of protecting our troops against this inhumane form of kidnapping consisted of increasing the number of security patrols and sentries, requiring the sentries to maintain constant contact with each other, establishing obstacles with alarm devices, laying minefields, and using trained watchdogs. These dogs, like setters, immediately indicated every movement in the vicinity of a sentry and attacked the Russians as they crept up or lurked in ambush. Despite such precautions, the endurance and ingenuity of the Red Army soldiers proved astonishing. Unable to realize his intention the first night, he continued to stalk our sentries every following night until he successfully acquired a victim. If he became aware of our countermeasures, he avoided them and went off in search of a spot that was better suited to his needs, and he continued to search relentlessly for such a spot until he found one. Often he would be rewarded by the carelessness of a German sentry, which he immediately noticed and exploited. In this strange and brutal manner the Soviets along the Donets managed (as they did on many other occasions) to obtain valuable information concerning the details of our defenses. Thus they determined that the positions of the 320th Infantry Division were particularly attenuated, owing to a shortage of troops, and that this was particularly true of the tree-covered hill sector north of A[——] Brook.[3]

As a result of this intelligence, the enemy selected this point for his first attempt to cross the river. Fortunately, the men of the battalion positioned here had remained vigilant. They had identified and mined the tracks of the Russian scouting parties and had adjusted their machine guns and mortars on the crossing points used by these parties, so that the weapons were ready for night firing. Thus prepared, they kept a close watch on the river throughout the night of 31 July–1 August. As expected, just before dawn, several companies of Red Army troops appeared and commenced crossing the Donets at three previously reconnoitered points, utilizing improvised equipment. The mines that exploded and killed the first Russian soldiers to land on the western bank took them by complete surprise. The companies near the river on the eastern bank came under heavy, preregistered fire from machine guns and mortars, scattering in panic with heavy losses. Our artillery finished the job by shelling and destroying the river-crossing equipment they abandoned as soon as the sun rose.

General Postel and his troops did not make the mistake of thinking that the Russians would abandon their intention to force a crossing at this location because of a single setback. On the contrary, they repeated the attack on the night of 1–2 August, at the very same crossing sites, employing stronger forces and new equipment. General Postel decided not to interfere immediately but to deliver a decisive blow at the most critical moment. He ordered several batteries to mass their fire on the bridge site to smash the construction work after it had progressed sufficiently. At a prearranged time, just before midnight, all the guns fired upon the bridge site simultaneously and then ceased as abruptly as they had begun. Observers on the ridge made out the silhouette of a bizarre tangle of beams and pillars in the flickering light of burning lumber on the eastern bank of the river. The partially completed bridge was a shambles in the midst of which wounded men were screaming for help as shadows and scurrying figures (presumably medical aid men) moved among them.

Scarcely half an hour had passed when our observers reported that full-scale construction activity had resumed. The sounds of intensive hammering and sawing induced General Postel to order another concentration fired shortly after midnight. The result was equally devastating, though this time silence followed the bursts of our projectiles, a silence interrupted only by explosions from a few ammunition dumps that caught fire after sustaining direct hits. Yet the fires soon died down, and after only a brief interval the Russians again resumed their efforts as if nothing had happened. Obviously, the commander on the opposite shore had positive orders that his bridge had to be complete by dawn.

To frustrate this intention without wasting ammunition, General Postel ordered one 210mm howitzer battery to deliver intermittent harassing fire on the bridge site. Flash observation confirmed that the projectiles had landed on or very close to their targets. After an hour of harassment fire the pattern of Soviet response became clear. When a round did major damage it cause a prolonged work stoppage, but after a near-miss the hammering resumed immediately. General Postel therefore concluded that under these circumstances the Russians might still be able to complete the bridge by dawn, harassing fire notwithstanding.

He therefore decided to employ some of our hidden machine guns to rake the construction site at short intervals with bursts of fire. Judging by the screams of those who were hit, and the immediate suspension of the bridging operation, the rapid precision fire of these weapons had a devastating effect. Even so, the Russians still attempted to continue with the construction, but high losses forced them to slow down and finally quit the work entirely.

At periodic intervals, our heavy howitzers resumed harassing fire to discourage the Soviets from resuming their project and to complete the destruction. Only after daybreak was it possible for our observers to obtain a true picture of the results achieved during the hours of darkness. A horrific sight presented itself. Splintered rafters pointed skyward, and in between hung grotesquely mutilated corpses of the brave men who had scorned death in the effort to accomplish their mission. Even more mangled bodies were strewn about in a wide circle around the bridge site or lay partially submerged in the mud holes formed by shell craters. Smashed vehicles, dead horses, and all kinds of ammunition and equipment littered the area. Live Russians, on the other hand, seemed to have vanished from the scene of their failure.

Nonetheless, a single small enemy group managed to escape destruction by clinging to the steep slope of the western bank, where our fire could not reach it. During the daylight hours of 2 August, however, combat patrols from the 320th Infantry drove this group into a nearby swamp, though even with mud reaching up to their chests and with the reeds providing scant cover this handful of Red Army soldiers kept fighting and held out until darkness again fell. To the astonishment of the German defenders, at dawn on 3 August not only did this ragged group of Russians still occupy its strip of swamp; it had been reinforced. At its side another one or two "swamp companies" had taken up positions. This was something that German or other European troops would never have done. The swamp was situated on the western bank just in front of the valley position, 300 meters back from the river. General Postel's regiment and battalion commanders had chosen to defend from the valley position because they considered the swamp in their front to be a very good obstacle to any enemy crossing attempt. None of these officers (and no German commander in a similar position) would have thought of placing his men within the swamp just to move them closer to the river.

Conversely, the Russians saw that boggy ground as the chance to gain a foothold on the western bank and so formed a "swamp bridgehead," placing their troops in a situation that the German defenders certainly did not envy. Our infantry frankly considered it impossible that the Russians could remain in the swamp for a long period of time. One observer, stationed in a nearby church tower, had an excellent view of the whole swamp bridgehead and watched incredulously as the helmet-covered heads of the Soviet defenders—their bodies concealed by the reeds—bobbed up and down like corks from the necks of champagne bottles. The Russians rested their rifles in the forks of branches or on boards and remained ready to fire at all times. By their side, the frogs of the swamp frolicked and peacefully croaked their monotonous evening song as an accompaniment to the conduct of the enemy, which seemed senseless to our troops. Yet we knew that the Russians must have taken this step as part of a plan. What could it be? Only subsequent events answered this question.[4]

Apparently thwarted in this crossing attempt, the Russians changed both the scene of action and their method of attack. It seemed plain to our officers that the Soviets felt they had fared badly in the swamp or they would not have abandoned this axis of attack after the second attempt. To change or abandon a plan once it had been adopted was not characteristic of the Russian way of thinking, and when such occurred, we always considered it an indication that the enemy felt himself to have suffered a serious defeat.

The enemy now therefore selected the battalion immediately adjacent to the north as the objective of his next attack on the afternoon of 3 August. This sector covered a group of wooded hills in an area where their elevation varied greatly, affording only a very limited field of view because of dense underbrush. The eastern edge of these hills—thirty to fifty meters high and situated along the western bank of the Donets—provided our defenders with good visibility and a chance to use their weapons effectively. However, the men of the battalion knew from prior experience that once the Soviets gained a foothold in the woods (which were difficult to defend) it would be nearly impossible to dislodge them.

We knew from two years of fighting that the only effective method of driving Red Army soldiers out of a wilderness such as this involved the use of massed troops or resorting to such extremely radical means as flamethrowers, flamethrowing tanks, or setting the forest on fire. Often it became necessary to encircle and destroy Russians in the woods in close combat, which necessarily resulted in severe losses on both sides. Russian tenacity surpassed anything previously known in other theaters of operation. The danger of becoming embroiled in a fight for these particular woods was all the greater because our line was so thinly manned. The Citadel offensive had left our line companies with scarcely half their assigned combat strength, and no adequate reserves existed in the rear.

At best the battalion had to rely on a few well-trained assault patrols and the slender regimental reserve (a company of sixty men) to eliminate any penetrations. To set fire to the young trees with their green leaves would have been impossible. Hence the officers on the scene regarded the future with grave concern. They knew they would have to collapse the Russian attack in front of the main battle line. Otherwise, we risked the loss of the wooded hill zone, which would make an excellent assembly area for the Soviets to concentrate for a strong thrust into our position. Only the 320th Infantry's divisional artillery (which was strong and still intact) and the Luftwaffe could enable us to thwart the enemy's plan. Both did all they could.

No sooner had the Russians readied their first stream-crossing equipment in the willows and reeds than our observers identified it, allowing us to destroy it by artillery fire despite its excellent concealment. Reconnaissance aircraft also spotted heavily manned trenches in the vicinity of the Donets. A short time afterward, Luftflotte Four's bomber wings arrived on the scene and smashed the enemy's troop concentrations and advanced heavy weapons in wave after wave of attacks. Even the Soviet batteries (which had previously adjusted their fire to target our positions along the edge of the hills) fell silent out of fear not only of German bombers but—even more—from dread of the 210mm howitzer battery from I Battalion, 213th Artillery Regiment, attached to our forward units. This battery had accurately determined the location of the supporting Russian guns by sound and flash ranging and took them under effective and precisely adjusted fire before they were able to change position. This success resulted in a further withdrawal and increased caution (one might say timidity) on the part of the Russian artillery, which served substantially to decrease its effectiveness.

On the other hand, periodic surprise fire from enemy *Stalinorgeln* proved extremely irksome.[5] These rocket launchers changed locations immediately after firing each salvo and hence could never be taken under fire by the 320th Infantry Division artillery. Only after our artillery observers determined that the rocket batteries repeatedly took up position—in irregular succession—at the same three or four crossroads did German artillery manage to silence them. Each of the available batteries from the II, III, and IV Battalions; 320th Artillery Regiment; and the attached 210mm howitzer battery adjusted its fire to one of the known rocket-launcher positions so that all the alternate positions could be hit simultaneously by a hail of fire as soon as the launchers fired a salvo. The fire from at least one of the ambush batteries then would certainly hit the target directly, and in fact many a rocket launcher was disabled by use of this method. The crews of the surviving rocket launchers stopped moving their launchers into the open and could no longer fire so freely on our infantry. Thus the rocket launchers ceased to constitute a threat, and this tactical solution once again proved the old saying that "necessity is the mother of invention."

Only after that incident did the troops enjoy a brief period of quiet, which proved to be the pleasant interlude before the storm, as the Russians now decided to capitalize on their proficiency at night operations. General Postel's artillery and heavy infantry weapons attempted in vain to interfere with or break up—by means of harassing fire—the new Soviet preparations for a night crossing of the Donets. This time the Russians intended to try their luck at two points simultaneously. In keeping with the Russian character, the first of these two was where they had suffered defeat the previous day. Yet simultaneously our observers also detected lively movement, the sound of logs dropping, and noise of heavy equipment several kilometers to the south, where a highway bridge had formerly spanned the river. It became quickly obvious that the Soviets intended not just to cross but to bridge the river and that this was where their main effort could be expected. Our troops passed a wearying and tense night, with every man realizing that the Russians planned to throw their full weight of men and equipment into the upcoming battle in order to achieve a quick decision, even if only by sheer weight of numbers.

With the first light of dawn on 4 August, relocated Red Army batteries hurled salvo after salvo across the Donets, devastating the bunker positions of the northern battalion along the edge of the hills. By the time all of the enemy's light batteries and a large number of heavy trench mortars had joined the firefight, it assumed the proportion of a regular witches' sabbath. Concentrated on a small area, this "infernal" fire demolished all the defense installations and shelters in the position. Uprooted and shattered tree trunks covered the ground, rendering all movement impossible for the surviving German defenders, who could only crouch resignedly in shell craters and await the inevitable assault by Russian infantry.

At length, after the barrage had raged for nearly two hours, the enemy shells began to whistle over the defenders' heads into a position situated in their rear. Our troops had scarcely discerned this shift of fire when the first Soviet infantry appeared, but after the paralyzing wait under nerve-racking fire the chance to fight back came as a welcome relief. Machine guns began to fire their volleys into the attackers, submachine guns started to rattle, and hand grenades burst on every side. All of these sounds were quickly drowned out, however, when the German counter-barrage opened. Concentrated fire from the 320th Artillery Regiment and attached batteries sent mud and columns of water spouting into the air, smashed the enemy's stream-crossing equipment, and inflicted murderous casualties on his forces.

Nevertheless, the Russians somehow succeeded in getting several rifle companies across the river, primarily because our defenses were no longer compact. The devastating Soviet preparatory fire had torn great gaps in the 320th Infantry's defenses, which had been thinly manned to begin with. Soon Red Army assault troops had penetrated through these gaps and enveloped several pockets of resistance—although these isolated posts put up the most desperate resistance. German troops thus fighting on could hear the enemy's cheering troops move farther and farther toward their own rear areas, and their fate appeared to be settled. Yet our encircled soldiers held their ground, even in this apparently hopeless situation, clinging to the chance that detachments from the adjoining units or the regimental reserves would come to their rescue. Until this happened, however, they were on their own; each hour seemed an eternity.

Suddenly German machine-gun fire raged in the forest to their rear, easily recognizable by its very high rate of fire. Soon the distinctive rattle of submachine guns joined in, the bullets whistling past the defenders' hedgehog positions. Volleys of hand grenades exploded, and a rousing "Hurrah!" echoed through the din of brutal fighting in the forest.

"Our reserves are attacking!" the encircled men cried out to each other as their hearts leaped. "They are coming, they are coming!" Soon the first few groups of Russians could be discerned in full flight through the trees, and their numbers kept increasing. Here and there the fighting flared up again at close range but subsided almost as quickly. The forces surrounding our cut-off troops decreased rapidly as they were caught up in the current of the retreat.

Close on their heels followed the rescuers, spearheaded by a heavily armed combat patrol, and by noon the entire position was back in German hands. This time it had still been possible, through the use of the last local reserves, to eliminate the Soviet penetration and thus avert calamity. Yet even though the Russians had suffered severe losses, they nonetheless clung tenaciously to a thin strip of the western riverbank. They held this narrow piece of ground thanks almost entirely to the weight of their artillery, which now threw down a protective curtain of fire. Such an action clearly indicated that the enemy intended to move up reinforcements and renew his attack.

The Russians assaulted the reformed German line that very afternoon, timing their attack to coincide with an attack farther south, which consumed the main efforts of our artillery and air support. To repulse this new attack, no more reserves were available, and the Soviets managed to achieve a deep penetration into the woods. Only the commitment of the divisional reserve (about a dozen assault guns and a 100-man company of combat engineers) succeeded in stopping the Russian thrust at the western edge of a gorge that traversed the forest from north to south. Fortunately, a variety of forest roads and narrow lanes through the woods facilitated the movement of the assault guns, which—in cooperation with the engineer company—provided critical support to the retiring, scattered units of the badly battered infantry battalion. Our retreating soldiers rapidly assembled along the rim of the gorge, which was a few meters in depth and conveniently situated for an improvised defensive line. There the battalion made its stand and, with the help of the assault guns and engineers, frustrated every Russian attempt to cross the gorge. Each time a Soviet machine gun appeared on the opposite rim of the gorge, our observers identified it as soon as it opened fire, and the deadly accurate fire of our assault guns destroyed it. With every passing hour the German battle line grew stronger as men returning from furloughs or the hospital made their way forward, along with soldiers from the division service and supply units, who were usually moved to focal points during a crisis. In addition, the engineers quickly mined the bottom of the gorge, as well as felling tree obstacles and erecting alarm devices. Taken all together these measures so greatly increased the strength of our resistance that even before sunset the threat of a Russian breakthrough had been eliminated.

In the meantime, however, the situation of the battalion farther south had taken a desperate turn. The northern flank of this battalion had been caught by the enemy push just described and was forced back into a weak oblique defensive line. Instead of pivoting heavy forces southward to expel the battalion from its dominating hill position (which necessarily would have weakened the attack toward the forest gorge), the Russians bypassed the thin German line, hoping to be able to take the defenders in the rear and collapse our entire valley position. Undaunted, this brave battalion frustrated those plans by holding fast in its critical position, despite the risk of encirclement.

All of a sudden a completely unexpected event occurred. In the gap between the battalion defending the gorge and the battalion on the hill, soldiers in German uniforms carrying German equipment appeared and, in good German, reported the arrival of reinforcements come to aid the threatened sector in the nick of time. Understandably, the troops received this news with great joy, and the story spread through the battalion with lightning speed. Before the battalion commander had time to ascertain the strength and origin of this seemingly providential reinforcement, the Soviets launched an assault along the battalion's entire front. In minutes the situation became critical, and the battalion committed every last man to the front line.

This was the moment when the "German" soldiers from the newly arrived companies poured out of the woods in dense columns and opened a murderous hail of fire against the battalion's flank and rear. Through the confusion that followed, shouts rang out: "Here are Germans!" "Don't fire!" "Cease fire!" "Madness!" "What's going on here?" For precious minutes no one among the defenders comprehended what had happened. Abruptly, all firing ceased as these new "Germans" had become hopelessly intermingled with the defenders. Now they unleashed ear-splitting yells of "Urrah! Urrah! Urrah!" and attacked at close quarters. In this bewildering situation it was impossible to distinguish friend from foe, and everyone in the forest began to fight everyone else. No one seemed to be able to help or even to disentangle the chaos.

The battalion commander suddenly grasped the purpose of the insidious attack and realized in a flash that only one decision could possibly save his unit and keep the entire valley position from being rolled up. He ordered an immediate retreat toward the northern edge of A[——] village, a call that had the effect of a kindling spark. Even in the midst of confused fighting our soldiers recognized their commander's voice and passed on the order; soon every German soldier understood exactly what had to be done. The order would not be easy to execute, but unless it was carried out every man and piece of equipment would soon be lost. Yet the commander held firm in his belief that his officers and his seasoned infantrymen could make it.

The battalion commander hastily gathered together a few officers and all the enlisted troops in his immediate vicinity and formed them into an assault detachment that he led personally. Holding submachine guns or rifles in front, ready to fire, or with daggers and hand grenades in clenched fists, this group killed the masquerading Russians wherever they met them, recognizing the enemy by his Mongolian features regardless of the uniform he wore. In this fashion the commander and his men pushed their way through the fighting soldiers, reading the forest edge in short bounds where they found the relative safety of the gullies and depressions that led into the village. Imitating their commander, other officers and senior NCOs [noncommissioned officers] formed their own detachments and fought their way back toward the village. As each contingent arrived, the commander immediately incorporated them into his improvised defensive positions alongside any soldiers from the rear services who happened to be present in the village already. Absolutely no regard was paid to anyone's unit of assignment—there was no time. In the meantime, regimental headquarters, having learned of the near-disaster, rushed a company of reinforcements to the village on trucks provided by division headquarters, along with a handful of assault guns.

Favored by the terrain, which sloped toward the village and afforded cover from both observation and fire, the commander had assembled the remains of his battalion into a coherent defensive position by late afternoon. When the Russians appeared on the edge of the forest soon thereafter, heavy machine-gun fire forced them back to the protection of the trees. Whenever the Soviets repeated their attempt to advance toward the village, artillery and assault-gun fire thwarted them. Time and again the fire of the defenders threw the enemy back into the woods with heavy losses. Gradually darkness fell, and in the twilight a surprising number of stragglers from the battalion found their way back to the village through various detours. By midnight the battalion had nearly reached the strength at which it started the day; in view of the crisis just past, its losses had been amazingly small. The commander's presence of mind and his ability to assert his will even in a chaotic situation, along with the initiative demonstrated by his officers and NCOs, had been all that saved the entire battalion from certain doom. The Red Army's gross violation of international law, though resulting in the loss of an important defensive bastion, failed to bring about the collapse of the German front along the Donets.

The speed with which this battalion recovered from the blow that it had received at the end of the day is indicated by the fact that the commander was able—that very night—to plan confidently on recapturing the lost position on the following morning. In this he demonstrated his confidence in the men who had passed with him through that black day. At dawn on 4 August he intended to strike the enemy (who was certain to try another advance) so hard with a surprise blow that the lost hill position might be recaptured.

At first light the Russian artillery and heavy mortars began shelling the village with a fire that quickly grew in intensity. With a deafening din, echoed over and over again throughout the forest, shells roared and whistled up to burst in the village and on the other side of the road. Under the protection of this wall of fire, wave after wave of Russians broke out of the forest and ran down through the meadow in front of the German positions.

The leading elements of the Russian attack had already come within storming distance when the German counterattack began. Ground attack and bomber wings appeared over the scene and struck the enemy on a continuous basis. The assault guns (whose number had been greatly increased overnight) moved forward against the Soviet line, all guns blazing. These guns and the machine guns being fired from trenches, foxholes, and houses, as well as the artillery, antitank guns, and flak, spread such havoc in the enemy ranks that the attack literally melted away. Caught in terrain that offered no cover, the Russian soldiers knew that their only chance to survive this hail of fire lay in an immediate retreat to the woods.

At the very moment, however, when the enemy started pulling back, the guns of the 320th Artillery Regiment began firing a deadly barrage into the edge of the forest, inflicting serious losses on the Russians and destroying their cohesion as a fighting force. Men ran in all directions, looking for some way to save themselves, but only battered remnants managed to find refuge in the forest. Even among the trees there was no safety to be found, and no time to reorganize, for the battalion commander now led his men in a spirited counterattack. His thin companies of infantry, still smarting from the enemy's trickery on the previous afternoon, followed the fleeing Russians, tracked them down in the forest, and—by pushing forward rapidly—prevented them from rallying on the original German hill position. Hardly two hours had passed since the beginning of the attack when the leading German infantrymen regained the positions held the previous day and secured them in short order.

The treacherous attack on 3 August had indeed created a perilous situation, but the counterattack on 4 August completely nullified any success that the Russians had unfairly gained. Heavy losses in men and equipment were the result of this operation on the Soviet side, including the deaths of the majority of Russian soldiers who had worn German uniforms. Unfortunately, our worn-out and depleted companies lacked the strength to push the enemy back across the Donets, though the 320th Infantry Division still held the critical hill positions in the south and the line of the forest gorge to the north.

Despite the heavy losses repeatedly suffered in bridge-building attempts at the southern bridgehead, the Russians resumed their efforts on the night of 4–5 August. Although we had not expected a resumption of construction at this point, our defensive system remained intact, and our harassing fire was guided by the experience gained earlier. Howitzers and machine guns began firing at the same targets as before. Again, machine guns were by far the most effective antipersonnel weapon, while the artillery fire was directed against vehicles and equipment. As on previous nights, the Russians refused to be discouraged and doggedly continued their bridge construction until just before midnight, when they apparently gave up and ceased working. The sound of track-laying vehicles coming from the eastern bank of the Donets gave the impression that prime movers had been moved up to recover disabled vehicles, stores of supplies, and bridging equipment.

In this instance we had arrived at entirely erroneous conclusions. To everyone's great surprise, the sounds of the tracked vehicles did not diminish as dawn approached; on the contrary, the noises came closer and grew louder. When our observers turned on their searchlights, they discovered that what they had taken to be prime movers were in fact tanks that had somehow crossed the river under the cover of darkness. While dawn was breaking the lead enemy tanks reached the outskirts of village B[——], through which they drove with guns firing against our defensive line just to the west. That movement was apparently the prearranged signal for a general attack, as Russian artillery then opened fire on the village from the eastern bank. Shells rained down upon our positions on the ridges and hills surrounding both sides of the valley of A[——] Brook in an obvious bid to neutralize the dominating defenses on the heights.

Our artillery immediately replied with fire aimed at the Russian forces in the valley and east of village A[——]. This barrage, combined with previously erected obstacles and mine fields, delayed the Soviet advance until there was sufficient light to permit more accurate firing. The full morning light revealed that the Russian tanks had cleared the roadblock east of the village and, accompanied by large infantry forces echeloned in depth, had penetrated into the center of the village. Other tanks had followed into the gap and then turned north and south to swing around and begin reducing our defensive positions one strongpoint at a time. Caught off-guard by this attack, the exhausted battalion (minus the assault guns and engineer company, which had been transferred to another sector of the front) had no choice but to fall back rapidly through the valley down which A[——] Brook flowed, yielding its defensive positions of the previous day in village A[——].

This was a critical moment, for the Russian penetration had reached a position from which it could either turn north—enveloping the defenders of the forest gorge—or plunge forward into the firing positions of the divisional artillery. General Postel immediately ordered the return of the assault guns and engineers to counterattack the enemy spearhead, and despite heavy pressure in the fighting along the Lopan River to the west, I released the II Battalion, 1st Heavy Mortar Regiment (equipped with the *Nebelwerfer* multiple rocket launchers), to support his operations. These forces, assembled by late morning, proved sufficient to halt the enemy's advance and then push him back to the eastern edge of village A[——].

During the initial Russian attack that morning, the "swamp battalion" along the riverbank attempted to make its presence felt again. With almost unimaginable tenacity, the Soviet defenders in that bog not only had held their position but also had been reinforced by at least several additional rifle companies. When the Russians launched their tank-supported assault down the valley, these troops tried to capture our strongpoint on the hill overlooking the river by a coup de main. To this end they had slipped down the riverbank and attacked the hill from the south. Fortunately, the German detachment posted there was not caught unawares and immediately pinned these "swamp soldiers" down with machine-gun fire. Moreover, an ambush battery from the III Battalion, 320th Artillery Regiment, had been established against just such an eventuality in complete concealment in a forested depression, from which it suddenly opened pointblank fire against the enemy's rear. As a result, the battalion was caught by fire from two sides, which was unbearable even by Russian standards, and which quickly wore out the resistance of even this battle-toughened unit.

By noon the general Soviet attack had been stopped everywhere and the enemy trapped in a deep, but very narrow, pocket in which he could move neither forward nor backward without sustaining heavy losses. His situation became even more unpleasant as all attempts to bring up reserves to force a new breakthrough failed due to formidable German artillery fire from his flank and rear. Only when darkness again fell would the Russians be able to move up sufficient numbers of troops to give their offensive a new impulse. That prospect deeply concerned General Postel and his subordinate commanders, who had already been obliged to employ their last man and their last weapon to stop the original advance. They could not afford to be satisfied with holding the Russians in place but would have to find a way to throw them back across the Donets before night.

Despite the disparity of forces, General Postel determined to employ his nine remaining assault guns and the engineer company in a frontal attack on both sides of the street running through the middle of the village. The combat engineers were stalwart fellows, "prepared to kidnap the Devil from hell," and well versed in working in cooperation with the assault guns. Supporting weapons on the flanks of the Russian penetration (machine guns, antitank guns, and flak) enjoyed a clear field of fire against the enemy positions, quite literally viewing the village in front of them as if it were situated on a raised table. This circumstance allowed for ideal coordination between the assault troops and their supports, to which could be added a few flights of ground attack aircraft that Luftflotte Four managed to make available. The attack began an hour after noon.

The engineers, it should be noted, were eager above all else to reach the Donets and learn how the Russians had managed to cross such a large number of tanks in spite of the fact that they had been prevented from building a bridge. This question puzzled everyone, all the way up through corps headquarters, because we had been defending this stretch of the river for months. We had measured its depth along all our defensive sectors and knew it to be an absolute tank obstacle, which during the Citadel offensive even our Pzkw VI Tigers and StG III assault guns had been unable to cross until a seventy-ton bridge had been constructed. Yet from the hill to the south (which had been successfully defended against the "swamp battalion"), our observers could plainly see tank tracks leading down to the eastern bank of the river and then emerging again on our side. Many officers on the scene therefore concluded that the tanks that appeared so suddenly must have been amphibious.

As the only officer present who had ever met amphibious Russian tanks, I disagreed. In July 1941, when commanding the 6th Motorized Brigade of the 6th Panzer Division, I had encountered and destroyed six light amphibious tanks on the Szilinia River south of Novoselye, which was located on the large *rollbahn* to Leningrad. At the time, having only a fleeting glance at these vehicles, I had assumed them to be of U.S. manufacture. The fact that such tanks were never to my knowledge encountered again, and having learned since the war that the United States had no such vehicles in production at the time, I now believe that these six tanks were test models of Soviet origin. Whatever their source, the critical question was one of size. The light amphibious tanks compared to the T-34s that the enemy had employed in this attack were as David compared to Goliath. As a result, I considered it impossible for the Russian tanks that had crossed the Donets without a bridge to have been amphibious.

How, then, did these T-34s, whose characteristics we knew quite well, manage to make their way across a river whose depth had recently been sounded at three meters? Although the T-34 had the greatest cross-country mobility of any tank on the continent and had often accomplished astonishing feats, it was the unanimous opinion of all the officers on the scene that no T-34 could have been driven across the Donets here. And yet their existence could not be denied.

Many hours of heavy fighting passed before we solved this riddle. First, it was necessary to reach the river, and though completely exposed to heavy flanking fire, the Russians offered heavy resistance at every step. Each house had to be wrested away from them in close-in, often hand-to-hand, fighting. Soviet infantry clung even to the ruins of buildings pounded into rubble by our artillery as long as their tanks remained in the vicinity. These T-34s now constituted the backbone of the defense, just as they had provided the momentum for the attack in the morning. Every weapon we could bring to bear was firing from all sides, but this had little effect unless an armor-piercing round chanced to score a direct hit and set one ablaze. Our assault guns, which represented the most dangerous threat to the T-34s, had a difficult mission to fulfill, as the enemy tanks—numerically superior—stubbornly held their ground and forced our StG IIIs to approach at pointblank range. Many of the assault guns suffered direct hits on their reinforced frontal armor before they could manage to incapacitate a single T-34. Once the top plate of the frontal armor on any given StG III was smashed, this vehicle had to be relegated to a secondary place in the rear of those of its fellows whose front armor remained intact.

Despite these difficulties, the assault guns gradually made headway; after an hour five T-34s were burning, whereas only a few of our StG IIIs had sustained light damage, and all remained in operation. Yet by the time our troops reached the center of the village, heavy Soviet losses had ironically created a balance of power. The resistance offered by the enemy infantry trapped in the valley actually stiffened as a result of more and more units being brought under direct fire while being caught in the flank by our advance. Those elements that could do so changed their front to face our assault troops directly. Only after the ground attack aircraft entered the fight, hitting these units with continual sorties while our artillery fire from the flanks and rear rose to unbearable proportions, did the Russians' will to fight begin to decrease noticeably. The T-34s, however, continued to offer extremely heavy resistance. Their crews realized that any withdrawal would result in certain defeat and ruinous losses. This refusal to yield could not prevent our victory but certainly delayed it; only by late afternoon had the last T-34 fallen victim to our remaining assault guns, whereupon enemy resistance completely collapsed.

Darkness fell as the German assault elements finally passed through the village, and our artillery observers could resume their old post in the "eagle's nest" at the top of the church tower that they had been forced to vacate that morning. In the last glow of twilight, assault guns accompanied by engineer patrols following the defeated Russians reached the riverbank where the T-34s had emerged through the morning mist. Even at very close range no sign of a bridge could be detected, and only when the confused engineers sounded the depth of the water could the riddle be solved. At a depth of half a meter, the engineers discovered a submarine bridge. The Russians had built such bridges on other occasions in order to shield river crossings from Luftwaffe aerial observation, and so the existence of such a bridge was less a cause for astonishment than the fact that it had been constructed in an incredibly short time during a devastating artillery fire. Only a closer inspection of the bridge foundations allowed this mystery to be unraveled. We discovered two rows of undamaged T-34s, which had been driven into the water one behind the other and which served as supports for the improvised submarine bridge. Planking had been hastily thrown on top of them and attached to the tanks with ropes. Thereafter the venture of allowing other tanks to cross the river on top of the submerged T-34s was immediately hazarded. To the Russians the fact that a few tanks overturned and plunged into the water in the process mattered little. The main objective—getting a majority of them across the Donets quickly enough to achieve tactical surprise—had been accomplished. Only our assault guns saved them the necessity of making a return trip over this strange bridge.

The enemy had obviously hoped to retrieve the submerged tanks from the water and utilize them again after a successful breakthrough. As matters stood, however, our combat engineers blasted them in place, sending another dozen T-34s to the same "tank graveyard" that their fellows had found on dry land. These demolitions constituted the last activity at the end of a day of grueling combat. Now the silence of night drew "a veil of peace over the scene."

Once again, an utterly unusual tactic employed by the Red Army had resulted in surprising success and threatened our entire defense with disaster. Only the immediate countermeasures instituted by commanders on the scene and the courageous bearing of General Postel's troops managed to nullify yet another potential Russian success. That such a small counterattack force—nine StG IIIs and about eighty engineers—managed to defeat a numerically superior opponent could in no small measure be attributed to the employment of a large number of automatic weapons, whose fire was coordinated with precision and struck the Russians with annihilating effect. The ultimate result of this small battle underscores what can be achieved by a minimum number of excellently trained men if they are supported by the most effective weapons.

In view of the continuously deteriorating situation on XI Corps's eastern flank, it is understandable that the Soviets, even after the repulse on 5 August, persisted in their attempts to force a breakthrough on the Donets front. By this time the Russians retained only one bridgehead over the river, along the wooded hills and bounded by the forest gorge that our troops nicknamed *Totenschlucht*—the "Gorge of Death." The enemy forces on the eastern rim of the gorge had remained inactive throughout the course of fighting on 5 August, but it seemed certain to everyone that the next Soviet offensive would have to take the form of an assault across the *Totenschlucht* despite all the inherent difficulties in such an attack.

Whether through coincidence or design, the Russians opened their attack on 6 August, at precisely the moment when XI Corps's left wing faced its most critical challenge, with enemy tank and infantry units attacking deep in the rear along the Lopan River. In effect, if the Soviets simultaneously penetrated our rear area there and forced a breakthrough along the Donets, five divisions would be encircled and destroyed. It was imperative that both the 106th and 320th Infantry Divisions hold their positions, even without any prospect whatsoever of additional reinforcements from corps headquarters.

General Postel found himself forced to resort to a desperate expedient in order to concentrate even minimal reserves. He stripped two battalions from thus-far quiet sectors on his far southern flank, replacing these veterans with a thin screen of recruits and replacements from the division's *Feldersatz* (Field Replacement) Battalion. Employing these young troops, inexperienced in battle as they were, side by side on a broad front without any reserve worth mentioning, constituted a serious risk, but the events of 6 August, as the redeployment of these units took place, proved that it had been imperative to do so.

After several unsuccessful assaults, the Russians managed to cross the minefields in the gorge by an unsparing and inhuman employment of their men. The method employed was very simple: Company after company was driven forward into the heavily mined gorge in front of the enemy lines until even the last mines had detonated. In the end, "fields of bodies" replaced the minefields. Then the next waves of the attack stepped over the bodies of their fallen comrades to climb the western edge of the gorge.

For hours, the devastating defensive fire of German machine guns thwarted every attempt to break over the edge of the ravine. This fire took such an ever-increasing bloody toll among the Russians that eventually an unbroken line of corpses lay at the rim of the gorge. Many a brave Soviet soldier still held his rifle in fire position while his head—pierced by bullets—rested on his weapon. Yet the enemy command needed a breakthrough at all costs, and again and again new waves marched into battle across a carpet of the dead until German resistance finally began to break as a result of the losses suffered and a lack of ammunition.

After the struggle for the *Totenschlucht* had consumed several hours, our infantry finally found itself obliged to withdraw, step by step. We nonetheless managed to maintain possession of the hotly contested western edge of the forest until evening, when reinforcements approached from the rear. Even though the Russians, at horrific cost, had substantially expanded their bridgehead, their efforts to achieve a breakthrough had failed. Not deterred, the Soviets ordered up additional battalions in order to gain a complete success on 7 August.

German reinforcements, however, had also arrived and begun preparing their own attack. The two battalions of the 320th Infantry withdrawn from the south, one battalion from the 106th Infantry, and our few remaining assault guns had the mission of regaining the forest in a concentric attack and throwing the Russians back into the river. A drumfire barrage delivered by all available artillery, reinforced by the *Nebelwerfer* battalion and several batteries of 88mm flak, would precede the attack. We could not, unfortunately, count on air support, because Luftflotte Four had to commit all its strength to support Fourth Panzer Army against the main Soviet breakthrough, whose masses of tanks had yet to be destroyed. This absence of the Luftwaffe, however, was essentially offset by the fact that the Red Army had also committed the overwhelming majority of its own air assets in trying to bring about a decision against Fourth Panzer Army.

Assembly for the counterattack went smoothly, and at the prescribed hour the *Nebelwerfers* and the concentrated artillery of both infantry divisions opened fire. Causing a terrific din, these shells detonated amid the massed troops that the Russians had concentrated for their own attack, shattering them. Heavy howitzer shells roared down into the *Totenschlucht* itself, landing among the troops and staff that had gathered there. Any danger that the German barrage delivered into the forest might hit our own front line had been eliminated by a systematic withdrawal minutes before the artillery opened fire. This brief retirement had been scheduled precisely according to the clock, went as far as the western edge of the woods, and had been immediately preceded by infantry fire that simulated an attack.

Simultaneously with the surprise concentration of fire that struck the Soviet front line, our real infantry attack commenced. Gradually the artillery concentration moved east, as far as the *Totenschlucht*, which, having now been taken under fire from all directions, turned into a mass grave for Russian soldiers and Russian hopes. Such a heavy artillery preparation not only lifted the morale of our assault troops but also did such damage to the enemy that the attack made rapid progress. With assault guns and strong combat patrols forming the spearhead, General Postel's troops reached the *Totenschlucht* before noon and crossed it a short while afterward. Even to our experienced veterans, the gorge offered a ghastly picture of death and ruin.

The single battalion of the 106th Infantry Division, attacking from the north with the support of a few assault guns, also advanced rapidly and pushed ever more deeply into the Soviet flank. Even the battalion on the southern hills, which had been so battered over the past several days, now joined the fight with gunfire and combat patrols. Everywhere the

Russians appeared to be in full retreat. By noon the concentrically attacking battalions had gained direct contact with each other's flanks in all sectors, and the iron ring around the enemy's decimated force drew tighter and tighter. General Postel intended to encircle and destroy the Russians before they could reach the river. By early afternoon the Soviet line had become so constricted that considerable elements of the attacking force, including most of the assault guns, had to be withdrawn from the front for lack of space. Certainly, everyone agreed, in no more than a few hours the entire western bank of the Donets would be back in our hands.

All of a sudden, however, Russian resistance stiffened again. Our spearheads quite unexpectedly encountered heavily mined tree-branch obstacles, tied together with barbed wire, that proved impossible to overcome. Attempts to blast these obstacles showed that behind the initial line rows and rows of additional mines had been deployed, which could not be removed because they were covered by heavy enemy defensive fire. For the first time that day the Soviets also opened a lively artillery barrage, reinforced by the fire of heavy trench mortars, which made any further German advance impossible. Soon it became evident that during the past few days the Russians had established a heavily fortified area on the western bank of the Donets. In the event of a tactical reverse, which the Red Army commanders had to consider as a possibility in light of their experiences over the previous week, they needed an area that could be held under all circumstances. This area represented sort of an "emergency bridgehead," or a "bridgehead within a bridgehead," whose purpose was to save them another costly river crossing if worse came to worst.

Indeed, every German attempt to remove this thorn from our side failed. The assault guns could not keep pace with the other troops in this very uneven and heavily wooded terrain. Nor could our artillery—even the *Nebelwerfers*—effectively "soften up" this small area a few hundred meters in diameter, despite the fact that their hail of fire did dislodge many of the tree-branch obstacles, tear gaps in the minefields, and batter the woods. Not even a single combat patrol managed to break into this position. Even employing flamethrowers proved unsuccessful, as the Russians were crouched in small dugouts and bunkers, against which even this terrible weapon proved ineffective. Although a few bunkers were destroyed and a number of dugouts buried under falling earth, enough remained on the other side and in their rear to forestall our advance.

Prisoner interrogations subsequently informed us that a "security garrison," which had been taken from a choice unit commanded by commissars and which had not taken part in the preceding battle, occupied this fortified bridgehead. These men had been faced with the alternative of holding their positions to the last man or being shot in the back of the neck. Another part of their mission (which they failed to perform) had been to stop any retreating Russian battalions on the west side of the river. These battalions, however, had been so thoroughly battered by the impact of our preparation and the ferocity with which our troops attacked that they eluded the grasp of their commanders. In terrain with such limited visibility, neither the draconian measure of the Russian officers or their commissars nor the fire opened on the troops by the security garrison in the interior bridgehead could stem the tide of the retreat. Instead, they only managed to add to the bewilderment of the panic-stricken rifle companies and increase their losses.

Nevertheless, the Soviets' unusual measure of building a small, heavily fortified "defensive bridgehead" within a large "offensive bridgehead" repaid the effort. Through it the enemy managed to retain one foot on the western bank of the Donets in spite of all the reverses suffered since 3 August. Moreover, this "bridgehead within a bridgehead" remained a thorn in our side while providing a continual ray of hope to the Russians. (It may also have made it easier for many a Red Army commander to transmit the bad news of the final crushing defeat in the woods to higher headquarters.) Eventually, General Postel decided to seal off the bridgehead and cease attacking it in order to avoid unnecessary casualties. Because the Russians also needed time to regroup after the severe losses just suffered, they also refrained from any offensive action, resulting in a brief rest during which both opponents had a chance to recover.

In the meantime, as will be described below, the situation in the rear of the Donets Front had greatly deteriorated due to Fourth Panzer Army's rapid withdrawal on our western flank. Red Army tank units along the Lopan River plunged ever deeper in their effort to envelop XI Corps, which caused me to order a phased withdrawal toward Kharkov. This, of course, necessitated the abandonment of much of the Donets River line. At the last minute, the Russians tried to push forward from their small bridgehead to hit the corps in the rear. Once again they reached the *Totenschlucht*, where so many of their comrades had fallen in vain. But a few hours later, when the Soviets launched their decisive attack across the gorge, they discovered that only German rear guards remained to face them. Having successfully simulated a strong defensive line, these rear guards now pulled out and followed the rest of the 320th Infantry Division, which had moved without interference from the river to its newly assigned position. Thus the Red Army's last hope of rup-

turing the Belgorod-Kharkov *rollbahn*—XI Corps's vital supply artery—
had been shattered.

Retreat to Kharkov, 9–12 August

On the northern front we held a position south of Belgorod for one day,
and abandoned it after the Russians had deployed their forces. Continued resistance in any one position would have led to heavy casualties
and the annihilation of the isolated XI Corps. Continuous Soviet attempts
to outflank our left wing submitted the command to a severe nervous
strain and made extreme demands on the physical endurance of the
troops. Yet however great the sacrifices, they had to be made if worse disaster was to be averted. On 9 August the limits of endurance seemed to
have been exceeded when, after an all-night evacuation, our troops failed
to reach the new phase-line by dawn. Enemy spearheads broke through
along the *rollbahn*, and the location of the entire 168th Infantry Division
was uncertain. Equally alarming news arrived from the Donets and
Lopan sectors. Russian tanks had broken out of the Donets bridgehead,
still other Russian forces had crossed the Lopan, and the assault-gun battalion from Kharkov had failed to arrive. Low-flying hostile planes in
great numbers dropped fragmentation bombs and machine-gunned
troops on the march. Suffering heavy casualties, our soldiers edged toward panic.

A few division commanders came to my corps command post, which
by then was situated close to the front line, and requested authorization
for an immediate speedy withdrawal to Kharkov in view of the critical
situation and the low morale of their forces. Suddenly several trucks
loaded with stragglers came tearing down the highway, ignoring all stop
signals. When the trucks were finally halted, the stragglers explained that
they had become separated from their 168th Infantry Division unit and
had been seized by panic when subjected to a tank attack farther up the
road. They intended to drive straight through to Kharkov, at that time
more than sixty kilometers behind our front. They reported that their entire division had been wiped out and added that the 88mm flak batteries
detailed to block the highway were no longer in place.

Every experienced combat commander is familiar with this sort of
panic, which, in a crisis, may seize an entire body of troops. Mass hyste-
ria of this type can be overcome only by energetic actions and a display
of perfect composure. The example set by a true leader can have miracu-
lous results. He must stay with his troops, remain cool, issue precise orders, and inspire confidence by his behavior. Good soldiers never desert
such a leader. News of the presence of high-ranking commanders up

front travels like wildfire along the entire front line, bolstering everyone's morale. It means a sudden change from gloom to hope, from imminent defeat to victory.

This is exactly what happened. I placed myself at a crucial point along the *rollbahn*, orienting unit commanders and assigning them a mission in the new defensive system I was attempting to improvise. Some self-propelled antitank guns, fortuitously arriving at this instant, I immediately committed to block the highway against a tank breakthrough, which seemed imminent as the fire from approaching Soviet armor crept ever closer. I then quickly drove out past this newly established line toward the din of battle to find out for myself whether the flak batteries were holding the line. Driving around a curve, I suddenly witnessed the destruction of a Russian tank by the improvised antitank front. I counted eleven more disabled tanks and saw the remaining enemy armor withdraw straight into an extensive minefield, where one tank after another was blown up.

On my return I found a fully consolidated front manned by soldiers inspired with fresh confidence. My report on the events at the advanced flak battalion caused a spontaneous outburst of jubilation, which rose to wild enthusiasm when, shortly thereafter, Luftwaffe fighters appeared and shot down more than a dozen Soviet aircraft, clearing the air over XI Corps's front. When enemy rifle divisions advanced on a broad front, our heavy weapons and artillery pinned them to the ground, firing salvo after salvo of shells just over the heads of our infantry. Here and there our heavy machine guns began to spit fire. It was not without reason that the Russians so dreaded these weapons. None could hope to escape their swift rate of fire (1,000 rounds per minute). They systematically liquidated enemy patrols creeping out of hollows and depressions, then fell silent, awaiting their next opportunity. To the left, down below the railroad, our flak batteries returned from the far front in accordance with my orders and reinforced the antitank units at Miranovka. The Soviets, having lost a total of sixteen tanks to the heavy flak (and even more to our antitank mines), turned back with the armor remaining to them. Thus the threat of a breakthrough along the *rollbahn* was eliminated and our lines held.

Meanwhile 6th Panzer Division faced a difficult situation on the corps's left flank when, in addition to its own sector, it had to take over the one previously held by the missing 168th Infantry Division. The Russians exerted heavy pressure against the new line, and 6th Panzer Division requested immediate antitank support. I dispatched twelve self-propelled antitank guns and arranged for an air strike on the Soviet tank column advancing east of the Lopan River. These combined efforts prevented the immediate collapse of XI Corps's flank cover.

Delayed by traffic jams, the long-awaited assault gun battalion did not arrive until noon. After refueling in some gullies covered with underbrush, it was committed in a counterattack against the enemy tanks still threatening the left flank. The mass attack of forty-two assault guns surprised the Russians and hit them hard. The battalion destroyed all enemy tanks and antitank guns on the eastern bank of the Lopan, shattered the Soviet bridgehead, and drove the remaining enemy forces back across the river. By early afternoon the situation was back under control. Reports from the Donets sector indicated that the enemy had been unable to enlarge his bridgehead there in the face of stubborn resistance from the 320th Infantry Division and its supporting assault guns.

It was only after noon that the Russian artillery finally entered the battle in full force along the northern front. The Soviet guns, though certainly very numerous, lacked a unified command and dispersed their fire in many directions, chiefly seeking targets of opportunity. During late afternoon, the enemy artillery fired a preparation designed to presage a big infantry attack to the east of the main road. We promptly recognized what was happening and, having our own completely intact batteries prepared, crushed their bombardment with counterbattery fire. A single Russian attack made with strong forces and tank support reached our front lines but again collapsed under the fire of all our weapons.

Also in the course of the afternoon, the Russian tanks that had turned aside from the main road then reappeared along the high road leading directly south from Belgorod. This attack proved just as unfortunate, however, as they were unable to penetrate the swiftly consolidated antitank position of the 106th Infantry Division, and the marshy ground did not permit them to undertake a flanking maneuver. At roughly the same time, we received word from the Donets that the 320th Infantry Division had managed to hold its ground against the surprise attack of Soviet T-34s across the river. Even though the entire 168th Infantry Division was still missing, XI Corps had scored an initial defensive success. The Red Army's intention to annihilate us by a concentric attack from three sides had failed. Heavy Russian losses in personnel and equipment, including sixty disabled tanks, resulted from the day's operations.

During the night of 9–10 August XI Corps made an unobserved withdrawal to a hastily prepared position about ten kilometers to the south, the salient points of which had already been occupied by advance detachments. Weak rear guards, left behind in the former position, led the Soviets to believe that the line remained fully manned. The next morning, when Russian infantry attacked the position after a heavy artillery bombardment, they found only the rear party maintaining contact. Our troops, who had been thoroughly exhausted by the previous day's fighting and the subsequent night march, were able to recuperate during the morning hours. By noon the first enemy patrols cautiously approached the new position. Its gun emplacements and strongpoints were well camouflaged; Soviet ground and air reconnaissance failed to locate them. The 106th, 198th, and 320th Infantry Divisions held this line, the latter having been pulled back from its positions along the Donets to rejoin the corps.

Russian attacks resumed during the afternoon with increasing violence. The most dangerous Soviet arm by this point was not badly mauled tanks or close air support but powerful artillery. Fortunately, in this particular instance the effect of the heavy artillery concentration was not so devastating as it might have been because the excellent camouflage of potential German targets forced the Russians to deliver flat trajectory fire. Whenever our machine guns or heavy weapons made the mistake of firing from open terrain, however, they were spotted by hostile observers and quickly neutralized. In order to escape destruction, our gun crews had to employ well-concealed and readily accessible alternate and dummy firing positions.

By the evening of 10 August the Russian attacks had lost some of their sting. Having learned from experience over the past few days, the Soviets made probing attacks after dusk to maintain contact with XI Corps in case of another German night withdrawal. We gave these probes a hot reception and—after all such attacks had been repulsed—withdrew unmolested to the next prepared position. By the time that the infantry arrived to occupy the new line, the bulk of the artillery and antitank guns were already in position and ready to fire. (This was achieved because artillery fire positions and observation posts, as well as those for the heavy antitank batteries, had already been reconnoitered and occupied with single-control guns [*Leitgeschuuetze*].) Forming another solid block, XI Corps remained unshaken by renewed enemy onslaughts.

We employed the same delaying tactics during the following days. The withdrawal to successive positions exhausted the troops, but the casualty rate stayed low. The Russians suffered disproportionately high losses, which forced them gradually to relax their pressure on German lines. As the corps front could be shortened and strengthened by units no longer required for flank protection, reserves were formed. The 168th Infantry Division, missing for several days, was found in a well-concealed area when I made a personal reconnaissance trip north of Kharkov. The division commander, Major General Walter Chales de Beaulieu, explained that he had understood his unit was to act as corps reserve and that he had therefore withdrawn to the forests forty kilometers behind the front. Though I recognized that this general had suffered a nervous breakdown, there was no time to be lost. After castigating his conduct in no uncertain terms, I ordered him to commit his division as the covering force in the next position to be occupied. This made it possible to pull out the 6th Panzer Division, designate it as corps reserve, and move it to the forest area for a well-deserved rest.

General Franz Mattenklott's XLII Corps, adjacent to our right, was forced to join the XI Corps withdrawal during the night of 11–12 August because its defensive line along the Donets now formed a deep salient into Russian-held territory. The 282nd Infantry Division on XLII Corps's left wing had not previously been engaged in a tank battle; it offered little resistance to strong Soviet tank forces, which broke through without difficulty and suddenly appeared in our rear outside Kharkov. The situation grew even more critical when the recruits of the newly arrived Grenadier Regiment 848, overcome by fear of the approaching Red Army tanks, ran for their lives until stopped at the bridges in the suburbs of Kharkov. Strong enemy rifle units poured into the wide gap to exploit the initial breakthrough their tanks had achieved. The 6th Panzer Division had to be immediately alerted, and its spearheads intercepted the Russians on the southeastern outskirts of Kharkov, where they had seized the big tractor plant. Counterattacking, 6th Panzer Division dislodged the Soviets from the factory after fierce fighting, destroyed many tanks, dispersed the Russian infantry, and closed the gap. This action, plus the arrival of 3rd Panzer Division to strengthen our flank, meant that the danger of a breakthrough into Kharkov had been eliminated for the time being.

Tank fright is frequent among newly activated infantry divisions when training in antitank defense has been neglected. Combined arms training with panzer or assault-gun units is essential to give each soldier the experience of being overrun by a tank while in his foxhole and to acquaint him with the use of antitank weapons. The regiment of recruits was subordinated to the 320th Infantry Division and soon overcame its "tank panic" to fight gallantly in the upcoming days.

The Battle for Kharkov, 13–25 August

Kharkov now constituted a deep German salient to the east, which prevented the Red Army from making use of this vital traffic and supply center. All previous Russian attempts to take the city had failed. Neither tank assaults nor infantry mass attacks had succeeded in bringing about the fall of Kharkov. Boastful reports made by Soviet radio—as well as erroneous ones by some Luftwaffe pilots—announced the entry of Russian troops into the city at a time when XI Corps's front stood unwavering, but these did not alter the facts. When the STAVKA perceived its mistake (the Russians seen entering the city were merely several thousand POWs), Marshal Joseph Stalin personally ordered the immediate capture of Kharkov.

The rehabilitated Fifth Guards Tank Army received this mission. It was clear that the Russians would not make a frontal assault on the projecting Kharkov salient but would attempt to break through the narrowest part of XI Corps's defensive arc west of the city (the so-called bottleneck) in order to encircle the town. We deployed all available antitank guns on the northern edge of the bottleneck, which rose like a bastion, and emplaced numerous 88mm flak guns in depth on the high ground. This antitank defense alone would not have been sufficient to repulse the expected Soviet mass tank attack, but at the last moment the reinforcements we had so long been requesting—in the form of the *Das Reich* SS Panzergrenadier Division—arrived with a strong panzer component; I immediately dispatched it to the most endangered sector.

The ninety-six Pzkw V Panthers, thirty-two Pzkw VI Tigers, and twenty-five StG III self-propelled assault guns had hardly taken their assigned positions on 19 August when the first large-scale attack of the Fifth Guards Tank Army got under way. The first hard German blow, however, hit the masses of Russian tanks, which had been recognized while they were still assembling in the villages and floodplains of a brook valley. Escorted by Luftwaffe fighters, which cleared the sky of Soviet aircraft within a few minutes, wings of heavily laden Ju 87 "Stukas" came on in wedge formation and unloaded their cargoes of destruction in well-timed dives on the enemy tanks caught in this congested area. Dark fountains of earth erupted skyward and were followed by heavy thunderclaps and shocks that resembled an earthquake. These were the heaviest, two-ton bombs, designed for use against battleships, which were all that Luftflotte Four had left to counter the Russian attack. Wing after wing approached with majestic calm and carried out its work of destruction without interference. Soon all the villages occupied by Soviet tanks lay in flames. A sea of dust and smoke clouds illuminated by the setting sun hung over the brook valley while dark mushrooms of smoke from burning tanks—the victims of our aerial attacks—stood out in sharp contrast. This gruesome picture bore witness to an undertaking that left death and destruction in its wake, hitting the Russians so hard that they could no longer launch their projected attack that day, regardless of Stalin's imperative order. Such a severe blow inflicted on the Soviets had purchased badly needed time for XI Corps to reorganize.

On 20 August the Russians avoided mass groupings of tanks, crossed the brook valley simultaneously in a number of places, and disappeared into the broad cornfields that were located ahead of our lines, ending at the east-west *rollbahn* several hundred meters in front of our main battle line. During the night Soviet motorized infantry had infiltrated through our defense lines in several places and made a surprise penetration near Lyubotin into the artillery position. Because our infantry units were so far understrength, this sort of infiltration had become common; our artillery positions therefore had to be fortified and constructed as strongpoints in the depth of our defensive zone. The gunners had to be given advanced infantry training, after which they were issued extra machine guns and hand grenades whenever possible. Nonetheless, after stubborn fighting with the gun crews, twelve howitzers (without breechlocks, which the crews took with them) fell into enemy hands. The spearhead of the infiltrating units then began shooting it out with local security forces in the woods adjoining the XI Corps command post.

Throughout the morning Soviet tanks worked their way forward in the hollows up to the southern edges of the cornfields, then made a mass dash across the road in full sight. *Das Reich's* Panthers caught the leading waves of T-34s with fierce defensive fire before they could reach our main battle line. Yet wave after wave followed, until Russian tanks flowed across in the protecting hollows and pushed forward into our battle positions. Here a net of antitank and flak guns, Hornet 88mm tank destroyers, and Wasp self-propelled 105mm field howitzers trapped the T-34s, split them into small groups, and put large numbers out of action. The final waves were still attempting to force a breakthrough in concentrated masses when the Tigers and StG III self-propelled assault guns, which represented our mobile reserves behind the front, attacked the Russian armor and repulsed it with heavy losses. The price paid by the Fifth Guards Tank Army for this mass assault amounted to 184 knocked-out T-34s.

In the meantime German infantry reserves supported by self-propelled assault guns from the 3rd Panzer Division had recaptured the lost battery positions, together with all twelve howitzers, and bottled up the battalion of infiltrating motorized infantry west of Lyubotin behind our main line. Stubbornly defending themselves, the trapped Russians awaited the help that their radio promised.

Fifth Guards Tank Army changed tactics on 21 August, attacking farther east in a single deep wedge, employing several hundred tanks simultaneously. But even while they moved across the open terrain along the railroad, numerous T-34s were set on fire at a range of over 3,000 meters by the long-range weapons of the Tigers and Hornets. Thus the enemy did not manage to launch his large-scale attack until late in the forenoon, and as the Russian tanks emerged from the cornfields this time they met the concentrated defensive fire of all Tigers, Hornets, Panthers, StG III assault guns, 88mm flak, and antitank guns. The attack collapsed in a short time, with the loss of another 154 Soviet tanks. The weak rifle units following the armored wedge were mowed down by the concentrated fire of our infantry and artillery as they emerged from the cornfields.

Meanwhile the encircled motorized infantry battalion behind our lines waited in vain for aid. Though it continued the fight with incredible tenacity, by late afternoon its radio announced the unit's defeat and then fell silent forever. After forty-eight hours of heroic defense, this Soviet battalion was killed to the last man—including the radio operators.

Russian losses incurred thus far were enormous, yet Fifth Guards Tank Army still possessed more than 100 tanks, and experience had taught us that further attacks were to be expected, even though such attacks appeared predestined to failure in view of the now vastly superior defense. The few tankers we took prisoner were aware that death or—if they were lucky—capture awaited every one of their comrades.

Contrary to all expectations, an eerie calm prevailed throughout 22 August. Several Russian tanks crawled about in the cornfields and towed damaged tanks away in order to reinforce their greatly depleted ranks. Summer heat shimmered over the bloody fields of the past several days of battle. A last glow of sunset brought the peaceful day to a close. Might the Russians have given up their plans, or even refused to obey the imperative order to attack? No, never! The Red Army would return even if it had to pay for the city with the last man and the last tank: That was clear to everyone.

Fifth Guards Tank Army, in fact, resumed the attack and did so on the same day. Before midnight, considerable noise from tanks in the cornfield betrayed a new approach. The enemy intended to achieve during the night what he had failed to gain by daylight attacks.

We were ready for them. Before the Russian tanks had reached the foot of the elevated terrain, numerous flashes from firing tanks had ripped the pitch-black darkness of the night and illuminated a mass attack of the entire Fifth Guards Tank Army on a broad front. Tanks knocked out at close range already were burning like torches and lit up portions of the battlefield. Our antitank guns could not fire properly, as they could hardly distinguish between friend and foe: *Das Reich*'s Panthers and Tigers had entered the fray, ramming Soviet tanks in a counterthrust or piercing them with shells at gun-barrel range in order to block the breakthrough. A steady increase in the flash and thunder of tank, antitank, and flak guns could be perceived after midnight as our main force of tanks launched a coordinated counterattack. As many tanks and farm buildings went up in flames, the contested plateau was illuminated by their pale light. This finally made it possible to recognize the contours of the T-34s at distances of more than 100 meters and to shell them. The thunderous roll turned into a din like the crescendo of kettledrums as the two main tank forces clashed. Gun flashes ripped the darkness from all around throughout an extensive area. For miles, armor-piercing rounds whizzed into the night in all directions. Gradually the pandemonium of the tank battle shifted to the north, even though flashes also appeared farther and farther behind our front and fiery torches stood out against the night sky. Not until two or three hours later was calm restored in the depth of XI Corps's front. The conflict gradually subsided throughout the entire battle position.

After daybreak on 23 August we could feel the battle had been won, though Russian tanks and motorized infantry still remained in and behind our main battle line, while here and there a small gap needed to be closed. The foremost of the Soviet tanks that had made the forward deep thrust was captured at the western outskirts of Kharkov by a divisional headquarters and the crew members taken prisoner. Though the process of mopping up the battlefield required all morning, by noon the position was back in our hands, and XI Corps was again ready for defense.

Only a small patch of woodland close behind our main line was still occupied by a force of Soviet motorized infantry, supported by a few tanks and antitank guns. All attempts to retake this patch of woods failed with heavy losses. Even heavy, concentrated fires by strong artillery units could not force these Russians to yield. Only an attack by flamethrowing tanks finally ended their tenacious resistance by burning the entire strip of woods to the ground.

The Soviet attempt to seize Kharkov by a large-scale night attack of the entire Fifth Guards Tank Army had failed. Their losses totaled more than eighty burned-out tanks, many hundreds of dead, thousands of wounded, and a considerable amount of equipment destroyed in a single night of battle. Fifth Guards Tank Army's effort to recapture Kharkov had cost 420 tanks in three days of fighting; as an effective combat formation it ceased to be a factor for the foreseeable future. Kharkov remained in our hands.

Blunders on the part of Russian leaders were only partially responsible for the fact that every one of the Fifth Guards Tank Army armored attacks failed, though the Red Army troops fought with extraordinary bravery. I was struck by the fact that the enemy had only weak infantry and artillery forces and that his air forces did not participate effectively at any point during these operations. With these deficiencies the tank forces could not be adequately supported, and any tactical successes could not be exploited. I suspect that Fifth Guards Tank Army had been forced into premature action for reasons of prestige by the well-publicized STAVKA orders.

Despite our defensive victory, Kharkov's evacuation became necessary because of unfavorable developments farther south. Our withdrawal was carried out without difficulty on the night of 23–24 August, and XI Corps occupied a previously prepared position a few miles to the west. Situated on high ground and protected by a swampy valley cutting across the approach roads, the new position was considerably shorter than the defense line skirting Kharkov and could therefore be held more efficiently.

During the withdrawal of our rear guard, the only bridge across the marshes that had been left intact collapsed under the weight of some Hornets, cutting off an infantry battalion of the 106th Infantry Division and eight Hornets on the eastern bank. Russian attempts to annihilate this force were frustrated by our units supporting the bridgehead from the western bank. After holding out for twenty-four hours so that the bridge could be repaired, the rear guard crossed under the cover of darkness on 24–25 August.

APPENDIX 10A

Order of Battle: Eighth Army, 24 August 1943[6]

(Note: due to the extreme exhaustion of most of these units, which had been repeatedly combined and re-combined into *Kampfgruppen* of various strengths, accurate divisional sub-organizations for the period cannot be derived.)

General of Infantry Otto Woehler
XLVIII Panzer Corps
General of Panzer Troops Otto von Knobelsdorff
7th Panzer Division (reduced to Kampfgruppe)
Lieutenant General Hans Freiherr von Funck

Grossdeutschland *Panzergrenadier Division*
Lieutenant General Walter Hoernlein
Totenkopf *SS Panzergrenadier Division*
Brigadefuehrer *Hermann Preiss*
Artillery Commander 130
    Engineer Battalion (Motorized) 127
    Bridge Column Sector Staff 8
    Bridge Columns 297, 2/410

III Panzer Corps
General of Panzer Troops Hermann Breith

223rd Infantry Division
Major General Christian Usinger

Wiking *SS Panzergrenadier Division*
Gruppenfuehrer *Felix Steiner*
Headquarters, 10th Panzer Brigade
    Tiger Battalion 503

Artillery Commander 3
    II/Mortar Regiment 52
    Engineer Regimental Staff 674

Engineer Battalion (Motorized) 627
Bridge Columns 7, 20, 842

XI Corps
General of Panzer Troops Erhard Rauş
198th Infantry Division (reduced to Kampfgruppe*)*
Major General Hans-Jaochim von Horn

106th Infantry Division
Lieutenant General Werner Forst

320th Infantry Division
Major General Georg Postel

Das Reich *SS Panzergrenadier Division*
Brigadefuehrer *Willi Bittrich*

3rd Panzer Division (reduced to Kampfgruppe*)*
Lieutenant General Franz Westhoven

Headquarters, 167th Infantry Division
Lieutenant General Wolf Trierenberg

Headquarters, 168th Infantry Division
Major General Walter Chales de Beaulieu

　Mortar Regiment 54
　Mortar Training Regiment 1
　Artillery Regiment 48
　Artillery Battalions I/19, I/61, II/Training
　Artillery Regiment 7
　Artillery Battalions I/35, I/4, 96
　Artillery Commander 411
　Artillery Regimental Staffs 781, 817
　Artillery Battalions I/213, II/54 III/818, II/62, 857 (−1 batt.)
　Observation Battalion 3
　Self-propelled Panzerjaeger Battalion 393
　Engineer Regimental Staff 601
　Bridge Columns 2/415, 8
　Construction Battalion 112

XLII Corps
General of Infantry Franz Mattenklott
282nd Infantry Division
Major General Wilhelm Kohler

Attached:
   Assault Gun Battalion 905

39th Infantry Division (reduced to Kampfgruppe*)*
Lieutenant General Ludwig Loeweneck

161st Infantry Division
Lieutenant General Heinrich Recke

355th Infantry Division
Lieutenant General Dietrich Kraiss

SS Cavalry Division
Brigadefuehrer *Hermann Fegelein*

6th Panzer Division (reduced to Kampfgruppe*)*
Colonel Rudolf Freiherr von Waldenfels
Heavy Mortar Regiment 1
   Sturm Battalion 8
   Artillery Regiment 99
   Artillery Battalions I/38, II/38, II/43, I/25, 81
   Artillery Commander 107
   Artillery Regimental Staff 612
   Artillery Battalions I/77, II/71
   Artillery Batteries 2/800, 2/857
   Light Observation Battalion 13
   Assault Gun Battalion 228
   Engineer Regiment (Motorized) 620
   Construction Battalion (POWs) 153
   Bridge Column 603

Army Troops:

   Tiger Battalion 560
   Senior Artillery Commander 310
   Commander of Mortar Troops 1
   Commandant, Poltava
   Engineer Battalions (Motorized) 651, 22
   Bridge Column (Motorized) 923
   Bridge Construction Battalion 531
   Bridge Column Sector Staff 8
   Bridge Columns 7, 9, 2/60, 110, 2/407
   Construction Battalion 26
   Bicycle Construction Battalion 676
   Organization Todt Regiment Heidenriech
   Organization Todt Battalions 30, 40

APPENDIX 10B

Combat Strength Report: Eighth Army, 24–25 August[7]

XLVIII Panzer Corps

7th Panzer Division (reduced to Kampfgruppe*)*

Unit strength: 11,528
Combat strength: 4,268
Panzers (operational): 17
Panzers (in repair): 44
Light Field Artillery: 8
Heavy Field Artillery: 3
88mm Flak: 5
Medium Antitank guns: 14
Heavy Antitank guns: 21

Grossdeutschland Panzergrenadier Division

Not reported

Totenkopf *SS Panzergrenadier Division*

Unit strength: 8,976
Combat strength: 4,805
Panzers (operational): 31
Panzers (in repair): 124
Light Field Artillery: 22
Heavy Field Artillery: 14
100mm Cannon: 4
20mm Flak: 38
37mm Flak: 8
88mm Flak: 12
Medium antitank guns: 30
Heavy antitank guns: 25

III Panzer Corps

223rd Infantry Division

Unit strength: 7,787
Combat strength: 4,717

Light Field Artillery: 31
Heavy Field Artillery: 6
Medium antitank guns: 16
Heavy antitank guns: 24

Wiking *SS Panzergrenadier Division*

Unit strength: 8,611
Combat strength: 3,761
Panzers (operational): 27
Panzers (in repair): 20
Assault guns (operational): 4
Assault guns (in repair): 0
Light Field Artillery: 23
Heavy Field Artillery: 8
100mm Cannon: 4
20mm Flak: 25
37mm Flak: 3
88mm Flak: 7
Medium antitank guns: 30
Heavy antitank guns: 17

Tiger Battalion 503

Unit strength: 1,092
Combat strength: 355
Panzers (operational): 25
Panzers (in repair): 17
20mm Flak: 6

XI Corps

198th Infantry Division (reduced to Kampfgruppe*)*

Unit strength: 10,794
Combat strength: 3,202
Light Field Artillery: 17
Heavy Field Artillery: 3
Medium antitank guns: 8
Heavy antitank guns: 13

106th Infantry Division

Unit strength: 10,238
Combat strength: 3,867
Light Field Artillery: 21
Heavy Field Artillery: 6
20mm Flak: 12
Medium antitank guns: 10
Heavy antitank guns: 17

320th Infantry Division

Unit strength: 9,945
Combat strength: 2,430
Light Field Artillery: 24
Heavy Field Artillery: 8
Medium antitank guns: 21
Heavy antitank guns: 21

Das Reich SS Panzergrenadier Division

Unit strength: 13,592
Combat strength: 5,692
Panzers (operational): 22
Panzers (in repair): 138
Assault guns (operational): 22
Assault guns (in repair): 6
Light Field Artillery: 36
Heavy Field Artillery: 12
100mm Cannon: 4
20mm Flak: 37
37mm Flak: 6
88mm Flak: 12
Medium antitank guns: 34
Heavy antitank guns: 18

3rd Panzer Division (reduced to Kampfgruppe)

Unit strength: 10,218
Combat strength: 3,991
Panzers (operational): 30
Panzers (in repair): 58
Light Field Artillery: 23
Heavy Field Artillery: 8
100mm Cannon: 4
20mm Flak: 39
88mm Flak: 8
Medium antitank guns: 14
Heavy antitank guns: 26

167th Infantry Division (reduced to Kampfgruppe)

Unit strength: 5,747
Combat strength: 1,749
Light Field Artillery: 20
Heavy Field Artillery: 7
20mm Flak: 11
Medium antitank guns: 8
Heavy antitank guns: 1

168th Infantry Division (reduced to **Kampfgruppe**)

Unit strength: 9,193
Combat strength: 2,471
Light Field Artillery: 17
Heavy Field Artillery: 5
150mm Mortars: 10
Medium antitank guns: 5
Heavy antitank guns: 8

Self-propelled Panzerjaeger Battalion 393

Unit strength: no report
Combat strength: no report
Assault Guns (operational): 0
Assault Guns (in repair): 7

XLII Corps

282nd Infantry Division

Unit strength: 8,711
Combat strength: 2,669
Light Field Artillery: 12
Heavy Field Artillery: 6
Medium antitank guns: 2
Heavy antitank guns: 4

Attached:
Assault Gun Battalion 905
Unit Strength: 430
Combat Strength: 150
Assault Guns (operational): 2
Assault Guns (in repair): 21

39th Infantry Division (reduced to **Kampfgruppe***)*

Unit strength: 6,424
Combat strength: 1,579
Light Field Artillery: 21
Heavy Field Artillery: 7
Medium antitank guns: 13
Heavy antitank guns: 14

161st Infantry Division

Unit strength: 6,257
Combat strength: 2,422
Light Field Artillery: 32
Heavy Field Artillery: 11
Medium antitank guns: 12
Heavy antitank guns: 13

355th Infantry Division

Unit strength: 7,500
Combat strength: 3,855
Light Field Artillery: 24
Heavy Field Artillery: 6
100mm Cannon: 3
Medium antitank guns: 13
Heavy antitank guns: 26

SS Cavalry Division

Unit strength: 7,500
Combat strength: 2,500
Assault guns (operational): 4
Assault guns (in repair): 3
Light Field Artillery: 8
Heavy Field Artillery: 3
20mm Flak: 11
88mm Flak: 4
Medium antitank guns: 8
Heavy antitank guns: 12

6th Panzer Division (reduced to Kampfgruppe)

Unit strength: 9,777
Combat strength: 3,883
Panzers (operational): 6
Panzers (in repair): 48
Light Field Artillery: 23
Heavy Field Artillery: 12
100mm Cannon: 4
20mm Flak: 39
88mm Flak: 8
Medium antitank guns: 14
Heavy antitank guns: 26

Assault Gun Battalion 228

Unit strength: 470
Combat Strength: 165
Assault Guns (operational): 4
Assault Guns (in repair): 26

Army Troops:

Tiger Battalion 560
Unit Strength: 648
Combat Strength: 312
Panzers (operational): 13

Panzers (in repair): 18
20mm Flak: 3

Eighth Army totals (excluding *Grossdeutschland*)

(Note: This report detailed only the strength organic to the divisions and that of independent panzer, assault gun, and panzerjaeger battalions, omitting all other artillery and engineer troops.)

Unit strength: 159,598
Combat strength: 61,327
Panzers (operational): 158
Panzers (in repair): 449
Assault guns (operational): 51
Assault guns (in repair): 82
Light Field Artillery: 406
Heavy Field Artillery: 137
100mm Cannon: 27
150mm Mortars: 10
20mm Flak: 222
37mm Flak: 17
88mm Flak: 54
Medium antitank guns: 253
Heavy antitank guns: 292

APPENDIX 10C

Changes in Combat Strength: XI Corps, 4 July–25 August 1943[8]

(Note: this report covered the divisions actually assigned to XI Corps on 25 August. Of these, only the 106th and 320th Infantry Divisions had been under corps control at the beginning of Operation Citadel. Nonetheless, this report provides a useful sampling of combat strength among a sample of infantry and panzer divisions in Army Group South during the period.)

Combat strength (*Gefechtstarke*) equals infantry, engineer, reconnaissance (fusilier), and *Feldersatz* (Field Replacement) battalions.

Division	Combat Strength 4 July	Combat Strength 25 Aug.	Casualties Off.	+	Men	Replacements Off.	+	Men
106th Inf.	6,577	2,752	147		5,933	60		2,722
167th Inf.	6,776	476	148		5,784	65		589
168th Inf.	5,515	569	193		7,281	78		486
198th Inf.	5,572	1,591	99		4,421	63		600
320th Inf.	5,995	1,515	134		6,335	59		1,948
3rd Pz.	5,170	331	161		3,934	101		959
DR Pz. Gr.	7,350	5,128	152		5,208	11		180
Totals	42,955	12,362	1,034		39,436	437		7,484

This report is marred by a number of glaring discrepancies. It is almost a certainty that 3rd Panzer Division's 25 August combat strength as shown here represents a typographical error, as the division was credited in two other reports with just shy of 4,000 combat troops on the same day. Moreover, the strength and losses columns of this report substantiate the assumption that the 331 figure is erroneous. The 3rd Panzer Division entered Operation Citadel with a combat strength of 5,170, took 4,095 casualties, and received 1,060 replacements. Even assuming that every single casualty occurred in the panzergrenadier, engineer, reconnaissance, and *Feldersatz* units (which was virtually impossible), by 25 August 3rd Panzer Division should have been able to report a combat strength of at least

2,135. The fact that the strength documented in other reports was about 1,800 higher suggests that the division's panzer regiment, artillery regiment, and panzerjaeger battalion had between themselves suffered about that many casualties.

There is also reason to suspect that the number of replacements apparently received by *Das Reich* is incorrect as well. Aside from the fact that the SS divisions normally received replacements at a steadier rate than Wehrmacht units, the numbers otherwise make no sense. *Das Reich* began the period with a combat strength of 7,350 and ended it with 5,128, for a decline of 2,222, yet suffered 5,360 casualties and received only 191 replacements. For this to have been possible, *Das Reich* would either have had to take nearly 3,000 casualties in the panzer regiment, artillery regiment, assault gun battalion, and panzerjaeger battalion while suffering almost 800 fewer losses in its infantry-type elements, or else have suffered so many minor casualties that literally thousands of men managed to return to the ranks within six weeks. Occam's razor and common sense suggest that a more realistic answer is a reporting error.

APPENDIX 10D

Combat Strength Report: XI Corps, 26 August 1943[9]

(Note: This report is somewhat at odds with the previous day's report for the entire Eighth Army. Strength figures fluctuated almost every day due to a variety of reporting irregularities during heavy fighting. It should also be recognized that XI Corps took significant casualties during the withdrawal from Kharkov, which do not seem to have appeared in the reports until 26 August. These reports starkly delineate the losses suffered by XI Corps, especially those in combat strength and antitank guns, during the Kharkov evacuation.)

320TH INFANTRY DIVISION

Grenadier Regiment 585:	379 Officers and men
Grenadier Regiment 586:	390
Grenadier Regiment 587:	384
Reconnaissance Bn. 320:	167
Detachment, 167th Inf.:	12
Feldersatz Battalion 320:	48
Total:	1,380

Light field artillery: 24
Heavy field artillery: 8
Medium antitank guns: 7
Medium antitank guns (Russian): 3
   Note: two of these guns lacked ammunition
Heavy Antitank guns: 14

106TH INFANTRY DIVISION

Grenadier Regiments 113, 239, 240:	2,277 Officers and men
Reconnaissance Battalion 106:	208
Feldersatz Battalion 106:	687
Total:	3,172

Light field artillery: 21
Heavy field artillery: 6
20mm Flak: 12
Medium antitank guns: 25
Heavy antitank guns: 8

198TH INFANTRY DIVISION

Grenadier Regiment 305:	450 Officers and Men
Grenadier Regiment 308:	451
Grenadier Regiment 326:	521
Reconnaissance Battalion 235:	93
Artillery *Kampfgruppe*:	115
(167th Infantry Division)	
Feldersatz Battalion 235:	220
Total:	*1,850*

Light field artillery: 17
Heavy field artillery: 3
Medium antitank guns: 6
Heavy antitank guns: 5

DAS REICH SS PANZERGRENADIER DIVISION

Division combat strength:	7,365
Panzers (operational):	4 Pzkw III, 32 Pzkw IV, 27 Pzkw V, 7 Pzkw VI, 6 *BefehlPz*. (Command tanks), 6 StG III
Total:	*92 Armored Fighting Vehicles*

Light field artillery: 36
Heavy field artillery: 12
100mm Cannon: 4
20mm Flak: 37
37mm Flak: 6
88mm Flak: 12
Medium antitank guns (Motorized): 20
Heavy antitank guns (Motorized): 14
Heavy antitank guns (Russian): 1

3RD PANZER DIVISION

Divisional combat strength:	3,991
Panzers (operational):	2 Pzkw III, 9 Pzkw III (75mm), 19 Pzkw IV

Light field artillery: 23
Heavy field artillery: 8
100mm Cannon: 4
20mm Flak: 39
88mm Flak: 8
Medium antitank guns (Motorized): 11
Heavy antitank guns (Motorized): 8

APPENDIX 10E

Report of Enemy Tanks Destroyed: 198th Infantry Division, 19 July–14 August 1943[10]

Date	Number of Russian tanks/ assault guns destroyed
19 July	5
24 July	4
4 August	6
5 August	32
6 August	16
7 August	8
8 August	3
10 August	2
11 August	10
12 August	4
14 August	22
Total:	*112*

11

Sixth Army Defends the Mius River Line

by Major Dr. Martin Francke
War Diarist, Sixth Army

Editor's Introduction

The Red Army launched three counteroffensives between 11 and 18 July 1943 to divert the Germans from pressing forward with the attack on the Kursk salient: against the Orel salient, from the Izyum bridgehead, and across the Mius River. The two-pronged assault toward Orel has drawn the most attention from historians, primarily due to its proximity to the Kursk offensive, the strategic stakes, and the participation of some of the German army's most elite units and well-known generals. The attempt to break out of the Izyum bridgehead was contained fairly handily, though it did have an impact on Operation Citadel in that the operation required the commitment of the XXIV Panzer Corps, which was Army Group South's final mobile reserve.

The Soviet effort to crack open the Mius River line in late July–early August has fallen into the shadows, obscuring an interesting and important battle. One reason for this lack of attention is the personalities involved. Karl-Adolph Hollidt, Willi Schneckenburger, Erich Brandenberger, Walter Nehring, and Paul Hausser—the senior generals who directed the battle—were all highly respected professionals, and the latter three are well known to students of the Russian front and World War II in general. None of them, however, left significant writings in regard to the fight for the Mius River line. Worse still, the hard-fought victory won by Sixth Army in the immediate aftermath of the battle of Kursk was not one that was destined to be celebrated for long. Within weeks the Soviets attacked again—this time in overwhelming force—shattering Hollidt's lines like an eggshell. The encirclement, breakout, and retreat of his army toward the lower Dnepr immediately eclipsed the earlier triumph.[1]

Nonetheless, Sixth Army's July–August battle for the Mius River line, however ephemeral the victory, should not be ignored. It is both a fascinating study on the impact of terrain on tactics (the area was divided between deeply cut ravines and high, narrow ridgelines) and a protracted opportunity to examine the intricacies of the evolving tactics of infantry-armor cooperation on both sides in the middle of the war. The battle also provides a necessary corrective to the idea that the ferocity of the fighting at Kursk was somehow unparalleled: Day by day the two panzer-grenadier divisions of II SS Panzer Corps suffered higher casualties, both in terms of men and machines, at the Mius River than they did in the drive toward Prokhorovka.

Major Dr. Martin Francke, the staff officer tasked with keeping Sixth Army's war diary (the *Kriegstagebuch*), was particularly well placed to follow the battle at all levels. He had access to the reports of the fighting transmitted to headquarters by the individual divisions and all relevant situation maps, which he combed for details to include in his official narrative. Privy to the conversations of Hollidt, his chief of staff, as well as corps commanders, Francke understood the reasoning behind most of the operational decisions taken during the battle.

Even more significant, Francke's manuscript, unlike almost all of the others in the historical program, was not written after the war. Francke composed his study of Sixth Army's battle within two weeks of its culmination, in early August 1943. When the original document, *Der Juli-Abwehrschlacht Der 6.Armee Am Mius vom 17.7–2.8.1943* (preserved in T-312, Reel 1467, at the National Archives), is compared to the German typescript translated by the U.S. Army in 1947, it is immediately evident that they are identical. The fact that Francke's document is therefore contemporary to the events described rather than a later reconstruction explains why, in the opening segments, he betrays no awareness that the overt indications of an imminent offensive were actually part of an elaborate Soviet *mashirovka* [deception] program designed to make the Germans pull units out of the Citadel offensive.[2]

Sixth Army Defends the Mius River Line
by Major Dr. Martin Francke
War Diarist, Sixth Army

The Russian Strategic Concentration in Front of Sixth Army

Until 9 July 1943 the Russian strategic reserve opposite the Mius River sector, consisting of Second Guards Army (two rifle corps, four tank/mechanized corps, and three cavalry corps), remained distributed in depth. The advance elements of Second Guards Army, which directly confronted our Sixth Army, had been maintained close enough to the front lines that that they could feasibly be assembled for a large-scale attack within three to five days. We had observed no withdrawal of units on our front to reinforce the fighting on the battlefield between Belgorod and Orel nor any change in the disposition or density of the Russian artillery.

Nevertheless, 10 July marked a turning point for Sixth Army. By early afternoon there began such a movement of infantry and mechanized forces in front of Lieutenant General Erich Brandenberger's XXIX and General of Infantry Willi Schneckenburger's XVII Corps that by the following day there could be no doubt but that the Soviets were concentrating their troops for action. Weather unfortunately rendered our air reconnaissance ineffective between 11 and 14 July. On the other hand, our troops had been trained in ground observation for weeks, and in conjunction with the 623rd Signal Intercept Company (long-range) and the 549th Military Intelligence Company (short-range) we had obtained much accurate information about the enemy's movements and intentions. As early as 11 July it became apparent that the main Russian concentrations had been assembled east of Kuibyshevo and around Dmitrievka (the boundary between XXIX and XVII Corps and the center of XVII Corps). On 12 July an additional Russian group appeared near the boundary between XVII and IV Corps around Malaya Nikolsevka while another small group surfaced opposite the right sector of the 17th Infantry Division near Ryazhanaya.[3]

The carelessness of the lower-echelon Red Army commanders provided us with many clues. Examples of this carelessness included the II Guards Mechanized Corps driving into the Nagolnaya Valley with their headlights turned on; artillery moving and infantry arriving at the front in broad daylight; and high-burst artillery ranging near Dmitrievka. Additional though less striking observations than these helped us complete the picture. For example, messenger pigeons were seen rising from two of the Soviet concentration areas, flying both east and west, and small groups of officers, maps in hand, could be observed acting as guides. Our combat patrols suddenly encountered no opposition: Russian front-line trenches were either empty or the men had been withdrawn as our patrols approached, in order to keep prisoners or deserters from betraying any information. Finally, our listening posts reported tank noises on the last day of the concentration.

From division headquarters down, Russian radio discipline was poor. Consequently, up through 14 July Sixth Army signal intelligence (both long- and short-range) intercepted most Soviet radio traffic, which allowed us to evaluate both encoded messages and those sent in clear. Radio direction-finding allowed us to pinpoint key Red Army headquarters, discovering, for example, that the Second Guards Army had been brought up immediately behind the Fifth Shock Army. We also discerned that the Fifth Shock and Twenty-eighth Armies had each improvised its own strategic mortar group by diverting resources from quiet sectors, each consisting of the equivalent of two or three Guards mortar regiments. Mentions of these two groups appeared with great frequency in radio traffic because of numerous changes in their chain of command.

Radio intercepts also provided Sixth Army with an increasingly accurate order of battle for the Soviet forces arrayed against it. We first identified the XLI Rifle Corps and 221st Rifle Division as belonging to the Fifth Shock Army on 11 July. Two days later it became possible to assign the 347th and 271st Rifle Divisions to the Second Guards Army. On 14 July Russian traffic revealed that the II Guards Mechanized Corps, 34th Guards Rifle Division, and 13th Guards Mortar Brigade had appeared east of Dmitrievka. This confirmed the results of radio direction-finding, which on the same day spotted II Guards Mechanized Corps's elements in the western part of Dyakovo and in the Nagolnaya and Nagolchik; we also affirmed the presence of five rifle divisions in the Second Guards Army area. Our operators on 15 July intercepted the first orders requiring the II Guards Mechanized Corps to reconnoiter in the direction of Dmitrievka, Stepanovka, and Artemovka (the presumable direction of its subsequent attack). This information agreed with the sudden and quite noticeable absence of all troop movements on our front that began on 14 July and led inevitably to the conclusion that the Soviet concentration had required exactly five days to complete, precisely as our intelligence service predicted.

When effective Luftwaffe reconnaissance flights resumed on 15 July, our pilots reported the Kuibyshevo-Dyakovo-Dmitrievka sectors as the main concentration centers for Soviet mechanized forces (including tanks). Once aerial photographs confirmed that the villages were bristling with Red Army troops and that at least 119 guns had been emplaced near Dmitrievka, there could no longer be any doubt as to the location of the Russian point of main effort when the offensive opened.

The Soviet Southern Front headquarters transferred forward from Novochaktinsk to the northern edge of Darievka on 16 July. Simultaneously, II Guards Mechanized Corps completed its concentration northwest of Dubrovsky (in other words, closer to Dmitrievka), and those elements already near Kuibyshevo moved closer to the front. The results of our long-range aerial reconnaissance, taken together with deserter statements, fixed 17 July as the first day of the attack.

Again it should be emphasized that—because conditions remained unfavorable for aerial reconnaissance throughout most of this period—ground observations and signal intelligence deserved credit for the detailed information Sixth Army headquarters received. The particular reliability and importance of these two branches of reconnaissance, even for operations on a fairly large strategic scale, were definitely proved by this example.

General of Infantry Karl Hollidt, commander of Sixth Army, effectively countered these enemy concentrations through artillery interdiction fire, air strikes, and his own regrouping of forces between 11 and 16 July as we became more certain of Soviet intentions. The 16th Panzergrenadier Division, from Army Group South's reserve, received orders for an increased state of readiness on 11 July. General Hollidt personally briefed Lieutenant General Gerhard Graf von Schwerin, commander of the 16th Panzergrenadier Division, and his officers on their tasks as his army reserve. During the night of 15–16 July, after having been formally attached to Sixth Army, this division moved into the assembly area around Malo-Christyakovo at the center of the XVII Corps sector. By the morning of 12 July XXIX and IV Corps each had been required to detach and place at the disposal of army headquarters one motorized regimental *Kampfgruppe* consisting of one artillery battalion, one engineer battalion, and one antitank company. These two *Kampfgruppen* were placed on a two-hour alert status. Sixth Army also reinforced General Schneckenburger's XVII Corps with heavy antitank, artillery, and assault-gun battalions that had been detached from other corps. On 15 July General Hollidt went forward not only to the XVII Corps command post but also to Major General Johannes Block's 294th Infantry Division and the front-line regiments of the 294th and 336th Infantry Divisions on the boundary between XVII and XXIX Corps. There he discussed future tasks in the upcoming battle with the officers and men.

At 2235 hours, 16 July, Army Group South authorized General Hollidt to alert Lieutenant General Nikolaus von Vormann's 23rd Panzer Division (currently in reserve behind First Panzer Army on our left) to be prepared to serve again as Sixth Army reserve and to expect early commitment in the sector of Major General Carl Casper's 335th Infantry Division. At the moment issued, this order was only precautionary, though it seemed highly probable that this division would soon be needed by Sixth Army. General Hollidt issued a basic order informing the troops about the conduct of battle in the event of a major attack, which stressed the conditions of their commitment, defense in depth, and economy of force. General Hollidt and Major General Max Bork, Sixth Army's chief of staff, personally supervised a final map exercise at the headquarters of General of Infantry Friedrich Mieth's IV Corps, during which the general staff officers of all corps and divisions received instructions regarding the probable commitment of their units as far as could be foreseen from our picture of Soviet preparations.

The hour of decision for both the commanders and their troops had arrived.

Russian Penetration of the Mius River Position, 17–25 July

In the early morning hours of 17 July the Russians unleashed a sudden, heavy artillery preparation, supported by the fire from automatic weapons. This signaled the opening of their major attack against Sixth Army's Mius River front in the Russkoye-Kuibyshevo-Dmitrievka area with the infantry and tank forces previously concentrated forward of the Lyssogorka-Dyakovo-Nish-Nagolchik line. The initial brunt of the attack fell on the Krynka sector between Uspenskaya and Artemovka.

OKH had expected a strong attack against Sixth Army's northern flank, but this did not materialize. Only from the land bridge at Izyum did the Red Army initiate a fairly strong infantry and tank attack against the front of First Panzer Army's XL Panzer Corps. This attack, with respect to both time and place, was strategically unified with the offensive against Sixth Army's eastern front. Given the direction of the two attacks, it may well have been the enemy's intention, after breaking through our defenses, to link up in the Stalino-Postyshevo area. If we are to believe what Russian officers told soldiers who later became our prisoners, the final objective of this offensive was the Dnepr River. At the very least, the Soviets intended to contain strong German forces at the south end of the Russian front in order to relieve the pressure against them in the Belgorod area.

The Russian command more than likely believed that the forces committed in this offensive would be strong enough to crush both wings of Sixth Army. The concentrations opposite our southern sector supported such an interpretation. The Soviets apparently thought that a flanking attack from the Donets toward the south would require them to drive more deeply into our rear, with less prospect of success.

Containing Attacks

Along Sixth Army's northern front, therefore, the Russians restricted themselves to general containing attacks and diversions. By far the strongest of these issued from Malo-Nikolaevka along a narrow front at the boundary of XVII and IV Corps between Ivanovka and Shterovka.

The LIV Rifle Corps of the Third Guards Army committed the 50th Guards Rifle Division; the 67th, 302nd, and 346th Rifle Divisions; one tank brigade; and one or two mortar regiments along a four-kilometer-wide front. The direction of this attack threatened the industrial district of Krasny Luch–Debaltsevo.

The Soviets overran our outer trench line in their initial onrush, seizing Hills 278.5 (northeast of Promandirovka), 223.2, and 207.0 on the eastern edge of the Yelizavetovka Reservoir. They followed up with an attack by mounted infantry and thirty to forty tanks along the Malya Nikolsevka-Ivanovka road and the ravine cutting through Rodkina. Though delayed at the eastern exit of the ravine by minefields (in which several tanks were lost), the Russians continued a seemingly inexorable step-by-step advance against our front-line regiments: Grenadier Regiment 571 of the 302nd Infantry Division and Grenadier Regiment 575 of the 306th Infantry Division. Fierce and prolonged fighting ensued—attacks alternated with counterattacks—and another eight Soviet tanks were put out of action. Thanks to the tenacity of our defending battalions, the Russian penetration was contained along a line passed through the small forest near Hill 243.8 (Swch. Petrovsli), Hill 274.0 (the eastern edge of Shterovka), and Hills 247.2 and 205.2.

Our defenses stymied all further Soviet attempts to break through in this sector on 18 July with the loss of additional tanks. To ensure unity of command, control of Grenadier Regiment 571 on the far left flank of XVII Corps was handed over to IV Corps. That same day, II Battalion/Grenadier Regiment 571—having been reinforced with additional troops and heavy weapons and designated *Kampfgruppe* Wandtke—led a spirited and successful counterattack against the enemy.

For two days German grenadiers struggled in the oppressive heat for control of hills, coal mines, ravines, and underbrush against tanks and the apparently inexhaustible Russian infantry reserves. *Kampfgruppe* Gruber, consisting of two infantry battalions and the Assault Gun Battalion 20, had to fight the entire day of 19 July before it succeeded in clearing the Redkino ravine of the Red Army soldiers stubbornly clinging to its walls. In a night attack II Battalion/Grenadier Regiment 575 threw the enemy off Hill 207.0, and by the end of 20 July the entire main battle line had been recovered. This successful defense—which would assume great importance with regard to the large, overall situation of Sixth Army—could be ascribed to the determination of the command and the courage of the troops. Thankfully, our losses were not excessive; the Russians lost about twenty tanks and more than 200 prisoners.

The Soviets attempted other containing attacks on the Donets River north of Nizhnaya and in the extreme left sector of Sixth Army southeast of Belaya Gora. In both locations a rifle regiment tried to establish a bridge-head on the opposite bank of the river in order to bring up the infantry and tank elements assembled farther to the rear. The objective of these attacks appeared to be to gain control of the southern railroad net behind our front. Within forty-eight hours, however, the Russian intentions had also been frustrated in both areas, thanks to two determined counterattacks by the 335th Infantry Division. Near Belaya Gora, Major General Carl Casper's grenadiers crushed the entire Soviet 1001st Rifle Regiment, taking more than 300 prisoners and much equipment, while around Nizhnoye we captured fifty prisoners and inflicted heavy losses on the Russians who tried to retreat across the Donets in rafts or by swimming.

Soviet Penetration South of Kuibyshevo

Although their containing attacks failed, the Russians launched their main assault in two locations from assembly areas, including Dyakovo, Dmitrievka, Kuibyshevo, and Russki. The southern sector of this attack targeted the area between Yassinovski and Kuibyshevo while the north-ern wing struck a sector extending north of Kuibyshevo as far as Dmitrievka. The southern strip—where the Twenty-eighth Army at-tacked—was the narrower of the two sectors, and the axis of the attack hit the boundary between XXIX and XVII Corps. Seven rifle divisions (151st, 347th, 320th, 271st, 118th, 127th, and 387th) and one tank brigade were committed along a front ten kilometers wide. The Soviets enjoyed a six-to-one or even eight-to-one numerical superiority, and their advan-tage in weapons and equipment was also considerable. Forty Russian batteries laid a heavy barrage on the foxholes, trenches, and shelters of the six front-line battalions of Grenadier Regiment 686 (336th Infantry Division) and Grenadier Regiment 515 (294th Infantry Division) as the at-tack began. Rolling salvos from the enemy's *Katyusha* multiple rocket launchers shook the air, and a thick cloud of dust and smoke obscured the flats along the Mius.

Initially we had difficulty discerning whether the Russians hoped for greater initial success here or in the Dmitrievka sector; they had appar-ently committed roughly equal infantry forces to both attacks. Because the Soviets adhered to rigid rules regarding the commitment and dispo-sition of their mobile troops, we could not expect to see them until their infantry had either achieved a breakthrough or at least penetrated deeply enough into our defensive system to gain sufficient room for tank units to deploy. Until the Russians thought they had reached the moment for their tanks to advance and complete the breakthrough into the depth of our defensive zone, it would be difficult to locate their main attack.

For achieving the initial penetration, tanks accompanied the Russian rifle regiments, which had also been liberally supplied with automatic weapons. The Russian air force supported its infantry with incessant bombing (employing ordinary explosives and phosphorus bombs) and strafing attacks. Thus the attack near Russki developed in this manner: continuous attacks by low-flying aircraft, rolling artillery barrages, and showers of phosphorus, high-explosives, and smoke.

South of Russki and near Skelyanski, however, our minefields delayed the Soviet tanks accompanying the lead assault regiments, probably disabling several. The combined defensive fire of the two front-line regiments and their supporting artillery (firing virtually every gun in both divisions) caused the Russians heavy casualties even during their initial assault. Local reserves staged immediate counterattacks against initial enemy penetrations, knocking out six tanks that tried to reach the high ground east of Gustavfeld and Novo Bakhmutski. Such a counterattack recaptured the village of Petropole, in which the II Battalion/Grenadier Regiment 686 had been encircled for several hours. As our defensive fire grew heavier and heavier, confusion broke out among the Soviet assault units, and none of their objectives could be attained. After an advance of only two kilometers, our front-line regiments stopped the Russians along the chain of hills east of Gustavfeld and Novo Bakhmutski, far short of XXIX Corps's support positions.

The insignificant depth of this penetration and the greater success enjoyed by the enemy in the attack on Dmitrievka prevented the commitment of the bulk of the tank brigade that had been concentrated southeast of Kuibyshevo for a breakthrough near Russki. This decision was made unwillingly, because the Russians tried again on 18 July to make good the failure of the preceding day. This attack proved even less successful, for the Soviet rifle regiments attacked with so much hesitation that our defensive fire decimated them. No new ground was lost, and ten more Russian tanks were put out of action.

Because boundary positions between units are often neglected (or operations there poorly coordinated), General Hollidt immediately shifted the boundary of General Brandenberger's XXIX Corps toward the north to the line passing through Kainovo, Novo Olkhovski, and the center of Kuibyshevo. He also attached all units of the 294th Infantry Division (assigned to XVII Corps) committed in that area to XXIX Corps.

In the meantime, General Brandenberger had been able to reinforce his front-line infantry and artillery, primarily by bringing up elements of the 111th Infantry Division. Allowing only a brief period of time for assembling the troops, *Gruppe* Recknagel (Lieutenant General Hermann Recknagel, commander, 111th Infantry) counterattacked the Russian penetrations with elements of the 111th and 294th Infantry Divisions. This attack jumped off from the area of Marienheim Kol on the morning of 19 July. In the first impetus of the attack, *Gruppe* Recknagel recaptured the ravines at Kholodnaya and Skelyanski, which gave our troops confidence that they would be able to regain the original main battle line. Russian infantry, accompanied by tanks, suddenly launched such a fierce counterthrust, however, that most of the captured ground had to be abandoned again. This attack, which issued from a mine west of Golubyachi, could only be stopped at the western exit of the Kholodnaya ravine. All further Russian attempts to improve their position in this sector through flanking attacks with tank support against Kucherovo or frontal assaults against Podgorny proved futile. Thus even though *Gruppe* Recknagel had to forfeit most of its initial gains, the southern Soviet attack group suffered such heavy losses from our concentrated defensive fire and creative use of antitank weapons that it completely broke the Russian offensive impetus. From 20 July onward the Red Army made hardly any offensive moves in this sector.

The steadfastness of the battalions in the front line, coupled with determined leadership from the XXIX Corps (and attached elements of the XVII Corps), wrested the initiative from the Russian Twenty-eighth Army. Because the Twenty-eighth Army found itself forced to discontinue attacks in this area, Sixth Army was enabled to shift the mass of defensive forces and weapons to the Dmitrievka sector where the Russians *had* achieved a breakthrough.

German losses in this fighting had fortunately been light. The two divisions that bore the brunt of the attack suffered the following losses from 17 to 19 July:

	336th Infantry Division				111th Infantry Division			
	KIA	WIA	MIA	Total	KIA	WIA	MIA	Total
Officers	1	10	0	11	2	6	0	8
Enlisted	73	444	41	558	49	191	37	277
Total	74	454	41	569	51	197	37	285

In addition, elements of the 294th Infantry Division of XVII Corps also suffered casualties in this sector of the front.

The Russian command very quickly drew the logical conclusions from this situation. As early as 18 July we observed columns marching north toward the Dmitrievka sector, and radio intercepts confirmed these movements. By 21 July five rifle divisions remained along the front of the penetration, but four of them had been badly mauled and possessed no offensive potential. The tank brigade and two or three intact rifle divisions had been transferred to the zone of penetration around Dmitrievka, a clear indication that the enemy had shifted his main effort into that zone.

Soviet Penetration Around Dmitrievka

The Soviets considered the terrain around Dmitrievka the most suitable for an attack and therefore concentrated their strongest forces there. Along an attack sector thirteen kilometers wide the Red Army sent in a first wave consisting of eight rifle divisions and the II Guards Mechanized Corps (with an authorized strength of 120 T-34s and eighty T-70s), as well as the 32nd Independent Tank Brigade (with a strength of forty-six T-70s). Counting the tanks assigned in regiments and battalions to accompany the rifle divisions, more than 300 tanks had been concentrated for this attack. In addition, we had observed forty or fifty Russian batteries and a strategic mortar group consisting of three Guards mortar regiments, heavily equipped with multiple rocket launchers. Approaching from the depths of the Soviet position another 150–200 tanks of the IV Guards Mechanized Corps moved forward. The Fifth Shock and Twenty-eighth Armies spearheaded the assault, both probably under the operational control of the Second Guards Army.

Confronting this massed strength, General Schneckenburger's XVII Corps had four front-line and two reserve infantry battalions from Major General Johannes Block's 294th Infantry Division and Lieutenant General Karl-Erik Koehler's 306th Infantry Division. General Schneckenburger's combined divisional and corps artillery numbered (by the most optimistic estimates) about two-thirds of the strength of the Russian guns. The XVII Corps did have General von Schwerin's 16th Panzergrenadier Division placed in its area by General Hollidt as a mobile reserve. This division possessed a single panzer battalion with a strength, as reported on 10 July, of twenty-nine Pzkw IIIs and seven long-barrel Pzkw IVs.

The ratio of forces in this attack thus favored the Russians by a factor of six- or eight-to-one. Because of this numerical advantage, and with their tank forces drawn up in very close formation at the point of main effort, the Soviets probably felt confident about the outcome of the operation.

The Magic of the Landscape

A certain magic about the landscape pervades military life, an intangible influence that the terrain of a battlefield exerts on the troops, so that for apparently inexplicable reasons they are attracted to one point and repelled by another, as by a hill with a single tree sitting atop it in maneu-

ver terrain. The village of Dmitrievka stretched like a worm, adorned by
its many fruit trees, for seven kilometers along the Mius River valley. The
town's western group of houses pointed like a finger toward the Gerasimova Balka, a deep ravine winding toward the northwest. Near Grushevy this ravine disappeared into the Snezhnoe hills. A few kilometers
south and almost parallel to this ravine lay the Olkhovchik, a stream that
in the course of the past thousand years had hollowed out a gorge in
which lay hidden the villages of Malinovka and Stepanovka. Between
these two ravines lay a ridge, the summit of which was Hill 213.9. Innumerable small lateral ravines and draws led up to the ridge, along whose
summit ran the road connecting Snezhnoe to Kuibyshevo. Hill 213.9
dominated all elevated terrain in the area, which was bounded to the
south by a lateral ravine of the Olkhovchik near Kalinovka. The only position that could potentially rival Hill 213.9 was Hill 277.9, farther to the
west, which guarded the Savostyanovka Valley like Fort Donaumont had
been the cornerstone of the French defenses at Verdun. It was at the foot
of this hill that the Russian penetration would eventually be brought to a
standstill.

As past masters of the art of infiltration, the Russians found themselves quite naturally drawn to these meandering ravines, through
which they hoped to make their way into the rear of our positions on
the high ground. Thus they inclined to favor valley tactics, considering
it to be a distinct advantage to possess the Mius flats and the village of
Dmitrievka. Red Army tanks rolled into these ravines at night and at
dawn ascended the slopes of the *balkas* [i.e., ravines]. Russian spearheads advanced everywhere as far as the ends of the ravines near Kalinovka, Stepanovka, Grushevski, and Paradrievo. The mud-colored figures of Soviet rifle troops emerged from the ravines of Gerasimova and
Olkhovchik, ascended the heights behind their tanks, and—despite
many casualties taken in the underbrush of the lateral valleys—
flooded forward in apparently limitless numbers. In the course of 17
July the Russians eventually succeeded in seizing the intermediate
heights, including Hill 213.9. Everywhere else, however, German
troops managed to stop the Russian attack at the outlets of the ravines.
A careful examination of the conduct of the Soviet attack through 23
July provides the careful observer a deep insight into the psychology
of the Russian soldier.

The course of the fighting also proves, on the other hand, that our
troops were not attracted by the valleys and the poor, battered villages
hidden in them. Our grenadiers clearly realized that these villages represented nothing more than deathtraps. For them, the magic of the landscape lay in the heights, possession of which they saw as decisive.

Initial Soviet Attack, 17 July

German radio intelligence had confirmed by 17 July that the Soviets planned to follow up a successful infantry penetration in the Dmitrievka-Stepanovka area with the II Guards Mechanized Corps. This corps had received orders to advance westward toward Artemovka in order to widen the breakthrough toward the north and northwest.

The Nagolnaya Valley east of Dmitrievka and the extensive village itself offered an attacker excellent possibilities for troop concentration, although our positions on the high western bank of the Mius allowed us to observe them clearly. The Russians had taken advantage of literally thousands of small depressions in the terrain to emplace their artillery, as well as on the heights and in the valleys around Dubrovka and Dobrovsky. Together with their rocket launchers, this artillery was capable of covering the German positions on the heights and in the valleys with a hail of shells. The troops likened their drumfire barrages and the huge shell holes to those of World War I as the Russians hammered away with their heavy guns in the initial preparation. We had to admit that the Red Army's artillery not only had become stronger but also had gained considerable experience, as evidenced by the admirable sophistication of their fire plan, which integrated mortars and rocket launchers with the heavy and field artillery. On the other hand, the Russians knew as well as we did that only under cover of such a barrage could they get their infantry to advance against our defenses.

Unfortunately, the front-line battalions of the XVII Corps had not been able to entrench themselves very deeply because of the rocky nature of the soil. Neither had the troops slept well in many nights, having suffered incessant air raids, which caused heavy losses in personnel and equipment, greatly decreasing their powers of resistance.

At dawn, as the infantry of the XXXI Rifle Corps, accompanied by tanks, began to attack, they were received by the defensive fire of our own artillery and mortars. Machine-gunners of Grenadier Regiment 513 (294th Infantry Division) and Grenadier Regiment 581 (306th Infantry Division) inflicted heavy losses on them. The Russians held undisputed air superiority, with swarms of up to 100 planes simultaneously bombing the comparatively narrow battlefield. Once the German defensive system had been severely hit in many places by these raids, the resistance of the battalions on the line became so much weaker that the Soviets managed to penetrate into the Gerasimova and Vodyakava ravines, advancing in the direction of the Olkhovchik ravine.

The Russians had targeted this as the weak point of the German defenses and decided early on to deploy their tanks in the first wave, stationed in Dmitrievka, for this attack. On their broad treads the T-34s drove out of Dmitrievka and into the ravines, which extended toward the west like a fan, from which they began ascending the heights. At 1630 hours, however, waves of the Luftwaffe's Ju 87 *Stukas*, heavy anti-tank guns, and local reserves combined to stop this attack with repeated counterthrusts.

By evening General Schneckenburger's troops had succeeded in blunting the Russian breakthrough attack, limiting the depth of the enemy penetration to about four kilometers. The new line passed through Hill 168.5, Hill 194.3, Gerasimova, and Hill 173.4. A Soviet flanking attack with tanks had been launched from the Gerasimova ravine, but was stopped near Hill 213.9. The hill remained in German hands on the evening of 17 July. Hills 168.5, 194.3, 121.7, and 173.4 (the last two changing hands several times) became the core of XVII Corps's stiffening resistance. The Russians had lost fifteen tanks and taken heavy personnel losses as well. On the other hand, losses in the 294th and 306th Infantry Divisions were also heavy: fifty officers and 2,061 enlisted men.

Critical Days, 18–19 July

By the evening of 17 July XVII Corps reported its situation as follows: the Soviets had only committed about 150 tanks—not by any means their full strength. Uncommitted reserves still lay close to the front, which suggested strongly that the Russians would develop their full strength over the following days. On the other hand, General Schneckenburger had to reckon with the fact that his local reserves would quickly be used up in an engagement with such superior enemy forces. For this reason General Hollidt ordered the 16th Panzergrenadier Division to move through Artemovka-Kolpakovka into an assembly area in the vicinity of Kalinovka. The division's Panzer Reconnaissance Battalion 116 moved forward to the high ground southwest of Stepanovka, as well as to Hill 202 west of Marinovka, in order to cover the German assembly and to carry out reconnaissance.

General Hollidt intended to throw the Russians back into the Mius River valley. For this purpose he ordered an attack by the 16th Panzergrenadier Division across the Olkhovchik Valley and against Hills 168.5 and 194.3—the southern flank of the Soviet penetration. If *Feldersatz* [Replacement and Training] Battalion 306, which had so far stoutly defended Hill 213.9, could hold its current position, the situation in XVII Corps sector could be stabilized. Such an intent ran directly counter to plans of the Russians, who expected II Guards Mechanized Corps to continue its westward thrust through the Olkhovchik Valley and roll over Hill 213.9.

By committing a great number of tanks to this attack, the Soviet command expected to widen the breach in our defenses to the north and threaten a breakthrough.

The initial encounter with the Russian main effort attack would therefore take place on 18 July. We would then discover whether German weapons and personnel, especially our antitank defenses, possessed sufficient strength to resist a massed commitment of Soviet tank forces. Generals Hollidt and Schneckenburger had resolved to conduct an aggressive defense, which anticipated the Russian main attack against Marinovka and Hill 213.9 (which commenced at dawn), by having General von Schwerin's 16th Panzergrenadier Division execute a quick thrust into the enemy's southern flank. Such a maneuver represented our only hope for preventing a numerically superior enemy from gaining the central ridge and for beginning the process of restoring our original main battle line. Simultaneous attacks on both flanks would obviously have been preferable, but serious time constraints prohibited General Hollidt from awaiting the arrival of General von Vormann's 23rd Panzer Division, which had already begun moving toward Sixth Army from First Panzer Army, pursuant to orders from Army Group South.

At first General von Schwerin's attack seemed to be developing favorably. Panzergrenadier Regiment 60 and Panzer Battalion 116 launched a dawn attack from their assembly areas south of Kalinovka. Supported by the division's forty-odd panzers, the panzergrenadiers crossed the Olkhovchik Valley near Yelizavetinski and attacked their initial objective, Hill 168.5. Seizing this hill would threaten the flank of the Russian units assembled in Olkhovchik Valley south of Marinovka. Soon, however, this wing of the attack became embroiled in heavy fighting. Meanwhile, Panzergrenadier Regiment 156 also appeared to make good progress at first. Advancing southeast of Marinovka, the regiment retook Hill 203.4 and thrust northeast (at the time Marinovka remained in German hands) through the Olkhovchik Valley toward Hill 114.3. This was the hill across which the Russians had been launching their own attacks against Hill 213.9 since early morning.

At Olkhovchik ravine the 156th Panzergrenadiers ran into bad luck. A strong Soviet tank attack issuing from the valley hit the regiment's right flank southwest of Hill 203.4 and forced the Germans onto the defensive. The Russians came so close to breaking through toward Garany that, at the very last moment, the regiment had to summon Panzer Battalion 116 to its assistance. The panzer battalion left its position on the western bank of the Olkhovchik, and without tank support the attack of Panzergrenadier Regiment 60 quickly stalled. The II Guards Mechanized Corps now threw its entire weight—more than 100 tanks—against General von

Schwerin's division, and although the 16th Panzergrenadier Division attempted another counterattack at 1530 hours that afternoon, it was clear that Sixth Army's original objectives could no longer be achieved. The best that could be said was that the panzergrenadiers held their ground, repulsing all Soviet attacks and inflicting heavy tank losses.

By the second day of battle, many of General Schneckenburger's front-line units had been scattered or dispersed, and XVII Corps had to conduct its defense largely with improvised *Kampfgruppen*. Consequently, following the failure of the 16th Panzergrenadier's attack, the corps quickly lost Hill 213.9 and the villages of Marinovka and Stepanovka. All Russian forces not directly confronted by the 16th Panzergrenadier Division had achieved freedom of action. Supported by ground attack aircraft, the Soviets redoubled their efforts to widen the breach to the north rather than attack toward the south where General von Schwerin's men made it too hot for them.

Near Hill 173.4 the Russians thrust as far as the southern edge of Grushevi and took Gerasimova, pushing tanks up the valley and through two ravines toward the west against the Snezhnoye-Marinovka road between Hills 222.0 and 214.0. Along this road existed an admirable system of defenses built for training purposes by the headquarters, Engineer Regiment 520; these extensive defenses included not only antitank ditches but also communications and support trenches. Now these training works suddenly acquired decisive importance, as our troops utilized them to make a firm stand. There, for ten days, they repelled the heaviest Russian tank and infantry attacks, thus securing for Sixth Army the critical assembly areas in which to muster forces for its subsequent counterattack. The hulls of innumerable burned-out and exploded T-34s lay in front of this small position or scattered in the narrow ravines approaching it. Behind the slopes, hundreds if not thousands of slain Russians were piled. The Soviet penetration into the depth of our main defensive zone cost the II Guards Mechanized Corps eighty-six tanks on 18 July alone when it met XVII Corps's medium antitank and assault guns.

Despite this check, however, the capture of Hill 213.9, Stepanovka, and Marinovka justified the Russian command's decision to continue its tank attacks with the hope of creating a breakthrough on 19 July. The battered Red Army units regrouped during the night of 18–19 July near Marinovka, where they received reinforcements both from the rear and from the failed Russki attack. Across the lines, General Schneckenburger and his subordinates awaited an enemy attack from the Marinovka-Stepanovka area toward Artemovka. Sixth Army considered a night attack possible and an early-morning assault a certainty; General Hollidt resolved to anticipate a Soviet breakthrough with a German counterattack.

Counterattack, 19 July

General von Vormann's 23rd Panzer Division reached its assembly areas near Removka and Pervomaisk late in the evening of 18 July, immediately deploying Panzer Reconnaissance Battalion 23 on Hills 253.5 and 256.8, as well as southeast of the area, to protect the division against surprise attacks. Moreover, XVII Corps had received *Sturm* [Assault] Battalion 6 from the Army Weapons School at Ordzhonikidze as an additional reinforcement. This heavily armed battalion General Schneckenburger assigned to defend the northern sector of the penetration.

Once IV Flieger Corps had promised the necessary support of fighters, dive-bombers, and ground attack aircraft, General Hollidt issued orders that the Soviet penetration should be eliminated by another counterattack beginning at 0700 hours, 19 July, which would have the objective of rolling up both enemy flanks. The difficult task of recapturing Hill 213.9 fell to the 23rd Panzer Division, whose panzer element would make an attack along the central ridge while passing north of Stepanovka. Hill 173.4 in turn dominated this ridge from the other side of the Gerasimova ravine, so the threat of a flank attack was to be eliminated by a parallel attack by elements of General Koehler's 306th Infantry Division and *Sturm* Battalion 6 against that hill. General von Schwerin's 16th Panzergrenadier Division would relieve pressure along the 23rd Panzer's right flank by conducting its own simultaneous attack against Stepanovka. If these units cooperated well—and received the necessary artillery support—there was every reason to believe it possible to push the Russians off of Hill 213.9, even considering their numerical superiority.

Unfortunately, the attack quickly misfired. Everything would have to have occurred according to plan, given the relative weakness of the forces committed by the Germans to this operation, and this did not happen. One regiment of the 23rd Panzer Division failed to advance in the direction of the main thrust due to improper commitment.[4] At almost the exact moment the counterattack jumped off, Russian reinforcements—including the IV Guards Mechanized Corps and an additional rifle division—had already entered the area of penetration.

Nonetheless, when Panzergrenadier Regiments 126 and 128 advanced toward their objectives at 0700 hours, they made good progress at first. Panzergrenadier Regiment 126 attacked past the northwestern edge of Stepanovka; Panzergrenadier Regiment 128 struck southeast after crossing the Olkhovchik Valley. Both regiments, however, had already been handicapped by the fact that Panzerjaeger [Antitank] Battalion 128 had been held up by Russian antitank artillery near Hill 214.3.

At 0830 hours the 201st Panzer Regiment pushed forward for a concentric attack against Hill 213.9, advancing to the left of Panzergrenadier Regiment 128 along the critical ridge.[5] Our panzers soon received flanking fire from the high ground beyond the Gerasimova ravine, where the attack of the 306th Infantry Division had not successfully dislodged the enemy. Even so, Panzer Regiment 201 established communications with Panzergrenadier Regiment 128, which in spite of initial heavy losses was now driving the Soviet reserves up the slopes of Hill 213.9 after forcing them to abandon the Olkhovchik Valley. In accomplishing this, however, the regiment had lost contact with Panzergrenadier Regiment 126. The 126th Panzergrenadiers, like Panzerjaeger Battalion 126 attached to it, had not been able to advance toward the southeast because of the flanking fire from Hill 203.9 and the northern edge of Stepanovka. A Russian counterthrust from Stepanovka led to fierce fighting and succeeded in throwing Panzergrenadier Regiment 126 onto the defensive. This allowed the Soviets to resist the attack against Hill 213.9 by delivering flanking fire with heavy guns from the southwest.

Among the corn and sunflowers that grew in the fields to more than a man's height around Hill 213.9, the Russians had erected a real defensive wall of antitank guns, dug-in T-34s, and concealed antitank rifles. Panzer Regiment 201 ran headlong into this wall at close range. Meanwhile, as the leading platoons of Panzergrenadier Regiment 128 climbed the slopes of Hill 213.9, they received a devastating fire from infantry and antitank guns, supported by mortars. Twenty-five Soviet 76.2mm antitank guns engaged the Germans from across the ravine as T-34s rolled forward to initiate a tank battle. Panzer Regiment 201 had twenty-eight tanks knocked out, ten of which were total losses, against Russian losses of fourteen tanks, twenty antitank guns, and seven infantry guns. Hill 213.9 remained in Soviet hands, and at noon Panzer Regiment 201 had to withdraw. Further attacks appeared impossible against the massed commitment of artillery and ground attack aircraft that the Russians directed from their observation posts atop the hill.

The 16th Panzergrenadier Division's supporting attack toward Stepanovka was spearheaded by the weak Panzer Battalion 116, which entered the battle with only twenty operable tanks. This attack also ran into such a strong antitank defense that, following the engagement, the battalion was reduced to only five tanks ready for immediate employment. Red Army antitank units had conclusively proven how much they had learned about opening surprise fire and adapting themselves to changing circumstances.

Yet it was not the defeat of the 116th Panzer Battalion but another event that proved decisive in this sector. Thirty minutes after the opening of the attack, a fan-shaped Russian attack (supported by strong tank forces) out of Stepanovka hit the center of General von Schwerin's division, pushing it rapidly back to the west. Soviet tanks broke into the position of the German engineer battalion stationed along the two hills southwest of Stepanovka. Despite bloody resistance by our combat engineers, the Russians succeeded in capturing the remaining ruins of what had once been the village of Garany. The stationary howitzers (French equipment) emplaced there had fired their last shells before the crews left them lying with their barrels blasted. Thus a dangerous gap had been created that our troops could not close, even by a counterthrust from Saur Mogilski. The troops committed in this action suffered very heavy losses, and our tactical situation became more critical by the hour. The day that had begun with the hope of crushing the Russian penetration now threatened to end in disaster.

Fortunately, our defenses on Hills 202 and 230.9 held, repulsing the Soviets with heavy losses—most importantly knocking out a significant number of enemy tanks. The situation perceptibly eased. With fifty tanks having been put out of action on 19 July, this brought the total of Red Army tanks lost from 17 to 19 July up to 159 vehicles. Soviet personnel losses had also been heavy. At 1530 hours, following a strong artillery preparation and dive-bomber attacks, the 23rd Panzer Division attempted to give the day a favorable ending by recapturing Stepanovka. With the 16th Panzergrenadier Division tied up dealing with the Russian penetration to Garany, this unsupported attack also proved unsuccessful.

Soviet numerical superiority had become so great that the skill and bravery of our troops could not compensate for it. Worse, Luftwaffe reconnaissance flights confirmed that the Russians continued to detrain even more reinforcements at Rovenki, Lutogino, and Vodino. Clearly, any future counterattack would require substantially stronger forces than those currently available to Sixth Army, but Army Group South informed us that no reinforcements could be expected within less than a week. Until then, our troops would have to hold the line with the forces now available.

General Hollidt therefore determined to change tactics. Because it had become necessary to economize forces, he ruled out counterattacks as a means of defense in all but the most favorable situations. Instead, he ordered our soldiers to cling tenaciously to all important points and to let the Russians dash themselves against our antitank defenses. Ammunition would be made liberally available. By utilizing all means of antitank defense available, General Hollidt proposed to break the Soviet tank superiority in a battle of attrition.

In order to have adequate reserves available for this type of defensive fighting, General Hollidt ordered all divisions that had not so far been attacked to form *Alarmeinheiten* [emergency alert units] out of all men not already committed in the main defensive zone. These improvised units replaced front-line battalions in quiet sectors during the night of 19–20 July, which allowed us—through a system of what might be called "mutual assistance"—to provide General Schneckenburger's XVII Corps with considerable infantry reserves. After days of the highest tension, the enlisted ranks of XVII Corps now felt inspired with a new spirit, as help came from all sides. Medium antitank guns, flak units, and assault guns appeared from other corps areas to reinforce their antitank defenses. To relieve General Schneckenburger of extraneous details and to ensure uniformity in the combat operations still ongoing around Kuibyshevo, the sector of Grenadier Regiment 515 (294th Infantry Division) reverted to the control of General Brandenberger's XXIX Corps; that corps accordingly shifted its boundary to the north.

General Hollidt also requested that Army Group South send him General of Panzer Troops Walter Nehring's XXIV Panzer Corps headquarters. General Nehring arrived the following day and took over command of the right sector of XVII Corps (23rd Panzer Division, 16th Panzergrenadier Division, and the bulk of the 294th Infantry Division). The XXIV Panzer Corps had the mission of preventing—at all costs—a widening of the enemy penetration in any direction from Stepanovka and to hold the high ground on both sides of Hill 277.9. The formal change of command in this sector took place on the night of 21–22 July.

Culmination of the Defensive Battle

On 20 July, without awaiting the arrival of the entire IV Guards Mechanized Corps, the Soviets attempted to force a breakthrough with the forces at hand. These included the remaining tank elements of the II Guards Mechanized Corps and 32nd Independent Tank Brigade and an infantry force increased from six to nine rifle divisions (including the 118th and 387th Rifle Divisions recently shifted from the Russki sector). The Russians made the maximum possible use of artillery, rocket launchers, and air support for the attack. Despite these measures the attack did not score any great success, due to stiffening German resistance and the heavy casualties already suffered by the Red Army units participating.

The Russians did succeed in capturing Saur Mogilski and in forcing Panzer Reconnaissance Battalion 116 to give up Hill 230.9 in the face of a heavy tank attack. Northwest of Saur Mogilski, however, Engineer Battalion 675 began the process of breaking up the attack by checking the enemy at Hill 277.9. This battalion's tenacious defense bought time for the 23rd Panzer Division to launch a quick and dexterous counterthrust into the Soviet infantry regaining Hill 214.3 initially, and following up this success by recapturing Saur Mogilski itself that evening.

German resistance had stiffened along the entire defensive line. More and more Soviet tanks fell victim to close-combat weapons, and it seemed that our troops had lost their initial fear of Russian armor. Thus elements of the 306th Infantry Division repulsed a tank attack from Garany, two attacks against Hill 196.0, and another against the commanding heights south of Paradrievo. Meanwhile the aircraft of IV Flieger Corps returned to the air in support of our troops, who knocked out seventy-one Russian tanks on 20 July. By itself, Assault Gun Battalion 210 had accounted for fifty-one Soviet tanks since the beginning of the battle. We estimated total Russian tank losses in the sector to have risen to at least 240—three-quarters of their starting strength. The remaining vehicles were not sufficient, on their own, to force a breakthrough.

Unfortunately, such a situation could not last. On 21 July the IV Guards Mechanized Corps (consisting of the 12th, 13th, and 15th Guards Mechanized Brigades) entered the fight with another 200–250 tanks. This raised Red Army tank strength, on the fifth day of battle, back to more than 300 vehicles. Conversely, Sixth Army possessed only nineteen Pzkw IIIs and seventeen long-barrel Pzkw IVs ready for action. Aside from nine identified rifle divisions already in the sector, intelligence believed four others to be present and had firm knowledge that the 45th and 87th Guards Rifle Divisions, as well as the 320th Rifle Division, had been brought up as reinforcements. Thus the balance of forces in the sector on 21 July appeared as follows:

Soviet	German
IV Guards Mechanized Corps	23rd Panzer Division
II Guards Mechanized Corps	16th Panzergrenadier Division
32nd Independent Tank Brigade	336th Infantry Division
sixteen rifle divisions	306th Infantry Division

On the Russian side, the II Guards Mechanized Corps and 32nd Tank Brigade were both far below strength, but the IV Guards Mechanized Corps and at least half of the rifle divisions were fresh. Sixth Army's units not only were numerically inferior by a wide margin but also were overtired from four days and nights of incessant fighting. The oppressive heat had worn down their stamina while the unceasing fire from artillery and rocket launchers, as well as air raids, had thinned their ranks. Dozens of experienced officers and hundreds of NCOs—all of whom it was impossible to replace—had fallen.

The IV Guards Mechanized Corps directed its first attacks on 21 July southwest toward Uspenskaya; a concentrated attack against Panzergrenadier Regiment 156 (16th Panzergrenadier Division) northeast of Kalinovka resulted in a deep penetration. XVII Corps hurriedly scraped together elements of the 16th Panzergrenadier and 294th Infantry Divisions for a counterattack that destroyed the Russian spearheads and restored the original battle line. Meanwhile the Soviets had captured Grigoryevka and the high ground to the northeast, from which they launched a tank attack east of Kalinovka. Yelizavetinski was one moment in Russian hands and another moment possessed by the Germans. Soviet attacks from Saur Mogilski against Hill 196.0, attacks north of Stepanovka, and attacks against Nikiferov and Paradrievo failed with the loss of thirty to forty enemy tanks. Russian attacks reached their culmination on 22 July with the commitment of the entire IV Guards Mechanized Corps for a breakthrough in the direction of Artemovka-Kolpakovica.

By this time General Nehring's XXIV Panzer Corps had taken control of this highly critical sector and before noon on 22 July had regrouped its armor-piercing weapons and handful of panzers to block the expected Russian advance. General Hollidt had committed such reinforcements as were available. The XXIX Corps brought a regimental *Kampfgruppe* built around the headquarters of Grenadier Regiment 70 (111th Infantry Division) to Alexeyevka to join the 294th Infantry Division. Assault Gun Battalion 236, just arrived, was attached to the 16th Panzergrenadier Division. General Mieth's IV Corps turned over to the XVII Corps the mechanized battalion, which had been held available for the army's use.

The Russians opened their attack against the front of XXIV Panzer Corps, as expected, between Grigoryevka and Saur Mogilski at 1530 hours. The axis of attack pointed southwest, with the spearhead consisting of approximately 150 tanks, supported by enormous amounts of artillery and aircraft. The magnitude of this attack—after four days of battle—clearly indicated the intention of the Soviets to force a decision. According to prisoner statements taken later, IV Guards Mechanized Corps had been assigned the mission of achieving a breakthrough as deep as the Krynka sector near Uspenskaya and Sukhaya Krynka—a penetration of seventeen kilometers.

As the fury of the fighting increased, it became obvious that the Russian tankers had learned many lessons from the previous days. In the initial attacks on 17 July the Soviets had already known to used concealed and irregular terrain for tank attacks, rather than following straight roads. Now, on the uncovered heights, they did not let their tank waves attack our defenses openly. Instead, they made good use of the dust towering above the withered ground, which had been stirred up by marching soldiers, tank treads, wheels, and the wind. The yellow dust clouds mixed with the smoke from the burning steppe, kindled by aerial spraying of phosphorus and mingling with the debris thrown into the air by thousands of shell and bomb impacts. At any point where this cover seemed insufficient, the Russians fired smoke shells or dropped smoke bombs. Behind this nearly impenetrable curtain of smoke and dust, the Soviet tanks approached our defenses. The superior range of our antitank weapons had been neutralized; gunners at the antitank guns, assault guns, and flak batteries could not discern the approaching T-34s until the very last minute. Nerves strained to the breaking point, our gunners and grenadiers could hardly breathe, their eyes burned, and their faces became encrusted with a thick layer of dirt and soot. Temperatures inside our tanks and assault guns rose to the level of a blast furnace, and the wounded, in particular, suffered horribly from the terrible heat and dust.

The dust and smoke also blinded artillery observation posts, made it difficult for our fighter pilots to find Soviet planes in the sky, and severely decreased the accuracy of our dive-bombers. The showers of phosphorus arcing through the smoke and dust created the picture of an infernal battle of attrition on the plains of Hell, as the first pestilential stench of putrefaction filled the torrid air. With the assistance of such formidable weapons as these, the Russian tanks succeeded for the first time in simply rolling past the German defenders and achieving a deep penetration in the direction of Krinichka.

This success, however, cost the IV Guards Mechanized Corps dearly, as our troops had also learned some important tactical lessons over the past week. We realized that the fighting qualities of the Soviet infantry had deteriorated to such a point that a battle was already half-won if it became possible to separate the rifle troops from their tank supports. On 22 July this factor decided the day's battle. Once Russian tanks rolled across our lines, they were isolated from their supports and lured into the prepared antitank defenses established by XXIV Panzer Corps. Tank after tank was annihilated on the western hill slopes in the rear of our thin line of grenadiers—after an hour no more than a handful of the enemy tanks that had penetrated our positions still survived. The Soviet tanks thrusting against Kalinovka suffered the same fate, with the 294th Infantry and 16th Panzergrenadier Divisions reporting that they had knocked out ninety-three enemy vehicles in a short time.

Thus the major attack of the IV Guards Mechanized Corps, though it succeeded in capturing Kalinovka, cost the Red Army another 130 tanks. This brought total Soviet tanks losses since 17 July to 400 and meant that the Russian attempt to break through on the Mius had more and more degenerated into a battle of attrition. Now that the Soviets had lost the greater part of their tanks and the danger of further concentrated tank attacks had been so greatly diminished, another factor assumed greater importance. While the IV Guards Mechanized Corps had been grinding its way toward Kalinovka, XVII Corps succeeded in completely repulsing all Russian attacks from the northern edge of the penetration zone near Hill 214.0 and Nikiferov. For General Hollidt, therefore, 22 July stood out as a decisive defensive success, which had to be ascribed primarily to the bravery of General von Schwerin's 16th Panzergrenadier Division.

Declining Strength of the Russian Attack

Because Luftwaffe reconnaissance flights had reported the arrival of additional Soviet reinforcements into the zone of operations, General Hollidt expected another major attack on 23 July. He ordered every possible measure taken to reform a continuous defensive line where our infantry had been forced back. The resulting line ran southwest of the Olkhovchik ravine and as far as Hill 188.4, southwest of Kalinovka. General Nehring, at XXIV Panzer Corps headquarters, received orders to take one panzergrenadier regiment (reinforced with tanks) from the 23rd Panzer Division to form a mobile reserve. Because General Nehring had experienced difficulties maintaining communications and contact with General Brandenberger's XXIX Corps, General Hollidt attached the entire 294th Infantry Division back to the XXIX Corps. This required the boundary between the two corps to be shifted to run along a line passing through Kolpakovka, Grigoryevka, and the southern tip of Dmitrievka.

The losses of 22 July had apparently so weakened the IV Guards Mechanized Corps that it became unable to make concentrated tank attacks. Presumably its commander had developed a healthy fear of running into more antitank defenses like the ones encountered the previous afternoon. Consequently, attacks made by the IV Guards on 23 July were spread widely apart, both in terms of time and space—the Russians simply dissipated their forces. We took these partial attacks as a sign of growing Soviet uneasiness regarding their ultimate prospects of success.

The Russians launched the first in a series of disjointed thrusts as early as 0300 hours out of the Yelizavetinski-Kalinovka sector. By sunrise ten enemy tanks had penetrated into Semenovski, but the 16th Panzergrenadier Division destroyed eight and sent the other two packing. Simultaneously, the 294th Infantry Division turned back another attack in heavy fighting south of Kalinovka at Hills 5.0 and 175.5 and the road junction north of them. After both of these attacks failed, the Soviets threw new, stronger—though equally unsuccessful—attacks against the

XXIV Panzer Corps front near Semonovksi and Hill 277.9 northwest of Saur Mogilski. Along the axis of the IV Guards Mechanized Corps's main attack of 22 July, the Soviets attempted nothing but did try additional partial attacks (once again without success) from Stepanovka against Hills 214.3 and 214.0. Despite all of these efforts, the Russians gained no ground on 23 July.

Aside from the weakness and lack of coordination in the enemy attacks, our troops also benefited tremendously from a change in the weather. The oppressive dry heat had lessened, and clouds appeared in the sky. Thundershowers came pouring down in some locations, much to the relief of our fatigued soldiers.

Although the Soviets had not concentrated their tanks in these attacks, they had not been spared heavy losses. Seventy more tanks were put out of action on 23 July, which meant that the Russians—as the culmination of the commitment of the IV Guards Mechanized Corps from 21 to 23 July—had lost 270 tanks. This figure represented the entire assigned tank strength of a mechanized corps. According to prisoner statements, infantry losses had also been severe, and by the end of that day none of the sixteen rifle divisions in the zone of penetration could be considered battleworthy.

The OKW [German Armed Forces High Command] bulletin for 25 July read:

> In the engagement along the Mius River, the 16th Panzergrenadier Division, from Rhineland-Westphalia, has greatly distinguished itself.
>
> The bravery of Panzerjaeger Battalion 661 also deserves special mention, for the guns and their crews of this battalion often remained in their positions on 22–23 July during Russian tank attacks even after their infantry supports had been overrun. With cool resolution, these gunners put out of action a high percentage of the enemy tanks destroyed.

How had it been possible to prevent a Russian breakthrough, when the enemy often attacked with six- or eightfold superiority in personnel, tanks, and artillery? One must inescapably attribute this victory to the high fighting qualities of the troops from all branches of the service and to the heroism consistently displayed by officers, NCOs, and enlisted soldiers alike. Intelligent leadership allowed the results of battlefield observations and reconnaissance to be transformed rapidly into combat orders, which led time after time to the flexible concentration of our slim resources precisely where they were most needed. Our field artillery provided lightning-fast concentrations of fire on demand, our antitank gunners stood their ground, and efforts of the Luftwaffe provided a textbook model for the conduct of ground support operations. In this manner we managed to overcome critical situations that followed, one after the other, like links in a chain.

These achievements, however, came at a heavy price. Those units that had been forced to bear the brunt of the fighting for several days—especially the 16th Panzergrenadier and 294th Infantry Divisions—had become so exhausted that their strength had reached the breaking point. As a single example, by the end of 23 July the infantry strength of the 16th Panzergrenadier Division (including four panzergrenadier battalions, one engineer battalion, and one *Feldersatz* battalion) totaled only 550 men.

General Hollidt, as he had done on 19 July, spent the critical hours of 23 July in the forward areas of the XXIV Panzer and XVII Corps. He had taken an active role in the fighting by issuing orders, bringing up reinforcements, and procuring extra ammunition. Having been an eyewitness to the battle, he could state a firm opinion that the troops in the penetration area had done their utmost. In answer to inquiries from Army Group South, General Hollidt reiterated this view, as well as warning Field Marshal von Manstein that his troops, if not substantially reinforced, would be able to defend their existing line only for a little longer and could do that only under the following circumstances:

1. The Russians in the area were not reinforced.
2. The Russians continued to make scattered attacks.
3. Sixth Army's ammunition supply held out.

The tension of the past few days, therefore, had not relaxed, especially because we knew that the Soviets had already moved reinforcements forward and that additional, concentrated attacks could be expected.

General Hollidt ruthlessly denuded the quiet sectors of his front line by scraping up every last man in the rear areas—including engineer and construction battalions—for employment at the front. He made it a point of honor for his other corps to reinforce the XXIV Panzer Corps. In this manner it became possible to supply General Nehring with three complete infantry battalions, supported by medium artillery, during the evening of 23 July. Moreover, in comparison to 21 July the tank situation of both the 16th Panzergrenadier and 23rd Panzer Divisions had improved as the result of reinforcements. The two divisions had, ready for employment on 24 July:

	On 21 July	On 23 July
16th Panzergrenadier Division	4	12
23rd Panzer Division	27 (13)	33 (18)

Note: numbers in parenthesis refer to long-barrel Pzkw IVs.

The relative losses suffered by our assault gun units had also been favorable if compared to the number of Russian tanks put out of action. Assault Gun Battalion 210, which sustained twelve losses among its guns (which represented almost our entire losses in assault guns) had done so in exchange for the destruction of eighty-two enemy tanks. Sixth Army's four assault gun battalions had, on hand and ready for employment on 24 July:

	Available	Operational
Assault Gun Battalion 209	28	10
Assault Gun Battalion 210	18	10
Assault Gun Battalion 236	10	10
Assault Gun Battalion 243	31	17
Total	87	47

Diminishing Attacks

As expected, the Soviets attacked the southern flank of the Dmitrievka penetration during the night of 23–24 July and again during the morning of 24 July. Though we lost the village of Semenovski, Russian attacks out of Yelizavetinski and Grigoryevka and against Hill 188.4 all failed. The 306th Infantry Division also repelled a diversionary probe west of Shelobok.

During 24 and 25 July the Soviets lost additional tanks and failed to gain any ground in a series of disjointed day and night attacks. Obviously regrouping, the Russians apparently used the time to relieve the IV Guards Mechanized Corps with the I and XIII Guards Rifle Corps. General Hollidt suspected that the enemy intended to concentrate his remaining tanks for an attack out of the northern flank of the penetration zone, but this assumption proved inaccurate. *Gruppe* von Vormann of the 23rd Panzer Division, which had been brought up behind the XVII Corps front line as a precaution against such an attack, never had to be committed.

On 26 July the Russians made two stronger attacks, in a new effort to create a breakthrough toward the south or southwest, committing the armored remnants of the II and IV Guards Mechanized Corps for this purpose. The first thrust hit the left sector of the 111th and 294th Infantry Divisions and consisted of infantry supported by ten tanks and close-support aircraft. Our troops knocked out nine of the ten Soviet tanks in defeating this attack. Two rifle divisions, supported by approximately 100 close-support aircraft, thirty tanks, and thirty rocket launchers, made a much stronger push west from the Garany area. The tanks advanced in successive waves of eight vehicles, but the entire assault collapsed under the defensive fire of the 16th Panzergrenadier Division. Our antitank weapons accounted for seven enemy tanks, and the only Soviet gain—a small penetration near Krinichka—was quickly mopped up.

Even weaker attacks in the same areas occurred on 27 July—again uniformly unsuccessful and costly in terms of Russian tank losses. The Soviets also attempted two diversionary attacks (supported by tanks), most likely because they had learned that the II SS Panzer Corps was being brought up. The first diversion targeted Ryazhanaya in the XXIX Corps sector, to no one's particular surprise, while the second occurred northwest of Krasnaya Polyana on the left flank of the XVII Corps. The first collapsed in front of our wire entanglements, and the second resulted in an insignificant penetration and the loss of Hill 290.8. Sixth Army's entire front remained quiet on 28 and 29 July. The enemy forces committed at Ryazhanaya marched off to the north. On the other hand, anticipating a German concentration and counteroffensive, the Russians reinforced their Dmitrievka penetration with tanks, rocket launchers, and fresh infantry (including the 315th Rifle Division).

Final Situation on 29 July

The Russian offensive in the Dmitrievka sector had been ground to a halt. The assault divisions were exhausted, and the danger of a breakthrough no longer existed. So many tanks had been lost by the II and IV Guards Mechanized Corps, as well as two independent tank brigades, that the scant remainder was concentrated as two small brigades, which were then attached to the I and XIII Guards Rifle Corps. All in all, our troops had destroyed or put out of action about 580 Soviet tanks, including two German Pzkw IIIs that had been previously captured by the enemy. We had to presume, of course, that scores of tanks reported to have been knocked out had probably been repaired during the course of the thirteen-day battle. This circumstance made it quite probable that we counted some tanks twice, that is, when they were knocked out of action a second time. Without doubt, however, only a fraction of the authorized strength of the Russian tank units committed at Dmitrievka managed to escape destruction. Between 17 and 29 July Sixth Army took 3,972 prisoners and processed 597 deserters. We also captured seventeen pieces of field artillery, three rocket launchers, fifty-four mortars, sixteen antitank guns, 504 machine guns, 105 antitank rifles, and 222 submachine guns.

German losses from 17–29 July may be itemized as follows:

XXIX CORPS

	Officers	Enlisted	Total
KIA	15	334	369
WIA	47	1663	1710
MIA	1	91	92
Totals	63	2108	2071

XVII CORPS

	Officers	Enlisted	Total
KIA	47	1087	1134
WIA	174	5289	5463
MIA	21	1515	1536
Totals	242	7891	8133

XXIV PANZER CORPS

	Officers	Enlisted	Total
KIA	19	435	454
WIA	83	2468	2551
MIA	3	248	251
Totals	105	3151	3256

MISCELLANEOUS

	Officers	Enlisted	Total
KIA	10	392	402
WIA	31	1391	1402
MIA	4	118	122
Totals	45	1881	1926

SIXTH ARMY TOTALS

	Officers	Enlisted	Total
KIA	91	2268	2359
WIA	335	10991	11126
MIA	29	1972	2001
Totals	455	15031	15486

With regard to infantry strength, the Russians in the Dmitrievka penetration zone remained numerically far superior despite their heavy losses. On the other hand, it was evident that they needed a pause in operations to rehabilitate—at least on a small scale—their tank units in the rear. We could not afford to grant them that opportunity.

On 30 July, therefore, the second phase of the battle began in conjunction with the forces of *Obergruppenfuehrer* Paul Hausser's II SS Panzer

Corps, which spearheaded Sixth Army's large-scale counterattack. In the interim it had been the task of our exhausted front-line divisions to forestall a Russian breakthrough until the onset of the counterattack. Despite heavy losses and many critical moments, they had succeeded in carrying out this mission.

East or West of the Mius?

General Hollidt's intention to destroy the Soviet forces in the Dmitrievka penetration zone and restore the old main battle line permitted two different solutions. He could possibly have ordered a breakthrough by our panzer forces toward the south and southeast. This would have entailed an initial attack north of the penetration area on both sides of Nizhni Nagolchik and then across the Mius River. Capturing Dyakovo and then turning west, our panzer divisions could have attacked the Russians deep in their rear. Such an operation undoubtedly promised a decisive success but also required twice as many troops as Sixth Army had available, not to mention the extra time necessary for attacking Soviet field positions that had been arrayed in depth along the potential axis of attack. Equally critical, such a wide swing east would have extended our flanks in a dangerous manner.

General Hollidt therefore decided to adopt a second option. He would attempt to envelop the Russian main forces in the penetration zone on the near side of the Mius River and to destroy them so thoroughly that—by the operation's end—Sixth Army would be able to defend that stretch of river with roughly the same amount of force as before.

Because this attack had a limited objective in a battle area only twelve kilometers deep, the enemy could be prevented from escaping only if we conducted it with lightning speed. The nature of the terrain, combined with the limitations on the force at our disposal, ruled out a simultaneous pincer attack with tanks from north and south. This meant that it was only possible for German panzers to attack from the west and northwest, on a broad front parallel to the three ridges already mentioned. These ridges extended from Nikiferov to Hills 173.4 and 121.7; from Removski mine by way of Hill 222 to Hill 312.9; and from the area northeast of Saur Mogilski over Hill 230.9 to Hill 223.7, or Hills 202 and 196 east and southeast of Garany. The two large ravines lying between these ridges—the big Gerasimova ravine and the Olkhovchik Valley—had to be rolled up completely in order to contain all Russian forces from the beginning and in order to avoid disaster due to a flanking movement. From the south and southwest we intended to drive the Soviets through the Olkhovchik Valley toward the northeast—preventing their escape to the south—with a *Kampfgruppe* composed of units form the 111th and 294th Infantry Divisions and the 15th Luftwaffe Field Division.

The essential prerequisite for success—especially because the Russians certainly knew we would attack—was speed. Our forces had to engage the Soviets quickly and adroitly, drive rapidly beyond the initial attack objectives, and separate the enemy in the penetration zone from their communications. In order to do so, our infantry had to be able to keep closely behind our panzer spearheads, using mutual assistance and their medium-caliber infantry guns to mop up pockets of resistance and clear the ravines. The effectiveness of our artillery preparation also assumed critical importance, with priorities assigned to neutralizing the Russian artillery, screening enemy observation posts, and direct combat support of our infantry and panzers in their struggle to dominate the high ground. The Luftwaffe's task necessarily resembled that of the field artillery. Coordination between the ground-support elements of IV Flieger Corps and Sixth Army—especially with regard to the timing of aerial attacks and the ground assault—had been carefully worked out in face-to-face discussions at the highest level.

Our attack divisions had to be deeply echeloned in narrow attack sectors in order to counteract the defensive advantages of the terrain, which we had to expect the Russians would exploit to the fullest, digging in their infantry and artillery for tenacious defensive fighting. General Hollidt decided, as a result of these factors, not to hold back a significant attack reserve but instead to commit all available divisions side by side. Aside from its own divisions, Sixth Army had been assigned the II SS Panzer Corps, which had been transferred from First Panzer Army on 25 July. Thus the distribution of friendly and enemy forces can be summarized as follows:

Attack Group, XXIX Corps (between Olkhovski and Kalinovka), consisting of elements from the 294th Infantry Division, one regiment from the 111th Infantry Division, and one battalion of the 15th Luftwaffe Field Division. Their first objective was to clear the Olkhovchik Valley and carry the hill east of Yelizavetski. Confronting this group we estimated there were four Russian rifle divisions, supported by the remaining tanks of the II Guards Mechanized Corps.

Attack Group, XXIV Panzer Corps (between Kalinovka and Saur Mogilski), consisting of the 16th Panzergrenadier and 23rd Panzer Divisions. This group had been assigned the mission of capturing Kalinovka; containing the enemy with attacks from Hill 277.9 against Saur Mogilski and Garany; and preventing the main effort attack by II SS Panzer Corps from being hit in the flank. Confronting these divisions we estimated that in the Kalinovka-Garany-Saur Mogilski area the Russians deployed five rifle divisions, half of an antitank brigade, and some elements of the II Guards Mechanized Corps.

II SS Panzer Corps (between Nikiferov and Stepanovka), consisting of SS *Das Reich* and *Totenkopf* Panzergrenadier Divisions and the 3rd Panzer Division. The II SS Panzer Corps had the initial objective of achieving the line passing through Hill 223.7 (south of Stepanovka), Hill 213.9, and Hill 174.4. From there the corps had to turn southwest and destroy the enemy near Marinovka with the assistance of the other attack groups. Confronting our main attack, we believed there were five and one-half rifle divisions, one and one-half antitank brigades, and elements of the IV Guards Mechanized Corps.

Attack Group, XVII Corps (between Nikiferov and the Mius River), consisting of two battalions of the 306th Infantry Division, two battalions of the 3rd Mountain Division, one battalion of the 335th Infantry Division, and *Sturm* Battalion 6 from the army reserve. This attack group had the assignment of capturing Hill 173.4 and the old main battle line north of Dmitrievka. Confronting XVII Corps we had identified one and one-half rifle divisions.

We believed that the Russians still had about 200 tanks available, either in the penetration zone or immediately east of the Mius, held in reserve for a counterthrust. Opposing this, the panzer divisions assigned to Sixth Army reported the following strength on 29 July:

Division	Pzkw III	Pzkw IV	Pzkw VI	T-34	Total
SS *Das Reich*	39	34	6	6	85
SS *Totenkopf*	22	58	9	0	89
3rd Panzer	26	11	0	0	37
16th Panzergren.	9	4	0	0	13
23rd Panzer	14	20	0	0	34
Total	*110*	*127*	*15*	*6*	*258*

The artillery forces had been distributed as follows: In the entire sector from Yassinovski to the left flank of the 306th Infantry Division on the Mius, the Russians had committed 160 batteries (twenty-five medium batteries, ninety-eight light batteries, and thirty-seven whose calibers could not be determined). Against the main effort of the II SS Panzer Corps in the Marinovka-Stepanovka area and Hill 213.9, the Soviets had thirty-one batteries; around the Yerassimova-Dmitrievka ravine they had twenty-one batteries. Sixth Army had concentrated 144 batteries throughout the sector. Of these, 106 had been committed in the Olkhovski-Paradrievo area, including forty-four medium [*scwhere*] and twelve light-medium [*mittlere*] batteries. Supporting the main-effort attack by II SS Panzer Corps, General Hollidt had committed *Nebelwerfer* Regiments 1 and 52, Howitzer Battalion 735, and II Battalion/Artillery Regiment 52.

The Counterattack

On 27 and 28 July the three divisions of *Obergruppenfuehrer* Hausser's II SS Panzer Corps moved up from their assembly areas around Makeyevka (*Das Reich*), Ordzhonikidze (*Totenkopf*), and Krasnaya Zvezda (3rd Panzer) to the vicinity of their line of departure. (Note: the SS *Liebstandarte Adolph Hitler* Panzergrenadier Division was halted at this point on the orders of OKH and sent back by rail.) The main bodies of these divisions reached their tactical assembly areas between 26 and 27 July. The motorized elements of the corps moved by day, the tracked elements by night; the final elements reached their destination by dawn on 29 July. The line of departure for each division was as follows:

> SS *Das Reich* Panzergrenadier Division: the line passing through the area comprising Mauilovo, Christyakovo, Olkhovchik, and Prokhorov.
>
> SS *Totenkopf* Panzergrenadier Division: the line passing through the area comprising Snezhnoe and Krasnaya Zvezda.
>
> 3rd Panzer Division: the line passing through the area around Sofina Brodskaya, Vessaloye, and Novy Donban.

These divisions entered their attack sectors during the night of 29–30 July.

At 0600 hours, 30 July, General Hollidt and the *Fuehrungsabteilung* (Operations group of General Staff officers) of Sixth Army moved into a forward command post close around Krasnaya Zvezda in order to be close to the front.

The First Day of the Attack, 30 July

Sixth Army opened its artillery preparation in coordination with Luftwaffe ground attacks at 0710 hours; the assault troops advanced at 0810 hours. The weather was sunny and very warm, and our troops made good progress at the outset. In the sector of General Brandenberger's XXIX Corps, the reinforced Grenadier Regiment 685 (336th Infantry Division) penetrated through the Olkhovchik Valley to capture the hill east of

Yelizavetinski, despite stubborn Russian resistance. Likewise, II Battalion/Grenadier Regiment 95 (17th Infantry Division) slowly gained ground toward the northwest through the same valley.

Considering the later course of the battle, General Nehring's XXIV Panzer Corps scored the best initial success. *Kampfgruppe* Major Schaegger (panzer elements from Panzer Regiment 201, II Battalion/Panzergrenadier Regiment 126, and Panzer Reconnaissance Battalion 23) forged rapidly through the forest north of Saur Mogilski and succeeded in capturing the ruins of Garany as well as the commanding Hills 202 and 196.0. Simultaneously, elements of the General von Schwerin's 16th Panzergrenadier Division captured the hill northeast of Seminvoski after fierce fighting for the remaining squalid huts in the village. Thus General Nehring's two divisions managed to form a pocket west of Garany and Hill 196.0 (the old tank battleground of 22–23 July), into which had been driven elements of five Guards rifle divisions. By late afternoon we had recaptured Saur Mogilski and began mopping up the pocket.

Gruppenfuehrer Walter Krueger's SS *Das Reich* Panzergrenadier Division carried Hill 230.9 with its first assault, and its spearheads penetrated farther inside the valley into the village of Stepanovka. As furious house-to-house fighting ensued in Stepanovka, the panzer elements of the division drove farther toward the southeast, securing the hill one and a half kilometers south of Stepanovka; capturing this hill was a prerequisite for a further advance on Marinovka. By this time, however, *Das Reich* had lost twenty-five of its eighty-five tanks through mechanical problems or antitank fire.

For the attack along the central ridge toward Hill 213.9, *Brigadefuehrer* Hermann Preiss's SS *Totenkopf* Panzergrenadier Division had to depend on the parallel attacks of *Das Reich* and the 3rd Panzer Division to eliminate Soviet flanking fire from Stepanovka and Hill 173.4. Unfortunately, the Russians had spent the previous forty-eight hours preparing extensive defenses for Hill 213.9, with pockets of resistance hidden between the fields of very high corn and sunflowers; dug-in T-34s; antitank gun positions distributed in depth; and stray minefields. They had also prepared to make tactical counterthrusts with their remaining tanks. It became quickly obvious that the Red Army troops defending Hill 213.9 had not been alarmed in the least by the fact that *Totenkopf*'s left flank elements had been able to penetrate into the Gerasimova ravine and capture the village, because the neighboring hills in the southeast and northwest thoroughly protected their flanks.

Although Lieutenant General Franz Westhoven had employed engineers to clear routes through the Russian minefields, his 3rd Panzer Division did not manage to push farther than Grushevy in the face of strong antitank defenses. The Soviet defenses also stalled the assault elements of General Koehler's 306th Infantry Division outside Paradrievo. As a consequence of all these factors, *Totenkopf* did not achieve much success in its attack against Hill 213.9 and found itself forced to pull back its tanks. The panzer regiment had lost forty-eight of eighty-nine tanks that day, though only one vehicle constituted a total write-off.

In spite of the early successes achieved by XXIX and XXIV Panzer Corps, the results of the first day's attack were anything but encouraging. Although our troops had captured 3,000 prisoners and inflicted the loss of sixteen tanks, twenty-three guns, 112 antitank guns, and numerous machine guns, antitank rifles, and mortars, it had to be admitted that the Russians had put up surprisingly strong resistance. They had employed fire from strongly held flanking positions and tactical counterthrusts to delay the advance of the II SS Panzer Corps. Contrary to our expectations, only a small portion of the Soviet infantry and artillery in the penetration zone appeared to be attempting to withdraw toward the eastern bank of the Mius River. Such withdrawals they did attempt, however, cost the enemy dearly as our dive-bombers relentlessly pounded the southern bridges across the Mius.

By evening there could be no doubt that Sixth Army would face continued strong resistance on the second day of its attack.

The Deadlock, 31 July

During the night General Hollidt ordered a regrouping of II SS Panzer Corps in order to reinforce *Obergruppenfuehrer* Hausser's southern flank for the continuation of the attack on 31 July.

In XXIX Corps's sector several Russian counterattacks against the high ground seized the previous day had to be defeated before General Brandenberger's troops could return to the attack. Once six enemy tanks had been knocked out, his troops succeeded in clearing the southern part of the Olkhovchik Valley near Yelizavetinski and in capturing the southern end of the village.

General Nehring's XXIV Panzer Corps continued to enjoy hard-fought success. Early in the morning, the 16th Panzergrenadier Division captured Kalinovka and—after breaking tenacious Russian resistance—also took Grigoryevka.

At sunrise General von Vormann's 23rd Panzer Division began a concentric attack against the Soviet units trapped south of Saur Mogilski, employing Panzergrenadier Regiment 128, Panzer Reconnaissance Battalion 23, *Kampfgruppe* Sander, and *Panzergruppe* Albert. The enemy made desperate attempts to break out of the pocket, and the Russian command launched a rescuing attack across Hill 202 with two rifle divisions supported by tanks. The 23rd Panzer Division, however, repulsed this attack with assistance from *Das Reich*. More than 3,000 prisoners fell into our hands, bringing the 23rd Panzer's two-day total to 267 officers and 3,928 enlisted men. General von Vormann's troops also captured or destroyed fifty-two antitank guns, eleven rocket launchers, and twenty-four pieces of field artillery. German losses in this sector on 31 July included thirty-one enlisted men killed, with ten officers and 133 enlisted men wounded. The 23rd Panzer Division followed up this success by crossing Hill 202 and advancing toward Marinovka. During this march the division captured its first Russian 150mm assault gun.

Obergruppenfuehrer Hausser continued his attack in its original direction, but tenacious Soviet resistance—including counterattacks assisted by close-support aircraft, tanks, and strong artillery—kept the progress of his divisions to a minimum. *Das Reich* had to remain on the defensive all day, repulsing at least fourteen tank-supported counterattacks during the afternoon. In the process, *Gruppenfuehrer* Krueger's division destroyed sixty Russian tanks and took numerous prisoners but proved unable to continue its attack.

Totenkopf's frontal attacks against Hill 213.9—the key Soviet position east of Stepanovka—broke down in the face of dogged enemy resistance, particularly on the part of the antitank brigade covering the four Guards rifle divisions concentrated in the area. Because the 3rd Panzer Division, like *Das Reich*, could not push forward, flanking fire from Stepanovka and the north could not be suppressed.

The II SS Panzer Corps had lost 1,300 officers and men in two days. In addition, the three divisions had lost thirty-seven Pzkw IIIs (ten completely destroyed); fifty-nine Pzkw IVs (fourteen completely destroyed); and nine Tigers (none completely destroyed), reducing the armored strength of the corps from 211 to 111. Further sacrifice by continuing to attack on this line appeared senseless; we did not possess the strength to break the deadlock on this axis of attack. The Soviets, whose main defensive effort obviously centered on Stepanovka and Hill 213.9, had lost another 6,000 prisoners, sixty-eight tanks, sixty-four guns, and hundreds of antitank guns. Yet despite these losses, the Russians remained strong, having committed fifteen rifle divisions, two antitank brigades, and numerous tanks to defend their penetration zone, and the Luftwaffe reported additional reserves being moved up.

General Hollidt had spent most of the day with the five panzer and panzergrenadier divisions and made his decisions based on that experience as well as the overall picture of the enemy situation. He resolved to continue the attack on 1 August but to redirect the main effort to the inner sector of the II SS Panzer Corps and the zone of the XXIV Panzer

Corps in an effort to capture the high ground east of Marinovka, having bypassed the village in the south. He also decided not to touch Stepanovka and Hill 213.9. The orders to II SS Panzer Corps went out at 1815 hours, requiring *Obergruppenfuehrer* Hausser to concentrate the overwhelming bulk of his forces in the far-right sector (*Das Reich*), leaving nothing but the most urgently needed covering forces around Stepanovka. The attack in the northern sector (XVII Corps) was to be discontinued altogether. During the night the 3rd Panzer Division withdrew from its former attack sector, moving into the Artemovka area as army reserve in the rear of the 23rd Panzer Division.

The XXIV Panzer Corps (to which the artillery of the 3rd Panzer Division had been attached) had been ordered to join in the attack spearheaded by *Das Reich* while also maintaining flank security to the south. The left attack group of *Totenkopf* had been instructed to continue its attack in the same direction, making as much use as possible of its remaining panzer elements for small-scale raids. *Brigadefuehrer* Preiss also had the assignment to use his division's artillery to suppress Russian flanking fire from the high ground east of the Gerasimova ravine. Meanwhile, the XXIX and XVII Corps on the outer flanks of the penetration zone received orders to hold the positions already gained but to be ready—once the main attack had begun to be successful—to cooperate with the advance of II SS and XXIV Panzer Corps. IV Flieger Corps and all other available artillery would directly support the main effort south of Marinovka.

Initially, General Hollidt ordered the new attack to be made chiefly with infantry in order to traverse the ravines. As soon as the situation in the center warranted, troops on the southern flank were to join the attack as assault detachments simultaneously stormed Hill 213.9. The following day would quickly reveal whether the Soviets' powers of resistance had in fact been seriously weakened and whether a more flexible conduct of operations would allow us to find their weakest points.

The Third Day of the Attack, 1 August

Sixth Army resumed its offensive at 0600 hours, immediately scoring small but nevertheless important successes. In the XXIX Corps sector, despite Russian flanking fire from the area north of Kuibyshevo, General Block's 294th Infantry Division, together with *Kampfgruppe* Haus (based on Grenadier Regiment 55 of the 17th Infantry Division, commanded by Colonel Georg Haus), captured the southern part of Yelizavetinski and a strongly entrenched antitank gun position. Assisted by II Battalion/ Grenadier Regiment 95 (17th Infantry Division), these units also seized Hill 168.5, which controlled access to the entrance to the Olkhovchik Valley.

In this operation the XXIX Corps took 600 Soviet prisoners. As had been consistently the case, the youngest Red Army soldiers remained the most courageous in both attack and defense. Concentrated German artillery and infantry fire, however, sufficed to break up any Russian counterattacks. Following the capture of Hill 168.5, the attack groups of General Brandenberger's corps prepared to continue their limited attacks toward the north.

General Nehring's XXIV Panzer Corps opened its attack against the Krutaya ravine, east of Hill 202, at 0600 hours. General von Vormann's 23rd Panzer Division had struggled to make its attack as scheduled, losing much time in the assembly area due to muddy roads and inundated fords. The 16th Panzergrenadier Division more than made up for this delay: General von Schwerin's troops quickly closed the gap between the boundary hill and the spot where the Krivaya opened into the Olkhovchik ravine.

In *Obergruppenfuehrer* Hausser's sector, the reinforced Panzergrenadier Regiment *Der Fuehrer* of *Das Reich* captured Hill 203.9 by 0830 hours. Following this success, however, long, stubborn fighting—both house-to-house and bunker-to-bunker—developed in Stepanovka, where fresh Russian infantry had reinforced existing positions. Meanwhile, the division's reinforced Panzergrenadier Regiment *Deutschland* pushed its forward elements as far as the western edge of the ravine running east from Stepanovka.

Major General Max Bork, Sixth Army chief of staff, visited *Das Reich*'s attack sector at 1030 hours and received the impression that Soviet resistance there, as well as directly in front of the 23rd Panzer Division, had weakened perceptibly. General Hollidt authorized him to order both *Das Reich* and the 23rd Panzer to make a sharp thrust directly east through the Olkhovchik ravine against the hill east of Marinovka. The divisions would advance as rapidly as possible, without any regard to the success or failure of the units on their flanks.

The 23rd Panzer Division set the pace for this attack. With the single exception of Hill 203.9 on its left, Panzergrenadier Regiment 126 reached the hedgerows two kilometers south of Marinovka by 1230 hours. The advance of Panzer Regiment 201 stalled in a minefield between the Krutaya ravine and Hill 203.4, but Panzergrenadier Regiment 126 and *Kampfgruppe* Henneberg of Grenadier Regiment 513 (294th Infantry Division) braved heavy Soviet fire to break through into the Krutaya ravine and storm the eastern slopes. After clearing the Olkhovchik ravine, Panzergrenadier Regiment 128 captured the twenty-four-ton bridge across that stream at 1745 hours, extending a bridgehead toward the east. Well-directed German artillery fire scattered massed concentrations of Soviet infantry, neutralized the enemy artillery east of Marinovka, and thus contributed significantly to the advances made by *Das Reich* in the adjoining sector. Taken together with the efforts of the 294th Infantry Division at boundary hill, the 23rd Panzer Division's initial success for the first time so threatened the Russians' line of communications that their front-line resistance began to weaken.

All of the foregoing set the stage for *Das Reich* (aided by concentrated artillery fire and strong air support) to gain a decisive offensive success that afternoon. *Gruppenfuehrer* Krueger's right attack group (on the immediate left of the 23rd Panzer) penetrated into the Olkhovchik valley and by 1600 hours reached the eastern bank of the stream two kilometers south of Marinovka. While this segment of the division prepared for a further drive to the east, *Das Reich*'s left-flank elements cleared the Soviets out of Stepanovka. Reinforced by an assault group from *Totenkopf*, these elements smashed a strong Russian antitank position at the road junction directly northeast of the village. By 1730 hours *Das Reich* was already advancing along the west bank of the Olkhovchik sector (which is to say, along the ridge immediately east of Stepanovka).

Russian resistance, by this time, had noticeably slackened along the entire line. General Bork, having returned to the army's forward headquarters, now ordered II SS Panzer Corps to throw the main body of *Totenkopf* into the attack, which he instructed *Obergruppenfuehrer* Hausser to continue toward the southeast. These orders quickly bore fruit, as *Totenkopf* assault detachments broke through the Russian main battle line in front of Hill 213.9 at 1430 hours. Following two and a half hours of heavy fighting, with our troops supported by the concentrated artillery fire from both division and corps, Hill 213.9 fell back into our hands at 1700 hours. The Russians grudgingly pulled back to the rear slope of the hill, improvising a new defensive line anchored by antitank guns. In a last-ditch effort to blunt our offensive, the Soviets tried to cobble together a new main battle line on the high ground east of the road between Marinovka and Hill 213.9, bringing up one of their last available rifle divisions for the purpose.

Possession of Hill 213.9, however, proved to be the key to the battle, and the Russians had lost it. While *Totenkopf* maintained its pressure to the front, the 23rd Panzer Division and the right-flank group of *Das Reich* threatened to envelop the enemy in the Marinovka area. The Soviet defensive line now simply showed too many gaps to be held on its current line. The Russians faced a choice between committing new strategic reserves of sufficient force to reconquer the lost terrain or withdrawing across the Mius.

Outcome

The Red Army no longer possessed the strength along the Mius River to stage a major counterattack. The difficulties of such a proposition on 1 August were overwhelming, considering both their heavy losses and the inadequacy of their improvised defensive line east of Hill 213.9 as the base for a counteroffensive. That day alone the Soviets had lost 3,600 prisoners, twenty-two tanks, eight guns, and forty-six antitank guns. We had finally broken the Russians west of the Mius River.

IV Flieger Corps dive-bombers attacked the Soviets as they attempted to withdraw east of the Mius, and our medium artillery was able to shell the northern bridges near Dmitrievka.

For the morning of 2 August General Hollidt ordered a general advance by all of our divisions. This attack broke the final enemy resistance and recovered our old positions on the western bank of the river by evening. Despite the heavy numerical superiority that the Russians committed to their Mius River breakthrough attempt, the Sixth Army had first held out with a minimum of forces and finally—when reinforced—decisively defeated the enemy with a prolonged counterattack. Although the Red Army had been able withdraw large forces at the last moment, there could be no doubt about the severity of the Russian defeat: Just the number of corpses left behind when the Soviets fled amounted to the full strength of several rifle divisions. To those gruesome totals could be added 17,762 prisoners (including 955 deserters) that General Hollidt's troops captured between 17 July and 3 August. Moreover, at least 732 enemy tanks were either destroyed or knocked out of action. Captured equipment (excluding tanks), included:

Guns	197	Machine guns	1,780
Anti-tank guns	522	Submachine guns	1,656
Mortars	438	Anti-aircraft guns	5
Anti-tank rifles	733		

Sixth Army's losses during the entire battle were:

	KIA	WIA	MIA	Total
Officers	130	480	24	634
Enlisted	3,168	15,337	2,230	20,735
Totals	3,298	15,817	2,254	21,369

The OKW bulletin for 4 August read as follows:

In the battle on the Mius, infantry and panzer units of the Army and Waffen SS, under the leadership of Field Marshal von Manstein and General of Infantry Hollidt, excellently supported by units of the Luftwaffe, led by General of Fliers Dessloch, foiled the repeated attempts of strong enemy forces to break through and in a spirited counterattack defeated the enemy forces that had penetrated into the area north of Kuibyshevo.

By 2 August, 17,895 prisoners had been captured in this engagements; 730 tanks, 703 guns, and 398 mortars, as well as numerous other weapons and great amounts of equipment were captured or destroyed. The number of Red Army soldiers killed in action is many times that of the prisoners.

In the days immediately following, after rapidly bringing up reinforcements and reorganizing the II Guards Mechanized Corps with sixty new tanks, the Russians tried once more to effect a penetration in the Dmitrievka sector. The objective of this attack appeared to be forcing the recall of the II SS Panzer Corps, which had already begun its march north. Utilizing some of the new tanks, and supported by air attacks, the Soviets managed on 4–5 August to make local breakthroughs against the 23rd Panzer, 16th Panzergrenadier, and 294th Infantry Divisions. Capitalizing on their tactical surprise, some T-34s even reached the outskirts of Stepanovka. These tanks, however, had been committed in small groups, and once separated from their infantry supports our assault and antitank guns destroyed them. In this manner forty-nine of the sixty new tanks—almost the entire armored strength of the II Guards Mechanized Corps—were put out of action during those two days. The Russian infantry attacks achieved even less success, collapsing under the concentrated defensive fire of all weapons; Sixth Army took 130 prisoners.

Enemy movements and radio traffic in front of the 17th, 336th, and 111th Infantry Divisions suggested that the Russians might make additional containing attacks in one or more of these sectors on 6 August. Our observers also noted tanks assembling the Dmitrievka area. Despite these signs, the Russians made attacks only in battalion strength in the old area of penetration.

Between 9 and 10 August, General Brandenberger's XXIX Corps succeeded in throwing the Soviets completely out of the penetration zone south of Kuibyshevo by a spirited attack. Once regained, our troops held the main battle line against all counterattacks. That this attack could be launched at all—given the exhaustion of our troops—required a heroic effort by officers and soldiers alike. Nonetheless, by 10 August General Hollidt's Sixth Army had entirely regained its old defensive line along the Mius River.

The following teletype message arrived from Army Group South on 3 August:

I congratulate the Sixth Army upon its fine success, and express my thanks for the achievements of the troops and their commanders.

The Commander-in-Chief

[signed] von Manstein

Field Marshal

A congratulatory teletype message arrived from the Fuehrer and Supreme Commander of the Wehrmacht on 4 August:

The attack by the Sixth Army against the area of penetration around Dmitrievka, prepared and ordered by the Commander-in-Chief of Army Group South and executed by the 111th Infantry Division, 294th Infantry Division, 306th Infantry Division, 3rd Panzer Division, 23rd Panzer Division, 16th Panzergrenadier Division, SS Das Reich, SS Totenkopf and attached units under the command of the XVII Corps, XXIX Corps, XXIV Panzer Corps, and II SS Panzer Corps, has resulted in a surprisingly great success and great amounted of captured material.

I assure the command and the troops of my full appreciation.

[signed] Adolph Hitler

Sixth Army headquarters issued its own congratulatory order of the day on 6 August:

Order of the Day

Soldiers of the Sixth Army

The July defensive battle on the Mius front has ended with your victory!

In a fortnight of heavy defensive engagements, the front-line divisions, the reserves that were rapidly brought up, and the Alarmeinheiten *succeeded in sealing off the penetration around Dmitrievka against the resistance of enemy troops eight times their strength. These enemy units attacked in overwhelming numbers and suffered heavy losses in personnel and equipment. Of tanks alone, 585 were knocked out of action, some of these at close quarters. Thanks to the heroic fighting of the troops mentioned above, and after bringing forward new forces, the army managed to begin a counterattack on the front of the penetration zone on 30 July. The old main battle line was regained after four days of heavy fighting. Enemy forces that had penetrated in other front sectors had been beaten back earlier by courageous counterattacks.*

The Commander-in-Chief of Army Group South, Field Marshal von Manstein, has expressed his thanks to me today for the performance of the troops of the Sixth Army and their officers.

I desire to express my personal thanks to the officers and men of all the units concerned for their tenacity in defense and for the model élan with which they carried out their attacks, overcoming all difficulties in their missions. Faithful to the last, every foot of ground, every village, and every hill was defended. The deeply distributed enemy defensive system was destroyed in a daring attack and a methodical advance. In spite of the burning sun, our soldiers held out as long as orders required it of them, and attacked with undaunted spirits as soon as they were given the opportunity. Here many a new stanza was added to the epic of German heroism.

The enemy penetration attempt has failed; strong enemy forces have been annihilated!

As usual, the cooperation from our comrades in the Luftwaffe was ideal. Continuously flying against our foes; attacking him just in front of our lines or in the depths of the battlefield; vigilantly following his movements; the Luftwaffe brought the army constant relief in its heavy struggle. In grateful and appreciative words I have again confirmed the comradely assistance of our sister service to the Commander-in-Chief of Luftflotte Four, the Commanding General of IV Flieger Corps, and the Commander of the 15th Flak Division.

The army bows reverently before those of its comrades who gave their blood and their lives in this heavy fighting. Their sacrifices guarantee our final victory.

The main point now, soldiers of the Sixth Army, is to keep what has been won, and to defend it stubbornly when our enemies attack again. I know that you will hold the Mius-Donets front and protect the Donets industrial region which is so important to our war effort.

Sieg heil *to the* Fuehrer!

The Commander-in-Chief

[signed] Hollidt

General of Infantry

The following annex, covering issues of logistics and supply for the period 17 July–5 August, was appended to Sixth Army's report of operations:

1. Ammunition expenditure

Average expenditure of heavy weapons ammunition during the defensive and offensive engagements:

Weapon	7/17–7/29 Defensive Avg. Daily Expend.*	7/30–8/2 Offensive Avg. Daily Expend.*
Machine guns	3.8	1.9
Heavy mortars	8.3	6.6
Lt. Inf. Guns	15.6	10.5
Hvy. Inf. Guns	11.8	12.6
Lt. Field Howitzer 16	31.0	36.8
Lt. Field Howitzer 18	21.4	25.4
Hvy. Field Howitzers	22.4	26.4
Hvy. Field Howitzers (French)	18.4	17.1
Hvy. 100mm Cannon	30.8	42.1
210mm Howitzers	22.5	36.8
Total average	*9.7*	*10.6*

*In percentage of initial issue of ammunition per weapon.

It is especially noteworthy that the expenditure of machine-gun ammunition was twice as high during the defensive engagements as during the offensive. Expenditures of mortar and light infantry gun ammunition was one-third less during the attack than during the defense. The expenditure of medium artillery ammunition rose considerably during the attack phase. The total ammunition expenditure (in tons) was:

Month	Tons
May	2,329
June	3,870
July	19,753

The days of highest expenditure for July and August were:

Day	Tons
7/17	1,430
7/19	1,450
7/23	1,250
7/30	1,700
7/31	1,600
8/1	1,350
8/2	1,300

It was characteristic of this fighting that total expenditures of artillery ammunition on 22 July—a day of large-scale defensive fighting—only reached

830 tons, while the expenditure of heavy mortar ammunition on the same day rose to 100 tons (as compared to thirty-six tons on 21 July and thirty to thirty-five tons on 23 and 24 July).

The heaviest expenditures of light field howitzer 16 ammunition was 11 tons on 17 July and sixty-five tons on 30 July—always on the first day of combat operations (either offensive or defensive). The same applied to light field howitzer 18 ammunition, although here the curve of expenditures reached a second high on 22 July.

2. Fuel consumption

The average daily fuel consumption in Sixth Army's zone of operations amounted to roughly 135 cubic meters between 17 June–2 July. During the period 17 July–29 July (defensive fighting), the average daily consumption was 586 cubic meters. During 30 July–2 August (attack phase) a total of 1,870 cubic meters—467.5 per day. The total fuel available to Sixth Army amounted to 11,062 cubic meters; the consumption was about 10,000 cubic meters. Supplies were therefore adequate to the situation.

The noticeable increase of fuel consumption in the defensive fighting was due to the forward movement of II SS Panzer Corps, the transfers involved in the army's defensive measures, and increased supply train traffic.

3. Supply train traffic

Between 17 and 29 July, 5,313 tons of ammunition, 167 tons of fuel, and personnel requiring 330 tons of cargo space were moved. Between 30 July and 2 August, 3,124 tons of ammunition, 105 tons of fuel, and twenty tons of signal supplies were moved. In seventeen days, therefore, 9,129 tons of supplies or personnel were transported, as compared to a monthly average of 5,321 tons in June.

Sixth Army transport space available for these shipments (including reinforcements), amounted to 2,160 tons of lift. Of these, 422 tons (truck capacity) were placed at the disposal of attached units (e.g., II SS Panzer Corps when moving forward), leaving 1,738 tons available to the army for all other uses.

4. Rail traffic

Railway traffic from 17 July–2 August amounted to:

Category	Tons
Ammunition	42,492
Supplies	17,509
Fuel	28,342
Coal	7,698
Total	96,041

APPENDIX 11A

Order of Battle: Sixth Army, 17 July 1943 (including reinforcements received during the next two weeks)

Colonel General Karl Adolf Hollidt

XXIX Corps
Lieutenant General Erich Brandenberger
111th Infantry Division
Lieutenant General Hermann Recknagel

Grenadier Regiments 50, 70, 117
Artillery Regiment 111
Reconnaissance Battalion 111
Panzerjaeger Battalion 111
Engineer Battalion 111

15th Luftwaffe Field Division
Lieutenant General Willibald Spang

Field Infantry Regiments 29, 30
Field Artillery Regiment 15
Field Fusilier Company 15
Field Panzerjaeger Battalion 15
Field Engineer Battalion 15
Field Flak Battalion 15

17th Infantry Division
Major General Richard Zimmer

Grenadier Regiments 21, 55, 95
Artillery Regiment 17
Reconnaissance Battalion 17
Panzerjaeger Battalion 17
Engineer Battalion 17

336th Infantry Division

Lieutenant General Walther Lucht

> Grenadier Regiments 685, 686, 687
> Artillery Regiment 336
> Reconnaissance Company 336
> Panzerjaeger Battalion 336
> Engineer Battalion 336

Battle Commander, Taganrog

> Artillery Commander 102
> Artillery Battalion I/53

XVII Corps

General of Infantry Willi Schneckenburger

294th Infantry Division

Major General Johannes Block

> Grenadier Regiments 513, 514, 515
> Artillery Regiment 294
> Reconnaissance Battalion 294
> Panzerjaeger Battalion 294
> Engineer Battalion 294

302nd Infantry Division

Major General Otto Elfeldt

> Grenadier Regiments 570, 571, 572
> Artillery Regiment 302
> Reconnaissance Battalion 302
> Panzerjaeger Battalion 302
> Engineer Battalion 302

306th Infantry Division

Major General Carl-Erik Koehler

> Grenadier Regiments 579, 580, 581
> Artillery Regiment 306
> Reconnaissance Company 306
> Panzerjaeger Battalion 306
> Engineer Battalion 306

Corps "Mieth" (IV Corps Headquarters)

(Formed from Commander of Security Troops and Rear Area Army Group Don in Feb 43)

General of Infantry Friedrich Mieth

> 3rd Mountain Division

Lieutenant General Hans Kreysing
Mountain Infantry Regiments 138, 139
Mountain Artillery Regiment 112
Bicycle Battalion 83
Panzerjaeger Battalion 95
Mountain Engineer Battalion 83

304th Infantry Division
Major General Ernst Sieler

Grenadier Regiments 573, 574, 575
Artillery Regiment 304
Reconnaissance Company 304
Panzerjaeger Battalion 304
Engineer Battalion 304

335th Infantry Division
Major General Carl Casper

Grenadier Regiments 866, 867, 868
Artillery Regiment 355
Fusilier Battalion 355
Panzerjaeger Battalion 355
Engineer Battalion 355

Artillery Commander 404

Army Reserve:

16th Panzergrenadier Division
Lieutenant General Gerhard Graf von Schwerin

Panzer Battalion 116
Panzergrenadier Regiments 60, 156
Panzer Artillery Regiment 146
Panzer Reconnaissance Battalion 341
Panzerjaeger Battalion 228
Panzer Engineer Battalion 675

Senior Artillery Commander 306
Major General Richard Metz

Artillery Battalions II/52, 735
Nebelwerfer Regiments 1, 52
Panzerjaeger Battalion 661
Assault Gun Battalions 209, 210, 236, 243, 277

Sturm *Battalion 6 (Army Weapons School Ordzhonikidze)*

Engineer Regimental Staff 520

Engineer Battalions 520, 675

Signal Intercept Company 623

Military Intelligence Company 549

Koeruck 540

Koeruck 585

Arrived 18 July
23rd Panzer Division
Lieutenant General Nikolaus von Vormann
Panzer Regiment 201
Panzergrenadier Regiments 126, 128
Panzer Artillery Regiment 128
Panzer Reconnaissance Battalion 23
Panzerjaeger Battalion 128
Panzer Engineer Battalion 51

Arrived 21 July
XXIV Panzer Corps headquarters
General of Panzer Troops Walter Nehring

Arrived 25 July
II SS Panzer Corps
Obergruppenfuehrer *Paul Hausser*
Das Reich *SS Panzergrenadier Division*
Gruppenfuehrer *Walter Krueger*
SS Panzer Regiment 2
SS Panzergrenadier Regiment 3 *Deutschland*
SS Panzergrenadier Regiment 4 *Der Fuehrer*
SS Panzer Reconnaissance Battalion 2
SS Panzer Artillery Regiment 2
SS Flak Battalion 2
SS Mortar Battalion 2
SS Panzerjaeger Battalion 2
SS Engineer Battalion 2

Totenkopf *SS Panzergrenadier Division*
Brigadefuehrer *Hermann Preiss*
SS Panzer Regiment 3 *Danmark*
SS Panzergrenadier Regiment 5 *Thule*

SS Panzergrenadier Regiment 6 *Theodor Eicke*
SS Panzer Reconnaissance Battalion 3
SS Panzer Artillery Regiment 3
SS Assault Gun Battery 3
SS Flak Battalion 3
SS Mortar Battalion 3
SS Panzerjaeger Battalion 3
SS Engineer Battalion 3

3rd Panzer Division

Lieutenant General Franz Westhoven

Panzer Regiment 6 (one battalion only)
Panzergrenadier Regiments 3, 394
Panzer Reconnaissance Battalion 3
Panzer Artillery Regiment 75
Panzerjaeger Battalion 543
Panzer Engineer Battalion 39
Flak Battalion 314

PART 3

Operation Citadel

An Analysis of Its Critical Aspects

STEVEN H. NEWTON

12

Hoth, von Manstein, and Prokhorovka: A Revision in Need of Revising

The apparent climax of the battle of Kursk—at least from the German perspective—occurred around Prokhorovka with the great roiling tank battle from 10 to 17 July 1943. There, despite Ninth Army's failure to crack Central Front's defenses north of Kursk, Field Marshal Erich von Manstein, Colonel General Hermann Hoth, and *Obergruppenfuehrer* Paul Hausser all sensed the opportunity to utilize German tactical superiority in the handling of great masses of armor to deal the Red Army's strategic reserve a staggering blow. Even as the Soviets opened Operation Kutuzov, their long-planned counteroffensive against Army Group Center in the Orel salient, von Manstein insisted to Adolf Hitler on 13 July that "victory on the southern front of the Kursk salient is within reach. The enemy has thrown in nearly his entire strategic reserves and is badly mauled. Breaking off action now would be throwing away victory!"[1]

Faced with additional Russian offensives at the Izyum River bridgehead against First Panzer Army and along Sixth Army's Mius River front, as well as the Anglo-Allied invasion of Sicily, Hitler refused to countenance the long-term continuation of the Citadel offensive. By 17 July Hausser's II SS Panzer Corps had been pulled out of the line, two divisions headed for the Mius and the third for Italy. The *Grossdeutschland* Panzergrenadier Division and 3rd Panzer Division soon followed. With the exhausted forces remaining to Fourth Panzer Army and *Armeeabteilung* Kempf, von Manstein knew that he could not hope to hold the advances he had made into the Soviet defenses south of Kursk. He reluctantly initiated a phased withdrawal toward a more defensible line near Belgorod.

The consequences of the renowned Greatest Tank Battle of All Time at Prokhorovka are still being debated. George M. Nipe Jr. has made a compelling case that most postwar accounts of the battle, upon which the vast majority of Kursk narratives depends, are erroneous with respect to German strength and losses, especially those of the II SS Panzer Corps. "It has long been an accepted belief that Hausser's SS-Panzerkorps lost hundreds of its tanks to the valiantly charging T-34s of Romitstrov's 5th Guards Tank army," Nipe writes, and that "with the loss of 300 or 400 panzers, including 70 or 100 'Tiger,' (depending on which account you read), the SS divisions were driven from the field of battle, leaving their destroyed tanks scattered all over the battlefield." With diligent research among archival materials, Nipe reconstructs a much more intricate (if somewhat smaller-scale) battle than has usually been depicted and concludes that "two divisions of a single German panzer corps, in one day of fighting, knocked out 600–650 Soviet tanks in the Prokhorovka sector, essentially eliminating major elements of the Soviet strategic reserve in the south." Incorporating many (though not all) of Nipe's assessments in their larger work, David M. Glantz and Jonathan House attempt to place Prokhorovka in perspective with the observation that "rather than the climactic battle at Prokhorovka, it was the incessant Soviet pressure against the flanks of the XXXXVIII and II SS Panzer Corps, together with Soviet denial of air superiority to the Germans, that conditioned ultimate German defeat."[2]

So much for the end; what about the beginning? Why was there even a battle at Prokhorovka at all? In one of their most provocative and revisionist arguments, Glantz and House assert that the armored dogfight between the II SS Panzer Corps and Fifth Guards Tank Army occurred in large measure because "late in the afternoon of 9 July, Hoth fundamentally and, in retrospect, fatally altered his plans." Fourth Panzer Army's original offensive plan, according to this argument, had envisioned a concerted thrust north from the Belgorod area, with both XLVIII and II SS Panzer Corps driving side by side across the Psel River for Oboyan. The left flank was to be covered by LII Corps, the right by the III Panzer Corps and Provisional Corps Raus of *Armeeabteilung* Kempf. The tenacious Soviet defense south of the Psel against XLVIII Panzer Corps, the failure of weak flank-protection forces, and the rapid commitment of the Fifth Guards Tank Army from Steppe Front reserves upset this design. "Thwarted in the center and preoccupied with the threats to his flanks," Hoth denuded his center by allowing XLVIII Panzer Corps to divert the *Grossdeutschland* Panzergrenadier Division to the west and sent II SS Panzer Corps toward Prokhorovka to deal with the Red Army's strategic armored reserves. "By attacking through Prokhorovka," Glantz and

House argue, "Hoth was convinced that the still-powerful SS corps, with concentrated air support, could smash the armored threat to its east, unlock the advance of the III Panzer Corps, and open a new, albeit longer, approach route to the key city of Kursk."[3]

The fact that this interpretation is a radical shift from the generally accepted view is evident from Hoth's postwar claim that he had always believed that "it would be better to deal first with the enemy to be expected via Prokhorovka before continuing our northward thrust in the direction of Kursk." Thus the commander of Fourth Panzer Army denied that swinging II SS Panzer Corps toward Prokhorovka represented any fundamental change to his original attack plans: He had always calculated on the necessity of defeating Soviet armored reserves in that area as a prerequisite to the advance on Oboyan and Kursk. Paul Carell, whose Kursk narrative in *Scorched Earth* long held sway as the definitive pro-German account of the battle, endorses this view, concluding that "Hoth's calculation proved correct. His plan of attack upset the Soviet High Command's plan of defence on the southern front of the Kursk salient and might well have brought about a turn in the battle." Most other writers have either accepted Carell's viewpoint or simply avoided dealing with the issue at all.[4]

Resolving the question of Hoth's original operational plan and the nature of his decision to commit the II SS Panzer Corps toward Prokhorovka on 9 July is critical to an understanding of the overall German conduct of the battle. If Hoth—and Hoth alone, for it should be noted that no one attributes any share of this decision to von Manstein—committed a major tactical error with an improvisational decision, then historians have long been paying far too much attention to tank ratios and the impact of multiple Soviet defensive lines as primary causes of the German defeat. Yet *if* Hoth had always planned to fight it out in the vicinity of Prokhorovka, and *if* George M. Nipe Jr. is correct in asserting that the Germans were on the verge of victory when the offensive was called off, the revision offered by Glantz and House requires a little revising of its own.

What evidence is offered by Glantz and House to support their position? First, there is the pertinent section of Hitler's 15 April 1943 Operations Order No. 6, which laid out the general objectives of the attack from Belgorod:

> Army Group South will jump off with strongly concentrated forces from the Belgorod-Tomarovka line, break through the Prilepy-Oboyan line, and link up with the attacking armies of Army Group Center at east of Kursk. The line Nezhegol–Korocha sector–Skordnoye–Tim must be reached as soon as

possible to protect the attack from the east without jeopardizing the concentration of forces on the main effort in the direction of Prilepy-Oboyan. Forces will be committed to protect the attack in the west; they will later be used to attack into the pocket.[5]

Though this order did not formally break down the two diverging objectives between Fourth Panzer Army and *Armeeabteilung* Kempf, Hitler and OKH obviously envisioned Hoth's army as "the main effort in the direction of Prilepy-Oboyan" and Kempf's force as the one assigned "to protect the attack from the east." This is the document that Glantz and House accept—quite correctly—as representing the expectations of German higher headquarters, and they make the implicit assumption that it also represents the parameters within which Hoth planned his battle. In fact, the authors follow traditionally accepted narrative lines in their examination of German battle preparations, concentrating almost exclusively on questions of equipment and the recurrent delays in launching Operation Citadel to the complete exclusion of any analysis of Army Group South's operational planning. Thus Hoth set off directly from Belgorod to Kursk via the Psel River and Oboyan because that was what Hitler demanded.

With respect to Hoth's 9 July orders for an attack toward Prokhorovka, Glantz and House rely on three German sources. Two of these, Rudolf Lehmann's divisional history of the *Liebstandarte Adolph Hitler* and Sylvester Stadler's *Die Offensive gegen Kursk 1943: II. SS-Panzerkorps als Stosskeil im Grosskampf,* are cited primarily (one is tempted to say exclusively) as sources for key operations orders of II SS Panzer Corps.[6] The third is a postwar study of the battle of Kursk conducted under the auspices of the U.S. Army Historical Program and authored by German generals Gotthard Heinrici and Friedrich Wilhelm Hauck. The authors cite this work as "the extensive memoir by the German defensive specialist, G. Heinrici," which they categorize as having "particular importance for this volume." It is important to note in this context, however, that while the use of the term "memoir" to describe the Heinrici study suggests some reliance on personal experience, when Operation Citadel occurred Colonel General Heinrici was commanding Army Group Center's Fourth Army, north of the Orel salient, hundreds of kilometers removed from the events around Prokhorovka. His knowledge of the planning and conduct of Fourth Panzer Army's battle accrued from a study of the records available to him at the time, and he should thus be considered a secondary rather than primary source.[7]

What Heinrici says of Hoth's original plans for 9 July is quoted at length by Glantz and House in their notes:

Before the 4th Panzer Army, in cooperation with *Armeeabteilung* Kempf, could remove the enemy on its eastern flank and continue its advance to the northeast, they believed that the threat in the west from the Oboyan and Pena salient area would first have to be eliminated. With the approval of the army group on 9 July, they decided to advance their two panzer corps to the north across the Psel—instead of further to the northeast toward Prokhorovka—in order to gain sufficient space to turn elements to the southwest and destroy the enemy in the Pena salient in cooperation with the LII Corps. This diversion would necessarily cause a two-day delay in the continuation of the attack in the main direction.[8]

After detailing the Soviet pressure on both flanks that they believe caused Hoth to give up a direct advance north across the Psel in favor of the diversion toward Prokhorovka, Glantz and House next cite "the fateful order to the II SS Panzer Corps, which was passed on [to] its subordinate divisions late on 9 July." What the authors actually quote as "the Prokhorovka order" is neither the directive from Fourth Panzer Army nor that of II SS Panzer Corps but the tactical order (Division Order No. 17, issued at 2215 on 9 July) of *Liebstandarte Adolph Hitler*. This order, which is quoted from the Lehmann divisional history, details in great depth the specific assignments of each regiment and battalion of the division and clearly lays out that "The II. SS-Panzerkorps is to move out at 10.7.1943 with the LSSAH to the right and SS-Panzergrenadier Division Totenkopf to the left on both sides of the Pssel and head northeast. Attack objective: Prochorowka/East." "With these changes in Hoth's plan, the German Kursk offensive was approaching its climax," the authors contend. Yet what this order did not do—and would not have been expected to do—was lay out the reasoning behind the assignment of this objective.[9]

In light of the fact that few historians have focused even this much attention on Hoth's decision making at Kursk, Glantz and House appear to have made at least a prima facie case for their interpretation. Though one might quibble with the depth of research (not a single archival source consulted or any testimony from eyewitnesses, much less a direct refutation of Hoth's postwar account), their premises and deductions appear both logical and consistent with the documents they use. In short, if unchallenged, there appears to be no reason for the Glantz and House revision not to become the new standard interpretation of the genesis of the Prokhorovka battle: Hoth made a tactical error in modifying his plans.

Enter Friedrich Fangohr, Hoth's chief of staff and the author of the chapter on Fourth Panzer Army for the Busse Citadel study presented in this volume. Fangohr, writing in 1947 (long before any of this material had become controversial), presented an entirely different view of

Hoth's plans at Kursk. Fangohr confirmed that Army Group South's original operations order echoed Hitler's plan: "Fourth Panzer Army would attack out of the area west of Belgorod along a straight line running due north via Oboyan to seek contact with Ninth Army near Kursk." But Fangohr also insisted that Hoth had not accepted this concept, noting that the army commander had "discussed the commitment of forces and the execution of the attack in detail" during a 10–11 May meeting at Fourth Panzer Army's headquarters. "General Hoth had developed several new ideas regarding the attack," Fangohr reported, "and Field Marshal von Manstein accepted them as the basis for all further operational planning."

Hoth's preexisting concern about the deployment and strength of Soviet strategic armored reserves had increased over the past several weeks. He "concluded that the Russians had presumably become aware of our intention, and had shifted elements of their strategic reserve toward the west in order to have them more readily available," and "on the basis of this estimate, General Hoth decided that the order to attack due north along a straight route via Oboyan was not to be interpreted literally." Hoth based his arguments on terrain, the layout of potential Psel River crossing sites, and his forecast of how the Russian strategic reserves would move into battle. This final factor was, for the panzer general, decisive. According to Fangohr, "General Hoth also had to assume that Soviet strategic reserves—including several tank corps—would enter the battle by pushing quickly through the narrow passage between the Donets and Psel Rivers at Prokhorovka (about fifty kilometers northeast of Belgorod)." If XLVIII and II SS Panzer Corps faced stiff opposition while fighting for bridgeheads on the Psel, "then a Russian tank attack would hit our right flank at exactly the moment in which the panzer divisions had their freedom of movement extremely limited."

Fearing that "such a situation could quickly turn into a disaster, General Hoth realized that his plans must anticipate an engagement with Soviet armored reserves near Prokhorovka prior to continuing the attack toward Kursk." Hoth told von Manstein that it was "vital to employ the strongest possible force in such a fight, so that we could compel the enemy to meet us on terrain of our choosing in which the panzer divisions could fully exploit their superior mobility, unhampered by the Psel River." This caused Fourth Panzer Army's commander to press for a modification in the assignments of both the XLVIII and II SS Panzer Corps. Hausser's three SS divisions, having pierced the initial Soviet defensive belts, "would not advance due north across the Psel, but veer sharply northeast toward Prokhorovka to destroy the Russian tank forces we expected to find there." Simultaneously, von Knobelsdorff's panzer divisions, following their "initial breakthrough on either side of Cherkasskoe, . . . would not push north to the Psel, but keep abreast of II SS Panzer Corps as it wheeled northeast. Such a maneuver would cover Obergruppenfuehrer Hausser's flank as he advanced toward the decisive battle, and potentially provide additional reinforcements for that engagement."

Fangohr's account was supported by von Manstein's chief of staff, Theodor Busse, who wrote in his introductory chapter that Soviet armored reserves "would have to be engaged in the vicinity of Prokhorovka had been recognized as a prerequisite for the overall success of the operation. Thus II SS Panzer Corps . . . was deployed in a parallel echelon to the right on both sides of Volkhovets, ready to push to Prokhorovka." Busse also acknowledged the change in von Knobelsdorff's orders: "XLVIII Panzer Corps' primary mission, upon reaching the Pena River, was to cover the left flank of II SS Panzer Corps against strong Soviet tank forces presumed to be in the vicinity of Oboyan."

Such postwar comments could be discounted as self-serving attempts to present the battle as having been fought as planned, and to accept the Glantz and House interpretation this is exactly what a reader would have to believe. Yet the details in Fangohr's account argue against such a conclusion: He presents not only Hoth's rationale but also a recounting of the army commander's discussions with von Manstein, as well as alluding to the outcome of several map exercises. Given the voluminous archival material available for Fourth Panzer Army and its subordinate units during the preparations for Operation Citadel, Fangohr—intentionally or not—provides ample information to allow the researcher to check his veracity.

Fourth Panzer Army's war diary [*Kriegstagebuch*] for 10–11 May 1943 confirms that von Manstein visited Hoth's headquarters for a discussion of the tactical details of the upcoming offensive.[10] Part of the reason for the field marshal's visit apparently stemmed from a rather caustic analysis Hoth had recently written of the proposed Operations Panther and Habicht. These were the two attacks that Hitler and OKH originally saw as preliminaries to the Kursk offensive. Habicht, ordered by Hitler on 22 March, was to be a two-pronged thrust by *Armeeabteilung* Kempf and First Panzer Army to clear the Chuguev-Izyum bulge in the Donets River front southeast of Kharkov. The Fuehrer then mandated planning for Panther, an even more ambitious attack by First and Fourth Panzer Armies to push the Red Army completely off the central Donets and back to a line running from Volchansk through Kupyansk to Svatovo.[11] According to the draft operations order from Army Group South headquarters, dated 23 March 1943, von Manstein envisioned the employment of all eleven panzer or panzergrenadier divisions that had been earmarked for Operation Citadel. He further predicated his plans on the army group receiving as reinforcements no fewer than nine additional infantry divisions, courtesy of OKH or other army groups.[12]

Hoth's undated response to this proposal (by context written in early April) raised pointed questions about the strength and dispositions for the attack. He was openly skeptical that OKH would actually keep its promise with regard to the reinforcements and worried about the panzer divisions' taking heavy losses prior to the main offensive. The core of the army commander's opposition to these subsidiary offensives, however, was his concern about Soviet strategic tank reserves. Hoth agreed, for example, that the five panzer or panzergrenadier divisions assigned to Fourth Panzer Army for Panther could break open the Russian front line but were woefully inadequate for the purpose of engaging enemy armored reserves. Hoth estimated that immediately opposite his own front the Red Army had concentrated one tank and one Guards mechanized corps. Available from enemy groupings facing Sixth Army on the Mius River were an additional two tank corps, and there was a force of equal size just north of Belgorod. Even more critical, Hoth noted that Luftwaffe reconnaissance and other intelligence sources placed three additional tank and one mechanized corps in strategic reserve north of Kupyansk. Aside from any tanks in independent regiments or brigades, this meant that the eleven German mobile divisions, which then averaged only about seventy panzers each, divided into three separate lines of attack, would have to contend with ten Soviet tank or mechanized corps. For this, Hoth flatly stated, Army Group South would need not only all the infantry divisions promised by higher headquarters but three to four more panzer divisions as well.[13]

Hoth's response clarifies two important points. First, it is obvious that finding some way to defeat the Soviet strategic armored reserves had become a critical question for him long before Operation Citadel jumped off. As he conceptualized the upcoming campaign, it is clear from this appreciation and other documents that the commander of Fourth Panzer Army saw dealing with those reserves as a prerequisite for attempting major territorial gains. In addition, Hoth's quick and forceful rejoinder provides considerable insight regarding his relationship with von Manstein. Hoth's arguments would be adopted by the army group commander, who used them to argue against the conduct of Panther and Habicht, and this interchange would set a tone for future interactions between the two men.[14]

Field Marshal Erich von Manstein was not the first commander to discover that Hermann Hoth was a strong-willed subordinate. During the planning stages for Operation Barbarossa (the German invasion of the Soviet Union) in early 1941, when Hoth commanded Panzer Group 3, both Colonel General Franz Halder (chief of the Army General Staff) and Field Marshal Fedor von Bock (commander, Army Group Center) were struck by the tenacity with which Hoth advanced his own tactical conceptions. The original attack plan called for Hoth's panzer group to be subordinated to Colonel General Adolf Strauss's Ninth Army and for Panzer Group 3 in turn to intermix infantry and panzer divisions in the initial assault. At a late February war game, von Bock characterized Hoth as having "made difficulties" over the issue. The army group commander realized that "if [he] gave in to Hoth's demand" the entire structure of the attack would be altered, and thus he refused to change the orders. Hoth did not let the matter die and continued to argue his point, with von Bock noting in mid-March that "Hoth is casting his eyes beyond the Dneiper and Dvina from the very outset and is paying scant attention to the possibility of attacking and defeating enemy forces which stand and fight somewhat further forward." Considering the larger picture and the demands of OKH, von Bock wrote that "I will have to reject Hoth's solution, even though there is much to be said in its favor. That won't happen without a lot of sparring." So certain was von Bock that Hoth would not easily accept "no" for an answer that he dispatched a senior staff officer "to Berlin to ascertain in advance whether Army Command intends to stick to its guns." Halder recorded not quite two weeks later that "Ninth Army and Hoth will need direct orders to get them to team up infantry divisions with armored group in the jump-off."[15]

The following summer, during the initial stages of Operation Blue, which would ultimately lead to the Stalingrad disaster, Hoth commanded Fourth Panzer Army, von Bock led Army Group A, and Halder remained chief of the Army General Staff. In early July OKH instructed von Bock to push forward Hoth's army to seize Voronezh. From the ensuing cloud of communications and evasion on Hoth's part, Halder concluded on 5 July 1942 about the headstrong panzer general's ability to influence his immediate superiors: "To me the situation looks this way: Hoth had the mission to strike for Voronezh, but did not relish the idea and so approached the operation with reluctance. Being directed to keep together all his forces in that direction, he asked von Bock to the protection of this southern flank. Von Bock has become completely dependent on Hoth's initiative and so has oriented the offensive toward Voronezh, to a great degree than he could answer for." Field Marshal von Bock, who later discovered that his support for Hoth's modifications of the offensive was a major factor in his relief a week later, also realized on 5 July just how obstinate the panzer general could be in pursuit of his own agenda. Having been formally called to heel, Hoth was vocally unrepentant, and his "old aversion against the attack was expressed in an intercepted radio communication by the Army High Command's liaison officer with him."[16]

It comes as no surprise, then, to discover Hoth in the spring of 1943 arguing with von Manstein for unauthorized changes in the Kursk attack plan. First, Hoth insisted that the XLVIII Panzer Corps was too weak to carry out its penetration mission and hold its western flank in the initial thrust to the Psel River. The panzer army commander had no faith at all that the very weak Second Army along the western face of the Kursk salient would be able to provide any pressure against the Soviets menacing von Knobelsdorff's left wing. When Operation Citadel had originally been scheduled for an early May jump-off, only *Grossdeutschland* and the 11th Panzer Division had been earmarked as its armored components. Hoth now raised the question of using the additional time occasioned by the delay in the offensive to refit the 3rd Panzer Division as a reinforcement. He did not, at that time, intend to commit the division in the initial assault but to hold it in reserve for flank defense or exploitation purposes. Field Marshal von Manstein agreed to this proposal.[17]

Hoth also braced his commander for a change in the boundary line separating Fourth Panzer Army's area of operations from that of *Armeeabteilung* Kempf. Because both Hitler's original order and the first operations plan emanating from Army Group South had envisioned a straight thrust north across the Psel River by both XLVIII and II SS Panzer Corps, Kempf's III Panzer Corps had been assigned a left-flank boundary that ran almost due north from Belgorod and encompassed the entire Prokhorovka area. Hoth convinced von Manstein to modify this boundary by placing "the land bridge west and northwest of Prokhorovka" in his army's sector. Both of these changes formed the basis for revised operations orders issued by Fourth Panzer Army four days later, which Hausser reiterated in his own 31 May operations order, requiring that II SS Panzer Corps, upon breaking through the second Soviet line of defenses, "make its main effort south of the Psel toward Prokhorovka."[18]

Examining those changes formed the basis of a series of late May–early June map exercises. General of Panzer Troops Werner Kempf held the first war game on 29 May, coordinated by Erhard Raus, who commanded the infantry corps responsible for the far right flank of the entire penetration; von Manstein attended and spent several hours with the participants before touring the line units to speak with the troops. On 2 June Hoth invited the army commander to a Fourth Panzer Army war game whose participants included the commanders, chiefs of staff, and operations officers of both XLVIII and II SS Panzer Corps; the key division commanders; and the operations officer of VIII Flieger Corps. The III Panzer Corps engaged in another war game on 2 June, and several days later both Hausser and von Knobelsdorff held their own exercises that extended down to regimental and battalion commanders. Hoth and von Manstein attended these exercises as well. Finally, having settled on a general operational design, each spearhead division held its own exercise in the latter half of June, involving officers as junior as platoon leaders.[19]

The barely decipherable handwritten notes from the XLVIII Panzer Corps (sans maps) exercise still survive. Probably scrawled by the corps chief of staff, Colonel Friedrich-Wilhelm von Mellenthin, these notes indicate that Fourth Panzer Army, a full month before the offensive started, envisioned the *Grossdeutschland* Panzergrenadier Division as the spearhead unit to drive straight north toward the Psel River crossings and directly threaten Oboyan. *Grossdeutschland*'s advance, however, was to be linked to that of the II SS Panzer Corps on its right, and the exercise assumed that the three SS panzergrenadier divisions would turn northeast toward Prokhorovka just as XLVIII Panzer Corps reached the Psel River line. By 27 June the Fourth Panzer Army war diary reported that Hoth and von Manstein had "settled in principle" on this as the final plan, to include the requirement that *Armeeabteilung* Kempf's III Panzer Corps turn more north than northeast (as Hitler's Operations Order No. 6 had required) to strike Prokhorovka from the southern flank when Hausser hit the area from the southwest. Negotiations between Hoth, Hausser, and von Knobelsdorff regarding the boundary lines and daily objectives for XLVIII and II SS Panzer Corps had been finalized. The strong brigade of Pzkw V Panthers would be under the control of XLVIII Panzer Corps at the start, but the possibility was held out to Hausser that at least part of the unit might be made available to support his drive toward Prokhorovka.[20]

This intent was clearly reflected in Hoth's final attack orders, issued on 28 June and 3 July. Fourth Panzer Army needed rapidly to "smash all resistance in the second enemy line, destroy the tank forces thrown at it, and to move on Kursk and the area to the east, *going around Oboyan to the east*" [emphasis added]. The 6th Panzer Division, the lead element of *Armeeabteilung* Kempf's III Panzer Corps, was "to attack from Belgorod via Ssabynino toward Prokhorovka." As for Hausser's II SS Panzer Corps, "after breaking through the second line, the Corps is to stand ready to move the bulk of its forces in rear echelon formation to the right south of the Psel sector toward the northeast, with the right wing moving on Prokhorovka."[21]

Neither did Hoth waver in his intent even though the Soviet defensive lines proved far more tenacious than expected. Prokhorovka as the immediate objective of II SS Panzer Corps was confirmed again in orders on 7 July, and even Fourth Panzer Army's original orders for 9 July emphasized that Hausser's primary mission the following day was to keep pushing *Liebstandarte Adolph Hitler* and *Das Reich* toward Prokhorovka, though Hoth expected the corps to keep close contact with *Grossdeutschland* on the left. The panzer army commander did expect Hausser's third division, *Totenkopf*, to push across the Psel River and seize some heights that commanded Prokhorovka. Hoth's primary anxiety at this point did not revolve around his original strategy to force a battle at Prokhorovka but instead focused on the constant pressure on his flanks that had sapped "a significant portion of the II SS Panzer Corps' strength" away from "the area of Prokhorovka."[22]

Fourth Panzer Army's war diary for 9 July indicates, however, that it was von Manstein, not Hoth, who wanted elements of II SS Panzer Corps to drive across the Psel prior to engaging the Fifth Guards Tank Army at Prokhorovka. Concerned by the failure of *Armeeabteilung* Kempf to provide flank security for the II SS Panzer Corps and the increasing pressure against von Knobelsdorff's left flank, the army group commander apparently favored a narrow penetration of the Psel in an attempt to gain the more favorable "panzer country" north of the river. This he may have envisioned as driving a wedge between the Soviet First Tank and Fifth Guards Tank Armies to enable Hoth to deal with them successively from a central position. Hoth preferred to strike west (XLVIII Panzer Corps) and northeast (II SS Panzer Corps) and destroy the Russian tank reserves before crossing the river in force. He was, as Fangohr observed, haunted by the prospect that "a Russian tank attack would hit our right flank at exactly the moment in which the panzer divisions had their freedom of movement extremely limited by the Psel River" and that "such a situation could quickly turn into a disaster." By early that afternoon Hoth had again brought von Manstein around to his way of thinking.[23]

Conditions were not as Hoth would have ideally preferred for the advance on Prokhorovka. He had originally hoped to have XLVIII Panzer Corps force the Psel River line by 7 or 8 July, and he had expected Kempf's III Panzer Corps to be covering Hausser's right flank. The panzer general had also planned on being able to support the SS panzergrenadier divisions with a significant contingent of Pzkw V Panthers. None of these prerequisites had been met. The First Tank Army was clinging to von Knobelsdorff's left, III Panzer Corps remained mired in Seventh Guards Army's defenses, and 10th Panzer Brigade had only fourteen operational Panthers. But the Fifth Guards Tank Army, reinforced by two additional tank corps, *had* rushed up from deep reserve and was positioning itself to strike in exactly the fashion Hoth most feared. Hoth believed that XLVIII Panzer Corps *could*, given another twenty-four to forty-eight hours, clean up its flank and prepare to force the Psel; he *hoped* that III Panzer Corps would break free in the same period to reinforce Hausser. Yet on 9 July the grim reality was that the only force available to challenge the Soviet armored reserve consisted of the three SS divisions. Hoth's real choice was whether to have II SS Panzer Corps meet the Russian tanks head-on, on ground at least partly of his own choosing, or to hold in place and weather the blow. In the universe of German panzer tactics this hardly even represented a choice.

In accepting battle at Prokhorovka, Hoth knowingly gambled on the tactical skills and technical superiority of the outnumbered and unsupported divisions of II SS Panzer Corps. Although the odds had shifted against him since he created his initial attack plan, Hoth had never been swayed from his belief that the decisive engagement in the campaign would be fought at Prokhorovka. He held to this conviction so strongly that the panzer army commander, not once but at least twice, managed to impress his own ideas on von Manstein, something he would achieve on numerous occasions during the year that the two men worked together in their ultimately unsuccessful attempt to retrieve the fortunes of the German army between the Volga River and the Carpathian Mountains.

13

Ninth Army and the "Numbers Game": A Fatal Delay?

Colonel General Walter Model, commander of Ninth Army, holds a peculiar position in the highly developed postwar mythology surrounding Operation Citadel. As the commander of the attack force on the northern face of the Kursk salient, Model, not Army Group Center commander Field Marshal Gunther von Kluge, supervised the operational planning for the assault. On 3 May, when the question of launching or postponing the offensive was discussed by Adolf Hitler, Kurt Zeitzler, von Kluge, and Erich von Manstein, it was a pessimistic report on the state of Russian defenses prepared by Model that swayed the dictator's decision over the protests of both army group commanders.[1] If Operation Citadel was fatally injured by the two-month delay in its execution, then Model—along with Hitler and Heinz Guderian—deserves to be assigned responsibility as one of the chief architects of the defeat. Surprisingly, however, Model's reasoning and the effects of the multiple postponements of Ninth Army's eventual attack have never been comprehensively analyzed.

A specialist in the kind of tenacious not-one-step-backward type of defense that Hitler favored, Model had first come to the Fuehrer's attention during the Soviet winter counteroffensive of 1941–1942. Newly appointed as army commander, Model scraped together an attack force to free his encircled XXVI Corps, only to find that Hitler intended to interfere with his operational planning, insisting on a two-pronged assault on diverging lines. Aghast at the idea of his weakened army being forced to attack in different directions, the general boarded a plane for East Prussia. Bypassing his immediate superior, Model sought a personal confrontation with Hitler. At first he attempted to lay out his reasons in the best, dispassionate General Staff manner, only to find the Fuehrer unmoved by logic.

Finally, desperate and disgusted, Model uttered the words that would initiate his moral ascendancy over his commander-in-chief. Glaring at Hitler through his monocle, Model brusquely demanded to know: "*Mein Fuehrer*, who commands Ninth Army, you or I?" Hitler, shocked at this show of open defiance from his newest army commander, attempted to cut the discussion short by issuing a direct order to include his changes in the assault plan. Model shook his head: "That must not stand for me." "Good, Model," the dictator finally responded, exasperated. "You do it as you please, but it will be your head at risk."[2]

It was the first time that a German general had so bluntly confronted his Fuehrer, and the lesson was not lost on Walter Model: Hitler respected strength and determination, and he could be intimidated. Ninth Army's successful, yearlong defense of the exposed Rzhev salient, including the orchestration of what historian David Glantz has termed "Zhukov's greatest defeat," cemented Model's prestige in Hitler's eyes, and the fact the army commander appeared far warmer toward the tenets of national socialism than either von Kluge or von Manstein did not diminish his influence. In October 1942, at the Fuehrer's behest, Model was placed on a short list of four younger generals preselected for future army group commands when such positions opened.[3]

When Model spoke, Hitler listened.

In order to comprehend what Model was saying in May 1943 with regard to Operation Citadel, it is critical to understand the situation at Ninth Army. Following its February withdrawal from the Rzhev salient (Operation Buffalo), the army's constituent divisions had been refitting, absorbing replacements, and hunting down partisans in the Army Group Center rear area. Model's divisions badly needed such a hiatus: Against a ration strength of 324,924 officers and men in twenty-four divisions, Ninth Army could place just 67,188 combat troops (21 percent) in the trenches. Only two of these divisions were anywhere near their authorized infantry strength, with the remainder hovering at or below 50 percent, most having dissolved at least three of their original nine infantry battalions. Field artillery batteries had been officially reduced from four guns to three, but many deployed only one or two. The army's two panzer divisions could not muster a complete tank battalion between them, and as far as supply and transport were concerned, Ninth Army lacked the thousands of trucks and horses needed to make its units even partly mobile.[4]

Fourteen of these understrength divisions were parceled out to other armies in Army Group Center (most to Fourth Army), and two went to the southern end of the front, leaving Model a nucleus of eight divisions (6th, 72nd, 86th, 102nd, 216th, and 251st Infantry Divisions; 2nd and 9th

Panzer Divisions), to which would be gradually added another seven infantry divisions, four panzer divisions, and one panzergrenadier division to build the northern assault force for Operation Citadel. None of these divisions could be considered in any sense fresh or at full combat strength when Model received them, all having been pulled out of the line for refitting at about the same time the Rzhev salient had been evacuated. The case of 4th Panzer Division illustrates the condition of these reinforcements. Engaged in almost continuous fighting in the Kursk, Mzensk, Novgorod Severski, and Sevsk from late January 1943 through 27 March, the division lost more than 3,550 men and had only about thirty operational armored fighting vehicles (which consisted of a motley collection of obsolete tanks, a handful of Pzkw IVs, StG IIIs, Marder II self-propelled antitank guns, and even a few captured T-34s). Nearly half of the artillery pieces available to Panzer Artillery Regiment 103 were captured Russian or French pieces, and the unit lacked so many trucks that it had been assigned 2,500 horses. Neither could the unit be fully rested, having to take part in antipartisan sweeps during April. By 31 May, when Lieutenant General Dietrich von Saucken took command, 4th Panzer Division contained only about seventy tanks and 2,840 combat troops (slightly more than half of its authorized strength in both categories).[5]

In his chapter on Ninth Army for the Busse study, Peter von der Groeben actually underemphasized the difficulties Model faced in turning his worn-out divisions into an assault force capable of breaching three successive lines of Soviet defenses. "Seasoned veterans," observed von der Groeben, "composed the divisions earmarked to spearhead the offensive," which "reorganized in rear areas in early spring, filling their ranks with new soldiers and—to some extent—receiving new weapons and equipment." The staff officer cited the most vexing problem with these hastily refurbished units as the need to integrate the cadre of veterans with the newly arrived replacements: "In their new organization and composition these divisions completely lacked combat experience and—to be more specific—experience in staging attacks through heavily fortified defenses. It was absolutely necessary that these divisions receive this kind of training."

It should be recalled, however, that during this period von der Groeben actually served on staff at Second Army, and when he wrote his postwar essay he had no access to the pre-Kursk strength reports filed by Ninth Army. He undoubtedly assumed that the gaps in the ranks of Model's heavily decimated divisions in mid-July (when he was transferred to the staff of Army Group Center) resulted primarily from the ferocity of the opening rounds of Operation Citadel. In this assumption von der Groeben was only partly correct.

In reality, the number of replacements Model had received by even mid-May amounted to no more than a trickle when he needed a flood. Comparing the early February combat strengths of the seven divisions Ninth Army brought out of the Rzhev salient for the Kursk attack with their situation on 16 May (two weeks *after* Model argued for a postponement of the offensive) highlights the seriousness of the manpower problem:

Combat strength (*Gefechtstarke*) in Selected Divisions, Ninth Army, February and May 1943[6]

Unit	Combat Strength, 7 February 1943	Combat Strength, 16 May 1943	Change
251st ID	2,602	2,591	−11
72nd ID	2,783	3,063	+280
102nd ID	3,004	2,683	−321
86th ID	3,277	3,610	+333
9th PzD	2,708	2,872	+164
216th ID	1,951	2,714	+763
2nd PzD	2,411	4,093	+1,682
6th ID	2,630	2,768*	+138
Totals	21,366	24,934	+3,028

*6th ID combat strength was not reported on 16 May; this figure represents the unit's 6 June 1943 strength.

The modest 3,028-man gain in combat strength achieved among eight divisions pulled out of the front line during the quietest three-month period in the entire war cannot even be completely attributed to the efforts of the Replacement Army (*Ersatzheer*) because a significant percentage of that increase (possibly as much as one-third) represented returning convalescents rather than new soldiers. Neither was the situation any better among the divisions Model had received from other armies. The twenty divisions assigned to Ninth Army on 16 May had a combined combat strength of 66,137 and an average divisional combat strength of just 3,306 (roughly 60 percent of the authorized strength, even for six-battalion infantry divisions). According to the standards employed by the German Army, deficiencies in combat strength would have kept all but four of Model's twenty division-equivalents (2nd and 12th Panzer Divisions, 10th Panzergrenadier Division, and 78th Assault Division) from being rated as capable of executing even limited offensive missions. This was hardly the force with which to crack the strongest defensive line that the Red Army had yet erected.[7]

The situation was equally dismal with respect to artillery. Ninth Army's twenty divisions should have had—by authorized strength—a total of 1,080 pieces of field artillery: 648 medium 105mm guns and 432 heavy 150mm guns. On 16 May, however, Model's divisions contained only 520 medium and 186 heavy pieces, a shortfall of nearly 35 percent. Army Group Center had been able to only partly compensate Ninth Army with the addition of forty-seven medium and seventy-one heavy pieces in nondivisional artillery battalions. No heavy mortar battalions or *Nebelwerfer* multiple rocket launchers had yet been made available to support the assault. Worse still, of the guns the army did possess, at least 15 percent (about 124 pieces) were effectively immobile for lack of prime movers or even horses to shift them from one firing position to the next.[8]

Ninth Army's transport situation remained mediocre. On 16 May Model's divisions reported their vehicle situation (cars, trucks, and prime movers) in terms that could best be described as marginal. Thirteen infantry divisions reported themselves about 2,000 vehicles short of their combined establishment, with infantry battalions possessing only 69.2 percent and artillery regiments only 79.2 percent of assigned transport. In the panzer and panzergrenadier divisions prospects were somewhat better: Five of the six reported their artillery as completely mobile, but the transport readiness of their infantry battalions hovered around 80 percent. The 18th Panzer Division still had horse-drawn wagons assigned to its panzer battalion, the 4th Panzer Division had not yet received the self-propelled artillery to replace its towed (captured) guns, and the 10th Panzergrenadier Division had an entire infantry battalion capable of moving only on foot.[9]

The trains coming from Germany had been bringing large numbers of tanks to Ninth Army, and in armored fighting vehicles, at least, Model's strength had grown impressively. His panzer divisions each contained between seventy-five and 100 tanks, and he had received several battalions of assault guns. Of the heavy Tiger tanks, however, not more than half a dozen vehicles from the promised battalion had arrived, and Ninth Army had yet to see the first of the new Panthers.[10] As the army commander calculated the attrition his panzers would undoubtedly experience in penetrating a defensive system more than thirty-five kilometers deep, his tank stocks still looked on the underside of adequate.

If such was the strength of Ninth Army in mid-May—66,000 combat troops, 824 guns, and about 800 tanks and assault guns—what were the odds Model's soldiers faced as they fought their way south toward Kursk? Immediately in front of his trenches, Model estimated that the Soviets had concentrated the following forces:

German Estimates of Red Army Strength Opposite Ninth Army, May/June 1943[11]

Unit type	Front-line troops	Army reserves	Front reserves	Strategic reserves	Total
Rifle div.	17	6	5	3	31
Airb. div.				3	3
Mortar Regts.	9				9
Artillery brigs.	1				1
Artillery div.	2	2	2		6
Rocket-launcher regts.	1		3		4
Rocket-launcher brigs.	1				1
Antitank brigs.		1			1
Tank regts.		5	3		8
Tank brigs.		2	1		3
Tank corps			1	3	4
Tank armies				1	1

German intelligence officers guessed that these organizations contained at least 124,000 infantry, 1,200 guns, 200 rocket launchers, and 1,500 tanks, which meant that Ninth Army would be outnumbered by nearly two-to-one in every major category while the Russians would also have the benefit of entrenchments and several hundred antitank guns emplaced in hardened positions. (If anything, the Germans underestimated Soviet strength.) As he examined the reconnaissance photographs delivered by the Luftwaffe, Model became more and more certain that an attack in May or even early June would end in almost immediate disaster. He suggested to von Kluge that the two armies in the Orel bulge (Ninth and Second Panzer) should start digging intermediate defense lines against the possibility of an immediate Russian offensive. When the army group commander, fully aware that Hitler did not want to hear about defensive measures, refused to give the order, Model quietly had his own engineers begin surveying anyway.[12]

Thus, given the condition of Ninth Army and the strength of the Red Army's Central Front, it is hardly surprising that Model lobbied for a delay in the offensive. Indeed, as von der Groeben implies, Ninth Army's commander may well have hoped that enough successive postponements would lead to a decision to cancel the attack altogether. Then the Ninth and Second Panzer Armies could have husbanded their combined resources to wage a defensive struggle for the Orel salient, hopefully inflicting such severe Russian casualties as to render the Soviets incapable of achieving major strategic gains for the rest of the year. If this was, in fact, what Model hoped, he was destined to be disappointed.

Two months later, when Operation Citadel belatedly commenced on 5 July, how much stronger and better prepared was Ninth Army to achieve the objectives set for it? The army's combat strength had risen from 66,137 to 75,713 (a gain of 9,576), but this increase was deceiving. More than two-thirds of the additional strength (6,670 men) resulted not from replacements or reinforcements to the existing divisions but as the result of the addition of the 6th Infantry and 4th Panzer Divisions to the Ninth Army's administrative reporting system; only 2,906 new soldiers and returning convalescents had joined the ranks in the intervening two months. When the four divisions of XX Corps, which were assigned to hold Model's far right flank and take no part in the initial breakthrough phase of the battle, are discounted, Ninth Army jumped off toward Kursk on 5 July with a combat strength of only 68,747 troops.[13]

A direct comparison with the assault divisions in Army Group South clearly indicates Model's critical weakness in combat troops. Whereas the total strength of Ninth Army's divisions remained low (an average of 11,134 for the infantry divisions and 12,966 for the panzer/panzergrenadier divisions), von Manstein's divisions were much stronger. Between Fourth Panzer Army and *Armeeabteilung* Kempf the infantry divisions averaged 17,369 and the mobile divisions 18,410. These differences become even more accentuated when only combat strength is considered. Model's fifteen infantry divisions averaged only 3,296 combat troops each; von Manstein's eight infantry divisions boasted roughly 6,344.[14] Each of Army Group South's infantry divisions was nearly twice as strong where it counted as each of Ninth Army's. Plainly the additional weeks of delay had not been a good investment for Model in this regard.

Yet Model's artillery holdings greatly expanded during May and June. According to returns for 4 July, which included virtually all the weapons in the three divisions held in reserve by Army Group Center, Ninth Army disposed over an impressive artillery force, including among its nondivisional units six assault gun battalions, two heavy self-propelled antitank battalions, ten mortar or *Nebelwerfer* battalions, and the equivalent of twenty-one independent artillery battalions. Along with the organic pieces in Model's divisional artillery regiments and antitank battalions, Ninth Army's holdings are summarized below:

Ninth Army Field Artillery, Heavy Mortars, and Antitank Guns, 4 July 1943[15]

Corps	Field artillery/heavy mortars			Antitank guns		
	Lt.	Hvy.	Tot.	Md.	Hvy.	Tot.
XX	120	41	161	55	17	72
XLVI Pz.	147	66	213	62	33	95
XLVII Pz.	115	123	238	81	96	177
XLI Pz.	127	109	236	34	36	70
XXIII	111	138	249	34	90	124
Total	620	477	1,097	266	272	538
Reserves	—	10	10	30	105	135
Grand total	620	487	1,107	296	377	673

To this total of 1,780 guns should be added 1,588 mortars (81mm and higher) organic to Model's divisions, for a guns-and-mortars total of 3,368. This guns-and-mortars figure is essential for meaningful comparisons to Red Army numbers, which habitually lumped together everything larger than 45mm antitank guns (with the exception of 50mm mortars). In terms of field artillery, heavy mortars, and antitank guns, the army had gained 362 pieces, at least 263 of which were heavy guns, heavy mortars, or *Nebelwerfers*. Weaker in all other categories than the assault elements of Army Group South, Ninth Army attacked toward Kursk with the support of 500–700 more guns and mortars than Fourth Panzer Army and *Armeeabteilung* Kempf. Thus from an artillery perspective Model appeared justified in arguing for a postponement of the offensive.

Ninth Army's transport situation improved only slightly between May and July. Model appears to have received about 1,200 additional motor vehicles in two months. Many undoubtedly were not new but stripped away from other units on Army Group Center's defensive fronts. Although the figure looks impressive at first glance, the actual gain in tactical mobility was only about 4–5 percent in each division. Calculated another way, each of the infantry divisions gained fewer than thirty vehicles; each of the panzer divisions received about 120.[16]

Model received approximately 100–120 more tanks and perhaps eighty assault or self-propelled antitank guns before 4 July, the most significant of which were twenty-six heavy tanks for Tiger Battalion 503.[17] More significant, however, were the tanks that did not arrive. The Ninth Army commander argued vigorously for the attachment of the 200 new Panthers (or at least a significant percentage of them) to his assault force. At one point Hitler and OKH seemed close to meeting this demand but ultimately diverted all of the Panthers to Army Group South. Hindsight suggests that Model would have been terribly disappointed in the battlefield performance of the new tanks, but there was no way for him to know that at the time.

To summarize, the relative strength of Ninth Army on 16 May and 4 July appeared as follows:

Change in Ninth Army Strength, May–July 1943

	Combat troops	Guns and mortars	Tanks and assault guns
16 May	66,137	3,006	800
4 July	75,713	3,368	1,014
Change	+9,576	+362	+214

To evaluate whether these increases were sufficient to warrant the repeated delay in launching Operation Citadel, inquiries must also be made into the extent to which the Red Army had reinforced opposite Ninth Army and—equally important—the success that the Germans had in recognizing that buildup. According to later intelligence reports, Army Group Center believed that the Soviets had increased their infantry strength north of Kursk from 124,000 to about 161,000 during the eight-week hiatus.[18] The overall quality of the new troops (many of whom were recent conscripts) was doubtful but, that caveat aside, these estimates meant that relative German combat strength had declined significantly due to the postponements of the attack. In May Ninth Army's combat strength by its own accounting was roughly 53.4 percent of that arrayed against it; by 4 July German strength as a percentage of Soviet numbers had dropped to just 47 percent. From an infantry perspective, attacking at a later date was a losing proposition.

Neither had Ninth Army's artillery buildup, as impressive as it may have seemed at the time, materially improved the odds of the offensive. The two armies holding the first defensive system immediately in Model's front (Thirteenth and Seventieth Armies), contained fewer than 3,000 guns and mortars as the Soviets enumerated them, the entire Central Front deploying less than 8,000. By 4 July, however, the Thirteenth and Seventieth Armies boasted 4,592 pieces of artillery, and Central Front's batteries had swollen to 12,453. Stated in the simplest terms, during the eight weeks in which the Germans moved up 362 new guns, the Russians brought forward 1,500 in the front line and 4,500 overall; as weak as Ninth Army had been in early May, it would have enjoyed far better prospects then for ultimate success.[19]

The story was much the same for armored fighting vehicles (AFVs). Contrary to German intelligence estimates, the Soviet Central Front had deployed only about 1,000 tanks and assault guns in late April–early May, rather than 1,500. This was a critical misinterpretation that explains much about Model's insistence on delaying the offensive. With 800 AFVs facing 1,500, the army commander had a legitimate case for arguing that additional panzers, especially Panthers and Tigers, were absolutely necessary for the assault. Had Model realized that Russian armored superiority was only about 200 vehicles, he would have been far more willing to proceed. By waiting, Ninth Army augmented its AFV holdings by about 25 percent, but the Soviets nearly doubled theirs. In early July, Central Front's advantage in tanks and self-propelled guns had increased from 200 to 700.

The overall conclusion must therefore be that the two-month delay materially contributed to the early failure of Ninth Army's attack. In all three critical categories—combat troops, artillery, and armor—the modest gains in strength that the Germans managed were more than offset by Soviet reinforcements. Model diminished his own army's chance of breaking through Central Front's defenses by convincing Hitler to postpone Operation Citadel. Given the faulty intelligence estimates with which he was working, however, the army commander's reasoning appeared to have merit, and in late spring 1943 few German officers yet realized the depth of Soviet resources.

14

Army Group South's Initial Assault: Analysis and Critique

When Fourth Panzer Army and *Armeeabteilung* Kempf advanced into battle on 5 July 1943, German planners were optimistic that they would succeed in cracking the first two Soviet defensive lines in short order. Thunderous artillery preparations would soften the defenders. Combat engineers would mark assault lanes through the minefields, along which the infantry would attack in narrow sectors, supported by StG III assault guns and Tigers. Once the front was breached, exploitation groups built around medium tanks, accompanied by infantry in armored personnel carriers, stood ready to race into the Russian rear. Most divisions had been assigned Psel River bridges some forty-five kilometers distant as their first-day final objectives.[1] Based on the experiences of 1939–1942 these expectations did not appear to be excessive, despite the repeated delays in launching the operation and the well-documented Soviet concentrations of men and equipment.

To suggest that the day turned out far differently than Erich von Manstein, Hermann Hoth, or Werner Kempf planned does not begin to capture the shock that permeated command posts from colonels leading the assault regiments all the way up to the headquarters of Army Group South. The deepest penetration scored by XLVIII Panzer Corps was a five-kilometer advance by 3rd Panzer Division on the corps's left flank; *Grossdeutschland*'s main-effort attack stalled in embarrassing fashion with heavy losses in men and equipment. Only late-afternoon assistance provided by the 11th Panzer Division around Cherkasskoe made it possible for *Grossdeutschland* to get anywhere close to its initial tactical objectives. Plainly unhappy with this performance, Fourth Panzer Army's war diary groused at length about the three hours *Grossdeutschland* had needed to make its initial penetration and the additional ten hours required to fight its way to Cherkasskoe, which was supposed to have fallen before 0900. Hausser's II SS Panzer Corps fared better, with *Liebstandarte Adolph Hitler* (*LAH*) punching twenty kilometers straight through the first Russian defensive line and coming to rest in front of the second system. Echeloned to the left, both *Das Reich* and *Totenkopf* managed significant though less impressive gains. Yet even by SS standards the cost appeared close to prohibitive: The *Liebstandarte* lost 602 men and about 30 tanks, nearly 25 percent of the total loss the division would sustain over the entire thirteen days of the battle. *Das Reich* lost 290 men, the largest single daily loss for the division at Kursk. On the far right flank, *Armeeabteilung* Kempf's III Panzer Corps posted an uneven record. Near Belgorod, the attack in front of 6th Panzer Division made so little headway that the division could not be committed. Farther south, 19th Panzer Division finally pushed a few kilometers into the Soviet defenses and 7th Panzer Division penetrated six kilometers deep. The 106th and 320th Infantry Divisions of Provisional Corps Raus, assigned to the far right flank, succeeded in advancing roughly three kilometers to the east to seize the railroad line that was the day's initial (but not, according to plan, final) objective.[2]

The strength of Soviet defenses, the lack of tactical surprise, the technical deficiencies of the new Panther tanks, and the willingness of Russian pilots to contest the Luftwaffe's air supremacy have all been offered as reasons for the German failure to shatter the Red Army along the Tomarovka-Belgorod front. All of those factors played important roles, but they should not be allowed to mask serious deficiencies in German tactical and operational planning that contributed to the opening-day misfire. Some of these misjudgments and planning errors were so profound that they raise real questions about the quasimythical image of German operational expertise.

Fourth Panzer Army's Plan of Attack

Hoth's operational plan for Fourth Panzer Army envisioned parallel forward thrusts by XLVIII and II SS Panzer Corps. The main-effort attack (*Schwerpunkt*) in each corps was to be made by a single division. In General Otto von Knobelsdorff's case, *Grossdeutschland* would spearhead the assault with the 3rd and 11th Panzer Divisions covering its flanks. *Obergruppenfuehrer* Hausser placed the weight of his attack with the *Liebstandarte* on the left of his line, with *Das Reich* and *Totenkopf* both echeloned to the right. In order to assure success in the XLVIII Panzer Corps sector, Hoth attached the 200 Panthers of the 10th Panzer Brigade to *Grossdeutschland*, creating a divisional armored juggernaut of nearly 350 panzers and assault guns that he expected to roll through any defense the

Russians might have erected. The tank assets available to the *Liebstandarte* were only slightly more than one-third that large; indeed, *Grossdeutschland* alone controlled nearly as many tanks on 5 July as the entire II SS Panzer Corps. To improve Hausser's odds, however, Hoth arranged for the overwhelming bulk of VIII Flieger Corps's sorties to be flown in support of his attack.[3] This curious either-or commitment of the Panthers and the Luftwaffe would have a significant effect on the course of the day's battle.

A more telling and almost universally overlooked aspect of Hoth's attack plan was the complete absence of anything but tactical reserves. To some extent the commitment of all six mobile divisions in the opening assault was conditioned by the shortage of infantry divisions. As will become apparent below, the few infantry divisions Army Group South possessed for use in the main attack zone were spread thinly across the front in a risky and quite unorthodox manner. Moreover, either Hoth or Fangohr would certainly have argued that—with only limited strength to make their first inroads into the Soviet defenses—they had to gamble on placing all of the panzer divisions in the front line on Day One. The view, though superficially logical, ignores the fact that such a deployment, in exchange for an initial (and transitory) tactical advantage, placed Hoth in a long-term operational straightjacket from which he never escaped.

Because Fourth Panzer Army kept not even a single division in reserve on 5 July, Hoth was committed to continuing to batter ahead in each division's assigned sector, regardless of the strength of the Russian defenses. For example, when *Grossdeutschland*'s spearhead attack floundered, it made little practical difference to XLVIII Panzer Corps that 3rd Panzer Division captured Korovino and then used its own armor to exploit the breach to Krasnyi Pochinok, cracking open the 71st Guards Rifle Division's first- and second-line defenses. General von Knobelsdorff could not capitalize on this success because it occurred on his left, and all of his resources had already been thrown into the center. The very hallmark of blitzkrieg was the concept of reinforcing success wherever it happened and maintaining flexible enough command arrangements to reorient the axis of attack at a moment's notice.

Yet what could Hoth have done differently, given the realities of his limited resources? The most radical solution would have been to launch XLVIII Panzer Corps's attack with only *Grossdeutschland* and one of the other two panzer divisions. In such a scenario 11th Panzer Division might have committed a single panzergrenadier regiment to assist the 167th Infantry Division in holding the extended line between XLVIII and II SS Panzer Corps and its artillery to support *Grossdeutschland*'s attack but otherwise would have been held in reserve. Once a tactical success such as 3rd Panzer Division achieved at Pochinok occurred, 11th Panzer's 102 tanks and assault guns, combined with infantry in armored personnel carriers, engineers, and panzerjaegers, could have passed forward during the night of 5–6 July and forced the Soviets to deal with a strong attack by fresh forces on the second day of battle.

Of course, it might be argued that in the absence of 11th Panzer Division's actual attack the Soviets might have taken advantage of that quiet sector to redeploy their own tactical reserves against *Grossdeutschland*, turning a bad day into an outright disaster. That objection is difficult to sustain for two reasons. First, throughout the early stages of the battle Voronezh Front and its subordinate armies conducted no more lateral movement than they could not possibly avoid. Reserves generally moved forward from the rear, and once they found a place in the front line those units remained there until successful or destroyed. Even had the Soviets attempted such a shift, an uncommitted 11th Panzer Division would have been more than able to take advantage of the resultant weakness in the front—a weakness that would hardly have gone unreported by the extensive Luftwaffe reconnaissance flights saturating the entire battlefield.

Second, a less radical though still workable plan for creating at least a modest operational reserve involved the 10th Panzer Brigade. Most analysts have become so fixated with the mechanical problems of the Panthers and their continued misfortunes with mud and minefields throughout the day that the obvious has been ignored: XLVIII Panzer Corps committed *too many* tanks in a constricted sector. Placing 350 tanks and assault guns in a three-kilometer-wide attack, with more than 250 of them supporting a regimental attack spearheaded by a single battalion, was a recipe for lumbering offensive impotence. With attack frontage so narrow, half that many tanks actually stood a better chance of achieving a breakthrough. As a result, either one of 10th Panzer Brigade's two battalions, along with headquarters of Panzer Regiment 39, could have been withheld from *Grossdeutschland*'s assault without making any appreciable difference. This would have provided the nucleus around which to build a reserve *Kampfgruppe*, for which the corps could surely have scraped up an infantry battalion, a company of engineers, and a battery of panzerjaegers. Again, such a decision would have left XLVIII Panzer Corps with the tactical flexibility to reinforce whatever success it achieved rather than to be condemned to battering ahead regardless of the outcome.

What is truly interesting about these options is that Hoth and Fangohr actually discussed them and apparently discounted each in turn. Having originally discussed the idea of retaining 3rd Panzer Division as a reserve to be committed on the second day of the attack with von Manstein on 10 May, Hoth changed his mind on 27 June. Fangohr had a fairly detailed entry made in the panzer army's war diary covering the new logic for the division's employment, the gist of which was that army headquarters had become worried that *Grossdeutschland* would not be able to force a breakthrough quickly enough without tank-supported attacks on both flanks. The fact that the command staff at Fourth Panzer Army still had serious concerns with XLVIII Panzer Corps's ability to breach the Soviet defenses quickly enough to enter the exploitation phase of the attack was a very bad sign indeed.[4]

XLVIII Panzer Corps Attack Dispositions

Everything in General von Knobelsdorff's sector was subordinated to *Grossdeutschland*'s effort to tear open the front of the 67th Guards Rifle Division. The opening artillery preparation involved not only *Grossdeutschland*'s organic divisional artillery and three battalions of corps artillery but also the artillery regiments of the 3rd and 11th Panzer Divisions, for a total of 100–125 guns of 105mm–210mm pounding a section of enemy trenches only three kilometers wide. Moreover, to *Grossdeutschland*'s already impressive total of 124 tanks and assault guns (including fourteen Tigers), von Knobelsdorff added the full weight of his 204 Panthers. Given the fact that the division possessed six battalions of seasoned infantrymen instead of the four owned by standard panzer divisions, all of the requisite elements of success appeared to have been added to the mix. Appearances can be deceiving: XLVIII Panzer Corps's concentration of resources overshadowed several serious flaws (each potentially fatal).

Grossdeutschland's artillery preparation, planned and coordinated by Artillery Commander 122 and Artillery Regimental Staff (Special Employment) 70, represented a seat-of-the-pants improvisation from the very beginning. Because the range of hills immediately in front of the Soviet lines could not be taken until 4 July in a preliminary attack, Lieutenant Colonel Karl Albrecht of Artillery Regiment *Grossdeutschland* later recalled that "no one, none of the responsible infantry or artillery leaders, had ever really seen the enemy positions!" In a desperate attempt to compensate for this shortcoming, the gunners requested Luftwaffe aerial reconnaissance photographs, which were "very pretty, but unfortunately taken from a considerable height. A maze of trenches. Which were manned and which were dummy positions?" Even as the batteries fired their ranging and final adjustment rounds, no one knew with certainty that the barrage would fall on the critical points.[5]

Not that there was much time to worry about accuracy: Firing the 5 July artillery preparation at all represented a major feat. The old firing positions of the 167th Infantry Division, which had been holding the front line, were located too far back to provide effective support as the attack progressed. As a result, more than 100 guns had to be hustled forward into new positions during the afternoon and evening of 4 July, after the outlying hills had been taken. The movement schedule was tight (adjustment fire had to begin no later than 0300, but some skeptic at army group headquarters placed a large question mark in the fire plan's margins), and the Red Army had left large sections of the area covered with mines and had obviously preregistered likely battery emplacements for its own counterbattery fire. Before 0300, in Artillery Regiment *Grossdeutschland*, one battalion commander's vehicle had been destroyed passing over a mine, the operations officer of another battalion had his head torn off by shrapnel, and at least one battery commander was killed by a mine explosion. So many signal vehicles were lost that the regimental signals officer only managed to patch together a tenuous telephone network minutes prior to the beginning of the artillery preparation.[6]

The schedule called for ranging and final adjustment fire between 0300 and 0430. This was probably unavoidable but decidedly unfortunate. Normally, in such a set-piece attack on a previously static front, ranging would have been completed over a period of days or weeks and done in a fashion that disguised the artillery's intended point of main effort. At Kursk, the Germans telegraphed the location of the division attack sector by waiting to seize the hills until the day before the main assault and then pinpointed the primary attack sectors by firing a flurry of adjustment rounds just before the infantry jumped off. Neither Major General I. M. Baksov, commanding the 67th Guards Rifle Division, or his superiors had to be tactical geniuses to realize by 0330 that *Grossdeutschland* was about to attempt to overrun the 196th Guards Rifle Regiment, which was why the 245th Tank Regiment and 27th Antitank Brigade moved up from their reserve positions so quickly.

Finally, there was the issue of ammunition. Colonel Albrecht's guns had an ammunition allotment sufficient only to fire a whirlwind barrage of fifteen to twenty minutes' duration: "There would be no sustained bombardment, and the actual barrage would last only so many minutes! We repeatedly emphasized that it had to be exploited." To make matters worse, the divisional artillery of 3rd and 11th Panzer Divisions immediately thereafter had to shift back to their own respective sectors, and at least a portion of the three corps artillery battalions had to be reallocated to them then. If the fury of the initial barrage did not blast a hole in Soviet defenses or if the timing of the tank-infantry assault was botched, *Grossdeutschland's* organic artillery would not possess sufficient strength to intervene decisively in the battle.[7]

The command arrangements for the assault were equally problematic. *Grossdeutschland's* two infantry regiments were to attack side by side, the fusiliers on the left, the grenadiers on the right. Curiously, both attacks were to be spearheaded by the respective regiment's III Battalion. Unfortunately, in the case of III Battalion, Fusiliers, the original commander lost a leg in the 4 July preliminary attack and had to be succeeded by the senior company commander. This was especially significant because within the three-kilometer attack sector the Fusilier Regiment's assault represented the *Schwerpunkt*. One battalion from Panzer Regiment *Grossdeutschland*, as well as both battalions of Panthers, had been assigned to support the fusilier attack, and therein lay a most serious command problem.[8]

The Panthers of Panzer Battalions 51 and 52 fell under Panzer Regiment 39 (Major Meinrad von Lauchert) and 10th Panzer Brigade (Colonel Karl Decker); Colonel Hyazinth Graf von Strachwitz led Panzer Regiment *Grossdeutschland*. Panzer Regimental Staff 39 and Panzer Battalion 51 arrived by rail from Germany on 1 July; Panzer Battalion 52 appeared on 3 July. The bulk of Colonel Decker's staff had not arrived by the time the battle opened. Few of the crews or commanding officers were veterans, much less possessed of combat experience in Russia. Aside from the known technical deficiencies of the Panthers, neither unit had ever conducted battalion maneuvers or even exercised its tactical radio network. Decker, however, ranked von Strachwitz, and despite the fact that *Grossdeutschland's* "Panzer Lion" had already begun developing a reputation as one of the army's finest armored tacticians, the inexorable logic of military seniority resulted in von Strachwitz being subordinated to Decker.[9]

The resulting comedy of errors had nothing to do with the infamous teething problems experienced by the Panthers and everything to do with the inexperience of their crews and the ineptitude of their commander. In a summary report, one observer noted that the two battalions moved to attack without either Decker or von Lauchert "issuing situational orders. The companies knew absolutely nothing about the attack plans. Confusion set in from the start, since neither objectives, formation, or direction were ordered." Lumbering awkwardly out of their assembly area in the dark, the Panthers first ran headlong into a minefield covered by Soviet antitank guns and antitank rifle platoons. Without training above the platoon level or effective radios, the new tanks took their first losses while trying to extricate themselves. Charging forward to make up lost time, Colonel Decker then ran his brigade into a hopeless bog, across which the combat engineers would have to spend critical hours building a bridge.

Because the Panthers had taken the lead, and because there were so many of them packed into such a small area, von Strachwitz with the divisional panzer battalion of Pzkw IVs could not bypass them, and thus the acting commander of III Battalion, Fusiliers, had no tank support when the artillery barrage opened. Caught between two imperatives—the knowledge that the division could only fire a brief artillery preparation and the absence of his tank support—and unable to contact his regimental headquarters by telephone or radio, the captain hesitated. He then committed his three assault companies several minutes after the artillery preparation had ended. It was the worst decision he could have made, because the Soviet defenders had been granted the critical time necessary to race back to their firing positions as the artillery fire walked past them, the German troops still did not have tank support, and—in the nearly complete absence of the Luftwaffe—Russian fighter-bombers appeared overhead. Within less than two hours the battalion had suffered more than 150 casualties without denting the Russian lines.

Colonel von Strachwitz was furious, and his anger only intensified when orders came down to divert the mass of armor to support the more successful attack by III Battalion, Grenadiers, on the right. Decker's two novice battalions moved in such ungainly fashion that they not only failed to get into proper position or cross the enemy anti-tank ditch at the edge of the Soviet defenses but also interfered with the commitment of the follow-up infantry battalions, delaying them for at least an hour. Unable to stomach any more of this farce, von Strachwitz took matters into his own hands. As Decker later complained, "He [von Strachwitz] simply did not come on the radio and operated independently." Von Strachwitz took his own complaint up the chain of command, and on the afternoon of 6 July General von Knobelsdorff personally sidelined Decker for four days, leaving the Panthers completely under the division's control. Unfortunately, in terms of the initial assault, the damage had already been done.[10]

The attack by III Battalion, Grenadiers, by comparison, looked like a textbook example of a successful assault. *Grossdeutschland*'s Assault Gun Battalion, Tiger company, and a company of the new eighty-ton Ferdinand self-propelled antitank guns all arrived on time, allowing the infantry battalion to follow closely on the heels of the creeping barrage. The II Battalion of von Strachwitz's regiment remained far enough to the rear to keep the sector uncongested but was then available to support the attack on Cherkasskoe once the defensive crust had been pierced. This result only served to highlight the mistake of committing too many tanks in the western attack sector, and by that point any question of reaching the Psel River had long since become moot.

Where did the responsibility for these accumulated miscues lay, and what could have been done to avoid them? The decision to attack all along the line, without operational reserves, was Hoth's, as was the commitment of the entire 10th Panzer Brigade in a single division sector. As late as 3 July, Hausser had attempted to convince Hoth to divide the Panthers between XLVIII and II SS Panzer Corps, but the panzer army commander (who was more of a "pure tank" enthusiast than has usually been recognized) held firmly to his vision of a wave of Panthers rumbling at speed through the Soviet defenses.[11] Once Hoth had chosen this deployment, only the direct intervention of von Manstein could have forced him to reconsider, and such intervention was unlikely for two reasons. Hoth had already established a pattern of influencing his army group commander with the change of direction in the larger operational plan, and only rarely would von Manstein assert himself in the face of his strong-willed subordinate's opinions. Worse, Hitler (supported by Guderian) wanted to see the Panthers employed en masse and might not have supported von Manstein in any other decision.

The completely senseless decision not to allow the assault divisions to seize the hills immediately in front of them sometime well prior to the main attack came from Hitler and OKH. Neither von Manstein nor Hoth had the ability to change or circumvent this order, though it must be admitted that there is very little evidence to suggest that either officer even tried to do so. In light of the handicap thus created for the corps artillery units, the gunners should receive credit for working a near-miracle by producing even a brief barrage exactly on schedule. Deficiencies in ammunition reflected the increasingly impoverished state of supply in the German army.

The unwieldy organization of the attack in the sector of III Battalion, Fusiliers, must be ascribed to the division commander, Lieutenant General Walter Hoernlein, and operations officer Colonel Oldwig von Natzmer. Hoernlein was a beloved figure within the division, but his tactical skills more closely resembled those of Sepp Dietrich than those of Hermann Balck. To cite only a single, telling example: On the morning of 5 July Hoernlein was not even aware of the extent of the division's ammunition shortage. Colonel von Natzmer demonstrated outstanding tactical and operational qualifications throughout the war, yet during the preparations for Operation Citadel he appeared strangely detached from the entire planning process. During the successive June map exercises, for instance, he is not recorded as ever having raised a single question regarding the wisdom of concentrating 250 tanks on such narrow frontage, restricted by minefields and marshy ground. And neither of these two officers challenged, before the battle opened, the unwise decision that effectively superceded their own veteran panzer commander with the unknown leader of a green unit.

The division command element simply could have done a much better job, even shackled as it was by certain constraints from higher headquarters.[12] The fact that Hoth insisted on the entire Panther brigade being deployed in the *Grossdeutschland* sector did not mean that he dictated the manner in which it would be committed. As the commanders of the 3rd and 11th Panzer Divisions managed, as did the commanders of all three SS panzergrenadier divisions, Hoernlein and von Natzmer could have limited the introduction of armor into the assault to tactically effective numbers, reserving the remainder to exploit breakthroughs. They also could have finessed the question of command to give von Strachwitz direct control over the first wave of panzers entering the battle.

What is critical to note in this prolonged consideration of the shortcomings of XLVIII Panzer Corps's *Schwerpunkt* attack is the fact that—even allowing for everything that went wrong—*Grossdeutschland* still penetrated the first line of Soviet defenses and in cooperation with 11th Panzer Division seized Cherkasskoe. The 67th Guards Rifle Division was wrecked as a combat formation; Glantz and House speak of "pitiful remnants" and "depleted ranks" pulling back after dark "to the northeast and the temporary safety of the 90th Guards Rifle Division's lines along the Pena River."[13] The Russians in front of Cherkasskoe had fought tenaciously and would have exacted a heavy toll of casualties under any conditions, but it is difficult to escape the conclusion that *Grossdeutschland* failed to achieve its scheduled breakthrough in the early hours of 5 July more because of German failures than the strength of the Soviet defenses.

II SS Panzer Corps Attack Dispositions

In comparing the relative success achieved by II SS Panzer Corps on 5 July 1943 to the mediocre results scored by XLVIII Panzer Corps, it is necessary to dispense with several deep-seated myths regarding the Waffen SS divisions in Operation Citadel. Many writers, like Robin Cross, tend to emphasize weight of numbers and the fanaticism of the troops, speaking of II SS Panzer Corps as "the ideological battering ram of Nazism, [which] was poised to strike with over 400 armoured fighting vehicles, including forty-two Tigers, and a *Nebelwerfer* brigade." In reality, XLVIII Panzer Corps was significantly stronger by almost any measure, as illustrated by the table below:

Comparative Strength, XLVIII and II SS Panzer Corps, 5 July 1943[14]

	XLVIII Panzer Corps	*II SS Panzer Corps*
Total strength:	86,381	74,863
(Divisions only)		
Combat strength:	30,233	26,202
Tanks/assault guns:	553	451
(Operational)		
Artillery battalions:	21.25	18
(Organic and attached)		

Only in the number of Tigers (thirty-five in II SS Panzer Corps; fourteen in XLVIII Panzer Corps) and in the near-total dedication of VIII Flieger Corps air support for the morning of 5 July did Hausser's divisions possess important advantages that von Knobelsdorff's units lacked.

Neither were the three SS panzergrenadier divisions without their own internal shortcomings. The *Liebstandarte Adolph Hitler* had just lost Sepp Dietrich, whose departure represented a huge blow to morale even though "Obersepp" (as he was affectionately known to the troops) was no one's idea of a technically competent division commander. Dietrich had been transferred to organize a second SS Panzer Corps headquarters, and with him as cadre for the new *Hitler Jugend* Division he had taken thirty-five key officers, one company from the reconnaissance battalion, one panzer battalion, and one artillery battalion. The division entered Operation Citadel with a new commander and new men heading the panzer regiment, artillery regiment, both panzergrenadier regiments, and four other combat battalions. Moreover, in the fierce fighting around Kharkov during February and March, the *Liebstandarte* had taken more than 4,500 casualties. The only partial compensations that the division received for the bulk transfers and combat losses were a contingent of 2,500 involuntary transferees from the Luftwaffe and several hundred conscripts delivered by the SS replacement system (initially receiving the derisive label of "yank-alongs" in a unit formerly proud to have been completely composed of volunteers). Both *Das Reich* and *Totenkopf* to a somewhat lesser extent suffered from the same problems.[15]

Neither had the Red Army intentionally slighted the defenses in front of the II SS Panzer Corps. It is instructive to examine the relative strengths of the two Soviet rifle divisions poised to take the brunt of Fourth Panzer Army's penetration attack. Colonel I. M. Nekrasov's 52nd Guards Rifle Division faced the *Schwerpunkt* of the II SS Panzer Corps assault, as did Major General I. M. Baksov's 67th Guards Rifle Division in the XLVIII Panzer Corps sector. Both divisions held a fourteen-kilometer front, and each had an organic strength of about 8,000 men, thirty-six guns, 167 mortars, and forty-eight antitank guns. Both divisions had been substantially reinforced with corps or army troops. Nekrasov's 52nd Guards Rifle Division had the support of an antitank rifle battalion (270 antitank rifles); twenty-four antitank guns from the 538th and 1008th Antitank Artillery Regiments; forty-six tanks (half of them T-34s) of the 230th Tank Regiment; thirty-six guns of the 142nd Artillery Regiment; and one battalion of the 5th Guards Mortar Regiment. Army headquarters had also promised Nekrasov immediate reinforcement by the 28th Antitank Brigade, with seventy-two more antitank guns. Thus across his fourteen-kilometer front Nekrasov's division deployed roughly seventy-two pieces of field artillery, 250 mortars, 270 antitank rifles, 144 antitank guns, and forty-six tanks. Baksov's 67th Guards Rifle Division enjoyed the support of the 868th and 611th Antitank Regiments; the 1440th Self-Propelled Artillery Regiment; the 159th Artillery Regiment; two battalions of the 5th Guards Mortar Regiment; and the 245th Tank Regiment. Army headquarters had promised Baksov reinforcement by the 27th Antitank Brigade and 496th Antitank Regiment. Though precise comparisons are difficult, the 52nd Guards Rifle Division in front of the II SS Panzer Corps appears to have been slightly stronger than its neighbor in terms of tank-killing systems, though it was weaker in mortars and light field artillery. These differences, however, were more statistical than tactically significant: Neither Hausser nor von Knobelsdorff faced an easy tactical problem.[16]

The one major relative advantage the SS panzergrenadier divisions did possess was the absence of any high ground in their immediate front. Thus whereas XLVIII Panzer Corps had to conduct a two-stage assault (the preliminary seizure of the heights on 4 July) that telegraphed the corps *Schwerpunkt*, caused some critical casualties, and impaired the effectiveness of the main artillery preparation, II SS Panzer Corps had the luxury of focusing all of its operational planning on the main assault. Though this circumstance of terrain played a part in the greater SS success on 5 July (and buttresses the observation made above that XLVIII Panzer Corps should have been allowed to capture the heights much earlier), it should not obscure the critical fact that the operations staffs of II SS Panzer Corps and its subordinate divisions indisputably created an attack plan far superior to that generated by XLVIII Panzer Corps.

With its three SS panzergrenadier divisions and a reinforced regiment from the 167th Infantry Division on the left flank, Hausser focused on creating one wide breach in the defenses of the 52nd Guards Rifle Division, through which the *Liebstandarte* spearheads would push first for Bykovka (roughly fourteen kilometers behind the front), then Yakovlevo (twenty kilometers distant), seizing Psel River crossings another ten kilometers north of that town. The plan envisioned reconnaissance units, "after the breakthrough across the enemy's second line of defense," reaching as far as "nine kilometers north of Prochorowka."[17] To accomplish these ambitious objectives, II SS Panzer Corps coordinated a series of sharp, successive blows designed to crack open the Russian defenses.

Das Reich and *Totenkopf*, which had supporting roles in the attack, were each organized along similar lines, with three tactical elements: assault, exploitation, reserve, and main body. The assault element consisted of one panzergrenadier regiment (minus the battalion mounted in armored personnel carriers), an engineer company, several batteries of assault guns, and the divisional Tiger company. In *Das Reich* the assault group was organized around *Deutschland*; in *Totenkopf* the central unit was *Thule*. The panzer regiment of the respective division, the armored personnel carrier–mounted battalion, a battalion of self-propelled artillery, and an engineer company composed the armored group with the mission of passing through the assault group as soon as the Russian first line had been breached. The *Das Reich* exploitation group had the primary responsibility of veering northwest toward Bykovka in case it became necessary to assist the *Liebstandarte* in blowing past that town. In *Totenkopf*'s case, the corps operations order suggested the possibility that the armored exploitation group might also end up being committed in *Das Reich*'s sector. In both divisions the second panzergrenadier regiment, the panzerjaeger battalion, the panzer reconnaissance battalion, and the rest of the engineer battalion constituted the tactical reserve while all artillery and support elements were grouped in the division's main body.[18]

The *Liebstandarte*, as the corps *Schwerpunkt*, having been reinforced by the *Regimentsgruppe* of the 167th Infantry Division, had been organized to attack on a wider front. The division employed three assault elements, an armored exploitation element, a small reserve, and an artillery group, organized as follows:

LEFT FLANK ASSAULT GROUP:
Grenadier Regiment 315
II Battalion, Artillery Regiment 238
1st Company, Engineer Battalion 238
one battery, Mortar Regiment 55
(later, one battery, Assault Gun Battalion *LAH*)

CENTER ASSAULT GROUP:
Panzergrenadier Regiment 2 *LAH* (minus III Battalion)
Assault Gun Battalion 1 *LAH*
Tiger Company, Panzer Regiment 1 *LAH*

5th Battery (medium), Flak Battalion 1 *LAH*
one company, Engineer Battalion 1 *LAH*
(note: one assault gun battery moves to support Grenadier Regiment 315
after the initial attack)

RIGHT ASSAULT GROUP (*SCHWERPUNKT*):
Panzergrenadier Regiment 1 *LAH*
one company, Panzerjaeger Battalion 1 *LAH*
4th Battery (medium), Flak Battalion 1 *LAH*

ARMORED GROUP:
Panzer Regiment 1 *LAH* (minus Tiger Company)
III (APC) Battalion, Panzergrenadier Regiment 2 *LAH*
one company, Panzerjaeger Battalion 1 *LAH*
II (Armored) Battalion, Panzer Artillery Regiment 1 *LAH*
6th Battery (light), Flak Battalion 1 *LAH*

RESERVE:
Panzer Reconnaissance Battalion 1 *LAH*
Headquarters plus one company, Panzerjaeger Battalion 1 *LAH*
Engineer Battalion 1 *LAH* (minus one company)
(Subordinated as necessary to the armored group)

ARTILLERY:
Panzer Artillery Regiment 1 *LAH* (minus II Battalion)
Artillery Battalion 861
Mortar Regiment 55 (minus one battery)

At 2300 on 4 July advance assault groups from all three divisions were
to move silently forward, without artillery support, to seize Soviet outposts forward of the main defensive line. Grenadier Regiment 315 and
Totenkopf sent companies in their respective sectors to capture high
ground for artillery observers, but in reality they did so to camouflage
the corps *Schwerpunkt*. *Das Reich* sent two companies ahead to reach
jump-off positions for the assault on Yakhontov from the east, as Panzergrenadier Regiment 1 *LAH* committed a company to infiltrate the ravine
northwest of the town. Panzergrenadier Regiment 2 *LAH* assigned an entire battalion under the cover of darkness to take the critical Hill 228.6.
Engineers attached to this group were "to create and mark paths through
the mine fields and crossings over the tank trenches along as broad a
front as possible," in order for the Tigers and assault guns to move up to
Hill 228.6 the moment the artillery preparation opened.[19]

The remaining units of the assault regiments were to begin moving up to these forward positions at 0300, fifteen minutes prior to the initial artillery barrage. This preparation had been organized in a carefully sequenced series of fires to support individual attacks while confusing the Russians with regard to the German point of main effort. At 0315, just as the Tigers and assault guns were starting forward for Hill 228.6, the *Liebstandarte* artillery (plus Artillery Battalion 861) opened a two-minute "hurricane" barrage immediately north of the hill; from 0317 to 0335 this fire walked steadily north to hit Soviet positions on either side of the Bykovka road. Also at 0300 *Das Reich's* artillery and two regiments of *Nebelwerfer* multiple rocket launchers fired a twenty-minute concentration on Yakhontov in support of the two-regiment attack on that village. Along both flanks the artillery attached to Grenadier Regiment 315 and *Totenkopf* fired local concentrations to support their attacks.[20]

Abruptly at 0335 the main artillery fire in *Liebstandarte/Das Reich* sector was scheduled to cease for ten minutes. This pause served three purposes: allowing the gunners to prepare new target concentrations, providing the assault groups time to overrun their initial objectives, and further confusing the defenders with regard to the thrust of the attack. The firing was to resume exactly at 0345, when the combined divisional artillery of *Liebstandarte* and *Das Reich*, reinforced by Artillery Battalion 861 and one *Nebelwerfer* battalion, were to strike to main Russian defenses along the road to Bykovka again, as Panzergrenadier Regiment 2 *LAH* moved to the attack. This direct attack toward Bykovka was to focus Soviet attention in the center of the sector. Moments later, however, an even more powerful artillery grouping (two artillery battalions, one mortar battalion, and five *Nebelwerfer* battalions) were to strike first in support of Grenadier Regiment 315's attack along the Vorskla River toward Bykovka from the southwest, then shift without warning in favor of the combined Panzergrenadier Regiment 1 *LAH* and *Deutschland* attack north from Yakhontov. Twenty minutes thereafter, at 0405, the preplanned portion of the barrage would be complete, and further fire missions would be fired as needed to support the *Schwerpunkt* units.[21]

The purpose of this admittedly complicated scheme (with its unforgiving schedule) was to draw Russian attention to the parallel attacks by Grenadier Regiment 315 and Panzergrenadier Regiment 2 *LAH* against the seam between the 153rd and 151st Guards Rifle Regiments defending the southwestern approaches to Bykovka. All these two regiments were expected to do during 5 July was to fight their way through to Bykovka, with their assault guns and Tigers hopefully acting as magnets to pull in the Soviet tactical reserves. As the Russians concentrated against this threat, Panzergrenadier Regiments 1 *LAH* and *Deutschland* were to drive from Yakhontov around Berezov and then thrust past Bykovka from the east. *Deutschland* and the armored elements of *Das Reich* would veer sharply east to broaden the hole in the defenses. Panzergrenadier Regiment 1 *LAH* would push forward to Yakovlevo and the second Russian defensive line. As soon as the spearhead bypassed Bykovka, the *Liebstandarte* armored group would be committed, hopefully to pass through the assault group at Yakovlevo and race ahead to seize the Psel River crossings. If everything proceeded according to plan, by the evening of 5 July II SS Panzer Corps would have torn a rent in the Soviet defenses nearly thirty kilometers deep and half that wide.[22]

The 52nd Guards Rifle Division proved to be a much tougher nut to crack than anyone had anticipated. By 1230 both of the *Liebstandarte's* panzergrenadier regiments were still struggling north, having just captured Hill 215.4, roughly two and a half kilometers to the south of Bykovka, according to records. Their combined assault did not manage to push the Russian defenders out of the town until after 1615, and the *Deutschland* assault group from *Das Reich* did not manage to pull even with *Liebstandarte's* right flank until after 1800. That was about the time that *Liebstandarte's* armored group (committed as the division spearhead passed north of Bykovka) "just as night was falling ran into an antitank front near [Yakovlevo]." At the cost of roughly 1,000 casualties and as many as thirty-five tanks, II SS Panzer Corps had broken through the first Soviet defensive system and driven all the way to the edge of the second line. If *Obergruppenfuehrer* Hausser's terse order for 6 July "to attack the enemy position southeast of [Yakovlevo] . . . to reach those objectives already ordered," suggests something of his frustration, it is important to realize that had XLVIII Panzer Corps done equally well on 5 July the gains so dearly bought by *Liebstandarte* and *Das Reich* would have been sufficient to keep the Germans in the game for a quick penetration toward Oboyan and Kursk.[23]

III Panzer Corps Attack Dispositions

Compared to the results achieved by the two panzer corps of Hoth's army, *Armeeabteilung* Kempf's initial assault represented an almost unmitigated disaster that may have—on the first day of the battle—fatally wounded any chance for the Germans to achieve a rapid penetration on the southern face of the Kursk salient. Unrealistic expectations certainly played a major role in the *Armeeabteilung's* failure: With only three panzer and three infantry divisions, III Panzer Corps and Provisional Corps Raus had been assigned to assault the Seventh Guards Army along a twenty-five-kilometer front as a prelude to driving sharply northeast sixty-five kilometers toward Skordnoye to protect Fourth Panzer Army's right flank. With respect to the forces available, the scope of its assigned objectives, and the strength of the Red Army in its path, the *Armeeabteilung* faced the longest odds in the high-stakes gamble known as Operation Citadel.

For the attack, General of Panzer Troops Werner Kempf deployed fewer than 100,000 men (roughly 32,000–34,000 of whom were combat troops by the German definition); about 825 guns and mortars; and slightly more than 500 tanks and assault guns. The *Armeeabteilung* did enjoy the attachment of forty-eight Tigers and 216 flak guns (seventy-two of which were motorized 88mm types) specially assigned in a ground support role. Of the six attack divisions, four (6th and 7th Panzer, 106th and 320th Infantry) had been transferred from France in late 1942, and with refitting after the battle for Kharkov in March they were in excellent condition. The 168th Infantry and 19th Panzer Divisions had been battered quite heavily during the Stalingrad debacle, and their reorganization had been much less thorough.[24] Nonetheless, this was a relatively impressive concentration of force for a flank protection role, especially post-Stalingrad, but it fell far short of what was necessary to accomplish the mission. Opposite Kempf's front, holding the first Russian defensive line, the Seventh Guards Army contained 76,800 men; 1,573 guns and mortars; 246 tanks and assault guns; and forty-seven multiple rocket launchers. Included in the artillery were approximately 336 divisional and 144 attached antitank guns, as well as more than 1,000 antitank rifles, totals to which Voronezh Front would add another seventy-two antitank guns on 6 July.[25]

The *Armeeabteilung* would have faced a difficult problem regardless of the balance of forces because of the Donets River. The III Panzer Corps held only two small bridgeheads (near Mikailovka) over the river north of Belgorod, and a slightly larger one just south of the city (opposite Razumnoye). These bridgeheads were subject to Russian observation and so cramped that the elements of the 168th Infantry Division holding them could not be relieved or reinforced by the panzer divisions prior to 5 July without alerting the enemy. If all three panzer divisions were to be committed on the first day of the attack, at least one of them would have to assault directly across the Donets. Moreover, the original operations order, prepared for Kempf by his chief of staff, Major General Hans Speidel, insisted that General of Panzer Troops Hermann Breith's III Panzer Corps place its *Schwerpunkt* in the three Belgorod-area bridgeheads. Speidel considered such a deployment necessary in order to place Breith's panzer divisions on the shortest possible route to Skordnoye and keep them tightly against II SS Panzer Corps's right flank. These tactical imperatives dominated III Panzer Corps's planning from the start.[26]

Working within this framework, Breith laid out his concept for the assault at the 3 June map exercise, attended not only by the senior officer corps of the *Armeeabteilung* but also by von Manstein, his chief of staff (Major General Theodor Busse) and his senior engineer officer (Major General Gustav Boehringer). He [Breith] assigned responsibility for breaking out of the two small bridgeheads north of Belgorod to the 6th Panzer Division, allocated the southern bridgehead to the 19th Panzer Division, and tasked the 7th Panzer Division with forcing a Donets crossing farther south in the vicinity of Solomino. The most unorthodox component in the III Panzer Corps plan was the deployment of the 168th Infantry Division, whose subunits were all to be attached either to the three panzer divisions or subordinated to Artillery Commander 3, leaving Major General Walter Chales de Beaulieu's headquarters nothing to control during the first thirty-six hours of the offensive. Each panzer division received a *Kampfgruppe* consisting of a grenadier regiment, a company of combat engineers, and one or two artillery battalions from the 168th Infantry Division. In addition, Major General Walther von Huenersdorff's 6th Panzer Division acquired the infantry division's reconnaissance battalion.[27]

In the 6th and 19th Panzer Division sectors, Breith envisioned the reinforced regiments of the 168th Infantry making the initial breach in the first Soviet defensive line. This, he thought, would alleviate the problem of overcrowding the bridgeheads because the first *Kampfgruppen* from the panzer divisions would cross the river only as the infantrymen moved out of their trenches for the assault. Recognizing that the infantry would require armored support, Breith's plan called for an assault-gun battalion (in 6th Panzer Division's sector) and a Tiger company (in 19th Panzer Division's sector) to move into the bridgeheads during the artillery preparation. Once the grenadiers had scored an initial penetration (corps headquarters appeared to expect a forward thrust of two or three kilometers), tank-heavy *Kampfgruppen* from the panzer divisions would pass through their lines and continue to drive into the Soviet defenses. The 168th Infantry Division's regiments were to reform as a division behind the panzer spearheads by the early morning of 7 July, then move northwest to establish contact with *Totenkopf* on Hausser's flank.[28]

Ironically, the lack of a bridgehead over the Donets provided Lieutenant General Hans Freiherr von Funck's 7th Panzer Division a greater degree of flexibility in its initial attack. The high ground on the German side of the river completely dominated the flats along the eastern bank, and the Soviet 78th Guards Rifle Division had not even attempted to anchor its defense at the waterline. In his four-kilometer-wide sector, von Funck opted for a two-pronged assault in which he committed a battalion of Grenadier Regiment 442 in the southern half of his operational area during the early morning hours of 5 July, at what easily appeared to be the most favorable river-crossing site. Once the infantrymen had effected a lodgment and attracted the attention of the Russian tactical reserves, elements of Panzergrenadier Regiments 6 and 7 would leapfrog the river not quite two kilometers to the north near Solomino at 1300. Engineers stood ready to erect a bridge capable of supporting armor, across which a company from Tiger Battalion 503 would immediately cross. With the heavy tanks as their spearhead, the panzergrenadiers were to flank the Russian defenders facing the original bridgehead as Panzer Regiment 25 passed over the Donets to become the spearhead for a drive due east through Krutoi Log.[29]

At the III Panzer Corps map exercise it became readily apparent that there were serious concerns with Breith's plan. Kempf wondered if the regiments of the 168th Infantry Division, even supported by assault guns, Tigers, and corps artillery assets, would have the strength to penetrate the first Soviet defensive line quickly enough to expand the existing bridgeheads for the commitment of the main bodies of the 6th and 19th Panzer Divisions. He questioned Breith's decision not to attach a Tiger company to 6th Panzer Division and mandated an increase in the infantry attachment to 7th Panzer (Breith had originally allocated von Funck only a single battalion). Field Marshal von Manstein expressed his own doubts about a tactical plan that required the 168th Infantry Division to be dismantled and then reassembled in the middle of the battle; he pointed to the absolute necessity of having that division available to relieve the pressure on II SS Panzer Corps's eastern flank. He also voiced concerns about the fire plan being employed to support the attack. Arguing that Russian camouflage and broken terrain "made identification of enemy positions difficult in spite of careful reconnaissance," Breith believed that "under such circumstances a long artillery preparation would have been a complete waste of ammunition, without producing concrete results." Though the summary of comments after the map exercise suggests that no one found this argument especially compelling, other than haggling over a few matters of detail neither the *Armeeabteilung* nor the army group commander required substantive changes to Breith's plans.[30]

On the day of reckoning, everyone's worst fears were confirmed. In 6th Panzer Division's sector, one *Kampfgruppe* built around I Battalion, Panzergrenadier Regiment 114, and a company from Panzer Engineer Battalion 57 (under the command of Major Konstantin Rogalla von Bieberstein) had crossed into the Mikailovka bridgehead soon after

midnight on 4–5 July to reinforce Grenadier Regiment 417 and its attached elements in the initial assault. *Kampfgruppe* von Oppeln-
Bronikowski, consisting of Panzer Regiment 11, a panzergrenadier battalion in armored personnel carriers, and an engineer company, was to
traverse the Donets on a twenty-four ton bridge just after dawn for
commitment through the infantry's penetration. As Panzer Regiment
11's war diary noted, however, the bridge "had been destroyed by a direct hit from artillery fire," and after a four-hour delay the *Kampfgruppe*
had to be rerouted "to cross over a different bridge." Lieutenant
Colonel Hermann von Oppeln-Bronikowski's panzers received yet another set of orders around 1700, before they had managed to cross the
second bridge. The attack by *Kampfgruppe* von Bieberstein and *Regimentsgruppe* 417, even supported by a battalion of assault guns, had
been halted dead in its tracks. Mired in previously unidentified minefields, harassed incessantly by enemy artillery and aircraft, and confronted by fierce Russian resistance at every strongpoint and bunker,
the infantry had simply been unable to penetrate the Soviet defenses
while fighting without benefit of either artillery or air support. The 6th
Panzer Division's attack had been a dismal failure.[31]

Lieutenant General Gustav Schmidt's 19th Panzer Division fared only
slightly better. Breith and Schmidt had pinned their hopes on the fourteen Tigers spearheading the attack out of the bridgehead by *Regimentsgruppe* 429 and Panzergrenadier Regiment 74. Unfortunately, liaison between the regimental commander from the 168th Infantry Division and
the headquarters of the 19th Panzer Division proved nonexistent. Captain Clemens Graf von Kageneck, commander of Tiger Battalion 503, reported that "there wasn't a single map available showing the location of
the mines that had been laid by the German units in front of the bridgehead. Two completely contradictory mine plans were available, and both
were incorrect." Kageneck's company lost nine tanks disabled by
mines—seven of them to German mines! Four more Tigers fell victim to
Soviet antitank fire because of what Kageneck characterized as the "result of carelessness or tactically incorrect employment." The heavy tanks
had been intended "to advance in direct contact" with the assault troops,
"directly behind the mine-detecting sections," but faced by extraordinarily heavy Russian fire the grenadiers lagged back, and "by the evening of
5 July, four Tigers stood 50 to 80 meters in front of the infantry elements,"
where they became the target of massed antitank fire. By nightfall only
one of the fourteen Tigers committed to support 19th Panzer Division remained undamaged. "The loss of the *Tiger-Kompanie*, which was the
Schwerpunkt of the attacking division," admitted Breith two weeks later,
"was very detrimental to directing the battle." When 100 vehicles from

the division's own Panzer Regiment 27 executed their own attack at 1300, Red Army antitank gunners destroyed nineteen Pzkw IIIs and IVs. The best that could be said for Schmidt's division by day's end was that the 19th Panzer Division had paid heavily to shatter the 228th Guards Rifle Regiment and had expanded its bridgehead by an unimpressive two kilometers.[32]

Positioned on III Panzer Corps's right flank, 7th Panzer Division's attack proved far more successful, though it gained considerably less ground than its orders envisioned. The initial attack by the infantry battalion of the 168th Infantry Division succeeded in riveting the defenders' attention, allowing von Funck to seize his second bridgehead in late morning and quickly throw a tank bridge across the Donets. As planned (though more slowly and at a higher cost than expected), this maneuver allowed him to pry open the Soviet defensives and send Panzer Regiment 25 into the breach. The German tanks cleared the first Russian fortified line, thrust eight kilometers northeast, and seized the critical ridge between Razumnoye and Krutoi Log.[33]

Unfortunately, as with the advance made by 3rd Panzer Division in the XLVIII Panzer Corps sector, 7th Panzer Division represented the outside flank of Breith's attack, not the *Schwerpunkt*. Nothing had been achieved that covered II SS Panzer Corps's flank, which meant that *Totenkopf*, instead of moving north to reinforce Hausser's spearhead divisions on 6 July, would have to assume complete responsibility for screening Fourth Panzer Army against attacks from the east. The 168th Infantry Division remained fragmented between Breith's three panzer divisions until 8 July, serving no useful purpose at all. Worse still, during the afternoon of 5 July the Germans committed a tactical deployment error with regard to 6th Panzer Division so egregious that its repercussions would be felt at Prokhorovka more than a week later.

It was a basic tenet of German armored doctrine that success should be reinforced and that panzer divisions should seek the line of least resistance into the enemy rear in order to gain freedom of movement. By midafternoon on 5 July, when it had become obvious that 6th Panzer Division was not going to force its way out of the Mikailovka bridgeheads, someone (the record is unclear whether this was Breith or Kempf) decided to redeploy Huenersdorff's division (reinforced by a Tiger company) behind the more successful 7th Panzer Division on the III Panzer Corps's right flank.[34] Inching its way along the crowded roads east of the Donets, *Kampfgruppe* Oppeln-Bronikowski did not manage to reach the bridge feeding into 7th Panzer Division's sector until 1300 on 5 July and did not enter the battle until 1430. Thus the strongest division in III Panzer Corps did not effectively engage the Russians until thirty-six hours after Operation Citadel commenced, and it did so at the cost of completely abdicating the *Armeeabteilung's* responsibility for guarding Fourth Panzer Army's right wing. As Erhard Raus observed in his contribution to the Busse study, "The Belgorod bastion . . . expanded as a result of the *Armeeabteilung's* continued advance" to the east, "until it formed a deep wedge pointing south and lodged between *Armeeabteilung* Kempf and Fourth Panzer Army." Raus further noted that "fresh enemy forces were already pouring into this wedge" during the night of 5–6 July.

What should have occurred instead? A much more promising move would have been to reassign the 6th Panzer Division to II SS Panzer Corps, tasking it to slide north-northwest into *Totenkopf's* area. This maneuver would have permitted Hoth and Hausser to utilize the division in one of two ways. The 6th Panzer Division could have taken advantage of the hole punched in the Soviet defenses by *Totenkopf's* subsidiary attack to push east and then south in the attempt to create a small pocket across the Donets from Belgorod, meeting the 7th and 19th Panzer Divisions as they attacked north from the Razumnoye–Krutoi Log area. The other option would have involved using the 6th Panzer Division to take over *Totenkopf's* defensive position, increasing the strength of Hausser's attack toward Prokhorovka by one-third on the afternoon of 6 July, which would have been a full seventy hours earlier than what happened in the actual battle. Either choice would clearly have been preferable to 6th Panzer Division's diversion nearly ten kilometers to the south.

Transferring one-third of Kempf's understrength armor to Hoth's army was a decision that would have had to be made by von Manstein himself. No substantive evidence has been found to suggest this option was even considered. Fourth Panzer Army's war diary and Friedrich Fangohr's account of the battle both suggest that Hoth's headquarters did not have a clear idea of just how badly the battle had developed for *Armeeabteilung* Kempf until the middle of 6 July or even the following morning. The war diary kept at Kempf's command post implies, though it does not state conclusively, that the decision to move 6th Panzer Division to the opposite flank of III Panzer Corps was made internally: Von Manstein and Busse seem to have been informed rather than consulted.[35] Even if that supposition is correct, however, it does not relieve Army Group South of the responsibility for the decision. Given the slow progress that *Kampfgruppe* Oppeln-Bronikowski made moving toward 7th Panzer Division's sector, ample time existed for von Manstein to countermand the orders had he been so inclined.

Why did the commander of Army Group South passively acquiesce to the *Armeeabteilung's* disastrous decision? Two possibilities immediately present themselves. First, it is important to consider precisely how little had gone according to German plans during the morning of 5 July. By noon it remained an open question whether II SS Panzer Corps would even wrest Bykovka from the Soviets (let alone Yakovlevo), and the chances of XLVIII Panzer Corps seizing Cherkasskoe (much less moving beyond it) appeared even slimmer. As the field marshal sat down to his lunch on the first day of Operation Citadel, the details were only beginning to trickle in, but it was already obvious that his panzers would not be establishing themselves in bridgeheads on the Psel River by nightfall. It is very possible that von Manstein simply did not have enough information to realize that the Mikailovka attack had been significantly less successful than those in other sectors.

Second, equally important is the observation that Erich von Manstein was a strategist, first and foremost, rather than a tactician. As the case with Hoth and the Prokhorovka revision to the original operations order illustrates, the field marshal was a firm believer in allowing his subordinates wide latitude to accomplish their objectives. Perhaps, as the detailed examination of the attack dispositions of Army Group South's three panzer corps has suggested, von Manstein permitted his commander too much latitude. The stunning lack of oversight by army group headquarters over the assault plans for 5 July calls many aspects of German tactical and operational planning into question. In the case of XLVIII Panzer Corps, von Manstein and Busse allowed the entire success of the *Schwerpunkt* to depend on the recently arrived, completely inexperienced, and technically unprepared brigade of Panthers. With respect to III Panzer Corps, von Manstein himself had voiced objections to Breith's plan of attack, but he did not insist on its being changed.

Conclusion

At Kursk the Red Army built defenses in depth, Soviet intelligence efforts deprived the Germans of tactical surprise, and—as Glantz and House have so carefully documented—Russian commanders at the army and front levels fought a tactically sound battle that made full use of their superior resources in men and machines. None of these factors, however, should divert attention from what the Germans themselves did, in a tactical sense, to contribute to their own defeat. Because the panzer divisions had never failed to break through Soviet defenses at the outset of any major battle, officers like Hoth, Kempf, von Knobelsdorff, and Breith appear to have suffered from a considerable case of overconfidence, at least as far as the initial assault was concerned. Ironically, only the Waffen SS units, often derided for a supposed lack of technical military expertise, planned meticulously enough to fight their way close to 5 July's assigned objectives. It is worth reiterating that had XLVIII and III Panzer Corps planned as carefully as Hausser and company, then the outcome of Operation Citadel might have been very different.

The most egregious error in Army Group South's planning for the initial assault was the absolute lack of any operational reserve. XXIV Panzer Corps (17th and 23rd Panzer Divisions and *Wiking* SS Panzergrenadier Division) technically constituted the reserve for the southern wing of Operation Citadel yet had to remain distant from the battlefield, serving as the emergency reserve for First Panzer and Sixth Armies, whose fronts had been dangerously thinned to achieve an offensive concentration around Belgorod. Commitment of this corps required at least forty-eight hours' notice, rendering it useless during 5–6 July. As has already been argued above, XLVIII Panzer Corps could have withheld either the 3rd or 11th Panzer Divisions from the initial assault, and it is not difficult to argue that, in III Panzer Corps's sector, 6th Panzer Division would have been better kept in reserve than committed to the fruitless attack from the Mikailovka bridgehead. With one or two panzer divisions still uncommitted on 6 July, von Manstein would have possessed many more tactical options than simply plugging doggedly ahead in the hope that Soviet resistance might abruptly slacken.

Almost as bad were the decisions by von Knobelsdorff and Breith, each of whom ordered their three panzer divisions to assault directly forward in parallel lanes with little provision for cooperation. Essentially such a deployment meant that neither the XLVIII nor the III Panzer Corps had a true *Schwerpunkt*; in addition, the Russians facing each division found themselves free to concentrate on defending against a direct frontal assault without much need to worry about the flanks. This made it possible for the Soviets to frustrate the advances of *Grossdeutschland* and the 6th Panzer Divisions in key sectors at an acceptable cost of penetrations by the 3rd and 7th Panzer Divisions on the far flanks. Here again the conduct of II SS Panzer Corps is instructive, with the entire corps effort subordinated to creating a wide breach in the *Liebstandarte* area. Had *Grossdeutschland* and the 11th Panzer Division cooperated in a similar attack (rather than coordinating their efforts on an improvised basis later in the day), it is quite possible that XLVIII Panzer Corps could have penetrated as deeply as did Hausser's spearheads.

A whole host of smaller miscues combined to reduce the chance of a successful initial assault even further. From the misidentified minefields in front of the 168th Infantry Division to the unrealistic reliance on the 10th Panzer Brigade to plunge through the Red Army's defenses, German staff officers at the division, corps, and army levels allowed incremental mistakes to multiply to the point that they became major factors in the battle. The vastly different artillery fire plans of the three panzer corps alone merit a detailed study of the technical and administrative deficiencies in the coordination of artillery preparations. Reading the planning documents, one is struck by the absence of any consistent doctrinal approach: The senior artillery officer in each corps appears to have reinvented his own wheel.

The fact that the Germans themselves were aware that the opening assault of Operation Citadel had been far less successful than it should have been (even allowing for the strength of the Russian defenses) becomes evident upon reading the postwar accounts of key officers. Theodor Busse insisted that on 5 July "the attack penetrated the enemy line at all but a few points" and that the inability of Army Group South to achieve its initial objectives had to be attributed to the Soviets "clinging tenaciously to their positions" and "the lack of a sufficient number of infantry divisions in the attack." In his only oblique reference to planning errors, Busse complained that the panzer divisions "expended their strength in the course of unaccustomed fighting in the system of fortifications before they could develop their primary assets—mobility and speed—in open terrain."

Concerning XLVIII Panzer Corps, Friedrich Fangohr blamed "formidable terrain obstacles" as much as Russian resistance for the fact that von Knobelsdorff's corps "had a tough fight on the first day of the attack, suffering losses that were far from negligible." Friedrich-Wilhelm von Mellenthin, the XLVIII Panzer Corps chief of staff, likewise considered meteorological "bad luck"—cloudbursts resulting in muddy ground—as the most significant obstacle to German progress. (In his postwar account *Panzer Battles*, von Mellenthin also somewhat disingenuously characterizes the limited 4 July attack on the heights as the opening of the offensive, which allowed him to describe events on 5 July by saying, "On the second day of the attack we met our first setback.") Breith singled out Soviet mines, counterbattery fire against his bridges, and the fact that the 168th Infantry Division "was unable to advance against strong enemy resistance" as reasons for the III Panzer Corps's disappointing performance while defending his flawed decision to forego any artillery preparation in support of the assault.[36] Raus echoed these sentiments in his contribution to the Busse study.

Simply stated, in their postwar analyses of their own campaigns, senior German commanders and staff officers naturally preferred to highlight the difficulties under which they labored rather than their own mistakes. In these narratives, the commanders' defeats inevitably resulted from inadequate resources, difficulties of weather and terrain, or the unreasonable dictates of Adolf Hitler. The fact that these men often donned rose-colored monocles while writing about their operations is not surprising; what is truly astounding is that the quasimythical level of excellence attributed to German operational and tactical planning has endured for so long in the face of voluminous archival evidence to the contrary. It is long past time for students of the war in Russia to come to grips with the reality that—when one is apportioning responsibility for the Wehrmacht's defeat—the cumulative battlefield mistakes of army, corps, and division commanders (and their respective staff officers) had a lot to do with why the war ended in the sack of Berlin instead of Moscow.

15

Was Kursk a Decisive Battle?

Unprecedented access to Soviet archival material has allowed David Glantz and Jonathan House to challenge many of the firmly established myths surrounding Operation Citadel, but they do not in the end disagree with the longstanding consensus that Kursk marked a turning point in the war strategically, operationally, and tactically. An important dissent to this conclusion, however, has recently been raised by Niklas Zetterling and Anders Frankson in their landmark study *Kursk 1943: A Statistical Analysis*. Zetterling and Frankson have published the first comprehensive examination of the strength and losses of the contending armies based completely on archival sources, both German and Russian. Eschewing drama for meticulous detail, the authors have created an important (one is tempted to say definitive) reference work that deserves to have a serious impact on all subsequent writing about Kursk. In their final chapter, "Consequences of the Battle," Zetterling and Frankson examine the strategic, operational, and tactical significance of the battle and—in light of the information they have unearthed—declare that it is not "possible to claim that [Citadel] produced an outcome which was decisive to the war in the east."[1]

Zetterling and Frankson base their contention on analysis of five major factors: German personnel losses, German tank losses, Soviet tank losses, changing force ratios, and long-term patterns of German attrition. In order to assess the validity of their argument, each category must be reviewed in turn. Before undertaking that task, it should also be noted that Zetterling and Frankson, when speaking of the battle of Kursk, refer only to operations between 5 and 17 July, which covers the period of the German offensive. Soviet writers, however, have long contended that both the Orel and Kharkov counteroffensives should be considered, along with the earlier defensive phase, as one long battle, running from 5 July to 23 August (the date of the Russian capture of Kharkov). Glantz and House, along with most modern military historians, have come to accept the broader view. As will become apparent below, the distinction involves more than the name of a battle.

German casualties at Kursk, according to the authors, "were quite small" and "cannot be seen as decisive, at least not in the context of the struggle on the eastern front." Total German losses sustained by Army Groups Center and South in the attack were 56,827 men, which amounted to roughly 3 percent of the total 1,601,454 men the Germans lost in Russia during 1943. Moreover, Zetterling and Frankson point out that the 89,480 replacements sent into the Soviet Union during July 1943 "were more than sufficient to cover the losses suffered during [Citadel]."[2] This argument is somewhat misleading, for it assumes that all troops lost in combat and all replacements sent forward are equal, and such was not the case. To make matters worse, the authors often engage in somewhat circular logic in their analysis of the numbers.

Consider the case of Model's Ninth Army. Zetterling and Frankson have this to say:

> The German 9th Army suffered 22,273 casualties from 5 July to 11 July. . . . 9th Army's losses were most severe on the first day of the offensive and subsequently loss rates declined. Compared to the ration strength of the army at the beginning of the offensive, losses up to 9 July (inclusive) constituted about 5 per cent, while losses for the entire month constituted about 10 per cent of the ration strength at the beginning of the month.[3]

What is wrong with this analysis is that although Ninth Army's ration strength on 5 July was approximately 335,000, its combat strength (including troops held in army group reserve) was only 75,713. By 9 July the army's combat strength had declined to 55,931, a reduction of 19,782. Thus all but 2,491 of the 22,273 total casualties had occurred in the army's infantry, engineer, reconnaissance, and *Feldersatz* units. Thus even though the overall casualty rate of the army was just 6.6 percent, the casualty rate among the combat troops was a staggering 26.1 percent! Even the most cursory glance at division-by-division combat strengths on 4 and 9 July reveals the extent to which some units had been gutted:

Comparative Combat Strengths, Ninth Army Units, 4 and 9 July 1943[4]

	4 July	*9 July*	*Loss rate*
XX Corps			
251st Infantry Division	2,736	2,698	0.1%
137th Infantry Division	2,826	2,789	0.1%
45th Infantry Division	3,747	3,721	.1%
72nd Infantry Division	3,309	3,319	NL
Corps total	12,618	12,527	.1%
XLVI Panzer Corps			
102nd Infantry Division	2,930	2,441	0.9%
258th Infantry Division	3,392	1,869	45%
7th Infantry Division	3,532	1,573	55%
31st Infantry Division	3,068	1,939	37%
Gruppe von Mantueffel	2,025	1,901	0.6%
Corps total	14,947	9,723	35%
XLVII Panzer Corps			
20th Panzer Division	2,831	1,751	38%
4th Panzer Division	3,549	3,142	11%
2nd Panzer Division	4,062	1,040	74%
6th Infantry Division	3,121	1,604	49%
9th Panzer Division	3,571	2,255	37%
Corps total	17,134	9,792	43%
XLI Panzer Corps			
18th Panzer Division	3,479	3,014	13%
10th Panzergrenadier Division	4,322	4,135	4%
86th Infantry Division	3,650	2,481	32%
292nd Infantry Division	3,714	1,710	54%
Corps total	15,165	11,340	25%
XXIII Corps			
78th *Sturm* Division	4,545	2,322	49%
Jaeger Battalions 8, 13	1,407	883	37%
216th Infantry Division	2,802	2,076	26%
383rd Infantry Division	2,633	3,036	NL
12th Panzer Division	4,462	4,242	5%
Corps total	15,849	12,559	21%
Total	75,713	55,941	26%

Note that these figures are skewed by the fact that XX Corps, on Ninth Army's far left flank, had seen no fighting and that several divisions (notably 4th and 12th Panzer Divisions and 10th Panzergrenadier

Division) had been engaged after 5 July. For example, the 11 percent losses reported by the 4th Panzer Division represented only a single day of combat. Among the eleven divisions that had seen continuous fighting between 5 and 9 July, the average loss rate was a debilitating 45 percent in combat troops. Thus for Zetterling and Frankson to down-play Ninth Army's losses during 5–9 July by categorizing them as merely a fraction of the army's ration strength is to present a distorted picture of the conflagration Model's troops endured during their short-lived offensive.

The authors are equally, if unintentionally, misleading with regard to Ninth Army's losses for the remainder of July during the defensive battle for the Orel salient. They assert that Model's army, in losing another 13,362 troops between 12 and 31 July, suffered only another 5 percent loss against "the ration strength at the beginning of the month."[5] As has al-ready been demonstrated, measuring combat losses against ration strengths rather than combat strengths is a chancy proposition. Worse, however, is that the authors ignore the fact that at least half of the divi-sions assigned to Ninth Army on 1 July had, by the middle of the month, been transferred to Second Panzer Army. Thus to measure percentage losses for the end of the month against the ration strength at the outset is guaranteed to return a deflated figure.

A more accurate method of examining German losses on the northern face of the Kursk salient is to combine the casualties of Ninth and Second Panzer Armies for the entire month of July. When that is done, German losses come into better focus. For the month of July, Ninth Army lost 37,355 soldiers while Second Panzer Army took 45,928 casualties, for a grand total of 83,283. The chronological spread of these losses between the two armies, as illustrated in the table below, makes the point about the transfer of the main responsibility for the fighting between the two armies that occurred in mid-month:

Comparative Casualties, Ninth and Second Panzer Armies, 1–31 July 1943[6]

	1–10 July	11–20 July	21–31 July	Total
Ninth	20,189	8,258	8,908	37,355
Second Panzer	1,059	10,120	34,749	45,928

The two armies on 1 July had an estimated combined ration strength of 495,000 men, which would return a figure of 16.8 percent losses. Yet, as demonstrated above, losses against combat strength were several orders of magnitude above losses against ration strength. Although precise figures for Second Panzer Army are not available, a best-guess estimate for that army's 1 July combat strength would land in the neighborhood of 36,000.[7] If losses among combat troops accounted for 75 percent of the total losses suffered (during Model's attack such losses equaled nearly 90 percent, but in defensive combat greater casualties befell support and service troops), then these would have amounted to about 62,400. That figure, compared to the estimate of 111,713 combat troops in both armies on 1 July, suggests that Ninth and Second Panzer Armies lost nearly 56 percent of their combat strength in a single month. Such loss ratios, whether the period under consideration is early July (Ninth Army alone) or the entire month (both armies), can hardly be characterized as "quite small." Similar calculations could be performed regarding the losses sustained by Fourth Panzer Army and *Armeeabteilung* Kempf.

The argument with respect to tank losses presented by Zetterling and Frankson is equally unsound. The authors suggest that German AFV losses during Operation Citadel, which they calculate at roughly 300, "were not extraordinarily high . . . nor were they impossible to replace." Citing statistics on tank production, shipments of armor to the armies, and the total number of AFVs on the Eastern Front at the end of December 1943, they conclude:

> It could of course be inferred . . . that a trend was reversed by [Citadel] and certainly there is some truth to this. However, what is remarkable in the figure is the long period of build-up before [Citadel]. Also it must not be forgotten that the quality of the tanks on the eastern front steadily rose, which is indicated by the growth in the number of Tigers, Panthers, and later-model Panzer IV. . . . Thus it can be argued that the *Ostheer* was better equipped with tanks at the end of the year than it had been before [Citadel].[8]

Specifically, the authors base their final statement on a comparison of the 30 June and 31 December AFV holdings on the Eastern Front. Recapitulated in the table below, "Specialty" tanks refers to all command and flamethrowing tanks; "Obsolete" tanks includes all Pzkw IIs, IIIs, and IVs that were equipped with the L24 gun; "Modern" tanks consist of all late-model Pzkw IVs, Panthers, and Tigers; and "Assault Guns" incorporates all StG IIIs, StuHs, and StuPz IVs.

German AFV holdings in Russia, 30 June and 31 December 1943[9]

	Obsolete	Speciality	Modern	Assault Guns	Total
30 June	1,028	157	1,213	1,036	3,434
	(29.9%)	(4.6%)	(35.3%)	(30.2%)	
31 Dec.	290	156	1,403	1,507	3,356
	(8.6%)	(4.6%)	(41.8%)	(44.9%)	

Clearly, in purely numerical terms, Zetterling and Frankson appear to have a point, as the total number of AFVs available at each date was very close while the number of modern tanks and assault guns in the mix rose from 65.7 percent to 86.7 percent.

The appearance, however, is deceiving, for two reasons: the increasing concentration of AFVs in nondivisional units, and steadily declining operational percentages. Note that the increase in the percentage of assault guns was actually greater than that of the modern tanks. In December 1943 there were thirty-nine assault gun battalions in Russia. Thirteen of these belonged to panzer or panzergrenadier divisions, serving as surrogate tank battalions, which also meant that twenty-six (66.7 percent) of the assault guns were in battalions normally attached to infantry corps and divisions and utilized in a tactical role as self-propelled antitank guns.[10] As David Glantz has pointed out, the increasing flood of Soviet tanks had left German infantry divisions—if they depended on the relatively slow towed antitank guns—almost defenseless against armored attack.[11] The fact that two-thirds of the assault guns were being used in such a capacity meant that they were not available for use in large or even medium-sized armored operations. The same was true, albeit to a lesser extent, of the Tigers. These heavy tanks, though often attached to panzer divisions for specific missions, outside the Waffen SS and Grossdeutschland divisions, were organized into independent battalions.[12]

This was a significant change from the situation in late June, when a far higher percentage of tanks and assault guns existed in battalions organic to the panzer divisions. Armored strength across the front had been significantly diluted into small packets by December, useable only for tactical purposes, and the panzer divisions that could be massed for operational counterstrokes grew weaker and weaker. Thus any conclusions that take into account only the total numbers of tanks available will necessarily distort the true picture.

Incorporating consideration of operational readiness hits the Zetterling-Frankson thesis even harder. As logic would suggest, the Germans managed to improve on their operational readiness during quiet periods of the war, but as active campaigning began it grew increasingly difficult to return broken-down or battle-damaged vehicles to the front lines. As the table below demonstrates clearly, the period of unceasing mobile combat that began at Kursk and swept the Wehrmacht out of the Ukraine and into Galicia by year's end had played hell with the workshop companies' ability to keep up with battlefield attrition:

Tank and Assault-Gun Operational Readiness, Eastern Front, March–December 1943[13]

Month	Tanks	Assault Guns
Mar	53.5%	77.0%
Apr	74.6	81.4
May	83.6	85.6
June	88.5	90.5
July	51.7	72.9
Aug	40.6	67.9
Sept	31.0	48.3
Oct	43.8	55.7
Nov	35.7	46.2
Dec	50.8	58.3

The difference, therefore, between armor "on hand" and "operational" was quite significant, as shown by the comparison of 30 June and 31 December AFV strengths modified to take this factor into account:

German AFVs in Russia, Available Versus Operational, 30 June and 31 December 1943

Tanks	Available	Operational
30 June	2,398	2,122
31 December	1,849	939
Assault guns		
30 June	1,036	938
31 December	1,507	879
Total AFVs		
30 June	3,434	3,060
31 December	3,356	1,818

Instead of AFV holdings similar in size but improved in quality, as Zetterling and Frankson suggest, the German army on the last day of 1943 could actually field 1,242 fewer tanks and assault guns than it had at the outset of Operation Citadel. It strains credulity to the breaking point to assert that a 41 percent drop in operational armor strength left Hitler's army "better equipped with tanks at the end of the year than it had been before [Citadel]."[14]

Zetterling and Frankson appear to have a much stronger argument with regard to Soviet armored losses. The authors note that:

> On 1 July, the Red Army had a tank strength of 9,888 in the front armies and 2,688 in STAVKA reserves. Six months later the Red Army had less than half that number in [its] field units and STAVKA reserves. During those six months 11,890 tanks and assault guns had been produced. It must be emphasized that when a force suffers such extensive losses as the Red Army armoured forces did during the second half of 1943, production of tanks will not suffice to replace losses. There will also be delays before the new tanks are issued to combat units owing to the need for training new crews.[15]

As has become evident when discussing German armor, operational readiness is critical to examining relative battlefield strength; unfortunately, the best authorities on Soviet tanks are vague concerning percentages of available versus operational AFVs. A poor best-guess estimate of Soviet operational readiness prior to the Battle of Kursk is that it approached 80 percent; German documents from the end of the year portray the Red Army in western Ukraine and Galicia as struggling to maintain a readiness rate of 40 percent.[16] If, for the sake of argument, these figures are provisionally extended to encompass Russian armored strength across the front on both dates, then the following picture emerges:

	Soviet		German	
Date	Avail.	Operational	Avail.	Operational
30 June	12,576	10,060	3,434	3,060
31 Dec.	5,643	2,413	3,356	1,818

Soviet tank losses during the period easily exceeded 15,000, and possibly approached 19,000, against German losses of only 3,841, a kill ratio in favor of the defenders of four- or five-to-one.[17] From this purely numerical standpoint Zetterling and Frankson would appear to have made an unassailable case that the Soviets were losing the battle of armored attrition.

Zetterling and Frankson's figures for field forces and STAVKA reserves, however, do not take into account total Soviet AFV holdings. At the beginning of 1943, according to G. F. Krivosheev, the Red Army possessed 12,500 vehicles not in the hands of organizing units; by year's end this total had risen to 18,600 despite prodigious losses.[18] The fact that the size of the Red Army's tank park could have increased by one-third during the same period that the number of AFVs available to the field forces declined by 55 percent suggests that—as Zetterling and Frankson argue—the true bottleneck lay in training new tank crews, not the supply of machines. This problem was obviously ironed out during the winter of 1943–1944, as Soviet tank availability, despite continued heavy losses, resumed a steady march upward early the next year.

What Zetterling and Frankson have actually documented is the extreme low point hit by the tank strength of the Soviet field forces at the end of successive offensives between July and December 1943, just prior to large waves of replacements arriving at the front. Moreover, Soviet armored losses must be weighed against what the Red Army had gained, especially in the south. German troops had been pushed almost completely out of Ukraine, the Wehrmacht had sustained irreplaceable casualties in trained manpower, and the Third Reich had been forced to concentrate heavily on producing AFVs (Tigers and assault guns) suited to the tactical defensive rather than the sweeping mobile operations of 1941–1942. This continuous if costly sweep to the west had begun at Kursk.

The final argument made by the two authors is that "using documents on monthly casualties on the eastern front it is possible to draw up a graph on the accumulated personnel losses . . . [that] shows a steady increase in accumulated German casualties without any distinctive or sudden rises in losses. In fact, this graph displays a rather even attrition which may gradually have worn the German forces down."[19] In other words, Zetterling and Frankson contend that, for Kursk to be considered decisive, some sort of spike should appear in the data during the six months following the battle, indicating a dramatic diminution of German strength; otherwise, Operation Citadel becomes merely one more nudge in the downward spiral of German strength.

Again the authors have focused exclusively on numbers at the expense of other considerations, in this case the length of the front. Prior to Operation Citadel the Russo-German front (excluding Finland and the Crimea) had temporarily solidified into one of the shorter lines held by the Wehrmacht during the course of the war: roughly 2,350 kilometers. By year's end that front had stretched to more than 2,640 kilometers, with minor shortenings of the northern and central sectors more than offset by the expansion of Army Group South's front line from 700 to 1,450 kilometers. Simultaneously, German Army strength declined from 3,138,000 to 2,528,000, a diminution of 610,000 men.[20] When Operation Citadel opened, the Germans could deploy roughly 1,335 troops per kilometer of front; a week after Christmas that average had dropped by 28 percent to only 957 soldiers per kilometer. In terms of combat strength this situation was far worse. Citadel had represented Hitler's final chance to stabilize—more or less permanently—the most economical front line he could achieve; the attack's failure led inevitably to progressively longer fronts that had to be defended with weaker and weaker forces. Yet to associate the beginning of the long, seemingly inexorable Soviet tide to Berlin with the battle of Kursk is not the same as proving that the battle itself was decisive. This appears, on balance, to be one of the points Zetterling and Frankson are attempting to make, and they are completely correct.

Any serious attempt to label Kursk—either in the limited 5–14 July sense that Zetterling and Frankson use or the larger 5 July–23 August context—as a decisive operation has to examine several key criteria:

1. The physical and moral effects of a failed German summer offensive;
2. The extent to which the short-term losses in Operation Citadel (whether or not they could be replaced in the long run) critically weakened the German capacity for resisting the Soviet counteroffensives directed at Orel and Kharkov;
3. The impact of losses in manpower, equipment, and territory to those Soviet counteroffensives and the retreat west of the Dnepr River;
4. The extent to which their losses reduced the qualitative edge of the German forces and decreased their capacity for operational concentrations; and
5. The consequences of maintaining an increased operational tempo across a lengthening front for six months.

When each of these considerations have been weighed and evaluated in their turn, then and only then will historians be able to supply a final answer to the question of whether or not Kursk represented a decisive battle. In the meantime there are literally tens of thousands of pages of German records from the period that deserve examination and analysis before a definitive portrait of the Wehrmacht's perspective on the battle can be presented. This book represents only a few tentative steps along that road.

ATLAS

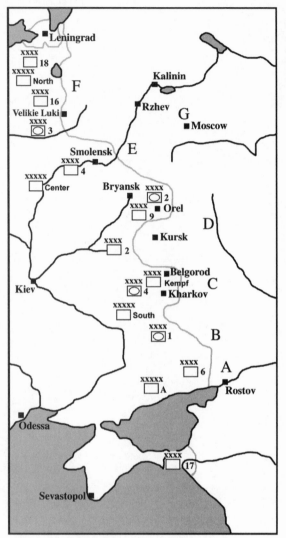

**Map 1-1
German Intelligence
Estimate of Major
Soviet Concentrations
to Late April 1943**

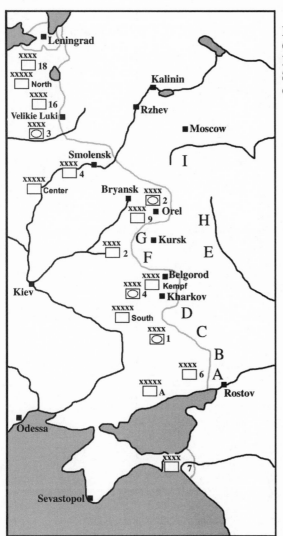

**Map 1-2
German Intelligence
Estimate of Soviet
Strategic Reserves
on 5 July 1943**

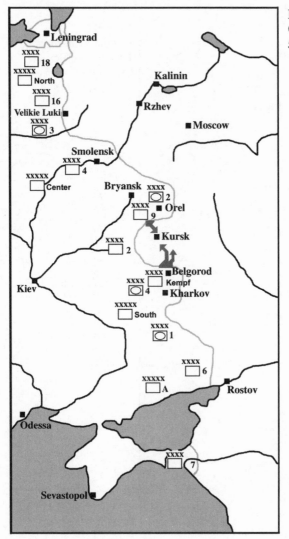

Map 1-3
Operation "Citadel"
5 July 1943

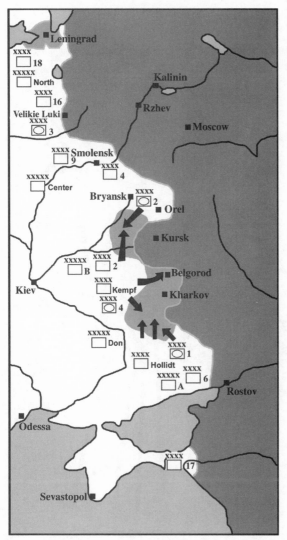

**Map 1-4
German
Counteroffensive
February-March 1943**

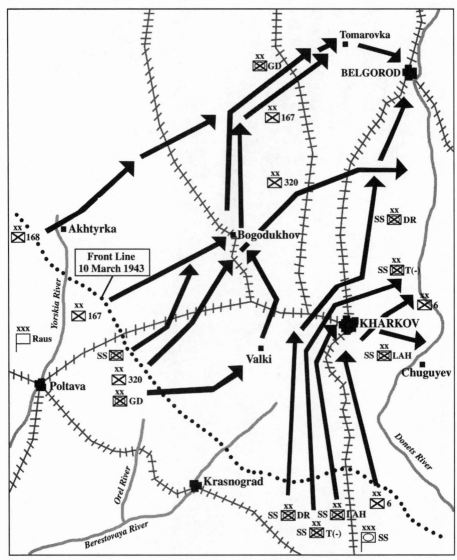

Map 2-1: Provisional corps Raus and SS Panzer Corps retake the Kharkov-Belgorod area, 10-17 March 1943

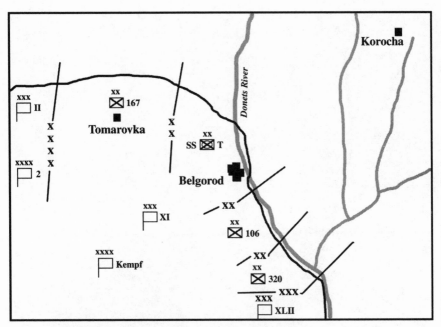

Map 2-2: *Armeeabteilung* **Kempf Sector, 10 April 1943**

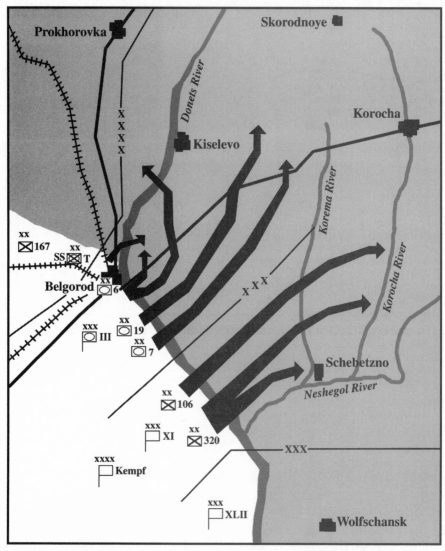

Map 2-3: Initial attack objectives: *Armeeabteilung*
Kempf, 5 July 1943

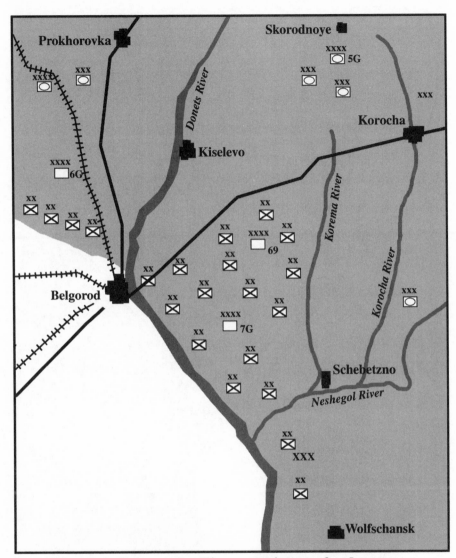

**Map 2-4: German intelligence estimate of red army
units in the front line and immediate reserves in
the area of *Armeeabteilung* Kempf, 5 July 1943**

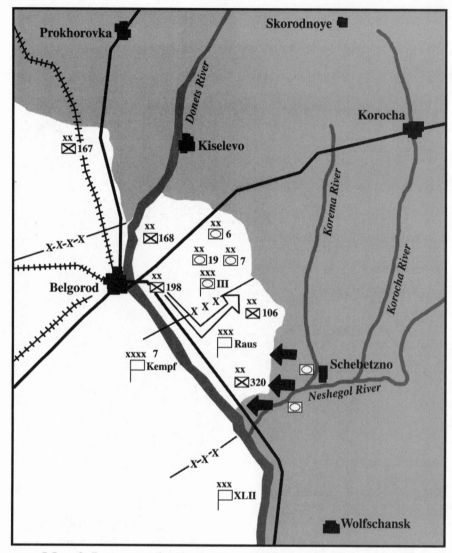

Map 2-5: *Armeeabteilung* **Kempf, Situation 10 July 1943**

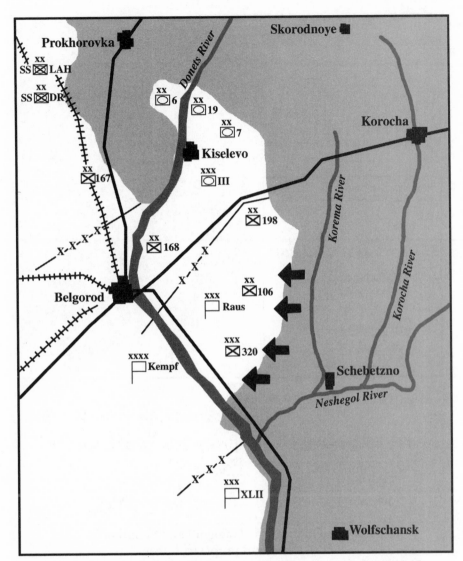

Map 2-6: *Armeeabteilung* **Kempf, Situation 12 July 1943**

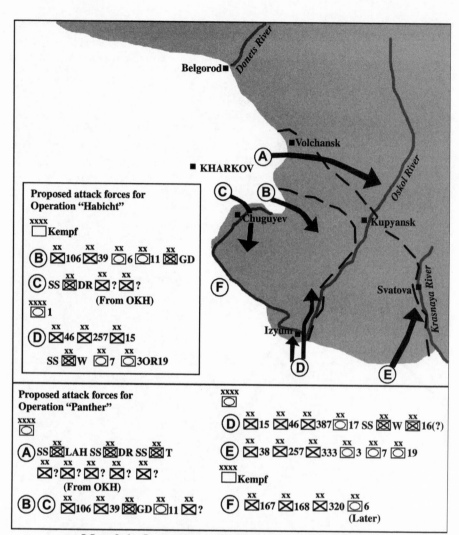

Map 3-1: Operations "Habicht" and "Panther"
Objectives and proposed forces

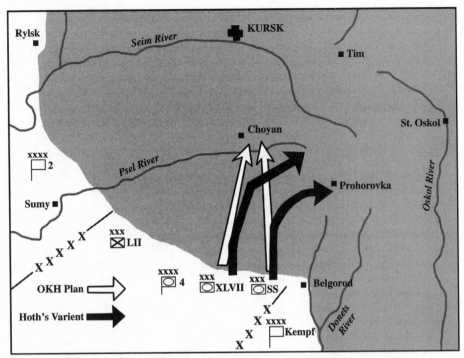

Map 3-2: Hoth modifies Fourth Panzer Army's attack plan

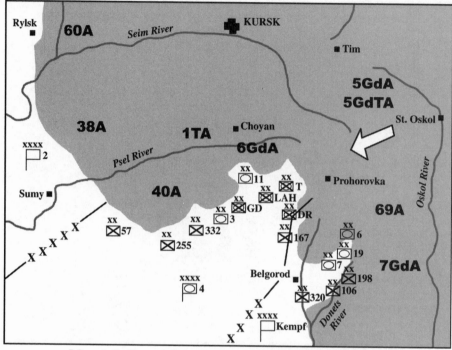

Map 3-3: Fourth Panzer Army, Situation 9 July 1943

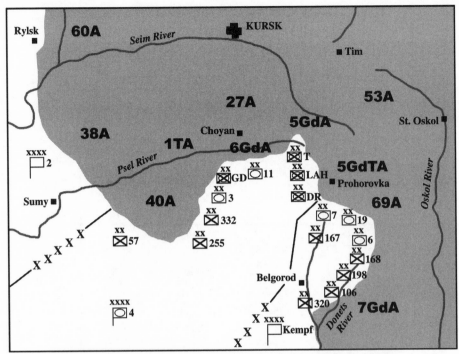

Map 3-4: Fourth Panzer Army, Situation 15 July 1943

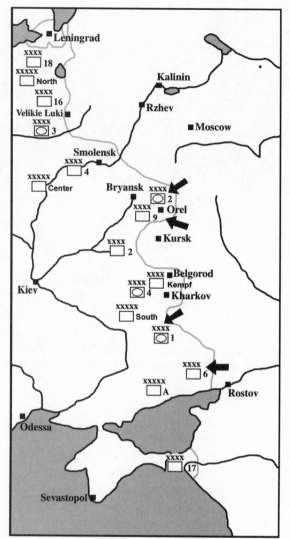

**Map 3-5: Soviet Counteroffensives
Mid July 1943**

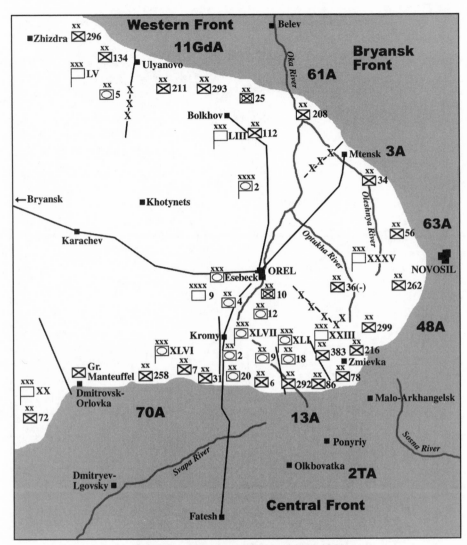

Map 4-1: The Orel Salient, 4 July 1943

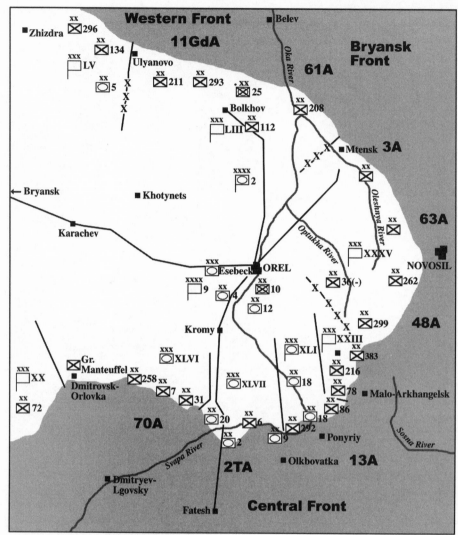

Map 4-2: The Orel Salient, Situation 5-6 July 1943

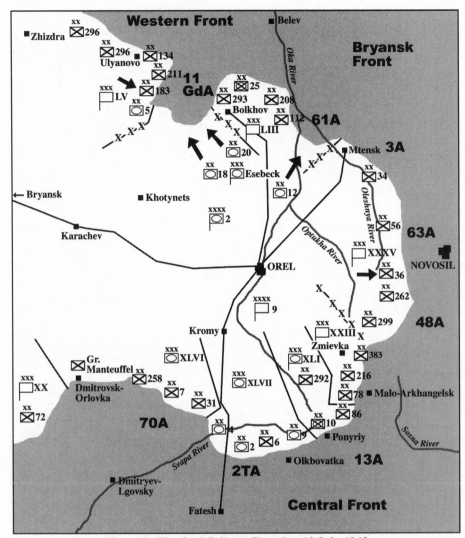

Map 4-3: The Orel Salient, Situation 13 July 1943

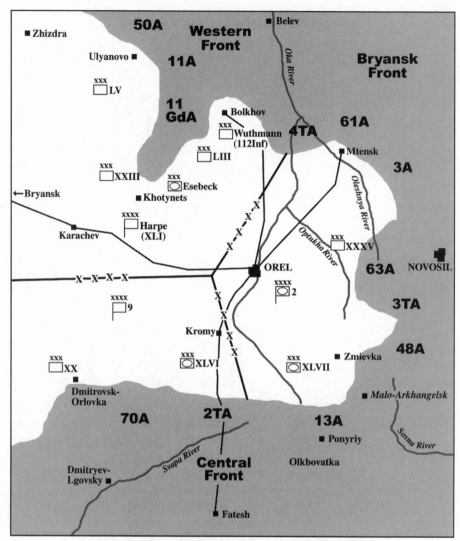

Map 4-4: The Orel Salient, Situation 21 July 1943
(German divisions too intermixed to depict separately)

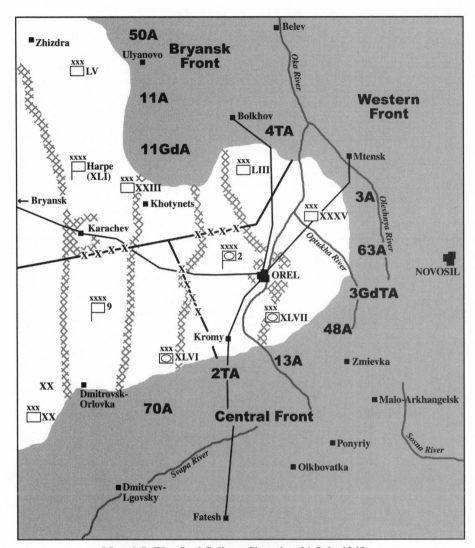

Map 4-5: The Orel Salient, Situation 31 July 1943
(Showing defensive phase lines for withdrawal)

NOTES

Introduction

1. The best historiographical account of Western treatments of the Russian front (albeit one now dated by more than a decade) is David M. Glantz, "American Perspectives on Eastern Front Operations in World War II," first published in the August 1987 issue of *Voprosy Istorii* [Questions of History] and currently available in English at the website of the Foreign Military Studies Office [note that when websites are mentioned in these notes and the bibliography, they will be cited by the name of the sponsoring organization rather than by an Internet address. Search engines will easily pick up the current site address, and the reference—hopefully—will not become dated].

2. Carell's work, though widely read and appreciated by Russian front aficionados and war-gamers, is often dismissed too quickly by academics. There are four reasons for this, not the least of which may be the unsavory personal past lurking behind the author's pseudonym. The book is also unambiguously pro-German, so much so that a reader once noted dryly that when the 16th Motorized Division's leading elements reached Astrakhan (marking the extreme eastern limit of the German advance) "my heart fairly burst with pride for the young sons of the Reich." Carell's breezy, journalistic style, though it carries its readers along breathlessly, tends also to cause historians to discount the value of the book. Then there is the most damning characteristic of all (at least to academics): All of Carell's works lack footnotes. Recently, however, opinions about the quality of Carell's books have undergone a positive shift. David Glantz notes in his "American Perspectives" article that Carell "tapped numerous accounts by individual German officers and soldiers who served in tactical units" and that Carell's work contained "an increased amount of Soviet materials" when compared to other works. Indeed, a careful examination of Carell's bibliographies will find listed almost every Soviet book that was available in the early 1960s, as well as several dozen articles from Soviet military journals. It goes without saying that no Western historian could have enjoyed access to the Soviet archives when Carell was doing his research. Moreover, as I discovered during the research for this book (specifically while working on the Raus material), Carell was extremely faithful to his source material. As an author, Carell would breathe as much life and drama as possible into his combat narratives, but he was rigorously faithful to the facts in his sources. The most recent edition of the second half of Carell's history of the Russo-German war is Paul Carell, *Scorched Earth: The Russo-German War, 1943–1944* (Atglen, PA: Schiffer, 1996).

3. Geoffrey Jukes, *Kursk: The Clash of Armour* (New York: Ballantine, 1968); Martin Caidin, *The Tigers Are Burning* (New York: Hawthorn, 1974); Mark Healey, *Kursk 1943: The Tide Turns in the East* (London: Osprey, 1992); Janusz Piekalkiewics, *Operation "Citadel," Kursk, and Orel: The Greatest Tank Battle of the Second World War*, translated by Michaela Nierhaus (Novata, CA: Presidio, 1987); George M. Nipe Jr., *Decision in the Ukraine, Summer 1943: IISS. and III. Panzerkorps* (Winnipeg, Canada: J.J. Fedorowicz, 1996); Walter S. Dunn Jr., *Kursk: Hitler's Gamble, 1943* (Westport, CT: Praeger, 1997).

4. Two German studies of Kursk continue to be so influential (either directly or filtered through secondary sources) on the U.S. view of the battle that they should be cited: Ernst Klink, *Das Gesetz des Handelns die Operation "Zitadelle," 1943* (Stuttgart: Deutsche Verlag-Anstalt, 1966); and Silvester Stadler, *Die Offensive Gegen Kursk* (Coburg: Nation Europa, 1998; reprint of 1980 edition).

5. The uncontested accomplishments and stature of the authors (especially Glantz) make it difficult to level this criticism at this work, but it is nonetheless merited. In terms of German sources, Glantz and House lean heavily on Carell, Helmuth Spaeter's history of the Grossdeutschland Division, Nipe's book, and Stadler's study of the IISS Panzer Corps. Strangely absent are a number of key unit histories, including those of the three SS divisions and the 19th Panzer. Only the U.S. edition of von Manstein's memoirs (with an abridged chapter on Kursk) is cited, and key articles and memoirs by officers such as Hermann Breith, Johannes Friessner, Hermann Hoth, Erhard Raus, and Lothar Rendulic do not appear in the bibliography. Worse still, in a number of places Carell is quoted as if *Scorched Earth* were a primary source. One such quotation opens with the misleading sentences, "It was already apparent to German general and infantryman alike that this battle was unlike any previous encounter. As one observer poignantly noted. . . " (p. 90). This introduction would surely lead any reader to expect what followed to be a first-person account, and there is nothing in the quotation, given the manner in which it is framed, that suggests otherwise. By any legitimate standard of source citation, however, Carell could not be considered an "observer" to the events in the passage. Unfortunately, this is not an isolated example. Among archival sources the authors cite a staff study by Gottfried Heinrici and Wilhelm Hauck, completed after the war under the auspices of the U.S. Army, claiming that it "has just been rediscovered" and that it is the "most prominent in this extensive group of German language manuscripts." In point of fact it would be difficult to rediscover Heinrici and Hauck, as Charles W. Sydnor Jr. utilized the work in his *Soldiers of Destruction: The SS Death's Head Division, 1933–1945* (Princeton, NJ: Princeton University, 1977), esp. p. 280n. Carell also used the material. Perhaps the reason that Glantz and House missed this is that Sydnor and Carell cite not the typescript in the National Archives but the version of the study that Heinrici and Hauck published under the title "Zitadelle" in *Wehrwissenschaftliche Rundschau*, vol. 15 (August-October 1965), pp. 463–482, 529–544, 582–604. Glantz and House also apparently missed the Busse Kursk study, as well as articles by Hermann Breith (commander, III Panzer Corps), Friedrich Poppe (commander, 293rd Infantry Division), and Karl Arndt (commander, 255th Infantry Division). In terms of captured German records, primarily map sets and schematic order-of-battle charts figure into the research done by Glantz and House. They assert that "surviving German records are fragmentary," due to intentional destruction and Soviet captures, and that "the most important of these missing records for the Kursk period are many of the records of the German Ninth Army" (pp. 431–432). In another section, they argue that "Ninth Army's participation in the Battle of Kursk is particularly difficult to reconstruct because the Red Army captured Ninth Army's records for this period. Although the au-

thor [presumably Glantz] has seen the appropriate Tagebuchen, the Russians have not yet returned them to the German archives" (p. 394). Several comments need to be made here. First, there is a wealth of information—poorly organized and indexed as it is—in the National Archives holdings covering the battle of Kursk at every level, from army group down to division. The notes throughout the rest of this book are only a small sampling. Second, though it is true that Ninth Army's *Tagebuchen* (war diaries) for the period are missing, this is hardly the impediment that Glantz and House portray it to be. Among the many pertinent documents regarding Ninth Army that do survive are extensive morning and day reports (*Morgenmeldungen* and *Tagmeldungen*), as well as a significant amount of the raw *Notz fur Kriegtagebuch*, which became the source material from which those missing documents were written. Moreover, extensive materials for both Army Group Center and Second Panzer Army cover this period, often with duplicates of messages sent from Ninth Army. At this point I have only begun to scratch the surface of the corps- and division-level sources available, but they are huge. Even more perplexing in a work marked by such groundbreaking research on the Soviet side, Glantz and House get many niggling details about the German Army at Kursk wrong. Many German division (and even corps!) commanders are presented in the order of battle with incomplete ranks and only surnames. Several are simply incorrect (listing the commander of the 19th Panzer Division as Rudolf Schmidt—in reality Gustav Schmidt—or mangling Walter Chales de Beaulieu's name into "Charles de Beaulieu"). These details are easily available in numerous published sources, and it is perplexing that the authors should not have gotten them correct. David M. Glantz and Jonathan House, *The Battle of Kursk* (Lawrence: University Press of Kansas, 1999).

6. Niklas Zetterling and Anders Frankson, *Kursk 1943: A Statistical Analysis* (London: Frank Cass, 2000).

7. The evidence for the identity of each of the authors is presented in the chapter introductions.

8. At this and several subsequent places it may seem that the point concerning the originality of the appendices is being driven home rather relentlessly. By way of explanation, my failure to do so explicitly in *German Battle Tactics on the Russian Front, 1941–1945*, led to at least one author assuming that the material printed therein was in the public domain and publishing it not once, but twice, as his own work and without attribution. Compare Appendix II in Steven H. Newton, *German Battle Tactics on the Russian Front, 1941–1945* (Atglen, PA: Schiffer, 1992), with Dirk Blennemann, "German Corps Organization in World War II," first published in *Command*, no. 32 (January–February 1994): 7–8, and later included in a *Command* anthology, *Hitler's Army* (Conshohocken, PA: Combined Books, 1999).

Chapter 1

1. Erich von Manstein, *Lost Victories* (Novato, CA: Presidio, 1982), p. 361.

2. Alexander Stahlberg, *Bounden Duty: The Memoirs of a German Officer, 1932–1945* (London: Brassey's, 1990), p. 210.

3. Wolf Keilig, *Das Deutsche Heer, 1939–1945*, 3 vols. (Frankfort: Podzun Verlag, 1958), vol. 3, pp. 211–252; Charles Burdick and Hans-Adolf Jacobsen, eds., *The Halder War Diary, 1939–1942* (Novato, CA: Presidio, 1988), pp. 152–201.

4. Albert Seaton, *The German Army, 1933–1945* (New York: Meridian, 1982), pp. 157, 170, 175; Matthew Cooper, *The German Army, 1933–1945: Its Political and Military Failure* (New York: Stein and Day, 1978), pp. 73–74, 270.

5. Stahlberg, *Bounden Duty*, pp. 256–258; Manstein, *Lost Victories*, p. 68.

6. R. T. Paget, *Manstein: His Campaigns and His Trial* (London: Collins, 1951), pp. 35, 37; Stahlberg, *Bounden Duty*, p. 215.

7. Peter Padfield, *Himmler* (New York: Henry Holt, 1990), pp. 546, 562, 598, 600; Walter Goerlitz, ed., *The Memoirs of Field Marshal Keitel* (New York: Stein and Day, 1966), pp. 190, 194, 207; Heinz Guderian, *Panzer Leader* (London: Michael Joseph, 1952), pp. 340–342, 346, 364, 382, 400, 406, 416, 429, 452; Stahlberg, *Bounden Duty*, pp. 257, 374–36, 396.

8. There is some discrepancy regarding the dates upon which Busse left the army group (then renamed North Ukraine) and took over the 112th Infantry Division. Keilig lists him as taking over the 112th on 10 July 1944, but von Siegler shows him as chief of staff until 20 July. Keilig also shows Busse's successor as taking the reins on 21 July. Because it was normal practice for the incumbent to remain—at least for a few days— to brief his successor, the dates suggested by von Siegler have been used here. Other than the chance concatenation of the changeover with the assassination attempt, there is no special significance to either sequence. Keilig, *Das Deutsche Heer*, vol. 3, pp. 211–252, 211–373; Fritz Freiherr von Siegler, *Die Hoeheren Dienstellen der Deutschen Wehrmacht, 1933–1945* (Frankfurt: Institut fuer Zeitgeschichte, 1957), p. 42.

9. Cornelius Ryan, *The Last Battle* (New York: Simon and Schuster, 1966), pp. 93–94, 110, 225–225, 438, 509–510; Guderian, *Panzer Leader*, pp. 427–428; Hugh Trevor-Roper, ed., *Final Entries, 1945: The Diaries of Joseph Goebbels* (New York: G.P. Putnam's Sons, 1978), pp. 211, 215.

10. Donald S. Detweiler, ed., *World War II German Military Studies*, 23 vols. (New York: Garland, 1979), vol. 1 [pages not numbered; see index entry for Busse and specific entries regarding P-143(a)(11) and P-211].

11. The extent to which Fremde Heer Ost and other intelligence-gathering agencies misread the Soviet buildup at Central Front is discussed in Appendix 1A.

12. It is interesting here that Busse does not place Walter Model in the group of officers supporting the idea of waiting for the Soviet offensive to strike. It is possible, of course, that he simply did not carry his assessment down to army level, although the inclusion of Heusinger (junior to all army commanders) would argue against that interpretation. Model's entire career was based on the tenacious defense of territory.

13. As an indication of the failure of the initial U.S. Army translation of the Busse study, the first clause of this sentence is therein rendered as "this failure must be ascribed to the troops or to front-line leadership."

14. Glantz and House, *Kursk*, pp. 290–335.

15. David M. Glantz, *The Role of Intelligence in Soviet Military Strategy in World War II* (Novato, CA: Presidio, 1990), p. 85.

Chapter 2

1. The numbers with regard to the relative strength of the opposing forces in this sector can be deceiving. Glantz and House cite the *Armeeabteilung* as possessing 126,000 men and 499–512 armored fighting vehicles (AFVs), while placing the strength of the Seventh Guards Army at 78,600 men and 246 AFVs, which would seem to give the Germans a 3:2 superiority in troops and 2:1 in armor. This is misleading, however, because the figures for the *Armeeabteilung* include the three infantry divisions of the XLII Corps that held the long flank south along the Donets and did not figure into the attack; thus at least 30,000 should be subtracted from the German manpower total.

The German superiority in tanks was numerically real but fails to take into account the fact that the Seventh Guards Army deployed seven antitank regiments (with an establishment of 168 76mm antitank guns), which were immediately reinforced by three more on 6 July, bringing the total antitank strength to 240—many of which were dug-in. Neither did this take into account five battalions of soldiers armed with antitank rifles, which even though suicidal in the best of conditions did manage to whittle down German strength. Moreover, a rough estimate of German artillery strength totals 1,200–1,300 pieces of field, flak, and antitank artillery, as well as mortars, against a reported Seventh Guards Army total of nearly 1,600. When it is also considered that absolutely no tactical air support was available to Kempf during the first forty-eight hours of the attack, what actually becomes amazing is that the Soviets failed to stop his assault in its tracks and throw him back across the river. See Glantz and House, *Kursk*, pp. 287–289, 309–311, 336, and 338; *Tageseinsaetzen (4–6 July 1943), Fleigerverbindungsoffizier beim AOK 2, Auszugweise Lutfwaffenubersicht 6 July–24 August 1943; Einsats des VIII Fl.Korps und Luftflotte 6*, in T-312, Reel 1253, National Archives and Records Administration, Washington, DC. All T-series microforms cited throughout the book are from the National Archives.

2. For whatever reasons, Breith's narrative is completely misleading about the initial deployment of III Panzer Corps, specifically with respect to the role of the 168th Infantry Division. He places the 168th Infantry Division leading the attack of the 6th Panzer Division around Belgorod, and he places the blame for the 6th Panzer's inability to break into the Russian defenses that day squarely on the shoulders of the infantry unit ("its frontal attacks had failed"). As Appendix 2B clearly shows, this is a complete misrepresentation of the facts, as the 168th Infantry Division did not even control a division sector on 5 or 6 July. The entire division had been broken up and attached to the three panzer divisions and the corps artillery commander, leaving the headquarters presiding over nothing more than the supply trains. See Newton, *German Battle Tactics*, pp. 152–158.

3. The only complete biography of Raus is Karl Heinrich Sperker, *Generaloberst Erhard Raus: Ein Truppenfuehrer im Ostfeldzug* (Osnabrueck: Biblio Verlag, 1988). The best biographical essay available in English is provided by Peter Tsouras in his introduction to the reprint of some of the government publications to which Raus contributed. See Peter G. Tsouras, ed., *The Anvil of War: German Generalship in Defense on the Eastern Front* (London: Greenhill, 1994), and Peter G. Tsouras, ed., *Fighting in Hell: The German Ordeal on the Eastern Front* (New York: Ballantine, 1995). Of studies attributed to Erhard Raus, the former includes "Military Improvisations During the Russian Campaign" and "German Defense Tactics against Russian Break-throughs." The second volume presents "Russian Combat Methods in World War II" and "Effects of Climate in Combat in European Russia." See also Erhard Raus, "Winterkampf an der Bistraja and Kalitwa," *Allgemeine Schweizerische Militarzeitschrifte* (January 1954), and Erhard Raus, "Zweimal Charkow," *Allgemeine Schweizerische Militarzeitschrifte* (December 1964).

4. Raus inaccurately understood the genesis of Corps Cramer, which was actually established in late December 1942—prior to the collapse of the Second Hungarian Army, to which it was subordinated. The corps originally controlled two-thirds of the 168th Infantry Division, 26th Infantry Division, 1st Hungarian Panzer Division, Panzer Detachment 700, and Assault Gun Battalion 190. *Corps Cramer, Ia Nr. 4824/31 December 1942 in Anlage zum KTB des Gen.Kdo.z.b.V. Raus (ab 20.7: Ge.Kdo. XI AK) Ein u. Ausgänge*, T-314, Reel 489, National Archives, Washington, DC.

5. Units designations during this period are extremely confusing. The corps Raus commanded had been known as Corps Cramer *zbV* (literally "for special employment," though a better translation might be "provisional"), which then became Corps Raus *zbV*. Some documents already refer to it as XI Corps—or XI Corps headquarters—as early as March, but the corps was not officially so redesignated until 20 July. Here, for the sake of the reader attempting to follow the action, it has been consistently rendered as XI Corps. There is likewise a problem with Hausser's SS command, which was actually I (not II) SS Panzer Corps until midspring. At that point, Hitler decided to organize a second SS panzer corps for Sepp Dietrich and—wanting his old crony to have pride of place—awarded the designation I SS Panzer Corps to him, "demoting" Hausser's command to II SS Panzer Corps. Again, for the sake of readability and consistency, Hausser's command has been listed as II SS Panzer Corps throughout this narrative.

6. In this anecdote, Raus apparently combines the experiences of two different divisions into one story. The 298th Infantry Division—not the 320th—had stood on the Don River as a "corset" unit for the Eighth Italian Army and had endured several weeks of running battles and encirclements to reach the reformed German lines. The 320th had arrived from France in January and had been placed in line adjacent to the surviving *kampfgruppe* of the 298th. In the Soviet push to envelop Kharkov at the beginning of February, the 320th was surrounded and did constitute a mobile pocket as it fought its way back toward the friendly lines held by II SS Panzer Corps around Kharkov. This retreat, however, consumed one week, not the "several" alluded to in the text. See David M. Glantz, *From the Don to the Dnepr: Soviet Offensive Operations, December 1941 to August 1943* (London: Frank Cass, 1991), pp. 43, 91–105; Werner Haupt, *Army Group South: The Wehrmacht in Russia, 1941–1945* (Atglen, PA: Schiffer, 1998), pp. 232–233; Eugenio Corti, *Few Returned: Twenty-eight Days on the Russian Front, Winter 1942–1943* (Columbia: University of Missouri Press, 1997), pp. 3, 21.

7. Precisely how much strength the 320th Infantry Division added to the German forces around Kharkov has been an open question. Citing both Soviet sources and edited war diaries for *Armeeabteilung* Lanz, David Glantz argues that Postel's retreat involved the loss of at least 4,000 men. This seems somewhat unlikely, as by 8 March 1943 the division mustered 11,670 men of all arms (2,700 front-line infantry). At most points, in fact, the Glantz study of operations in the Donets region between January and March 1943 tends to underestimate German strength. He places the strength of the *Armeeabteilung* in January–February at no higher than 50,000 men, when contemporary records suggest that the four divisions assigned to the *Armeeabteilung* by the end of February numbered more than 57,500 men, a figure that does not take into account at least another 3,000 troops in nondivisional units. See Glantz, *From the Don to the Dnepr*, pp. 88, 97, 153; *Gliederung XI AK, 2 March 1943; Az. 622 (Korpsintendant), 8 March 1943*; both in *Anlage des KTB Gen.Kdo. XI AK*, T-314, Reel 489.

8. Postel was awarded the Oak Leaves to his Knight's Cross on 28 March 1943 for his leadership through this period; John R. Angolia, *On the Field of Honor: A History of the Knight's Cross Bearers*, 2 vols. (No location given: Bender, 1979–1980), vol. 1, p. 163.

9. Here Raus confused two different Red Army formations and their commanders. The Third Tank Army, which was operating south of Kharkov as described in the text, had General Pavel S. Rybalko as its commander. Mobile Group Popov, led by General Markian M. Popov, was operating in the area southeast of Izyum. See Glantz, *From the Don to the Dnepr*, pp. 382–384; Richard N. Armstrong, *Red Army Tank Commanders: The Armored Guards* (Atglen, PA: Schiffer, 1994), pp. 168–175.

10. Note that the estimate of the number of rifle divisions listed as being in the forward area in the text (eight divisions) includes only the Seventh Guards Army and does not take into account the Sixty-ninth Army as shown on the map. This is a contradiction in the original manuscript.

11. Raus did not know it either in 1943 or after the war when he wrote this manuscript, but much of *Armeeabteilung* Kempf's deception effort was wasted. Recently published files of the KGB (Soviet intelligence) indicate that Red Army signal intelligence units had correctly located the assembly areas and command posts for both the 6th and 7th Panzer Divisions. Christopher Andrew and Vasili Mitrokhin, *The Sword and the Shield: The Mitrokhin Archive and the Secret History of the KGB* (New York: Basic Books, 1999), p. 103.

12. In the original manuscript, working without source material, Raus was much more general (though surprisingly accurate) in his listing of the fire-support elements available to III Panzer and XI Corps; these designations have been derived from Glantz and House, *The Battle of Kursk*, pp. 287–289.

13. Though Raus places this regimental staff with III Panzer Corps at the outset, contemporary records show it as still assigned directly to the *Armeeabteilung* until several days after the offensive began. *Kriegsgliederungen Armeeabteilung Kempf, July-August 1943*, T-312, Reel 55.

14. In this interpretation of events on the III Panzer Corps front, Raus follows the postwar account of Hermann Breith, the corps commander. For whatever reason, however, contemporary documents portray a different story. Instead of the 6th Panzer Division supporting the attack by the 168th Infantry Division near Belgorod, Breith had completely disassembled the infantry division into three regimental *Kampfgruppen*, each composed of one infantry regiment, one or two companies of engineers, and one or two artillery battalions. The staff of Artillery Regiment 248 was subordinated to Arko (Artillery Commander) 3 at the corps level, and the staff of the 168th Infantry Division did nothing but preside over the division support troops and trains on 5 July. Beginning on 6 July, especially after 6th Panzer Division's initial attack misfired, Breith began regrouping the 168th elements back under their own headquarters, but the process was not completed until at least 9 or 10 July. See *Gliederung des III Panzerkorps Gen.Kdo. for 1–10 July 1943* (beginning with Ia Nr. 1355/43), in T-314, Reel 197.

15. The order of battle for the three infantry divisions is drawn from *Corps Raus zbV Stand 2.3.43*, in T-314, Reel 489. The composition of Kampfgruppe Strachwitz is from Helmuth Spaeter, *The History of the Panzerkorps Grossdeutschland*, vol. 2 (Manitoba, Canada: J. J. Fedorowicz, 1995), p. 55.

16. *Korpsintendant Az. 622, 8 March 1943*, in T-314, Reel 489.

17. *Corps Raus zbV, Ia, 87/43, 7 March 1943*, in T-314, Reel 489.

18. *Armeeabteilung Kempf Kriegsgliederung, 18 July August 1943*, T-312, Reel 55; *III Panzerkorps Gliederung, 1 July 1943*, T-314, Reel 197.

19. Incorrectly listed in Glantz and House, *Kursk*, p. 288, as Rudolf Schmidt.

20. Incorrectly listed in Glantz and House, *Kursk*, p. 288, as "Charles de Beaulieu."

Chapter 3

1. Keilig, *Das Deutsche Heer*, vol. 3, pp. 211–280.

2. Friedrich Wilhelm von Mellenthin, *Panzer Battles: A Study of the Employment of Armour in the Second World War* (New York: Ballantine, 1971; reprint of 1956 edition), p. 190.

3. It must be admitted that Hoth's memoirs—Hermann Hoth, *Panzer-Operationen* (Heidelberg: Scharnorst Buchkameradschaft, 1956)—are singularly disappointing and unenlightening, deservedly obscure, and rarely cited. See Carell, *Scorched Earth*, pp. 78, 129–130, 212, 426; Manstein, *Lost Victories*, p. 386.

4. At a guess, which will require further research to substantiate, Fangohr probably left Fourth Panzer Army in mid-June 1944, after receiving the Knight's Cross in recognition of his service there. It was not at all unusual for such an award for service (as opposed to recognition in combat) to be given at the very end of an officer's assignment. Hermann Plocher, who is not always reliable with regard to biographical notes, dates Fangohr's relief at Fourth Panzer Army as 15 June. Keilig, *Das Deutsche Heer*, vol. 3, pp. 211–280; Earl F. Ziemke, *Stalingrad to Berlin: The German Defeat in the East* (Washington, DC: Center of Military History, 1966), p. 212.

5. *Panzerarmeeoberkommando 4, Kreigsgliederung, Ia, 1103/43, 12 March 1943*, T-313, Reel 369.

6. *Panzerarmeeoberkommando 4 Gleiderung, 6 July 1943*, T-313, Reel 369.

Chapter 4

1. Details of von der Groeben's career and postings are from Keilig, *Das Deutsche Heer*, vol. 3, sec. 211, p. 109; the comments by von der Groeben are taken from his foreword to Klaus Gerbet, ed., *Generalfeldmarschall Fedor von Bock: The War Diary, 1939–1945* (Atglen, PA: Schiffer, 1996), pp. 7, 211–212.

2. Second Panzer Army had a total strength of 160,000 men in early July, which was just over 54,000 below the establishment for fifteen line divisions; the combat strength of these divisions was much lower, probably in the neighborhood of 45,000–50,000. The infantry divisions possessed between four and eight combat battalions. A combat battalion was defined as an infantry, engineer, reconnaissance (fusilier), or *Feldersatz* (Field Training) battalion. Under the old establishment (1939–1941), each division should have owned twelve such battalions. Likewise, the army was short of its artillery establishment by 119 light and thirty-two field howitzers; all batteries in the infantry divisions had been reduced from four to three guns. Transport had been cut to the bone in order to augment Ninth Army. Of fifteen divisions, then, only eight carried a rating of "attack-capable" while four were rated "capable of limited attacks only." One division was categorized as "defensive-capable only" and two as "limited-defensive," the lowest category for a line division. Walther Nehring, *Die Geschichte Der Deutschen Panzerwaffe, 1916 bis 1945* (Berlin: Propylaeen Verlag, 1969), pp. 296–297.

3. Between 25 April and 18 July Model's Ninth Army received sixty-nine Pzkw IIIs, 228 Pzkw IVs, eleven Pzkw Vs, forty-seven StG IIIs, forty-two self-propelled field howitzers, and eighteen flamethrowing tanks; much more had been promised. Nehring, *Der Deutschen Panzerwaffe*, pp. 297–298.

4. The 18th Panzer Division provides an example of the replacement and equipment problems faced by Ninth Army during the buildup for Operation Citadel. Always considered something of a hard-luck unit with a mediocre fighting record, the 18th Panzer had been reduced to a total strength of 6,904 in April 1943, against an establishment of roughly 14,000. The combat strength of the division had declined to 3,906 against an establishment of 5,500. Although total strength figures for the division in July are somewhat elusive, it is known that the combat strength of the 18th Panzer had been reconstituted to nearly full strength (5,432). The quality of these re-

placements, however, was very much at issue. During the Kursk offensive, Major General Karl Wilhelm von Schlieben reported that in his division "it has happened that [entire] companies, on hearing the cry 'enemy tanks,' spring on their vehicles . . . and drive away to the rear in wild confusion." Moreover, the division lacked the tank strength to give it real striking power, deploying only seventy-two tanks in July, less than half of which were Pzkw IVs, the rest being obsolete lighter models. In both the panzer battalion (18th Panzer Division only had a single panzer battalion) and at least one of the panzergrenadier regiments, all of the support vehicles for this supposedly swift-moving mobile division were horsedrawn. Nehring, *Geschichte der Deutschen Panzerwaffe*, p. 297; Thomas L. Jentz, ed., *Panzer Truppen: The Complete Guide to the Creation and Combat Employment of Germany's Tank Force*, 2 vols. (Atglen, PA: Schiffer, 1996), vol. 2, p. 80; Omer Bartov, *The Eastern Front, 1941–1945: German Troops and the Barbarisation of Warfare* (London: MacMillan, 1985), pp. 18–21, 33–35.

5. Note in original: "Main axis of motor transportation from which all animal transport and marching columns are normally barred."

6. *Untersellungskalender, Panzerarmeeoberkommando 2, vom 1.1.–13.8.1943*, in T-313, Reel 153.

7. *HARKO 305, Ia, 2030/43, 3 July 1943*, in T-313, Reel 153.

8. *Artilleriefuehrer, Gruppe Weiss, Ia, 465/43, 27 June 1943*, in T-312, Reel 322.

9. Soviet artillery estimates are from Glantz and House, *Kursk*, p. 336. It should be noted that the authors allow for the fact that the artillery strength of the Thirteenth Army may have been underreported by 400 pieces.

10. *Gruppe Weiss, Ia/PzOffz, 3884/43, 2 July 1943*, in T-312, Reel 322.

Chapter 5

1. Herman Plocher, *The German Air Force Versus Russia, 1943*, edited by Harry R. Fletcher (New York: Arno, 1967; reprint of 1966 edition), p. x.

2. See James S. Corum, *The Luftwaffe: Creating the Operational Air War, 1918–1940* (Lawrence: University Press of Kansas, 1997); E. R. Hooten, *Eagle in Flames: The Fall of the Luftwaffe* (London: Arms and Armour, 1997); Richard Muller, *The German Air War in Russia* (Baltimore: Naval and Aviation, 1992); Williamson Murray, *Strategy for Defeat: The Luftwaffe, 1933–1945* (Maxwell Air Force Base, Maxwell, AL: Air University Press, 1983); Joel S. A. Hayward, *Stopped at Stalingrad: The Luftwaffe and Hitler's Defeat in the East, 1942–1943* (Lawrence: University Press of Kansas, 1998).

Chapter 6

1. Samuel W. Mitcham Jr., *Men of the Luftwaffe* (Novato CA: Presidio, 1988), p. 209; Plocher, *German Air Force Versus Russia, 1943*, pp. 318, 335.

2. Muller, *German Air War in Russia*, p. 137.

Chapter 7

1. William B. Folkestad, ed., *Panzerjaeger: Tank Hunter* (Shippensburg, PA: Burd Street Press, 2000), pp. 18, 43.

2. Nigel Thomas and Carlos Caballero Jurado, *Wehrmacht Auxiliary Forces* (London: Osprey, 1992), pp. 5–8.

3. See Edgar M. Howell, *The Soviet Partisan Movement, 1941–1944* (Washington, DC: Department of the Army, 1956), pp. 161–169; John A. Armstrong, ed., *Soviet Partisans in World War II* (Madison: University of Wisconsin Press, 1964), pp. 456, 465–466, 470–471; Matthew Cooper, *The Nazi War Against Soviet Partisans, 1941–1944* (New York: Stein and Day, 1979), pp. 132–139.

Chapter 8

1. Glantz and House, *Kursk*, pp. 230, 342.

2. Interestingly enough, Glantz and House utilize neither of these sources, preferring to cite the version in Albert Seaton, *The Russo-German War, 1841–1945* (Novato, CA: Presidio, 1990; reprint of 1971 edition), pp. 366–367, which is dependent upon Lothar Rendulic, *Gekampft, Gesiegt, Geschlagen* (Munich: "Welsermuehl" Wels, 1958), pp. 366–367.

Chapter 9

1. A far larger number of officers served for long tenures in a single corps or division command than is generally realized, especially in infantry commands. Keilig, *Das Deutsche Heer*, vol. 3, pp. 211–276; Angolia, *On the Field of Honor*, p. 266.

2. Already weakened prior to Operation Citadel, the 7th Infantry Division suffered more than 2,300 casualties between 5 and 19 July and indeterminate though heavy losses during the next five weeks. By the time of its commitment to the fighting around Sevsk, General von Rappard's combat elements had already been reorganized from formal regiments into three weak *Kampfgruppen*, each about the strength of a normal infantry battalion. Wilhelm Hertlein, *Chronik der 7. Infanterie-Division* (Munich: Bruckmann, 1984), pp. 177, 184, 219–220.

3. As has been noted in some of the earlier chapters, Roman is not implying that his infantry divisions, with a assigned strength of 12,300 men, had been reduced to barely 700 men each. The term that translates as "combat strength" is the German reporting category *Gefechtstarke*, which could be more accurately (though not completely so) rendered as "infantry strength." *Gefechtstarke* included men in the infantry, engineer, reconnaissance (sometimes fusilier), and *Feldersatz* battalions. For a typical infantry division in late 1943, the authorized strength of these units average in total about 5,200–5,800, depending on the precise division composition and the highly variable strength of the *Feldersatz* battalion. Thus while Roman is not arguing that his divisions had been completely wiped out, as the first glance at the 700-man figure would suggest, he is asserting that the line infantry strength available to division commanders had diminished to about 13.7 percent of authorized strength—or roughly the strength of one full-strength infantry battalion. If such divisions still possessed their artillery, antitank weapons, and supporting arms, they would be classified as capable of limited defensive combat but almost completely worthless for any offensive missions whatsoever.

4. *Gliederung, XX Armeekorps, 9 August 1943*, in T-314, Reel 656.

Chapter 10

1. Paul Carell's narrative in *Scorched Earth* is gripping but too disjointed to follow at the operational level. For a general Soviet overview of the operation (with excellent

maps), see Glantz, *From the Don to the Dnepr*, pp. 215–365. Nipe, *Decision in the Ukraine*, pp. 259–330, covers the operations of II SS and III Panzer Corps on XI Corps's immediate left flank. Farther to the left, with respect to operations around Akhtyrka, the best reference is still Spaeter's *Grossdeutschland*, vol. 2, pp. 146–205.

2. When writing this section of the manuscript, Raus apparently lacked the names of several villages and streams; they are referred to herein by the same letter designations he utilized. To this point it has been impossible to reconcile the exact locations against specific towns or rivers on the surviving situation maps in the National Archives.

3. For a detailed examination of this practice from Russian sources, which the Red Army termed "hunting tongues," see Richard N. Armstrong, *Red Army Legacies: Essays on Forces, Capabilities, and Personalities* (Atglen, PA: Schiffer, 1995), pp. 79–96.

4. This particular method of forcing and maintaining a bridgehead achieved by even the smallest group of soldiers was one in which the Red Army came to excel. It is especially enlightening to compare Raus's description of the Russian crossing of the Donets into the "swamp bridgehead" with Paul Carell's account of the Lyutzeh bridgehead on the Dnepr almost exactly two months later. Although the similarities are uncanny, the differences between the two narratives are also instructive. Carell describes the Germans as well aware of this Soviet tactic and understanding that "it was the same old story—a resolute leader with a handful of determined Soviet soldiers. Every single man would have to be forced out of his firing pit separately." Raus, on the contrary, depicts the soldiers of the 106th Infantry Division as being completely befuddled by the tactic and slow to understand its significance. See Carell, *Scorched Earth*, pp. 413–416.

5. The Germans called the truck-mounted multiple rocket launchers employed by the Red Army "Stalin Organs," while the Russians named them *Katyusha*.

6. *Kreigsgliederung, Armeeoberkommando 8, 25 August 1943*, in T-312, Reel 55.

7. *Anlag zu Kreigsgliederung, Armeeoberkommando 8, 25 August 1943*, in T-312, Reel 55.

8. *Generalkommando XI Corps, Ubersicht uber die Gefechtsstarken, 25 August 1943*, in T-314, Reel 493.

9. *Generalkommando XI Corps, Korps Gefecthsstand, Ia —/43, 25 August 1943*, in T-314, Reel 493.

10. *Anlag 1 zu 198.I.D. Ia, 17 August 1943*, in T-314, Reel 493.

Chapter 11

1. Some of the obscurity has fallen away from the Mius River battle with the publication of Nipe, *Decision in the Ukraine*, which chronicles II SS Panzer Corps's participation in the fight (and which draws heavily on the Francke manuscript). Tim Ripley, *Steel Storm: Waffen-SS Panzer Battles on the Eastern Front, 1943–1945* (Osceola WI: MBI, 2000), pp. 112–125, also describes the battle. Ripley, however, follows Nipe rather than referring directly to Francke, even though several paragraphs (notably the description of Soviet *mashirovka* [deception] efforts on p. 118) seem to be nearly direct paraphrases of Francke's work.

2. The discovery of the original document in the files relating to Sixth Army also raises an interesting, if minor, question: Was Francke ever in fact a participant in the U.S. Army's historical program, or was his manuscript merely translated? The fact that there is absolutely no biographical material on Francke appended to the official translation is at variance with normal practice, and no other documents in the pro-

gram are attributed to Francke. Although this is a seemingly trivial point, it opens the door to the possibility that many other manuscripts in the program may well represent contemporary accounts rather than recollections and reconstructions.

3. In the original manuscript, IV Corps is initially designated "Corps 'Mieth,'" a term that apparently stymied the translators and reviewers of the document. Major F. D. Cronin appended the following note to the first such reference: "This corps is later referred to as Gen.Kdo. z.b.V. Mieth (Corps Headquarters for Special Employment Mieth), probably indicating that this was in some sense, a provisional corps. Its commander has not been identified." In reality, Corps "Mieth" was one of a number of headquarters improvised during the dark days of January–February 1943 to control the scattered German divisions attempting to hold a battered front in the Donets Basin. General of Infantry Friedrich Mieth had, until early February, been commander of security troops and rear area, Army Group Don. His command was first redesignated Gruppe "Mieth" and then Corps "Mieth" in much the same fashion that Corps "Raus" would be created in the Kharkov area. Along with several other such provisional headquarters, Corps "Mieth" was elevated to full status on 20 July, receiving the designation IV Corps (a corps headquarters lost at Stalingrad). Because this chapter opens on 9 July, and almost all the action takes place after 16 July, for consistency's sake the organization has been rendered throughout as IV Corps. See Keilig, *Das Deutsche Heer*, vol. 2, sec. 90, subsec. IV, p. 2.

4. Francke's description of the organization of the 23rd Panzer Division's attack leaves much to be desired. General von Vormann apparently divided his maneuver units into two *Kampfgruppen*, one built around the 128th Panzergrenadier Regiment and the 201st Panzer Regiment, the other around the 126th Panzergrenadier Regiment and the 128th Panzerjaeger Battalion. The subsequent description of the battle in this manuscript renders it nearly impossible by context to determine which regiment had "failed to advance in the direction of the main thrust due to improper commitment," but the situation maps suggest strongly that the errant force was the 126th Panzergrenadiers.

5. Francke apparently did not possess the statistics for the strength of the 23rd Panzer Division when he drafted this manuscript. In reality, the 23rd Panzer was little, if any, stronger than the 16th Panzergrenadier Division. About a week before this attack, the 201st Panzer Regiment (which was really a four-company panzer battalion with a single battery of assault guns attached) mustered between fifty-five and sixty tanks (only thirty of which were long-barrel Pzkw IVs) and about seven StG III assault guns. Haupt, *Army Group South*, p. 261; Jentz, *Panzer Truppen*, vol. 2, p. 81.

Chapter 12

1. Quoted in Carell, *Scorched Earth*, p. 88.

2. Nipe, *Decision in the Ukraine*, pp. 64, 359; Glantz and House, *Kursk*, p. 272.

3. Glantz and House, *Kursk*, pp. 138–147.

4. The original Hoth statement is from Hermann Hoth, *Panzeroperationen* (Heidelberg: Vowinckel, 1966), p. 32; it also appears in Carell, *Scorched Earth*, along with that author's conclusions on pp. 42–43.

5. Cited in full in Glantz and House, *Kursk*, p. 356.

6. Stadler's work is an excellent source, including the KTB (war diary) for II SS Panzer Corps and key Fourth Panzer Army orders, but it should be used with some care. For example, the fire plans shown in the back of the book as appendixes are somewhat different from the draft and approved fire plans by which Hausser's corps

actually controlled its artillery on 5 July. The ones Stadler uses appear to have been polished quite a bit after the fact (see Chapter 14 in this book); Stadler, *Die Offensive Gegen Kursk*, pp. 217–224.

7. Glantz and House, *Kursk*, p. 432.

8. Quoted in ibid., p. 412.

9. Rudolf Lehmann, *The Liebstandarte III* (Winnipeg, Canada: J. J. Fedorowicz, 1990), pp. 224–227; Glantz and House, *Kursk*, pp. 146, 358–360.

10. *KTB, 4.PzAOK, 11 May 1943*, in T-313, Reel 365, National Archives, Washington, DC.

11. Ziemke, *Stalingrad to Berlin*, pp. 124–128.

12. *Ia Nr. 111/43, 4.PzAOK, 23 March 1943*, in T-313, Reel 382.

13. *Ia Nrs. 112/43 and 114/43, 4.PzAOK*, undated, in T-313, Reel 382.

14. *KTB, 4.PzAOK, 23–26 April 1943*, in T-313, Reel 365.

15. *Bock War Diary*, pp. 201–203; *Halder War Diary*, p. 341.

16. *Halder War Diary*, pp. 633–634; *Bock War Diary*, p. 516.

17. The participation of the 3rd Panzer Division in Operation Citadel had been discussed but not finalized prior to the meeting between Hoth and von Manstein. After having seen the optimistic force allocations for Habicht and Panther, Fourth Panzer Army headquarters appears to have taken a skeptical (almost wait-and-see) view of whether or not the division would be released to them for the campaign. No specific references to 3rd Panzer Division in army operational documents appear until 6 May, and the context there is tentative. See *Ia Nr.—/43, Auffrischungsstab Chrkow, 6 May 1943*, in T-313, Reel 370; *Ia Nr. 151/43 Oberkommando der 4. Panzerarmee, Durchfuehrung der Operation "Zitadelle," 14 May 1943*, in T-313, Reel 370; *KTB, 4.PzAOK, 10 May 1943*, in T-313, Reel 365.

18. These changes caused considerable rewriting throughout the army group. *Armeeabteilung* Kempf had just issued its basic operations order for the attack, which included the old boundary lines, and apparently did not become aware for nearly two weeks thereafter that von Manstein had agreed to the change. Army Group South's operations staff marked the pertinent section (paragraph 4) for revision and sent it back to Kempf; *Ia Nr. 800/43, Armee-Abteilung Kempf, 1 May 1943, Operationsbefehl for "Zitadelle" Nr. 1*, in T-312, Reel 51; *Ia Nr. 0505/43, Oberkommando der Heeresgruppe Sud, 20 March 1943, Operationsbefehl fur "Zitadelle" Nr. 1 (Neufassung)*, in T-312, Reel 51; *KTB, 4.PzAOK, 10 May 1943*, in T-313, Reel 365; *Ia Nr. 151/43 Oberkommando der 4. Panzerarmee, Durchfuehrung der Operation "Zitadelle," 14 May 1943*, in T-313, Reel 370; *Ia Nr. 462/43. Generalkommando I. SS-Panzer-Korps, 31 May 1943*, in T-313, Reel 370.

19. *Uber Planspiel "Zitadelle" beim Gen.Kdo.xbV Raus am 29.5.43, 9.00 bis 12.45 Uhr*, in T-312, Reel 51; *Niederschrift Uber Planspiel "Zitadelle" beim III.Pz.Korps am 3.6.1943, 900 Uhr bis 12.45*, in T-312, Reel 51; *Planspiel, XXXXVIII. Pz-Korps, 5 June 1943*, in T-313, Reel 382; *KTB, 4.PzAOK, 25 May 1943, 2 June 1943, 6 June 1943, 8 June 1943*, in T-313, Reel 365; Ralf Tiemann, *Chronicle of the 7. Panzer-Kompanie 1. SS-Panzer Division "Liebstandarte"* (Atglen, PA: Schiffer, 1998), p. 52; Lehmann, *Liebstandarte III*, p. 198.

20. *Planspiel, XXXXVIII. Pz-Korps, 5 June 1943*, in T-313, Reel 382; *KTB, 4.PzAOK, 27 June 1943, 3 July 1943*, in T-313, Reel 365.

21. *Ia Nr. 194/43, Oberkommando der 4. Panzerarmee, Operationsbefehl "Zitadelle," 28 June 1943*, in T-313, Reel 370; *Panzerarmeebefehl Nr. 1, 4.PzAOK, 3 July 1943*, in T-313, Reel 366; see also the translated excerpt in Lehmann, *Liebstandarte III*, p. 202.

22. *Panzerarmeebefehlen Nrs. 3–5, 7 July 1943, 8 July 1943, 9 July 1943*, in T-313, Reel 366; *KTB, 4.PzAOK, 9 July 1943*, in T-313, Reel 365.

23. *KTB, 4.PzAOK, 9 July 1943, 3 July 1943*, in T-313, Reel 365; Fangohr is quoted from Chapter 3 of this book. Glantz and House argue that the 9 July orders were disseminated from Fourth Panzer Army "late on 9 July," because the *Liebstandarte Adolf Hitler* division order they quote was issued at 2215. Division operations officer Rudolf Lehmann, however, specifies that Headquarters, II SS Panzer Corps, briefed him on the plan at 1630. Although there is not a precise "time hack" on Hoth's Panzerarmeebefehl Nr. 5, for it to have penetrated through corps down to division suggests a bare minimum of two hours in the transmission. Allowing for the time necessary to write and duplicate the Fourth Panzer Army order places what Glantz and House would characterize as the "Prokhorovka decision" at least as early as 1330 and potentially back as far as noon. This is an important consideration, as Glantz and House build their case for Hoth changing his mind about an attack across the Psel River at least partly on events that would have occurred after his orders were written. See *Panzerarmeebefehl Nr. 5, 9 July 1943*, in T-313, Reel 366; Lehmann, *Liebstandarte III*, p. 224.

Chapter 13

1. Ziemke, *Stalingrad to Berlin*, pp. 128–129; von Manstein, *Lost Victories*, p. 445; *KTB, 4.PzAOK, 3 May 1943*, in T-313, Reel 365.

2. Walter Goerlitz, *MODEL: Strategie der Defensive* (Wiesbaden: Limes Verlag, 1975), p. 116; see also James Lucas, *Hitler's Enforcers: Leaders of the German War Machine, 1939–1945* (London: Arms and Armour, 1996), pp. 92–93.

3. David M. Glantz, *Zhukov's Greatest Defeat: The Red Army's Epic Disaster in Operation Mars, 1942* (Lawrence: University Press of Kansas, 1999), pp. 289, 323; *OKH Heerespersonalamt/1.Staffel, Nr. 75/43, 19 January 1943; OKH Heerespersonalamt/1.Staffel, Nr. 1200/43, 5 July 1943*, both in T-78, Reel 39; *Tatigsseitsbericht des Chefs des Heerespersonalamts, General der Infanterie Schmundt, 5 October 1942, 9 October 1942*, in T-78, Reel 39.

4. *Armeeoberkommando 9, Ia Nr. 852/43, 7 February 1943*, in T-312, Reel 308.

5. Andrej Kin´ski, Tomasz Nowakowski, Mariusz Skotnicki, and Robert Sawicki, *4.Dywizja Pancerma Kursk 1943* (Warsaw: Wydawnictwo "Militaria," 1999), pp. 6–7, 18; Robert Michulec, *4.Panzer-Division on the Eastern Front (1) 1941–1943*, Hong Kong: Concord, 1999), pp. 5–6.

6. *Armeeoberkommando 9, Ia Nr. 852/43, 7 February 1943*, in T-312, Reel 308; *Gruppe Weiss, Ia Nr. 3052/43, 16 May 1943*, in T-315, Reel 321.

7. *Gruppe Weiss, Ia Nr. 3196/43, 23 May 1943*, in T-315, Reel 321.

8. *Gruppe Weiss, Ia Nr. 3052/43, 16 May 1943; Gruppe Weiss, Ia Nr. 3196/43, 23 May 1943*, both in T-315, Reel 321.

9. Ibid.; Michulec, *4.Panzer-Division*, p. 6; Bartov, *Eastern Front*, pp. 18–21, 33–35.

10. Zetterling and Frankson, *Kursk 1943*, pp. 181–184.

11. Information in this table and the numerical estimates below have been derived from Gruppe Weiss, *Ia Nr. 119/43, 9 June 1943; Gruppe Weiss, Ia Nr. 0142/43, 20 June 1943*, both in T-315, Reel 321.

12. See Chapter 4 in this book.

13. *Gruppe Weiss, Ia Nr. 3898/43, 4 July 1943; Armeeoberkommando 9, Ia Nr. 3898 (II), 10 July 1943*, both in T-315, Reel 321.

14. Ibid.; *XI Corps, Ubersicht uber die Gefechtsstarken, 28 August 1943*, in T-314, Reel 493; *Armeeintendant Pz.AOK 4Nr. 532/43, 5 July 1943*, in T-313, Reel 370.

15. The numbers in this table are derived from *Gruppe Weiss, Ia Nr. 3898/43, 4 July 1943*, in T-315, Reel 321; *Artilleriefuehrer, Gruppe Weiss, Ia, 465/43, 27 June 1943*, in T-312, Reel 322. The numbers for the mortars organic to the divisions are taken from TO&E estimates; see Zetterling and Frankson, *Kursk 1943*, p. 18. The discrepancy between the figures offered in this work (3,368) and those provided by Zetterling and Frankson (3,630) are in fact relatively minor and center around the estimation of mortars and the question of whether heavy self-propelled antitank guns are counted as artillery or AFVs. The problem is that German records are in fact too voluminous to provide a definitive number.

16. These figures are derived by examining the mobility percentages in *Gruppe Weiss, Ia Nr. 3898/43, 4 July 1943*, in T-315, Reel 321, and estimating against the authorized vehicle strengths for the units. This is admittedly only a best-guess estimate.

17. Zetterling and Frankson, *Kursk 1943*, pp. 181–184.

18. These very rough figures for Soviet combat strength are based on an examination of *Gruppe Weiss, Ia Nr. 119/43, 9 June 1943; Gruppe Weiss, Ia Nr. 0142/43, 20 June 1943*, both in T-315, Reel 321.

19. Glantz and House, *Kursk*, pp. 58–60, 336–337; Zetterling and Frankson, *Kursk 1943*, pp. 11, 20; Konstantin K. Rokossovsky, *A Soldier's Duty* (Moscow: Progress Publishers, 1970), pp. 184–189.

Chapter 14

1. *Anlage zu Auffrischungsstab Charkow, Ia Nr. 186/43, 23 June 1943*, in T-313, Reel 370.

2. *KTB, 4.PzAOK, 5 July 1943*, in T-313, Reel 365; Lehman, *Liebstandarte III*, p. 215; Haupt, *Army Group South*, pp. 280–281; Glantz and House, *Kursk*, pp. 94–104; Zetterling and Frankson, *Kursk 1943*, p. 207.

3. Jentz, *Panzer Truppen*, vol. 2, pp. 78–82; *Ia Nr. 181/43, Oberkommando der 4. Panzerarmee, 16 June 1943*, in T-313, Reel 370.

4. *KTB, 4.PzAOK, 10 May 1943, 11 May 1943, 27 June 1943*, in T-313, Reel 365.

5. *Anlage B, Ia Nr. 20/43, Generalkommando 48.Pz.Korps, 1 June 1943*, in T-313, Reel 370; Spaeter, *Grossdeutschland*, vol. 2, p. 114; Spaeter rather uncritically accepts Albrecht's claim that he coordinated and supervised the entire artillery plan, an assertion not borne out by contemporary records.

6. See the fire plan attached to Anlage B, *Ia Nr. 20/43, Generalkommando 48.Pz.Korps, 1 June 1943*, in T-313, Reel 370; Spaeter, *Grossdeutschland*, vol. 2, pp. 113–116.

7. Ibid.

8. *Ia Nr. 20/43, Gen.Kdo. 48. Panzer Korps, Angriffsplan des 48. Panzer Korps, 1 July 1943*, in T-313, Reel 370; Spaeter, *Grossdeutschland*, vol. 2, pp. 114–116.

9. *KTB, 4.PzAOK, 27 June 1943*, in T-313, Reel 365; *Ia Nr. 195/43, Auffrischungsstab Charkow, 28 June 1943*, in T-313, Reel 370; Jentz, *Panzer Truppen*, vol. 2, pp. 95–96.

10. Jentz, *Panzer Truppen*, vol. 2, pp. 96–97; Spaeter, *Grossdeutschland*, vol. 2, pp. 116–119.

11. *KTB, 4.PzAOK, 27 June 1943, 3 July 1943*, in T-313, Reel 365; *Ia Nr. 195/43, Auffrischungsstab Charkow, 28 June 1943*, in T-313, Reel 370.

12. It should also be noted in passing that von Knobelsdorff and his chief of staff, von Mellenthin, appear to have given Hoernlein and von Natzmer a much freer hand in their tactical planning than was allowed to the 167th and 332nd Infantry Divisions or the 3rd and 11th Panzer Divisions. The corps operations order for the attack dictates the deployment and even *Kampfgruppe* composition in all four of those divisions

in great detail while leaving similar decisions with regard to Grossdeutschland to the division's planners. See *Ia Nr. 20/43, Gen.Kdo. 48. Panzer Korps, Angriffsplan des 48. Panzer Korps, 1 July 1943,* in T-313, Reel 370.

13. Glantz and House, *Kursk,* pp. 98–99.

14. *Armeeintendant Pz.AOK.4 532/43, Verpflegungsstarken nach dem Stand vom 1.7.43, 5 July 1943,* in T-313, Reel 370; *Kreigsgleiderung der 4. Panzerarmee ohne Versorgungnstruppen (Stand: 5.7.1943), 28 June 1943,* in T-313, Reel 370; *Ia, Gen.Kdo XI Corps, Ubersicht uber die Gefecthsstarken, 28 August 1943,* in T-314, Reel 493; Jentz, *Panzer Truppen,* vol. 2, pp. 78–82.

15. Lehmann, *Liebstandarte III,* pp. 194–200; James Lucas, *Das Reich: The Military Role of the 2nd SS Division* (London: Arms and Armour, 1991), pp. 103–104; Sydnor, *Soldiers of Destruction,* pp. 270–271, 280–281; Paul Hausser, *Waffen SS im Einsatz* (Goettingen: Plesse Verlag, 1953), pp. 87–88.

16. The descriptions of these two sector defenses have been taken entirely from Glantz and House, *Kursk,* pp. 68–73, 307–308. The authors' unparalleled access to Soviet archival sources has given us the clearest picture ever drawn of the Red Army's frontline defenses.

17. Lehmann, *Liebstandarte III,* p. 208; *Generalkommando I. SS-Panzer-Korps, Ia Nr. 462/43, 31 May 1943,* in T-313, Reel 370; see also Stadler, *Offensive Gegen Kursk,* p. 23.

18. *Generalkommando I. SS-Panzer-Korps, Ia Nr. 462/43, 31 May 1943,* in T-313, Reel 370; see also Wolfgang Vopersal, *Soldaten, Kampfer, Kameraden, Marsch, und Kampfe der SS-Totenkopfdivision,* vol. 3B (Biefeld: Biblio Verlag, 1987), pp. 321–326.

19. Lehmann, *Liebstandarte III,* pp. 206–208.

20. *Uberblick zum Feuerplan, Generalkommando I. SS-Panzer-Korps, Ia Nr. 462/43, 31 May 1943,* in T-313, Reel 370; compare with Stadler, *Offensive Gegen Kursk,* pp. 217–224.

21. Ibid.

22. *Anlage im Auffrischunggstab Charkow, Ia Nr. 186/43, 23 June 1943,* in T-313, Reel 370.

23. *KTB, 4.PzAOK, 5 July 1943,* in T-313, Reel 365; Lehmann, *Liebstandarte III,* pp. 208–213; Stadler, *Offensive Gegen Kursk,* pp. 40–41.

24. These estimates differ slightly from the figures presented by Zetterling and Frankson, calculating the total ("ration") strength of the attacking elements of the *Armeeabteilung* a bit lower and converting the figures given by the Germans for "field artillery" into a comparable form for the "guns and mortars" (typically any weapon over 45mm except the 52mm mortar). See *Kriegsgliederung der Armee-Abt. KEMPF fur "Zitadelle," Ia Nr. 183/43,* undated, in T-312, Reel 51; *Anlage, Flak—Kampfgruppe Koeppen, Uber Planzpiel "Zitadelle" beim Gen.Kdo.zbV Ruas am 29.5.43, 9.00 bis 12.45 Uhr,* in T-312, Reel 51; *Anlage 3 zu Gen.Kdo.III.Pz.Korps, Ia Nr. 21/43, 4 June 1943,* in T-312, Reel 51; *Ia, XI Corps, Ubersickt uber die Gefechtsstarken,* undated, in T-314, Reel 493; Wolfgang Paul, *Brenpunkte, Die Geschichte der 6.Panzerdivision (1.liechte), 1937–1945* (Osnabrueck: Biblio Verlag, 1993; reprint of 1984 edition), p. 303; Jentz, *Panzer Truppen,* vol. 2, pp. 78–82; Zetterling and Frankson, *Kursk 1943,* pp. 18–19, 23, 32.

25. Glantz and House, *Kursk,* pp. 309–311, 336.

26. *Armee-Abteilung Kempf, Operationsbefehl fur "Zitadelle" Nr. 1, Ia Nr. 800.43, 1 May 1943,* in T-312, Reel 51.

27. *Ia Nr. 1355/43, Generalkommando III-Pz.Korps, Gliederung, 1 July 1943,* in T-314, Reel 197; *Niederschrift uber Planspiel "Zitadelle" beim III. Pz.Korps am 3.6.1943, 9,00 Uhr bis 12.45,* in T-312, Reel 51.

28. *Niederschrift uber Planspiel "Zitadelle" beim III. Pz.Korps am 3.6.1943, 9,00 Uhr bis 12.45*, in T-312, Reel 51.

29. *Niederschrift uber Planspiel "Zitadelle" beim III. Pz.Korps am 3.6.1943, 9,00 Uhr bis 12.45*, in T-312, Reel 51; *Anlage zu Armee-Abt. Kempf, Ia Nr. 78.43*, undated, in T-312, Reel 51.

30. Hermann Breith, "Breakthrough of III Panzer Corps Through Deeply Echeloned Russian Defenses (Kharkov, July 1943)," in Newton, *German Battle Tactics*, pp. 168–169; *Niederschrift uber Planspiel "Zitadelle" beim III. Pz.Korps am 3.6.1943, 9,00 Uhr bis 12.45*, in T-312, Reel 51.

31. Paul, *Brennpunkt*, pp. 305–306; Jentz, *Panzer Truppen*, vol. 2, pp. 87–88.

32. *KTB, Armeeabteilung Kempf, 5 July 1943*, in T-312, Reel 51; Jentz, *Panzer Truppen*, vol. 2, pp. 92–93; Thomas L. Jentz, *Germany's Tiger Tanks, Tiger I and II: Combat Tactics* (Atglen, PA: Schiffer, 1997), pp. 88–89.

33. *KTB, Armeeabteilung Kempf, 5 July 1943*, in T-312, Reel 51.

34. Breith claimed after the war that he had made the deployment decision, which he strongly defended on tactical grounds; the war diary of the *Armeeabteilung* for 5 July is ambiguous; Breith, "Breakthrough," p. 158; *KTB, Armeeabteilung Kempf, 5 July 1943*, in T-312, Reel 51.

35. *KTB, 4.PzAOK, 5 July 1943*, in T-313, Reel 365; *KTB, Armeeabteilung Kempf, 5 July 1943*, in T-312, Reel 51.

36. Mellenthin, *Panzer Battles*, p. 267; Breith, "Breakthrough," p. 158.

Chapter 15

1. Glantz and House, *Kursk*, p. 280; Zetterling and Frankson, *Kursk 1943*, p. 149.

2. Zetterling and Frankson, *Kursk 1943*, p. 145.

3. Ibid., p. 112.

4. *Armeeoberkommando 9, Ia Nr. 4007/43, 13 July 1943, Ist- und Gefectsstarken, Verlust (Nach dem Stand vom 4. und 9.5.43)*, in T-315, Reel 322.

5. Zetterling and Frankson, *Kursk 1943*, p. 112.

6. Ibid., p. 117.

7. This assumes that the ration strength–to–combat strength ratio for the Ninth Army held true for the Second Panzer Army.

8. Zetterling and Frankson, *Kursk 1943*, pp. 145–147.

9. Ibid., p. 195.

10. The thirteen divisions that included assault-gun battalions in December 1943 were the 14th, 16th, and 24th Panzer Divisions; 10th, 18th, 20th, and 25th Panzergrenadier Divisions; *Grossdeutschland*; and the SS divisions *Liebstandarte Adolph Hitler*, *Das Reich*, *Totenkopf*, and *Wiking*. See Jentz, *Panzer Truppen*, vol. 2, pp. 68–70; Walter J. Spielberger, *Sturmgeschutz and Its Variants* (Atglen, PA: Schiffer, 1993), pp. 243–245.

11. David M. Glantz and Jonathan House, *When Titans Clashed: How the Red Army Stopped Hitler* (Lawrence: University Press of Kansas, 1995), p. 179.

12. Jentz, *Germany's Tiger Tanks*, pp. 27–28, 124.

13. Operational readiness for tanks is drawn from Jentz, *Panzer Truppen*, vol. 2, p. 110; rates for assault guns are depicted in Spielberger, *Sturmgeschutz*, p. 249. Note that the Spielberger table has to be read very carefully, as several of the column headings have slipped (at least in the first edition) over the wrong columns.

14. Zetterling and Frankson, *Kursk 1943*, p. 147.

15. Ibid., p. 148.

16. This conjectural process starts from the assumption that the larger numbers for Soviet tank strength cited in the General Staff study reflect "available" vehicles while the much lower figures that Glantz, House, Zetterling, and Frankson derived from a wide variety of Russian archival and semiarchival sources are "on-hand" or "operational." See Zetterling and Frankson, *Kursk 1943*, p. 48; Glantz and House, *Kursk*, pp. 336–345; David M. Glantz and Harold S. Orenstein, eds., *The Battle for Kursk 1943: The Soviet General Staff Study* (London: Frank Cass, 1999), pp. 197, 208, 222. A representative German intelligence assessment that includes Soviet operational rates for late 1943 is *4.Pz.AOK, Ic, Nr. 2296* (undated but by context early December 1943), *Kampfwert der vor der Front der 4.Panzerarmee stehenden Feinverbande*, in T-313, Reel 376.

17. Glantz and House, *When Titans Clashed*, pp. 296–297, 306; Zetterling and Frankson, *Kursk 1943*, p. 148.

18. Ibid.

19. Zetterling and Frankson, *Kursk 1943*, pp. 149–151.

20. Burkhart Mueller-Hillebrand, *Das Heer, 1933–1945*, 3 vols. (Frankfurt am Main: E. S. Mittler and Sohn, 1969), vol. 3, pp. 124, 133, 149, 217.

BIBLIOGRAPHY

Manuscript Sources

Captured German Records, National Archives, Washington, D.C.

2.Panzerarmee
4.Panzerarmee
Armeeabteilung Kempf
Armeeoberkommando 2
Armeeoberkommando 6
Armeeoberkommando 8
Armeeoberkommando 9
Generalkommando Corps Raus a.b.V.
Generalkommando III.Pz.Korps
Generalkommando XI Corps
Generalkommando XX.Korps
Generalkommando XXV.Korps
Generalkommando XXXXVIII.Pz.Korps
Heeresgruppe Sud
Heeresgruppe Mitte
Heerespersonalamts

Foreign Military Studies, National Archives, Washington, D.C.

C-078 (1950). Francke, Martin. "Sixth Army, Russia."

D-153 (1947). von Roman, Rudolf. "XX Corps in the Defense of the Area Southwest of Orel (Summer 1943)."

D-229 (1947). Arndt, Karl. "293rd Infantry Division (July 11–August 18, 1943)."

D-258 (1947). Breith, Hermann. "Breakthrough of III Panzer Corps Through Deeply Echeloned Russian Defenses (Kharkov, July 1943)."

D-336 (undated). Poppe, Friedrich. "255th Infantry Division (1943)."

D-369 (1948). Teske, Hermann. "Railroad Transportation: Operation Zitadelle (1943)."

P-060g Part III (1953). Raus, Erhard. "Small Unit Tactics—Unusual Situations, Stalingrad Area."

P-060g Part IV (1952). Raus, Erhard. "Small Unit Tactics—Unusual Situations."
P-079 (1951). Rendulic, Lothar. "The Russian Command in World War II."
T-9 (undated). Heinrici, Gotthard, and Wilhelm Hauck. *The Axis Campaign in the East, November 1942–May 1945.* Chapter 12: "'Citadel': The Attack Against Russian Positions Near Kursk, July 4–15, 1943."
T-10 (1951). Raus, Erhard. "German Defense Tactics Against Russian Breakthroughs."
T-21 (1951). Raus, Erhard. "Military Improvisations During the Russian Campaign."
T-22 (1950). Raus, Erhard. "Russian Combat Methods in World War II."
T-26 (1947). Busse, Theodor, et al. "The Zitadelle Offensive, July 1943."

Published Works

Andrew, Christopher, and Vasili Mitrokhin. *The Sword and the Shield: The Mitrokhin Archive and the Secret History of the KGB.* New York: Basic Books, 1999.
Angolia, John R. *On the Field of Honor: A History of the Knight's Cross Bearers.* 2 vols. No location given: Bender, 1979–1980.
Armstrong, John A., ed. *Soviet Partisans in World War II.* Madison: University of Wisconsin Press, 1964.
Armstrong, Richard N. *Red Army Legacies: Essays on Forces, Capabilities, and Personalities.* Atglen, PA: Schiffer, 1995.
_____. *Red Army Tank Commanders: The Armored Guards.* Atglen, PA: Schiffer, 1994.
Bartov, Omer. *The Eastern Front, 1941–1945: German Troops and the Barbarisation of Warfare.* London: MacMillan, 1985.
Blennemann, Dirk. "German Corps Organization in World War II." *Command,* No. 32. January–February 1994.
Burdick, Charles, and Hans-Adolf Jacobsen, eds. *The Halder War Diary, 1939–1942.* Novato, CA: Presidio, 1988.
Caidin, Martin. *The Tigers Are Burning.* New York: Hawthorn, 1974.
Carell, Paul. *Scorched Earth: The Russo-German War, 1943–1944.* Atglen, PA: Schiffer, 1996.
Cooper, Matthew. *The German Army, 1933–1945: Its Political and Military Failure.* New York: Stein and Day, 1978.
_____. *The Nazi War Against Soviet Partisans, 1941–1944.* New York: Stein and Day, 1979.
Corti, Eugenio. *Few Returned: Twenty-eight Days on the Russian Front, Winter 1942–1943.* Columbia: University of Missouri Press, 1997.
Corum, James S. *The Luftwaffe: Creating the Operational Air War, 1918–1940.* Lawrence: University Press of Kansas, 1997.
Detweiler, Donald E., ed. *World War II German Military Studies.* 23 vols. New York: Garland, 1979.
Dunn, Walter S. Jr. *Kursk: Hitler's Gamble, 1943.* Westport, CT: Praeger, 1997.

Folkestad, William B., ed. *Panzerjaeger: Tank Hunter*. Shippensburg, PA: Burd Street Press, 2000.

Gerbet, Klaus, ed. *Generalfeldmarschall Fedor von Bock: The War Diary, 1939–1945*. Atglen, PA: Schiffer, 1996.

Glantz, David M. "American Perspectives on Eastern Front Operations in World War II." *Voprosy Istorii [Questions of History]*. August 1987.

Glantz, David M., and Harold S. Orenstein, eds. *The Battle for Kursk, 1943: The Soviet General Staff Study*. London: Frank Cass, 1999.

_____. *From the Don to the Dnepr: Soviet Offensive Operations, December 1941 to August 1943*. London: Frank Cass, 1991.

_____. *The Role of Intelligence in Soviet Military Strategy in World War II*. Novato, CA: Presidio, 1990.

_____. *Zhukov's Greatest Defeat: The Red Army's Epic Disaster in Operation Mars, 1942*. Lawrence: University Press of Kansas, 1999.

Glantz, David M., and Jonathan House. *The Battle of Kursk*. Lawrence: University Press of Kansas, 1999.

_____. *When Titans Clashed: How the Red Army Stopped Hitler*. Lawrence: University Press of Kansas, 1995.

Goerlitz, Walter, ed. *The Memoirs of Field Marshal Keitel*. New York: Stein and Day, 1966.

_____. *MODEL: Strategie der Defensive*. Wiesbaden: Limes Verlag, 1975.

Guderian, Heinz. *Panzer Leader*. London: Michael Joseph, 1952.

Haupt, Werner. *Army Group South: The Wehrmacht in Russia, 1941–1945*. Atglen, PA: Schiffer, 1998.

Hausser, Paul. *Waffen SS im Einsatz*. Goettingen: Plesse Verlag, 1953.

Hayward, Joel S. A. *Stopped at Stalingrad: The Luftwaffe and Hitler's Defeat in the East, 1942–1943*. Lawrence: University Press of Kansas, 1998.

Healey, Mark. *Kursk 1943: The Tide Turns in the East*. London: Osprey, 1992.

Heinrici, Gottfried, and Wilhelm Hauck. "*Zitadelle*" *Wehrwissenschaftliche Rundschau*. Vol. 15. August–October 1965.

Hertlein, Wilhelm. *Chronik der 7. Infanterie-Division*. Munich: Bruckmann, 1984.

Hooten, E. R. *Eagle in Flames: The Fall of the Luftwaffe*. London: Arms and Armour, 1997.

Hoth, Hermann. *Panzeroperationen*. Heidelberg: Vowinckel, 1966.

Howell, Edgar M. *The Soviet Partisan Movement, 1941–1944*. Washington, DC: Department of the Army, 1956.

Jentz, Thomas L. *Germany's Tiger Tanks, Tiger I and II: Combat Tactics*. Atglen, PA: Schiffer, 1997.

_____, ed. *Panzer Truppen: The Complete Guide to the Creation and Combat Employment of Germany's Tank Force*. 2 vols. Atglen, PA: Schiffer, 1996.

Jukes, Geoffrey. *Kursk: The Clash of Armour*. New York: Ballantine, 1968.

Keilig, Wolf. *Das Deutsche Heer, 1939–1945*. 3 vols. Frankfort: Podzun Verlag, 1958.

Kin'ski, Andrej, Tomasz Nowakowski, Mariusz Skotnicki, and Robert Sawicki. *4.Dywizja Pancerma Kursk 1943*. Warsaw: Wydawnictwo "Militaria," 1999.

Klink, Ernst. *Das Gesetz des Handelns die Operation "Zitadelle," 1943*. Stuttgart: Deutsche Verlag-Anstalt, 1966.

von Knobelsdorff, Otto. *19.Panzer-Division*. Bad Neuheim: Verlag Hans-Menning Podzun, 1958.

Lehmann, Rudolf. *The Liebstandarte III*. Winnipeg, Canada: J. J. Fedorowicz, 1990.

Lucas, James. *Das Reich: The Military Role of the 2nd SS Division*. London: Arms and Armour, 1991.

_____. *Hitler's Enforcers: Leaders of the German War Machine, 1939–1945*. London: Arms and Armour, 1996.

von Manstein, Eric. *Lost Victories*. Novato, CA: Presidio, 1982.

von Mellenthin, Friedrich Wilhelm. *Panzer Battles: A Study of the Employment of Armour in the Second World War*. New York: Ballantine, 1971; reprint of 1956 edition.

Michulec, Robert. *4.Panzer-Division on the Eastern Front (1) 1941–1943*. Hong Kong: Concord, 1999.

Mitcham, Samuel W. Jr. *Men of the Luftwaffe*. Novato, CA: Presidio, 1988.

Mueller-Hillebrand, Burkhart. *Das Heer, 1933–1945*. 3 vols. Frankfurt am Main: E. S. Mittler and Sohn, 1969.

Muller, Richard. *The German Air War in Russia*. Baltimore: Naval and Aviation, 1992.

Murray, Williamson. *Strategy for Defeat: The Luftwaffe, 1933–1945*. Maxwell, AL: Air University Press, 1983.

Nehring, Walther. *Die Geschichtite Der Deutschen Panzerwaffe, 1916 bis 1945*. Berlin: Propylaeen Verlag, 1969.

Newton, Steven H. *German Battle Tactics on the Russian Front, 1941–1945*. Atglen, PA: Schiffer, 1994.

Nipe, George M. Jr. *Decision in the Ukraine, Summer 1943: IISS. and III. Panzerkorps*. Winnipeg, Canada: J. J. Fedorowicz, 1996.

Padfield, Peter. *Himmler*. New York: Henry Holt, 1990.

Paget, R. T. *Manstein: His Campaigns and His Trial*. London: Collins, 1951.

Paul, Wolfgang. *Brennpunkt: Die Geschichte der 6.Panzerdivision (1.leichte), 1937–1945*. Osnabrueck: Biblio Verlag, 1993.

Piekalkiewics, Janusz. *Operation "Citadel," Kursk, and Orel: The Greatest Tank Battle of the Second World War*. Trans. Michaela Nierhaus. Novato, CA: Presidio, 1987.

Plocher, Herman. *The German Air Force Versus Russia, 1943*. Ed. Harry R. Fletcher. New York: Arno, 1968; reprint of 1967 edition.

Raus, Erhard. "Winterkampf an der Bistraja and Kalitwa." *Allgemeine Schweizerische Militarzeitschrifte*. January 1954.

_____. "Zweimal Charkow." *Allgemeine Schweizerische Militarzeitschrifte*. December 1964.

Rendulic, Lothar. *Gekampft, Gesiegt, Geschlagen*. Munich: "Welsermuehl" Wels, 1958.

Ripley, Tim. *Steel Storm: Waffen-SS Panzer Battles on the Eastern Front, 1943–1945*. Osceola, WI: MBI, 2000.

Rokossovsky, Konstantin K. *A Soldier's Duty*. Moscow: Progress Publishers, 1970.

Ryan, Cornelius. *The Last Battle*. New York: Simon and Schuster, 1966.

Seaton, Albert. *The German Army, 1933–1945*. New York: Meridian, 1982.

_____. *The Russo-German War, 1841–1945*. Novato CA: Presidio, 1990; reprint of 1971 edition.

von Siegler, Fritz Freiherr. *Die Hoeheren Dienstellen der Deutschen Wehrmacht, 1933–1945*. Frankfurt: Institut fuer Zeitgeschichte, 1957.

Spaeter, Helmuth. *The History of the Panzerkorps Grossdeutschland*. Manitoba, Canada: J. J. Fedorowicz, 1995.

Sperker, Karl Heinrich. *Generaloberst Erhard Raus: Ein Truppenfuehrer im Ostfeldzug*. Osnabrueck: Biblio Verlag, 1988.

Spielberger, Walter J. *Sturmgeschutz and Its Variants*. Atglen, PA: Schiffer, 1993.

Stadler, Silvester. *Die Offensive Gegen Kursk*. Coburg: Nation Europa, 1998; reprint of 1980 edition.

Stahlberg, Alexander. *Bounden Duty: The Memoirs of a German Officer, 1932–1945*. London: Brassey's, 1990.

Sydnor, Charles W. Jr. *Soldiers of Destruction: The SS Death's Head Division, 1933–1945*. Princeton, NJ: Princeton University, 1977.

Thomas, Nigel, and Carlos Caballero Jurado. *Wehrmacht Auxiliary Forces*. London: Osprey, 1992.

Tiemann, Ralf. *Chronicle of the 7. Panzer-Kompanie 1. SS-Panzer Division "Liebstandarte."* Atglen, PA: Schiffer, 1998.

Trevor-Roper, Hugh, ed. *Final Entries, 1945: The Diaries of Joseph Goebbels*. New York: G. P. Putnam's Sons, 1978.

Tsouras, Peter G., ed. *Fighting in Hell: The German Ordeal on the Eastern Front*. New York: Ballantine, 1995.

_____, ed. *The Anvil of War: German Generalship in Defense on the Eastern Front*. London: Greenhill, 1994.

Vopersal, Wolfgang. *Soldaten, Kampfer, Kameraden, Marsch, und Kampfe der SS-Totenkopfdivision*. Vol. 3B. Biefeld: Biblio Verlag, 1987.

Weidinger, Otto. *Division Das Reich*. Vol. 4. Osnabrueck: Munin Verlag, 1986.

Zetterling, Niklas, and Anders Frankson. *Kursk 1943: A Statistical Analysis*. London: Frank Cass, 2000.

Ziemke, Earl F. *Stalingrad to Berlin: The German Defeat in the East*. Washington, DC: Center of Military History, 1966.

INDEX